GAME PLAN

KAREN L. WALL

GAME

A SOCIAL HISTORY OF **SPORT IN ALBERTA**

PLAN

THE UNIVERSITY OF ALBERTA PRESS

Published by

The University of Alberta Press
Ring House 2
Edmonton, Alberta, Canada T6G 2E1
www.uap.ualberta.ca

LIBRARY AND ARCHIVES CANADA
CATALOGUING IN PUBLICATION

Wall, Karen L. (Karen Linda), 1955-
     Game plan : a social history of sport in
Alberta / Karen L. Wall.

Includes bibliographical references and index.
Issued also in electronic formats.
ISBN 978-0-88864-594-4

     1. Sports—Social aspects—Alberta—
History. 2. Sports—Alberta—History.
3. Alberta--Social conditions. I. Title.

GV706.5.W24 2012   306.4'83097123
C2012-902674-3

First edition, first printing, 2012.
Printed and bound in Canada by Houghton
Boston Printers, Saskatoon, Saskatchewan.
Copyediting and proofreading by
Joanne Muzak.
Indexing by Noeline Bridge.

The University of Alberta Press is committed
to protecting our natural environment. As
part of our efforts, this book is printed on
Enviro Paper: it contains 100% post-consumer
recycled fibres and is acid- and chlorine-free.

The University of Alberta Press gratefully
acknowledges the support received for its
publishing program from The Canada Council
for the Arts. The University of Alberta Press also
gratefully acknowledges the financial support
of the Government of Canada through the
Canada Book Fund (CBF) and the Government
of Alberta through the Alberta Multimedia
Development Fund (AMDF) for its publishing
activities.

Government
of Alberta ■

To my mother, Jane Wall, tireless athlete, coach, and sports fan, who kept me in motion.

And my father, John Wall, storyteller and history aficionado, who stopped at every roadside monument.

Maybe that did it, I thought—maybe that was one of the things that
turned me into a writer—my playing [softball] far out in the field...
The being isolated, out there in the prairie wind and the summer light;
my striking up a conversation with a nearby gopher...The caring so much,
so enduringly, for the movements of small creatures, for the ongoing
game, for all the shouting and the laughter that are some of the various
names of love.

—ROBERT KROETSCH

"Alberta, Twenty-Five Years after Alberta," preface to Alberta, *2nd ed.*

CONTENTS

Acknowledgements XI

Abbreviations XIII

PART I

INVENTING ALBERTA SPORTS CULTURE

1   Sport as Cultural Identity 5

2   From Indigenous Games to Cities of Champions 15
    A Basic Chronology

3   Fencing the Fields 33
    Organizing Principles and Social Order

PART II

WRITING THE RULE BOOK
FROM PASTIMES TO ORGANIZATIONS

4 "The West has Made Fairly Good Headway" 59
Core Summer Team Sports

5 "Love and Hometown Glory" 95
Core Winter Team Sports

6 Sport and the Single Athlete 133
Mavericks, Knights, and Knickerbockers

PART III

THE SOCIAL BODY
FREEDOM AND CONTROL

7 "A Vain Shadow" 191
Fitness, Discipline, and Social Control

8 "Red-blooded Sports" and "Masculine Facsimiles" 225
Gender and Sexuality

9 A "Great Slaughter on the Field" 263
Aggression, Risk, and High Performance

10 "The Rain Upon Our Senses" 291
Sport, the Mass Media, and Marketing

11 Getting on the Map 331
Sport Raises the Rafters

Notes 365

Archival Sources 435

Bibliography 439

Index 479

ACKNOWLEDGEMENTS

THIS BOOK IS THE RESULT of a wide network of support and encouragement. Bruce McGillivray and Jane Ross conceived of the project
and, working with the Friends of Royal Alberta Museum Society,
secured funding for it from the Alberta Community Development,
Sport and Recreation Branch and the Alberta Sport, Recreation, Parks
and Wildlife Foundation. Cathy Roy of the Royal Alberta Museum
co-ordinated later development. The manuscript evolved significantly
after the research project ended, and any errors or omissions are my
responsibility.

David Whitson of the University of Alberta introduced me to the
history and culture of sport as a professor, colleague, and exemplar
of scholarship in the area. For the opportunity to explore the topic as
an instructor of leisure history and philosophy, thanks are due Darrel
Morrow and students at Red Deer College and students of Canadian
Studies and of Recreation and Leisure Studies at the University of

Alberta. Athabasca University, through the President's Award for Research and Scholarly Excellence, made it possible to complete the manuscript; and thanks go to many inspiring colleagues, particularly the very supportive Friday morning Alicean Research Group.

Ultimately, research in local and regional history is directly dependent on the expertise and commitment of museums and archives staff, and I am grateful for assistance from institutions large and small, urban and rural, throughout the province of Alberta. Thanks to staff of the University of Alberta Press, especially Peter Midgley, Mary Lou Roy, Alan Brownoff, and copyeditor Joanne Muzak. Not least, my family (sports fans and otherwise) kindly attended to random narratives of sport or explained why they would rather not; thanks especially to Cliff Vallentgoed, bicycle guru and true sporting gentleman.

ACKNOWLEDGEMENTS

ABBREVIATIONS

AA	Athabasca Archives
AAA	Alberta Amateur Association
AAFL	Alberta Association Football League
AAAU	Alberta Amateur Athletic Union
AAHA	Alberta Amateur Hockey Association
AAUC	Amateur Athletic Union of Canada
ACA	Alberta Cricket Association
ACAC	Alberta Colleges Athletic Conference
AFG	Alberta Francophone Games
AGA	Alberta Golf Association
AIRCA	All Indian Rodeo Cowboys Association
AJHL	Alberta Junior Hockey League
ARGRA	Alberta Rockies Gay Rodeo Association
ARU	Alberta Rugby Union

ASAA	Alberta Schools' Athletic Association
ATB	Alberta Treasury Branches
BEG	British Empire Games
CAAU	Canadian Amateur Athletic Union
CAAWS	Canadian Association for the Advancement for Women and Sport and Physical Activity
CABA	Canadian Amateur Basketball Association
CAHA	Canadian Amateur Hockey Association
CBAA	Calgary Buffalo Athletic Association
CEA	City of Edmonton Archives
CFL	Canadian Football League
CFR	Canadian Finals Rodeo
CFSA	Canadian Figure Skating Association
CGRA	Canadian Girls' Rodeo Association
CIAU	Canadian Interuniversity Athletic Union
CIRCA	Canadian Indian Rodeo Cowboys Association
CIS	Canadian Interuniversity Sport
CLGU	Canadian Ladies Golf Union
CNGR	Canadian National Gay Rodeo
CWA	City of Wetaskiwin Archives
CWIAU	Canadian Women's Intercollegiate Athletic Union
CWUAA	Canada West Universities Athletic Association
DFC	Division Football Club
EEA	Edmonton Exhibition Association
EFCL	Edmonton Federation of Community Leagues
EFSC	Edmonton Figure Skating Club
ESC	Eskimo Ski Club
FC	Football Club
FIFA	Fédération Internationale de Football Association
FJA	Francophonie jeunesse de l'Alberta

GA	Glenbow Archives
GMA	Galt Museum Archives
GLISA	Gay and Lesbian International Sport Association
GWG	Great Western Garment Company
HBC	Hudson's Bay Company
IRCA	Indian Rodeo Cowboy Association
ISU	International Skating Union
JYMA	Jasper Yellowhead Museum and Archives
LABA	Lethbridge Amateur Boxing Association
NASL	North American Soccer League
NHL	National Hockey League
NPAC	National Parks Association of Canada
NWMP	North West Mounted Police
PCHL	Pacific Coast Hockey League
PCL	Pacific Coast League
RCA	Rodeo Cowboys Association
RCCC	Royal Caledonian Curling Club
RDDA	Red Deer and District Archives
SPRA	South Peace Regional Archives
WAAF	Women's Amateur Athletic Foundation
WCBL	Western Canada Baseball League
WCH/RAM	Western Canada History/Royal Alberta Museum
WCHL	Western Canada Hockey League
WCIAA	Western Canadian Intercollegiate Athletic Association
WCJHL	Western Canada Junior Hockey League
WCRFU	Western Canada Rugby Football Union

WHA	World Hockey Association
WHL	Western Hockey League
WIAA	Western Intercollegiate Athletic Association
WIAU	Women's Intercollegiate Athletic Union
WIFU	Western Interprovincial Football Union
WIL	Western International League
WSA	Workers' Sports Association
UCA	University of Calgary Archives
YCL	Young Communist League

PART I

**INVENTING ALBERTA
SPORTS CULTURE**

Overleaf: School sports competitor, Edmonton, October 1926. Photo: McDermid Studio, Edmonton. [GA NC-6-11903B] "they reshaped the Canadian landscape from a disjointed collection of communities into a people with a common history and mythology. They all ask us to be part of something larger than ourselves that extends from sea to sea to sea."

AROUND THE WORLD, the symbolic meanings of sport "evince a life passion not generally observable in other cultural domains."[1] A Canadian public school lesson plan asks students to look at selected athletes as national heroes, not simply for their skills or victories but because "they reshaped the Canadian landscape from a disjointed collection of communities into a people with a common history and mythology. They all ask us to be part of something larger than ourselves that extends from sea to sea to sea."[2] With countless variations, the core expectations and experiences of sport endure through time and across cultures. This book focuses on the ways that those experiences have been managed and organized in the Prairie province of Alberta in western Canada. It considers the presence of sport in Alberta society not from the position of a dedicated fan but of a resident's fascination with its power and endurance in the province's culture and its claim on our attentions for well over a century.

1

SPORT AS CULTURAL IDENTITY

LIKE OTHER MODERN SOCIETIES developed in relation to imperial, metropolitan centres, Alberta's history is a collision of pragmatism and mythologies. Developing from the eighteenth-century fur trade and the arrival of missionaries in the mid-nineteenth century, full control of the Prairie region passed from the Hudson's Bay Company to the Dominion of Canada in 1870. Then known as the North-West Territories, there were four districts (Athabasca, Assiniboia, Alberta, and Saskatchewan) until 1905, when the provinces of Alberta and Saskatchewan were established.[1]

From Indigenous, trading, and settler communities to a province of ever-increasing urbanization and oil wealth, sport has played important roles in constructing and defining Alberta society. It has provided a realm for acting out heroic fantasy and engaging competitive energies for both individuals and communities. Sport has been pastime,

passion, business, metaphor, and a good excuse for a party or civic celebration. On the other hand, for many it has been an irritating drain on
community resources, an incomprehensible distraction from other
cultural possibilities, or the monster that ate your family's free time.

Why, out of the range of possible stories to be told about the history
of Alberta, should we attend to those that have to do with the games
people have played and watched, in camps, fields, towns, and cities?
What can the history of sport in Alberta tell us about ourselves, our
passions, and our ways of life? In what tangible and intangible ways
has sport shaped our urban landscapes and use of time? How has sport
in Alberta been similar and different to sport in other modern social
contexts? How has it changed over the decades as other ideas about
social life have changed?

Eric Dunning includes sport with religion and war as one of the
most successful means of collective mobilization humans have
devised.[2] Raymond Williams insisted that, as part of the social sphere
of culture, which consists of a particular way of life that expresses
certain meanings and values, the need for sport is "as real as the need
for art."[3] Viewed as popular culture, the history of sport and leisure
illuminates enduring social tensions between freedom and control
and offers insights into core ideas about myth and identity. Sport is a
set of cultural phenomena woven together from, and actively consti-
tuting, not only games, athletes, and organizations, but wider aspects
of everyday life, technologies, broad social movements, and political
and economic realities.[4] A sense of social identity in a community or
country is forged only in part on the rational, organizational levels of
policy, legislation, and public programs. It grows and thrives in the
more fluid spheres of emotion and sensation, and sporting culture is
one of its dynamic forces. Shared games and spectacles alike dramatize the relationships between people, and between humans and
environment.[5]

Stories about sport situate small details of everyday life in the
larger sphere of meaning determined by a society's cultural, social,
and economic relations. Outdoor curling, for instance, focuses the

struggle with the winter environment; baseball fever evokes the pride and spirit of a small but ambitious town. Women find new places on public fields, and men selectively allow certain people into club-houses. Grandees from the old country invite, or forbid, their hired hands to join in the polo game. A First Nations lacrosse player watches British men invent new rules and borders. And recent arrivals from America and Ontario gather teams together and scheme to sell tickets. Meanwhile, on the edge of the fields and behind the bleachers, others have other ideas about when, where, why, by whom, and how games will be played.

⋮ SPORT IN WESTERN SOCIETIES

TRADITION TO MODERNITY

In the summer of 1940, as the people of Drumheller enjoyed fresh air in a city park, conflict arose. Groups of youth were randomly occupying open areas to play spontaneous ball games, making it impossible for picnickers and children to share the space. Besides that, their rowdy play left marks on the grass and disrupted the landscaping. The city quickly responded by creating a dedicated sports field in an adjacent waste ground, where events could be scheduled and contained, and order brought to these impulsive athletics.[6]

This simple incident, not unusual in urban space, echoes recurring themes of space and time in the social history of sport. A central issue is the use and control of public space; in this case, grounds selected for certain purposes were marked out within a city that itself delineated civilization amidst the vast unmonitored distances beyond. Second, designated public spaces come with the imposition of time constraints on activities there, either directly scheduled or enforced by limits to daylight and leisure hours. From the late nineteenth through the twen-tieth century, new technologies of control over time and space accompanied an unprecedented rate of change in economies and social structures in Western societies. In the context of modern industrial development of Euro-Canadian resource bases in western Canada,

Governor General Lord Tweedsmuir acting as the starter for an Indian race at the annual
Calgary Exhibition and Stampede, 1936. [GA NB-16-103]

sport developed as a regional instance of the widely shared "story of
the modern emergence of free time."[7]

Most organized forms of sport came to Alberta from European countries via central and eastern Canada and the United States. Historians
of sport and leisure practices in modern Western societies have typically discerned three main eras: traditional, or pre-industrial (usually
agrarian) life until the late eighteenth century, followed by the reform
period that coincided with accelerating industrialization and urbanization during the mid-to late nineteenth, and the present dominance of
commercial, professional entertainment industries evolving over the
twentieth century. In agrarian societies, for example, traditional sport
was typically spontaneous and relatively unorganized, occurring as
games or, more formally, contests around seasonal or ritual occasions.

Sport and games often also had allegorical, ritualistic meanings closer to what we think of as art and religion, both in Europe and among Native North Americans.[8] But the process known as modernization is central to the nature of sport as it developed in North American societies from the latter part of the nineteenth century onward.

In modern sport, as in other areas of experience, the traditional fusion of sacred, or ritual, and everyday practices gradually gave way to values of quantification, or the rationalized control of data, people, and action.[9] Modern working life and leisure hours would harmonize in the focus on mass production of entertainment for mass audiences of consumers. On the community level, organizers of popular pastimes could influence social norms and behaviours in ways suited to the efficient operation of urban-based economies. In this context, acceptable activities and attitudes were those subject to reform through regulation and efficient packaging that could be easily and predictably reproduced from place to place and group to group. Common public space and unruly activity were domesticated by civic authorities through legitimated community sport grounds, while the eventual construction of designated facilities was intended to produce high-level, high-profile athletics as well as serve the general public.[10] In this way, organized sport directly affected the urban landscape.

Social networks and other conditions must be in place to develop markets for sport as it shifts from elite practice for amateurs to become professional spectacle and commodity. Middle-class ideals of sportsmanship, including fair play, character, and rule observance, were also values relevant to capitalism, in which winning scores and records equate to worth and profit, and designated organizations shape efficiency and minimize risks.[11] In developing sport as a cultural vehicle as well as a commercial product, prairie organizations struggled for local control in relation to central, national organizations; in turn, athletes and teams dealt with constraints handed down by regional branches of amateur or professional organizations; and rivalries between northern and southern areas of the province played out in the founding of groups and events.

Although the paradigm of modernization is a helpful set of truths about Western history, it is not a deterministic process whereby rules, skills, competitions, and leagues spring up as if the expression of some magical logic.[12] Active human engagement is as important as such economic trends as modernization and urbanization in explaining socio-cultural developments in leisure and sport, so that we consider the continuities in sporting culture over time, or the ways that patterns and interests recur in a dynamic relationship of power interests in society. Naturally, there were, and are, tensions and inconsistencies in this process. People tend to resist the pruning of untidy, unruly, and generally unworthy pastimes and to find ways to get around rules and challenge expectations. Amateur ideals and community allegiances clashed with the developing professional star system; debates about local priorities are still with us today. But in Alberta we can follow a familiar pattern of transition from traditional (unorganized or spontaneous games, as well as Indigenous forms of sport) to reform (with European settlement and education systems developing) to professional and commercial forms of the early twentieth century and beyond.

Regions in Canada have functioned as political, economic, and cultural resources supporting national development, and Alberta has a well-developed social identity, part of which is a historically entrenched sense of regional alienation.[13] Aritha van Herk's 2002 book and a related exhibit at Calgary's Glenbow Museum presented Albertans as "mavericks," suggesting that "there is something special, though vague, about Alberta which shapes larger than life residents and sensibilities."[14] In its capacity to produce and celebrate not only talented team players but eccentrics, individualists, and capitalists, as well as fiercely loyal fans, sport has offered a medium of identity formation for a wide range of Albertans.

Popular sport histories, like sport journalism, have typically echoed themes of linear progress toward achievement and victory, the conflicts of powerful opponents, the triumph of the maverick individual or leader, and the telling details of statistics that establish hierarchies of significance. Accounts of Canadian sport intended for popular audiences, in particular, have focused on the institutionalization of sport among Indigenous and immigrant peoples, the emergence of sport heroes, and the urban organization of sport as professional product. Like origin myths of the Euro-Canadian west that include the familiar conquering of distances, climate, and frontier conditions, these often heroic narratives tend to omit the background stories about how audiences were formed, how sport merged into other components of leisure time and everyday working life, and how people both contributed to and struggled against an evolving sport culture. In contrast, the critical sociology of sport has explored sport as social and cultural practice, a perspective that extends beyond academia to those engaged with issues of the relevance of sport to community development, social services, and urban economic competition.[15]

Canadian sport scholarship has predominantly focused on the national level, particularly on the development of organized sport in central and eastern Canada. There is also much material specifically on the Maritime provinces, Ontario, and Quebec. This book represents, first, the effort to survey, compile, and expand upon widely distributed scholarly and popular resources concerning sport history in Alberta. Within these particular temporal and geographic boundaries, its goals are twofold. First, it aims to provide a broad chronological narrative as a foundation of understanding how core sports and sport cultures in the province evolved. Of course, from the beginning of Euro-Canadian trade and settlement, sport in Alberta has been part of an evolving metropolitan and global sport culture and, in general, as a branch of the British Empire, followed contemporary patterns of colonial cultural development with regional variations. To great extent, it is impossible to isolate one region, demarcated by arbitrarily designated boundaries, from national and international contexts, but the scope of the present discussion remains as far as possible within the province from the period of its formation as such; the reader wishing to consult other background material on sport or social and cultural history at the national and international levels is directed to the footnotes and reference list, which point to comprehensive sources on these topics.

The second goal of this book is to expand the edges of the developmental chronology of mainstream sports and to introduce the people, teams, spectators, and lesser-known games that have remained on the margins of most sport histories. Research originated as a compilation of exhibit resource data for the Royal Alberta Museum. As such it was grounded in collecting and structuring material drawn from scattered, often ephemeral archival collections including photographs, scrapbooks, souvenirs, and organizational records. Community and oral histories are sources of local memory in which sport often figures prominently, and popular magazines and newspapers outline events and players through both sport coverage and editorial perspectives. The study samples news sources selected as representative of coverage in specific decades and locations, ranging over more than one hundred years. Primary sources are integrated with published material about social history and sport in the province, including works with a national focus that contain scattered references to Alberta and works that deal with other aspects of history and culture in Alberta.

The chronological introductory sections of this book, then, move from pre-industrial tradition to the era of late modernity, which considered the era of industrialized capitalism, and to postmodernity, or the latter twentieth century, to the present. In the next sections, this conventional sequence of historical periods is reviewed, questioned, and supplemented with perspectives that examine historical assumptions of sport as organizational progress, heroic achievement, and shared community celebration. Here, the study circles back to consider sport as a set of multifaceted social phenomena, much as one might circle a game in progress to get a sense of what different players experience. We begin with the premise that sport is a human social and cultural product created over time that reflects important truths about and insights into society—more than simply a collection of pastimes, a mythic expression of national or local character, or a profitable industry.

2

FROM INDIGENOUS GAMES TO CITIES OF CHAMPIONS

A BASIC CHRONOLOGY

IN 1910, Emily Murphy wrote of the Edmonton area, "there is much tea and tennis...mobiling, dancing, dining and wild riding across the hills; for when people are healthy and prosperous they are instinctively hospitable."[1] Settlers did not arrive to a landscape featuring level playing fields and marked ice surfaces, though the region was relatively flat and unforested. Nor did they have so much free time that their first thoughts were of play. Why, under challenging living and working conditions, did sporting activity become a mainstay of both urban and rural community life? The immediate answer is, of course, that people simply enjoyed playing and watching others play. But sport was also a powerful medium of social interaction and cultural expression. Team sport was woven into other spheres of leisure activity, with games and contests routinely supplemented by dancing, dining, and various side-show entertainments.

This chapter sketches the chronological framework of some of the development of mainstream sport culture in Alberta starting with an overview of Aboriginal games of the pre- and post-contact eras and moving to leisure and physical training in trade and military posts, followed by pastimes of social life in the settlement period and industrialization. Sport took an important role as entertainment and social capital in immigrant communities and growing cities. Economic and demographic conditions were amenable to supporting a "golden age" of sport and commercial culture in the 1920s and 1930s, followed by significant organizational change with technological and economic shifts from the 1950s through the 1970s. By the 1980s, sport in Canada was increasingly bureaucratized and directed toward elite athletics and international prestige, while over the next decades public recreational participation in sport declined steadily. Alberta's dependence on the oil economy, and shifts in political ideologies concerning public services, has shaped the involvement in sport of civic and provincial governments over intermittent periods of prosperity into the early 2000s.

Casual, popular activities that flourish to this day in the province have emerged, almost from the beginning of European settlement, alongside more formal organizing strategies. Beginning mainly in the mid-1870s, virtually every mainstream amateur sport followed patterns of order set out earlier by central Canadian organizations.[2] Meanwhile, commercial, professional versions emerged by 1905 as new technologies and urban cultures fostered the pleasures of spectatorship. Amateur and recreational activities were definitively divided from elite professional sport, but all levels of play were subject to centralized administration at civic, regional, or national levels. As the twentieth century progressed, advances in transportation and communication carried games and their audiences beyond their hometowns. Particularly in team sport, the broadened scope of participation and competition meant the formation of allegiances, tensions, and mythic rivalries that sometimes endure to the present. All of these factors raise questions about the nature of cultural development in a region that, while in many respects a frontier, was essentially a product of modernity. A history of sport is one way that we can trace how the concurrence of circumstances shapes local culture.

⦙ FIRST NATIONS
DISPLACED TRADITIONS

As is the case in the rest of the country, the history of sport in the region begins with traditional Aboriginal games and ceremonies and the way these were adapted and merged into the sports of colonists and settlers. A lack of written records limits mainstream understanding of these histories, but oral tradition and observation suggests that First Nations peoples of the Prairies valued physical endurance, strength, stoicism, and skill. Sport was a way to toughen men and to develop skills and bravery for combat. There were special games for women, and children's games prepared them for adult roles. The role of sport in these communities appears to have been very like that in late medieval Europe, where games had an informal and communal character with rules legitimated by tradition. Often elders were referees, but a high level of physical contact and rough play was tolerated and expected.[3]

Lacrosse, in particular, developed skills useful in combat and provided a means to resolve conflict without war. Traditionally, there were few set rules governing play. The shape of the stick, the size of the ball, the number of players, the size of the field, the goals, and the length of the game were all decided by those involved. Euro-Canadians, who encountered the game without a cultural understanding of the integration of sport into broader dimensions of Aboriginal culture, typically viewed it as a frivolous distraction from useful labour and assimilation into mainstream society. An interest in lacrosse grew in the mid-nineteenth century and settlers adopted the game, as they did others such as foot racing, according to principles and rules that directly or tacitly excluded First Nations and Métis men from partici-pating (not incidentally because they usually won.)[4]

Federal governments also controlled Aboriginal access to sport, mainly in the service of national assimilation. For example, early-twentieth-century legislation constrained Alberta Aboriginal peoples' leisure time activities by restricting their attendance at dances, rodeos, and fairs, where sports were usually integral. Traditional gatherings, which also involved games, were repressed, and Euro-Canadian sports days were substituted in First Nations communities. Such events became more significant after off-reserve dancing was banned in 1914. Officially approved sports days were opportunities to gather for friendly competition at a time when First Nations people were largely confined to reservation territories. These events would also divert spectators from the clandestine religious ceremonies and other traditional pursuits made possible by larger gatherings.[5]

As federal regulations discouraging Aboriginal sports participation have largely been repealed, today's First Nations leaders have linked participation in sport to the well-being of individuals and communities. In 2007, teacher and lacrosse coach Russ Sheppard and an Inuit student named Aviak organized youth lacrosse in the reserve community of Hobbema. For Louis Bull band children, it was the first team sport available, and, as they took to it with a passion, school attendance improved significantly. Many went on to organize other activities both entrepreneurial and recreational.[6] Other programs also attest to the power of organized sport to benefit Aboriginal youth, and through them, entire communities. As Janice Forsyth and Kevin B. Wamsley point out, Aboriginal leaders have inverted the process of assimilation through sport by achieving self-determination through their organization of Indigenous Games events.[7] A 2003 Canada-Alberta funding initiative established the Indigenous Sport Council Alberta in an effort to increase grassroots participation. Sport is a key component of the Alberta Future Leaders program, which brings programs to youth in Métis and First Nations communities.[8] Alberta also participates in related community programs supported by Canadian Heritage. In sport, as in other spheres, then, Aboriginal peoples applied expertise and endurance in adapting to changing circumstances. Many

Aboriginal athletes made their mark in sport history in the twentieth century, particularly as runners, rodeo and later hockey stars. The history of Aboriginal sport in Alberta remains to be written, and Aboriginal women's sport has been particularly overlooked, but upcoming chapters discuss modern and contemporary phenomena.[9]

FROM FORTS TO FACILITIES

1870s–1930s

Howard Palmer and Tamara Palmer divide the Alberta settlement era into civilizing (1870–1885), frontier (1880–1896), and immigration and "boom" periods (1896–1913).[10] The roots of regional sport developed even earlier among men stationed at remote North West Mounted Police (NWMP) and Hudson's Bay Company (HBC) posts, where Mounties and traders organized games as physical and social outlets for homesick, restless men. Pastimes at Fort Macleod, Fort Edmonton, Fort Saskatchewan, and Fort Calgary variously included rugby, cricket, baseball, track and field, soccer, polo, lacrosse, hockey, and horse racing. They also established the social role of team sports and competition in nearby small communities. Occasionally, there were incentives to participation; in 1876 the Fort Macleod garrison awarded cash prizes totalling $280 to police, settlers, and Native people.[11] In Medicine Hat, 1886, the NWMP won the first North-West Territories organized cricket tournament; four years later, a civilian club involving most of the town's rising young businessmen was formed to promote the sport.[12]

Developing a sports culture in often inhospitable circumstances presented unique challenges as people created tennis courts, cricket pitches, curling ice, and baseball fields out of harsh landscapes and climates. Young males, the majority of the first wave of settlers, tirelessly expended considerable resources in "constantly searching for new and exciting ways to enjoy their new home."[13] Amid unpredictable conditions, an "intense desire to organize their lives" was reflected in the establishment of numerous teams, alongside fraternities, lodges, schools, and churches. Small towns often had trouble sustaining

Blackfoot people race riders at the High River races, n.d. [GA NA-466-28]

literary societies or libraries but the "sociability starved" enthusiastically met at sports fields and arenas.[14] In areas that served a high proportion of transient workers, such as oil and coal communities like Turner Valley, organized sports joined gambling and drinking as social highlights. For small centres, such as Hanna, sport helped to create solidarity and a sense of place, bringing diverse people together in a common interest and helping to ameliorate the difficult conditions of rural life.[15]

Leisure developed within an infrastructure that included a large rural population, certain types of work and available resources of time, money, and technologies. As settlement expanded in 1880s Alberta, community sport reflected an imported British upper-middle-class leisure culture that involved fox hunting, polo, cricket, and tennis; this cultural focus continued into the 1940s.[16] One of the first sports taken up by settlers in the south was horse racing. Local Blackfoot (Siksika) people participated in races such as those at High River around the turn of the century. Ranch life was especially occupied with sports, to the point where they dominated social life. A visiting woman complained in a letter home that "polo and cricket and hockey and tennis...seem to embrace about all the capabilities of most of the Sheep Creek people."[17]

Non-British sport such as hockey, baseball, or skating gradually became more accessible to working people in the late nineteenth century. The Irish focused on rugby, field hockey, and lacrosse. The Scots influence, particularly evident at early NWMP and HBC posts, is reflected in golf and curling, and by the Highland Games held inter- mittently in Alberta since Edmonton's first annual Caledonian Games in 1909.[18] By the late 1880s, there was so much sporting activity in southwest Alberta that the *Macleod Gazette* presciently advised towns to compose non-conflicting schedules. In Red Deer, a town of less than 400 people, competitive team sports started in 1897 with cricket, baseball, and football, followed by organized lawn tennis and skating competitions (to say nothing of the informal games played by both adults and children). Fairgrounds and agricultural exhibitions across the province featured hockey, football, cricket, and lacrosse matches, as well as basketball and horse racing.[19]

In the early twentieth century, sport culture generated the inven- tion of new rules, techniques, and equipment supporting a wide range of opportunities to participate in (or watch) hockey, curling, ski jumping, boxing, basketball, bowling, pool and billiards, skating, snow- shoeing, volleyball, badminton, table tennis, swimming, wrestling, and other sports. Larger centres supported various leagues for men, women, boys, and girls. Organization was made possible, as well as necessary, by a rapid population increase from the late 1890s as the agricultural economy expanded rapidly; the province's population grew and waned with economic conditions, but in 1911 it numbered 274,000 people— Calgary with 44,000 and Edmonton 31,000.[20]

The pre–World War I enthusiasm that had Albertans involved in nearly thirty different organized sports was undermined by the Prairie-wide economic recession of 1913 and, within a few years, the loss of a majority of able athletes to the military. Following the war, "the political stability and relative prosperity of Alberta no doubt did much to secure the concurrence, albeit passive, of the non-British peoples with this circumstance, in particular migrants from the devastated regions of Eastern Europe."[21] As the province became more culturally and socially diverse, participation in major sports began to cut across class, ethnic, and rural-urban lines. For many immigrants in developing towns and rural areas, sport offered a route to equality and social acceptance.

Postwar economic stability nurtured the revival of interest in sports as the transition from pioneer life brought shorter urban working hours and improvements in agricultural technology yielded more rural leisure. Access to private vehicles and new highways extended the range of team travel and freed game schedules from the older network of fixed railways. In an emerging mass leisure culture, larger formal organizations and established playing circuits superseded small-scale neighbourhood matches. Growing cities could also (sometimes just barely) support professional teams. The special facilities that were built for both amateur and professional team sport energized a new urban sports culture. Indoor arenas and other venues, for instance, meant that cities could schedule competitions year-round.

With the expansion of a commercial entertainment industry, new mass audiences developed, both for live games and the new medium of radio. Professional sport's decline after the 1920s has been attributed in part to the effect of radio drawing away increasing numbers of spectators from live games, local teams losing players to the pros, and the Depression's curtailing effects on leisure spending and travel for competition.[22] However, amateur and minor sport continued to be a central part of recreational social life in both small towns and cities.

BOOMS AND BUSTS

1945–1980s

For players and spectators, organized sport may satisfy needs for focus and continuity during times of social uncertainty; during the mid-century decline in adherence to traditional religion and the continuing expansion of leisure time, sport became even more central to popular culture in North America.[23] In Alberta, population numbers increased significantly following World War II; Edmonton, for instance, grew by almost 80,000 people after 1945, reaching almost 200,000 by 1955. This population combined with the new oil-driven prosperity after 1947 meant that more middle-class urban people took up recreational and spectator sports, and professional teams became a symbol of a city's new confidence and affluence. The Calgary Stampeders' Grey Cup victory of 1948 and the Edmonton Eskimos' dynasty of the 1950s inspired fervent fan loyalties. Several athletes and organizers built on their public profiles to become political leaders and public figures, including Peter Lougheed, Don Getty, and Norman (Normie) Kwong, all of the Eskimos, and Percy Page, who headed the Edmonton Grads basketball organization.[24]

The oil boom of the 1970s saw unprecedented government investment in cultural development and recreation, both to occupy the energies of large numbers of "baby boomer" youth and to project modern metropolitan status.[25] Although a severe recession followed in the 1980s, Alberta boosted its international profile by hosting several major sporting events, including the Commonwealth Games in Edmonton in 1978 and Universiade in 1983; Calgary's successful production of the Winter Olympics in 1988 publicized the province worldwide. The promoters of these mega-events broadcast the image of Alberta's evolution from a remote frontier to a complex, modern society plugged into a global culture. Edmonton's profile was also enhanced by successful professional hockey and football dynasties in the 1970s and 1980s.[26] But by the end of the century the bleak economic realities of sustaining "world-class" teams and infrastructure in relatively small markets had become apparent.

FEMALES ON THE FIELD
WOMEN AND ORGANIZED SPORT

The authors of a 1994 local history of Lethbridge describe a 1925 photograph of a group of women playing softball in a field outside the city. It was a common pastime for old and young, male and female, and no one paid much mind to this game except for a few observers who looked more closely at the players. Suspicion arose that this was the "sporting subculture" of prostitutes about which alarm had recently been raised in the city. It remains unknown whether these were local prostitutes or, according to another interpretation, a church group.[27]

Whoever these women were, the sport would have been a way for them to assemble as a group, and to enjoy exercise and friendly competition during periods when both were curtailed for women in their daily public lives. Although sportswomen were expected to stay modest, polite, and feminine both on and off the field, and those who did enter elite competition were barred from professional status, most found that within these constraints they were free to enjoy sports of their choice. Sport has been an important, though often unrecognized, site of negotiation for women's rights to involvement in the public sphere. The progress toward equity in sports for North American women has been attributed to factors including the rise of feminism, the supportive role of government and sporting organizations, and the increase in female sporting role models.[28] In Alberta, specific characteristics of European settlement and climate, and vagaries of history, including war and economic depression, also shaped the level and nature of athletic pursuits for women.

Mixed softball team playing in the river valley, Lethbridge, 1925. [GMA 19760235007]

While fighting for suffrage and temperance between 1867 and 1914, middle-class North American women also found time to advocate for parks, playgrounds, recreation, and public health programs. But neither health nor emancipation campaigns typically addressed the realm of sport.[29] Some men, such as basketball inventor James Naismith, supported the participation of women in competitive sport, but many organizers and institutions resisted the notion. Women's hockey, baseball, and basketball teams, though they often attracted large numbers of spectators, were not taken as seriously by organizers and sponsors as were men's teams. Prior to World War I, in any case, most middle- and working-class women could not afford the time or money for serious involvement and were unlikely to have been overly concerned about access. In the next decades though, urban life and new technologies freed more women to pursue leisure pursuits, and choices of what to do and how to do it looked more important.

World War I was a turning point for women's entry into public life. Different kinds of workplaces and sports facilities were opened to females, often for the first time, and they started grassroots clubs, organizations, and leagues. Most popular were basketball, curling, golf, ice hockey, and tennis, which became organized to the point of supporting championship competition.[30] Social institutions successfully channeled physical activity into approved formats. Public schools consistently provided platforms for girls' participation in sport, as did their increasing enrolment in secondary and post-secondary institutions with organized teams. As was the case for men, elite-level amateur and professional sport brought increasing restrictions and regulations. In 1914, the Amateur Athletic Union of Canada (AAUC) segregated women's sports and advised them to limit themselves to respectable, non-contact pastimes.

The YWCA organization, originally offering urban women shelter, education, and a place to gather "between shopping tours and the luncheon hour," promoted physical fitness for moral well-being and the "upbuilding of perfect womanhood."[31] As well as providing indoor space and urban facilities, Calgary's YWCA built a chalet in Banff in the 1920s to provide for outdoor excursions and fresh air to counter the negative effects of city life. Though empowering for many women, YWCAS continued for decades to bar non-Anglo immigrant and African-Canadian women, among others. In the 1930s, working-class women were finally invited to join when fitness became viewed as an instrument to increase physical efficiency and improve their service abilities.[32]

The rising popularity of women's sport in the 1920s was evident in the scope of media coverage, higher than at any other time in the century. Women's polo, for instance, was followed seriously by sportswriters and spectators. By this time, Alberta women had access to provincial, regional, and Dominion championships in various events. These did not involve contact or rough play; women interested in such competitive team sports "were thought to be ahead of their time,"[33] an uncomplimentary sentiment. These barriers became more entrenched with the contemporary boom in men's professional and spectator sport. As a mass popular culture emerged in North America, the cultural production of sport as a realm of power and status furthered what Bruce Kidd calls a "symbolic annihilation" of women within it.[34] This was, of course, a familiar pattern affecting women's presence in many activities in the public sphere, but the institutions and systems of codified rules in organized sport makes those threads particularly visible.

Despite broadly restrictive practices, women remained keen participants in recreational and amateur sports. And as athletic opportunities developed in the interwar period, female athletes worked to take control of administering and shaping their own sports organizations. In 1931, women members of the Alberta Amateur Hockey Association, called the Ladies Hockey Club, made plans to form their own organization "in order to function to a greater advantage."[35] The Women's Amateur Athletic Foundation (WAAF), established in 1926, built a coast-to-coast network in seven sports. Although women's clubs were less concerned with producing victorious teams and star individuals than with organizational autonomy, the WAAF laid the foundation for international successes, such as the track team entry in the 1928 Olympics. By 1939, the organization was larger than the male-run AAUC.[36]

During the 1920s, the Canadian sport media were far more supportive of women athletes than was the case in the United States where the media were more male-dominated.[37] But despite (or possibly due to) successes in organizing a parallel universe of sport, by the mid-1930s it was rare to see extensive coverage of women's sports in newspapers. Three pages on sports in a July 1938 edition of the *Albertan* included only three items on women's activities: a track meet in Toronto, softball in British Columbia, and lawn tennis in Dublin.[38] Apparently continuing to assume the absence of public interest, by 1955 the *Edmonton Journal* sports section ran articles on hockey, cricket, curling, boxing, football, baseball, golf—but typically very few of them mentioned women.[39] What coverage there was tended to be accompanied by photographs designed to showcase well-groomed beauty and sexual appeal. The image of Pat Fleming, a track star of the 1940s, is a case in point.

In 1961, Marjorie Eustace, the first woman to be chosen as "athlete of the year" by the Calgary Booster Club, had to have her husband accept her trophy because women were still barred from the club's premises. But after a decline in advocacy for women's sport since the Depression period, the growth of the women's movement in the 1960s extended to challenging social barriers to "the most male dominated sphere of all."[40] Covering the Calgary Sports Women Association's fifth annual awards dinner for Alberta junior and senior athletes in April 1966, the *Herald*'s magazine editor (also a sportswriter) commented that their achievements contradicted any suggestion that "the West is, and always has been nothing but rugged, he-man country." By the mid-1960s, this news would seem to have been common knowledge. Judy LaMarsh, then secretary of state, was guest speaker at the event, as was Charlotte Whitten, past mayor of Ottawa, in a previous year.[41]

In the following decades, women's team sport flourished at the grassroots level, and government support was institutionalized following landmark events such as the 1970 Royal Commission on the Status of Women in Canada and the first National Conference on Women and Sport in 1974.[42] Although news coverage of women's sport remained sparse in the 1960s, and growing fitness movements of the 1970s targeted appearance more than physical strength and competitive edge, by the 1980s the growth of female team sports increased participation and media attention. The semi-governmental agency, the Canadian Association for the Advancement for Women and Sport and Physical Activity (CAAWS), was founded in 1981 to foster participation in competitive sport. In the 1990s, women's sports moved from a concern with equality of opportunity to one of equity, or a focus on changing the sports system itself to accommodate women. As more established organizations opened to girls and women, CAAWS became a national advocacy group.[43]

Generally, women have excelled in amateur and recreational team sports and individual performance sports, but not had many

Pat Fleming at the Canadian Track and Field Championships in Edmonton, July 25, 1947.

[CEA EA-600-260C]

opportunities to pursue professional careers. There have been a few exceptions—hockey and basketball teams well-known in their time, and individual stars in swimming, skating, tennis, and curling—but after World War II women involved in sport did not receive the legitimation through media coverage or popular recognition that would have ensured an ongoing high profile. Kidd, in a discussion of official sports museum narratives, notes that women are underrepresented in halls of fame. As mainstream sport became a commercial cultural production, the focus was ever stronger on men's sport as consumer product. The interests of continental and metropolitan capitalism, according to Kidd, helped to smother the brand of "assertive womanhood encouraged by the WAAF."[44]

Outside any statistical accounting of victories, Alberta women athletes have helped to challenge the social construction of male superiority by entering sports and succeeding in competition in great numbers.[45] Although Canadian women may have entered sport in fewer numbers, when the scope of events and team size are considered they have usually outperformed the country's men in international competition.[46] Their inability to pursue professional athletic careers may have actually encouraged them into a range of different sports rather than focusing on one specialty.

⋮ CONCLUSION

The perceived social value of sport rests on rationales of social cohesion, civic identity, public health, and so on to support its entitlement to collective community resources. Undermining these broad appeals are arguments that organized sport supports private, elite, and patriarchal powers, and, on the other hand, weakens democracy by diverting public attention from pressing social issues with gladiatorial circuses. As state support and funding increases to broaden access to cultural activity, and official institutions co-ordinate the boundaries and opportunities provided, knowledge and attitudes are organized in specific ways. Institutions and organizations appear increasingly neutral and natural in their activities, while citizens are represented as an aggregate, or social body, made up of varied but interdependent domains of interest.[47] These broad patterns are apparent in the early development of Alberta's sports culture in the context of British influences on ways of thinking about and managing leisure activity. The next chapter traces social institutions and ideologies at work in this process.

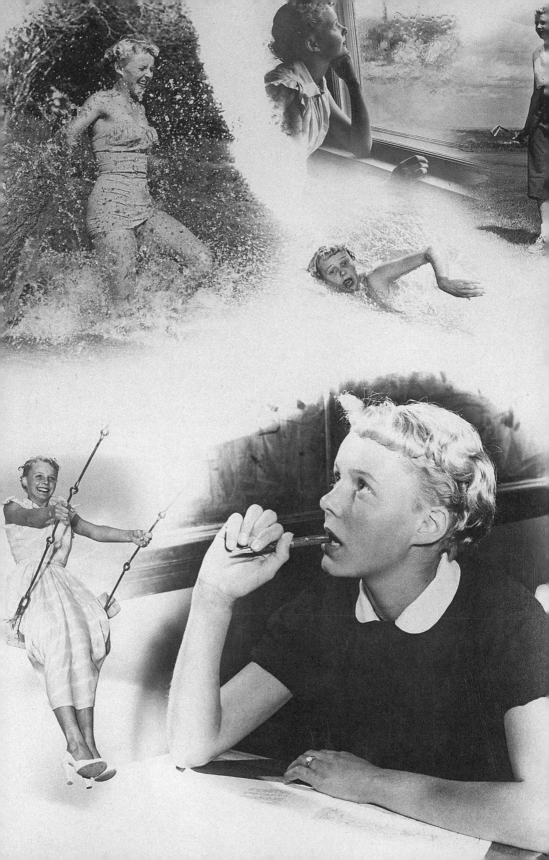

3

FENCING THE FIELDS
ORGANIZING PRINCIPLES AND SOCIAL ORDER

ONE SCHOOL RECESS PERIOD in the 1940s, young Denny May and
Jerry Hyndman of Edmonton were "sitting on the teeter-totter—
talking about important things—sharing experiences and ideas. The
principal, Mr. Stockwell, came out one day and said to us 'if you two
don't participate in sports you will never amount to anything' and he
gave us a baseball. We invented our own sport—sitting on the teeter-
totter, throwing the ball back and forth. Mr. Stockwell gave up."[1]

The social order within which a sporting culture develops deter-
mines the acquisition of cultural and economic capital, including
appropriate values and opportunities to pursue leisure activities. In
school settings, for example, sport functions as cultural capital as it
socializes youth into preferred behaviours; participating in group
activities also develops social capital, defined by Pierre Bourdieu as
"the aggregate of the actual or potential resources which are linked

to possession of a durable network...which provides each of its members with the backing of the collectivity-owned capital."[2] Codes of discipline, self-restraint, and fair play that now seem intrinsic to Anglo-American sport were shaped largely in a crucial nexus of culture, politics, and economics in the Victorian era. Mr. Stockwell was the bearer of, not only a baseball, but a powerful legacy of thought concerning the role of sport in socializing children.

From the late nineteenth century into the twentieth, ideals of amateur "sport for sport's sake" aligned with tenets of rational recreation, moral improvement, and social control derived from British urban contexts. The "playground movement" targeting urban children was part of the notion that leisure time, like other aspects of public culture, was a vehicle for improving the health and morality of the urban working classes. To those concerned with public life in an industrial, urbanizing culture, people of the working classes appeared to be undisciplined, unhealthy, and potentially unruly. Sports and games had particular potential for uncontrolled physicality, which could be made orderly with the imposition of rationalized rules, codes of teamwork, and appropriately controlled time and playing space. So-called "play discipline" refined the unruly pastimes of everyday life and turned leisure time into a useful tool for the proper socialization of both children and adults.[3] The structures and practices of modern sport, largely a British invention, followed the empire in the late nineteenth century and "went forth to conquer the world."[4]

Anglo-American notions, elaborated and adapted in Canada, sent out flexible but tenacious roots into the popular leisure culture of what would become the province of Alberta. By the early twentieth century, though, North American organizers viewed recreational team sports more as forces for social levelling or democratic leisure. The contemporary doctrine of environmentalism suggested that social institutions directly instilled character and behaviours, and recreation policies aimed to nurture correct moral standards and citizenship. Idleness could undermine and sport could reinforce preferred British norms of good character, which included specific criteria of "manliness" and honour.

Properly supervised physical activity was a key ingredient in networks of moral reform, public health, and leisure disciplines. Their significance extended far beyond the provision of choices for unoccupied time. In the summer of 1912, for example, Elizabeth Bailey, an influential local writer and journalist interested in progressive social reform, advised the mothers of Calgary to keep their children away from the "lure of the streets." This was particularly dire for older children who were likely to turn to, among other things, moving picture shows for entertainment. There they would encounter degrading, rough, and probably grotesque matters, as they would in rough spontaneous play. Bailey commended the city's action in providing playgrounds suitable, instead, for "the highest mental and physical development."[5]

These ideals were prevalent, not only in ideas about raising children, but by extension in thought about the role of sport in developing a cohesive modern culture out of a dynamic and evolving new society. The process was not uniform or universal, but for the most part the co-ordination of sport was anchored by family life, churches, schools, and leisure organizations. Public recreation and educational institutions co-ordinated relationships between games, players, and passions at a key point in the transition to urban industrial society. By 1885, Canadian sports culture comprised aspects of recreation, amateur competition, and commercial spectacle. The Queen's Birthday sports days held across the country, for example, offered events for all community members in the context of socializing and celebration. At fairs like these, sport helped to link local cultural life to national custom and identity, while providing welcome popular diversion. National industrial development policies brought settlers and railroads to western Canada. Work was central to everyday life, but leisure was also medium of community formation. Institutions such as schools, churches, and community organizations espoused immediate goals of public health and vitality, but in the long term were also deeply concerned to shape understandings of the social body through the ordering of categories of class, ethnicity, race, and gender. Both results benefited those with a stake in building prosperous, cohesive communities.[6]

⋮ SPORT AND SOCIAL INSTITUTIONS

CHURCHES

Doctrines of "muscular Christianity" were influential in Alberta as in Protestant cultures in Britain and America. Between roughly 1880 and 1920, many Alberta Protestant churches propounded versions of the philosophy, a value-centred concept of sport that linked virtue and athleticism. Invigorating exercise and competitive games would refine the physical temple of the spirit, and selected team activities were considered wholesome. Reverend Robert Pearson, for example, was active in promoting and administering sport in Alberta, and in 1914 addressed an audience in Calgary on the connection between physical health, a "wholesome life," and the development of moral conscience. Pearson warned that "the boy who goes wrong is not the leader in sport, but the quiet lad who wanders around by himself. Social progress and athletics should always go hand in hand." The *Journal*'s report praised the gospel of muscular Christianity's capacity to shape the citizens of tomorrow into "a source of strength to the state" and happiness to themselves.[7] Bruce Kidd points out that, although muscular Christianity is often associated with right-wing politics, in Canada it was linked to the left through the social gospel movement, and influenced progressive social change. It was central to the mission of the original YMCAs, for instance, and its influence is still evident in the holistic philosophies of Canadian amateur organizations.[8]

Church-sponsored sports events and facilities also happened to attract men to the pews, particularly when they allowed Sunday play.[9] Church-organized sports clubs in Alberta often became launching grounds for broader participation and training. Churches sponsored baseball, basketball, and hockey for both males and females. In 1916, for instance, the Victoria Girls' Hockey Team of First Presbyterian Church played the National Girls' Team at Edmonton's Diamond Park. And building on church support for tennis, the entire province was divided into tennis districts of dozens of towns holding interclub games. Mormons were the first Americans to bring basketball training and facilities to the region beginning in the 1870s, after emigrating from Utah to avoid persecution for polygamy. The *Vancouver Sun* noted that in 1924 Edmonton was a "great basketball centre." Anticipating a tournament that attracted nearly 400 entries, the writer described the Alberta team as a "polygamous quintette" of "five strapping Mormons" all over six feet tall. Although the church abandoned the practice in 1890, the *Sun*'s reference suggests that stereotypes endured.[10]

Protestant groups were particularly supportive of curling. The *Canadian Curler's Manual* praised the sport as appropriately Christian, calling up "none of the low and degrading passions of our nature,"[11] and special curlers' church services were common in prairie centres. Bonspiel sermons across North America at the time, and up to the 1970s in some places, explored the spiritual significance of curling as a metaphor for daily life (and death). A typical exhortation from 1896 New York urged "more of community of feeling, more brotherhood... have feeling for the tramps, for they, too, are in the bonspiel...I fear a great many men play the game of life with no thought, no calculation...Out with such aimlessness!...Better pursue a mistake boldly, courageously, deathlessly, as King James IV of Scotland did when he played the last bonspiel on Flodden field and died in glorious defeat."[12] Virtually every curling club on the Prairies appointed a chaplain to provide moral and spiritual direction to players, as well as to pitch in on the ice. The 1909 Calgary church parade featured forty-three curling teams marching from the Alberta Rink to Knox Church to hear a sermon by the Reverend Fortune. Reverend Dr. MacRae, at the 1909 annual meeting of the Alberta Branch of the Canadian Curling Association, appealed for less commercialism in the "royal game," so far not entirely permeated by professionalism and crookedness (usually considered interchangeable). One of the first appointments to the Alberta Curling Association, established in 1917, was that of Reverend Dr. McQueen, the only remaining member of the original 1891 Edmonton Curling Club.[13]

Church sponsorship did not dampen curling's social aspects. In 1898, Norman McLeod and three friends from Lethbridge decided to attend the Calgary bonspiel, wearing "big blue fishermen's jerseys with 'Use Galt Coal' emblazoned on the breasts...We arrived safely and put up at the Alberta, which I am sure we shall all gratefully remember because of the strong spiritual encouragement furnished us by Fred Adams and Tom Speers in the bar."[14] Bonspiel sermons eventually dropped from schedules, but social events remained important. In 1920, when an Edgerton team won the Wainwright bonspiel, local women raised funds for the prize of buffalo meat by selling dinner tickets.[15] When Beiseker's Mayor Lount opened the town's first curling club in 1940, he praised the sport as "a game of friendliness, a game that creates much kindness and establishes a brotherhood, resulting in a healthy, moral and spiritual relationship in our community."[16]

PUBLIC RECREATION

Other foundational early-twentieth-century organizations including YWCAS and YMCAS, Scouting, Guiding, and community leagues also co-ordinated youth programs in physical education, gymnastics, and games on the Prairies. Ideals of moral improvement were lashed into institutional programming, but for those patrons given a choice, Bible instruction played to a lot of empty seats.[17] The most successful adult-organized activities for youth in 1920s Edmonton were team sports and related events. Young males, and many females, took up baseball, basketball, and hockey in large numbers.

Edmonton was the first Canadian city to establish community leagues (1907), and the Edmonton Federation of Community Leagues (EFCL) formed in 1921. Based on the American model of social centres, a politically focused socialistic movement for grassroots empower-ment, Canadian community leagues were usually supported by public funds and tended to emphasize social unity through collective play and "sports for all." With sports a priority, the EFCL started a hockey program in 1917, and various leagues went on to sponsor football, baseball, basketball, and other activities. In 1922, Crestwood Community League was the first neighbourhood to win municipal designation of recreational land, and eventually established its own curling rink for Jewish people, who at the time were excluded from other clubs. By 1924 the city had twenty community leagues, mostly sports-oriented, that incorporated many commercial and private sports clubs. In the name of widespread access, the federation convinced the school board to raise grant monies for rinks and in 1933 even approved Sunday hockey playing.[18]

Civic and provincial governments also directly supported teams and public facilities, including the country's first municipal golf courses in first decades of the century. Government workers of the 1920s were organized as the Civil Services Athletic Association,[19] in part a response to a strong postwar citizens' movement lobbying for provincial administration of sport and recreation. Since the 1970s, the Alberta ministry responsible for culture has included the portfolio of community recreation and sport, and cultural and athletic activities are both funded through lottery grants.

EDUCATION

Public educational systems across the country were influenced by the ideas of Egerton Ryerson, who, as Ontario's first supervisor of education in the 1840s, promoted physical training to cultivate mental prowess. Western provinces focused on drill and calisthenics in the late nineteenth century, and no Canadian school curricula offered games or sports. Following World War I, Alberta school curricula emphasized physical health, morality, and a commitment to democratic citizenship, loosely identified with "sportsmanlike" behaviour such as individual achievement, fair competition, and co-operation.[20] Alberta public schools also employed sport as a powerful medium for assimilating non-English immigrants. Sport "Canadianized immigrant children, [establishing] connections between objects and words through practical experience…The children were quick to learn words such as 'bat, ball, base.'"[21] According to a contemporary education official, school games were considered beneficial "both because of the effect of dissipating the stolidness of [Slavic] pupils…and in making them more approachable and amenable to the subtle influences of comradeship and rivalry."[22] As children adopted the prescribed language, emotional attitudes, and social behaviours of games, they were socialized as members of mainstream society.

Most high schools and training institutes sponsored and coached teams at all levels for both boys and girls, and in 1927 Calgary Normal Schools sponsored six ladies' hockey teams of future teachers.[23] A developing network of competitions and championships mirrored a developing professional sport culture. Various supervisory groups formed and re-formed, and the Alberta Schools' Athletic Association (ASAA) emerged in Calgary in March 1956 to co-ordinate school sport in the province. In the decades following, supported by provincial government and corporations, the ASAA co-ordinated athletic programs in educational settings; as of 2010, the ASAA sponsored thirty-two provincial championships, directly involving over 8,000 participants in twelve activities.[24]

Building on the public school foundation, post-secondary institutions have proved to be important training grounds for elite amateur and professional athletes, as well as for coaches and teachers. Both men and women in university athletics could progress from informal to intramural to intercollegiate competition, and some elite athletes have gone on to professional or amateur careers. University sport developed across Canada from 1906 to 1919; composed only of universities from Ontario and Quebec, the original Canadian Interuniversity Athletic Union (CIAU) Central was founded in 1906 and existed until 1955. The Universities of Manitoba, Saskatchewan, and Alberta were charter members of the 1920 Western Intercollegiate Athletic Association (WIAA), the first recognized western-based post-secondary athletic organization in Canada. Intervarsity exhibition play began in 1922.[25]

School closing montage published in The Albertan, *June 30, 1954. Although a schoolgirl is portrayed as the daydreamer, the images are of grown women, probably the intended readership.*

[GA NA-5600-7623A]

Patrick Harrigan suggests that the history of intercollegiate sport is particularly relevant to how the traditional gender role expectations of women students (until recently, mainly white and middle-class) influenced their athletic experiences. Since 1908, women have been involved in sport in Alberta colleges and the University of Alberta, including its southern branch, which was established in 1960 and became the University of Calgary in 1966. Despite obstacles such as inadequate facilities, male-dominated press, limited spectator support, and insufficient funding, varsity sports provided women with good training and competition. Although Canadian women's intercollegiate sport was influenced by this shift in priorities, it was not curtailed. However, the goals of competition were de-emphasized for several decades to come.[26]

The U of A's women's intervarsity hockey team, known as the "Puckettes," endured from 1922 until World War II, when women's sports virtually vanished from campus until a resurgence in the 1970s. After operating at the club level, women's hockey again became a varsity sport in 1997.[27] Basketball was strong in the 1920s, the men's team winning the provincial championship in 1922 and 1923. Several women basketball players went on to join the legendary Edmonton Grads, though varsity players were responsible for one of the rare losses by the star team. In 1925, a team called the Varsconas, which included women from previous university squads, beat them by a score of 22 to 18. The *Edmonton Journal* called the event "basketball history."[28] Helen Beny Gibson, a star member of the varsity basketball team and later the Varsconas, later served as alderman in Medicine Hat and in 1967 received an honorary doctorate of laws from the University of Alberta, and in 1973 the Order of Canada.[29] Star track athlete Ethel Barnett set two new records for female Alberta athletes at the Dominion Day provincial track and field meet in 1932, although they were not credited since "none of the women's events carded were championship affairs."[30]

As contemporary news reports indicate, university athletes and sport teams were in the Alberta public eye consistently in the pre-World War II years, competing with junior and senior amateur athletes and teams in their communities. But the public visibility of university sport declined with the advent of televised international sport in the 1950s. Nevertheless, interuniversity sport developed rapidly from late in the decade, and enrolments in Canadian post-secondary institutions tripled in the 1960s.[31] Alberta's total undergraduate university enrolment grew from 7,777 in 1961 to 26,314 in 1970. The modern CIAU formed in 1961 as an umbrella organization for provincial associations, and its parallel, Canadian Women's Intercollegiate Athletic Union (CWIAU), was established in 1969. The west, like the Maritimes, had no independent women's organization and a Western Canadian Intercollegiate Athletic Association (WCIAA) meeting in Alberta in 1965 called for the Women's Intercollegiate Athletic Union (WIAU) to hold women's national intercollegiate championships. Harrigan reports that competitive ideals were stronger in the west, and westerners also were the first to promote national men's championships.[32]

Canadian women's university enrolment quadrupled in the 1960s, and numbers in Alberta grew from 2,525 to 10,693.[33] College enrolment also increased, and the Western Inter-College Conference was founded in 1964 (Alberta Colleges Athletic Conference, or ACAC, as of 1969) with five member colleges. The only officially designated activity was men's basketball, with others such as hockey and tennis at exhibition status.[34] During this period, significant numbers of both male and females rejected stereotypical constraints on female athleticism, and in 1968 the WCIAA again advocated high-level competition to the WIAU. Although many educators argued that sports were as important for women as they were for men, in 1962, Maury Van Vliet, then dean of Physical Education at the University of Alberta, introduced a motion to exclude women from the WCIAA. Although the motion was defeated, women were not influential in the organization, and women's varsity sport in the west continued to decline in the early 1970s with cutbacks to all "minor sports."[35]

The 1970 report of the Royal Commission on Women set out a framework for change, recommending, like Title IX in the United States, that principles of gender equality be applied to sport in educational institutions.[36] Canadian national intercollegiate women's championships were inaugurated in 1971. The CWIAU merged with the CIAU in 1978 (now Canadian Interuniversity Sport [CIS]), but progress remained slow; although there were over a hundred women's club teams in 1994–1995, few received financial support or access to university facilities. Harrigan concludes that "the sense of a distinctive mission and cultural imperative that female [sport] be directed by women has been subsumed into the dominant male model of competition and commercialization" in the drive to gain fans, money, television coverage, and sponsorship.[37] Male athletes tended to dominate press coverage, funding, and the better facilities at all institutions of higher education, including the University of Alberta.[38]

Within these constraints, both Alberta university women and men have excelled in intervarsity competition. Championship women's teams have come from both Edmonton and Calgary. The University of Calgary has won more Borden Ladner Gervais Awards for top male and female varsity athletes than any other school in the country. The University of Alberta is the only one to have won a national championship in each of the eleven team sports administered by the CIS, as well as the most national championships in major sports since the early 1980s.[39] The University of Alberta Pandas women's teams have also been very successful, amassing numerous awards, including two Canadian Interuniversity Athletic Union (CIAU) Coach of the Year Awards, ten CIAU All-Canadians, four CIAU Player of the Year Awards, one CIAU Rookie of the Year Award, twenty-four Canada West All-Stars, and four CWUAA Championships. Between 2008 and 2011, the *Gateway* listed Calgary as the best all-round Canadian university in sports.[40]

The University of Alberta has also produced widely influential teachers and coaches. W.H. Hardy arrived to teach classics in 1920, and linked his interest in sport to the classical importance of balancing athletic and intellectual pursuit. Hardy coached the hockey team, raised funds for the Varsity Arena (1927 to the late 1950s) and gave his name to the Hardy Cup for western Canadian university sport. Another key university figure was Clare Drake. Drake coached of the Golden

Bears hockey team for twenty-eight years. He was also the head coach
of Canada's 1980 Olympic team and originated many of the tactics and
philosophies used in today's NHL.[41] In the 1970s, the university established the first Faculty of Physical Education in the Commonwealth. In
2005, several members of the university's Faculty of Physical Education
and Recreation, and one from the University of Calgary, received a
special Centennial award given to 100 Albertans for contributions to
sport and recreation during the province's first century.[42]

Beyond the records and achievements cited by varsity sports
programs, the history of university sport provides insight into the
ongoing social debate over amateurism and core rationales for public
support of sport, as well as evidence of dissent to its uncritical promotion as a component of higher education. As North American practices
of mass physical education devoted to moulding well-balanced good
citizens diverged from those for training elite athletes by the turn of
the twentieth century, the main foci of funding and coaching turned
to cultivating superior performance for intervarsity competition. The
Carnegie Commission praised Canadian universities in the 1920s for
preserving the idea of the balanced scholar-athlete; women's sport,
in particular, was seen at the time as a sphere that should avoid the
professional, commercial character that had corrupted men's sport.[43]
North American collegiate and varsity sport developed into a prestigious public relations instrument and a symbol of institutional vitality.

Countering voices of the 1920s and 1930s, the University of Alberta's
Gateway newspaper questioned the role of sport in producing balanced,
well-developed youth. In 1920, one writer divided students into "those
who take an interest in athletics, and those...who care for studies
alone...and those who take an interest in neither."[44] Others worried
about the distraction from serious learning and other campus activities offered by spectator sports, perhaps demonstrating a certain
respect for Reverend Pearson's "quiet lad who wanders around by
himself." But a 1930 columnist complained that students were "notice-
ably lax" about showing up at weekly hockey games, and some
proposed to cancel the competing Saturday night dance (a suggestion

immediately dismissed).[45] Another argued that the ongoing lack of school spirit pointed to a sensible attitude toward athletes who were, after all, merely other students who were "better built...and...passed more time at some essential exercise."[46]

The benefits to spectators of varsity competitions, such as a healthy emotional outlet, were also questioned in comparison to those accruing to the athletes themselves.[47] Student fans may "lose their senses" and succumb to "an ecstasy of emotion" causing "our quiet, sober, intelligent, and educated men and women" to become a frenzied crowd "drunk with...a passion essentially selfish and ultimately self-glorifying."[48] And four decades later, a *Gateway* sports columnist complained of such prevalent alcohol consumption at games that university football spectators were at risk of having "a trumpet jabbed into your stomach by a falling drunk...an empty bottle...bounce off your head...[and] to have to leave the game...because your girl is afraid to stay."[49]

Those who rejected the administration's rationales for what they considered disproportionate varsity sports funding admitted in 1961 that "athletics are the most convenient means of providing a sense of belonging" but that the exchange of ideas should take precedence over the exchange of blows on a field. A mature, self-confident institution should be known primarily for academic achievement. Part of the issue was the relative value placed on recreational sport as opposed to the more elite, publicized versions; at the time, intercollegiate sport had a budget of $65,000 and involved 300 students, whereas intramural sports included ten times that many and operated at a tenth of the cost. Fine arts competitions were also in the original mandate of the ACAC, but due to lack of interest and support the cultural program ended in 1969.[50] The argument continues. J.E. Smyth, for instance, insists that athletics is still central to academe's broader purpose of producing balanced individuals, not only elite international competitors.[51]

For most people in the formative years of the province and after, sport remained a recreational pursuit deeply imbricated with everyday life and social institutions. But for athletes participating in the more elite competitions, recreational activity, sports days, and gatherings were launching pads for higher-profile events and occasionally careers. In Edmonton, for instance, the 1908 Victoria Day marathon served as the Alberta trial race for that summer's Olympic Games in England.[52] The figure of the amateur became distinct from that of the casual recreationist as organizations that were distinctly dedicated to sport began to dictate access to competition at the turn of the twentieth century. The Canadian Amateur Athletic Union (CAAU) (later the Amateur Athletic Union of Canada) formed in 1884. In 1902, the CAAU defined an amateur as a person "who has never directly or indirectly received any...money considerations whatever for any services as an athlete except his actual travelling and hotel expenses."[53] In 1908, a group of Calgary men formed a committee to supervise local Olympic tryouts. They consolidated the committee as the Calgary Amateur Athletic Association and soon formed the Alberta Branch of the Canadian Amateur Athletic Union (AAAU), which was the province's first sports umbrella group. Three years later, according to the *Edmonton Capital*, the union had "a strong hold on the better elements of the sporting fraternities of every kind....Without the organization, athletics in the province would now be in a chaotic state."[54] The leaders of amateur sport co-ordinated not only activity but also social attitudes and development strategies.

In practice, amateur codes excluded certain kinds of people from recognized competitive events. Around 1900, official sporting culture was exclusively male and bourgeois; organizers selectively showcased the games and contests best suited to the requisite disciplined, team-playing British gentleman. A set of written and unwritten rules, social attitudes, and cultural distinctions correspondingly ordered participation in sport by the working class, women, non-British ethnic groups, and Aboriginal peoples. Edmonton captain Harold Burnham's letters home to Ontario around 1910 remark on the strong local press interest in football. At the time, amateur players were consistently evaluated as much for their behaviour as for their athletic skill. Burnham, who had played rugby at McGill University and was an owner of the Burnham-Frith Electric Company on Jasper Avenue, was reported as having "made a name for himself on the Canadian gridiron, not only as a good player but as a man who plays the game on the square."[55]

According to a 1911 newspaper, the efforts of the A A AU to educate provincial athletes "to an appreciation of strict amateur principles, where before there had existed practically no principle with relation to sport, and the attempt to bring together the various interests into one whole, was by no means an easy task."[56] Despite early conflicts over codes and practices, within the first year of the organization 180 men registered as amateurs, and the A A AU issued ten permits to hold athletic meets. Individual membership soon grew to 300, but ambivalence to organizational process may be detected in an announcement of a day of meetings of both the Alberta Amateur Hockey Association and the Amateur Athletic Union of Canada. The announcement reassured readers that "nothing of any great importance" was scheduled so the meetings should not take too much time; a rugby game was scheduled to follow.[57] By the 1920s the organization represented over 1,500 athletes and thirty-one different sports groups. It played an important role in amateur sports activities over many decades, organizing the first Alberta Winter Games in 1968. The A A AU disbanded in 1971 when its functions were adopted by Sport Alberta, a voluntary federation of provincial sport agencies, which was incorporated in 1972 and dissolved in 1986 when its programs were transferred to the Alberta Sports Council and government agencies.[58]

From the beginning, however, struggles for control at various levels continued. Across the country, resistance to organization tended to come from rural areas, and support mainly from urban centres, and Alberta was urbanized relatively late. The Prairies shared several pragmatic concerns. For example, players with jobs outnumbered those of independent means and naturally resisted the restrictions on receiving compensation for wages lost while training or competing. For organizers and promoters, excluding professionals from the relatively sparse population pool meant the loss of some of the most talented players, who could attract audiences and win games.[59] Western provinces urged changes to amateur rules and regulations to accommodate such differences to sport in central and eastern Canada, and throughout the Depression, sports rivalries were vehicles for western resentment. After World War II, many amateur regulations were altered or abandoned as central organizations found merit in changes long urged by western provinces.[60]

The discourse of amateurism held sway among sports organizations and political and social leaders, while other dominant voices, including newspaper editors, churches, and educators, condemned professional sport for its perceived violence, corruption, and, into the bargain, its capacity to distract spectators from productive work. In practice, of course, amateur and minor sports have always been routes to professional careers for elite athletes. As amateur sport was increasingly organized on an intercity and regional level, developing audiences and circuits fostered the formation of professional leagues. A strict amateur ideal in Alberta team sport was no longer viable as western Canadian cities became vehicles for "the development, complete packaging, and demonstration of the professional product, easily lured out of the west by superior markets and therefore superior resources elsewhere."[61] In 1928, the AAUC warned of the deterioration of the amateur code; within a decade, professional sport, especially hockey, thrived.

Stephen Brunt discusses the consequences for social connection and identity of these patterns of modernization in sport. At one time, there was an organic link between athlete and spectators, all of whom came from the same community. The players on a team "were family or friends or neighbours, or at the furthest remove, strangers who came from the place you called home. Gathering to support them was a shared, collective purpose, like church or temple, like grassroots politics, the act of being part of a larger whole...To celebrate one of our own in competition with athletes from a place near or far away was to celebrate [a common set of] core values...asserting your place in the universe."[62] For decades, while the big leagues were distant or seemed irrelevant, connections endured between town, players, and teams at all levels. As anyone who has encountered local hockey fans when the home team is in the Stanley Cup playoffs can testify, the essential spell remains despite the knowledge that pro sport has travelled far from organic representation of community.

⋮ CONCLUSION

Like other spheres of culture, sport works to shape individual character and collective imaginations. At every turn in the history of leisure, we encounter the drive for personal agency and freedom, even if simply expressed in a boisterous pick-up game on a day off. Just as consistently there arise forms of social control, exemplified by the concerted effort to manage amateur play early in the province's history.[63] In a utilitarian society concerned with establishing economic stability and growth, the advocates of leisure had to justify time and resources spent on sports. Accordingly, imported games were adapted to a new landscape and social agenda, linking athletics to concepts of citizenship, identity, and prosperity. But even as established standards of shared culture were disseminated through sport, ideas about sport became more open to social change. Some sports originally associated with the elite lost much of their exclusivity in the region, and, by necessity, rules of participation were often broken and social norms ignored in the spirit of play. But, in general, as centralized patterns of economic production established Alberta as one of many resource hinterlands, standardized organizations, team and league formations, and competition rules developed in the context of both amateurism and commercial enterprise.

As well as by broad international forces, sport in Alberta was shaped by settlement geography, ameliorated by technology, and constrained by local socio-economic factors.[64] Amid these conditions, the deliberate and focused actions of groups and individuals, from citizens looking for diversion to power brokers looking for profit and politicians looking for votes, provide some dramatic case studies in the ways sport has influenced our ways of thinking about each other, about our towns and cities, public life, and identities.

PART II

**WRITING THE
RULE BOOK**

FROM PASTIMES TO
ORGANIZATIONS

> "The organization
> of sport in Euro-
> Canadian society
> reflects the tensions
> between centre and
> margin as well as
> local dynamics of
> power and lifestyle."

IN THE LATE NINETEENTH CENTURY, the Dominion government attracted thousands of immigrants to homestead lands on the Prairies, and, in 1905, the North-West Territories became the provinces of Alberta and Saskatchewan. Elsewhere that year, the Trans-Siberian Railway opened, Einstein formulated the theory of relativity, and the Wright Brothers kept a plane in the air for over half an hour. The Canadian Northern Railway reached Edmonton and the Liberal party won Alberta's first election. Two years later, the National Council of Women made a formal demand for "equal pay for equal work." As industrial-scale agriculture expanded along with railroads, urban settlements, property values and economic investment, imported newspapers and new mass media were linking the region to the world. Although in an early stage of material development, the province was enmeshed in metropolitan power bases. The federal government in Ottawa continued to govern

Alberta and its minerals, timber, lands, and separate schools.

The organization of sport in Euro-Canadian society reflects the tensions between centre and margin as well as local dynamics of power and lifestyle. Politicians, merchants, and land developers used sport as a keen instrument of social formation. Athletic skill could offer the individual a route to mobility and prosperity, and for working people sport was an accessible diversion. We initially focus on team sports as nurtured through the interaction of athletes, partici-pants, audiences, and promoters. The following survey of the organizational period of sport in the province moves broadly from early recreational activity to amateur and profes-sional organization. The sharply defined seasons of the prairie climate, in the days before controlled facilities, meant that there were distinct summer and winter activities.

4

"THE WEST HAS MADE FAIRLY GOOD HEADWAY"

CORE SUMMER TEAM SPORTS

⋮ **LACROSSE**

FROM NATIVE SPORT TO "NATIVE SONS"

Euro-Canadians began to play lacrosse around the mid-1800s and developed specific rules and standards in 1867 when the National Lacrosse Association was formed and the number of clubs in Canada rose from six to eighty. Although several sources trace the declaration of lacrosse as Canada's national game to 1849, it did not become the official summer sport of Canada until 1994.[1] Lacrosse was never actually formally declared Canada's national sport by act of Parliament but had equivalent popular status until the 1994 declaration. Donald Fisher describes the duality of lacrosse in the nineteenth century as it became both a middle-class "gentleman's game" associated with Victorian science and civilization, while still evoking the "noble savage" as an icon of virile Canadian manhood.[2] Like snowshoeing and tobogganing, lacrosse was an Aboriginal cultural pursuit, which separated Canadian sport from American and British sports. In adopting lacrosse, colonizers appropriated Aboriginal identity and thus legitimized their claim to the country. In practice, Native people and cultural motifs appeared mainly as propaganda at civic celebrations, parades, and royal visits. But even in the context of games, as Gillian Poulter notes, sport is a public performance, always a dialectic process between actor and audience in certain contexts and producing preferred meanings.[3] After 1885, lacrosse lost its gentlemanly associations and was increasingly associated with the image of the barbarous savage. The idea of the "noble savage" who had introduced Europeans to lacrosse lost its currency as Aboriginal peoples lost power and status with the institution of the repressive reserve system. The North-West Rebellion, led by Louis Riel, spawned fears of further conflict as the west was settled by Europeans, and reminders of Indigenous culture and strength, such as the "little brother of war," were unwelcome.[4]

Native players were commonly excluded from competition as having unfair advantages in a supposedly innate superior ability. W. George Beers, a key organizer of the game, argued that "it is a lamentable fact, that Lacrosse, and the wind for running, which comes as natural to the red-skin as his dialect, has to be gained on the part of the pale-face, by a gradual course of practice and training."[5] The distinction here between concepts of spontaneous popular activity and scientifically-planned competitive approaches reflects a central drive of organized sporting culture in this period.

The National Lacrosse Association eventually permitted Native people to participate as sport became more competitive and as skilled players became more important than maintaining social divisions. Early organizers promoted lacrosse as a quasi-romantic tradition of a violent and savage race, paying Aboriginal players to provide "exotic" demonstrations alongside important tournaments and fundraising occasions both at home and on international tours. Aboriginal athletes likely recognized the fact of their exploitation but benefits, including remuneration, outweighed such exploitation. In the long term, though, these benefits were superseded by those accruing to settler peoples. The 1926 Edmonton team name "Native Sons" referred not, as we might imagine, to the historical roots of the game but to the contemporary movement to favour Canadian born citizens over immigrants in national life.[6]

General merchants and hardware stores sold lacrosse equipment in Edmonton in 1882. A city club was organized in 1883 but disbanded in 1885 for lack of competition. The Calgary Lacrosse Club formed in 1884 and the *Calgary Herald* reported thirty players at the "grand rally of lacrossists." Potential players were urged not to be "discouraged because you feel awkward and can't catch...or throw the ball" and promised training. The club soon folded, reorganizing in 1887.[7] Organized lacrosse in Alberta and Saskatchewan developed rapidly from the 1890s on the model of centralized league structures. As was the case with virtually all early organizations, leading professional and business people drove local interest. Barrister Pat McNamara was active in lacrosse in Calgary. When he moved to Edmonton in the early 1890s, he organized a new club and signed up seventy-six members within a week.[8] (McNamara, like many sportspeople of the day, was an all-round athlete and was also president of the Edmonton bicycle club.) Intercity, regional, and national levels of competition developed from leagues based in the larger centres. In 1900, Medicine Hat won the Dominion Championship, and a lacrosse game entertained crowds at the 1905 provincial inauguration celebrations in Edmonton. A Calgary team won the first championship of a new provincial lacrosse association launched in 1907; Calgary organized at least one team that played both lacrosse and hockey, which suggests either that there were too few lacrosse players for a separate team, that a new, combined game had been invented, or simply that players did not specialize in any one sport.

In 1913, the Alberta League included teams from Calgary, High River, Medicine Hat, Strathcona, Edmonton, and Lethbridge. The Calgary

Calgary lacrosse-hockey club, ca. 1907–1908. [GA NA-1280-5]

Chinooks were Senior Lacrosse Champions of Canada in 1914, but by
that point waning spectator interest along with tensions between
amateur and professional factions had undermined the sport's growth
and it declined in popularity.[9] Perhaps as a result, there is little in the
archival record on lacrosse in Alberta after World War II. Box lacrosse,
the indoor version, is the most common version of the game in Canada
and was invented to act as a summer sport for hockey players; it is
played in a hockey arena and is similar to hockey in that each team has
five players and a goalie on the floor. The game grew all over the province during the 1930s, but by the 1950s lacrosse had almost vanished as
communities that had supported thriving clubs turned their enthusiasm to hockey. In 1974, there was a junior lacrosse league in southern
Alberta, and another formed in 1979, though the sport died out in

Lethbridge in 1982.[10] Several minor and senior leagues now operate in the province, most of them in Calgary. However, the High River Lacrosse Association, which until recently had several minor to junior teams, had insufficient registrations to form even one team in 2009. That year, minor participation numbers were down 10 to 15 per cent across the province.[11] The sport had not developed promotional strategies or the kinds of rule changes that made the game exciting to watch on television, although lacrosse attracted renewed interest as a demonstration sport at the 1978 Commonwealth Games in Edmonton,[12] and Alberta teams have won six national championships since the 1980s.

For most of the twentieth century, since lacrosse was not promoted at the grassroots level, there were too few spectators interested to sustain investment in the pro game.[13] It was not until 2001 that Calgary acquired a pro team, and Edmonton followed in 2006. Edmonton Rush owner Bruce Urban claimed optimistically that "lacrosse is now the sport of the century with a cool factor."[14] The Calgary Roughnecks have played for "over 19,000 screaming fans,"[15] and both teams built respectable records. Plagued by financial issues, though, the 2008 season was cancelled after the National Lacrosse League rejected a union bid from players, who often also held full-time jobs, to raise the maximum salary cap.[16]

POLO

LEVELLING THE FIELD

Any follower of sports history will recognize the often-passionate debates around origins, and Alberta's story includes several points of contention. Tony Rees credits rancher E.M. Wilmot of Pincher Creek with introducing polo to Alberta in 1883 and starting the first polo club in Canada in 1889.[17] But according to Simon Evans, a group of retired army officers imported the game when they settled in the area. We know that a local team, active by 1892, has claims to have been the first in North America. However, Fort Macleod organized a club that played its first game in 1891.[18] The *Macleod Gazette* urged the formation of an association to settle interclub disputes in 1894. Within a few years, the sport had caught on in small southern ranch communities, where ample flat land and horses for play were available. Ranchers were focused in part on developing new stock, and some shipped a carload of polo ponies to England in 1899.[19]

Polo peaked in popularity in the region by 1915, when twenty clubs were centred around Pincher Creek alone. Around 1900, almost every community in southern Alberta had a team, and the Sheep Creek Polo Cup circulated between them from 1901 to 1939. High River won the Canadian championships in 1905, and Pincher Creek won the 1912 western Canada championship. A 1911 three-day match in High River attracted large crowds of spectators and yielded gate receipts of $120.75.[20]

As the culture of sport came to valorize victories and revenues over idealism about character and intrinsic rewards, the less wealthy were disadvantaged by the constant need for better equipment, facilities, and finances. Polo, perhaps surprisingly, was an exception. Since polo had come from India to Britain only in the 1870s, John Varty argues, it was not necessarily linked with old money and status for contemporary British immigrants to western Canada. Its success was in part due to the amenable prairie topography and the adaptability of the sport to the intermittent leisure hours of farmers and ranchers. With a relatively sparse population, the sport also bridged social divisions as wealthy players pooled resources to subsidize more team members. And polo was one of the first competitive sports played by women; a ladies' cup was offered in Alberta, and in 1928, a Toronto man sponsored a Calgary women's team travelling to Long Island for a game.[21]

Although highly skilled teams with names like Sons of England competed across the continent at large tournaments, polo was also played recreationally by working people. The Bar U Ranche team was known as the Pekisko Polo Club (1904–1914). A visiting Australian watching the cowboys playing polo after a working day in the saddle was reminded of a Queensland team called the Gee Bong Polo Club that had similar "irregular and rash" style on "unpolished" ponies. The Bar U polo team, which adopted the same name, won a match in California against opponents who underestimated "these very highly mobile and maneuverable little horses" who were quite ready to "barge them off the ball in a rather rough and uncouth fashion."[22]

There is evidence of other creative approaches to the game; an 1880s Calgary polo team played on roller skates.[23] In this period horses were inexpensive and widely available,[24] so non-equine loco-motion may have been adopted for novelty or challenge. However, the Depression limited popular participation. Clarence Patton's account of a 1930s polo match remarked upon "some of Calgary's elite maneu-vering their steeds in an exciting game."[25]

: CRICKET [26]

"WICKETS IN THE WEST"

Cricket was one of the most popular sports among Dominion mili-tary posts before 1870 and became a pastime of what a contemporary writer called "the superior sort of colonists."[27] From the late nine-teenth century, rules and protocols of cricket were supervised by upper-class members of London's Marylebone Cricket Club. But by this period cricket was not easily accessible in British urban working-class areas due to its requisite large space, dress code, and long game dura-tion.[28] In western Canada, the game was somewhat more accessible but retained emphasis on "gentlemanly" qualities including sports-manship, manliness, and amateur fair play. The Victoria *Daily Colonist* of March 16, 1863 reported approvingly on a friendly game of cricket by "lovers of this manly exercise" before "a large number of spectators."[29] In 1879, an American writer insisted that cricket "can never be subser-vient to the evil influences of the class of gambling 'sports' who have brought such odium of late years on the national game of baseball."[30] The 1926 program for the Western Canada Cricket Association tour-nament advocated a permanent games field in Edmonton to enhance "peace and concord in [the] city...there is no game to be compared with cricket—when played in the true cricket spirit—for bringing this about."[31] Amateur ideals endured; at the end of the 1957 season, Edmonton club members decided that "although we had not done too good on the field we had a very happy team and this was the more important feature of all."[32]

The first prairie cricket club formed in Winnipeg in 1864, and Lethbridge and Pincher Creek had clubs in 1886. The Edmonton Cricket Club, now one of the oldest in the country, formed in 1882, competing against Fort Saskatchewan (1884) and later Strathcona (1893); the Canadian Cricket Association was formed in 1892. In 1901, an Edmonton team played against Calgary on a cricket pitch inside the walls of Fort Edmonton. The Millarville Cricket Club won the 1900 NWT championships. Calgary had a team in 1908, and the Alberta provincial association was established in 1910.[33] In Calgary, Ezra H. Riley donated land for a park on the condition that only cricket be played there, and construction of three pitches was begun in 1919; others were built in three city parks over the next years. In 1922, the Interprovincial Cricket Tournament was held in Riley Park.[34]

While in other countries the British form of cricket was eventually subverted and adapted by local peoples, in Canada it remained firmly rooted in imperial ideologies and amateur philosophies. (An Edmonton team called Sons of England did change its name to Borden Park in 1930.) The Marylebone Cricket Club's "gentlemen-amateurs" toured North America in the summer of 1872, and again in 1937 brought greetings "from the Mother Country" to places including Riley Park in Calgary.[35] An array of Alberta's homegrown notables and politicians associated themselves with the sport. The first Edmonton club president, Dr. Wilson, was the speaker of the Legislative Assembly of what was then the North-West Territories. In 1926, Calgary M P (later prime minister) R.B. Bennett was official patron of the Western Canada Cricket Association.[36] The Marylebone Cricket Club was still "promoting hi-grade [sic] cricket in the outposts" when it stopped in Calgary on a 2005 tour.[37]

However, cricket's elite connotations and British associations contributed to a gradual decline in popular interest. For one thing,

Canadians were rejecting British models in their quest for distinct national identity after Confederation. In America, the British discouraged sustained organization and professionalization, and Alberta was strongly influenced by American culture's embrace of baseball after the Civil War years.[38] Cricket remained a game of elites, not included in the public programs of institutions like the YMCA and YWCA. Unlike cricket, hockey, and football, which were organized by the middle and upper classes, baseball was the working man's (and woman's) sport; it could be played at all levels of skill and income and needed only simple facilities and equipment. Baseball not only had fewer class barriers but allowed professionals and rule changes that accommodated changing lifestyles, and so succeeded as a spectator sport. As well, success as an organized sport depended on a dynamic balance of good players, a fan base, and skilled administrators and promoters, all of which were lacking in Canada.[39]

The popularity of cricket peaked in the 1930s as more neighbourhood organizations and businesses sponsored teams. Organization expanded from local clubs to competitive circuits supported minimally by municipal recreation and sport funding, and by private sponsors such as Birks jewellers in Edmonton. Despite the sport's elite associations, Alberta cricketers typically struggled with "a great dearth of equipment" and of playing grounds; the Edmonton and District Cricket League league was "eternally impoverished."[40] In 1930, the Calgary and District Cricket Association appealed for public support to improve playing grounds for the upcoming Western Canada Cricket Tournament. It was the first time such an appeal had been made since the North West Mounted Police established the game at their local post. Although there were now ten clubs in the city league, in Alberta cricket did not have the support that it had in other provinces. Subscriptions were offered and the first purchaser was E.W. Beatty, president of the Canadian Pacific Railway.[41] In 1946, the Edmonton league, noting that most of its members were returned servicemen and veterans, approached several military units and requested donations of unused equipment. The league had to negotiate access to playing grounds with the city from year to year; after three decades of lobbying, in 1979 Edmonton Parks and Recreation scheduled regular time at three sites.[42]

The 1930 Western Canada Cricket Tournament, the 1961 Dominion Interprovincial Cricket Tournament (where the Edmonton Cricket Club warned its players to "ensure that Calgary does not stage the whole show"[43]), and the 1975 Canadian Interprovincial Cricket Championship were all held in Calgary. An Alberta Cricket Association (ACA) has endured into the early twenty-first century. Non-British immigration has helped to keep cricket alive in Alberta cities among Fijians, Guyanese, Trinidadians, Ismailis, and Pakistanis; West Indians who immigrated to Alberta in the late 1960s and early 1970s found cricket to be the one thing that they had in common. The St. Kitts–Nevis–Edmonton Cricket Association was founded in 1983. And in 1984 the Alberta Sport Council (now Alberta Sport, Recreation, Parks and Wildlife Foundation, which grants financial assistance to develop recreation and sport) donated several thousand dollars to ACA for leadership and participation development programs. However, in general Alberta has lacked sufficient competition, coaching, and training opportunities. Successful sport requires sustained intergenerational interest, but Alberta teams have not done well in national competition since the mid-1990s. Nevertheless, according to the Alberta Cricket Association, "youth cricket participation...exploded" in the early 2000s.[44]

⁝ BASKETBALL

HOOPS FOR ALL

Basketball started in Alberta mainly as an indoor winter pastime in the pre-World War I period as western population and urbanization expanded. By the 1920s and 1930s, men's and ladies' basketball leagues were sponsored by businesses, schools, churches, and city agencies in the larger centres. In southern Alberta, indoor basketball was an alternative to outdoor sports on unpredictable ice, which technically makes

it a winter sport, though it was played outdoors in summer. Jessie
Embry cites a game in Stirling, 1901, as the first basketball game in the
province; a team from the town won the 1914 Alberta championship.[45]
Where there were no local teams, towns supported school sports, and
the Mormons were particularly active in the region. In towns such
as Raymond, Stirling, Cardston, and Magrath, Mormon-sponsored
programs produced a disproportionate number of good players and
local teams became championship training grounds. Raymond hired
athletic directors from Utah and built two facilities: a school gymnasium and an opera house with a dance floor that also served as a court.
The Raymond Union Jacks dominated senior men's basketball for
decades, winning fifteen provincial titles between 1921 and 1941, and
the national men's championship in 1923.[46] A high school girls' team
won the provincial championships in 1950 and 1952. In the 1980s, girls'
teams won three provincial championships and the small Raymond
High School's senior boys' team, the Comets, have won the provincial title seven times since 1960. The town is intensely involved in the
team's successes; Richard Bohne, a Raymond graduate and later star
of the University of Calgary team, commented that "the game has
brought the community closer together."[47]

The YMCA and YWCA promoted basketball across Alberta, along
with churches, community leagues, schools, athletic clubs, and the
military. Following World War I the national Canadian Amateur
Basketball Association was formed, with community senior teams its
initial focus. Several men's and ladies' leagues were active in Edmonton
in the 1920s, and the men's Central Community League team were
Northern Alberta champions in 1923–1924. The YWCA hosted events
such as the Ladies Basketball ABC Studio Trophy Series Doubleheader
on Tuesday nights and regular Girls' City League games on Friday
evenings during 1941–1942. YMCA Hoop League games also played to
large audiences, and local papers printed detailed accounts of games
and league standings.[48]

Men's senior amateur and semi-professional basketball was not a
central sport in the province in the era, though. In 1949, J.N. Murdoch,

athletic director of Lethbridge's recreation centre, called a meeting to discuss starting an international basketball league as a stimulant to the sport in the province. Although Lethbridge had adequate training facilities and an established audience, neither Calgary nor Edmonton did, and the costs of travel from Edmonton especially would work against that city joining. The league was established, with six Alberta towns and cities (including Edmonton) and seven from Montana.[49] By 1954, the league was struggling, with every club "on the financial ropes" due to low attendance, high player salaries, and competition for the entertainment dollar. American clubs suggested that without financial assistance from Edmonton and Calgary, they could no longer continue "making the long trips into the Alberta country."[50]

During the 1920s, twenty-nine teams participated in the Calgary public school girls' league, and provincial championships were held annually. In Edmonton, the Morris School of Physical Culture had ladies' A and B teams. The ladies' section of the city's Mercantile Basketball League, sponsored by local businesses and the Ys, played outdoors at the Hudson's Bay Company Athletic Grounds. (The Bay sponsored a team called the Fur Trappers.) These games involved serious competition and served as training grounds for many star athletes. Doris (Neale) Chapman, for instance, was a renowned sports-woman who went on to play for the Edmonton Grads from 1929 to 1936. Members of the 1924 H B C team included well-known local athletes such as Vera Gillespie, Jean Robertson, Violet Davis, Myrtle Strong, Bessie Semple, and Kate Macrae, several of whom also played for the Grads.[51] Smaller towns combined forces to build programs; several teachers formed a league for towns around Stony Plain, for instance, in 1928; games for both boys' and girls' teams were all played outdoors for lack of gymnasiums.[52]

In the 1930s and into the 1940s, teams like the Gibson Girls from Calgary, the Eskimo Girls of Edmonton and the Pats played in senior girls' basketball leagues. The Girls' City League played Friday evenings at the Y W C A gym. Businesses in small and large towns supported women's leagues. Even with company sponsorship, though, most women's leagues were not well funded. In 1930, Alexandrine Gibb, president of the Women's Amateur Athletic Association of Canada, recommended that softball organizations not be represented on the governing board because she felt that there were not enough leagues in the Dominion. The clause was not accepted at that year's annual meeting. In September 1936, two games in Edmonton between the senior Pats and the Eskimos at the Boyle Street Grounds were advertised as "Benefit Games in Aid of Expenses of our Girl Athletes."[53]

The success of the Edmonton Commercial Graduates, known as the Grads, inspired many other young women to join the sport in the 1920s and 1930s. Gladys Nagel attended Edmonton's McDougall Commercial high school, home of the Grads basketball team. After school, she recalls, "I would walk up to the YWCA to play basketball. There was about five or six teams. Some of the Grad basketball team players came and volunteered to coach us...The team I played with the first year won the trophy. The next year I was in a team in Edmonton City League and once again we won the Alfred Blythe Studios Trophy. I also played on a softball team. I was very fond of all kinds of sports and outdoors."[54]

Catherine Macdonald, among others, has called the Edmonton Commercial Graduates Canada's most successful team of either sex.[55] (A 1975 article entitled "Edmonton Grads: 25 Years of Basketball Championships, 1915-1940" notes that the Grads won 96.2 per cent of official games played.)[56] A brochure produced by the Grads organization, "Sitting on Top of the World, 1915-1940: The Amazing Record of the Edmonton 'Grads,'" holds that the Grads won 502 of 522 official games.[57] Organized by J. Percy Page in 1914 and comprised of students graduated from the John A. McDougall Commercial High School where he was principal, the team won the vast majority—93 per cent, according to MacDonald—of their games between 1915 and 1940. This included an unprecedented 147-game winning streak and forty-nine out of a possible fifty-one domestic titles. They won their first Canadian title in 1923. That year, the Underwood Trophy was inaugurated for international women's basketball competition and won by the Grads. It was equivalent to the Stanley Cup in significance, and when the Grads

disbanded two decades later it was retired in honour of their achievements. Team member Edith Stone Sutton remembers with pride that
"hockey was a dirty word back then. We were bigger than hockey." She
recalled, the Underwood Trophy was "just as famous as the Stanley
Cup and far more so than the Grey Cup."[58] The team also represented
Canada at four Olympics between 1924 and 1936, winning all twenty-
seven of their matches (but no medals since women's basketball was
not yet an official competition). Radio broadcasters and print journalists covered games played before packed houses; a May 5, 1930
game broke all previous records for attendance at Edmonton sporting
events.[59]

Most team members had full-time clerical careers, but the Grads
were recruited, trained, and coached according to a professional
model. New members were recruited over the years until the team
disbanded in 1940. A highly organized feeder system that took girls
through successive levels including the Cubs, Comets, and Gradettes
resulted in almost fifty women becoming Grads over the years. The
junior Cubs and intermediate Comets were, in effect, understudies for
the Gradettes, who substituted for the senior Grads when they were
unavailable as they defended their world championship during the
1936 Olympics.[60] The close control held by Page over every aspect of the
Grads' careers is well-known. Team captain Noel MacDonald remarked
on Page's insistence on discipline, noting that none of the team
members smoked or drank while on the team, and that this gave them
a distinct advantage over opponents who did since they could "run
them into the ground by halftime."[61]

When the Grads disbanded, Page attributed the decision to a lack of
fan attendance support for a team that had become "too successful,'"
as well as the time demanded by his new political career.[62] That year,
the Gradettes competed for the 1940 Canadian championship and the
Grads organization formed a new senior team called the Comets, who
would also draw upon "most of the material" for the team from the
same high school students.[63] Page was business manager for the new
organization, which had its own farm team, the Starlets, and which

had the goal of competing on a world championship level. The Comets, who "took over where the...Grads left off" were Alberta champions in 1941, and their first interprovincial game was "the first time in senior women's basketball history here that the famous Grads" would not be representing the city in interprovincials or involve Page as coach.[64] The next year, the team was known as the Grad-Comets, and former Grad captains Noel MacDonald and Etta Dan played an exhibition series raising funds for the "Milk for Britain" campaign.[65] There was never another women's team in any sport that attained the status of the Grads.

Today there are several college and university basketball teams and high school basketball leagues throughout the province. As is the case in other sports, though, community and minor league interest no longer translates to elite and professional team survival as it did for the Grads over a quarter century. Insufficient audiences and capitalization remain problems, as do the long travel distances for northern teams in American leagues. Semi-pro basketball teams in Alberta have all been short-lived, and all part of American Leagues, including the Alberta Dusters, Edmonton Skyhawks, Calgary 88s, and Calgary Outlaws. The Dusters were based in Lethbridge, playing in the Continental Basketball Association for one year in 1980-1981. The Calgary Outlaws played in 1984 only for the National Basketball League. The World Basketball League, established as the International Basketball Association in 1987, included only one Alberta professional team, the Calgary 88s, which folded in 1992 after leading the league in games won for all seasons but one.[66]

In 2004, Calgary acquired the semi-pro Drillers of the American Basketball Association, but they suspended operations the next year citing long travel distances. The Edmonton Skyhawks played in the National Basketball League in 1994; the Edmonton Chill (2008) of the International Basketball League changed its name to the Edmonton Energy in 2009 after eleven local business owners co-operated to sponsor the team. Despite qualifying for the 2010 playoffs in Portland, Oregon, the team did not participate due to lack of travel funds.[67]

Alan Metcalfe argues that by virtue of its presence throughout the country, it is baseball that should be known as the Canadian game.[68] Played since the 1870s, the game's popularity expanded into southern Alberta with American settlers and came east with the railways that reached Calgary in 1883 and Edmonton in 1891; the railway's arrival in small towns, such as Beiseker in 1912, also coincided with the first local ball games. Marshall McLuhan, who defined games as "extensions...of our social selves," considered baseball a relic of the pre-industrial era in that all the players perform the same non-specialized skills of catching, throwing, and batting.[69] This may help explain its wide popularity.

So many people played ball that the *Lethbridge News* deemed it necessary to organize a league to regulate tournaments as early as 1888. By 1899, the game was sufficiently established to be a feature attraction at local Dominion Day events. Virtually every community put together a team, equipment costs were low, and the game was popular across social and working classes. A group of travelling salesmen formed teams called the Edmonton Never Sweats and the Thirsty Thugs for a well-publicized game in 1903. In 1905, the Alberta Amateur League formed with teams from Edmonton, Banff, Anthracite, Wetaskiwin, Olds, and Medicine Hat. A contemporary Sunday ball league in Calgary made up of the Barbers, the Bar Tenders, and the Fire Department was disbanded after a stray ball broke the window of a funeral hearse.[70]

Softball was organized and played by North American women in cities, towns, and countryside from the turn of the century. The wide popularity and reach of game networks is evident in the trip made by the Boston Bloomers to play a Lethbridge team in July 1900.[71] Many businesses, such as the Hudson's Bay Company, sponsored women's recreational leagues in Alberta cities, including the Edmonton Senior Girls Baseball League that played on the Boyle Street Grounds to hundreds of spectators in the 1930s and 1940s. Teams included the Eskimo Girls, Army and Navy, Hudson's Bay, Eagle Toddies, Muttart

Lumber, South Side Terrors, and Eaton's. Calgary also supported a range of teams and leagues. In 1931, the ladies section of the Calgary Citywide Softball League broke away to form the Calgary Ladies Softball Association. Men's teams also played at the Boyle Street park, which over the years became a community institution. In 1930, the Edmonton Imperials and the Drumheller Athletics played for the senior men's provincial baseball championships. There had been an announcement that the games would go on at Diamond Park, which was distinguished by better facilities, including an enclosed field and no automobiles in the outfield, but the Edmonton Baseball Association ruled such a move unfair to the loyal patrons who had followed the season at the humbler east end park.[72]

By the 1920s, the men's game dominated summer sports in the province and "massive crowds" paid admission to see semi-pro and pro games.[73] Development, though uneven, followed the typical pattern from recreational pastime to organized leagues to professional teams. Boosters and investors adopted baseball as a medium for regional promotion, and, from the late 1800s into the twentieth century, towns seeking higher profiles supported senior amateur, semi-pro, and pro teams. Both Edmonton and Calgary acquired teams in the early 1900s in an effort to build a market for the sport. Professional ball on the Prairies is divided into the initial minor league era and, after World War II, the major league farm team system. Edmonton's Deacon White founded the semi-professional Western Canada Baseball League (WCBL) in 1907 and was instrumental in other leagues, coaching, and a variety of other sports promotions. Lethbridge, Calgary, Medicine Hat, and Edmonton played in the WCBL, a "compact, snug little circuit" that a Winnipeg reporter called typical of the energetic "spirit...of the west."[74]

Playing at the lowest pro level, the league's popularity and membership waxed and waned. Moose Jaw, Regina, Brandon, and Winnipeg joined the league, but it folded in 1908. Although play resumed in 1909, by 1912, only four WCBL teams existed: Edmonton, Calgary, Red Deer (financed by Calgary sponsors), and Bassano (population 1,400).

Bassano's mayor had invested his own funds into a team called the Boosters in hopes of raising the town's profile, and the town spent $3,000 on a new stadium. Only 500 spectators attended the first game, setting a downward trend for a season undermined by poor performance, bad weather, the distraction of farming, and rising ticket prices. That fall, the stadium was dismantled to build a new railway trestle. The long distances between communities—in its first year of operation the WCBL faced travel costs of over $7,000—and the unpredictable prairie weather played roles in bankrupting many other clubs.[75]

In 1914, a WCBL season opener in Edmonton drew a record 4,300 people but as wartime crowds diminished the league disbanded and reformed in 1919.[76] Edmonton's Diamond Park hosted publicity events such as a visit by the Prince of Wales, marked by World War I star pilot Wop May's biplane flight over the field to drop the first ball of the season. But in the 1920s, the lack of paying audiences, in part due to radio broadcasting, as well as loss of interest in low-stakes play meant the decline of the minor leagues; the "predominant mindset among the fans and the newspapers during the first two decades of the century was 'go big or not at all.'"[77] The WCBL folded again in 1921, next year becoming the minor Western International League (WIL). According to Brant Ducey, a central factor in the instability of professional and semi-professional prairie ball was the lack of comprehensive organization at the provincial and national levels. Leagues disbanded and reformed as resources permitted. Between 1907 and 1954, for instance, nine different versions of the WCBL operated in succession, each with a configuration of teams from cities including Medicine Hat, Edmonton, Lethbridge, Calgary, Saskatoon, Brandon, Regina, Moose Jaw, Bassano, and Red Deer.[78]

During the "golden era of baseball" in the 1920s, then, the Prairies had no professional team. But the sport remained strong in the minor Central Alberta Baseball League, which fielded teams from Red Deer, Ponoka, Lacombe, Blackfalds, Alix, Mirror, and other towns. Organized baseball thus survived the Great Depression. A contributor to Barry Broadfoot's oral history of the period noted that, after all, there was nothing else to do during the long drought in farming country but practice, play, and watch baseball. Tournaments were held every weekend all over the Prairies. Many of these offered prize money, some up to $500 and more, which attracted many teams, some with imported pro players when the pot was big enough. Other teams were ordinary prairie people "trying to make the best of a tough situation."[79]

Women continued to play as mothers passed on the baseball and softball passion to daughters. A 1937 *Edmonton Journal* article on public school sports reported that, because girls did not play hockey, and few schools had indoor basketball facilities, "the opening of the softball season [was] doubly welcome to the girls" and that "in swatting ability and enthusiasm," girls' teams "are just as good in proportion to their strength as the boys are."[80] That same year, so many girls came out for softball in Drumheller that they made up three teams and formed the city's first league.[81] Recreational tournaments between towns and villages were well-established, and informal rules of organization were often in play to accommodate local realities, such as population and distances. In the small farming hamlet of Carvel, for example, mixed boys' and girls' teams travelled to and hosted regular games with other schools from communities that were sometimes hours away by horse-drawn wagon.[82]

World War I, during which pro sport was discontinued, stimulated recreational spectator sports among locally-stationed servicemen. The Inter-Allied Sports Council organized games in Edmonton between local business-sponsored teams and those made up of army and navy men. During 1943, attendance records for these games were consistently broken at Renfrew (previously Diamond, later Ducey) Park, peaking on July 4 at 8,700 fans. The Prairies' first night baseball game under permanent lights was held at Renfrew Park in August 1947.[83]

During the World War II absence of men, more women played baseball and often developed elite skill levels. Originally intended as a novelty entertainment, the famed All-American Girls Professional Baseball League (which included nine Alberta players) was so successful that it influenced women all over North America to form

During the 1930s and 1940s, hundreds of spectators attended women's softball games at Edmonton's Boyle Street park. [CEA EA-160-512]

softball teams. The league became famous after a movie, *A League of Their Own*, was made in 1992. After the war, women's baseball lost its high profile as well as any opportunity for professional careers, although amateur baseball remained popular in Alberta.[84]

From the 1920s, barnstorming baseball teams travelled to villages and towns across the Prairies entertaining large crowds. John Ducey promoted a team called the Edmonton Oilers after his Big Four Inter City League (1947) folded in 1950. Both Edmonton and Saskatoon played in the independent Manitoba-Dakota League (1950), which included many players from the former Negro Leagues that declined after American pro ball integrated.[85] In 1953, Ducey brought organized pro ball back with the Class A WIL; the Moose Lodge Annual amateur tournament of the 1920s was revived in 1955 Camrose, and Lethbridge and Lacombe also established major tournaments. The WIL disbanded in

1961 but, by that time, the wcbl was operating again as a semi-pro league, and the Eskimos won the Canadian championship.[86]

As Canadian teams continued to acquire American talent, protests against unfair advantage on the field arose. There was also tension off the field because, as one player recalled, "there was a limited number of girls" to go around for both locals and newcomers.[87] In a response to the potential loss of imported talent, one club owner went out and ripped up the home plate saying, "I don't want any bushers [local minor league players]" crossing it.[88] The 1955 champions of the Western Canada Independent Baseball League, the Edmonton Eskimos, were tapped to represent Canada at the inaugural Global World Series in Milwaukee. When they refused to compete if the team included imported players, the second-place Saskatoon Gems went instead.[89]

In southern Alberta, the Big Six League at various times included teams from Taber, Magrath, Picture Butte, Spring Coulee, Raymond, and Lethbridge. The Lethbridge team, called the Nisseis, consisted of second-generation Japanese settlers.[90] The Brooks, Medicine Hat and District League also played ball, and George Wesley established the successful Granum clubs in the Foothills-Wheatbelt League.[91] In 1957, while Edmonton represented Canada in the Global World Series in Detroit, the Granum White Sox won their fourth straight Alberta title as well as three major tournaments, capping their streak by sharing "top money at Lacombe when the final was rained out."[92] The revolving declines and revivals of elite-level baseball in these years is a testament to a widely shared passion among organizers, an ability to ignore market and meteorological conditions, or both.

The popularity of baseball in southern Alberta endures. Minor pro ball returned to the Prairies in 1975 when Lethbridge joined the Pioneer League as a rookie team for the Montreal Expos. After leaving the league in 1983, the team returned in 1992 as the independent Lethbridge Mounties.[93] This meant that the four Alberta cities that had started the wcbl in 1907 were now the only ones with pro baseball teams on the Prairies. A Toronto Blue Jays farm team came to Medicine

Hat in 1976 but was sold in 2002. Two other Pioneer League franchises operated in Alberta; Medicine Hat and Calgary had teams starting in 1977.[94] In 1977 Calgary businessman Russ Parker, "the driving force behind pro baseball" in the city, spent one million dollars of his own money to acquire the Cardinals, but the team folded after two years. Parker acquired another team, the AAA Cannons, in 1984. He sold the team in 2002 after steady financial losses.[95] Edmonton, Lethbridge, Medicine Hat, and Okotoks have all recently had teams in the Western Major Baseball League, but, as of 2010, the Calgary Vipers were the only professional team in southern Alberta.

In 1979, Alberta's first women's professional softball team, the Edmonton Snowbirds, played their only season in the International Women's Professional Softball League's last year.[96] Meanwhile, amateur softball continued at high competitive levels. To name only one player, Shelley Berube Gadoury has won eight top pitcher awards and four MVP awards and has been inducted into both the Alberta Amateur Softball Association Hall of Fame and the Canadian Softball Hall of Fame. She learned the game from her father Emile Berube, a coach in Calahoo for over forty years. Gadoury played on teams that won twelve straight provincial championships, as well as gold, silver, and bronze medals between 1985 and 1996.[97]

Peter Pocklington, a local entrepreneur and sports promoter, brought men's pro ball back to the city when he imported the Trappers in 1981. Although the team attracted high fan numbers and won four Pacific Coast League (PCL) championships, they were sold in 2004. Columnist Marc Horton commented that for the Edmonton Eskimos, who then owned the franchise, "self-interest trumps community interest every time."[98] The minor league Cracker-Cats, the namesake of oil drilling equipment, arrived in 2006 and, with an average attendance figure of only 2,104 that season, were almost immediately termed "a lousy baseball team, a lousy draw and, in many obvious ways, a lousy idea whose time has come to an end."[99] The team was renamed the Edmonton Capitals when bought in 2009 by Daryl Katz, who had bought the Edmonton Oilers a year before.[100]

Despite the decline of public interest in pro and semi-pro ball, amateur and minor baseball has thrived under the supervision of Baseball Alberta since its organization as the Alberta Amateur Baseball Association in the early 1900s. The provincial government began to provide travel funds in 1970, supporting the establishment of intercity, regional, and national competition among over a hundred communities and 500 teams. Today the organization promotes and develops baseball locally and nationally and players range from age five to sixty-five in over 400 communities. Parker's son Brent recalled, "hockey was something we did until baseball season started again. And probably both ways. I loved both sports the same."[101]

RUGBY, SOCCER, AND FOOTBALL

"A STRONG HOLD ON THE PEOPLE"

While hockey, baseball, and basketball are all continental sports, Canadian football remains a distinct merger of British, European, and American games. Though Canadian football and soccer became more common than rugby, all three versions of the game generically called "football" remained in play over the years across Alberta.[102] Fort Edmonton hosted the first recorded football game in Alberta in 1869, but organized sport had to wait for arrival of the railway.[103] The railway brought not only enthusiasts and sports equipment, but, as Hugh Dempsey points out, raised the population of "young men who needed an outlet for their energies" in the region.[104] In Calgary, the CPR's arrival in 1883 was closely followed by the Mounted Police organizing football games with civilians. The town formed a regular team in the late 1880s, as did Lethbridge. Calgary played country teams from the surrounding region as well as the police and fire brigade, and usually lost "as we had not the same opportunity of practicing as the police had." However, recalled A.G. Wolley-Dod, "that did not worry us much, as the games were good and clean, and generally ended up with a smoker in the evening."[105]

Civilian Edmontonians played rugby against the Mounted Police and other local teams, and formed a club in 1891 that challenged any western club for a $3,000 prize.[106] The team was more organized and better outfitted than Calgary's for their first game that year, but Calgary won. For the return match ten days later, the team left Calgary two men short but managed to find two at Innisfail and another in Edmonton, where they also borrowed another from that club. After Edmonton won, they entertained the Calgary team "right royally." Though members on both teams were good friends, they nevertheless fought fiercely in some of the first "Battles of Alberta" for dominance between north and south.[107]

In the early organizational period, conflict between elite and workers' versions of rugby prevailed, and various groups developed rules and league systems to protect what they viewed as correct play. The amateur Canadian Rugby Football Union (renamed the Canadian Rugby Union in 1892) was formed in 1884. By the time of the first national competition, the Senior Amateur Football Championship of Canada in 1909, official rules of "Canadian rugby football" were substantially distinct from those of the original game. Players and coaches from central Canada and the northwestern United States influenced the shaping of rugby union football as Canadian football in Alberta, but rugby disappeared by World War II.[108]

In 1895, the Edmonton Rugby Football Club played their first organized games and won the first Alberta Rugby Football Union title. Calgary's first team was formed in 1907, reorganizing as the Tigers a year later, when the Calgary Rugby Football Union also formed. Edmonton's club became the Esquimaux and won the provincial championship in 1907 and 1908. The game drew large audiences, including a crowd of about 1,200 to a 1908 Edmonton game at which the lieutenant-governor kicked off the ball. In 1911, the Alberta Rugby Union (ARU), which also included the Calgary Tigers and YMCA teams, joined the new Western Canada Rugby Football Union. The championship went back and forth between Edmonton and Calgary over the next few years; the rivalry between the two cities in this sport, as in others,

Calgary Indian Industrial School versus Calgary Caledonians, football group. Founded in 1896 and closed in 1907, this was the last Canadian industrial school established by the Anglican Church. [GA NA-3-1]

The Calgary Tigers play football in the snow, ca. 1919–1939. [GA NB-16-511]

persisted.[109] The *Toronto Globe* admitted in 1912 that "the west has made fairly good headway in nearly every other line of sport, to wit—hockey, lacrosse and rowing. It is not inconceivable that some day the West... may duplicate in rugby football the triumphs that it has recently had in these other forms of athletics."[110]

After a suspension of play during the war, the ARU reorganized in 1919 with the Calgary Canucks, Tigers, Eskimos, and University of Alberta teams. Influenced by players and coaches from central Canada and the northwestern United States, the organization developed its own rules, sharing with other western groups goals of consistency in performance and interpretation of written rules. For western teams, geography played an important role in organization; travel costs were prohibitive, and the first Grey Cup game between east and west was not played until 1921 in Toronto by the Argonauts and Deacon White's Edmonton Eskimos. The introduction of the forward pass in 1931 intensified the search for skilled players. No western team won the cup until 1935, when the Winnipeg 'Pegs (later the Blue Bombers) won with a team that included nine American players. This inspired the Canadian Rugby Union, influenced in part by the Alberta Rugby Union, to draft rule changes to legalize American players in 1946, further eroding the concept of amateurism.[111]

After a hiatus of five years, the Alberta Rugby Union met in 1941 in response to the "sudden, enthusiastic support of junior football in Alberta."[112] Finances permitting, the ARU within a new western league would operate for the benefit and promotion of the junior game. But rugby was not revitalized until after the discovery of oil in 1947. During the immigration wave that followed, a group of British immigrants formed the Edmonton Rugby Football Club in 1953. The first Calgary teams, the Saints and the Saracens, organized, and a new Alberta Rugby Union was established in 1961, as was a strong rugby program in Calgary schools. In 1967, Alberta began to advocate for a stronger national rugby program, and, in the 1970s, new teams formed in Edmonton, Calgary, and, in the 1980s, Red Deer, Fort McMurray, Lethbridge, and Medicine Hat.[113]

Women's rugby is an Alberta success story. The first club in Edmonton came together as the Rockers with twenty-five members in 1977; another club, the Coven Women's Rugby Football Club, broke away in 1982. The Alberta Women's Rugby Union fielded a provincial team in 1983 that excelled at the inaugural Western Canadian Women's Rugby Championships. Growth at the club level was still slow, but in 1987 Alberta hosted the first Women's National Championship, winning the first title. The provincial team also hosted and won the first National Championships for Under 19 Women in 1993 and the Senior Women's Championship at the 2003 Rugby Canada National Festival. The University of Alberta adopted women's rugby as a varsity sport in 1999, and the team won the championship that year.[114] In the early twenty-first century, Alberta has women's rugby teams at minor, major, and university levels.

In 1906, the Alberta Football League was created in Red Deer; in 1909, two provincial organizations merged to form the Alberta Association Football League, which then became the Alberta Soccer Association in 1915. The first indoor soccer league in Canada was created in 1910 in Calgary although growth did not continue. The Alberta Football Association was incorporated the following year, organized the Alberta Association Football League (AAFL), and became the Alberta Soccer Association in 1915. The Canadian game built on the sport's popularity in Britain.[115] In 1911, after Calgary's Maple Leaf Football Club won the international championship, Reverend Dr. MacRae spoke of the "need of keeping young Britons," meaning British immigrants and descendants "interested in soccer, in order to keep the championship of Canada in Calgary."[116] Alberta players hosted English, Scots, and Australian teams before and after World War I, and in the 1920s Alberta newspapers still commonly posted British scores before local ones. In 1913, soccer had such a "strong hold on the people" that the *Calgary Daily Herald* expressed "no doubt that soccer will predominate in Canada" as long as the AAUC dropped its prohibition on amateurs playing with professionals as they had "in old country football."[117] But in 1920, a letter writer to the University of Alberta

Gateway urged the revival of the "once-popular" sport of soccer, which had lost many players to rugby. The writer urged "the boys" to "Ginger up!" and get into the game.[118]

All four western provinces formed the Western Intercollegiate Rugby Football Union in 1927. University teams, particularly in hockey and football, regularly played against senior and professional teams. When varsity football on the Prairies was disbanded from 1949 to 1958, the University of Alberta sold their green and gold jerseys to the recently formed Edmonton Eskimos professional team. After ten years' absence, western intervarsity football returned to the University of Alberta in 1959 as part of the Western Canadian Interuniversity Athletic Union, which included twelve major and minor sports, including hockey, basketball, tennis, golf, swimming, and curling. The football team bought equipment with the money that had been "collecting cobwebs and interest" since it was received from the sale to the Eskimos.[119] Steve Mendryk, the last of the original Eskimos team, and in 1958 the head of the university's physical education program, became head coach. In 1964, the Western Intercollegiate Football League formed, and play has continued, with periodic reorganization, to the present.[120]

The term "soccer" came into use in England during the 1880s, when association football was distinguished from rugby football by extending the second syllable of "association." The famed Calgary Caledonians soccer team formed in 1904 and became the first "soccer dynasty" in Canada, winning the People's Shield for the unofficial national championship in 1907, 1908, and 1909. The prize was presented by an English newspaper; it was no longer played for when the Connaught Cup was introduced in 1913. The Callies, as the team was popularly known, won the 1908 Alberta championship as well as the four following years. Play was suspended for the duration of war but when it resumed the team won again in 1923 and 1938. Other teams were also renowned; the Lethbridge Supinas, for example, won the Alberta championship in 1932, 1934, and 1935. Red Deer also produced championship teams. Jimmy Graham played for the Edmonton,

Members of the 1927 Red Deer Football (soccer) Club with trophies won that year.
[RDDA MG-193-1-21-1]

English, Welsh teams in the 1920s and the Alberta All-Stars in 1935. He was also a centre for the Edmonton Gainers Superiors hockey team in the 1930s, and he coached Edmonton's Waterloo Mercurys to the World Hockey Championship in London in 1950. Graham played baseball and was a championship golfer in the 1960s.[121]

Soccer declined in popularity as baseball became the dominant summer sport in Alberta by the 1920s, but popular participation increased after World War II as European immigrants played the sport they had loved at home. In 1949, the Alberta Football Association urged that soccer be promoted to young people in order to build the senior game in the province. Encouragingly, there were enthusiastic Ukrainian clubs in Edmonton and Lethbridge, and the University of Alberta found it "fast gaining popularity among students."[122] In 1951, German-Canadians formed the Victoria Soccer Club, fielded the first team in 1952 at Clarke Stadium; within three years, the club won the city championship, the Alberta championship, and three consecutive

Dragon Cups. (The club also organized table tennis, a band and, in 1964, a cycling club.)[123] Joe Petrone, the top male goal scorer in Alberta soccer history, came to Canada from Italy in 1957. He recalls the 1960s and 1970s as golden years for soccer, with top players from Europe, and in Edmonton spectators averaged 5,000 to 6,000 at Clarke Stadium (the Eskimos football team averaged 9,000). Players were paid well, but Petrone took up football at the advice of Eskimo Rollie Miles and became an all-star player, playing for the University of Calgary before joining the Dallas Cowboys, later moving to the University of Alberta Golden Bears. Petrone also made contributions to soccer as coach and manager.[124]

On a professional level, soccer came late to the province; the first pro circuit emerged in 1965 with teams from Edmonton, Calgary, Winnipeg, and Saskatoon.[125] Reflecting the relatively low national interest among audiences, with the exception of immigrant communities, pro soccer in the 1980s and 1990s attracted few fans. The history of pro soccer in Edmonton is a lengthy list of failures. Pocklington brought a professional North American Soccer League (NASL) franchise, the Drillers, to Edmonton in 1979. The team won the championship in 1981, and, in the first years, an average of over 10,000 people attended each game, but the 1982 season attracted an average of below half that number. When the outdoor team folded in 1982 due to low media support, huge operating losses, and bad business strategies, the whole league followed. The Drillers returned in 1996 as part of the National Professional Soccer League, but lost between $500,000 and $700,000 in their first season and folded again in 2000.[126]

The Brickmen, part of the professional Canadian Soccer League, also played in Edmonton from 1986 to 1990. This league folded in 1992, however, after only six years in operation. In 2004, a group of Edmonton investors launched men's A-League and women's W-League soccer teams called the Aviators. "Unlike every other professional team in Edmonton's history," the group had good resources and organization but faced the challenge of winning community goodwill.[127] A spokesman called previous failures the result of undercapitalized

ownership rather than a lack of popularity. The club also arranged
for the Edmonton Minor Soccer Association, which registered 29,000
players in 2003—over half of whom were female—to increase its registration fee and provide each player with season's passes. The U-19
FIFA World Women's Championships held in Edmonton in 2001 drew
more than 47,000 for the gold medal game, and the Aviators aimed to
capitalize on interest with as first women's soccer team in the city.[128]
They disbanded in 2004 due to financial problems compounded by low
attendance.

The Calgary Boomers, owned by Nelson Skalbania, played in the
NASL in 1981 and then folded; the Calgary Kickers lasted from 1987
to 1989. As host city for the Canadian national soccer team in 1994,
Edmonton produced the biggest crowd to ever watch a soccer game
in this country; 52,000 people watched a match between Brazil and
the nationals at Commonwealth Stadium. Based on this success,
Edmonton hosted the Canada Cup of Soccer in 1999. In 2007, Calgary
and Edmonton had teams in a new Canadian Major Indoor Soccer
League. In 2009, Edmonton won the Canadian Division championship.[129] The following year, FC Edmonton was established, playing in
the North American Soccer League.

The sport has been most successful at the minor and amateur level.
Participation rates have risen rapidly in the course of one generation to become what the Alberta Soccer Association, in 2004, called the
"largest grass-roots sport in history in this province."[130] A Calgarian,
Jack Taylor, created a provincial youth soccer program in the late 1940s.
Minor soccer membership rose steeply from the 1970s to the 1980s; the
Calgary Blizzard Soccer Club grew from three teams in 1977 to seventy-
two in 2003.[131] Women's teams were formed during the 1960s and '70s,
and Edmonton hosted the first western Canadian girls' soccer championships in 1977. As of 2010, the Alberta Women's Major Soccer League
had eight teams, one called the Calgary Callies. The Alberta Major
Soccer League, an amateur senior league with both men's and women's
teams, formed in the early 1990s with the goal of developing young
players to compete at higher levels.[132] After two years in operation,

women's indoor soccer had twenty-five teams in 1999, and 45 per cent of all players were female as the twenty-first century began. In 2009, over 150,000 youth and adults participated in organized soccer in Alberta; in 2010, the Alberta Soccer Association was the largest sport organization in the province with 90,000 members.[133]

As of 1999, 7,500 Edmonton kids were playing indoor soccer and another 1,300 were commuting to play in the city. In comparison, minor hockey had about 8,600 kids playing on thirty surfaces; the gap between hockey and soccer is closing. For a variety of reasons, including lower participation and equipment costs, more and more Alberta families are "converts to a game deemed a bastardized foreign sport not long ago."[134]

In the early years of organized football, eastern teams refused to undertake the long, expensive trip to compete with western teams, whom they considered inferior in any case. The Edmonton Eskimos became the first western team to go to the Grey Cup where they played before 9,000 spectators in Toronto in 1921. Although the Eskimos lost the game, the Regina *Leader* reminded readers that rugby was "only in its infancy in the western provinces"; that the team had come such a long distance and spent ten days "without anything but signal practice, step[ped] onto a strange field in a strange city, and [held] the greatest team ever assembled in Eastern Canada to as close a score as they did" boded well for the future.[135] Moreover, the *Manitoba Free Press* reported that "the contest was a triumph for the uniformity of playing rules."[136]

Clarence Richards, an Edmonton schoolteacher who founded the first Kinsmen Club of Edmonton in 1925, decided around that time that Edmonton needed another football team. He called the team he organized the Hi Grads in tribute to the iconic women's basketball team, dressed them in random pieces of uniforms, and gathered up equipment. They played teams from the University of Alberta, Calgary, and Lethbridge and formed the nucleus of a new version of the Edmonton Eskimos in 1938. The team folded again with the advent of another war.[137]

The Western Interprovincial Football Union (WIFU), composed of Winnipeg, Regina, Calgary, and sometimes Edmonton, replaced the Western Canada Rugby Football Union (WCRFU) in 1936 as the most important competition in the region. Both Calgary and Edmonton built major football stadiums in the 1930s, but financial problems and low attendance led to team and league failures. In 1938, the first game at the new Clarke Stadium in Edmonton, won by the Calgary Bronks (later the Stampeders), drew 2,500 spectators, but the Eskimos consistently found it impossible to raise the annual budget of $20,000. Future premier Peter Lougheed, who played on the Eskimos that year, was paid $250 for the season: $200 for university tuition and the rest for spending money. In 1940, Edmonton withdrew from the WIFU, and, as other teams folded, the WIFU closed in 1942.[138]

After the war, football was the first professional sport to reorganize, and, by 1948, the sport attracted capacity audiences. It was football, not hockey, that Prime Minister John Diefenbaker called "the greatest unifying force in Canada" at the time.[139] Junior league teams drew as many as 9,000 fans to regular season games, and players often went on to the pros. No pro football league existed in Alberta until 1946, but Calgary's 1948 Grey Cup win sealed the popularity and commercial viability of football in Alberta. Capacity audiences followed the game and with the postwar economic boom, social change, and the waning of the amateur ideal, the Edmonton Eskimos entered a revived, four-team WIFU, which became the Western Football Conference in 1961.[140] An all-time attendance record for a western stadium was set with 15,000 spectators for a 1952 game between Edmonton and Calgary in Clarke Stadium. Edmonton's Grey Cup wins in 1955 and 1956 entrenched the game as a fan favourite.[141]

The Eskimos went on to record more Grey Cup appearances and victories than any other team in Canadian football's modern era. The team was one of the first multiracial teams in professional sports with players of African, European, and Asian heritage.[142] Led by Jackie Parker, Johnny Bright, and Normie Kwong (who became Alberta's lieutenant-governor in 2010), the team won the cup in 1954, 1955, 1956, three straight Western Conference titles (1973, 1974, 1975), and another Grey Cup in 1975 before making history as the only team in Canadian Football League history to win five Grey Cups in a row from 1978 to 1982 and again in 1987, 1993, and 2003.[143] The Calgary Stampeders won the cup in 1971, 1992, 1998, and 2001. Edmonton Eskimo and Calgary Stampeder football fans still hold a much-hyped "Battle of Alberta" to start off each season, but fan interest declined in the 1980s and 1990s.

In 1952, the professional game was increasingly populated with imported American players.[144] Calgary mayor Don Mackay warned that sport was "going through an era of specialization and...coming to ruthless competition. We must determine whether sport is a business or a medium to produce better men in city, province and nation."[145] Although the CFL is unique in North American pro sports in that many teams are or were community-owned, Mackay's question has been answered; the business model prevailed. While interest in the pro game has declined amid the loss of football teams to the United States in the 1980s and 1990s, minor, high school, and other amateur football continues strong. Football Alberta, which oversees all amateur teams in the province, counted 400 teams and 12,000 players, coaches, officials, and volunteers in 2009.[146]

⋮ **CONCLUSION**

All the core summer sports have survived as popular pastimes into the present. Several are still major spectator attractions. But winter sports seem to remain central to the prairie imagination and community life, providing diversion, companionship, and excitement during the long cold months. The next chapter focuses on how winter sports were played, experienced, and organized in the province.

5

"LOVE AND HOMETOWN GLORY"
CORE WINTER TEAM SPORTS

In the little town of Khartoum, Alberta...they are thinking today of [a] little man—a simple unassuming cobbler who led his rink of three tried men and true—to grand slam victory in the Macdonald Brier Play-offs... Wullie stand for something fine in the Canadian character—Wullie stand for grim determination—Wullie, I salute you.

—W.O. MITCHELL,
The Black Bonspiel of Wullie MacCrimmon

CURLING
ROCKS ON THE ICE

In W.O. Mitchell's narrative, the popularity of curling inspires the Devil to install a rink in Hell and then to challenge Wullie to a match for his soul. According to the influential doctrine of a "northern character," the Canadian habit of cheerful adaptation to the winter environment would have nurtured many other quality souls as well. In 1840, the *Canadian Curler's Manual* recommended winter sport "to counteract the enfeebling influence of confinement to our close and heated...houses."[1] One manifested good character, at least in part, by gritty triumph over ice and snow. As a bonus, the energetic wielding of brooms, sticks, and blades made the climate seem an opportunity for play rather than an endurance test. To this day, as is made evident in contexts from television advertising to national currency, "the frozen pond is a key signifier of our national claims on winter and northernness, of our identity as a wholesome, hardy people."[2]

According to Vera Pezer, no sport in any area of the country has been as dominant as has curling on the Prairies. In Alberta, where it dates back to the 1880s, curling has long rivaled hockey as the favourite winter game. In 1998, Sandra Schmirler's rink—not the Grey Cup-winning Calgary Stampeders or a Canadian NHL team—was named "Canada's Team" after winning the Olympic gold medal.[3] Significant factors in curling's popular entrenchment have been ease of access, simple equipment, and the integration of sport and socializing that, though a common feature of other prairie sports cultures, seems to be especially characteristic of curling. Norman McLeod recalled a game held on a homemade rink in 1894 Lethbridge, after which the players retired to the town's hotel with the prize, a bottle of scotch. When two NWMP sergeants arrived after midnight, they all decided to hold another game immediately.

> We took Harry Mossop along with the hot water kettle in case anyone
> developed toothache or an attack of nerves. It has never yet been explained
> how three or four of the strongest temperance advocates accidentally
> found bottles of scotch about their persons on arrival at the rink...By and
> by, Harry Mossop, finding no demand for the hot water "in natura"
> thought he had better sterilize it by a small addition of scotch...it was not
> very long before the fumes began to affect the curlers and, foolishly, they

began to drink the horrible concoction; first a drink after every end, then after every shot, and, finally, go as you please.[4]

Formal organization of the sport began, as usual, among military men at forts, and the game remains strongly associated with the military to this day. Southern Alberta towns including Lethbridge, Fort Macleod, Anthracite, and Banff formed clubs in the late 1880s and Medicine Hat in 1896. In 1883, the *Calgary Herald* called for fans of the "roarin' game" to form a club.[5] They played at the outdoor Claxton's Star Rink from 1885 until 1890 when a joint stock company, largely composed of players and fans, raised funds for an enclosed facility. The Edmonton Curling Club was organized in 1888 in the law offices of McDonald and McLeod; the *Bulletin* reported the first curling match in Northern Alberta that year, held by a group of Scots celebrating St. Andrew's Day.[6] Teams had names like Calgary's Sons of Scotia, and the *Edmonton Bulletin* reported an 1884 match between "Canada" and "Scotland." As well as the Scots' influence, the promotion of curling in the west can be attributed to the railways and shrewd sponsors, beginning in 1925 with Macdonald Tobacco, which saw curling as a unifying force for the provinces of Canada as well as a good advertising venue.[7]

The climate and a ready supply of flat icy surfaces, of course, were also important factors in accessibility of the sport, but as Mary Louise Adams reminds us, "once there was simply ice: on lakes, ponds, rivers, canals. It froze or it didn't. The ice was hard or it was slushy. It bore or it broke. People…waited in vain for freeze-up."[8] The lack of artificial ice was a major obstacle to the development of organized hockey and curling, particularly in southern Alberta where warm chinook winds alternated with deep freezes. The fifth annual Calgary bonspiel (1900), for instance, was "not up to the mark of past years" due to "unfavourable" weather.[9] The fickle winter climate prevented Medicine Hat from organizing hockey until after most other sports were established; Lethbridge's first hockey team (1908) had its first league game cancelled due to rain.[10]

At best, early ice making was a creative but arduous task. After the 1909 Calgary bonspiel, the home club's icemaker fell ill after having worked almost around the clock for days to refine the frozen surface. In Millet, the curling rink was located eight feet from the town well. Water was pumped by hand to make an ice path between the rink and the well, and sleighs loaded with barrels of water were pulled to flood the rink. Volunteers "brought 14 eight-gallon cans of lukewarm water from the creamery...When the signal was given, water from all the cans was dumped at the same time onto the ice to provide the finishing layer for curling."[11]

Until 1904, Alberta clubs belonged to the Manitoba Branch of the Royal Caledonian Curling Club (RCCC). The 1899 Calgary bonspiel hosted several rinks from the area as well as from Edmonton and British Columbia. In 1904, the Alberta Branch of the RCCC was formed in Calgary with joint patrons Colonel James Walker, called Alberta's "Father of Curling" for his efforts in launching and sustaining the sport, and MLA Richard Secord of Edmonton. The organization was the world's third largest club at the time. In 1907, Alberta beat Saskatchewan to win the first interprovincial match.[12]

In the 1890s and early 1900s many curling facilities separated male and female spectators, and women served mainly as providers of bonspiel food. But after women began to curl around 1908, curling was one of the only sports to allow mixed gender teams—despite some initial argument that women might be too fragile to throw rocks. (Pezer reports that before mixed teams were accepted in regular competition, Calgary allowed them in charity bonspiels but a man playing opposite a woman had to deliver his rock left-handed as a chivalrous handicap.) The Thistle Club of Edmonton accepted women curlers by 1920. Smaller farm communities, which needed help to finance and maintain clubs and fill rosters, were quicker to grant fair access to rinks than were most urban clubs.[13] In 1910, a Lethbridge group erected a five-sheet curling rink; a ladies' club was organized within four years. In Millet, a ladies' club formed quickly after the town built an indoor curling rink in 1925.[14]

Lady curler, Edmonton, 1929. [GA NC-6-12356B]

Mixed teams were widely accepted, but direct competition between males and females was not. A separate women's bonspiel event was well-established in Calgary by 1925. At the 1933 Calgary Curling Club Men's Open Bonspiel, Jim Gorrie played on a team with three women as a joke entry. After they won five consecutive games, the executive voted the team ineligible for further competition.[15] Women were excluded from sport supposedly for their own good; the male domain of sport was said to be a location of potential abuse for women. Women's presence was also a threat to male-dominated, often crude locker room culture. In 1932, women were still refused membership to the Bowden curling club. The locker room fears proved accurate; three years later, when women were newly admitted, a man was banned from the club after they complained about his foul language.[16]

The ladies' section of the 1936 constitution and bylaws of the Calgary North Hill Curling Club emphasized civility in the sport: "While the main objective of matches between clubs is to determine their relative skill in the game...the ultimate object of curling is to develop a WOMANLY RECREATION and to promote good will, kindly feeling and honorable conduct among those who take part in it."[17] Although this may be read as another instance of accepting social pressure against serious athletic competition among women, we are actually assured by this example that the wider culture of curling sincerely prized social bonding and sportsmanship, or its female equivalent.

Rivalries between Edmonton and Calgary ran high, and a 1904 bonspiel between the two cities took over front pages for four days, trumping news of the Sino-Russian War. When Edmonton won all the trophies, the CPR ran a special non-stop train home from Calgary, an honour never before accorded to a sports team.[18] The first Alberta bonspiel was held in Edmonton in 1911, when the city had thirteen ice sheets and hosted seventy-nine teams. The following year, fifty-three teams attended the event in Calgary, but Edmonton curlers resented being controlled by the provincial organization in Calgary and, in 1913, after Edmonton had added six more sheets, the city petitioned to become permanent bonspiel host. When the bonspiel returned to Calgary in 1914, the one Edmonton team that had registered didn't bother to show up, and in 1915, the city, which had four curling clubs, ended its association with the Royal Caledonian Curling Club. Two years later, the Alberta Curling Association was established to promote curling north of Red Deer, and ninety-one rinks entered the organization's 1918 bonspiel, the biggest ever held west of Winnipeg at the time. In 1928, Alberta endorsed the formation of the Dominion Curling Association and joined in 1935; by 1945, there were thirty-seven participating clubs in the province.[19]

Play spread in rural areas by the 1920s, becoming a fixture in the social life of communities during the winter lull in the farming season. Covered rinks were built as soon as communities could afford them, and in most places electricity was available by the 1920s. As population and facility numbers expanded, artificial ice making supported longer seasons and formal organization.[20] Curlers persisted through obstacles of weather and misfortune. The Camrose Curling Club played in the local hockey arena until the roof collapsed under a heavy weight of snow in 1914. The curlers formed a joint stock company, sold shares for ten dollars each and built a new rink the next fall. A new five-sheet rink was built in 1936, financed by individual member subscriptions and a loan, and when it was lost to fire in 1942, the club constructed another rink, this time with insurance money, for that year's season. Sheets were added over the years until a new recreation complex was built in 1967.[21]

Even during World War I and the Depression, curling remained vigorous on the Prairies since the game was popular and accessible to people of both sexes, all ages and levels of fitness. With stereotypes of women's fragility faltering, new opportunities arose to throw rocks, but at various times curling was slightly less accessible for women. At the three-sheet Camrose Curling Club in 1914, ladies were given the use of one sheet for the morning and one for the afternoon for a fee of five dollars.[22] The sport also appealed to a range of social groups. The Jewish community of Edmonton supported a team at Crestwood Community League, and the Edmonton B'nai Brith Lodge opened a curling club in 1949, which became the Menorah Curling Club in 1947. The original club had fifty-six members, competed with other Jewish curling clubs in bonspiels across the western provinces, and raised its own building in 1951. The purpose of the club was to "to reunify Jewish families in a new land, regardless of wealth, social status or country of origin, and to provide fellowship and a social outlet for its membership."[23]

From the 1950s to the end of the 1970s, prairie people led the country in curling. In 1960-1961, for instance, the region held 17 per cent of Canada's population but 66 per cent of the nation's curling clubs and 48 per cent of all curlers.[24] The first Western Canada Women's Championship was sponsored by Eaton's at Calgary's Glencoe Club in 1951, significantly boosting women's curling in the region. By 1952 Eaton's sponsored all three prairie provincial ladies' championships, and, in 1954, Alberta claimed the largest membership on the

Prairies. Ethel Lees of Red Deer was provincial ladies' curling champion in 1957 and led the only undefeated rink in the 1960 Southern Alberta Playoffs; the following year, the team toured Scotland.[25] Although in 1959 two eastern Canadian curlers proposed a national event to be sponsored by Macdonald Tobacco, western women chose to remain with Eaton's on a regional level. Nevertheless, the national women's curling association was formed the following year.[26]

On December 14, 1960 the *Camrose Canadian* announced a future mixed curling event open to "any club member and/or his wife."[27] Whether local women were members of clubs in their own right or not, they organized their own annual provincial playdowns. By this time women were firmly in charge of their own organizations. Jack Reilly, supervisor of athletics for the City of Edmonton, promoted a city-run girls' curling program in the late 1950s but women's provincial clubs discouraged the idea. Instead, in 1958 Hazel Jamieson led a group initiating the Edmonton Girls' Curling Association. Calgary followed, and the Alberta Girls' Curling Association formed in 1960 to stage the first provincial championship. Between 1961 and 1971 Alberta ranked behind only Ontario in the numbers of women curlers. Calgary's Tournament of Roses and Edmonton's Tournament of Pearls became two of the most lucrative bonspiels. In 1968, heading a rink composed of her daughters, Jamieson won the first ever Canadian Ladies Curling Association championship in Winnipeg.[28] Prominent Alberta curlers since 1961 have included Cathy Borst, Susan Seitz, Myrna McQuarrie, and Gayle Lee. Alberta's Shelby MacKenzie won the first Canadian Junior Women's Championship in 1971. Alberta women's teams have won several national tournaments, including the Canada Cup and the Tournament of Hearts.[29]

A key factor in curling's success has been its association with corporate sponsors. Publicity and commercial development of the sport in mid-century meant that more bonspiels were held and sponsorships increased with innovations such as "Carspiels" that offered automobiles as prizes. In 1960, Massey-Ferguson announced its sponsorship of a national championship for curling farmers. Local agents, including the dealers in Camrose, organized local playdowns to choose the national participants.[30] Many competitive curlers took up the sport as children in small towns; three-time Canadian and World champion Ron Northcott and his team members, for example, began in Vulcan and other rural areas. Fred Storey came from Empress, and Bernie Sparkes from Claresholm, where his father was the local icemaker.[31]

The Brier national championship was established in 1927 and proved a catalyst for expanding provincial and regional organization. Cliff Manahan, who entered competitive curling in 1926 in Edmonton, won sixty-five championships in twenty-three years, and in 1933 was the first to bring the Brier to the city. At the time, however, curling champions did not have high public profiles as serious athletes. Later curlers have achieved wider fame. Matt Baldwin's rink won the 1954 Brier in Edmonton, and his athleticism at the event helped to change the public image of curling as a "sissy" sport. A "curling boom" ensued in the city. The Crestwood Curling Club was the first of about ten venues built following the event. Hector (Hec) Gervais, a potato farmer nicknamed the Friendly Giant for his size, may have been the first curling folk hero in Alberta. He entered the game after seeing Baldwin's Brier win.[32] The final game of the 1961 Brier between the rinks of Gervais and Saskatchewan's Jack Keys at the Calgary Corral attracted 8,124 fans, a one-game attendance record at the time. Gervais's rink won the Canada Cup and the Scotch Cup for international curling supremacy that year, and the Brier in 1973. He played competitively into the 1980s, while a team including his sons Stan and Hector won third place in the 1981 World Open Bonspiel in Edmonton.[33] Other Alberta curlers whose rinks have won the Brier and other championships since 1954 include Ron Northcott, Matt Baldwin, Ed Lukowich, and Pat Ryan, who won five Alberta championships, two Briers and, in 1989, a world championship.[34]

Although there have been men's world championships since 1957, there was little international interest in the sport until the early twenty-first century. By 2008 over thirty nations were members of the World Curling Federation, and, at elite levels, Alberta teams are particularly competitive and fans dedicated. Curling was a demonstration event at the 1988 Calgary Olympics; Ed Lukowich of Alberta won bronze. The province was dominant in the Brier in the early 2000s; whereas BC teams have won the Brier four times since 1948. For instance, Alberta's Randy Ferbey won the Brier four times since 2001. Kevin Martin was Brier champion four times as skip, including 2008 and 2009, and the Team Canada skip for a gold medal performance at the 2010 Olympics. A Brier attendance record was set in Edmonton in 2005 and more than 14,000 attended the opening of the 2009 event, where Martin's fans wore cowboy hats, rang cowbells, and waved Alberta flags in the crowd. Ferbey, referring to his longstanding rivalry with Martin, compared the two teams to the Calgary Flames and the Edmonton Oilers,[35] in effect borrowing the high status of professional hockey to enhance the image of curling.

Curling, like hockey, is an enduring example of the resonance between sport and cultural memory, illustrating the embedding of daily life within sporting cultures. On the Prairies especially, curling remains integral to community life, with a club in almost every small town and an estimated over one million participants. The sport has retained its spirit of collective celebration and the strong cohesive association of curling events with congenial, supportive community. While CBC has broadcast curling championships since 1946, viewership grew in the early twenty-first century, particularly during the 2005 NHL strike.[36] As the stakes get higher curling's image is changing; the Canadian Curling Association calls the sport's party reputation a mixed blessing, drawing players and fans but undermining its image as a serious sport.[37]

CBC Sports executive director Scott Moore dismisses the myth that curling "just attracts an older audience...There's a younger audience...and it's a very passionate audience. It's a hidden opportunity for marketers...to [reach] a wide variety of demographics."[38] Although Canadian high schools have dropped curling from their physical education programs, Alberta curling clubs and organizations promote youth programs. But compelling alternatives compete for the youth

market and participation expenses are increasing. Canada's relatively
low population cannot provide television or sponsorship revenue for
a professional curling circuit or sustain commercial growth for the
CFL, especially in light of generous funding for American equivalents.
Nevertheless, as Stephen Wieting and Danny Lamoureux observe,
there are still legions of curlers who would not shun the odds taken
by Wullie MacCrimmon in hopes of a championship.[39]

⋮ HOCKEY

ICE AND HOMEFIRES

MINOR, JUNIOR, AND SENIOR LEAGUE HOCKEY: STARS ARE BORN

*Where was I, one Saturday morning in December of 1961, just as the first
cold grey was starting to show us the hoarfrost on the trees, promising
a startling shock as we stepped out of doors? Where else? I was gettin'
ready to play hockey.*

—KEN BROWN, *Life After Hockey*

The silhouette of a hockey arena looms in almost every community
in the province, alongside "the schools and churches and homes...
an essential part of every town's life."[40] In 2005, the town of Viking's
Carena (so called because it was financed by a car raffle in 1950) burned
down. The town's Sutter brothers, of whom six later played in the
NHL, had practiced at the facility, but its significance went beyond
producing stars. Mayor Garry Wolosinka said, "the first year [without
the arena] was pretty bad because the hockey rink in the wintertime
was the focus for young and old."[41] The "hockey town" came out in
volunteer force to build a new multi-use facility that opened in 2007
with space for activities such as rodeos, graduations, and concerts, as
well as a library, and fitness centre. Mayerthorpe's thirty-year-old arena
was also used for a rodeo and agricultural fair until it burned down in
2006 to virtually identical discourse.[42]

Like the arena in the landscape of town life, the game of hockey figures large in the mythology of Canadian culture and collective identity. Even if Canadians "try their best to ignore it altogether...their disregard must be purposeful, done in conscious escape, for hockey's evidences are everywhere—on television and radio, in newspapers, in playgrounds and offices, on the streets, in sights and sounds, in the feeling of the season."[43] The federal Department of Canadian Heritage includes sport among its priorities alongside arts and multiculturalism. Although a 2001 documentary presents hockey as the quintessentially democratic populist game, "cameos by author Roch Carrier, Governor General Adrienne Clarkson and Prime Minister Jean Chrétien remind us that shinny [also] has the blessing of Canada's cultural and political authority figures."[44] In fact, Chrétien called his government's international trade committees "Team Canada." Hockey in this country was at first dominated by the same elite groups that controlled the organization of other sports. It attracted wide popular devotion partly in response to a powerful combination of economic and media interests. In order to command the scarce resources of time, energy, and money available in the late nineteenth and early twentieth century when it took root, the game needed focused support from businesses, institutions, and civic leaders to consolidate and organize popular interest.[45]

In its association with a nostalgic ideal of everyday national life, the game seems to have "developed almost magically out of an exposure to ice, snow, and open spaces."[46] Ken Dryden and Roy MacGregor suggest that, in the bleak white prairie expanses, hockey was particularly effective in creating a "communal way to help endure, even celebrate" winter. The "search for solidarity and entertainment" was enough to get prairie people to "slog ten miles through winter cold" to a game.[47] This is a convincing argument; however, it could as easily apply to curling or even potluck suppers in the community hall. It was not inevitable that hockey achieve a prize position in Alberta's sporting culture, nor that it remain there when game schedules no longer depend on outdoor conditions. This section traces the ascendance of

TOBBY IT, TOM.

Woodcut showing ice hockey, from Medicine Hat News, *December 20, 1894.* [GA NA-1754-2]

hockey in Alberta sports culture and the public imagination according to the major forces that selected, shaped, and produced its contemporary commercial forms from the original grassroots game.

In its long domination of winter sports coverage, hockey has generated archives and attics full of scrapbooks of newspaper clippings, programs, score cards, player cards, and other ephemera, not to mention multiple published volumes and films about famous teams, players, business, and the history of the game. As a result, we have relatively more detail on its organizational period than we do for many other sports. A Calgary newspaper of January 4, 1893 reported a "very exciting game of hockey was played at the Star skating rink between teams of town boys and one picked from the ranks of the tailors"; this game is now usually cited as the first recorded hockey game in the province.[48] Although there later was a Calgary team called the Town Boys, it is likely that this first game was literally between boys of the town and a group of tailors. In March of that year, a notice appeared that when the NWMP team had failed to appear for a hockey game

Ladies' hockey club, Edmonton, 1899. Note that the players are fastening skate blades to their everyday footwear. [GA NA-2750-36]

at the curling rink, a friendly game had taken place among the "town boys" instead.[49]

In fact, the designation of the game as the first in the province must be modified to specify male hockey, or hockey of a particular organized level. A contemporary newspaper account reports an Edmonton women's hockey team playing in 1890. Annie Laurie Robertson, daughter of Edmonton's first sheriff, was captain.[50] Women's teams generally played for recreation when men did not need the ice time; some barred spectators but most were open and drew good audiences since rivalries were fierce and teams played to win. Like Edmonton, Calgary had several women's hockey leagues with teams formed by community clubs, schools, and businesses. In 1899, the Edmonton

Ladies Hockey Team was the first Canadian women's hockey team with commercial endorsement, in this case by Starr Acme Club skates.[51]

In this early period, Calgarians, who were less interested in watching hockey than were Edmontonians, boasted more on-ice, populist participation. (Spectatorship grew; the first covered rink was built in the city in 1904, and in 1911, one Calgary hockey game turned away hundreds of spectators for lack of seats.)[52] The first Edmonton games were played on the river in the winter of 1894-1895. In 1896, the Thistles built an outdoor rink on Jasper Avenue and First Street and in 1902 built the covered Thistle Rink, which had a seating capacity of 2,000. After it burned down in 1913, the Edmonton Pavilion opened to replace it. The Shamrocks built the outdoor Strathcona rink in 1895 and a covered rink in 1904 with a seating capacity of 2,200. From the beginning, fans were so enthusiastic that crowd control was often necessary to keep them from physical involvement in games. Edmonton held its first hockey game on Christmas Day 1894; the senior home team Thistles beat Strathcona. Before travel between Edmonton and Calgary became more common, Edmonton and Strathcona took the roles of epic rivals. Terence O'Riordan argues that, at least for these two towns, hockey rivalry provided a unifying community experience.[53] The following year, for instance, the Thistles and the new South Edmonton Shamrocks all met after their game at the Strathcona Hotel "for the most important reason for hockey—dinner and socialising."[54]

Organized competition schedules developed around rematch challenges and the accompanying social activities. In men's hockey, a prevalent gambling system, common since the 1890s, raised the stakes for players and managers and nurtured an erratic observation of rules. Scandals attended standards of refereeing and amateurism since virtually all competitive "shamateur" teams used professionals. In 1907, the Alberta Amateur Hockey Association (AAHA) was founded in Red Deer for senior and quasi-pro teams, but intermediates and juniors later joined.[55] During the 1909 series for the Alberta championship, the Taber team eliminated the Edmonton Eskimos, who immediately called for an investigation by the Alberta Amateur Hockey Association. Taber was disqualified for using a professional player, but the Calgary Shermans refused the AAHA order to play the Eskimos in a new final. The Eskimos were awarded the championship without stepping on the ice for a single playoff game.[56] That year the National Hockey Association (later the NHL) formed as regulating body for professional hockey, and a great many skilled amateur players turned professional as hockey became a profitable spectator attraction in larger cities. The Stanley Cup, originally awarded for amateur hockey in 1893, was awarded to a fully professional team for the first time in 1908. That year the Edmonton Eskimos lost the cup to Montreal, despite acquiring stars Lester Patrick and Tom Phillips from the rival team for the game.[57]

The popular intercity rivalry between Edmonton and Strathcona and, later, between Edmonton and Calgary teams, also played out in women's sports. In 1901, South Edmonton had two women's teams, including the Shamrocks, who played for the Western Girls' Hockey trophy against Edmonton's "high-powered feminine aggregation."[58] In 1906, the first women's provincial tournament was held at the Banff Carnival, which hosted championships up to the end of the 1930s. In 1916, the city's Victorias high school team played the National Girls Team at Diamond Park, and the next year the Edmonton Monarchs played Calgary's Regents for the ladies' provincial championship. The Victorias were renamed the Monarchs in 1918 and, at that year's carnival, which they won, they were the only hockey team to be coached by a woman. After that date they were coached by a man, and did not win the Banff Carnival tournament again until 1926, when they defeated the Fernie Swastikas to win the Alpine Cup. They also won Alberta's Misener Cup for Women's hockey, and the Western Canadian Championship. (Not unusually for the time, team member Christina McKnight gave coach Potts Newman the credit for their success.)[59]

Calgary had a Swastika skating club in 1909, and both Edmonton and Fernie later had women's teams called the Swastikas after what was then a good luck symbol. The first Calgary city women's team, the Crescents, played teams from Red Deer, Okotoks, Canmore, Banff,

A renowned member of the Monarchs hockey team, Violet Davis of Edmonton poses at the
Banff Winter Carnival, 1932. Like male athletes of the period, women often participated in
several different sports. [GA ND-3-6539A]

and Medicine Hat. Another Calgary team called the Regents won the
Alpine Cup, the Banff Winter Carnival's provincial trophy in 1917, 1919,
1920, and 1921. In 1924, the team merged with several other players
and formed the Calgary Hollies, who went on to win four Banff tournaments and the Alpine Cup. In 1927, the top-ranked Hollies beat the
Monarchs for the Banff Carnival championships as well as for the
Alberta Ladies Championship. The following year the Monarchs took
back the title. The top western team, the Jasper Place Rustlers, won
the Edmonton Open City Women's Championship and the provincial
championship in 1932. In 1933, the team won the Western Canadian
Championship, the Dominion Women's Hockey Championship, and
the Canadian Senior Ladies championship. They won the latter title
again the following year, and held the Alberta and British Columbia
titles for 1934–1935. In 1937, the Calgary Avenue Grills were provincial
champions but never played for the national championship after being
barred for refusing to join the Dominion Women's Amateur Hockey
Association.[60]

Red Deer was another centre of women's hockey. A new skating
and curling rink hosted the first women's hockey teams, the Stars
and the Skookums, in 1904. The Red Deer Amazons were provincial
champions twice during the 1920s and Alberta Intermediate Champs
1933–1934. Smaller towns also had women's hockey teams in the 1890s,
and leagues and interurban competitions were organized by the early
1900s, increasing in number as ice rinks became more common into
the 1920s. In Medicine Hat, a women's game took place in 1897, with
spectators not allowed.[61] However, Robert Kossuth asserts that young
women challenged gender perception and reacted to male domination
in sports through playing hockey in southern Alberta before World
War II.[62]

Enthusiasm for women's hockey peaked in the 1930s, when all
provinces except Saskatchewan competed for the Dominion Women's
Amateur Hockey Association championship.[63] But after World War II,
women's hockey lost much of its fan base. As Alberta shifted from an
agricultural to industrial economy during the twentieth century, more

rural people migrated to cities, where audiences had turned their attention to high-profile men's teams. As hockey became more professional and elite, more ice time was given to boys and men on community rinks and indoor arenas; fewer recreational skaters had access.

Alberta women moved into the workplace after the war, supported in Alberta by the economic expansion following the discovery of oil in 1947. Laura Robinson attributes the marginalization of women's hockey in part to these shifts, concluding that as global economic forces and women's equality movements challenge traditional constructs of masculinity, spheres such as sport work "twice as hard at providing constant affirmation of male strength and aggression."[64] Women continued to play recreational hockey in community leagues and clubs, but not to the large crowds drawn by even minor and amateur men's teams.

Canadian girls successfully insisted on the right to join boys' hockey teams in the 1970s, and the base for serious organized competition at higher levels returned. In 1973, four Edmonton teams formed the Northern Alberta Ladies' Hockey League. The Edmonton Chimos dominated; classed as an A team, the Chimos took on Bantam and Midget boys' teams, Oldtimers, and other men's teams. They were Canadian Ladies champions in 1984–1985. In 1978, the Alberta Amateur Hockey Association formed a women's council.[65] Around this time, ringette, a version of indoor hockey played only by women, gained popularity. The Edmonton Ringette Club formed in 1984, and Alberta has contributed five team players at the national level. In 2002, the team won the World Ringette Championships; the national Woods Ringette Tournament was held in Edmonton in 2003.[66]

By the 1920s, as an emerging popular entertainment and mass media culture fostered hockey's success as a commercialized spectator sport, recreational hockey flourished in communities and regional and provincial organizations. The largest cities typically supported both men's and women's hockey teams, as did businesses, schools, colleges, churches, and service clubs. In 1921 Edmonton, a city of fewer than 60,000 people, there were juvenile, junior, intermediate, and senior city leagues, junior and senior church leagues and community leagues,

Doug and Fred Purvis looking at hockey equipment—a suggestion for Christmas presents.
Published in The Albertan, *December 21, 1954.* [GA NA-5600-7897C]

including one for girls. Recreational skaters and women's teams alike
began to lose priority on community ice time to male hockey teams
as an increasing emphasis on team profile, winning, and prestigious
contests exerted pressure for more practice time.[67]

Still, despite the game's popularity it had not yet achieved a central
national presence in everyday life and sports. In 1930, of a Canadian
population of ten million, fewer than 14,000 kids played hockey. A
journalist warned in 1948 that without nurturing young stars, high-
level hockey could not succeed. However, by that time, recruiting had
become systematic, with players from "open-air rinks, swept by winds
from the prairies" graduating to "big, heated, artificial ice arenas" in a

bid to build careers in hockey.[68] As amateur clubs regularly supplied talent to the professionals, NHL scouts came regularly to the province. As a *Calgary Herald* sportswriter put it, "if some player in some God-forsaken two-bit village 200 miles from nowhere shows the slightest signs of ability on ice," he could expect to see "two or three scouts, disguised behind dark glasses, handlebar mustaches, broad-brimmed hats and smelly stogies" checking him out.[69]

The postwar baby boom provided the population to fill minor hockey leagues, and television arrived soon after to expand the audience already created by radio. More varieties and brands of hockey equipment were available, and the visual images of hockey stars on television and in print helped to inspire young people's interest in the game and thus in related consumer goods. By the end of the 1950s, Canada's best male athletes were choosing hockey as their sport. With the population a little over sixteen million in 1957, almost 100,000 youth were involved in organized hockey, and memorial arenas and retail outlets were built across the country.[70] The Alberta Junior Hockey League (AJHL) was organized in 1963 with five teams after the Oil Kings won the Memorial Cup and suddenly "there were 10,000 kids wanting to play junior hockey in Alberta."[71] The success of the AJHL and other junior leagues also renewed interest in senior and professional hockey. In the early 1960s, there was still only "a handful of arenas" in Edmonton but Chief Commissioner George Hughes, an important champion of minor hockey, ensured the number of indoor arenas rose from four to twelve during the 1970s. As of 2007, Edmonton had nearly fifty indoor arenas, and Calgary around forty. Hughes was also involved in developing large arenas and organizing world championship events. The historic South Side Arena was renamed in his honour in 2008.[72]

The Edmonton Beavers won the first provincial junior title in 1915 and the Calgary Crystals in 1917. In 1924, the Calgary Canadians were the first Alberta team to compete for the national Memorial Cup; they lost, but won two years later.[73] The Edmonton Athletic Club, the first city team to win the Abbott Cup for the western Canada junior championship in 1935 was a training ground for senior hockey. Gordon Watt, who played with the team in their championship year, went on to play defence with the Eskimos in the Alberta Senior Hockey League and then to captain the famous Edmonton Flyers. As an amateur player, he held a day job as fireman, lending his double public hero status to public events and promotions for the city and the game.[74]

For young men, junior amateur play can be a stepping stone to senior or even professional status, but many clubs have won significant popular followings in their own right. In the 1940s, four Edmonton Athletic Clubs produced members of a junior team called the Capitals, renamed the Oil Kings in 1950 by team owner Jim Christiansen to reflect the city's new source of wealth. The team, along with Calgary's juniors, joined the Western Canada Junior Hockey League (WCJHL) in 1951 as it became the Western Hockey League (WHL). That season the Oil Kings attracted around 3,000 fans per game, the highest junior hockey attendance in western Canada. In 1954, the Edmonton Exhibition Association (EEA) adopted the club, whose players included John and Bill Bucyk, Gary Melnyk, Norm Ullman, and Ray Kinasewich. The team reached the Memorial Cup playoffs ten times and won twice before folding in 1976, reforming in 1978–1979 and again in 2007.[75]

After the Oil Kings' 1963 Memorial Cup win, gleeful fans poured onto the ice; the *Edmonton Journal* photographed team captain Roger Bourbonnais in robe and crown for the sports section. He played for the Olympic national team later that year, but Canada won bronze only retroactively when a recount was held in 2005, upon which a *Journal* columnist lamented the loss of "players of Bourbonnais's generation, back when hockey was played, not for millions, not for the corporate bottom line, but for love and hometown glory."[76] Such a mythic view of hockey history contains a thread of reality, because glory often had to suffice; the unstable bottom line was certainly always a factor. The Oil Kings established a pattern of financial losses, down $7,000 in their first season and $21,000 in 1953–1954. When the EEA took over, it tied players' salaries to gate receipts. As the Detroit Red Wings farm team, the Oil Kings continued to lose money, in part because Detroit took the best players. But in 1962, they played the first televised hockey game featuring a western Canadian team. The team was sold to investors for $10,000 and then simply turned over to Bill Hunter, the president and general manager.[77]

After the Oil Kings won the Memorial Cup again in 1966, the team moved to the more competitive senior league and were ruled ineligible for the junior cup by the Canadian Amateur Hockey Association (CAHA), which inspired Hunter to form the Western Canadian Major Junior Hockey League; it was renamed the Western Canada Hockey League (WCHL) in 1966-1967 with eleven teams. The CAHA, which westerners already resented for taking a percentage of the gate during playoffs, declared the league "outlaw." In keeping with this image, league play was marked by fights and occasional riots among teams from Calgary, Edmonton, and Medicine Hat, among others from Manitoba, Saskatchewan, and BC. In 1972, the Oil Kings won the WCHL title.[78]

As pro hockey came to Calgary, Edmonton, and Winnipeg, interest in junior hockey waned somewhat but play continued. In 1972, the Edmonton Movers and Edmonton Maple Leafs combined to become the Edmonton Mets, which became the Spruce Grove Mets in 1974. The team won several championships in the following years, and as the St. Albert Saints won four AJHL championships between 1980-1981 and 1997-1998. Now the Spruce Grove Saints, the team is the only extant franchise from the original league. AJHL players, including Mark Messier, have gone on to senior play and to the NHL, minor pro leagues in North America and Europe, varsity and collegiate leagues.[79] Lethbridge acquired a major junior hockey team, the Broncos, in 1975. The team reached the Memorial Cup finals with players such as Bryan Trottier and Brian Sutter who went on to play in the NHL.

For ambitious players, a place on a university or college team provides a step toward the majors and potentially professional levels. The University of Alberta Golden Bears, established 1908, joined the Western Intercollegiate Athletic Union in 1919 and went on to win seventeen straight titles until taking permanent possession of the trophy in 1950. The women's hockey team has also dominated, winning eight Canada West titles and four national championships as of 2005.[80] Since the mid-twentieth century, universities have adopted a commercial model and built large facilities in part to attract paying audiences, and teams represent their campuses like the pros represent cities.

For many years, senior amateur hockey in Alberta was more popular than the NHL, which represented only a few Canadian cities. Almost every sizeable community iced a senior amateur team, most consisting "of 'community players' born and raised where they played hockey."[81] There was no provincial governing body for senior amateur hockey until the 1907 formation of the AAHA, which excluded professionals, set residency rules, and divided senior amateur hockey into two tiers. In practice, A teams brought in "ringers" and professionals, paying them under the table to help win big games. Claiming that the AAHA favoured Edmonton teams, Calgary rejected membership and formed a new southern league in 1910. (In 1916, the Calgary Vics, then the top team in the province, refused to play in the provincial amateur finals against Edmonton if they were not paid.)[82]

Before World War I, the Edmonton Dominion Furriers club was the top senior team in the province, and 2,000 fans turned out to watch them play against the Eskimos in the first game of the 1913 season on Christmas Day at the Edmonton Gardens. The Canadian Hockey Association formed in 1914, and the Allan Cup soon became a major senior amateur prize. The best teams—the Eskimos, Dominions, Calgary Columbus, and Calgary Tigers—formed the Big Four league in 1919. Amateur in name only, it attracted professional players such as "Duke" Keats, who had been a star player for the NHL and later played for the Boston Bruins, Detroit Cougars (later Red Wings), and the Chicago Blackhawks. Internal disputes between Edmonton and Calgary over the use of pro players helped to undermine the league, which folded before two full seasons.[83] Alberta teams that have won the Allan Cup include the Calgary Stampeders, Edmonton Flyers, Stony Plain Eagles, and Drumheller Miners. Edmonton won the cup in 1984, 1985, 1987, 1988, and 1990, losing the conference final in 1986 to the Flames, who won the cup in 1989.[84]

Senior games were well-supported by local fans and media in the 1920s. On March 17, 1923 the *Edmonton Journal* reported that "seven thousand Edmonton citizens will tell their children and their children's children that it was on this night the Eskimos emblazoned their names large on the pages of hockey history by winning the championship of the WCHL in the most thrilling contest in the annals of the game in Western Canada."[85] In the early 1930s, after teams like the Tigers and Eskimos became professional, senior hockey was more affordable, more interesting to locals, and played to full houses. In their best season, 1936–1937, the Edmonton Dominions drew record crowds of 5,000 or more to the Gardens. The team reached the Allan Cup playoffs, helping to create a fan base that would contribute to the sport's postwar momentum.[86] One young fan later remembered watching games at the Gardens.

> *The Edmonton Gardens did not coddle its patrons. This was a building that made you work for the privilege of seeing what you'd come to see... From the nosebleed seats at the south end of the building, fully half the ice surface was obscured by the overhanging lights. Even the wealthier citizens further down were obliged to contort themselves in order to see around the many diagonal support posts holding the great building up. But this was not cause for complaint. Heck no. We knew nothing else, remember.*[87]

Senior hockey thrived in the 1930s and 1940s in part because local companies sponsored teams and made jobs for journeymen athletes. Teams and their sponsors reminded fans of their community linkages wherever possible. In 1946, the Calgary Stampeders wore cowboy outfits rather than team uniforms in a local parade. Managers could sign and keep good players with the promise of a steady wage earned close to home; players were paid between fifty to seventy dollars per week, which typically exceeded their day job salary. Harvey "Pug" Young of the Flyers, for instance, made sixty dollars per week as a player, while his City Telephone Department job paid under forty dollars per week.

Calgary Stampeders Allan Cup Champions hockey float, 1946. [GA NA-2785-18]

When he demanded a raise, coach Riley Mullen warned other officials such as Dave "Sweeney" Schriner not to encourage such "greedy"
players.[88] After the Edmonton Gainers Superiors became provincial
senior champs in 1931, captain John Beattie left his meat-packing plant
job to play for the professional Boston Bruins. In 1933, the Superiors
won "the city's first major international triumph," the International
Championships in Switzerland, as well as the Alberta Provincial
Championships. They won the Alberta championships again in 1935.[89]

Edmonton was the leading hockey city in Alberta for two decades
before the Calgary Vics became the top team in 1936, bringing new
attention to the game there. After 1945, the Stampeders and Flyers
became Alberta's senior amateur rivals, respectively winning the Allan
Cup in 1946 and 1948 before going to the minor pro Western Hockey

League in the 1950s. Senior hockey was just as popular in smaller centres. When the Lethbridge Maple Leafs won the Alberta Senior Hockey Championships in 1941 and 1942 they "were the toast of [a] hockey-mad city."[90]

As it later would for the junior Oil Kings, the EEA became sponsors of the senior Edmonton Flyers in 1937. The team, which consisted of local junior hockey veterans except for one player, attracted an average of almost 5,000 fans in its first season, later reaching a league attendance high of around 6,000. Nevertheless, interest in the pro game rose among fans and players who saw a chance to earn a living on the ice instead of a factory floor. The Flyers, who won the amateur Allan Cup in 1948, joined the professional Detroit Red Wings organization to become the senior WCHL farm team when minor pro hockey returned to Alberta in 1951. Captained by Doug Messier, later father of Mark Messier who would be a star player for the Edmonton Oilers and other teams in the 1980s, the Flyers won the WHL title in 1953, again in 1955 and 1962.[91] As professionals, the Flyers attracted capacity crowds but attendance dwindled as television's *Hockey Night in Canada* drew more attention to the NHL. The Flyers lost $15,426 in their first pro season, in part because of a significant drop in fan interest when the team cut local players in favour of imported professionals; many senior players, older and with roots in the city, decided to remain with amateur intermediate teams. By the end of the decade, previously full houses also dropped sharply for Calgary's minor pro Stampeders, and both teams folded in 1963.[92]

City senior and junior hockey teams were made up of an ever-shifting roster of local heroes who moved between organizations over the years. Star goalie Jack Manson went from the Edmonton Junior Hockey League to the Flyers and moved to the Mercurys in 1948. Owned and sponsored by Jim Christiansen's Waterloo Motors car dealership, the Mercurys lost in Allan Cup playoffs that season but won both the Western Intermediate A Championship and the world championship title in 1950. In 1952, the team was selected to represent Canada at the Oslo Olympics, in part because owner Christiansen,

unlike most amateur club sponsors, could afford the trip. One of the
players recalled that, for Christiansen, the trip "was all about pride.
He was always waving the Canadian flag. He wouldn't even let us
move our skates during the anthem."[93] The level of national pride may
have been somewhat diluted when, after collecting seventeen penalties in one of the games, the Mercurys had to be cautioned by the
International Amateur Ice Hockey Federation to modify their aggressive strategies on the ice.[94]

When they won the gold medal as predicted, though, only one
Canadian reporter was present, and the province's sports pages
provided little coverage. Only two weeks later was a parade held at
home in Edmonton. One player humbly recalled, "it was nice. They had
floats. And the mayor let the school kids out...We were all quite thrilled
by it."[95] It would be half a century before Canada again won Olympic
gold in men's hockey. The Mercurys were forgotten until they were
celebrated at the 1988 Calgary Olympics and named to the Canadian
Olympic Hall of Fame in 2001. The 2002 Canadian Olympic team
jackets, uniforms, and other apparel were modelled after the Mercurys'
original Olympics gear, though Team Canada wore the crest of the 1924
Toronto Granites, the first official Canadian Olympic team.[96]

Other Alberta teams achieved international acclaim. In 1951, the
Lethbridge Maple Leafs won the world amateur hockey championship with a team composed of local senior and junior hockey players
who held down day jobs. The intermediate Lacombe Rockets represented Canada in a 1965 exhibition tour of Europe, winning eleven out
of fifteen games.[97] The minor pro Lethbridge Native Sons (named for
local men serving in the war) won world championships in 1951 and
1952, the first time any Canadian province had won back-to-back international prizes. In 1954, the minor pro Calgary Stampeders won both
the WHL title and the Edinburgh Cup. The Drumheller Miners made it
to Allan Cup competition in 1967, as did the Stampeders in 1971. More
recently, cup winners have included only two Alberta teams, the Stony
Plain Eagles in 1999 and the Lloydminster Border Kings in 2001.[98]

Organized women's hockey declined after World War II, as men's
and boys' hockey took primary place in the cultural imagination
and in acquiring ice time. More recently, Alberta women's teams
have fared well; the Edmonton Chimos won the Canadian Women's
Championship in 1984, 1985, 1992, and 1997, and the Calgary Oval
X-tremes won in 1998, 2001, and 2003.

The five main periods of pro hockey in Alberta are the 1920s, 1930s,
1950–1960s, 1971–1979 (World Hockey Association), and 1979 to present
(National Hockey League). In the early decades, organized western
pro and amateur leagues were alternatives to the elite professional
game that dominated central Canada, but amateur and professional
hockey players increasingly moved back and forth between leagues. By
the early 1920s, hockey players were well-paid in comparison to other
professional athletes, and the presence of three official pro circuits in
the country meant a good market for their skills.

Minor pro leagues, some of them with NHL farm teams, formed in
Alberta cities by 1910, and pro hockey thrived in the early 1920s. The
Eskimos and the Calgary Tigers of the professional Western Canada
Hockey League (1921–1926) lost the Stanley Cup in 1923 and 1924 respectively. The Tigers won three regular season titles and two playoff
championships in their six years of play, but it would be sixty years
before either team challenged for the cup again. Nevertheless, when
Eskimos' revenues could not meet star player salaries, and owner
Kenny McKenzie considered moving the team to Regina, loyal fans
organized a successful ticket drive to keep them in the city.[99] The
debate about the ethics of paying star athletes to play on amateur
teams had consequences when Pacific Coast Hockey League (PCHL)
president Frank Patrick accused professional players, including "Duke"
Keats, of accepting bribes to play for the Edmonton Eskimos. In 1923,
the PCHL went professional.[100] The league was soon defunct, and in
1925 the WCHL acquired several teams from PCHL.

In the burgeoning new mass entertainment market, western Canadian teams mainly served to develop talent, which was then lured away to larger cities. "Edmonton Express" Eddie Shore was sold to the Boston Bruins in 1926. The whl folded later due to problems including low population and long distances to games, as well as a lack of artificial ice.[101] But minor pro leagues and teams continued intermittent cycles of revival; whl reformed in 1932-1933, the pchl reformed in 1936-1941 and again in 1944-1952. As hockey expanded in the 1950s, Calgary and Edmonton joined a new Western Hockey League formed from the pchl and the Western Canada Senior Hockey League, which operated until 1974.

In 1972, the World Hockey Association (wha) formed with the Alberta Oilers as founding members; the plan was to split the season between Calgary and Edmonton, but they combined to become the Edmonton Oilers the following year. The Calgary Cowboys were that city's first pro team, arriving in 1975. The wha collapsed in 1979, and Edmonton and Calgary joined the nhl. A group of Calgary investors headed by Nelson Skalbania bought the Flames from their Georgia equivalents; the logo image originally stood for not oil power but the Civil War burning of Atlanta. The team made the playoffs in their first eleven seasons and won the Stanley Cup in 1989. The Oilers won the Stanley Cup in 1984, 1985, 1987, 1988, and 1990.[102] As small-market teams began to leave Canada during the 1980s, partly because budgets would no longer cover star players' salaries, Oilers owner Peter Pocklington traded star player Wayne Gretzky to the Los Angeles Kings in 1988. The trade entered local and national mythology, casting Pocklington as the villain who destroyed local hockey pride.

The Oilers lost the playoffs in 1989 and several of their best players over the next years, finishing out of the playoffs for the first time in 1993. The team's performance and attendance at home games fell after the Gretzky trade, in part due to local resentment toward Pocklington. A 1996 ticket drive doubled the local season ticket base, but Pocklington, financially pressured by creditor the Alberta Treasury Branches (atb) (a Crown corporation owned by the province), put the team up for sale the next year. Premier Ralph Klein favoured keeping the team in Alberta, but because the ATB is owned by the provincial government, he was wary of appearing to subsidize a professional hockey team. However, a few years later when the Calgary Flames were also in financial trouble, Klein proposed an Alberta-wide lottery whereby those buying tickets would be spending their money to support both NHL teams.[103]

The local investors group that finally bought the Oilers in 1998 called the team "an asset we couldn't afford to lose for emotional and economic purposes...We really believed we were not buying a hockey team—we were buying into our city."[104] After the 2004-2005 NHL lockout season, a new NHL salary cap agreement and a better currency conversion rate from Canadian to US dollars meant that the Oilers were more financially viable, and although they did not qualify for the playoffs after the 2005-2006 season, they remained popular with local fans. In 2007-2008, Daryl Katz bought the Oilers.[105]

HOCKEY FUTURES

Radio and television broadcasting have successfully sold the idea of NHL hockey as a Canadian institution despite its foundation in an American cartel. Before 1914, commercialized hockey was based on a "developing maturity of infrastructure combined with increasing integration into the world of big money...the amateur gentleman had been replaced by the skilled professional."[106] As Alberta's economic base shifted from agriculture toward industry, oil production, and free market systems, the social conditions and shared experiences that forged community connections also changed. As social values became less rigid during the 1960s, hockey itself was transformed along scientific, profit-oriented lines. This evolution reflected increasing levels of state organization and bureaucracy by the power of extra-national capital.[107]

The myth that the home team represents the community and the nation has been shattered regularly by cultural theorists and business people since the early twentieth century but has remained compelling for sports fans. Still, Albertans now share in a national rethinking of hockey's role in our leisure lives and imaginations. Early in its organization, the game appealed to community leaders in part because it promised the catharsis of adolescent male energies within the constraints of rules and rinks. Paul Rutherford argues that, in the 1950s, the masculine mystique of the game still meshed well with a society "characterized by an excessive devotion to rules and conventions."[108] But ideals of masculinity are themselves in process of change. Edmonton poet Tim Bowling writes of rejecting the culture of pro hockey, whereby "many so-called sensitive, cultured men...are nonetheless fervent fans of a brutal, bone-breaking, blood-spattering sport." Why should he "follow...empty rhetoric around outdated and destructive notions of patriotism and manhood?"[109] Bowling admits that, although he commonly encounters youth indifferent to the tradition, the great narrative of hockey still has social functions of connecting high and mass culture and offering a common topic for conversation and community bonding. In 2006, during a rare Edmonton Oilers playoff run, young people with no previous interest in the sport found themselves fervently cheering night after night among friendly strangers, inspiring much reminiscing among their parents about the glory days of the 1980s.[110]

Though women have always played hockey on recreational and amateur levels, their primary and enduring role has been as supporters of male players. In the early 1970s, women's participation in the game was still viewed as a novelty for events such as mother-son hockey games. This attitude was on the edge of lasting change; girls were admitted to minor hockey organizations in the 1970s and received training at girls' hockey schools. However, attitudes were slow to change. The *Calgary Herald*'s report on girls' hockey in 1974 featured the headline annotation, "Some want to get off the bench and others want to get back there; and only their hairdressers know for sure."[111] In 2002–2003, a record 61,000 Canadian girls and women registered in hockey leagues, a fivefold increase over one decade. As many boys have moved into other sports such as soccer, girls are "now the main engine

Community centres' annual mother–son hockey match, Calgary, January 1971.

[GA NA-2864-18609]

of growth in the national game, and a critical source of the fees that keep its arenas open."[112]

Women's sports coverage once was far more extensive than it is now, where articles tend to focus primarily on tennis and golf. On one day in November 2010, for instance, the *Edmonton Journal* ran ten articles on men's sports and only one on women's soccer. The sole article, which noted the Canadian senior women's soccer win of the Confederation of North, Central American and Caribbean Association Football tournament for the first time since 1998, ran outside the sports pages. The Hockey Hall of Fame added two additional spots to those designated for women in 2010 in order to include Angela James, dominant Canadian female player in the 1970s and 1980s, and Cammi Granato, all-time leader in goals and points for the United States in world championships. A *Montreal Gazette* editorial urged more recognition for elite women athletes as a key to attracting more girls to the game and improving international competition.[113]

Alberta organizations and writers continue to produce men's hockey homages, from the Oilers Heritage website to new books, including one on the Edmonton–Calgary rivalry (Sandor, *Battle of Alberta*) and one on the 1954–1955 Flyers (Vantour, *The Fabulous Flyers*). The latter was published by the Hockey Alberta Foundation, which also released a new edition of collectibles featuring team greats Norm Ullman, Glenn Hall, and Johnny Bucyk.[114] Outside of the unsteady current trajectory of professional hockey, there has been a resurgence of interest at recreational and community levels and in lower-priced junior play. The fragments of national mythology are still discernible amid the clashing sticks, but events such as the 2005 NHL strike and the Olympic success of women's hockey teams have also introduced cracks in the ice.

In Alberta, minor hockey registration increased slightly in Edmonton in the early 2000s, partly due to improved access through equipment distribution programs. The city's Minor Hockey Week, the largest of its kind in North America, had its forty-ninth anniversary in 2012.[115] Calgary hosts the Mac's World Invitational AAA Midget Hockey Tournament, many participants of which have gone on to the NHL. In 2003, professional hockey scored one for public relations when the Heritage Classic game between the Oilers and the Canadiens was staged on an outdoor rink, evoking, at least for the local press, images of traditional prairie hockey.[116] The spectacle inspired a revived interest in Minor Hockey Week. Sponsor Lyle Best remarked, "when you think about it, how many events are there which touch so many people? Who isn't a parent, grandparent, aunt, uncle, brother or sister of a minor hockey player?"[117] The revival of pond hockey programs in Alberta also returns us to the immediacy of playing the game for fun on any convenient ice. Adult leagues draw good participation in the province.

Another sign of health is the strength of varsity hockey. The University of Alberta men's hockey team has won a record twelve national titles and forty-five Western Canada championships since its start in 1908. Thirteen members of the team have gone on to play in the NHL. The university's women's hockey team, the Pandas, have also won multiple national championships in the Canadian Interuniversity Sport league. The University of Calgary Dinos have won eight Canada West Championships since 1974 and played in the CIS finals ten times. The women's team won their first Canada West title in 2009 after seven years in the conference.[118]

The de-emphasis of the elite hockey culture that has been nurtured over decades in the province may point to the thawing of mythologies that for generations have implied that "any kid without an instinctive understanding of the game is genetically un-Canadian."[119] But, amidst the powerful currents of change in both amateur and professional levels of the sport, hockey has remained a fulcrum of emotion, business, memory, and urban planning in Alberta.

CONCLUSION

The pattern of team sport organization over the past century or so echoes the history of other realms of popular culture in which folk practices or grassroots production were taken under the auspices of an individual or group for a number of purposes, including the making of financial or cultural capital. Team sport organization might have been undertaken for both intrinsic love of the cultural form or for its exploitation. From the late nineteenth century on, in Alberta sports six themes prevail: (1) the value of the amateur ideal as opposed to professional organization and marketing; (2) relatedly, the vision of sport

as cultural vehicle as opposed to commercial product; (3) the centralized, metropolitan core of organization and administration in relation
to western adherence or resistance to those models; (4) the industrial
production of players as commodities from minor through professional levels of play; (5) the expansion of mass media and the growth
of audiences, which gave scope to intensified imaginative identification with players and teams; (6) accordingly, while sporting teams
became prestigious vehicles for intercity and international competition, communities continued to identify with them and they remain,
to varying extents, media of social cohesion.

These themes and patterns have been explored through histories
and narratives of team sport and of broad organizational dynamics
within the context of the developing province itself. The next chapter
considers the experiences of athletes engaged in competition as individuals in sports whose organizational processes both reflected and
diverged from those of baseball, hockey, football, and other team sports.

6

SPORT AND THE SINGLE ATHLETE

MAVERICKS, KNIGHTS, AND KNICKERBOCKERS

ALTHOUGH HOCKEY, BASEBALL, AND FOOTBALL TEAMS have typically commanded the public imagination, civic pride, and investment dollars, sports played by individual athletes reveal as much about the passions and patterns of Alberta society. Competitive forms of sport such as rodeo, track and field, swimming, and skating emerged from contexts of everyday work skills or leisure pastimes. Others, including cycling, downhill skiing, tennis and golf, first arrived with settlers and entrepreneurs who could afford specialized equipment and spaces before spreading to the mainstream. All, to varying extents, feature the compelling figure of a solo athlete challenging an opponent or simply the self and, often, forces of nature.

RODEO

CONTROLLED STAMPEDES

Aritha van Herk has observed that culture, sport, and spectacle in Alberta have always merged because "we don't like our culture lying on a plate, boring and passive. We want it alive, biting back, an articulation of our love for carnival, for excess and excitement."[1] On his first trip north in the 1950s, football player Jackie Parker passed through Calgary during Stampede week. Seeing herds of cattle in the street and hundreds of people dressed in cowboy gear, he figured that the province was still a wild frontier.[2] This impression of Alberta has been a common and persistent one, in part due to conscious exploitation. In 2008, Alberta Liberal Party leader Kevin Taft wore a black cowboy hat and bolo tie to a press conference that coincided with the annual, very popular, Canadian Finals Rodeo. Taft asked, "what is more Alberta than rodeo?" And he urged that rodeo become the official provincial sport.[3] By contrast, in 1965 a group of Quebec's Laval University students turned down a request from Alberta students to stage a rodeo, explaining that "we do not consider a rodeo, folkloric in nature, to be a serious matter."[4] Cultural stereotypes aside, the apparently maverick, recklessly individualistic quality of the rodeo rider does continue to strike regional chords.

Partly due to its North American origins and grounding in conditions and skills of working life, rodeo eludes some of the patterns prevalent in Alberta sport history. Spectators watching the feats of champion riders over the years have likely had little reason (other than occasional injuries and mayhem) to compare the events with more visibly organized sports. But as a hybrid of rural nostalgia and modern spectator entertainment, rodeo embodies a central aspect of sports culture: the ongoing dynamic between power, spontaneity, and energy and the constraints of commercialized, centralized organization. Competitive rodeo, along with its wild, frontier image, was produced quite deliberately as mass spectator entertainment, and there were no official amateur agencies supervising its development.[5] Small, local rodeos offered amateurs the opportunity to compete and develop their skills, while professionals were usually connected with larger prize meets and Wild West shows. But by the 1920s, increasing commercialization blurred the lines between amateur and professional status. Organized rodeo culture thus largely bypassed the "gentlemanly" amateurism of team sports development, the focus on professional rewards comparatively direct and transparent as compared to the rhetoric and ideals in other sports.

From the early days of regional ranch settlement, equestrian events such as race weeks, turf clubs, polo tournaments, gymkhanas (games played on horseback), and driving clubs have flourished. Horse racing was one of the first sports to be organized and was initially dominated by First Nations ponies. A regional network of tracks and intercity competitions was established from the 1890s. In southern Alberta, Mounties and constabulary held gymkhanas. Urbanites and ranchers alike supported gala race meetings; special trains took Calgarians out to Cochrane events in the early 1900s. There was, therefore, an established audience for organized rodeo as it emerged around the late 1880s. At first an informal, popular cowboy sport, rodeo competitions grew from variants of traditional Anglo-Canadian events at race meets, sports days, and agricultural fairs as skills and practices rooted in rural life were codified for competition.[6]

Southern Alberta rancher John Ware may have invented rodeo sport in 1892 when he wrestled a charging animal to the ground and later demonstrated his technique at a Calgary equestrian show. Ware, one of the first black settlers in the province, also won roping contests at the Calgary Exhibitions of 1893 and 1894. Over a century later, a documentary about Ware featured Leon Jamerson, known as western Canada's "last black cowboy." Descended from black pioneers who came to Alberta from Oklahoma in the early 1900s, Jamerson was a championship chuckwagon racer who, in his early seventies, competed at the Ponoka Stampede. In 2010 he won the sportsman of the year award from the Alberta Professional Chuckwagon and Chariot Association.[7]

Other legendary rodeo stars were Herman Linder and Pete Knight. Linder emigrated from Wisconsin to Cardston as a child and rode in his first event at the age of fourteen disguised as a cowgirl named "Alberta Pearl."[8] In 1924, at age seventeen, the "Kid from Cardston" began his professional career when he won the Canadian Bronc Riding and Bareback Bronc Riding Championship at the Calgary Stampede. He became a hero across North America before retiring in 1929, winning the prestigious Prince of Wales Cup three times and multiple other top awards, including four world titles for bronc riding and twenty-two titles in the Stampede.[9] Pete Knight, whose professional career began in 1918, also won numerous Stampede and national champion-ships and was World Champion Bronc Rider for four years in the 1930s. Knight's popularity also stemmed from his performances with the widely touring Alberta Stampede Company. Country singer Wilf Carter, a protegé of Knight, competed for a time in the Canadian rodeo circuit while writing tunes, including "Pete Knight, King of the Cowboys" and later "Pete Knight's Last Ride" after the cowboy star was killed at a California rodeo in 1937. Thousands mourned, and every provincial government sent flowers to the funeral, as did the majority of states.[10]

The town of Raymond claims to have held the first organized rodeo in Canada in 1902; Medicine Hat also claims original status with its 1917 institution. The Hand Hills Lake Stampede (1917), which has served as a practice ground for all the great contestants in the Calgary Stampede, is also cited as the first organized rodeo.[11] There is some dispute over where the first organized rodeo was held. The town of Raymond claims to have held the first organized rodeo in Canada in 1902. In their book *Useful Pleasures*, Donald Grant Wetherell and Irene Kmet note that Medicine Hat also claims original status with its 1917 institution. And Brock Silversides calls Hand Hills Rodeo the longest running organized event in the province with its first rodeo in 1917. Differences in size, scale, and impact of these events likely account for the discrepancy in what constitutes the first "organized" rodeo.

As a provincial circuit developed, rodeo events were kept affordable since so many fans were rural working people and farmers. Despite its new respectability, early rodeo was still dogged by its uncouth, frontier image. Paradoxically, the iconographic wildness from which rodeo drew much of its appeal needed to be tamed and contained by organized standards of quality control suitable to a modern, urbanizing culture. The Calgary Stampede was a key influence on the emergence of organized rodeo, effectively associating it with both a wholesome agrarian way of life and Calgary's urban identity. Maxwell Foran points out that the white Stetson, associated by now with cowboy culture, represents as well the rancher and oil executive. The Stampede organization has also played an important role in advancing other sports in the city, promoting hockey and providing the largest facilities in the city for local events and national championships between 1950 and 1981. Stampede organization directors typically represent a range of urban and oil interests.[12]

After a particularly brutal winter almost destroyed the open-range ranching industry in 1906–1907, the first Stampede in 1912 was planned as a nostalgic "one shot affair to celebrate heritage and...a dying way of life."[13] Wild West shows had treated cowboy skill demonstrations as frontier theatre, but Stampede organizer Guy Weadick presented rodeo as an organized sporting competition. Over the 1920s rodeo became an established public sport, meeting that definition because it "involved physical exertion, it measured skill against standards of performance, it was competitive, and it applied uniform rules...all within a recreational framework."[14] It proved so popular that in 1923 it was formalized within the Calgary Exhibition and became one of the top sporting events on the continent. Rodeo moved further toward social legitimacy as a local tradition as towns all over the province added events to annual sports days, usually renaming them "Stampedes." Edmonton had a Stampede Rodeo in 1925 but did not consolidate it as an annual event. Jasper's first rodeo was held at Henry House Flats in 1926. After a slight decrease in audiences during the Depression years, an improving "harvest outlook in the province" contributed to the biggest crowd since 1929 when 38,541 attended the July 11, 1938 Calgary Stampede.[15]

Organizations emerging from the 1920s to the 1940s consolidated trends toward event regulation and uniformity, further aligning rodeo with other sporting cultures. Cities participating in established circuits could attract top acts.[16] By the 1950s there was a well-organized circuit of management and promotion, which included the Edmonton Rodeo of Champions, whose management, the Edmonton Exhibition Association, staged regular information and social events for prominent sports journalists.[17] Although the first Edmonton rodeo in 1951 lost $4,000, there was much local interest, particularly in the chuckwagon races, and that same week a Cardston rodeo broke all previous attendance records. Rodeo impresario Herman Linder was "ready to gamble" by producing another show the next year.[18] Both 1952 and 1953 shows drew low attendance due to rain, and the EEA barely met expenses until attendance rose steadily after moving the event to April and an indoor venue.[19] However, although over 29,000 attended in 1960 as compared to 21,046 in 1951, rising costs meant that success was not reflected in profits. The national championship Canadian Finals Rodeo ("Bringing the Wild West to Edmonton!") has been held in Edmonton since 1974; attendance peaked in 2006 at 95,552.[20]

According to Wetherell, as the Stampede became more institutionalized and thus entrenched within a selective frontier mythology, the figure of the pioneer (and cowboy) as hardworking, risk-taking maverick easily transferred to the ethos of capitalism. Hardworking, risk-taking individualists proved their powers over market adversities in the shops and offices of downtown Calgary. So, over time, a complex Anglo-Canadian history of provincial development was distilled into an essentialist set of ideas about open-range ranching as crucible of identity and aspirations.[21] Meanwhile, cowboys organized for better working conditions, insurance, and pay. In 1936, Herman Linder was one of sixty-one cowboys who staged the first rodeo cowboy strike at the Boston Gardens; the action precipitated the birth of the Rodeo Cowboys' Association, renamed the Cowboys' Insurance Association and later the Canadian Pro Rodeo Association. Most rodeos have belonged to one of three major institutions: the

Canadian Stampede Manager's Association, the Rodeo Association of America, or the Canadian Rodeo Cowboys Association. The Canadian Girls' Rodeo Association serves female riders.[22] By 1950, there were so many rodeos and stampedes held that the Central Alberta Stampede Managers questioned whether spectators were being "rodeoed to death"; they concluded that too many events were scheduled too close to one another to ensure sufficient attendance. With the rising financial costs of production, in part due to competitors' demands for larger prizes, the proliferation of rodeo had endangered the survival of many smaller events.[23]

Separate women's rodeo organizations and competitions developed in mid-century.[24] Alberta women joined the Girls' Rodeo Association (now the Women's Professional Rodeo Association) when it formed in Colorado in 1948. The Canadian Girls' Rodeo Association (CGRA) formed in 1957 as the Canadian Barrel Racing Association. The 1981 Cowgirls' Super challenge was held in the Panee Memorial Agriplex in Hobbema. Built by the Ermineskin band in 1977 for $3 million following the discovery of oil on the reserve, the facility has 1,600 inside seats as well as outside bleachers and a racetrack. Chief Lawrence Wildcat proclaimed that it was "the way of the Indian Culture to encourage participation and the spirit of fair play."[25] In this period there were more contestants from Northern and Central Alberta, as well as the United States, including both professionals and amateurs competing for total prize money of $45,000. Putting a practical spin on feminine stereotypes, CGRA members contributed to their organization's finances by holding annual sales of domestic handicrafts in the 1980s. As of 2012, most sponsorship comes from regional small businesses.[26]

The process of codifying cowboy sport for crowds of civilized spectators fell into place along with the components of other potentially violent and unpredictable sports, such as hockey. The individual skater speeding over the frozen pond and the lone, self-reliant cowboy were both corralled within performance categories and systems of measurement. Nevertheless, the resonance between the mythic versions of hockey and rodeo stars persisted. In 1961, legendary hockey player

Maurice "Rocket" Richard in Calgary, February 4, 1961. [GA NA-5093-937]

Maurice Richard, known for his aggressive playing style, dressed in cowboy costume for a photograph while in Calgary. And when rodeo star Blaine Pedersen of Alberta won the World Champion Steer Wrestling title in 1994, he was wearing Wayne Gretzky's number 99 on his back in homage to his sports hero.[27]

One significant difference between rodeo and other organized, commercialized sport in the province has been its inclusion of a relatively high number of Aboriginal participants. Nevertheless, Euro-Canadian dominance of wild elements was a key underlying message of rodeo culture from the start. Promoters of Wild West shows and stampedes developed crowd-pleasing spectacles by controlling the roles played by people and animals. "Show Indians" were constrained within the motif of their "dying way of life" and had limited access to serious competition and prizes. This had, of course, been the case with lacrosse and foot racing organization. Some champion riders, such as Tom Three Persons, achieved wide recognition but without the same rewards as successful white cowboys and promoters.[28] It was not until 1955 that the Banff summer festival, Indian Days, turned over supervision of its rodeo events to a First Nations leader, Jake Two Youngman, who promised new "wild and wooly" broncos fresh from the Morley stampede. The event was publicized widely, and the association of Native people with rodeo was reinforced when the June issue of *Reader's Digest* that year featured an image of Indian Days.[29]

Elizabeth Furniss discusses BC's Williams Lake Stampede as a "ritual complex" in which competitive participation in the rodeo by First Nations cowboys are not of as much interest to organizers as the tourism appeal of Wild West stereotypes and cultural display. But while rodeo producers have profited from incorporating First Nations cultures as marketable imagery, rodeo has also offered scope for First Nations people to dramatize positive aspects of their cultures and identities. In a society that limits their access to symbolic resources, First Nations' stereotypical roles and marginalized performances have served as pragmatic opportunities to communicate with mainstream audiences.[30]

All Indian Rodeo, 1965. [GA M-8984-20]

However, the mid-twentieth century was also a period of Aboriginal activism in response to unfair adjudication in mainstream rodeo. Cowboys from the Kainai reserve in southern Alberta formed a rodeo club, whose executive formed the All Indian Rodeo Cowboys Association (AIRCA) for Treaty Indians in 1962. Later known as the Indian Rodeo Cowboy Association (IRCA), and expanded to allow non-Treaty Indians and Métis, the organization held its first international finals in 1969 in Lethbridge.[31] Jan Penrose argues that, while mainstream rodeo was an instrument to entrench a dualistic idea of cowboy versus Indian, denying the legitimacy of Indian cowboys, all-Indian rodeos responded by asserting their reality. Access and respect varied between events and locations, but over time the innovation of Indian rodeos met the needs of First Nation communities themselves.[32]

In the years between 1956 and 1976, "Native communities created a viable rodeo industry."[33] The Hobbema reserve, known as the "rodeo capital in Indian Country," hosted a major gathering in the late 1980s. Although Indian rodeo declined in Alberta in the twenty years afterward, the 2007 Canadian Indian Finals Rodeo was again held at Hobbema's Panee Memorial Agriplex. Albertans won most of the prize money among cowboys from the western provinces and states.[34] Rider Todd Buffalo of Hobbema commented in 1993 that rodeo is now part of First Nations heritage, and "you have to be proud to be a cowboy, but most important, you have to be proud to be an Indian cowboy."[35]

TRACK AND FIELD

THE FIRST SPECTATOR SPORTS?

Like rodeo, track athletics summons up the image of the individual passionately challenging boundaries of strength and endurance. Among early European travellers and settlers such activities were also a response to a lack of entertainment options, and van Herk observes that wagering probably inspired Alberta's first spectator sports. We do not know the motivation of expedition leader and sportsman John

Palliser when he proposed a foot race among several Blackfoot men in 1859, but the first track and field meet in the region was likely an informal contest set up in 1863 by John McDougall. He also was the first traveller to describe a game of football, held in 1883 on the river ice at Edmonton. The track contests included foot races, jumping, and stone throwing contests between McDougall's men and a group of Métis encountered on the trail. Aboriginal people continued their long traditions of foot racing as athletic events were organized. The first recorded organized contest in Alberta was held in Fort Macleod in 1876, where a First Nations man from Lac Ste. Anne named Mooswa won the mile race.[36] Deerfoot and Little Plume were famed Siksika runners of the 1880s.[37]

Alex Wuttunee Decoteau was born in 1887 on the Red Pheasant reserve and played sports at the Battleford Industrial School before moving to Edmonton to become the first full-blooded Aboriginal person to join a municipal police force in Canada. In 1909, as a member of the Irish Athletic Club, he came second in his first race in the city, and a month later he won the five-mile race at the Edmonton Exhibition. Two days later, Decoteau set a new western Canadian record in the same event, and in 1910, he won all four events he entered at the Alberta Provincial Championships in Lethbridge. He became the only Saskatchewan or Alberta athlete to qualify for the 1912 Olympic Games, where he finished sixth in his event. After the Olympics, Decoteau set two Alberta provincial records in the one- and two-mile events on July 1, 1914. On October 30, 1917, at the age of thirty, Decoteau's life ended at the battle of Passchendaele.[38]

Organized track and field, also known as athletics, grew out of the participatory events held all over the province to mark public holidays such as the Queen's Birthday from the late nineteenth century. Competitions continued to hold a central place in community life. In Wetaskiwin in 1931, for example, the Women's Dominion Championships and Boys' Provincial Championships were accompanied by "a parade of provinces in which decorated floats representing each province were drawn by Wetaskiwin children to the park. Former

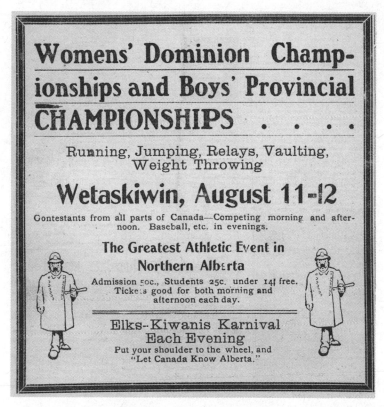

Free Press *advertisement for the Women's Dominion Championships and the Boys' Provincial Championships, Wetaskiwin, August 1931.* [CWA WET-98.10]

track and field star Norma Chiddy presided as queen of the contest." The event was opened by the lieutenant-governor of Alberta and the mayor.[39] In the 1930s, George Sutherland, Canada's top all-round track athlete for almost two decades, won numerous Canadian championships in both hammer and javelin throw as well as thirty-five Alberta championships in nine events. The Alberta track team that participated in the western division of the British Empire Games (BEG) in 1937 included Sutherland, Thelma Norris, Fay Peacock, who both set records, Sid Ashmead, and Bob Armitt, who won their events.[40]

Despite the prominence of these traditions, track athletes faced financial obstacles common to those participating at elite amateur levels. Jesse Jones was an Alberta short distance racing champion from

1915 to 1923. Although he qualified for the Canadian team for the 1924 Olympics, he could not get time off work to attend. Serious athletes on the Prairies in almost all sports faced problems due to distances and scarcity of competitors for training and practice. Since she was unable to find top competitors in the west, Edith Skitch travelled to a competition in Montreal in 1948 to prepare for the Dominion Championships and Olympic trials.[41]

The best-known Canadian female track athlete is probably pentathlete Diane Jones Konihowski, who has influenced Alberta amateur sport as an administrator. In 1985, she joined the Alberta Sport Council as director of the Alberta Olympic Game Plan, which was intended to put more provincial athletes on the 1988 Canadian Olympic Team. She went on to work with high performance athletes at the National Sport Centre in Calgary and held several other national administrative posts.[42] But women have been track and field stars in Alberta for decades. In the heyday of the sport, the 1930s and 1940s, Alberta produced several athletes, including Edmonton's Charlotte Dawes, "one of Canada's greatest girl sprinters."[43] Dawes entered the British Empire Games in Hamilton in August 1930, where women were allowed to compete in swimming and athletics. She won three events in the 1931 Ladies Open Championships in Calgary, where Nettie Anderson of Wetaskiwin also broke her own junior Dominion record in the discus pitch. The Canadian Women's Track and Field Championships of 1933 in New Westminster hosted Alberta competitors Dawes, Edith Hyatt, Kathleen Hyatt, Ethel Barnett, Patricia Page, Beatrice Gillespie, and Thelma Norris.[44]

News reports of women athletes typically mentioned their physical attributes, including small size relative to talent and, of course, to males in sport. Edith Skitch, known as "Mighty Mouse" won one Dominion and six Alberta championships, setting records in many events up to 1953. The "diminutive" Dawes was on the Canadian Olympic team in 1932, and later in the decade set Canadian women's and world track records.[45] Doreen (McLeod) Ryan of Edmonton, whose size was less remarked upon, was the "ace" player on the Victoria High School's girls' basketball team, scored the highest number of points at the 1947 Canadian Track and Field Championships in Edmonton, and also won top honours in that year's junior women's provincial speed skating championships. Vera (Barilko) Rivet won the City of Edmonton Track and Field award in the early 1940s, and played and coached soft-ball after serving in the Canadian Armed Forces during the war.[46]

Annabelle Murray won a bronze medal at the 1954 British Empire Games and the Canadian championships in 1955 and 1956, setting a new Canadian record in broad jump. In 1960, Murray was the first woman ever inducted into the Alberta Sports Hall of Fame for achieve-ments in track and field. It is likely that Murray's success reflects in part the significance of family and community support for young athletes of either sex. She was part of a sporting family from Okotoks where her father coached hockey teams, her mother curled, and her brother later became a well-known hockey trainer with the Calgary Flames.[47]

Athletics were a central component of education programs from the turn of the century.[48] Interscholastic competitions were held regularly and the Canadian Championships came to Edmonton in 1947. Although it has continued strong in school programs and college and universi-ties, popular track and field interest peaked in the late 1930s and by the mid-1950s had declined all over the province.[49] Several of the compet-itors at the interscholastic track meets at Mewata Stadium in Calgary in 1956 were in training for the Canadian Olympic team. The Highland Games, established as the Caledonian Games in 1909, are still held in towns and cities all over Alberta but there is little emphasis on track events. In 2001, Edmonton became the first North American city to host the International Association of Athletics Federation championship.

Like soccer and cricket, bicycle sports never achieved a high profile in North America. Alberta cycling history is of interest for the way it illustrates broader interactions of sport, community, social class, and technology. The British and American "bicycle mania" of the 1870s reached Alberta in the 1880s as improvements in communication and transportation brought metropolitan trends and commodities west, connected cyclists to established groups and competitions in eastern cities, and expanded paved surfaces. Bicycle riders seemed to transfer the rodeo spirit of freedom and daring to the vehicle when it first arrived. The highwheelers of the early 1880s appealed to elite youth since the machines were relatively dangerous and expensive, a status symbol used mainly for racing by so-called "knights of the cycle."[50] Still, Alberta's was a modest mania; one bicycle club formed in 1887 Calgary, its executive composed of businessmen and professionals, including jeweller L.H. Doll, hotel owner H.A. Perley, and an assortment of doctors and barristers. In 1892, this club was succeeded by another whose membership rose to thirty-eight over the following year. Five years later, though, the city of about 4,000 still hosted only 120 bicycles, most owned by affluent citizens.[51]

By the 1890s, the high wheeler had been replaced by the safety bicycle, broadening access to the sport across the province. Edmonton cyclists competed among each other for some time before the city's first official bicycle club was formed in June 1893. A few years later, the more exclusive North Star Cycle Club formed, affiliated with the Canadian Wheelmen's Association. The existence of rival clubs in the same city meant, for the *Journal*, that the sport truly had arrived. Smaller centres got involved as well as more roads were paved with asphalt. Lethbridge organized a club in 1893. Medicine Hat, inspired by local man Tom Botterill, who had become famous as a racer in the United States, organized a bicycle club the following year and sold subscriptions to build a half-mile track.[52] Clubs organized intertown competitions and tours such as the one Calgary staged in 1892 for racers from Winnipeg to the West Coast.

Ignoring initially disparaging public opinion, many Alberta women were keen cyclists but were slow to be accepted as equal athletes when cycle clubs were primarily intended for organizing competitive events. The North Star Cycle Club of Edmonton, established in 1896, admitted women as full members, although the original local club had restricted them to honorary membership only a few years before. Ladies of Calgary's first club were "honorary" members, not expected to ride but to attend social events. (More than half a century later, the Edmonton Cycle Club of 1965 included only three women, listed last on the roster of twenty-one members.)[53] Photographs of male cyclists in riding gear posed in studio settings are common from this era, but few such images of women exist; the two Edmonton women photographed by Ernest Brown in 1897 were associated with the cycling elite. The first, a Miss Calvert, was an employee of the first club founder Pat McNamara, and the second, Mrs. Fred Ross, was the wife of an owner of the Edmonton Hardware Company where the North Star Cycle Club met.[54]

Organizing bodies and competitive cyclists both demonstrated keen involvement in the sport. Cycling star Pat McNamara, Edmonton barrister, found his machine sabotaged by a rival (but he still won three medals). J.H. Wrigley of Lethbridge's Chinook Cycle Club won a championship in Regina in 1894 but was disqualified for unreported reasons. The Chinook club protested but Lethbridge may have been justified; Wrigley was soon afterward barred for two years by the Winnipeg Turf Association.[55] In happier events for Edmonton cyclists, Sam McNamara set a territorial racing record at the 1896 Canadian Wheelmen's Association championship. Two years later, his brother Pat won the Northwest Territorial Championship Bicycle Meet in Calgary.[56]

As the safety bicycle was mass-produced and became more affordable, elite interest in cycling as a sport waned.[57] By the turn of the century, older married men, young bachelors, women, and children were all riding bicycles for transportation and recreation, and many cyclists were less interested in competitive racing than in touring and

Bicycle races, Edmonton, 1915. [CEA EA-10-1189]

commuting. The bicycle was less associated with athletic speed and recklessness and more with respectability. The initial horror of the late 1800s concerning women roaming free on the machines gave way to tolerance and the hope that feminine participation could help to "civilize" reckless masculine energies. The proponents of rational recreation even managed to attribute Christian values to cycling, demonstrating real creativity given initial suspicion of the sport as a potential temptation to free-spiritedness.[58]

Cycling also contributed to popular access to other sporting events for players and spectators. The growing market of cyclists is reflected in the local advertising of the late nineteenth century, though it was not a main focus of newspaper sports pages. By 1895 cycling was a common sight in everyday Edmonton life. At a south side baseball game in June 1899, reported the *Edmonton Bulletin*, the "air was thick with bicycles."[59] Robert Hess, though, argues that while at this time a bicycle was often cheaper to own than a horse and thus offered democratic transport, the climate of Edmonton did not allow for year-round wheeling, and it is likely that only those who could afford a horse also owned bicycles.

One of the reasons that cycling became popular in industrial metropolitan centres was its ability to transport the rider out of city cores and into the clean air along country roads. But, as Hess suggests, in prairie cities the sport also represented not an escape from but a sign of urban behaviour. Numerous photographs of rural and small town houses suggest that bicycles were a common accoutrement of the domestic scene as useful transport to homesteads as well as to patients or congregations. Many of these photos, though, also point to the novelty and status components of bicycle ownership for some. In Alberta, cycling, like many other sports, represented another sign that metropolitan status and civilization had arrived, reflecting "a pioneer mentality that was characterized by metropolitan aspirations, financial prosperity and entrepreneurial spirit."[60] The bicycle was both a sporting instrument and an everyday tool of transportation and recreation. Although cycling was initially organized in clubs and competition circuits, it became primarily a recreational and practical mode of transport on the Prairies. Like other summer sports, it has been limited by the climate, but its marginal status is probably due to its greater limitation in appeal as a spectator sport.

By the early decades of the twentieth century, then, the bicycle had travelled from a position of privilege and mode of escape from social constraints to a convenience for everyday productive activities. In 1919, when numerous bicycle sales and repair shops dotted the larger cities, the bicycle business was "one of the sturdiest, steadiest" in the country; cities in Alberta participated in Canada Bicycle Week with sales and events.[61] Races continued to be staged at fairs and sponsored by businesses and newspapers, as did special competitions attended by stars such as Torchy Peden of British Columbia in the 1930s. In Edmonton, bicycle associations such as the Northern Alberta Bicycle Association of the 1930s continued, long distance races and events at athletic association tracks were held, and groups like the Silver Hawks

Bicycle Club participated in exhibition parades through the 1950s. Torchy Peden's nephew, Sandy Peden, rode with the Silver Hawks club.[62]

Interest in bicycle racing grew in the 1960s, probably due to the development of ten-speed models. A club was organized in Edmonton in 1963. Although it had few members, the club competed against Calgary's Juventus Club, which was established in 1957. Races were held on any available roads, which resulted in a controversy that conjured up the ghosts of reckless highwheelers past. Edmonton's Frank Ludtke was runner-up for the Alberta championship in 1966 and represented Canada at the World Championships in Sweden. Calgary's ace, Gerry de Jong, won the 224-mile Tour of Ontario in 1966. In 1965, the First Division Football Club (DFC) Victoria Soccer Club took over sponsorship of the Edmonton Cycling Club and the following year a new bike club, Velo-Sport Edmonton, formed.[63] Both Calgary and Edmonton built velodromes in the mid-1970s, as the new ten-speed bicycles renewed popular interest in the sport. In 1982, a group of Italian-Canadians established the Juventus Sports Club for soccer and cycling, and in 1993 the Juventus Cycling Club moved to the Argyll Velodrome. Most cycling clubs across the province are oriented to recreation, though many also participate in race events.

Although cycling clubs generally include women members, the only dedicated women's club in the province as of 2005 was the Dirt Girls, whose branches in Edmonton and Calgary operate competitions and recreational events.[64] These and other women's cycling clubs, such as Edmonton's Sirens, are hosted by sports clubs associated with bicycle retailers. Lori-Ann Muenzer trained with the Juventus Cycling Club in Edmonton and won eleven World Cup titles and numerous medals, including the Olympic gold in 2005. Named Canada's female athlete of the year by the Canadian Press and Broadcast News, and inducted into the Edmonton and Alberta sports halls of fame, Muenzer announced her retirement in 2006 after a career marked by ongoing struggles for financial support and reported indifference from the Canadian Cycling Association. She went on to develop several projects, including training programs for youth through the Juventus Club.[65] Tara Whitten won numerous medals for cycling in 2010, including gold at the Commonwealth Games and the World Track Cycling Championships. Whitten has managed to capitalize on her results with federal funding in the preparation for the 2012 Olympics, with a budget for the Canadian team much expanded from the 2008 season.[66]

The association of organized sport with the status of urban modernity echoes on Alberta tracks, fields, courts, and rinks down through the next century. The presence of high-profile team sport was a sure sign of a post-frontier society, but so were those relying on imported equipment such as bicycles. Elite colonial-era connotations around certain sports endured into the twentieth century. This was in part due to the activity itself, but also significant were the amount and nature of the space required for play, the appropriate costume, and attendant rituals. Sports like skiing, tennis, and golf were considered by athletic organizations into the mid-twentieth century as social sports, pursued without physical contact while generally dressed in approximations of street clothing and usually involving a well-appointed clubhouse and refreshments nearby.

TENNIS AND GOLF
FROM COUNTRY CLUBS TO CITY LANDS

Like so many other sports, tennis came to western Canada with the North West Mounted Police and followed much the same pattern of organization of other sports. Southern Alberta ranch lands provided free space for play and spectators. The privileged sectors played tennis first, but it was not as expensive as other elite sports such as golf, and the wider public took it up with the advent of cheaper equipment and public facilities. One factor in the success of tennis was that employers, perceiving the sport to be conducive both to propriety and productivity, often allowed players to leave work early to be able to play during daylight.[67] In Alberta and Saskatchewan, the last provinces to organize formal leagues, imported patterns and rules of play did not persist

Tennis group at Coalspur, September 1915. [GA NA-2623-8]

as strongly as they did in eastern Canada. As seen in the photograph of the Coalspur tennis players, the game was not limited to organized urban clubs. Nevertheless, the game remained associated with select levels of society and social mobility for some. Douglas Cameron, son of Vermilion pioneer, writer, and publisher W.B. Bleasdell, played competitive tennis in the 1930s. In 1938, he was a member of Canada's Davis Cup team, and a decade later his father reflected, "when you took to sport, I was glad...Your tennis brought you contacts which I'm sure have been valuable to you—among cultured men and women."[68]

Tennis, like softball and golf, was open to women participants from the turn of the century. Again, they could play in modest clothing in acceptable social surroundings such as urban country clubs and lawns. Some clubs, like the Jamboree in Lethbridge, established in 1908, at first prohibited women, but companies and community organizations sponsored tournaments that allowed women participants. A Canadian National Railway Tennis Club Tournament in Calgary, July 1938 attracted two women, including a former champion.[69]

In the early 1900s tennis was popular with upper-class students at most universities. Though it was a well-supported competitive sport at the University of Alberta during the 1920s, it became a primarily recreational pastime in the 1930s, and by the early 1970s lost its intercollegiate status. The game's popularity on campus was actually at its lowest during the North American tennis "boom" of the 1960s, which waned by the 1980s and 1990s when the university was investing far more resources in the Golden Bears hockey and football teams.[70] Nevertheless, a tennis centre was constructed for the international 1983 Universiade.

Most municipal councils and churches also approved of tennis, considered it a wholesome, Christian sport. City leagues of the era included church, YMCA and YWCA, civil service, commercial and private clubs, though no public courts were built until the early 1960s. The first lawn tennis club in Edmonton was established in 1891, and the Capital Tennis Championship was held in 1908. The Calgary Lawn Tennis Club was founded in 1889, lost its downtown court in 1897, and reorganized in 1905; the following year a city dentist organized a provincial championship tournament, played at the NWMP barracks at Fort Calgary. Twelve clubs joined a local league in 1919.[71]

The same enthusiasm prevailed in Edmonton. In June 1916 the *Bulletin* reported large numbers of ladies and gentlemen contestants in the Highlands Lawn Tennis Tourney. The June 17, 1921 sports page of the *Edmonton Bulletin* ran news of women's and other tennis tournaments on its first page. In 1926 the city allocated a block of land in North Garneau for recreation, and volunteers built four shale tennis courts for public use. Alberta government workers had their own tennis club. By this time, the entire province was divided into tennis districts composed of dozens of towns. Regular provincial championships were held each year beginning in the early 1920s; although the event attracted nearly 400 entries on July 25, 1924, the tournament attracted only eighty-five competitors in 1939, which was a rise of five players over the year before.[72]

Alberta produced several star players of both sexes, and it was common at the time for athletes who excelled in one sport to also play on elite levels in others. Tennis champion Lindsay Carver, who won the provincial title several times in the 1930s, was also a hockey star for the intermediate Luscar Indians in the Coal Branch area. At a time when athletes supported themselves by playing on professional teams in one sport while maintaining amateur status in another, Carver made more money playing in the Coal Branch than he could have in the N H L. But tennis largely avoided contemporary conflicts over professional status, as players remained strictly amateur well into the twentieth century. While this may have reflected lack of opportunity as much as idealism, the professionals hired to instruct for the first clubs were generally considered socially inferior to the members.[73]

Newspaper coverage of the 1920s and 1930s notes women involved in tennis around the province. Marjorie Collinge Eustace of Calgary was a championship player beginning in the 1920s. In 1922 she won her first Junior Provincial Ladies Championship at Edmonton's University Courts, and that year also won the Senior Open Ladies Championship. Between 1924 and 1945, she won forty-nine open championships, twenty-one provincial championships, and four western Canadian championships. Eustace later built a career, which she called a "hobby," volunteering with the St. John Ambulance organization; in 1947 she was part of the winning team in the Dominion First Aid Competitions. A 1970s newspaper article focused on her volunteer work. Of her athletic achievements, the article noted only that she had been an "avid tennis player."[74]

Between 1958 and 1969, Edmontonian sisters Gail Foran-Woodward and Shannon Foran-Lindenberg, who had established careers as speed skaters, each won several national and provincial tennis champion-ships as well as the provincial doubles championship in 1964 and 1965. Shannon won provincial doubles titles with other partners in 1966, 1967, 1968, and 1969. Each also won 1965 provincial ten-pin bowling championships.

The trajectory of the golf ball has left a visible impact on both urban and rural Alberta landscapes. Golf may have been first played in the HBC outposts of the west in the seventeenth century, rather than, like most sports, in the east of the country. In any case, the enthusiasm of the NWMP made golf immediately popular in Alberta in the late nineteenth century, where a growing urban society supported its growth. Outdoor leisure appealed to a new middle class of clerks and office workers who wanted to play in the open air and had more time for it, thanks to new labour laws. The introduction of urban trolley systems and bicycles made it easier to reach the clubs, usually set at a distance from town centres.

Increasingly supported by public fitness movements and more independently mobile with access to bicycles, women adopted golf in large numbers in the 1890s. The fact that the clothing worn for golf was conservative and ladylike was probably a factor in their acceptance, though they faced various restrictions at most clubs. In 1905, at Edmonton's upper-middle-class Mayfair Golf Club, women were allowed to join but could not be elected to executive committee positions or considered for pro positions. Dress codes, such as long skirts for players, were enforced, and playing time was also restricted. Attitudes changed over the years; in 1931, when the Lethbridge Municipal Golf Club reserved ladies' golf time to Saturdays before 1 P.M., enough people were offended that they created the Lethbridge Country Club in 1932.[75]

When the Alberta Golf Association was formed in 1907, a Mrs. Clark of Calgary won the first provincial award, the Mackay Trophy. In 1908, Edmonton's Miss Brown won the ladies' title. Nora Polkinghorn and a Mr. Arnison of the Calgary Golf and Country Club won the mixed championship that year.[76] A separate Canadian Ladies Golf Union (CLGU) formed in 1913, and the *Calgary Daily Herald* of April 19, 1928, reported the formation of the Alberta branch of the CLGU. Alberta was the last province to join the union, and it meant that the organization would control tournaments, which would not be held at the same

Two men playing golf in Edmonton, likely at Victoria Park, 1920. [GA NC-6-6207]

time as men's so that more attention could be directed to the women's championships.[77]

Calgary had a Golf and Country Club in 1897. The first golf club in Edmonton was organized the previous year with a five-hole course and Fort Edmonton's "Big House" as its clubhouse, a grand landmark "emblematic of the club's elite status."[78] The Hudson's Bay Company donated one of the oldest competitive trophies in western Canada in 1898 for the club championship. R.A. Ruttan, the city's Dominion land agent, was the first club president. The first female member and "patroness" of the club was Mrs. J.M. Lay, wife of the Imperial Bank accountant. Equipment was available from an outfitting business that advertised "a supply of golfers' requisites in the shape of sticks and balls."[79] The club was the precursor of both the Edmonton Country Club and the Victoria Municipal Golf Course, which opened as the country's first municipal course in 1914.

The Edmonton Country Club was founded in 1910 when Golf Club members began to look for a permanent location as the city expanded. Original shareholders included the lieutenant-governor, two Alberta premiers, four chief justices and other judges, as well as cabinet ministers, MLAs, the attorney general, the mayor, and the president of the Board of Trade among others. Six shareholders were women; their names and occupations are unrecorded but they are likely to have been wives of prominent male shareholders. When the club was established in the west end of the city, realtors rejoiced, predicting that "there will be springing up a good class of homes in which will live the men who can afford to leave their work early in the afternoon, and who will enjoy their favourite game in the immediate vicinity of their home."[80] Clearly, golf was still associated with the elite of society.

The newer Mayfair Golf and Country Club officially opened in 1922, and University of Alberta President Dr. H.M. Tory and leading merchant James Ramsay played the first game. The club membership included so many bankers that they once formed a team to compete against everyone else. When the Lieutenant-Governor of Alberta William Egbert golfed at the club, his caddy grew restless while waiting for the golfers at the green after the last shot and nudged the ball into the cup. Egbert was roundly celebrated for his hole-in-one.[81] The course was remodelled in 1927 by Stanley Thompson, designer of the Banff and Jasper golf courses. Bobby Locke, winner of four British Open Golf Championships, praised it in the 1930s as the "best Canadian course by a long way." Upon learning that it was used for skiing in the winter, Locke was amazed at "how so many Canadians reached such a high standard of golf when their playing time is so restricted."[82]

The Alberta Golf Association (AGA) was established in 1907, incorporated in 1912, and merged with the Alberta Ladies Golf Association in 2000, becoming Alberta Golf. The first provincial award, the Mackay Trophy for ladies' golf, was awarded to a Calgary woman whose name is recorded only as Mrs. Clark. The first provincial men's championship was held in 1908 Calgary according to Royal and Ancient Golf Club of St. Andrews Scotland rules, and alternated between Calgary and Edmonton until 1914. It was won by C.W. Hague of Calgary, and Edmonton's Miss Brown won the ladies' title. After 1912, the AGA included five member clubs: Lethbridge, Fort Macleod, Calgary, St. Andrews (also in Calgary), and Edmonton. The association conducted provincial amateur and interclub competitions.[83]

The game was well-established by 1911 when a Scots expert converted a Banff garbage dump into what would become an iconic course for the CPR hotel. Locals commented on a "fellow in knickerbockers...always hitting a ball wherever we saw him. We all thought he was crazy."[84] Another national park golf course opened over a decade later in 1925 at the Jasper Park Lodge. The number of clubs in the country had doubled between 1919 and 1922. The sport diffused to the general public, and many new courses were developed in Alberta once public lands were made available. Edmonton's first public course, Victoria Park, was the first in Canada. Victoria Park became the model for other public facilities, including the second one in the country in Medicine Hat in 1916. The Shaganappi Club in Calgary opened to the public in 1915, planned in part as a way to boost the profits of the street railway that ran to the west end location. Calgary provided land to expand the public golf course in 1925, following the notion that a city should have "a large number of citizens actively participating in the forms of recreation provided [rather] than to have a few providing spectacles for a large crowd of onlookers."[85] Golf also found favour in smaller centres. In Hanna, enthusiasts formed a club in 1921 with a membership of thirty men and ten women. Turner Valley's golf club was built in 1930 by employees of oil companies developing the local industry.

The 1930s was an important organizational period for women's golf. A Banff Springs club ladies' division was established in 1931. Local community leaders continued to shape developments. The Banff Ladies Golf Club included luminaries such as Fern Brewster, Eleanor Luxton, and Mrs. Byron Harmon, who gave a cup for "best approaching and putting" in 1933. They were also privileged enough to occasionally play against men at the Banff Springs Golf Club. In 1960, the club invited Calgary women to play, followed by tea. The women reported, "although perhaps our Golf wasn't at its best, the social visit was extremely pleasant."[86] Smaller cities and towns were also active in golf; Camrose established its first Ladies Tournament in 1948, mailing invitations to neighbouring towns and Edmonton clubs in hopes of a high turnout.[87]

Edmonton's member-owned Highlands Golf Course was constructed in 1929 and has been an important centre for the sport's development. The only junior girls' club in the city started at Highlands in 1938. Not until 1953, an especially bad year for mosquitoes, were women allowed to wear slacks instead of skirts while playing. Police officer and amateur golf star Henry Martell, who won the first Canadian Amateur Championship for Alberta, became club pro in 1948. Martell dominated the game from the 1930s to the 1950s, winning four Alberta and Saskatchewan Opens, nine Alberta Amateurs, and two Canadian Professional Golf Association championships, among many other victories. Other stars have included Doug Silverberg of Red Deer and Keith Alexander. By 1972 there were sixty-eight golf clubs in Alberta.[88]

Martell is also noted as an important teacher of successful golfers, among them Betty Stanhope Cole of Edmonton, who won the first

Canadian Ladies Junior Championship in 1956. She also won twenty-five amateur Edmonton and seventeen provincial championships, nine senior ladies' titles, and the 1957 Canadian Ladies' Open; she played on four national world championship teams and in two Commonwealth Games and during the winter, she skipped three Alberta rinks in Canadian women's curling. Among other honours, Stanhope Cole was named Edmonton's Outstanding Athlete in 1957. She was later inducted into several sports halls of fame, including the Alberta Sports Hall of Fame in 1980, Edmonton's Sports Hall of Fame in 1993, and the Canadian Golf Hall of Fame in 1991. In 2011, she was honoured with the opening of a park named after her, overlooking the Highlands Golf Course.[89] Other championship women golfers from Alberta since the 1940s include Paddy Arnold, who won six Alberta Provincial Championships between 1938 and 1949, Rae Milligan Simpson, Pat Heisler, Marilyn O'Connor, and Cathy Galusha. But women were still not necessarily considered seriously as golfers; in 1963, the executive of the new Canmore golf course extended an invitation to any Calgarian "who wants to play golf while his wife and children go on to Banff for a swim."[90]

SWIMMING

POOLS IN A DRY LAND

The sport of swimming has had a relatively low public profile, but several international stars have emerged from Alberta waters. The development of the sport illustrates the significance of local facility development for year-round training as well as the ways in which athletes progress from recreational performance to elite status. Edmonton had three outdoor pools when the Edmonton YWCA opened the city's first enclosed pool in 1907, and swimming instructor H.H. Corsan arrived in town to give lessons to boys and men. In 1925 his father, George H. Corsan, visited and added girls and women to the student list.[91] The practical, life-preserving aspects of swimming meant that most children were encouraged to take lessons, and

George H. Webster, mayor of Calgary, centre; Helen Woodside, champion lady swimmer of Alberta, right. Taken at opening of swimming pool, Chateau Lake Louise, May 12, 1926. [GA NA-4108-1]

citywide public campaigns were organized, such as the *Edmonton Journal*'s Learn to Swim event in 1934. The University of Alberta also offered swim lessons. Diving events and social activities were held in conjunction with swimming.

The Canadian Amateur Swimming Association formed in 1909, and Calgary's YMCA pool held the first provincial championships.[92] Swimming was particularly popular before the 1920s, and both Edmonton and Calgary had pools in 1916. That year, while attendance at sports and fitness classes fell, 500 women signed up for swimming in Calgary,[93] which suggests that women still valued physical exercise (or feared drowning), if not necessarily through organized games. Helen Woodside of Calgary was one of the most consistent swimming stars in the province's history. In 1922, the thirteen-year-old "aquatic marvel" won the

YWCA fifty-yard swimming race and continued to win championships and set records. Since Calgary had no natural swimming facilities, the YWCA indoor pool was a crucial factor in her training. In 1926 she won all thirty-four of competitions she entered. By that time, she had won five provincial championships, two city titles, the Calgary club crown, the Banff Winter Carnival championship (where the city's "swimmers clean[ed] up"), the Alberta fifty- and hundred-yard championships and more. She also played on the Central Collegiate Institute basketball team, which won provincial intermediate championships in 1923–1924.[94]

During the Depression years, interest in competitive swimming grew in Edmonton due to two factors: an enthusiastic rivalry between teams from different city-owned pools, and the economic accessibility of the sport. Even smaller centres such as Ponoka held fundraising campaigns in the 1920s and 1930s to build public swimming pools. Competitive swimming in the province began with the first provincial championships at the Calgary YMCA in 1909. In Calgary's Bowness Park, a large public pool was built in 1919. In this period Calgary had one indoor and one outdoor poor, whereas Edmonton had four pools by 1925. The following year Calgary city council found a proposal to convert the city market building to a pool unfeasible. A subsequent suggestion to create natural pools along the rivers also led nowhere. When interest in competitive swimming rose in the 1930s, the YMCA provided pool time, and several swimming holes were built along the river.[95]

Interest in swimming declined in the 1940s and early 1950s but rose again later in the decade as new indoor pools in both urban and rural areas fostered programs and competition, and automobiles made transportation to tournaments easier. The 1955 Jubilee celebrations brought funding for cultural and athletic infrastructure, including a Calgary pool sponsored by the Kiwanis Club. The first Alberta Open Swimming and Diving Championships were held at Mill Creek Pool in Edmonton in 1959. That year, thirteen Alberta clubs were affiliated with the Canadian Amateur Swimming Association.[96]

Many swim clubs fostered elite competitors, such as Carman Bradley and Bill Patrick of the Mewata Swim Club in Calgary. Patrick was an outstanding diver, winning ten Canadian championships and representing Canada in the British Empire Games in 1954 and 1958. He was a member of the 1956 Canadian Olympic Team and also excelled in gymnastics, winning the YMCA Tri-Provincial Championship in 1950 and excelling in both sports at Ohio State University. Later in his career, he coached Calgary high school teams and clubs in football, basketball, track and field, and gymnastics as well as swimming. Helen Woodside was a noted Calgary athletic star who won numerous swimming records from the 1920s to the 1940s. At various times she also held the city and provincial badminton singles championships and was a member of Calgary's basketball team the Central Grads, which played Edmonton's Commercial Grads for the provincial title in 1928.[97]

Edmonton's South Side Swim Club, founded in 1928 at the outdoor South Side Pool (later Queen Elizabeth Pool), the oldest municipal pool in western Canada, also produced star athletes. By the early 1960s, the club was participating in provincial, regional, national, and international events, including the First Alberta Open Swimming and Diving Championships, in Edmonton on August 22, 1959. Its members set several records. In 1968 the club took to indoor pools under the direction of Dr. W. Donald Smith, professor of physical education at the University of Alberta. Access to year-round training raised the level of achievement and the club, later renamed Keyano, produced many international competitors and champions.[98] The baby boom pressure of significant numbers of youth accelerated recreational facility development in the 1960s and 1970s. By 1975, there were twenty recreational facilities operating in Edmonton.

The Smith family became particularly prominent as competitors and champions in the 1960s and 1970s. Graham Smith, for instance, won a record six gold medals at the 1978 Edmonton Commonwealth Games (the most by a single athlete in Commonwealth Games history) in the pool named after his father, who had died shortly before the opening ceremonies. Graham established seventeen Canadian, three

Commonwealth, and two world records during his career, and he won the 1978 Lou Marsh Award as Canadian Male Athlete of the Year and became a Member of the Order of Canada and the Alberta Sports Hall of Fame. His sisters, Sue, Sandra, and Rebecca, set records and won championships in the 1960s and 1970s.[99] Mark Tewksbury was born in Calgary in 1968, and began swimming eight years later. He joined the national swim team in 1984, won gold medals at the 1986 and 1990 Commonwealth Games, and silver at both the 1988 Olympics and 1991 World Aquatic Championships. In 1992, he won the gold medal with an Olympic record time of 53.98 seconds, five one hundredths of a second short of a new world record.[100]

The recognized varieties of competitive swimming expanded when synchronized swimming became an Olympic sport in 1984. The Alberta section of the Amateur Synchronized Swimming Association of Canada (now known as Synchro Swim Alberta) was formed in 1957. Jean Ross, inducted into the Alberta Amateur Sports Hall of Fame in 1967, coached the Edmonton Aquadettes Synchronized Swimming Club, which won a Canadian national title and twenty Alberta titles in the 1960s.[101]

The Calgary Aquabelles, sponsored by the YWCA, was established in 1966 by Mary Ann Reeves, a former synchronized swimming champion. Debbie Muir joined the Calgary Aquabelles in 1965 and was a team member in 1973 when the team won Canada's first World Aquatic Championships silver medal in the sport. In 1974, she began coaching the team and, as head coach from 1976 to 1986, she guided the club's swimmers to twenty-two national titles and, at the 1978 world championships, two gold medals. As national team coach from 1981 to 1991, Muir won gold medals at the 1988 Olympics, the 1986 and 1990 Commonwealth Games, and the 1983 and 1987 Pan-American Games. Caroline Waldo of the Aquabelles won three gold medals at the 1985 World Cup, and in 1988, to the relief of many Canadians in the wake of the Ben Johnson Olympic drug scandal, her solo performance garnered the country's first gold medal at the games. With Calgary's Michelle Cameron, she also won gold in the duet event.[102]

Olga (Ollie) Currie worked for over forty years to build the swimming as a sport at local, provincial, and national levels. Beginning as a volunteer in Edmonton in 1970, Currie went on to manage the Canadian national team at numerous international competitions, including the 1988 Olympics and three Paralympics. She chaired many other competitions. She has also served as board director of all the leading swimming organizations and was named to the Order of Canada for her long service to youth and to the sport.[103]

SKATING AND SKIING

FANCY FOOTWORK

In 1887 the country's first sport association, the Amateur Skating Association of Canada (the Amateur Speed Skating Association of Canada as of 1967), formed to organize official competitions. In 1914 a separate organization for figure skating was established and its first national championships held; it became the Canadian Figure Skating Association (CFSA) in 1939, joined the International Skating Union in 1947, and became Skate Canada in 2000.[104] Short track speed skating originated in 1905. Alberta men and women alike have distinguished themselves in the sport. Kevin Sirois was a Red Deer speed skater and cyclist who held several Canadian records in both sports, competing in the 1972 Winter Olympics and, at the time of his death later that year, training for the Summer Olympics.[105] Pierre Trudeau was the first, and very likely the last, prime minister to wear speed skates at an athletic event when he attended the opening of the 1975 Canada Winter Games in Lethbridge, Alberta.

Women's speed skating developed in Alberta in the context of community winter carnivals, such as the carnival at Banff, which hosted interclub and intercity meets. Doreen McLeod Ryan, for instance, started racing in an Edmonton community league carnival. She excelled in both speed skating and track and field, winning Canadian junior championships in both sports in 1947. She went on to win fourteen skating championships between 1951 and 1959 and participated on Olympic teams in 1948, 1960, and 1964. At one point, she held every Canadian women's record. McLeod Ryan was the first woman admitted to the Edmonton Sports Hall of Fame. In 2001, she received a CAAWS award recognizing her long-term achievements and influence on females in sport for her athletics, coaching, teaching, and volunteering.[106] When Don Wynn and McLeod Ryan won the Canadian Championships in 1947, Edmonton built a track. In 1960, the city built a 400-metre oval for the competitive circuit. Women's speed skating has been an Olympic sport since 1960, and the first Olympic championships held indoors were in Calgary's Olympic Oval in 1988.[107] Both McLeod Ryan and Pat Underhill competed in the provincial speed skating championships held in Red Deer in 1953. Underhill, who held numerous Canadian, provincial and national titles and records, started the Red Deer speed skating club in 1950; by 1955 its members achieved national recognition. She was the first of three female presidents of Speed Skating Canada. As an athlete, however, Underhill found that one of her greatest barriers to high-level competion "was raising the funds necessary to cover the travel costs...Women were not part of the Olympic structure and national funding support system until 1960."[108] Underhill did manage to attend the 1957 Worlds but never competed in the Olympics. Doreen Ryan, similarly, was never able to compete in the World Championships due to lack of funding. Male amateur athletes based in the west traditionally have also been challenged financially, but women may have been particularly affected by inadequate funding for a longer time.

With some improvement in funding programs over the years, athletes have had more access to international competition. Based in Calgary, speed skater Catriona Le May Doan has amassed a long list of wins and world records. In 1998 and 2002 she won Olympic gold medals; in 1998 and 1999 she topped the World Cup standings in her events. In 2002, she won World and World Cup championships in the 500-metre event and became the first Canadian athlete to defend a gold medal. Le May Doan won the 2002 Lou Marsh Award as Canada's

Athlete of the Year and is a three-time recipient (1998, 2001, 2002) of the Canadian Female Athlete of the Year award. Today, speed skating awards are named after Le May Doan, Underhill, and Ryan. Susan Auch, also based in Calgary, is another Olympian speed skater; Auch started speed skating at the age of twelve. She won silver in the 500-metre Olympic race in 1994.[109]

The popularity of figure skating helped drive the invention of artificial ice and indoor rinks. Calgary had fifty-eight ice surfaces in the 1920s.[110] Since the 1930s, Canada has won more than 500 international figure skating medals, and promoters, including media networks, represent the sport as a "national pastime," despite the fact that only 0.5 per cent of Canadians actually figure skate.[111] Enthusiasm for figure skating in Alberta followed the rise of Canadian stars such as Barbara Ann Scott. Many urban community leagues began offering figure skating lessons in the late 1940s, coinciding with the intense media attention to Scott's championship career. A visit by Scott to Wetaskiwin in 1949 brought out over 500 people, including the mayor, Kinsmen and Skating Club members. Smaller towns started skating clubs in the 1940s, and by the late 1950s there was a circuit of performance and competition held in local rinks. The Stettler Figure Skating Club, for example, was established in 1947. A Ponoka revue of 1959 featured 125 young people staging a visit by a rocket ship to the planet Earth.[112] The Medicine Hat Figure Skating Club attracted approximately 3,000 people to its first Carnival performance in 1961.[113]

Figure skating in Alberta developed in great part due to the efforts of dedicated teachers and promoters, who travelled the province teaching and organizing. Walter Kaasa put himself through university in the 1940s and 1950s by holding figure skating carnivals and teaching figure skating in small towns around Edmonton. Later, Kaasa acted in local theatre and tirelessly promoted the arts as a volunteer.[114] The growth of hockey in the 1940s usurped recreational skaters' rink time, which led to exclusionary divisions of sport. This division occurred along class and gender lines, and figure skating was associated mainly with females.[115] On December 12, 1961, Mrs. Lilley of the

North Glenora Community League wrote to young performer Archie Zarisky that his recent performance on an outdoor rink would greatly encourage "young community league figure skaters" even though at minus forty degrees Fahrenheit the bitter cold meant few spectators.[116] Until the early 1960s Edmonton had two clubs, the Edmonton Figure Skating Club (EFSC), which operated under Canadian Figure Skating Association sanctions, and the Federation Figure Skating Club, which was operated by the community leagues. There were only two indoor rinks—the Edmonton Gardens and the Varsity Rink.

Peggy Currie, whose husband Frank coached the Edmonton Flyers, coached figure skating for the EFSC and at the Calgary and Stettler Summer Schools. Calgary's skating school, organized by the Curries, opened in 1957; the school offered both figure skating and hockey programs. Although there had been summer schools in Edmonton for several years prior to its opening, the Curries' school was only one in the Prairie region at that time. The Curries' daughter Sonja was a championship figure skater in the 1950s, and many of Curries' students went on to elite performance. Gail Donaldson, for example, was a seventeen-year-old star basketball player from Hanna who joined the Ice Capades in 1960 after working with Currie in Calgary.[117] Calgary also had the Glencoe Club, which opened in 1931 with a display of "fancy skating."[118]

One of the signs of postwar and oil strike affluence in Alberta was "an outbreak of country club fever." New clubs like the Derrick and the Royal Glenora provided sports and socializing facilities for shareholder members.[119] The Royal Glenora Club opened officially in 1961 as an amalgamation of three earlier clubs—Royal Curling Club, the Glenora Skating and Tennis Club and the Braemar Badminton Club. The Royal Glenora offered an indoor training venue for elite skaters. Neil Primrose, son of Lieutenant-Governor Philip Primrose, was a founding member of the club. By the mid-1960s there were four active clubs in Edmonton, although skaters still had to order specialized equipment such as custom made boots from Toronto or Vancouver, which, with many more indoor rinks, dominated figure skating nationally.

With the popularity of amateur figure skating in the Prairie region, the local press followed news of competitions and published human-interest features about local star skaters. While elite performance was linked to training facilities, media attention to championship performances was key to raising interest among young people across the country.[120] Among other major events, the Canadian Figure Skating Championships, previously held at the Glencoe Club in Calgary, came to the Royal Glenora for the first time in 1963. The North American Championships in 1951 and the World Championships in 1972 were held at Calgary's Stampede Corral and the Worlds in Edmonton's Coliseum in 1996.

Both Calgary and Edmonton have generated champion skaters. The Royal Glenora "figure skating factory" has turned out champions including Kurt Browning, Jamie Sale and David Pelletier, Kristy Sargent, and Kristi Yamaguchi. Browning won the Canadian and World championships in 1989, successfully defended both titles in 1990 and 1991 (as well as the World title again in 1993), and became the first figure skater to win the 1990 Lionel Conacher Award as Canada's outstanding male athlete.[121] Since there are no professional leagues in the sport, the typical post-athletic career path is into commercial entertainment such as the Stars on Ice touring show in which Browning, Sale and Pelletier, Yamaguchi, and others have appeared.

After the 1994 Olympics, the popularity of figure skating rose swiftly. The 1996 World Figure Skating Championships was the largest sporting event held to that date in Edmonton, with a television audience of 177 million viewers, 220 athletes, over 600 media representatives, and approximately 20,000 visitors to the city. Edmonton also set live attendance records for the event. The competition roused local ire when International Skating Union (ISU) rules prevented Albertan Kurt Browning, who was ineligible to compete, from giving an exhibition at the rink. Alberta takes its sports seriously, and "insulted by the idea that their national hero would not be allowed to skate," fans regularly booed during medal ceremonies, embarrassing local organizers. At day four of "Kurtgate" the ISU president made a special concession to allow Browning and Kristi Yamaguchi to skate an exhibition performance.[122]

Canadian public interest in figure skating declined in the years after the event, due in part to the sport's overexposure and, later, the 2002 Olympic judging scandal. After a technically superior performance at the 2002 Olympics, Canadian figure skaters Jamie Sale and David Pelletier were denied the gold medal in favour of the Russian pair. After days of public outrage and intense pressure on the International Olympic Committee to investigate formal allegations of vote tampering by the French judge, Sale and Pelletier were awarded their own gold medals and designated co-medallists with the Russians.[123] In 2001 Skate Canada announced that figure skating was second only to hockey as Canada's most popular spectator sport, but the most other sources cite football in this position.[124]

Norwegians provided much of the initial impetus for skiing in Camrose, Edmonton, and Calgary, organizing meets and tournaments as early as 1910.[125] Skiing was introduced in Banff in 1890, and Austrian Conrad Kain built the first jump on Tunnel Mountain in 1910. Around the same time, Jack Stanley began to manufacture skis at his lumber mill near Lake Minnewanka. Although the sport declined when Kain left in 1912, the formation of the Banff Ski Club in 1917 inspired the establishment of the Banff Winter Carnival, where ski jumping was featured. Competitors came from all over the continent, including Gus Johnson of Camrose, who stayed in town and organized the Banff Ski Club the next year. Of twenty-nine members, all by five were young men. By 1920 the club had over thirty members.[126] In the early years, women usually took part in cross-country events. Typically, they were also involved in organizing and fundraising, but later participated in downhill racing as successful athletes in their own right.

A larger ski jump, built in 1919, became part of the increasingly popular and lucrative North American professional tournament circuit for elite skiers, but for most local people, it was still a spectator sport. When Clifford Whyte became president of the Banff Ski Club in 1930, he started a competitive ski development program. The Ski Runners of the Canadian Rockies was established in 1931 to foster competition and raise the status of downhill skiing. The club took it upon themselves to regulate the sport, insisting that all race entrants hold both amateur cards and memberships in registered clubs. One reason was to control access; in 1954 the organization recommended that memberships on Mount Norquay be sold to Banff residents only. This effectively prevented Calgarians from getting the special club rates.[127] The sport's development depended on local capacity in equipment, facilities, and transportation, and proceeded slowly for several decades. Mount Norquay was the region's first developed ski hill in 1926. By 1935 there were still no facilities in Banff during the winter. In 1969 the Banff Springs Hotel began to stay open year-round, but the Chateau Lake Louise did not open for the winter season until 1982.[128]

Meanwhile, prairie skiers were forced to exercise ingenuity. As the *Calgary Herald* put it in 1950, the growing enthusiasm for skiing in small, flat prairie towns and cities was "almost miraculous...positive proof that there must be something tremendously attractive about the sport." At the time, for example, there were clubs in Red Deer, Turner Valley, Castor, and Nanton, operating in "depressions in the flatlands."[129] Grande Prairie and Edmonton were among the cities that built wooden ski jumps for lack of sufficient hill elevation. The Calgary Ski Club was formed in 1920 and overcame obstacles of terrain and climate to hold a jumping contest that year on a ramp leading down from the roof of the Stampede Grandstand in Elbow Park. Another jump was built in Victoria Park in 1921; according to one observer, the ski jump had a 100-foot wide hole at the bottom that skiers had to manoeuvre to avoid.[130]

In November 1922 Calgary hosted the World Ski Jumping Championships but, due to a chinook melt, they had to import snow from Lake Louise. There were reportedly only about five people in the city who owned skis at the time, but the *Calgary Herald* owner John Southam took up the cause and was the driving force behind the club's efforts "to facilitate...transportation and ski accommodation in the mountains."[131] The first ski special busses and trains to Banff, and the first racing competition, were organized in 1935, and the CPR inaugurated its snow train service two years later. In 1939, new projects were also developing in Jasper led by Swedish skier Peter Vajda and Canadian ski champion Gertrude Wepsala; Mount Whistler had the country's longest downhill ski course.[132] Jim Morrison of Banff built the first rope tow in the west by connecting a bull wheel to a McLaughlin Buick car engine. These measures helped open the mountain parks to national and international tourism, promoted by CPR pamphlets on "Skiing in the Canadian Rockies." The special trains ran until around 1950, when more private automobiles were available.[133]

The impact of a hundred or so Calgary Ski Club members arriving each weekend helped to inspire Banff's development as a major resort in the 1930s and 1940s, involving both commercial operators and federal government agencies. The Lake Louise and Canmore clubs also promoted the sport. In 1937 the Dominion Championships, the first in the Canadian Rockies, were held at Norquay, as were subsequent national, regional, and local competitions. The mass popularity of skiing in the Rockies ultimately depended on access by automobile as well as train. When new highways east and west, as well as between Jasper and Banff, opened in the early 1940s, sport tourism from eastern Canada and the United States expanded. New facilities were built in both resort centres as the "barriers of mountain and forest which long marked the travel frontiers of Canada" were overcome, and skiing was the fastest-growing sport in the country in 1959, a trend that continued in the next decades.[134] Prime Minister Pierre Trudeau helped to promote the sport when he skied at Lake Louise and Sunshine in 1975, just before the day he opened the Canada Winter Games at Lethbridge and met with Alberta Premier Peter Lougheed on national oil policy.[135]

After World War II, with over 1,000 members and more recreationists with disposable income, the Calgary club joined the Western Canadian Ski Association. The club followed established Alberta tradition in rejecting the national association, this time for its bias in preferring eastern racers to westerners for sponsorships. The J.B. Cross slalom trophy was given for skiing competitions between Edmonton and Calgary in the 1930s and 1940s; the Calgary Ski Club slalom team won in 1938. At the time, Cross was president of the Calgary Brewing Company, known for its support of local sport. In 1941, the Edmonton Saskatchewan River Bank Snowbirds won the trophy at Norquay.[136] Annual competition between the Edmonton and Calgary clubs continued in the early 1950s, but Calgary regularly dominated (reportedly due to the northern city's lack of good nearby practice hills, despite its more reliable snow cover), and many Edmonton skiers lost interest.[137] A second Calgary club, the Skimeisters, formed in 1961 to train young skiers in slalom and downhill.[138]

The city maintained a vigorous ski culture, however. A group of "ski-obsessed, ex-pat Norwegians" founded the Edmonton Ski Club in the river valley in 1911. The club built a ski jump, but the structure was demolished in 1924 for safety reasons. The club experimented with other locations, including the river bank near the Highlands Golf Course, which took skiers onto river ice usually covered with six or more inches of water. In the 1940s the club built a full-sized world championship ski jump spanning the main road down Connor's Hill. A thriving ski culture developed. Bruce Mcgavin recalls night exhibitions in which skiers went down the jump with blazing fireworks attached to their skis and through a hoop set on fire with kerosene. After its reconstruction, Edmonton's Winter Carnival, which ran from the mid-1930s until after World War II, featured skiing events in which "you had to be a real skier to stay alive" through daredevil displays such as the "Heigh-Ho Silver" in which one skier rode downhill on the backs of two crouched one behind the other.[139] Although the jump was "slightly dilapidated" by 1962, the club hosted major championships such as the Alberta Nordic Juniors that year. The ski jump was dismantled as an eyesore when Queen Elizabeth visited Edmonton in its 2005 centennial year. The club generated generations of skiers, clubs, and programs in the city, including the Varsity Ski Club, the Eskimo Ski Club (ESC), and Rabbit Hill, the latter the only surviving program. Alumni of the ESC include Jenn Heil, Olympic medallist, among others.[140]

Alberta skiers, including Jim Hunter, Cary Mullen, Edi Podivinsky, and Thomas Grandi, have achieved international recognition. Dorothy (Dee) Read won the Dominion Ski Championships at Mount Norquay, Alberta, in 1948, competing in several events. In the 1992 Olympics, Kerrin Lee-Gartner of Calgary skied the world's most difficult women's downhill course and gave Canada its first Olympic gold medal in women's alpine skiing since 1984. Karen Percy won four World Championships and seven Canadian National Championships from 1983 to 1989, as well as two bronze medals at the 1988 Olympics. On the way to the medal ceremony, Percy remembers, "I sat in this van riding into Calgary all by myself. I had just won an Olympic medal. It was kind of surreal. But that's how individual sport is."[141]

As we have seen in this chapter, athletes in solo sport are motivated by passion for competition against their own best efforts, against opponents, and, in some cases, against unpredictable natural elements, including snow, ice, and animals. All the stories that hit the headlines and the record books begin with someone who wanted to play and others who wanted to make it happen. The successes of these individuals and of their sports, however, transcend solo performance; as in the case of team sport, collective organization has proved essential. The culture of sport also depends on backstage performances. Coaches, community facilities, clubs, and organizations at various levels have built the foundations that launch star athletes. These efforts may or may not lead to elite levels of performance, but they are consistently considered crucial when they do. To name only one example, Dorothy "Dee" Read "was considered the matriarch of alpine ski racing in Canada, a one-time champion racer who remained devoted to the sport for six decades and instilled a love of skiing in her prodigious family." All four Read children made it to the provincial ski team, and two, Jim and Ken, competed at the Olympics. Ken Read was a member of the Canadian Ski Team (known as the Crazy Canucks) from 1974 to 1983 and won the Canadian Championships and the World Cup on multiple occasions. Read was named Canada's Athlete of the

Year in 1978, Calgary's Athlete of the Year in 1979, and Canadian Male Amateur Athlete of the Year in 1979 and 1980. Dee Read volunteered at the 1988 Winter Olympics and was the second woman ever to be named Sportsman of the Year by the Calgary Booster Club; in 2001 she was inducted into the Canadian Ski Hall of Fame as both athlete and builder of the sport.[142]

Community groups such as booster and service clubs also play important roles in developing sport, as they have since earlier decades of community promotion. The Edmonton Kinsmen, like other branches across the province, supported local sports and recreation, building outdoor sporting fields in 1953 on city land on the south bank of the river.[143] The Calgary Booster Club also donated volunteer hours and raised funds to promote access to sport as well as to directly support teams such as the Calgary Bronks in the Western Canada Rugby Football Union during the 1930s. The Booster Club became a driving force for amateur sport in the 1950s. In the 1960s and 1970s, for instance, the group sponsored high school and junior golf, speed skating, and swimming, supported an annual hockey school, and donated funds to the Alberta Special Games and national wheelchair sports, among other projects. In the 1980s the club supported Calgary's Olympic bid, and was still actively promoting sport in the city well into the twenty-first century.[144]

An evaluation of the roles of these community organizations in the broader development of sport in Alberta depends in great part on the perceived significance of amateur and minor activity in the everyday life of the population. It is easy to overlook this dimension of sport culture, distracted as we typically are by the spectacle and drama of international professional sport. In Alberta, historical challenges of climate, sparse population, and distances affect the high degree to which people have chosen to participate in organized sporting culture, which reflects sporting culture's broad social significance over more than a century of Euro-Canadian history in the region.

Various sports have captured the public imagination over time, super-seded by others, but most historical games are still played today. Why do some sports achieve commercial success, winning hearts, minds, and wallets, while others fade as popular recreations and spectacle? As discussed in previous chapters, for instance, cricket predates hockey in the North-West Territories, but waned in comparison as hockey, basketball, football, baseball, and lacrosse were played increasingly as working-class Canadians began to reject British-dominated sports. Public facilities and sports promoters also helped to direct popular interest with their sponsorship of certain sports. Sport's meanings and social roles changed as it became a commercial product in a complex of urban mass culture, within broad networks of national organization and resource distribution.[145] Throughout the defining organizational processes that launched today's sporting culture in Alberta, the spheres of recreational, amateur, and professional sport resonated together. The development of professional sport culture in Alberta reflects patterns typical to most areas of popular culture as they developed from unreg-ulated and non-commercial pastimes over the late nineteenth and twentieth centuries. Simply put, power brokers including adminis-trators, promoters, and owners ultimately prescribe the means and methods of play, the incentives to participate, and the time and spaces in which they occur. Accordingly, effective distinctions are estab-lished between the roles of spectators and performers, or amateurs and professionals.

Although the evolution of sports cultures situated within these global and national contexts, Alberta's history, demographics and geog-raphy have shaped some particular twists in the patterns. According to Bill Kirwin, the history of professional baseball, for example, reflects that of western Canada itself. The imperialistic fortunes of a model colony are based on the exchange of resources (players) from the hinterlands for marketable products (winning teams) that return capital to central Canada, so that it is difficult to sustain semi-pro or pro sport in smaller centres. Sports have in this way replicated the unequal relations between regions and economic centres. The "pattern of marginal franchises playing in shaky leagues" shaped most pro sports in Edmonton and Calgary.[146]

In following the developing history of sport, we also need to take into account the ways that shifts in demographics may interact with established influences on sport, such as regional climate and geography. For example, according to D.W. Calhoun, soccer has been mainly a game of the southern hemisphere, fluid and kinetic. On the other hand, hockey is traditionally a game of the North based in extremes and endurance, physically brutal within a confined space among players who, until recently, have been almost exclusively white.[147] In the twenty-first century, after a generation and more of increased immigration from countries without the tradition or ideology of winter sports, soccer's presence in everyday life is growing.[148] Both Ken Dryden and Gamal Abdel-Shehid see the hold of hockey on Canadian imaginations loosening in recent years, becoming more habit than passion.[149] Again, this may apply more to central Canada and the West Coast than to the Prairies. In comparison with major cities such as Toronto, Montreal, and Vancouver, for instance, Alberta has smaller centres and receives fewer immigrants. As of 2006, the population included fewer visible minorities (one index of non-traditional sources of sport) than Ontario and British Columbia.[150]

As demonstrated by numerous sources concerning both historical and contemporary sport in Canada, mainstream sports discourse has historically served dominant power interests.[151] However, alternatives to established hierarchies, such as women's organizations or immigrant sports clubs, have tended to replicate the same styles of organization and accreditation. If the nostalgic, romanticized discourse of sporting history tends to help produce normative standards and identities in a region or nation, it is the task of critical thinking about sport to challenge these boundaries as given categories of exclusion or inclusion. The themes of national mythologies, demographic and social change, masculinity and gender, cultural transmission, and the relationships between popular, elite, and mass sports culture will be investigated further in the next section.

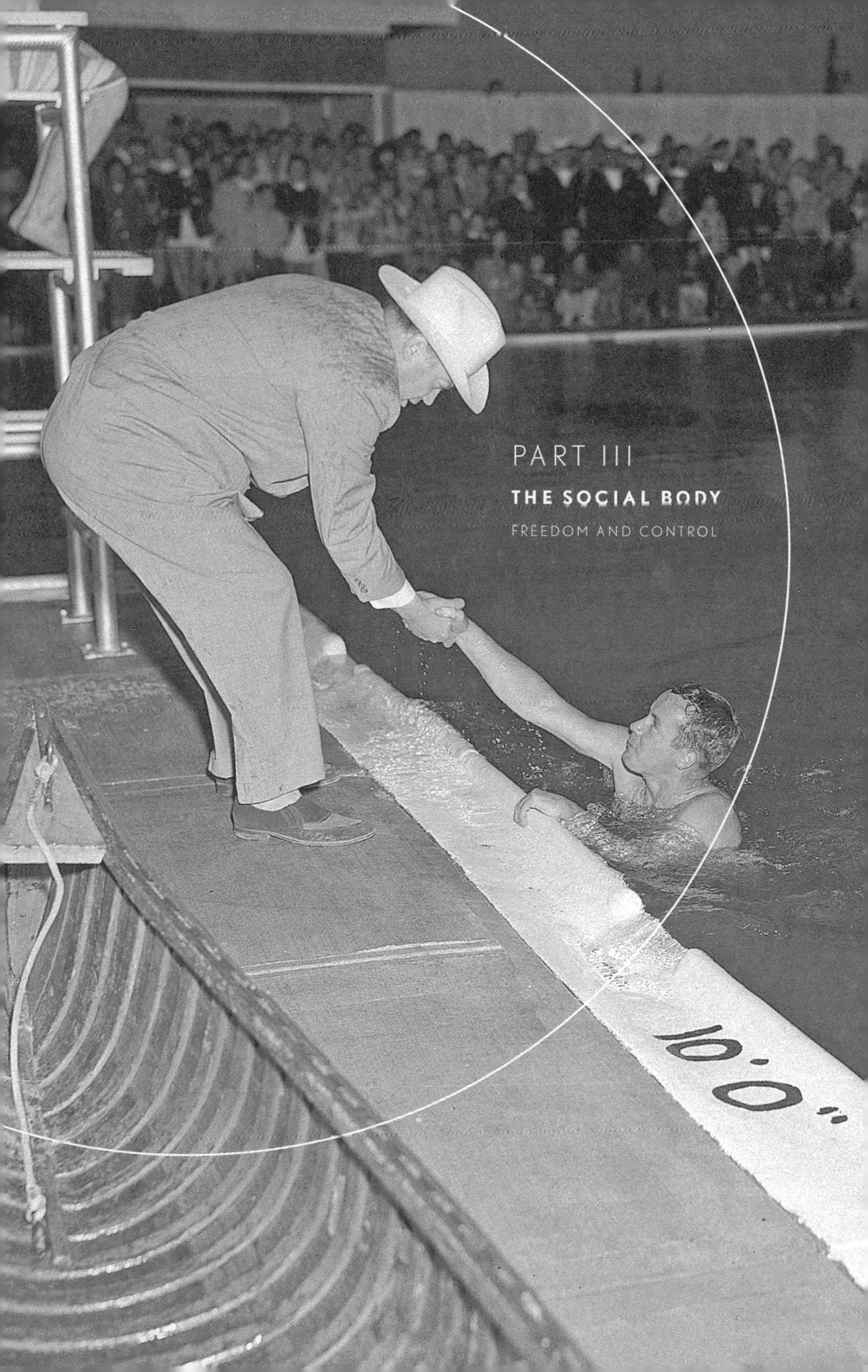

PART III

THE SOCIAL BODY

FREEDOM AND CONTROL

"Physical capital—the sporting body—connects with economic and cultural capital to express certain social principles and cultural meanings."

IN 2004 the *Edmonton Journal* published a list of the city's top ten historical events in sport. Eight involve professional or elite amateur male team sport; two are about women; and one concerns a member of a visible minority. None of the stories involve Aboriginal people (the "Eskimos" don't count), recognized gays and lesbians, disability athletes, or minor sports events. The list reads:

1. *Oilers win first Stanley Cup 1984*
2. *Eskimos win first Grey Cup 1954*
3. *Edmonton Grads' career 1915–1940*
4. *Edmonton Flyers win Allan Cup 1948*
5. *Wayne Gretzky trade 1988*
6. *Matt Baldwin's Brier wins 1950s*
7. *Diane Jones Konihowski, gold medal, Commonwealth Games 1978*
8. *Jackie Parker trade 1963*
9. *Heritage Classic 2003*
10. *World Championship in Athletics 2001.*[1]

In a 2006 study of sports coverage in the *Globe and Mail*, Romayne Fullerton found an almost exclusive focus on professional sports, while a similar survey of smaller community papers found a much higher rate of coverage of local and amateur sport. The focus on able-bodied men's sport keeps this demographic high in public awareness as winners, but the media preoccupation with male professional sport only developed in the 1920s, '30s, and '40s. Since World War II, the interdependence of professional sport and the mass media have worked together to almost eliminate the previously numerous stories about women's sports, for instance. Fullerton notes that both large and small newspapers concentrated on winning events, statistics, and scores; almost as numerous were references to money, owner-ship, coaching, and winning skills. In this value system, women and amateurs are marginalized, as are disabled and First Nations sports. These marginalized realms

have a demonstrated interest in sport participation as part of popular culture, rather
than as a scorecard or business. Just as
Lorna Robinson found in 1997, Fullerton's
2006 study showed that the sports pages are
still sexist, class-oriented, largely white, and
dominated by able-bodied people.[2]

To most of us, this is likely to seem a
neutral and inevitable reflection of popular
interest and engagement, but it more accurately reflects broader fundamental power
structures and discourses in society. Cultural
analysts have argued that selected tastes
and activities, or dispositions, are formed by
social influences rather than by arbitrary,
autonomous judgments and are used by
different classes to secure relative power
positions and boundaries. Elite tastes are
defined, and access to them controlled, while
popular tastes are reinforced as the territory
of lower socio-economic groups. As Pierre
Bourdieu suggests, cultural capital consists
of the knowledge and behaviours that

support access to certain areas of activity and production. Bourdieu views sport, like other realms of cultural activity and knowledge, as an instrument of social exclusivity and cultural distinction; dominant social groups promote certain games that reinforce the status quo. Physical capital—the sporting body—connects with economic and cultural capital to express certain social principles and cultural meanings.[3]

Colin Howell asserts that "the history of sport in twentieth-century Canada is a story of class and gender formation, capitalist transformation, and nation building in the broadest sense."[4] Class associations bestow social value on certain sports and certain approaches to them; the middle class may practice gymnastics for health and beauty, whereas the working class will practice for strength. Team sports, boxing, and wrestling demand endurance and collective discipline and are associated with working classes; the dominant classes favour aesthetic

contemplative sports like golf, skiing, and
tennis that involve individualistic competition, early training, specialized gear, and
social tradition. Participation also enhances
career opportunities and privileged social
contacts with little risk of injury. Boxing and
rodeo, on the other hand, are sports in which
one is likely to work with colleagues from
less powerful racial and ethnic groups; these
sports are dangerous and thus avoided by
those with a choice. While sports can be a
path to success for working-class people, the
necessary sponsors and funds are not under
their control.[5]

Relationships between economic and
cultural capital and sports consumption
vary by context and, as Bourdieu notes, no
one type of culture shapes all class
dynamics. Whereas Bourdieu argues that
rugby has been a sport of the popular
sectors, any organized sport now presents
economic obstacles to participation,
including the need for leisure time to play

and practice, and hidden entry requirements such as membership in specific schools or neighbourhoods. In Canada sports knowledge can serve to integrate rather than distinguish between social groups. However, judged by cost and participation rates, sports such as golf and downhill skiing may be instruments of social exclusion rather than social bridging.[6]

Gender and sexuality, race and social class, as well as bodily presentation, the star system, and mass media have all shaped how we understand, participate in, and watch sports in Alberta. But behind memories of famous games, events, and deals lie other stories. While official organization occurred within existing structures of power that welcomed and validated certain models of athletics and athletes, people have struggled not only for the right to play sports of their choice but for autonomy over the physical body and its meanings and to participate in activities in ways and places of their choice.

7

"A VAIN SHADOW"

FITNESS, DISCIPLINE, AND SOCIAL CONTROL

THE "BODY BEAUTIFUL" AND FITNESS AS SOCIAL DISCIPLINE

As Calgary grew, the YMCA was an affordable place for kids to play, exercise, and meet friends in the 1920s. They jumped into the pool without realizing that they would also be immersed in good citizenship lessons based on the conviction that sport helped to break down social barriers and build tolerance. In 1921, the organization reported that boys from the immigrant and working-class Riverside area were "playing in competitive games with boys from other parts of the city. Does this mean the breaking down gradually of that suspicion and prejudice that has existed? It does, and it means better citizens in the future."[1] Institutions such as the YWCA and YMCA incorporated agenda previously articulated by the playground movement of the late nineteenth century that aimed to improve the quality of urban working-class life through access to green space and rationally designed recreation. Although its proponents viewed recreation as a democratic right, with "sport for all" as the goal, the establishment and supervision of public playing spaces was also intended to prevent delinquency among youth. In 1921, Calgary's Children's Aid department attributed a reduction of 38 per cent in juvenile delinquency rates in

part to the YMCA's work to "promote civic righteousness." The promotion of sports in the inner city Riverside neighbourhood produced championship gymnastics teams as well as star athletes. Norman Kwong, a pro football player, and David "Sweeney" Schriner, a star hockey player and coach, were from the area.[2] The rhetoric of fitness, sport and good social order endured; forty years later, supporters of the new Killam Memorial Arena advised that athletics was "conducive to the physical, social and moral betterment of both present and future citizens."[3]

In linking sports with social values of tolerance and productivity, the Y drew upon powerful ideologies of physical culture that aligned stray individuals with a disciplined, conforming social body. The concept of the "social body" links the individual as cultural actor to society. In this perspective, the individual body is not a given biological state but a complex social creation and category whose meanings shift between eras and individuals. As an "inscribed surface of events" the body carries representations of nature, society, and culture and participates in contests and hierarchies of power and domination.[4] Bodies are regulated and controlled in areas of work, leisure, and health, shaping social life according to aggregated conditions organizing power. Individuals working for their own purposes are nevertheless influenced by ideals and aims of wider society; ideals, aims, and defects are all factors in driving society along certain paths for the well-being of the social body.[5]

Ideals of the "body beautiful" are entwined within these social connections and reflect a range of ideas about physicality that are not exclusive to but expressed perhaps most obviously in sporting culture.

The celebration of the human body is deeply entrenched in Western societies. The ancient Greeks famously valued a healthy mind in a healthy body, the ideal of beauty. Marble or bronze statues of famous athletes lined stadia and gymnasia to inspire the young, much as do posters of today's sports stars. Sparta, one of the most physically fit societies in history, directed exercise regimes toward producing male warriors and mothers of warriors. The Greek goals of individual and collective excellence, often in military terms, have come down to us in European cultures of fitness and holistic discipline.[6]

In seventeenth-century Germany, Johann GutsMuths's strong nationalist fervour drove his physical development programs for military preparedness. The Enlightenment push to measure more systematically and scientifically control human performance also fired the impulse to achieve physical perfection through sport.[7] In the nationalist climate of Europe between 1700 and 1850, physical education programs expanded and gymnastics regimes developed in Germany, Denmark, Sweden, and Great Britain. A gymnastics treatise of 1828 proclaimed that "as long as man has got a body here below... which enervates into a vain shadow without power and strength, without endurance and persistence, without agility and skills—the art of gymnastics will have to take up a large part of human education."[8] The "body beautiful" movement was influential in Europe from the eighteenth century, evolving into nineteenth-century cults of health and beauty that, in part, reflected a socially oriented quest for control and perfection. By the 1920s the beautiful body was a reflection of national discipline, virtue, and health, glorified through sport most infamously by the Nazi regime in its staging of the 1936 Olympics.[9]

Victorian writers, philosophers, and social reformers took a strong interest in maintaining a healthy body. John Ruskin and Herbert Spencer recommended exercise for children, though George Bernard Shaw suggested that the idea was motivated mainly by a desire to exhaust the noise and mischief out of the young. For others, such as Rugby School headmaster Thomas Arnold, team sport was intrinsically amoral because it distracted from the proper mental and spiritual concerns of the young.[10] It would be necessary to invent some means of producing a holistic blend of health, morality, and social conscious-ness. For those Britons advocating a strenuous physical life, muscular Christianity was an alternative to both an overly corporeal focus and the horrors of bodily weakness. The normalized versions of the move-ment spread across class, status, and gender lines and were cogs in the engine of British cultural colonialism.

Despite early American opposition, late-nineteenth-century Protestant fears of perilous effeminate influences helped to sustain the ideology into the 1920s, when a growing pacifism made suspect the militarism of muscular Christianity. In Canada, though, the movement was linked to the political left and influenced progressive social ideas, including democratic recreation and community support for amateur sport.[11] (Echoes of muscular Christianity occasionally recur in prairie culture. In 2005, a Winnipeg church innovated Christian-themed wrest-ling matches in an effort to update its image and attract membership. The congregation included those who found wrestling "a natural fit with religion because of the theme of good versus evil.")[12]

⦂ EXERCISING SOCIAL CONTROL

Ideals of bodily discipline also harmonized with secular interests. As suggested in the previous chapter, the values of industrial capitalist society are reflected in a culture of sport that has stressed competition, individual ambition, and elite privilege. Victorians prized goals of disci-pline achieved through organized, rational knowledge of individuals and collectives; like the machines that produced material goods, the disciplined body would obey certain predictable codes of time sched-uling and orderly behaviour. As industrial technologies and urban living purportedly threatened society with mass bodily degeneration, fitness promoters also associated exercise programs with decreased public health costs.

In Alberta, the social construction of the athlete and the athletic body was based on historical paradigms of health and fitness,

Pyramid group for Morris School of Physical Culture, Edmonton, June 1926. Photo: McDermid Studio, Edmonton. [GA NC-6-11866J]

articulated and mediated in part through discourses of physical culture. Alongside the rhetoric of social duty, a parallel commercialized discourse of the individual body emerged. Ideas about physical fitness and sport became ever more commercialized as the body in consumer culture became a commodity and professional sport demanded impressive performances and idealized physiques to ensure profits and audiences. By the early twentieth century, fitness was becoming a form of cultural capital for both sexes, distinguishing the educated middle class from those without the means to pursue time-consuming leisure activities.[13]

Business energies in Alberta connected fitness to social and financial success. A 1921 *Calgary Daily Herald* advertisement for bicycles advised readers that cyclists "earn more money because the healthful exercise of riding enables them to do better work and more of it. Do you?"[14] And the social pressure toward fitness, merged with messages about lifestyle management, generated a market for products and programs targeting body size. In the *Edmonton Bulletin* of January 1920, an ad for "overfatness" pills promised to "Take Off Excess Fat."[15] At the same time, women were criticized for developing larger, more muscular proportions through participation in sport. In this social context, bulk of any kind sent the wrong message about class; working-class women were not chastised for developing muscles through participation in labour.

In 1890s Alberta, businesses commonly promoted employee health, vigour, and productivity by allowing extra time off for sports participation. Many Lethbridge merchants, for example, closed early to allow tennis club members time to practice for upcoming matches.[16] Even those in relatively physical occupations were in danger of degeneration. At the end of the 1920s, the corpulence of the Edmonton police force's average member occasioned a new policy on fitness through exercise and sport. Constables worked out at the YMCA in preparation for possibly strenuous arrest manoeuvres. The police also had a softball team, which played on Boyle Street and won district tournaments.[17] Employers also organized team sports among workers to promote physical co-ordination and occupy leisure time. Unions recognized the bonds created by sports and promoted team participation as an arm of solidarity; a co-ordinated team could outperform a group of individualists. Businesses, including Drumheller valley coal mine operators, also saw the promotional benefits of sponsoring teams whose names and uniforms provided advertising; "industrial" teams and leagues were sponsored by companies all over the province.[18]

The regional demand for physical education lagged behind that in central Canada, where the effects of urbanization and labour-saving technologies were evident earlier. Although it was not part of the curriculum when the University of Alberta opened in 1908, physical education soon became compulsory. In 1909, the Men's Athletic Association was founded, followed by a women's organization, to encourage amateur physical culture and sport on campus; both were amalgamated as the University Athletic Board after 1946.[19] Communities and associations also promoted fitness for youth. Jack Rinehardt's physical culture classes for Wetaskiwin boys in the 1930s were offered free of charge with the reminder to parents that "a physically fit body makes for better study." (Classes for boys were subsidized by fees for "gentlemen" to take "private classes not subjected to public eyes during training.")[20] In 1938, the Canadian National Parks Association promoted the Rocky Mountain national parks by comparing the strong European government support for outdoor physical exercise with the Canadian state's general indifference to the "undernourishment and poor physique of so many of our children."[21] Those in the many families on relief were thought to be in particular danger.

The Edmonton YMCA, like the university, opened in 1908 and was equipped with a swimming pool, employment bureau, education classes including Bible study, a gymnasium, running track, and residence. Calgary's first YMCA building opened a year later. Leisure participation in fitness and sport has been an instrument of shaping social relationships, and the YMCA was concerned not only with integrating immigrant youth as good citizens but working-class people

Advertisement for Jack Rinehardt, physical instructor, sponsored by the Driard Hotel Gymnasium, Wetaskiwin, April 1, 1931. [CWA WET-FREE-1-4-31]

in general. In Britain, the institution targeted the spiritual and physical development of office and shop workers, but in North America it expanded its focus to manual labourers—whites only through the first decades of the twentieth century.[22]

James Martens describes the role of the YMCA in Depression-era Calgary as once plentiful jobs disappeared and middle-class men accustomed to the Protestant work (and leisure) ethic lost not only jobs but affordable activity options. The YMCA created a Leisure Time League to allow middle-aged men as well as youth access to facilities, hoping to draw patrons into employment counseling and organized programs. Most, though, availed themselves only of gyms and showers. When the masculinity defined by autonomy and making a good living was no longer economically viable, the YMCA offered a place where male physical strength and civilized cleanliness could be maintained.[23]

Immigrants sustained cultural networks in part by importing home country sports. Political ideologies were integrated into these communities as well. Many employers at the time were motivated to provide sports programs by a sense of social responsibility, but others instituted programs as a means of channeling workers' energies following strikes and workplace disputes. The Workers' Sports Association, a European socialist movement, was active in Canada from 1924 to 1935 through the Young Communist League (YCL) and ethnic-based sport associations. Operating mainly in small Ontario and British Columbia resource communities, the YCL organized children's camps and boxing and wrestling programs in several southern Alberta communities by 1925. The group started soccer teams and other sports programs in Lethbridge, Drumheller, Blairmore, Calgary, Edmonton, Sylvan Lake, Newcast, New Kiev, and Rosedale.[24]

Workers' Sports Association (WSA) leaders challenged bourgeois or "bosses' sport" provided by employers and the state, arguing that such programs were intended to forge commitment to the workforce, increase productivity, and train workers for war while distracting them from their exploitation. Sport and leisure, in this view, would maintain existing social orders and inequities. WSA affiliates promoted sports on terms of comradeship and vitality, and preparation for collective living, rather than commercial antagonism and individualism. Not only corporations but professional and amateur organizations, which still followed norms of upper-class control over participation and membership, were sites of conflict between social classes. The organization opposed the YMCA for strikebreaking and held counter events to protest Amateur Athletic Union championships and British Empire Games; they also lobbied for public facilities for working-class use.[25]

The WSA successfully established sports such as wrestling and cross-country skiing in Canada, but the main focus was on acrobatics and gymnastics, in which groups such as Ukrainian immigrants were particularly strong. They organized public displays of skill and strength by individuals and teams that dramatized propaganda ideals of workers' strength and class pyramids. Over time, the WSA had limited success. The focus on European sport and ideological demonstrations of strength, as well as a lack of resources and equipment, limited the

WSA's appeal to Canadian youth who were interested in more familiar pastimes, and not all workers were motivated by the prospect of sport as training for the revolution but by "sport for sport's sake." Political tensions also came into play. Lewis McDonald, a boxer involved in youth sports in Drumheller in the early 1920s, was active in the coal miner's union and the WSA. However, after a lengthy strike in 1925, McDonald was sentenced to prison on charges of assault, and no landlord with sufficient facilities would rent to the group. In the mid-1930s, the WSA Alberta secretary advised "a proper balance between propaganda and serious athletics," arguing that a successful team would itself be good publicity, but the organization folded in 1935.[26]

In the same period, a British Columbia education minister called for physical education classes for the unemployed to counter the degenerating effects of enforced idleness that undermined morale and character.[27] Jan Eisenhardt developed the British Columbia Provincial Recreation Programme starting in 1934, providing recreation centres and programs for unemployed and homeless people during the Depression. Aiming to make people fit for work and everyday life, Pro-Rec was the most accessible program in Canadian history and influenced other jurisdictions, including Alberta, where the recreation leadership training program was run by Pro-Rec staff. Eisenhardt went on to national positions and programming, including a program to develop sports and recreation in Aboriginal residential schools and on reserves that applied his ideas about remedial physical training to government assimilationist policy objectives.[28]

Perceptions of social class persisted into rural-urban sports rivalries in the mid-twentieth century. In 1956, when Edmonton and Lloydminster were the only Alberta teams in the semi-pro Western Canada Baseball League, the latter "was the tough country team with dirt on their uniforms...Many of their players were grizzled veterans from minor league baseball, in contrast to Ducey's clean-cut Yankee college boys from the big city."[29] Among rural or working-class men, those who excelled at sports could become local heroes attaining, at least symbolically, equal or superior status with the affluent.[30]

In part influenced by the Pro-Rec program, the National Physical Fitness Act passed in 1943 amid concern over perceived lack of fitness in young male Canadian soldiers entering the war. At the end of the 1940s, the National Parks Association of Canada (NPAC) linked outdoor exercise, good citizenship, and tourism development when it advised parks management to provide accommodation for the "residents of the crowded industrial areas" who needed health intervention in order to produce robust future generations.[31] In the 1950s, Alberta children could tune in to CBC fitness expert Lloyd Percival, who coined the term "TV legs" for children who failed a fitness test due to excessive viewing time. Percival's weekly broadcast lessons reached almost 800,000 correspondence students across the country, although the National Fitness Act was repealed in 1954.

As postwar Canadian economic development and middle-class leisure opportunity expanded, the rhetoric of democratic access to fitness and sport became somewhat subtler. Sport and fitness remained an engine to produce social capital, a strong and united citizenry, but governments and public agencies took on campaigns previously steered by reformers and communities. After lobbying by fitness advocates and alarm about declining Canadian sports performance in international competition, in 1961 the federal Fitness and Amateur Sport Act launched decades of federal funding, agencies, and research that legitimized national public support for sport.[32] The act included the rationale of mass participation as a route to generate better athletes. Emphasis on the production of morality and civic participation yielded to prescriptive programs for enhancing individual physical capacity and performance.

The same year that the act was passed, the Royal Canadian Air Force developed the 5BX (Five Basic Exercises) and 10BX (for women) programs to combat sedentary lifestyles, offering activities from level one, for "housewives" to level six for "champion athletes."[33] However, a 1968 report warned that Canadians were still committing "armchair suicide" through dependency on cars and passive amusements.[34] The 1970 federal policy paper on sport, *A Proposed Sports Policy for Canadians*, still asserted mass participation as a goal but directed programs and funding toward the development of elite athletes, and since large commercial sponsors were uninterested in amateur sport, the federal state was the main benefactor of high performance athletes.[35]

In this context, public physical education programs came to focus on sports and games rather than holistic fitness, leading to the separation of health and aesthetic training from elite sports performance. Sport Canada, Recreation Canada, and Participation Canada (later ParticipACTION) were all created in this period. ParticipACTION, established in 1972, pioneered the use of social marketing and health communication techniques with a seemingly ubiquitous barrage of television, radio, and print ads comparing, for example, unfit Canadians to an idealized athletic Swede, perhaps targeting a shared national mythology of northern hardiness.[36] The emphasis on personal rather than social or public initiative to cure society's ills was reinforced by the 1974 report *A New Perspective on the Health of Canadians* (also known as the Lalonde Report), which was the first in the Western world to recognize the role of lifestyle and behaviour in public health. The doctrine of self-discipline was well-entrenched by this period, when "fat camps" for children in Alberta were compared to army boot camp. From our current perspective, the majority of participants in the photographs that follow appear to be of normal weight, which suggests the gradual evolution of social constructions of body size. The province was one of the first to pass recreation legislation with the Recreation Development Act in 1980; in 2008–2009, funding for this sector was almost $50 million. But obesity rates in Alberta more than doubled between 1985 and 2000, despite public recreation, fitness, and sports programs.[37]

As spectator sports peaked in popularity and Alberta's population and oil wealth grew in the 1960s, the province developed programs to support amateur and minor sport, and municipal governments also sponsored activity and fitness infrastructure. The contemporary vogue in public health promotion and the state's connection with sport is evident in the array of social leaders who typically appeared at fitness

Camp Slim-Teen, Calgary. These two separate, cropped images were published in the Calgary Herald, *April 10, 1974. (top) Exercising on the spot, these teens are trying to slim themselves down at the camp. (bottom) Going for a run: Exercise program for girls is like a page torn out of an army fitness program.* [GA NA-2864-25088]

centre openings and events. The 1962 opening of what would become the University of Calgary gym was attended by the Honourable J. Percy Page, then lieutenant-governor of Alberta.[38] The association of public health with fitness and sport persisted; Mayor Ralph Klein and various dignitaries appeared at Calgary's Thornhill Fitness Centre's opening ceremonies in the early 1980s.[39]

Control over the body as an expression of deep anxieties about social issues has been a persistent thread in cults of health and fitness. Ideals of beauty, health, and sexuality shift with social change, as do convictions of their connections. One era or society may associate female physical beauty with robust health while suppressing women's sexual freedom, for example; another associates health with the free expression of sexuality. Ideologies of "exorcis[ing] the evils of modern society" through the prescription of a collectively disciplined, ascetic lifestyle gain force in times of economic and political upheaval, such as the economic recession and public spending cuts of the 1980s and early 1990s in Alberta.[40] Paradoxically, however, the period coincided with a continental fitness boom characterized by prominent references to and imagery of overt sexuality in contexts of advertising, education, and entertainment. Whereas the discourses of previous eras focused on health and discreet suggestions of social success through fitness, those of the latter twentieth century focused much more explicitly on the need to develop a sexually attractive body. Even public facilities, such as the Thornhill Fitness Centre in Calgary, often provided cosmetically oriented suntan units as well as exercise equipment. Despite the incentives of both health and beauty, however, Canadian participation in physical activity did not increase in the 1980s or 1990s, and sport participation among those age fifteen and older fell almost 11 per cent between 1992 and 1998.[41]

The practice of serious bodybuilding is one of the legacies of early health and fitness cults. Though the "strongman" was already a popular figure in Canadian sideshows in the Victorian and Edwardian eras, for most people admiration did not imply emulation. With the

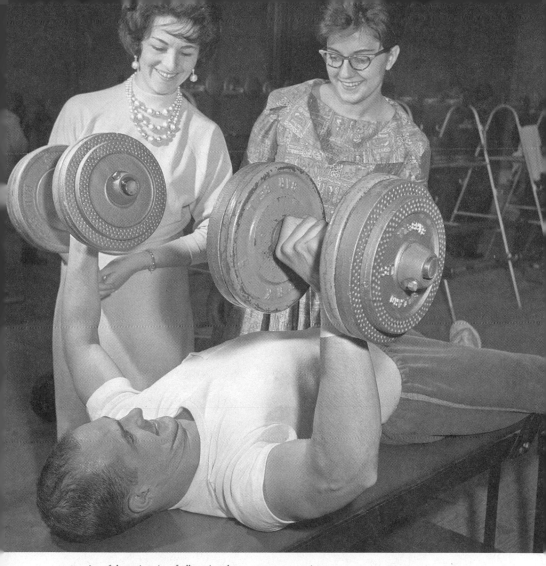

Opening of the University of Alberta's Calgary campus gymnasium, 1962. [UCA 82.010_1.19B]

so-called golden age of bodybuilding between 1940 and 1970, muscular
bullies appeared in Alberta magazine ads urging the spindly man
to bulk up to keep his women. But formidable though these figures
appeared, they usually remained within "normal" range for body fat
and strength. Over the past several decades, however, the typical body
size of serious athletes in all pro or semi-pro team sports has increased.

Even in the 1950s, the bodies of boxers and wrestlers tended to be less muscular than fleshy.

In 1953–1954, the biggest players in the N H L weighed around 180 pounds; some of the best players were significantly smaller. Edmonton Oilers team members of 2006 averaged about 205 pounds.[42] As sport infused marketing campaigns, television and film accelerated the associations of fit and muscular males with certain products such as automobiles and resorts; the objectification of male athletes as ideal body types and the production of the audience as consumers of these images went hand in hand.[43] The 1962 photograph of the weightlifter at the Calgary gym is a classic rendition of muscular masculinity and sexuality, realized by the presence of an admiring female audience. If any female bodybuilders performed at this event, no photograph exists.[44]

INCORPORATING "OTHERS" INTO THE SOCIAL BODY

Alberta has been characterized as a deeply conservative province but also a frontier where possibilities of difference have prevailed. As the social body has been shaped to fit the roles of modern life, amateur sportsmen and women who have resisted centralized control over associations and rulebooks have themselves resisted the incursion of "others" in their own activities. The pre-eminent sporting body in Anglo-American culture has typically been white, young, and male. Those outside the parameters of the idealized athletic body and its appropriate behaviours are sorted into various categories of distance from official sports culture. These categories, of course, reflect those in play in other social and cultural spheres. The problem comes when people want to break out of zones of segregation and compete on an equal basis.

Founding sports organizations defined amateur status to exclude working-class competitors, professionals, people who were adopted whose lineage was undocumented, or Aboriginal people. Events involving any group marked out as different from the white male athlete was understood to have mainly novelty value for entertainment or demonstration of skill, and public competition between whites and non-whites was strictly controlled. Sport, like other aspects of culture, continued to serve as an instrument of acculturation for youth and minorities as the twentieth century unfolded. In 1947, the minister of National Health and Welfare promoted fitness for national social integration.[45]

But, as in other areas of popular culture, "others" not fitting the traditional athletic ideal have found a way to manage and often resist assimilation in sport. Non-English speaking groups also maintained internal cohesion in community leisure circles. Sport has been a significant part of the resurgence of francophone cultural identity and expression in Alberta since the 1960s. The French youth organization Francophonie jeunesse de l'Alberta (FJA) was formed in 1972, and in 1992 held the first games for francophone youth as a week-long sporting and cultural event. In 2004, the Alberta Francophone Games (AFG) were organized for all ages. Like other comparable events, the AFG promotes francophone identity in young people and cultural pride in the community as an integrated whole. As is typical in most amateur sport organizations, there are clashes between sport-focused agendas and broader social goals. Christine Dallaire has suggested that the current focus on performance and management expertise, rather than on the promotion of francophoneness and participation, is to some extent reshaping the AFG.[46]

Although the constrained scope of non-English speaking groups activities made little impact on the dominant culture for most of the century, at various times immigrant expertise has sparked a wider interest in certain sports. In the more remote coal-mining towns with a largely male, transient population, ethnic divisions still prevailed in the 1920s and 1930s; new European immigrants played soccer while the local-born preferred hockey.[47] Many communities took up baseball as a route to integration, though separate teams were formed. Eric Solomon has discussed ways that baseball provided North American

Jews a mode of acculturation, countering the stereotypes of effete and bookish Europeans. For the Young Men's Hebrew Association base-ball team in 1912–1914 Calgary, for instance, league participation helped players integrate with other youth without threatening their core cultural identity.[48] An Edmonton team called the Jewish Hustlers played against a team called Invictus A in 1924. In Rumsey and Trochu, two of the largest Jewish farm colonies in Alberta, baseball was part of social life and teams entered competition around the region. Into the 1960s, half of Rumsey team members were still Jewish.[49]

Sport was part of the postwar period of cultural development in Alberta's Asian communities. The martial arts were a cultural accom-paniment to the Second World War immigration of Japanese-Canadians to southern Alberta, though at first some locals misinterpreted the practice as an enemy military plot. The prevailing public suspicion about sport practices was reflected more generally in unease about the practice of Buddhism in the region; a Raymond town hall meeting of May 24, 1942 petitioned the town council to close the local Buddhist temple, the first one in the province.[50] Despite these attitudes, Yoshio Katsuta, the founder of Alberta judo, opened the first club at Raymond in 1943 and often travelled to promote the sport across the province. The first annual YMCA judo tournament was held in Calgary with two teams from that city and others from Edmonton, Raymond, and Lethbridge.[51] Judo Alberta was formed in 1960. High levels of participa-tion have supported the development of successful national and international competitors. The Lethbridge Kyodokan Judo Club has won Alberta's only three senior national medals, and three competitors from Lethbridge won gold medals for judo at the 1974 Olympics.[52]

NHL hockey players Paul Kariya and Devin Setoguchi, both from Alberta, also descend from Japanese families who were sent to intern-ment camps during World War II. Devin's father, Dale Setoguchi, played junior hockey in Alberta and was the 1979 MVP in the AJHL.

Another prominent Asian sportsman was Kemo Inamasu, who settled in Calgary in 1905 and for many years operated cafés for Burns plant workers, farmers, ranchers, and railroad workers. From the 1930s, he turned to the track and found success breeding, training, and racing thoroughbreds in partnership with jockey Hiromi Uyeyama, the only such Japanese combination in North America. His horse, the Duchess of York, won thirty-eight races as well as numerous seconds and thirds throughout the continent and was elected to the Canadian Horse Racing Hall of Fame.[53] Probably the best-known Asian-Albertan athlete is the Honourable Norman L. Kwong, Alberta's sixteenth lieutenant-governor. Kwong played for both Edmonton and Calgary's pro football teams, the first Chinese-Canadian to play in the league. He was Canadian Male Athlete of the Year in 1955 and held over thirty records when he retired. He has also been president of the Calgary Stampeders, general manager of the CFL, and co-owner of the Calgary Flames hockey team.[54]

People of colour have been accepted more in some sports than in others in the region. Although John Ware's place in history seems to negate racist constraints, William McLennan mentions rancher John Ware's reputation as one of the "whitest" men in the west to indicate the local respect held for him, although he was also known as "Nigger" John. In 1960, his daughter requested that the Nigger John 4-H Beef Club named in his honour drop the "ghastly" moniker. The group explained that they had not even known his surname, but that like many sites with the same title in the area, it was intended as a respectful way to preserve a historical memory that they feared was endangered by the sensibilities of "the present generation."[55] (The club did change its name.)

In 1911, a New Zealand paper reported with surprise the animosity in Alberta toward African-American settlement. Since the sentiment was unusual in Canada, the reporter associated it with the over 100,000 wealthy Americans buying land in Alberta and settling there in great numbers in the past year alone, bringing their prejudices with them.[56] Almost all prairie newspapers, governments, and boards of trade in communities including Edmonton, Morinville, Strathcona, Fort Saskatchewan, and Calgary criticized the early-twentieth-century immigration of black people from Kansas and Oklahoma. Opposition rose with growing numbers of black settlers arriving in the province, partly based in fears of miscegenation and cultural change detrimental to the "White race."[57] In urban settings the majority of black people could find their places only in the spheres of entertainment and sport. Employment opportunities were limited to jobs such as railway porters. John Ware's son Bob, for example, was a Pullman porter on the midnight train from Calgary to Edmonton for many years.[58] Up until the mid-twentieth century, access to competitive sport was limited primarily to individual performance such as track or boxing. These sports offered routes to potential prosperity for black and working-class men. Alberta's best-known African-Canadian athletes prior to 1950 were usually boxers. Joe "Dad" Cotton, born a slave in 1853, became a prizefighter in the United States before moving to Edmonton in 1912 to open a boxing club to train young men and promote the sport. Other noted Alberta boxers have included Richard and Nathaniel Lipscombe in the 1920s; Harvey Bailey, who won the western Canadian featherweight championship in 1935; Benny Geary and Vern Escoe, champions of the 1940s; and Doug Harper, who was Canada's light-heavyweight champion in the early 1950s.[59]

The Gideons were an African-Canadian family who moved to Calgary from Nova Scotia in 1912 and lived in the Victoria Park district in 1920 at a time when residents unsuccessfully petitioned city council to designate the community a white-only district. Russ Gideon grew up amid other instances of organized resistance against African-Canadians, but participated in Calgary's sporting and cultural life from a young age. He played on championship baseball teams, including the Victoria Park Athletic Club and Calgary Dodgers, but was best known for football. He joined the Calgary Tigers in 1928 and may have been the first black player on a senior team in the country. In fact, in 1929 he played in the first Canadian game to use the forward pass between Calgary and Edmonton.[60]

In 1910 the Medicine Hat baseball team refused to play the Regina Bonepilers because the team included African-American player Dick Brookins. Despite Brookin's claim to be Native American (also subject

Amber Valley baseball team in the Northern Alberta Baseball League, Athabasca, ca. 1930s.
Top row, left to right: Cliff Brown, Fordie Medlock, Horace Hinton, J.B. Brown, unknown,
Alonzo Edwards, Ozzie Lipscombe. Front row, left to right: Booker Edwards, Arthur Saunders,
Kenny Edwards. [AA ATH-03237]

to prejudice but apparently less so), Calgary and Medicine Hat both
protested his "Negroid features" and the Western Canada League president banned the "alleged Negro" from play.[61] The incident reflects
the cultural and ethnic biases connecting selected kinds of play and
players with legitimate sport and the arbitrary development of codes
that, in this case, ranked the Aboriginal player above the black athlete.
Around the same time, though, the first black settlers to Alberta
emigrated from Oklahoma to Wildwood, and many later settled in
Amber Valley near Athabasca. An active local social life included an
annual sports day and picnic, and during the 1930s Amber Valley's all-
black team was one of the most successful ball teams in the province.

The Amber Valley Giants barnstormed widely, playing only against white teams, a practice banned in the United States at the time. They won respect and fans, but were not part of regular league play.[62]

In 1950, an Amber Valley team was listed among competitors in the "huge" 1950 Lacombe baseball tournament, as well as a team called the Athabasca Colored Giants. It is likely that another black team did not exist, however, as a report of the tournament stated that the "Amber Valley coloured giants from the Athabasca region" had failed to show.[63] Imported black teams that toured the province seem to have been viewed in part as novelty acts in the context of the barnstorming tradition. The *Camrose Canadian* promoted a local game featuring the Muskogee Cardinals in 1948: "The Cardinals, a darky club, were the champions of the Southwest from 1934 to 1947...Those who have seen them play report they put on the best show any touring ball club has ever shown. They play to win, but add enough comedy to the game to give you your money's worth."[64] In June 1952 the all-black Western Canada League team the Indian Head Rockets, barnstormers from Florida bought by a Saskatchewan town, won an exhibition match against the Pincher Creek Dominoes. Unlike regular barnstorming teams, the Rockets kept up their comedy routines. After seven innings, they "proceeded to unload numerous antics on the diamond that had the fans howling with laughter. The colored team introduced...a dice game back of the mound...with one player losing his glove, spikes, socks and almost his pants and shirt...while a Negro player called the balls and strikes." Half way through the game, "65-year-old Upton Williams...[performed] an imitation of a famous step dance routine by the late Bill Robinson, Negro tap-dancer."[65]

Apart from such novelty acts, American players are likely to have influenced Canadian styles of baseball to some extent. Steven Pope argues that, rather than a conservative tradition emphasizing racial conformity to white standards of performance, African-American sport such as baseball and basketball popularized a black style of play that became dominant. Baseball was faster and rougher, with more fluid and improvisational movements that improved the game for players and spectators. Similar stylistic development has been noted in other settler societies such as West India, India, and South Africa. Indigenous peoples in North America have also imported cultural styles of play into sports such as hockey.[66]

Following World War II, with support for civil rights growing, attitudes began to change, and anti-discrimination law was passed in Alberta in 1955. As ball teams and leagues thrived, declined, and reformed in communities all over the province, more imported talent exposed Alberta fans to new faces. With the integration of baseball in the United States, the Negro Leagues disbanded and Canadian teams had a larger pool of talent from which to draw. Players from American colleges were also brought to Alberta, including several Hawaiian players from California who played against the Picture Butte Indians in 1956. The 1956 Picture Butte Indians team was itself composed of several Asian, one white, and one black player (but no actual "Indians").[67]

Whereas tolerance for "others" in the sporting realm increased as the twentieth century went on, Aboriginal athletes have typically struggled for legitimacy and autonomy. Running had long been, in part, a spiritual activity among the Blackfoot, Peigan, and Blood peoples. The last of the Plains Indians to contact and adjust to Euro-Canadian culture, the Blackfoot Nation found the turn of the century to be one of disruption and trials that led to their near extinction. John Dewar points to the runners of this period for insight into the ways that frontier economics, policing, and reserve pass rules, among other factors, shaped the roles of two runners: Bad Dried Meat, a Peigan man, and Scabby Dried Meat, often mistaken for the same person.[68]

The latter, Api-Kai-Ees (Scabby Dried Meat), was a famed Siksika runner and nephew of Crowfoot, who worked as a foot messenger for the NWMP. A sports and gambling syndicate renamed him Deerfoot after a famed Native American runner and launched his career in competition in 1884. He ran amateur and professional races in Calgary until 1886, when he won a ten-mile race against runners from Winnipeg and Britain; when the British complained about miscounted laps, he ran the race and won again, though his own backers bet against him. Disillusioned, he left the syndicate to run as an independent. The next year, he returned to his reserve and, lacking sufficient supplies, stole two blankets from a settler's house. He eluded capture by the NWMP for two years before serving a short jail term. The tuberculosis he contracted in jail led to his death in 1897. Today he is remembered in the name of a Calgary freeway and the annual Deerfoot Classic Relay race.[69]

By the mid-twentieth century, skilled players of most backgrounds were welcome in local professional competition. Jimmy Rattlesnake, from Hobbema and often called "Chief" in baseball reports, was a star pitcher from the 1930s through the 1950s. He was the first Aboriginal baseball player from Canada to turn professional in the United States, but, like Deerfoot, he rejected a professional career that would have taken him far from his home. After a brief interlude with the New York Yankees in the 1930s, he played around Alberta and Saskatchewan in most of the money tournaments at various times with teams such as Edmonton's Stockyard Bulls, the Edmonton Royals, the Wetaskiwin Braves, and Wetaskiwin Old Stars. Rattlesnake died in 1972 and is a member of the Wetaskiwin Sports Hall of Fame.[70]

Sports that welcomed First Nations participants, such as rodeo, still maintained unwritten constraints. Often Aboriginal competitors were denied credit or prize money they had earned and were excluded from official record books. A champion Aboriginal cowboy from the Blood reserve in Standoff, Pete Bruised Head, was the first to finally ride the "outlaw" horse Midnight at the Midnight Rodeo in Fort Macleod. Despite hundreds of witnesses to the event, it was ultimately the non-Aboriginal Pete Knight who got the credit. During the 1930s, Aboriginal wins in Stampede competition were celebrated but labeled in distinction to the main, white cowboy contests.[71]

Tom Three Persons, a member of the Blood tribe, won first place in the 1909 bronc-busting competition at the Lethbridge Fair. At the first Calgary Stampede in 1912 he became the first Canadian to win a world championship in any major sporting event. In the booster tradition of sports reportage to this day, Three Persons's win was celebrated as a win "for Canada."[72] Meanwhile, he continued to be barred from United States rodeos, and his career was restricted at home by government regulations on professional performance. Candace Savage suggests that accounts of Three Persons's life have themselves been shaped to serve the image of the "mythic cowboy" rodeo star, despite evidence of the darker realities of "racism, violence and greed that underlay the appropriation of the West."[73]

There were also stories of co-operation and interaction. Although the Wild West show tradition dramatized Indian and Cowboy as historically oppositional figures, the fact was that in Alberta the earliest ranchers hired Aboriginal men to work for them. This racially diverse cowboy culture prevailed throughout the Americas. But western pageants were further segregated by race and gender after World War II—"cowboys in the rodeo arena, 'cowgirl' beauty queens at ceremonial places of honour, and Indians in the Stampede Parade."[74] Comments made by an observer of the Sundre Stampede around 1940 demonstrate that, while rodeos included Aboriginal participants, cultural distinctions continued to be made: "Some of the Indians took part in the competitions and enjoyed the excitement as much as their white brothers, though they didn't very often show it outwardly."[75] In the late 1960s, people of the Stoney reserve protested the suppression of the Indian rodeo at Banff Indian Days. The dispute led to the cancellation of the festival.[76]

In 1962, amid continued discrimination at mainstream rodeos, a provincial rodeo club established by Blood reserve members became the All Indian Rodeo Cowboys Association for treaty Indians (later the Indian Rodeo Cowboy Association [IRCA]). Aboriginal people organized and competed autonomously. The IRCA held its first international finals in Lethbridge in 1969, and in 1973 a second organization, the Northern Indian Cowboys Association, emerged. Indian cowboys also now competed in mainstream events on their own terms. After Blood Indian Jim Gladstone won the Calf Roping World Championship at the National Finals Rodeo in 1977, "a member of the

Blood tribe sang the flag song to honour a warrior who had returned from a victory."[77]

Albertans are active in national organizations. Former competitive cowgirl Shelli Yellowbird of Hobbema is the current rodeo administrator for the Canadian Indian Rodeo Cowboys Association (CIRCA); Stephen Fox, president of the Indian National Finals Rodeo, is originally from Standoff, Alberta. Local and regional rodeo associations have

formed, including the Northern Alberta Native Cowboys Association in Hobbema. The Panee Memorial Agriplex in Hobbema was built by the Ermineskin band in 1977 for $3 million, partly in order to host large rodeos. Chief Lawrence Wildcat proclaimed that it was "the way of the Indian Culture to encourage participation and the spirit of fair play."[78]

On reservations and in schools, the social function of sport was to undermine traditional culture, in part, through assimilation to Euro-Canadian models of discipline and teamwork. Residential schools, for instance, had hockey teams, as did Aboriginal communities, all of which were segregated from white community teams by custom if not by written code. For many First Nations children, sport was one of the few positive elements of residential schools. Sport was an important part of the program at St. Dunstan's Calgary Indian Industrial School, which operated from 1896 to 1907. Rufus Goodstriker, a pro rodeo rider and boxer in the 1940s, attended St. Paul's residential school on the Blood reserve near Lethbridge, and recalled the sports program with approval. The other reserve school, St. Mary's, had a strong sports program from the 1960 to the 1980s, winning two provincial high school basketball championships. The principal recalls that the sport was popular because "on the basketball courts, [the youth] were equal or superior to whites."[79]

Until the end of the twentieth century, very few Aboriginal youth continued to elite or professional levels of play. The federally-operated Native Sport and Recreation Program (1972–1981) was designed to train and assimilate Native athletes into the mainstream sport system, but after funding was cut, Aboriginal leaders resolved to foster their own vision of sport that integrated cultural values. Michael Robidoux, for instance, notes that in Indigenous hockey leagues athletes can often play creatively instead of within structured systems based on efficiency. Victoria Paraschak argues that in northern Canada this influence is more limited so that there is more potential for traditional practices to endure.[80] J. Wilton Littlechild, a lawyer, activist, and community leader from Hobbema, took his law degree and two degrees in physical education from the University of Alberta. He is an international human rights advocate, past member of Parliament and, in 2007, regional chief for Alberta in the Assembly of First Nations. As an athlete, Littlechild has won more than fifty provincial, regional, national, and international championships. In 1988, he was a founder of the first North American Indigenous Games; in 1990, approximately 3,000 athletes participated in the first event in Edmonton. Later editions of the games have attracted record numbers of participants from across North America. Littlechild also worked on the 2012 World Indigenous Games planning.[81] In the end, desegregation of sport in North America has paralleled the economic need to keep producing a large stock of star athletes and teams for commercial spectator sport.[82]

Sport is a realm of knowledge, activity, and resources comparable to other complexes of cultural phenomena related to entertainment. As in other fields, as well, those who command the power to shape value systems concerning performance and reward delineate patterns of social exclusivity and distinction. Dominant groups will act in ways that defend the status quo that benefits them, meaning that less powerful ethnic, class, and gender groups must work to challenge the system of ideas and values that position them within the cultural complex. As more minority individuals have achieved recognition in sport at both amateur and professional levels over the past century or so, patterns of social control over sport are shifting, but the process remains incomplete.

Disability sport also challenges assumptions of the standardized, ideal athletic body. In the past few decades, disability sport has moved from "a predominantly medical rehabilitative model to an elite sport model."[83] The International Paralympic Committee classifies athletes into categories according to functional ability rather than by medical diagnosis of disability, viewing them as legitimate competitors rather than patients in rehabilitation or with abilities outside the range of "normal."[84] The numbers of countries and athletes participating in the Paralympics, and its recognition and legitimization, has grown rapidly since 1960. Studies on leisure inequality have tended to omit discussion of disability, another socially constructed category, since many disabled people's situations are determined in part by social structures and policies.

What if you happen to be both a "crip" and a "queer," as Edmonton-born wheelchair athlete Danielle Peers puts it? She points out that oversimplified sporting categories, whether based on gender or physical condition, can themselves can be disabling. Girls and women with disabilities have competed in sports since the early 1900s, but this history is largely lost due to the focus on the male disability athletes and particularly men's wheelchair basketball. Although both women and men with disabilities have competed in major international sporting events such as the Olympics, it is typically very difficult for any athlete to cross lines between Paralympic and Olympic competition, for instance. Peers notes that "athletes with easily categorized disabilities are...compelled to compete in segregated, disability-specific competitions where athletes are assumed to be less competent and are therefore granted less status, funding, media coverage and athletic opportunities."[85]

After competing in mainstream college basketball, Peers developed muscular dystrophy, took up the wheelchair sport, and joined the Canadian national team. She later went on to win medals as part of the

Alberta Northern Lights men's team and a French team in the world's only professional wheelchair league. Because Peers can still walk, and sometimes is perceived as straight, she is interested in how expectations of normality are structured. For example, choosing to play a wheelchair sport can be viewed as a consequence of failure to qualify for "normal" basketball. At the same time, are those with greater lack of mobility to be considered more authentic wheelchair athletes? In terms of sexuality, Peers learned at one point that her status as a lesbian in fact earned her more acceptance as an athlete on an all-male team.[86] When female athletes are categorized as weaker and less economically and socially significant than male athletes, it is easier to sustain complacent assumptions about traditional gender roles in sport culture. Heterosexual women have had to battle for inclusion on men's teams against considerable resistance even where they demonstrate comparable levels of skill. A lesbian woman, on the other hand, may fit more comfortably into a less stringent set of ideas about clashing gender categories on a ball court.

Alberta had the first Canadian team to qualify for a National Wheelchair Basketball Tournament in the United States in the mid-1980s. Nine Albertans competed at the Vancouver 2010 Paralympic Winter Games taking place in Vancouver/Whistler from March 12 to 21.[87] Beyond competition, however, Albertans have made significant impacts in building disability sport. The first Alberta Special Games, sponsored by the Alberta Association for the Mentally Retarded, were held in Calgary in 1970; Special Olympics Alberta was incorporated in 1981.[88] The University of Alberta hosted the first national wheelchair games in 1968. In 1986, a meeting in Jasper laid the foundation for the Active Living Alliance, and, in 1994, the Moving to Inclusion series developed to integrate children with disabilities into mainstream physical education classes. Edmonton's Gary McPherson was an important advocate for disability sport. McPherson was a leader in adapted physical activity. He was president of the Canadian Wheelchair Basketball Association for eight years and served ten years as chairman of the premier's council on the status of people with disabilities.

International ski meet with physically challenged skiers, Calgary, ca. 1970s.
[GA NA-2864-16502]

Robert Steadward of the University of Alberta helped to organize the first wheelchair sport national championship, founded the Alberta Wheelchair Sports Association in 1971, and later coached the Paralympic Sports Association's swim, track, and wheelchair basketball teams. He also played a key part in convincing the Olympic movement to include the Paralympic Games and in 1989 became first president of the International Paralympic Committee, which established democratic national representation for disabled athletes. The university's Steadward Centre is a multi-disability fitness, research, and lifestyle facility. Steadward was inducted into Canada's Sports Hall of Fame in 2007. After a 2007 injury sustained while horseback riding, Steadward became a patient in the centre he established, and returned to riding after two years of recuperation.

Steadward has also been a strong supporter of rodeo, and after disappointment in Edmonton's profile at the 2010 Olympic Games, he decided that the city needed an iconic event like Calgary's Stampede. He spearheaded the revival of 2004's River City Roundup in which dozens of professional cowboys drove over a hundred head of cattle through the downtown streets to kick off the annual Canadian Finals Rodeo.[89]

Disability organizations and activists have made access to participation a civil rights issue but controversies continue. Although rights-based movements have brought positive recognition and advantages, as in the cases of ethnicity and gender, they do not change underlying concepts and categorizations of what it means to be "able" or "disabled." Disability athletes are typically constrained within narratives of extraordinary experience, rather than considered alongside the experiences and trials of other athletes. Peers, for example, has argued that the history of the Paralympic movement is characterized by its recurring emphasis on the empowerment of marginalized victims of misfortune. She finds that such histories, one of them by Steadward, represent Paralympians as passive and marginalize Paralympians' stories as part of the tragedy of disability.[90] Jay Coakley and Peter Donnelly suggest that media portraying disabled people as active free agents and events like the Paralympics help this sector of sport to be accepted but also glorifies the trained athletic body over that of the everyday person with a disability who wants equal access to local recreation opportunities.[91]

CONCLUSION

Complex social constructions of the human body have included associations between physical beauty, mental and moral health, and society as a collective, interactive body. The state has had a vested interest in the body as a term of social control to ensure the sustainability of civic life: maintaining capacity for work, war, and reproduction. Employers, unions, and regulating organizations have overseen team sport for related reasons, including the need to shape and influence social relationships. Defining differences and ideals in accordance to physical appearance can appear to be neutral or natural processes when evolving in the context of rules for games or participation. A normalized range of social types, faces, and bodies will be reflected but also perfected in team photographs or athletic spectacle. Participation in sport by marginalized groups can challenge these frames, either by eroding or invading them, by forming islands or bridges within a regional or national sporting culture. One of the most basic categories deployed in controlling the social body and its internal relationships is that of gender and the body's assumption of masculinity or femininity in specific contexts. These concepts are inextricable from sports history in Western societies, including that of Alberta.

8

"RED-BLOODED SPORTS" AND "MASCULINE FACSIMILES"

GENDER AND SEXUALITY

In the late 1940s my parents wanted to get me into sports...I was, again reluctantly, signed up for a boxing match—with great trepidation we went to the community hall—there were lots of parents and other kids and lots of shouting, bells clanging and kids limping out of the ring with bloody noses. I watched for a while and then my turn came. I did not like the idea of being beaten up in front of others and I kept seeing those bloody noses and finally...I told my Dad that I did not want to fight. I was driven home, quietly, my Dad was not talking to me.

—DENNY MAY

"The Sportsman, an Edmonton Childhood Memoir From the 1940s,"
in Edmonton: A City Called Home

YOUNG DENNY MAY got the message that refusing to box meant more than avoiding a bloody nose. His father, Wilfrid Reid "Wop" May, himself embodied a classic regional masculinity as a heroic bush pilot and World War I flying ace who may or may not have shot down the German Red Baron. Boxing, wrestling, and hockey have all been particularly associated with appropriate displays of "manliness" via physical engagement and injury. But even less directly combative sports have served to embody desired male qualities of endurance, courage, team play, and physical skills. American baseball star Ty Cobb called his game "a red-blooded sport for red-blooded men; it's a struggle for supremacy: a survival of the fittest." In turn-of-the-century Canada, Colin Howell claims, the "baseball diamond was a testing ground for manhood, offering boys a chance to prove their masculinity to their peers."[1]

Such models continue to thrive, but changing circumstances also offer new ones. Ideals of masculinity, like other notions of gender and power, are situated in specific cultural and historical contexts. Although classic frontier male or mountain man motifs may still be part of Albertans' cultural imagination, the historic range of masculine identities has also encompassed, among others, the First Nations leader, British gentleman, and the respectable professional or merchant. Masculinities are mobile across a continuum that spans the wild man of the frontier and the Mountie who brings him to order. And codes of masculinity shape the figure of the referee as much as they do the football star.

The masculine ideal of the European settlement era conflated the possession of physical courage or superior strength with that of restraint and control. As the structures of organized leisure evolved, social reformers had instilled sport with ideals of gentlemanly values. Ministers used sports analogies to prescribe the desired merging of courage, perseverance, and vigour needed to succeed in modern life, warning young men not to "become stranded on the third base of life. There is no heaven, not even a newspaper notice for the player who freezes on third base...it will take manhood to reach home plate."[2]

But you had to get there in a certain way. Just as a baseball player, for example, "could admittedly win with dirty tactics but this was unfair, unsportsmanlike, and a disservice to the game," manhood too should be attained through honesty and respect.[3]

Beyond home plate, coaches, officials, fans, and spectators also encountered expectations of behaviour. Not only would a young athlete benefit from a "manly, attractive disposition," good manners, strict mental control, and an outlet for the "superabundance of animal energy," the spectator was expected to respond to sporting action with appropriate masculine enthusiasm. In February 1912, University of Alberta students were urged to attend campus games or suffer the stigma of the arts-oriented: "he must indeed be a student of English IV if the excitement of the play does not...cause him to exercise his lungs and throat with a copious emission of his college yell." Athletic prowess did not exclude educational goals, of course; the well-rounded young man would inevitably bring intellectual as well as physical skill to the institution. Sport was a visible, audible "advertisement for any university which will bring to it the most virile type of student."[4]

This kind of rhetoric drew on the fusion of ascetic Protestantism and British-led sports organization that dictated invigorating but disciplined exercise, competitive sports, and physical education. On the University of Alberta campus, which was under snow for most of the school year, this ethos was probably exacerbated by the stubborn notion that the Canadian national character sprang from the rigours of the northern climate.[5] But there were other, eventually suppressed contributors to the Euro-Canadian masculine ideal. Michael Robidoux describes the way First Nations models of stoic and courageous masculinity were taken up by French fur traders and colonists as they adapted to a harsh environment. By the turn of the twentieth century, the mythos of manhood extolled Aboriginal activities such as snow-shoeing, canoeing, and lacrosse; however, the traditional aggression and violence in games were eventually modulated to suit decorous bourgeois sensibilities. According to Robidoux, the rationalized modifications to lacrosse in particular symbolized the taming of an uncivilized

Polo team, Fort Macleod, ca. 1890. [GA NA-967-26]

Indigenous population.[6] A photo of the well turned-out polo team circa 1890, above, posed in front of a distant tipi, recalls the ranks of uniformed mounted police patrolling Aboriginal life on the prairie landscape.

Both the adventurer and the frontier trader were models of masculine daring appropriate to an emerging hinterland capitalism in the nineteenth century. The untamed image of the coureurs de bois in the wilderness was balanced by the reality of their shrewd business skills. As associated pragmatic and material values twined through evolving social structures in western Canada, and as the constraints of industrial urban life relegated masculine energies into productive work or combat, sporting culture handily embodied both the wild and the civilized branches of masculine identity. Participation in sport could both release a fierce power and reinforce a necessary social discipline. Hockey was considered by a typical 1895 observer to be "one of the manliest of sports. Strength, speed, endurance, self-control, shrewdness, are the necessary qualities of one who would excel in it."[7] In 1924, when the senior Calgary Tigers lost the Allan Cup to Montreal, the *Calgary Herald* called for a "plainsman" athlete who could "put the effete East in its place."[8] Ignoring the fact that the stereotyped languishing, effeminate, often francophone easterners produced teams of excellent hockey players, the press presented western athletes as representatives of a specifically regional masculine strength.

According to Cecilia Danysk, two models of masculinity prevailed among pioneer farm workers. One was the stoic, hardworking, strong but uncivilized bachelor homesteader or labourer, contrasted to the farmer and landowner as the head of a successful, settled family. However, the first role was a transient one, tolerated because it would ultimately be contained in the second, the successful farmer with control of his patch of economic agrarian society.[9] The same dynamic of an eventually reformed, refined model of citizen is evident in the organization of sporting culture as it absorbs diverse characters. As frontiers closed, workplace and family roles narrowed and Anglo-American fears of the "feminization" (i.e., weakening) of society gained more rhetorical power in western Canada. Organized sport offered an expression of traditional male values as more men became urban office or factory workers. Sport was a way to validate a more regulated masculinity within established and recognized codes. The pursuit of well-ordered outdoor sport arose not so much as an escape from the bureaucratic world, though, but an attempt to impose its values on nature by managing bodily strength, discipline, and the conceptual knowledge of terrain.[10]

Sports, and contemporary training programs for youth such as the Boy Scouts, had grimmer implications with respect to the demands of imperial, colonial societies. In 1894 the *Calgary Herald* reported that an Englishman had escaped "the Matabole warriors" by dodging them with skills learned in football and recommended the game to all soldiers for that reason.[11] The British call for "manly courage...whether on the sports field or battlefield" during World War I makes clear the role of sport in conditioning young men for potential combat roles.[12] When William Sharples left the Shamrocks hockey team to serve in

Soccer team, 14th platoon, 56th Battalion, Canadian Expeditionary Force at Sarcee camp, Calgary, 1915. [GA NA-3232-78]

the Boer war in 1900, the *Alberta Plaindealer* reported that he had gone to "keep goal for the British [Empire]."[13] In the next world war period, approaches to fitness as obligatory activity pervaded leisure time, insisting that the individual has a duty to be fit for the sake of the greater welfare whether in contributing to a stable economy and civic life or by preparing for their more direct defence. Alberta participated in the "dominion-provincial youth training program" in 1941, and 400 participants presented a program of fitness exercises and displays of ability in Edmonton that year.[14]

The Edmonton Thanksgiving Day sports meet in 1941 drew around 12,000 people, the largest sports crowd in the city's history to that point. The Maple Leafs of the Edmonton Junior Rugby Football league defeated the Notre Dame hounds, but this was considered incidental to the "giant patriotic rally" and service. Notre Dame's Father Athol Murray "practically exploded in a dynamic" speech urging "our sports heroes" to take a leading role in war recruiting. Suggesting that "sportsman's battalions" could be operating all across the region, he specifically singled out "hockeyists" to do their part.[15] During World War II, as one division of Edmonton soldiers marched out, a young junior hockey fan called on them to beat the Nazis just like the local team had won the Allan Cup. Although women athletes were excluded from battle training, an admirer of the Edmonton Grads found that the team's stellar record of victories could also inspire as World War II began.

> Today we face a greater game;
> For life and freedom must we play,
> And we shall need the gallant flame
> The "Grads" have lit along the way.[16]

CURLERS OR COWBOYS

WHAT MAKES A "REAL" ATHLETE?

Good press is at least part of the answer to the question what makes a "real" athlete. Unlike rodeo, curling does not top the list of sports associated with machismo or even fitness. In photographs from the 1930s and 1950s, curlers appear in ordinary street clothes with a wide range of body types. Accessible to most recreational and amateur players, the sport does not insist on high-level athleticism and training. Even elite women curlers tend to retain accessible images as everyday wives and mothers, cleverly juggling family with competition while avoiding stereotypes of the female jock, as the masculine model inclines toward mannerly behaviour and methodical accuracy.

However, when in the 1970s old-style corn brooms were replaced by easier-to-handle artificial push brooms, Edmonton broadcaster Wes Montgomery called for a more conventional model of athletic masculinity. In an era predating openly gay sports stars, he commented, "who needs those fag push brooms. What sport makes it easier on an athlete? Give me athletes if it is an athletic sport."[17] At the time, though, curlers did not present themselves as typical aspiring jocks. Until relatively recently (1980 for the Brier and the mid-1990s for play-downs) they could, and did, smoke on the ice. Smoking while playing in the Brier was banned the year after Macdonald Tobacco ended its fifty-year sponsorship. Curling became an Olympic sport in 1998, and soon the Canadian Curling Association, fighting the image of overweight "men who smoked cigarettes after the fifth end" warned players to get in shape.[18]

Curlers traditionally also indulged in considerable amounts of liquor at bonspiels without compromising their credibility or that of their sport. Today, though curling remains a social game with players and fans mingling for beers in the breaks, the 2009 Brier competitors were "poster boys for health and fitness."[19] As world-level competitions and commercial incentives increase, the drive for professionalization means new training programs and standards of athletic legitimacy. For both men and women in curling, this trend arguably has narrowed the range of possible expressions of gender identity and social interaction in sport to more closely align with the model of the bodily elite.

Like the curler, the cowboy is not the most obvious version of a sporting hero. Nevertheless, the rodeo cowboy remains a powerful western archetype of masculinity in great part due to a history of excellent promotional strategies. Between 1878 and 1965, photography helped to create the widespread romantic image of the competi-tive cowboy as untamed outlaw, even as rodeo became a standardized entertainment business across the American and Canadian west. The early Calgary Stampede capitalized on the symbolic capital of western experience already established by popular writers, musicians, photog-raphers, Hollywood films, and visual artists. By the mid-twentieth century, Stampede advertising posters and other messages evoked a communal celebration of masculine dominance over savage nature—animals and Aboriginal peoples.[20]

"Why can't it be macho to be an 'Urban Indian'?" Cartoon by Everett Soop, published in Kainai News, *January 1, 1981. The "urban cowboy" look was popular at the time.* [GA M-9028-1405]

Canadian historical images and "cowboyography" tend to down-play violence and individualism relative to American versions. In 1884, for instance, the *Calgary Herald* described the Canadian cowboy as a gentleman who shunned bravado. The early imposition of struc-tures of law and order in western Canada meant that even cowboys from violent American backgrounds tended to behave themselves. The central figure of the cowboy as a representative of the Wild West contrasts sharply with the history of the Canadian frontier and the post-ranching agrarian development of the region. Sheila Bannerman asserts that, "prior to the first Calgary Stampede of 1912, there were no Canadian 'cowboys,' but ranchers, ranch hands and herders" and that the concept was mainly absent in southern Alberta. Privileging accounts of everyday life and workers disrupts mythologies of the Wild West. The first Calgary Stampede in 1912 was the first suggestion that Canadian ranch hands might identify as "cowboys." A ranch worker of the period was solicited to enter pony races but refused because racing was not one of the animal's responsibilities. But it was the wild, renegade cowboy that Albertans watched in popular Wild West shows and rodeo dramatizations after World War I.[21]

Rather than destabilizing notions of disciplined sportsmanship, however, rodeo's well-structured constraints of narrative, time, performance space, and event sequence helped to sustain its legitimacy. (In this respect rodeo and professional wrestling have much in common.) Since around the mid-twentieth century, the machismo of the cowboy in western Canada has been conveyed not through a display of rebellion enhanced by highly-trained musculature but through an association with frontier authenticity. This includes qualities of trustworthiness, practical skills, and community-mindedness as much as physical strength and courage. A Montreal article of 1935 described a contingent of Alberta cowboy champions on their way to London, UK, for a rodeo exhibition as extremely modest, "colorful young fellows with soft drawling voices" who "doffed their enormous hats...and said 'Howdy!'"[22] In comparison, a contemporary group of American cowboys visiting Venezuela "got to juggin' a little" and took the pants and guns of the police who came to settle them down; apparently "they just [didn't] understand cowboys."[23]

As GWG jeans ads running in Alberta rodeo programs of the 1960s and 1970s demonstrate, the authentic cowboy was also a well-groomed gentleman and all-round productive family supporter and citizen outside the ring. Established in Edmonton in 1911, Great Western Garment Company (GWG) was the largest work wear manufacturing company in Canada by World War II, and its advertising incorporated ideas of the frontier as a romantic, challenging zone demanding strength and integrity as well as work clothing. In ads from 1911 to the mid-1940s, men are portrayed as fit and clean-cut rather than rough. GWG turned to rodeo clothing after 1944 when the Cowboy's Protective

Hanna rodeo program, 1967. [WCH/RAM H08.17.244]

Association took over the management of rodeos and entrepreneurs no longer financed events. As a commercial sponsor, GWG was a major supporter of western Canadian rodeos in the 1950s, 1960s, and 1970s.[24]

⋮ "A PROPER, NORMAL ALBERTA IDENTITY"

Of course, the real cowboy may be brave, family-minded, tough but civilized, while also being homosexual. Issues around sexual preference and orientation in Alberta sport reflect in part a particularly conservative political and social context but are not substantially different than those affecting the experience of gay and lesbian athletes elsewhere.

During the early 1990s the Alberta government actively contested movements to establish legal rights for gay and lesbian citizens. The struggle was, and is, partly "over what constitutes a proper, normal Alberta identity and who rightfully belongs within the Alberta community/mosaic."[25] Meanwhile, as North American society shifted toward a relative liberalization of attitudes, several sports organizations emerged to champion the interests of gay and lesbian athletes. The 1990 Gay Games in Vancouver was the largest amateur sporting event in the world that year. The Gay and Lesbian International Sport Association (GLISA) promotes diversity in the Canadian sport system on the premise that discrimination based on sexuality is as unacceptable as that based on race, ethnicity, or religious grounds.[26]

In 2008 the City of Calgary announced its intention to become a gay and lesbian tourism destination, and sporting events appeared central to the campaign. In partnership with GLISA, Calgary was the host of the first North American OutGames in 2007. Organizers hoped to showcase the city as one of diversity and acceptance. Although the city's alignment of its interests with those of the Calgary Stampede organization helped to launch and sustain the event's popularity, it is not yet clear how much civic support will accrue directly to gay sport. OutGames have consistently lost money wherever they were held, and it can be difficult to get sponsorship. The estimated financial impact of the OutGames held in Calgary over eight days, with 600 participants, was $661,000. Of the 3,720 people who attended, 63 per cent identified as gay, 18 per cent as lesbian, and 14 per cent as heterosexual; 44 per cent that year also attended the Western Cup, sponsored since 1982 by Apollo Friends in Sport and now the longest running annual LGBT multi-sport event in North America. Surveyed as to their perceptions of the OutGames' legacy, a strong majority believed that they would positively affect Calgary's national and international image, but, given the low level of interest from straight audiences, respondents were skeptical of a corresponding local increase in appreciation of the city's GLBTQ community.[27]

A significant difference between mainstream and gay rodeo is that the latter allows men and women to compete in parallel events; for example, women ride bulls and men participate in barrel racing. The Alberta Rockies Gay Rodeo Association (ARGRA) was formed in 1991 with sponsorship from Edmonton and Calgary businesses. ARGRA held their first function, the Canadian National Gay Rodeo (CNGR) in 1993, later joining the International Gay Rodeo Association. ARGRA is actively involved in fundraising and charitable work.[28]

In 2007, Team Edmonton marked "new competition in the Battle of Alberta," when it entered the Western Cup, which has been associated with Calgary for over twenty-five years.[29] The 2007 event attracted over 500 athletes in six different events. Participants say it's about more than just sport; it's about values—"camaraderie over competition" and sportsmanship over skill. It's also not about segregation; straight competitors are welcome.[30] Phil Ivers runs the curling bonspiel and remarks that the all-straight Calgary Curling Club "just embraces us. We are so much fun, we are low maintenance and we drink a lot." Ivers also rejected the stereotype of a gay bonspiel as "flamboyant sissies curling" since the players are highly competitive, including one team that consistently excels in a competitive straight men's league in Toronto.[31] The director of the 2007 Western Cup suggested that, although Alberta is still a conservative province, homophobia tends to remain primarily in rural areas rather than among urban populations. Still, he added, sport is the last bastion of rampant homophobia.[32]

And some bastions are better fortified than others. In 2000 and 2001, the Ice Breaker tournament held in Edmonton offered several sports for gay and lesbian competitors, including volleyball, swimming, curling, bowling, and pool. In the same period, a summer camp for gay, lesbian, and transgendered youth, established in Edmonton in 2004 by researchers at the University of Alberta, proved successful and offered a model for several others across the country. However, a few years later, a 2007 University of Alberta research study found that while both male and female student athletes preferred women to men team doctors, homophobia drove some males' choice.[33] Conservative governments, in power in the province since the early 1970s, have been reluctant to support equality based on sexual orientation. In this context, activists for tolerance have struggled to normalize the recognition and inclusion of homosexuals in, among other fields, mainstream sport. In 2009, after years of resistance, Alberta became the last Canadian province to include sexual orientation in its human rights laws. At the same time, however, a provision was introduced to allow parents to exempt children from school discussions of the topic. Negotiations continue; in 2011, the Edmonton public school board became the first in the Prairie provinces to approve a policy for schools prohibiting discrimination based on sexual orientation. Since schools are powerful institutions of sport training and socialization, the future of athletics may be somewhat more inclusive.[34]

Although segregated sports events and organizations like gay rodeo and games are tolerated and even celebrated by communities, especially where they suit commercial and political purposes, in mainstream team sports homosexuality remains marginalized and obscured. Though some constraints on sexuality in sport have changed over time, hockey and football, for example, are especially silent on the subject despite recurring exposures from around the 1990s onward about the homosexual culture of minor hockey. In terms of professional careers, as one observer put it, sex sells—but only to a point.[35]

Even in sport not predicated on aggression and combat, individual athletes remain cautious in revealing sexuality. Although Alberta-born swimmer Mark Tewksbury was praised for his honesty in coming out in 1998, he felt able to do so only after retiring as a professional athlete, and he still lost a major speaking contract by coming out. Skaters like Kurt Browning and Elvis Stojko have had long-term endorsement contracts, but other world champions such as Brian Orser never received comparable offers. Orser, one of the few "out" gay athletes, has said that skaters "guard their gayness closely because of the likely effect of public disclosure on their careers."[36]

Initiatives to counter homophobia in sport include efforts by the Canadian Association for the Advancement of Women and Sport and

Physical Activity and the Canadian Association for Health, Physical Education and Recreation, in light of "the powerful potential of sport to contribute to personal, social and community development."[37] For the first time in history, the 2010 Olympics in Vancouver had a designated gathering place for gay and lesbian athletes. Sports historians Kevin Wamsley and Michael Heine commented that this is a significant move for the conservative and even homophobic Olympics, which has avoided the issue of sexuality in sport since the 1920s. Alberta sportsmen and women should benefit from these broader movements; granted, these movements are potentially hampered by a provincial legacy of homophobic attitudes and legislation.[38]

Just as men who avoid athletics are potentially suspect as queer, women athletes may be stereotyped as lesbian. By the 1930s, according to Susan Cahn, lesbianism was associated not with the (potentially alarming) expression of desire itself, but with a failure to perform normally in heterosexual society. These ideas and others were encoded in the persistent warnings that sport, or even exercise, would influence manlike behaviour and possibly damage female functions or, in other words, turn straight women into lesbians. Caitlin Cranshaw suggests that many straight female athletes brand themselves as feminine sex symbols in promotional activities in order to avoid falling into the lesbian stereotype.[39] But sport can also function as a form of cultural expression and activism. Gay teams and events "counter popular misconceptions that gays can't throw and lesbians can't dance while creating a space outside of nightlife for queers to be social and feel good about themselves."[40]

DRESS CODES AND PUBLIC PERFORMANCE

Ideals of "masculine" appearance and behaviour, of course, also establish their opposite values. For example, the muscularity and bulk considered desirable in male competitive team sport is discouraged in elite female athletes. From the late nineteenth century, the mass press in the North America circulated an athletic iconography in sports pages and advertisements that smoothly portrayed the norms distinguishing manly figures from working-class, Native, female and non-western Europeans.[41] These ideals of masculine and feminine attitudes to sport were supported in discourses of everyday life and leisure activities. While activity in the outdoors was considered essential to the healthy, normal North American boyhood, a contemporary appeal to the "Out-of-Doors Girl" to protect herself from the "unpleasant effects of sun and wind" with Pond's Extract points to a quite different set of criteria for women. Mass-market sports shoes were available in the 1920s, and in May 1922 the Montgomery Brothers store in Wetaskiwin filled a window with a display of Fleet Foot shoes manufactured by the Dominion Rubber Company in Montreal. There were shoes for men, women, and children, but boys in particular were targeted as hopeful sports stars with a newsletter "full of news about champions, athletes, big games and fights."[42]

As well as body type, apparel and accessories enhance the body's messages about social identity. Men's and women's sports clothing evolved as versions of streetwear and slowly became more practical in terms of fit and shape, at least for men. There were practical reasons for dress restrictions in western Canada before the emergence of a continental sporting goods industry. Bloomers for women cyclists, appropriately known as "rational costume," amidst contemporary movements for dress reform,[43] were famously contested in the 1880s, but bloomers were not available in Canadian prairie stores until the turn of the century. Eaton's catalogues were available in Winnipeg in 1905, with distribution centres in Saskatchewan in 1915; although they offered bicycle suits for men and boys, they did not cater to women. Sears Roebuck offered a women's bicycle suit comprising a jacket and bloomer pants but was not available in the region until 1916.[44] By 1910, the market provided men's stretchy golf sweaters and jackets with expanding pleats; Alberta women had access to knitting patterns for voluminous golfing suits and canoeing outfits.[45]

In 1917 *Vogue* advised women skiers to remove overskirts in favour of jodhpurs once on the slope,[46] but most female sportswomen made

Edmonton Swastikas Hockey Team, 1916. [Photo: WikiMedia Commons]

no sartorial concessions to physical exertion outside private spaces.
Alberta women wore bloomers for gymnasium activities and sports in
1912, but in public venues, including rodeo, most stuck to long divided
skirts.[47] A 1916 Edmonton women's hockey team called the Swastikas,
marked by what at that time was a popular good luck symbol, wore
a version of bloomer pantaloons. In the 1920s, women in organized
hockey, such as the Mount Royal College team of 1925, were allowed to
wear leggings rather than skirts, but these and the winter layers kept
them well-covered.[48]

American women were the first to adopt lighter, briefer styles of
athletic wear. When Edmonton's Grads played their first international
basketball competition in 1923, the champion Cleveland Favorite-Knits

wore trim shorts while the Grads appeared in heavy woolen stockings, knobby knee pads, and baggy knee-length bloomers. (Despite the weight of their uniforms, the Grads defeated the Favorite-Knits to capture the Underwood Trophy.) Even after the Grads adopted uniforms with short sleeves and pants, for several seasons they were worn only on the road to avoid alienating hometown supporters.[49]

For female athletes, constraining uniforms and conservative daywear have served in part to allay nervousness about "mannish" or unfettered women. With the organization of sport as public commercial spectacle, official and unwritten dress codes were ways to domesticate suggested sexuality and constrain moral panic around social fears of both women's exposed bodies and the powerfully trained young men roaming the streets. Although behavioural and dress restrictions on women were more overt, the community context of amateur and junior sport also involved social control over the public images of male athletes. In the 1950s, Oil Kings' manager Leo LeClerc was vigilant in insisting that the young men meet high local expectations of behaviour and appearance to avoid embarrassing the club. Bruce MacGregor, team captain in the 1960s, recalls that LeClerc knew everything and had spies everywhere; at one point he had an equipment manager crawl through the air duct to eavesdrop on conversations in the team dressing room.[50]

With the professionalization of sport, team uniforms also became linked to corporate identities that needed to be further controlled. More intense media attention to player behaviour made it necessary to maintain a civilized persona outside the game itself, a requirement currently manifest by the common pre-game sight of a bus full of giants wearing suits and ties. Stacy Lorenz and Rod Murray argue that, as in other spheres of society, this standard middle-class business attire carries strong connotations about race and class as well as gender. The NBA's 2005 ban on hip-hop style was widely seen as catering to white fans and advertisers who were uncomfortable with "gangsta" culture. A dress code worked to erase the spectre of thuggish black men,[51] just as it turns on-ice enforcers into reputable youth.

Women's district curling winners, Lethbridge, January 26, 1955. [GMA 19753806042]

Standards for athletic clothing were shaped not only by social attitudes and availability but by technological production methods. The clothing worn by cyclist Torchy Peden in 1938 and by school track athletes in 1954 was still loose and heavy, but postwar synthetic fibres introduced light, flexible textiles. The trend was inspired by competitive demand and also by the growing consumer market for practical leisure sportswear. Alberta's small garment industry, which had focused primarily on work clothing, moved increasingly into "sport clothing carrying the flamboyant 'cowboy' motif."[52] Curling, once again, was an exception to the prevailing sporting code. Men and women curlers for decades dressed exactly alike, in smart trousers and heavy, elaborately knitted patterned sweaters, usually hand-knit by the women.

As spectator sport and its fan subcultures grew in prominence, the "rough sex appeal" of sport was amenable to marketing in a mass

Norton Wait and Bunty Noble, skaters performing at the Glencoe Club, Calgary, ca. 1930s.
[GA NA-3852-7]

culture of consumption. In the 1950s, television exacerbated the objectification of idealized body types and physical performance.[53] By the
1960s, cotton or nylon tracksuits were available and became fashion
items in the 1970s and 1980s. Brightly coloured warm-up suits and
aerodynamic Lycra garments became acceptable as everyday wear
for both men and women, for reasons apart from enhancing athletic
performance. In 1966, the *Calgary Herald* announced that women
skiers' "stretch pants have been proclaimed as the greatest boon to
girl watchers since the bikini."[54] New materials also gave athletes an
edge in speed and performance, and sportswear was a lucrative business by the 1990s. Despite the contemporary use of revealing uniforms
worn by female athletes, both professional and amateur, outmoded
notions of propriety persisted. In late 2004, the University of Alberta
Pandas (women's) volleyball team was penalized for changing from

warm-up T-shirts to game uniforms at courtside. Coach Laurie Eisler argued that the trip back to the dressing rooms would break concentration and commented that the issue "goes beyond feminism. It's a humanist thing." Observers considered the rule obsolete in light of the fact that most women's teams already wear revealing spandex shorts and tops.[55]

Sports that involve solo or duet performance are particularly subject to evaluation based on aesthetic criteria. The discourse of figure skating has been particularly evocative of deeply held attitudes toward gender performance. In the photograph on page 244, skaters at Calgary's Glencoe in the 1930s are both wearing modest, functional costumes. Within several decades, as the sport became organized as a more commercial spectacle, skating costumes came to embody a romanticized or sexualized theatrical aesthetic for both men and women.

Karen McGarry argues that skating culture incorporates particular classes and races as appropriate skating bodies. The idealized perception of the female figure skater still tends to associate Victorian ideals of Nordic looks with perceived feminine qualities like virtue and discipline. In the summer of 1953, for the third year in a row, sixteen-year-old Rosemary Hall of Calgary skated eight hours a day for eight weeks to pass the highest test of the Canadian Figure Skating Association. Although a newspaper report noted her competitive ambition, it downplayed her athletic achievements in favour of the sport's cultivation of feminine qualities such as "poise and grace and... bouncing good health" as well as character and contacts with "nice people."[56] Historical notions that women of the working or lower classes generally lack control and discipline also persist. A contemporary Canadian coach has commented that her students, like those of the 1950s, must sustain standards of aesthetics, demeanour, and personal appearance to "pass as ladies."[57] The culture of figure skating, like that of tennis, then, has been associated with social conduct as much as performance.

Due to the aesthetic, non-contact nature of the sport, males have been subject to similar standards. In 1964, an *Edmonton Journal* story marveled that figure skating was "no sissy sport" but very hard work.[58] Promoters attempting to attract boys to the sport stressed the potential to meet girls, who vastly outnumbered them in the ranks of both recreational and competitive skaters; the *Journal* announced that "Ten Girls for Every Boy Makes Practicing a Joy." Club crests and programs of the time commonly displayed male figure skaters, though most members were female.[59] Nevertheless, most Alberta boys with skates took to the hockey rink in mid-century—and still do.

Despite these promotional efforts, men's figure skating has been particularly fraught with homophobia and innuendo. In 1970 the federal Department of Health and Welfare found it necessary to point out that figure skating was "definitely for the 'He-man' too. The amount of energy used...can easily equal that needed for a hard-played game of hockey."[60] The implication, as Mary Louise Adams points out, is that only certain kinds of male athletes deserve respect and that manly and supposedly effete pursuits are sharply divided. Popular skaters like Kurt Browning and Elvis Stojko have routinely been compared to hockey players in media reports using terms such as "crush" and "attack," or "gunning for a medal."[61] In 2009, as audience interest in the sport dwindled, Skate Canada introduced a new marketing campaign featuring its "rough-and-tumble aspects" with skaters posed at motorcycle dealerships telling stories of speed, danger, and risk. Meanwhile, the organization rejects accusations of fostering homophobia by promoting a countering masculine stereotype associated with hockey.[62]

"A DISTURBANCE OF THE SOCIAL ORDER"
FEMALES ON THE FIELD

Sporting bodies have been particularly equated with a conventional model of masculinity that encompasses power, strength, and competitive vigour.[63] Women adapted, or did not, to contrasting ideals and principles but worked with the same social and cultural instruments to carve out versions of gender identity. Both the formation and the destabilization of related gender categories around performance in the public sphere blurred and shifted over time with changing social conditions, regional experience, and economic imperatives. Because sport is a vessel of meaning implicated in broader male identity formation, whatever affects it will also threaten to engulf other social constructs. The "normal" place of women on the sport field has been as cheerleader or spectator of men; in the words of the early-twentieth-century press, a woman in an athletic uniform created "a disturbance of the social order."[64] As women entered public spheres of business and leisure, the possibility that they might perform athletically in front of spectators challenged not only the idea of sport as a male preserve but the idealized domestic enclosure of the female.

One source of revulsion toward female team sport was the prospect of an immodest spectacle erupting amid the "emotional excitement of an athletic contest."[65] In 1897, for instance, no male spectators were allowed to view the "unladylike" activity of one Alberta women's hockey game.[66] And not only was one's reputation in jeopardy; outdoor physical exertion threatened a desirable appearance as well as "a young girl's mind."[67] In other words, to engage in manly behaviour would directly endanger the female identity formation at all levels of being.

It might also undermine the nature and the future of the nation. Social anxiety in the late Victorian period articulated concerns around gender roles but was more deeply related to long-term focus on continuing the British Empire as populated by British rulers and citizens. In Canada, the healthy female was to be the vessel of national prosperity and "racial regeneration" that would be cultivated by virile outdoor sportsmanship. Convictions of the effect of physical activity on reproductive health appeared not only in direct condemnation of female sport but in more subtle cautions. A 1912 *Ladies' Home Journal* article feared that "female athleticism" would turn women into "masculine facsimiles," or, tellingly, that women might feminize sport.[68] As early as 1900, Alberta glove dealers announced that "golf, tennis, rowing, and driving" were responsible for the consistent increase in the size of women's hands, and an artist opined that women's indulgence in "athletic and outdoor life...has totally destroyed the form and shape of the hand."[69] In the coming decades, the femininity of sportswomen was consistently scrutinized and evaluated.

Although sport supports and reinforces the social constructions of gender roles, it also functions as a place in which to challenge these constructions. Nineteenth-century American politicians and educators worked to normalize regimes of physical fitness for women, though these regimes were to elicit the social graces as much as health. Catherine Beecher Howe predicted that "young girls will be trained in the class-rooms to move head, hands and arms gracefully; to sit, to stand, and to walk properly, and to pursue calisthenic exercises for physical development as a regular school duty."[70] Although the traditional domestic, passive image of womanhood prevailed later in nineteenth-century Anglo-American culture, there also arose a tradition of women's "purposive exercise" to foster social and intellectual empowerment. While regimes of both active gymnastics and more passive calisthenics persisted, the latter was the norm for women by the turn of the century.[71]

Nevertheless, many women of the era challenged the prevailing medical wisdom that females and their reproductive systems were dangerously fragile when exposed to education and exercise. For the young woman listening to baseball sermons or campus boosters, any serious prospect of being excluded from either heaven or team games for lack of virility would have been somewhat disconcerting. In practice, this kind of prescription was routinely ignored or challenged by those in positions to do so. Women in western Canada had some advantages when it came to abandoning metropolitan constraints. Settler society developed under frontier conditions where tidy dichotomies between male and female attributes and roles tended to collapse under challenges of new work and leisure settings. Farm and ranch women consistently countered claims that women lacked strength and stamina or could be ruled by imported strictures around sexuality. Emily Ferguson exclaimed in 1910, "Yes! I am riding astride. Most of us do. It is safer, more comfortable, more healthful, and in every way consistent with good taste. Besides, here is the wide and tolerant West; everyone knows that a woman's boots are not pinned to her skirts."[72]

In 1900, the *London Times'* colonial correspondent Miss Shaw listed the recommended qualities of a prairie farm wife. She should be lean, though not diseased, since the coarse foods would fatten her; tough, so as not to need expensive heat in winter; large and rangy to handle an axe; and with the proper stance to balance a canoe.[73] These were not the qualities prized by metropolitan style setters and ideologues of the day, but they were advantages to a sportswoman. Women cooked for and organized the social events—picnics, teas, and dinners— that accompanied virtually all sporting gatherings, but where girls and women wanted to play games like baseball, they went ahead and grabbed a bat; where they were needed as players, most teams in small towns and farm communities would not quibble about gender.[74]

The practicalities of equestrian life on ranches also prepared the way for the rodeo cowgirls of the 1920s and 1930s. At the Calgary Stampede, as the first successful female professional athletes, they were admired by audiences and the press alike.[75] Most cowgirls were travellers with American troupes and so were not as subject to criticism as local women might be, but others such as Flores Ladue, wife of Stampede founder Guy Weadick, were Albertans by immigration or marriage. Nevertheless, as in the case of other competitive sports, including hockey and baseball, women were typically the sideshows or novelty acts around the main attraction of the male competitions. By 1952 women's Stampede participation was curtailed to barrel racing, and the rodeo west was constructed as a masculine realm.[76]

For most people, though, the organization of sport in the modern era sharply distinguished the informal behaviours of people in their communities from those of officially designated mainstream clubs, which regulated performance. Although by the 1880s Canadian urban sports clubs often allowed women as honorary members, tennis was the only relatively vigorous sport in which they could compete publicly before 1900. Middle- and upper-class women were steered toward

Polo at Millarville, ca. 1910. Women served refreshments from the log building in the background. [GA NA-2520-35]

ice skating, horseback riding, croquet, and roller skating. Notably, female athleticism emerged alongside the early feminism of the "new woman," which led to an increasing involvement in sport among women.[77] Ladies were given a special invitation to the provincial swimming championships at the Calgary YMCA in 1911 because they had "taken a decided interest in the sport and attend [events] in large numbers."[78]

As the twentieth century went on, public commentary continued to focus on the feminine qualities of sportswomen, but their boundaries were expanding. A 1926 news article about Calgary swimming star Helen Woodside commented that the "pretty little western brunet is, like most of her generation, a girl of action and an all-round athlete."[79] Woodside herself commented that she was not one for remaining indoors sewing, and her engagement announcement in 1942 reminded readers that she held the city and provincial badminton singles titles and had been a swimming champion.[80]

The advances of the 1920s were eroded in the economic instability and associated social upheaval of the next decade. A growing condemnation of women in competitive team sport rested on a moral panic revival not unrelated to fears of their competition in the job market. Social leaders and journalists again cautioned that sport would foster "manly" behaviours in women and, doubtless the crux of the issue, encourage them to move into what were considered men's roles. Influenced by Americans, male and female physical educators and a great many male sportswriters in Canada advocated feminizing play, limiting aggression, and altering existing rules.[81]

Contemporary press coverage focused on competitive athletes' retention of traditional feminine qualities as members of the powerful Edmonton Monarchs hockey team were named Banff Winter Carnival Queen in 1932 and 1933. Margaret Stevenson, the "pretty little queen" of 1932, competed in carnival hockey and novelty events and won a dog sled race against famous professional wrangler Ike Mills. According to the *Edmonton Journal*, she "laughed merrily," discounting her win as luck. Violet Davis, queen in 1933, was an all-round sportswoman, excelling at hockey, skating, skiing, tennis, and riding; the *Journal* posed her sitting graciously on skis in the 1930s, but for decades to come images of female athletes actually in motion tended to feature long legs on women looking perfectly groomed, attractive, and cheerful. A 1971 ad in the *Calgary Herald* shows ski fashions on women sitting or standing rather than engaged in the sport for which the clothing is intended. Of course, most of the photographs discussed here would have been taken for publicity or advertising purposes rather than to document athletics, but the point remains that they construct a very selective vision of women in sport.

Sport as social capital is a persistent theme in all areas of Alberta sport history but is particularly explicit in discourse around women. Leisure and fitness organizations echoed the message that sport should enhance, rather than replace, feminine charms. In the 1940s, North American YWCA programmers appealed to vanity with one brochure arguing that a "sparkling person, with good posture, clear skin, and

a radiant smile is an ATTRACTIVE person, no matter her features or her color." After the war, as a reduced complement of eligible men returned to their jobs, a Darwinian battle loomed for women who were warned that they faced "increased competition in every field...and that includes matrimony...[which] puts the listless, lethargic lassie out of the running in no time flat...If you belong to this category, why not face the issue, take steps to improve...and then set out for a few scalps yourself?" Marissa Salcedo concludes that such imagery emphasized the YWCA's stress on heterosexual identity, which was also consistent with ideals of the domestic feminine of the era.[82]

Retailers targeting women also linked sport and social success. In the 1940s, the Calgary shop Premier Cycle and Sports urged consumers to "Stay Young and Lovely...Take up a lively, healthful sport...You find a zest in life...meet the right kind of people...that charming crowd that has learned to enjoy the great outdoors."[83] The Ski Runners of the Canadian Rockies in Banff also organized junior skiing, emphasizing safety, and ran pre-season exercise classes to condition skiers of both sexes. The "value of relaxed co-ordination" was promoted at lessons in "dry skiing," which also rewarded members with "limber muscles and lithe figures!"[84]

The evidence provided in ads and publicity photographs must be evaluated from the perspective of the motivations of those presenting them, rather than viewed as a monolithic set of boundaries on women's actual behaviour. In 1926 the Edmonton YWCA opened a new gymnasium and swimming pool, publicized with a photo of young women in swimsuits at the side of the pool, one of whom was demonstrating a diving pose over the empty tank. Snapshots taken by the women themselves demonstrate a more relaxed emphasis on socializing, mischief, and fun, but official photographs present a ideal model of respectable, wholesome, and disciplined young women. Contemporary records of YWCA interiors feature, besides exercise equipment and athletic spaces, the more domestic and feminine

< *Woman modelling ski fashions, 1971.* [GA NA-2864-19928]

areas of the building. Diana Pederson explains that the commissioned photos would have been used for fundraising among conservative businesses and churches, and so the image presented gives us a sense of how the notion of appropriate femininity was constructed.[85]

Women went on playing team sport but, by the 1950s, the focus of organizers and participants shifted to events in which the athlete was highly competent but maintained her femininity in all activities. Valda Burstyn suggests that the femininity market (including fitness regimes as well as diet products) promoting the physical shrinking of women has evolved in parallel to the male-enlarging masculinity market and has increasingly done so in association with feminine sports. In sports-related imagery, women would more likely appear as non-participants or involved in individual, aesthetic activities, and typically at a recreational level rather than in team competition.[86] Most amenable to this trend have been sports featuring beauty and grace, like gymnastics, figure skating, and synchronized swimming, as well as skiing, tennis, badminton, and golf. The most numerous female inductees for any one sport in the Alberta Sports Hall of Fame are in synchronized swimming. The Barbara Ann Scott figure skater doll was a bestseller in Canada until the mid-1950s, as were later blonde, blue-eyed figure skater dolls modelled on medallists Karen Magnussen (1974) and Elizabeth Manley (1989).[87]

When Dr. Ethel Taylor ran for Red Deer City Council in 1961, she objected to the fact that the city (no doubt like many others in the region) had no recreation facilities for women and girls.[88] In that decade feminists finally took up the issue of equal opportunity in sport, viewing progress in this area as a dimension of overall equality; in the interim, women's advocates recommended that women's fitness involve self-defence training. Advertising of the period continued to portray male athletes in active, vigorous poses and women as passive bearers of good hair and stylish gear. Women students at the University of Alberta in Calgary appeared in football helmets in 1964, but apparently only for novelty value; there was no women's football team, although the university did hold an annual Powder Puff Football game.

Freshman activities, University of Alberta at Calgary, September 1964. [UCA 82.010_1.53]

In 2007, though, the Alberta Female Football League had tackle football teams from Edmonton, Calgary, and Lethbridge. In 2011 the league combined with the Prairie Division to form the Western Women's Canadian Football League. Teams play by CFL rules, are competitive, and prove that "women can play up in the men's ranks with no problem at all at their level."[89] The difference, of course, is that these teams are unaffiliated with any varsity or professional organization.

⋮ "THE FINEST TYPE OF CANADIAN WOMANHOOD"

In 1915 a women's secondary-school team formed that was to prove a powerful challenge to myths of women's lesser ability. The Edmonton Commercial Graduates basketball team became the most successful

Connie Smith and Dot Johnson, two members of the Edmonton Commercial Graduates Basketball Team, 1926. Most of the extant photographs of the Grads are posed in uniform with coach Page at the centre; although this photograph was also posed for publicity, it is one of the comparative few showing the players in action. [CEA EB-27-67]

dynasty of any sports team in history and influenced many other women to take up the game. Over several decades of player turnover, coach Percy Page shaped a consistent team personality, in large part through his insistence on a set of behavioural criteria. Page famously called them ladies first and basketball players second.[90] (As was the case in other sports, this goal was aided by the imposition of special "girls' rules" developed to prevent female emulation of men's playing style.) James Naismith, who called the Grads "the greatest team that ever stepped on a basketball floor," admired the team as the model for all female athletes for retaining the womanly graces while also being superior athletes.[91]

A newspaper report that "Alberta, and particularly the Edmonton district, produces the finest type of Canadian womanhood," likely referred to a combination of strength and practicality with undiluted femininity.[92] Although selected features were celebrated in such reports, the model of femininity was constructed on a sliding scale. Page took the trouble to announce in a 1935 newspaper article that only one of the scores of girls who had played for the Grads was not a mother. (Before Wayne Gretzky and Janet Jones, the Alberta sports marriage sensation was the match between Eddie Shore of the Edmonton Eskimos hockey team and Kate Macrae, star of the Grads.[93]) Yet, in action, the Grads exhibited an intensely competitive style of play. Eastern and American sportswriters often remarked on the disparity between their ladylike image off the court and the athletic reality of the Grads. In 1926 a reporter noticed that they "do not run like girls...In three minutes, the old-fashioned man...found it very hard to pay attention to the charms of the young ladies, as such, owing to the astounding discovery that there was a mighty contest of skill being enacted before his eyes. These champions apparently do not depend upon the skin you love to touch for their success in life...They get scratched, bruised, sprained."[94]

Despite their recognized power as athletes, the disciplinary constraints imposed on team members by Page may have been considered acceptable in the context of the era, which prized "the concept [of lady] as the ultimate pinnacle of womankind."[95] Edith Stone Sutton later pointed out that women in sport "were kind of an oddity then... We had to be nice girls. And we were!...No young men got near us. And don't think they didn't want to, being famous, well known and well thought-of as players...I don't think any men's team would have toed the line like we did."[96]

However, Wamsley suspects that accounts such as Stone's reflect, not unquestioning acceptance of their assigned roles, but a sense of ongoing responsibility to perpetuate the historical narrative of the Grads as ladylike.[97] And at the time, the Grads appear to have had a pragmatic sense of the limitations of their public roles and to have

followed rules that would allow them to pursue their most important goals. Most of them held full-time day jobs as clerical workers,
and team membership allowed them not only to compete but to travel
and garner attention and social contacts that they would otherwise
not have had. In so doing they were instrumental in providing models
and mentorships for other women athletes, including girls who had
participated in the network of public school basketball leagues of the
era. Although most accounts credit Page's genius in forging a championship team out of a group of schoolgirls, in fact, at least seven of
them had attended Parkdale School where coach Olive Thomson "gave
them the skills that....J. Percy Page could use."[98] However, Page remains
central to the Grads' success story.

In assessing such phenomena, it is crucial to consider the social
context and local histories that shape potential access to positions of
power. As may be expected, Page's later career opportunities surpassed
those available to his team. While he had fostered the conditions
for them to excel, he also benefited from his public connection with
the team when he entered politics, eventually becoming lieutenant-
governor of Alberta from 1959 to 1966. Although several team members
went on to professional careers, such as Noel MacDonald who worked
as a journalist with the *Edmonton Journal*, none attained comparable
status in public life.[99]

Women's soccer demonstrates a successful challenge to dominant
myths and attitudes as women simply turned out in droves to play over
the decades, despite discouragement. In the 1920s, the Dominion Soccer
Association opposed Alberta women's attempts to form teams and
discouraged a tour by an American women's team.[100] It seems that not
much had changed by 1980 when the Vancouver *Province* called the idea
of females playing soccer "the ultimate sports obscenity."[101] But that
year, 317 Under-19 girls registered in youth soccer in BC, as compared
to three in 1973. The Canadian Soccer Association still denied interprovincial sport competition to women on the basis of low participation,
but in 1995, the Fédération Internationale de Football Association
(FIFA) secretary noted that "the future is feminine. Women's soccer

is growing so fast that we may justifiably expect that within the first decade of the next century, there will be as many women playing as men."[102] At the beginning of the twenty-first century, soccer is one of the most popular sports for women, and more than 45 per cent of Alberta Soccer Association players are women, though they continue to experience lower levels of spectators, funding, and practice time.[103]

⋮ CONCLUSION

At various times and into to the present, gender outlaws in Western cultures have stepped beyond the bounds of regulated desire as represented in images of hysterical women, overbreeding working classes and ethnic groups, and homosexuals. In Alberta sports history, we find traces of the broader social efforts to build and maintain those fences around public behaviours. An Alberta public health campaign of the 1920s included a poster, on which an apparently Arabian man rode a raging stallion, titled "Why is it necessary to control the sex impulse?"[104] Racist equations of non-Europeans with undisciplined recklessness aside, the message of generalized male power and the necessity for control over corporeal nature comes through. Public health authorities since the Victorians have promoted male exercise as one instrument of control over sexuality, and the ongoing containment of the masculine culture of sport within established social institutions was one aspect of the effort to control potential sexual outlaws. Correspondingly, rituals of sport also reinforced a sense of strength and position with respect to women and femininity.[105]

In the post-World War II period, Thomas Joyce argues, selected masculine virtues of order, rationality, and control came to prevail in an increasingly bureaucratic, white-collar economy. War veterans, among others, found that older ideals based on masculine duty and heroism, more primitive ideals of authentic manhood, were no longer as relevant. Factors of space are as important as those of changing time in reactions to gender images. In 1994, Budweiser found that its ads featuring a macho cowboy were working well in western Canada but not in Ontario. While the cowboy was still a valid choice for rugged masculine identity in one province, in other provinces he seemed irrelevant, a sad loner, and generally out of date.[106]

Despite the myriad ways we find to sketch out the limits of the possible, outlaws do continue to roam our imagination. As the province developed as an economic and political territory in the twentieth century, persistent mythologies of the Wild West grew comfortably in tandem with those of modern urban progress. It actually seems inevitable that the "wild" and "domesticated" versions of gender identities developed inseparably on the Prairies given the complex history of the region. Anglo-Celtic culture and gentlemanly conduct ideally embodied civilized aspirations on the Prairies in the agrarian settlement period. In practice, though, British "greenhorns" were generally considered to lack the locally desired masculine traits of physical toughness and know-how and were ridiculed for their dependence on maps and guidebooks.[107]

From a historical perspective, we can see that the man who relied on rationality, imperial codes of order, and central organization was marking the future, whatever actors happened to take front stage at any one time. Today, perceived hazards of unsupervised play in the streets are of less social concern than the campaign to produce elite performance. While fitness levels in the country are declining and obesity rising among the rest of us, for professional athletes, the production of the superb athletic body has often been dangerous in itself. The next chapter continues to consider themes of discipline and control over the energies and performances of individuals, along with the attempt to control the boundaries of acceptable behaviour and acceptable danger. This involves the development of regulations, training programs, and technologies of enhancing performance.

9

A "GREAT SLAUGHTER ON THE FIELD"

AGGRESSION, RISK, AND HIGH PERFORMANCE

ONE LATE AUGUST EVENING in Medicine Hat, 1890, locals were treated to "a great slaughter on the lacrosse field....Five men were knocked out."[1] Players may have been channeling lacrosse's cultural origins as the "little brother of war," but varying degrees of mayhem among both players and spectators were not unusual in other sports. In the years that followed, amateur regulations and professional restrictions concerning violence were ignored or manipulated as soon as they were drawn up. A Calgary baseball game of 1920 featured various "atrocities... inflicted on the public,"[2] and, we assume, the players. Violent infractions were so rife in a Canmore girls' basketball game that "if each player had been armed with a shillelagh the evening would have been complete."[3]

Despite the dangers of regulated violence in organized sport, far more injuries to young athletes tend to occur during informal activities.[4] All physical activity carries risk. In 1921, nine-year-old Ray Bagley of southern Alberta was killed by a baseball that struck him in the back of the head in a casual game.[5] In the end, there is no guarantee that even a mundane event can be controlled by the individual. In 1991, Margaret MacCabe tried a back flip in her Westlock gym class, missed the crash mat and became a quadriplegic. The Court of Queen's Bench later awarded MacCabe a precedent-setting $4 million, citing insufficient training and inexpert supervision.[6] Some observers saw the award as part of a cultural pattern that places all consequence of risk on society. Leon Craig, a professor of political philosophy at the University of Alberta, has commented that this trend is psychologically dangerous: "You cannot learn real courage without confronting things that call for courage, things which might involve some pain and reasonable risk. Cases like this make schools reluctant to undertake programs that have any risk."[7]

Risk will always accompany physical activity, but efforts to contain risk and aggression have contributed important characteristics to modern sporting culture. The influential argument that sport acts as cathartic release for strong emotion is increasingly controversial, and sport in routinized, constrained societies may actually provide models of, rather than substitutes for, the expression of violence. Sport is "perhaps the only setting in which acts of interpersonal aggression are not only tolerated but enthusiastically applauded by large segments of society."[8] Other segments enthusiastically disapprove. By the early twentieth century, Anglo-North American societies had constrained or banned popular leisure forms such as blood sport, public drinking, and spontaneous street parties. Potentially unruly spaces like rodeos, saloons, and arenas were licenced and supervised. Rowdy behaviour was replaced by more organized freedom outside of working hours, time scheduled and controlled. Stephen Brunt explains that spectator sports such as football thrive precisely because modern life involves the sublimation of aggression and taming of everyday behaviours to suit modern market production.[9] The bloodied but unbowed player and the watching sports fan are simply balanced on different spots along a continuum.

A culture that tolerates violence as rational in relation to achieving certain goals, such as victory in war, will commonly extend the same attitudes toward sport. Unlike war, sport must be integrated into the everyday life of societies, so regulators target the agon mentality, or the drive to competition arising in settings from the workplace to the arena. But just as the history of war has shaped diplomacy between nations, the threat of injury has shaped organized competitive sporting culture. In effect, the state or its representatives would set limits on violence by setting and enforcing regulations in sport as it does in law enforcement and military spheres. In *Rites of Men*, Valda Burstyn argues that core men's sports today maintain the male warrior ideal.[10]

Canadian regulatory agencies essentially had to resolve some of the central contradictions of sport between the need for control and the excitement of unruliness and unpredictability. The conceptual separation of the concepts of gentleman athlete (or amateur) and working-class "rowdy man" (and professional) was one way to do this. Discourse on behaviour ranged from condemnations of brutality and rough play to approval for "strenuous spectacle" and tough players.[11] Attitudes varied depending on the game, the crowd, and whatever stakes were involved for individuals. As the world of competitive sport expanded outside the leisured classes, abstract claims of the amateur's gentlemanly conduct (evidence to the contrary notwithstanding) supported amateur organizations' warnings that professional leagues would naturally nurture violence. As concerns about violent play grew more evident in sports discourse, new regulatory bodies formed, including the 1909 National Hockey Association (to become the NHL in 1917.)[12]

The demand for control over performance in competitive team sports is echoed in the drive to excel in non-contact sport, such as track, cycling, or skiing, where the athlete competes against him or herself. Violence here may be inflicted, not upon opponents, but on the self in the form of drugs or extreme training regimes intended to bypass bodily limits of performance. Other modes of expanding athletic performance capacity include ongoing adjustments to rules, equipment, and facilities. Such measures were necessary for sport to become an organized, predictable, commercial spectacle with a controlled end product depending on efficient, routinized quality control.[13] But without the promise of potential transgression in performance, the professional product itself would be less attractive to audiences, investors, and sponsors, so producers continued to bend the painted lines around the action. As these dynamics of transcendence and control emerged in Alberta's sport history, they reflected the ongoing tension between the rhetoric of sportsmanship and the reality of competitive conditions that shape and direct the drive for achievement.

⋮ ORDERING VIOLENCE, CONTAINING RISK, EXTENDING PERFORMANCE

The power of athletes as role models is especially strong in the context of elite sport, where combative behaviour can be justified by the high-stakes rewards of victory. Historically, higher emphasis on competitive spectacle and specialized training in elite sport corresponds to a rise in youth sports injuries. For a number of reasons, high school sport participants have been particularly vulnerable. An Edmonton study in 1969 showed that of the injuries to 40 per cent of football players at all levels, most incidents occurred in city high schools.[14] The North American drop in numbers of deaths and paralyzing injury in minor football since the 1960s has been attributed to improved rules and equipment. A 1985 study found an average of eighty-five deaths annually in minor league football. But a pediatrician warned in 1987 that "playing high-school football...is statistically as dangerous as being a deep-pit miner."[15] Due to high participation rates in ice hockey and baseball, a 1995 Alberta study found that these sports produced around one-fifth of all injuries. Although boxing, rodeo, and rugby were the most injurious activities in Alberta, they accounted for relatively few of the estimated injuries because of low participation levels.[16]

Technology has contributed to hazardous play insofar as new equipment permits increased speeds and risk-taking, sometimes exacerbated by the financial stakes involved in organized gambling on the outcome. At the same time that advances in technology have promised greater physical protection and control for athletes, efforts to ensure player safety and higher performance have been matched by the evolution of new forms of injury. Protective football gear for organized team play gained popularity in Canada after World War I. As hockey helmets and faceguards dramatically reduced brain, eye, and dental injuries in later decades, players hitting the boards headfirst received a higher frequency of spinal injuries.[17]

Part of the problem is that, since both athletes and fans prize stellar results, advances in safety equipment are matched by advances in performance enhancement. Development of new technology also means more devices to calibrate the action, which increases pressure on athletes to set and surpass records. In Alberta, inventors of equipment, games, and tools have attempted to make sports less risky and more accessible to non-experts. The safety bicycle and the pneumatic tire drew more people to cycling in the 1890s. Commercial opportunity also played a role in the advance of equipment quality and choice. Even before machines themselves were available in Edmonton, shops stocked specialized clothing including suits, caps, and shoes for athletes and cyclists.[18]

Over the following century or so, efforts continued to mould aids to both safety and performance. In 1894 a Calgary newspaper announced the invention of a bicycle rear-view mirror.[19] Horse racing helmets were used by a few hockey players for the first time in the 1930s; jockeys used them for the first time on a Canadian track in Calgary in May 1956. In 1963 Albertan E.B. Olson patented a curling ice shaver; in 1968 a Red Deer man patented a ski release harness.[20] In 2000 University of Alberta engineer Ken Fyfe invented a shoe-mounted sensor device that provides runners with instant digital feedback on performance.[21] But, just as Wes Montgomery pondered the athletic status of curlers, some have worried that more convenient and efficient equipment could result in a loss of refined skill. Recalling the historical romance of climate and vigour, speed skater Doreen Ryan warned that leaving the bracing outdoors for warmer indoor rinks meant that skaters could lose a certain toughness and speed.[22]

Direct contact with the environment could not be avoided by skiers as it eventually could by skaters, and specialized equipment and clothing for skiing was not easy to come by in early years. Banff skiers shopped at Compton's Sports, the Bay, Eaton's, and MacFarland's for equipment and outfits involving tweed plus-fours and jackets. The selection was small prior to market growth, and skiers commonly improvised. In Edmonton, blacksmiths made ski bindings in lieu of manufactured equipment. In the late 1940s, North American manufacturers moved from Harris tweed to lighter gabardine for ski pants and to stretch fabric in the mid-1950s. Banff shops were so well-stocked by this time that the Ski Runners of the Canadian Rockies held an annual fashion show with members of the club (including famous photographer Bruno Engler) modelling clothing from local retailers.[23] The 1960s, the space program produced new fabrics that, adapted for sports, at first were so slippery that a fallen skier was in danger of sliding uncontrollably for long distances.[24]

Although sport skiing was organized in Banff by amateur enthusiasts, commercial operators became involved as major technological changes made long-term economic planning and large investments necessary. Investment in machinery led to commercial investment in other amenities to recoup the original outlay. In 1959 downhill skiing was the country's fastest-growing sport. New equipment available in Banff ski areas meant an expansion in the sport's popularity; the number of skiers at Norquay was estimated to have doubled in the ten years leading up to 1969, when there were over ten ski areas with lifts. Even before the Rockies around Calgary were "literally crawling with lifts," the mountains were "infested with skiers" and hills were clogged.[25]

What has been called the "golfification" of skiing provides increased comfort and amenities for an aging skiing population. Frequently, massive modification of the terrain separates the experience from traditional skiing sites and the skier from the necessity to develop certain skills. In 1980, for example, the Sunshine Village gondola opened and attracted greater numbers of skiers with a speedy transfer from parking lot to mountain. Addressing perceptions that the quality of slopes like Norquay, Sunshine, and Lake Louise suffers due to park conservation restrictions, William Yeo argues that park authorities have actually rarely resisted new initiatives. To the balance of risk and safety for human beings, then, we have added the difficult task of moderating the effects of sport on the environment.[26]

The nineteenth-century notion that human performance capacity is limited, though somewhat manipulable by scientific training, shifted after the Cold War period to policies of setting higher goals for strength and endurance. After the 1960s, Canadian public policy trends moved away from supporting sport for community well-being and toward subsidizing individual achievement and high performance sport. As performance records are more clearly identified as priorities, competitive events, such as the 1983 Universiade in Edmonton, become significant not so much for themselves as for their role as "great development exercises for our athletes, getting up that ladder to the Olympic competition."[27] Today, Sport Canada supports training programs designed to produce "podium results."[28] Calgary was chosen for the country's first dedicated Canadian Sports Centre, an institution with the goal of "supporting high performance athletes to achieve podium performances in international competition."[29]

RODEO, BOXING, AND WRESTLING

RITUALIZED MAYHEM?

Rodeo announcers call bull riding the most dangerous eight seconds in sport, with "the highest injury rate of all major events in professional rodeo."[30] Part of rodeo's spectator appeal is the inherent unpredictability of contests between humans and animals. Successful rodeo had to be both exciting for viewers and worth the risk for contestants. The early Calgary Stampede's prize monies of $20,000 were quadruple those of any other championships of the day. But while risky tasks such as roping and riding are part of rodeo's ranching history, many more dangerous events such as the chuckwagon race, steer decorating, trick riding, and wild cow milking were invented purely to provide audience excitement.[31] Chuckwagon audiences, for instance, watch "sixteen horses, four drivers, and sixteen outriders thread the loop of two barrels and fight for the rail, wagons and horses and men locked in a dangerous thundering career around the half mile of hell."[32] The *Albertan* described a chuckwagon crash at the 1938 Calgary Stampede in which driver Jack Morton of Gleichen "flew high into the air and came down hard with several crushed ribs." The event was watched by 10,000 people and Stampede officials who later "reported the total attendance for the day as highly satisfactory."[33]

A high-profile Alberta rodeo injury was suffered by champion bronc rider Duane Daines in 1995 when a horse reared and crushed his back in the chute. Now without the use of his legs, Daines still rides with a special saddle and attends the Stampede with his wife Cheryl Daines, a barrel racer. Accepting risk to life and limb is part of the sport, because "that's what cowboys do."[34] University of Calgary sports epidemiologist Dale Butterwick asks, "How much is the death of one twenty-year-old cowboy worth?...What's the cost to the health care system for a cowboy crushed by a bull in competition who is paralyzed for the rest of his life?"[35] In 2007 the university opened a registry for catastrophic injuries in pro rodeo, a type of registry already in place for every other sport that documents and investigates life-changing injuries in support of implementing measures for increased safety for athletes. Meanwhile, though some riders now wear protective vests, very few have heeded medical advice to wear helmets, a fact blamed by at least one doctor on the machismo culture of rodeo.[36] It seems that there are some things cowboys don't do.

As a confrontational sport, boxing, like wrestling, has valorized both positive and negative models of masculinity. In the early years of the province, social reformers promoted amateur boxing as a medium of socializing fine young men through the manly art of self-defence. But others exploited the growth of mass media and spectator markets to popularize the sport in matches often orchestrated to dramatize ethnic, racial, and class tensions. Prize fighting was banned in Canada in 1881 but continued to be tolerated; western Canadian city officials, professionals, police and firemen, and businessmen all patronized matches and tended to view violence as legitimate in sport. In Calgary, ready audiences attended "intense and unprovoked matches [that] took place in smoke-filled basements or old barns, abandoned buildings or tents outside city limits...So popular was the sport that prizefighters would show up...and spread the word that they wanted a challenger."[37]

American boxing champion Tommy Burns retired from the ring and settled in Calgary around 1910. He became a promoter, touting boxing matches as powerful publicity vehicles for the city. Insisting that his fights were legitimate contests between manly and honourable fighters, he welcomed women spectators to "enhance the reputation of the sport in the community."[38] When Calgary city council voted to ban all professional boxing and sparring events that charged admission, Burns got around this by building a stadium just outside city limits. But following the death of one of the contestants in a 1913 Calgary match, boxing became a magnet for debates about violence, gender, race, class, science, and modernity itself.

Refusing a challenge from heavyweight African-American Jack Johnson to Luther McCarty, Burns instead promoted a fight between white contenders McCarty and Arthur Pelkey. An estimated 3,000 fans attended the Victoria Day bout. After one minute and forty-six seconds, McCarty, who had an undiagnosed skull condition, fell and never regained consciousness. He was the first boxer to be killed in the ring in Canada; four days later, pro boxing was banned (again) in Calgary. Pelkey was exonerated by a coroner's jury but arrested and charged with manslaughter by the N W M P, and Tommy Burns's arena was burned to the ground thirty-six hours after the match.[39]

Although the fight had been an illegal cash contest, both sportsmen and spectators objected to legal intervention, arguing that to penalize boxers or ban boxing matches would jeopardize amateur programs meant to foster healthy virility in youth. More significantly, middle-class boosters and community leaders recognized that Calgary's reputation as a "fight town" was good for business and that violence in sport attracted audiences. Support from this corner was bolstered by that of working-class white males, and charges against Burns were dropped later that year in favour of continued spectacles of physical domination.[40] Newspapers of the day continued to lament the failure of sportsmanship but others poked fun at amateur ideals propounded by the "simon pures."[41] In a 1936 Calgary event, Bobby Stewart tossed Harry Kent out of the rink and then kicked a spectator who booed him for foul tactics; in another match, Stewart and Bob Russell mauled each other's faces with their taped fists.[42]

But boxing also had a cleaner face, a recreational countenance of scientific training and discipline consistent with the norms of muscular Christianity, and amateur boxing was regulated by the Amateur Athletic Union of Canada (A A U C) from the 1920s to the 1970s. Far from being sanctioned for his role in pro boxing, promoter Burns was honorary president of the Y W C A, which organized bouts for boys. In Calgary, over thirty boxers entered a typical provincial amateur championship event in the 1920s. Large crowds of spectators attended "fast, snappy and wholesome exhibits," partly because of the cheap fifty-cent admission to benefit "strictly amateur sport."[43] Nine hundred fans turned out to a match at the Victoria Pavilion in 1922, and 3,300 came out in 1931.[44]

The Lethbridge Amateur Boxing Association (L A B A), founded in 1949, provided young boys with a "healthful and beneficial outlet for their surplus energy."[45] It was also a good outlet for surplus funds, as by early October that year local merchants, including confectioners and grocers, pharmacists, lumber and automobile merchants, had

Young men learning to box, Lethbridge, 1975. [GMA 19760235087]

donated almost $2,000 to the club's gym at the new city sports centre.
Community support was represented at the gym's opening by city
council members, the Chamber of Commerce president, the Alberta
vice-president of the Amateur Athletic Association of Canada, the
chief constable, a reverend, and the director of city school athletics.
Telegrams of congratulations came from Joe Louis and Jack Dempsey.
Any public concerns about safety were allayed by newspaper photos of
boys being examined by a doctor before joining.[46] As seen in the photograph above, young men were still training in the sport a generation
later. The rationale of catharsis and socialization persisted through the
years. Walter Twinn, longtime chief of the Sawridge Creek band and a
Canadian senator, was an accomplished boxer who became a promoter
in an effort to offer Aboriginal youth an outlet for aggression.[47]

For most of the twentieth century, professional wrestling was
promoted as a legitimate sport but, as Alberta's *Stampede Wrestling*

Women's tag team match, Sims Auction Mart, Red Deer, 1954. [RDDA MG-306-10-8]

broadcaster Ed Whalen observed, the action, once "straight," became
more manipulative and staged over time.[48] Pro wrestling has launched
a thousand debates about sportsmanship as it ritualizes elements of
good and evil, honest men versus cheaters, downtrodden versus privileged—"us" versus "them." It is true that hockey and football players
are also assigned theatrical roles as "goons" or "gentlemen," and teams
are taken to represent certain communities; spectators routinely react
as though the outcome of the game were a matter of life and death.
Jeffery Mondak suggests that pro wrestling's cyclical popularity corresponds to periods of confrontational political xenophobia and foreign
policy in the 1930s, 1950s, and 1980s. Roland Barthes compared wrestling to classical theatre, film, or opera, all of which offer narratives

Male wrestlers, Sims Auction Mart, Red Deer, 1953. [RDDA MG-306-10-85-4]

and images of passion, stories of suffering, defeat, and justice.[49] The key difference is that, in wrestling, the fight itself is supposed to be the main attraction—a rare contemporary throwback to pre-industrial "blood sports." By the 1950s, both male and female wrestlers toured the province in tag team matches that, to judge by the photographs in this section, amounted to a theatre of violence. Alberta did not invent pro wrestling, but, arguably, it contributed decisively to its current nature through the Hart family of Calgary and strong audiences throughout the province over the years.

Stu Hart was an amateur wrestler who took up wrestling when he joined the Edmonton YMCA in 1929. He won the Dominion Championship in 1940 after playing centre for the Edmonton Eskimos football team in the late 1930s. Hart competed for more than four decades as a professional wrestler and started Stampede Wrestling in 1948. The show, a forerunner of today's World Wrestling Entertainment, toured the province to sell-out crowds; Edmonton and Calgary "were probably the two best towns in Canada for wrestling."[50] The Harts also trained dozens of pro wrestlers at their Foothills Athletic Club, and Hart boasted of a "waiting list of big kids who wanted to be wrestlers."[51] Stampede Wrestling was censured for excessive violence by the Calgary Boxing and Wrestling Commission and sold to the World Wrestling Federation in 1984; revived a year later, it endured until Hart retired in 1990. Hart commented that "there's been chicanery, slight-of-hand tricks going on in wrestling for years, I suppose. Since Shakespeare's day. Since the gladiator days when fellows were wrestling lions and stuff."[52]

His twelve children, "all from the same wife," as he pointed out, and other relatives have also participated in the sport or its promotion.[53] Bret "Hitman" Hart built a successful career, won all three of Stampede Wrestling's recognized titles, and became a two-time British Commonwealth Mid-Heavyweight Champion and six-time North American Heavyweight Champion. Hart's persona in the ring was "emotionally vulnerable...an underdog," a classic Canadian hero defending social values and annoying Americans.[54] His career ended in 1999 when he was kicked in the back of the head by a motorcycle boot at a World Championship Wrestling match; he battled for an insurance settlement for years afterward. In 2004 he was named one of CBC's "Fifty Greatest Canadians." His brother Owen Hart, another star wrestler, died in the ring in 1999 when he fell eight stories during a stunt. Some observers blamed the event on the culture of pro wrestling, constantly increasing violence and danger to win audiences.[55]

Another popular Alberta wrestler was Gene Kiniski, who learned the sport at the Edmonton YWCA as a youth. Kiniski was also a football star with the Edmonton Eskimos until 1953 when he became a professional wrestler and a compelling celebrity character. Kiniski, known for his brutal and cantankerous ring persona and blustery ego, was in real life "the sweetest Canadian this side of Guy Lombardo's musicians," according to veteran sportswriter Jim Coleman. Kiniski became a co-promoter of All-Star Wrestling in Vancouver in 1962.[56] Writer and sportscaster Dick Beddoes once called Kiniski "Canada's Greatest Athlete," citing his prowess in several different sports. Kiniski held world wrestling titles in the 1960s, when, he recalled, violence was not limited to the ring: "The fans tried to decapitate me...They ignited newspapers, trying to suffocate me...What always bothered me was audience participation. They bought a ticket to see me, not for them to participate...I've been hit with chairs, stabbed. The lowest part of my career was in Fresno, CA, when a fan threw acid on me. I've had so many lawsuits, it's unbelievable."[57] There were rewards, though; one match between Kiniski and Whipper Billy Watson in the 1950s turned away 20,000 fans from the sold-out event; another match grossed $25,000 for one of the biggest paydays of the era.[58]

In the early years of Canadian television, boxing and wrestling were evening broadcast staples, but as sports coverage spread throughout the day many viewers rejected violent play intruding into family time and their popularity waned.[59] *Stampede Wrestling* was broadcast live in the afternoons; Ed Whalen was the television commentator for twenty-seven years, starting in 1957. Wrestling was more popular in Alberta than in Saskatchewan in the 1970s, and *Stampede Wrestling* drew steady audiences. At one point in the 1970s Whalen was interviewing Billy Robinson in the ring when the foreboding Abdullah the Butcher climbed in and began strangling Robinson with the microphone cord. Whalen grabbed it back and whacked Abdullah over the head, resulting in thirteen stitches. A small boy watching television at the time "laughed and laughed. I thought it was part of the show."[60] Of course, it was all planned, but nobody had informed Whalen, who preferred to hold his own microphone. He later retired spontaneously mid-broadcast in a reaction to a match in which "Bad News Allen was running around with a fork, and there was wall to wall blood...Stampede Wrestling became too bloody."[61]

HOCKEY: RULES BREAK OUT

Ice hockey has always been particularly rife with blood and bruises, despite an early attribution of courtly values to players of this sport. Not only were they presumed to be gentlemen amateurs but models of a Christian ideal of masculinity, particularly when leading players were members of the clergy, as was often the case. The N W M P certainly couldn't be counted on to keep order on the ice; the Mounties' team in 1897 Edmonton was so violent that audience disapproval discouraged the local team, the Thistles, from playing them. However, in the early 1900s when Strathcona played at the Thistle Rink in Edmonton they crossed the river on a special train and brought the police force, which consisted of one man, to guarantee fair play.[62]

Middle-class reformers, community leaders, and editorialists worried about the moral influence of poor sportsmanship on audiences. In 1911 the *Lethbridge News* called for a ban on foul language at sports events.[63] Around the same time, a letter writer to the *Edmonton Bulletin* asserted that hockey was "a fine manly game...but [when violent] it becomes a very vulgar spectacle...Brute force never wins in the world of sport and only brings down the censure of the public on the team resorting to it."[64] From players to do-gooders to journalists to citizens, the vast majority of these voices came from the middle class, those with the highest stakes in creating at least the appearance of a respectable modern civilization. In practice, enthusiastic audiences conveyed a sturdy ambivalence. When the Lacombe team came to town, at one point Edmonton fans would bring lumps of coal to throw into their path over the ice. Fans at the Thistle Rink were known to lean over the boards to join in the play with umbrellas aimed at both puck and players. In 1905 the *Medicine Hat News* reported that "the chief objection to hockey is its roughness...[but] the spectators cheer for any piece of rough play."[65]

Established rivalries raised the stakes; when the Thistles beat the Calgary Fire Brigade team in 1899, the *Herald* accused the crafty

Edmontonians of taking the southerners out on the town to sap their energies the night before. The game itself featured a brawl in which a Calgary player lost an eye.[66] We know this because although newspaper editorials overtly condemned violence, they didn't miss many chances to print descriptive accounts of altercation or rough play while also condemning it. The *Edmonton Bulletin* commented on the "cleanness of the game" several times in a 1913 account of a Dominions versus Shermans hockey match. The same day, several columns of the sports section were devoted to a round-by-round description of the blows and injuries that occurred in a boxing contest featuring Luther McCarty.[67]

While social elites championed control, they remained vague about how to exert it. Those directly involved drew much authority from their social status rather than expertise, since amateur ideals dictated that a game played by gentlemen be arbitrated by one of themselves. Peter Fortna describes a dispute over Dr. O.F. Strong's officiating at an Edmonton-Strathcona game in 1904. Accusations of bias prompted Strong to defend, not his specific decision as referee, but his gentlemanly status as final guarantor of his fair treatment of players. When the Alberta Amateur Hockey Association was founded in 1907, it paid little attention to the practical necessity of training and standardizing the decisions of referees; in fact, no training programs were available until the 1950s. In 1967, a provincial government report continued to appeal for "good men" to officiate on an unpaid, non-unionized—in other words, gentlemanly and non-professional—basis.[68]

But even by 1885 "both the development of official rules and growing hierarchies of teams and players anticipated the future."[69] The drive to regulate dangerous behaviours was inseparable from the campaign for centralized control amid the professionalization of sports. The formation of the NHL in 1909 was in part due to concern about unregulated violence; in 1919 the Canadian Amateur Hockey Association (CAHA) adopted a common set of rules on the subject. Between the wars, the game developed a set of rules to define acceptable body contact. Meanwhile, popular Edmonton Eskimos player Eddie

Shore was "one of the most-feared hockey players" of the mid-1920s; his "ability to lay out opponents with brute force" was encouraged to attract more fans as the Western Canada Hockey League foundered. Shore, known as "Old Blood and Guts," joined the N H L's Boston Bruins, and in a 1933 game he hit Toronto star Ace Bailey from behind, causing him a career-ending head injury. Hundreds of people, including Edmonton's mayor and the president of the Chamber of Commerce, signed a petition supporting Shore. After Bailey's injury, Shore became the first high-profile N H L player to wear a helmet regularly. The National Hockey League had rejected a prototype helmet in 1927.[70]

The C A H A introduced limits on body contact in 1923, but fighting was not addressed until the 1930s, and not until 1936-1937 was a rule introduced concerning the deliberate injury of an opponent. Violence and the potential for injury drew some crowds but it also slowed down the games, and there was a pragmatic element to prevention. In Alberta in 1958, the intermediate Big Six League and the professional Western Hockey League (W H L) took steps to reduce violence and injury and to speed up the action in the sport. The Big Six adopted international rules, and the W H L enforced existing ones concerning body checking in an effort to reverse several years of declining attendance. Other leagues were expected to follow because fighting on the ice "makes for better entertainment, which is the only reason fans come to the games at all," according to the Winnipeg Warriors' general manager. At the first game in Edmonton played under the new rules, the Flyers' general manager Bud Poile said, "Just listen to [the fans]. They like the idea."[71]

Helmets were not part of standard hockey gear until the 1970s.[72] The protective headgear proved to be a difficult sell for hockey teams above the juvenile level. The Oil Kings 1964-1965 program to institute helmets for all was quietly ignored by most players, and Coach Ray Kinasewich said that he also "kind of forgot it, probably because I never wore one myself." It would take a generation that grew up wearing helmets to continue doing so as adults.[73] Albertans cherishing the regional maverick image will happily recall that the last N H L player to shun a helmet was Craig MacTavish, with the Oilers and later St. Louis until his retirement in 1997. He later became the Oilers' coach.

At least one violent confrontation in twentieth-century Alberta hockey was attributed to racism. The Saddle Lake Warriors, the only team in their Junior B league composed mainly of Aboriginal players, made the national news in February 1998 when "racial taunts from the opposing [Wainwright] Bisons triggered a bench-clearing brawl."[74] The spectators joined in the action, throwing bottles, pounding drums, and shouting. By game three of the playoff series, fans were screaming, "We want blood!" Players screamed back, the Warriors' coach was ejected by officials, and the game ended early after Saddle Lake fans barely missed hitting one of the referees with a bottle. Only three Saddle Lake players were uninjured and without penalties at the end of the game. Local resident Larry Moosewah argued that the team's passionate audience reflects its central role as a source of pride and a centre for social life on the reserve, where "in the winter, hockey's all people live for. It's in our blood."[75] When nearby St. Paul's Junior B team folded for lack of fan support, several white players joined the Warriors, and the numbers of white fans increased.

Violence in amateur and minor hockey also includes spectator aggression; such behaviour can produce a culture of violence that is difficult to change. In 2001 the minor Foothills Hockey league in southern Alberta banned the Kainai team of the First Nations Hockey Association from league play due to various infractions by officials, players, and parents. Michael Robidoux argues that the problem was exacerbated by conflicting perceptions of appropriate play based in wider racialized discourses in the district. He views differences between mainstream and First Nations hockey as rooted in the latter's cultural construct of masculinity, which includes stoic modes of reacting to injury.[76] As of 2010, the Kainai Chiefs were part of the Ranchland Hockey League. There continue to be separate hockey leagues and competitions, though Aboriginal players are now represented on junior senior, professional, and NHL teams in Alberta.[77]

In the Western Hockey League, Colton Yellowhorn and Clay Plume play for the junior Lethbridge Hurricanes and Gary Gladue for the Calgary Hitmen. In the Alberta Junior Hockey League, Shawn Breaker and Dean Shade are on the Brooks team and MacKenzie Reid with the Calgary Royals. In the NHL, Scott Ferguson of the Edmonton Oilers serves as hockey mentor for the Alberta Native Provincial Championships; Chris Simon plays for the Calgary Flames. And Sheldon Souray, who was with the Oilers for a time, participates in Native youth hockey camps across Canada. Calgary Flames player Sandy McCarthy runs a hockey school in Calgary for First Nations children and regularly speaks to youth on reservations about the value of sport.[78]

When the stakes in minor hockey culture include hopes of a career in the pros, the difficulties of individuals, who are typically very young when entering elite levels of play, are compounded. In an environment that exploits male physical supremacy and the star system, analysts link documented victimization and power abuses within the sport to the central factor of ownership. The player's position as commodity and lack of power over his own career means that other aspects of life outside hockey, such as education and family life, are correspond-ingly devalued. In this context, junior hockey does not serve the needs of youth but ultimately those of the market.[79] These dynamics, of course, depend to an extent on the individuals involved. Leo LeClerc and Bill Hunter, manager and owner of the Edmonton Oil Kings in the 1950s and 1960s respectively, insisted that players finish high school or university and even paid for tutors where necessary. In 1966, the Oil Kings was the only team in western Canada known for promoting players' education, having produced twenty-one university graduates and thirty-three pros in twelve years.[80]

A 1968 committee appointed by the legislature to investigate amateur and minor hockey in Alberta reported that "amateur hockey and amateur players are being exploited," and that some organiza-tions had "induced minors to enter into contracts and agreements which have been unfair and injurious to them." The committee recom-mended legislation requiring a provincial commission to approve anyone under eighteen signing a contract; minor hockey was at the time virtually under the total control of the NHL. The Youth minister rejected the suggestion on the grounds that the provincial government was concerned not with professional development but with broadened participation in recreational hockey.[81]

BASEBALL AND BASKETBALL: NON-CONTACT?

Baseball is not usually associated with a "field of nightmares." In Alberta, baseball has been upheld as a gentleman's pastime, useful for character building in boys. The sport lacks the intrinsic threat of injury from body checking, speed, icy surfaces, or angry animals, but it shares the perceived high stakes of competition. At the same time, scorekeeping is inherently subjective, without visible goal lines or time limits on play. In practice, disputes and violence occur off the field among officials, coaches, and fans as much as among players. Baseball games could turn particularly nasty on the barnstorming circuit, which thrived in the 1930s, 1940s, and 1950s; players in Class D leagues like the Western Canada Baseball League were often transient and had little to lose in terms of their low or non-existent wages. In one of many incidents in the league's history, two Lethbridge players were fined for physically attacking an umpire in 1907. Gary Lucht describes a visit during the 1920s by an American barnstorming team to Moose Jaw where a fan and a player got into a fight; the Mounties ejected the fan, but later that night the player attacked the fan and the team had to leave quickly to prevent a riot.[82] The *Calgary Herald* lamented in 1920, "the 'baseball' game between the Cubs and the Kaysees last night was an absolute farce...the City Baseball League should be disbanded forth-with...It was an exhibition of poor sportsmanship such as seen happily enough rather rarely...What the fans demand is clean sport—games that have life, action and keenness."[83]

On the other hand, fans could give as good as they got. In 1946 teams from Nordegg, a mining town, and Eckville, in ranch country, competed in the central Alberta baseball championship in Rocky Mountain House. Irked by a call in the second game, women in the audience "took matters in their own hands and threw the base ump out of the park."[84] Attempts to regulate the sport during the 1950s included the Granum League's player contract prohibiting "drinking or partying" twenty-four hours before a game, or even for the whole season.[85] But the North Battleford Beavers of "the turbulent Western Canada Baseball League" were reputedly "the wildest and woolliest aggregation in all the riot-ridden records"; however, team coach Emile Francis proclaimed in June 1957 that the "roughneck era" had been replaced by "fast, clean baseball strictly supervised by better umpires."[86] Shortly thereafter, he was evicted from a game between the Beavers and the Edmonton Eskimos after throwing a pile of bats at the umpire and wrestling with police officers called to the field. When one officer recommended an apology, the Beavers refused on the grounds that it would injure the team's pride. As the game continued, two hurt players were carried off the field. Right fielder Johnny Ford punched a police officer and was arrested. Ford objected, while another player jumped on the officer with his cleats. Francis complained that the "umpire is a dud. There's no room in this league for both of us."[87]

Fans also occasionally joined the action. Edmonton baseball maven John Ducey described games in North Edmonton in the 1940s where "we'd go out in the Gainers' trucks...and we'd draw the truck up behind the grandstand...They had very rabid fans out there in North Edmonton...As we'd get to the last inning, particularly if we were in the lead, we'd turn the motors on and get them revved up...With the last out...we'd make a beeline for the trucks and just get out of there quick because those fans are after you, I tell you."[88]

Despite efforts to educate umpires and control players and fans, violence was never quite eliminated in major league and pro baseball. Alberta's longstanding rivalry between Edmonton and Calgary sports teams flared up in the 2006 minor league baseball season. After an Edmonton Cracker-Cats player was hit by a series of Calgary Viper pitches, a brawl broke out. It was so violent that the game was suspended. When Edmonton refused to return, Calgary was awarded the victory. Both managers and seven players were suspended for a total of seventy-nine games.[89]

The urge to protect athletes from themselves has been far more marked in women's sport, where rule adjustments in the early 1900s attempted to limit rough play and injuries. This was not an abstract concern, even in a non-contact sport like basketball. During the 1920s, Banff's Spark Plugs basketball team played on a circuit with the champion Canmore Red Wings. In one game between the two teams, a Banff player broke a finger, one sprained an ankle, and another injured her arm; on another occasion the local paper reported that the Spark Plugs "are not sparking very well these days owing to injuries to several players."[90]

Another Spark Plugs game in Canmore featured "shoestring tackles" and "necktie clutches," a fracas that "resembled the second battle of Ypres with a charge or two by the noble six hundred thrown in for good measure." The centralized distribution of rulebooks seemed ineffective. The Spark Plugs "didn't know men's rules, Canmore didn't know girls' rules and the referee didn't enforce either." A return match in Banff was scheduled to be played by men's rules and a good crowd of spectators was anticipated.[91] In a game between the Canmore Bluebirds and the Banff team, the referee "did very well, but he might work a little harder to keep down the rough stuff, as rough play doesn't help to establish friendly relations between the players."[92] Another story details frequent penalties for both teams as players "checked hard and in the excitement of the game overdid the job on numerous occasions."[93] At the 1930 meeting of the Women's Amateur Athletic Association of Canada, a representative of the Dominion Basketball Association argued strongly for men's rules in women's basketball, but the group ruled against this.[94]

As the stakes rise for individuals and nations, the scientific approach to regulating bodily performance capacity has extended to the use of drugs. Critics such as Donna Haraway and John Hoberman have suggested that drug use is a logical technological outcome of an obsession with performance. As early as the 1860s, cyclists were accused of using stimulants, including heroin, cocaine, and caffeine, for speed and endurance. Marathon runners at the 1904 Olympics used strychnine.[95] *The Futurist Manifesto* of 1909 advocated a cult of sport and physical strength, speed and heroism, and author Filippo Marinetti lauded the fusion of body and machine. Almost a century later, the Canadian Prairies had the highest proportion (5 per cent) of athletes admitting to using performance-enhancing drugs; a small percentage of preadolescents used steroids and other substances that can have devastating side effects.[96] In a high-profile event in June 2007, professional wrestler Chris Benoit killed his family and himself in Calgary. Although the World Wrestling Entertainment organization at first denied any connection to mood swings caused by steroid use, Chairman Vince McMahon later admitted that steroids were found in the home and were a factor. Benoit's career began in Alberta, where he trained with the Hart family and got his start in Stampede Wrestling; when he headlined a wrestling show in Edmonton in 2004, the mayor declared it Chris Benoit Day.[97]

Objections to drugs centre partly on unfair advantage accruing to users. When Alberta swimmer Graham Smith was inducted into the Canadian Olympic Hall of Fame in 2002, his mother Gwen Smith reflected on the experience of raising a family of competitive athletes from the 1960s to the 1990s. Referring to the prevalence of drugs in high performance sport, she said, "If I had it to do over again, knowing what I know now, I doubt very much if I'd put my kids in a sport like that again...There will never be an even playing field."[98] It becomes news when an athlete resists this pressure. Cross-country skier Beckie Scott of Alberta was awarded an Olympic gold medal in 2002 after her competitor was found guilty of doping. The Canadian Olympic Committee president called Scott "an icon for fair play."[99] But as Brunt asks, if performance-enhancing drugs offer the hope of a break-through in performance, "how would the risk/benefit analysis work for someone who believes...that they're on the brink?"[100] The rules of fair play become increasingly abstract where the professional athlete may also be pressured to succeed by team owners and sponsors. The public condemnation of drug use in sport parallels the historical pattern of rejecting violence in play while it helps to sell newspapers and tickets; calls for purity are undermined by market forces privileging elite performance. At the same time, according to Stacy Lorenz, a focus on drugs obscures other problems in a sport culture that is based in compromised health, safety, and sanity.[101]

The inherent unpredictability of sporting outcomes attracts strate-gies of control, but also strategies of profit. As a clandestine activity, the history of gambling in the province is not well documented, but, in the 1880s, Deerfoot was managed by a group of backers who organized racing wagers. Despite strong public opposition and moral condemna-tion as the province grew, police failed to eliminate the practice largely due to a lack of political will, and gambling accompanied both informal and organized sport. Paul Voisey suggests that gambling was so popular in the west, transcending social and racial divisions, because it reflected the prairie pioneer experience that life itself was a gamble played against high odds; in fact, one reason for the early popularity of baseball was that it provided a gambling opportunity.[102]

Advancing communication technologies permitted more sophis-ticated, pervasive information networks. A major incentive for better measurement and record keeping in sport was the popularity of gambling as the cash stakes got higher. Team sponsors at all levels could boost returns on their investments through gambling. In 1903 local Olds businessmen sponsored a local hockey team to play at Lacombe, the game to be followed a meal at the best café in town. The players encouraged the sponsors to bet against them and at first seemed to be throwing the game, but when the sign came that "the money was up" they went ahead to win. The angry sponsors abandoned the team in town and "the tired hungry hockeyists waited in the darkness for the train that carried them home."[103] In 2004 an estimated $24 million per year was spent on hockey wagering.[104]

Horse racing has figured large in the province's sport history. Serious betting was prevalent among Southern Alberta ranchers from the start. By 1894 bigger crowds of spectators could bet on roping and bucking horses at the Calgary Exhibition. A June 1907 issue of the *Calgary Eye Opener* carried a horse racing program at the top of its front page.[105] Edmonton's Northlands Park officially organized and sanctioned racing in 1907 and parimutuel betting in 1913. The Edmonton Exhibition Association became managers of thoroughbred racing in 1957 when the Canadian Derby came permanently to the park. The popularity of betting on horse racing grew in the 1920s; in the 1930s gambling in Alberta was still illegal and still pervasive. In June 1955, the *Camrose Canadian* reported that a man who had won over $3,000 on a horse and then dropped dead of a heart attack was robbed of the winning tickets by funeral parlour employees. They were arrested when they tried to cash in at a track window. Millarville, where horse racing has been a tradition since 1905, held one of the first quarter horse races in Canada in 1957, and the *Calgary Herald* predicted that the sport would become a lucrative business as the event combined parimutuel betting with "one of the most scenic spots in the foothills."[106]

Today Alberta has more horses than any other province, and Edmonton has set world records for per capita betting. Parimutuel betting, the only legalized form of gambling, has sustained the long-term popularity of horse racing at the Edmonton Exhibition grounds. In the early twenty-first century, far from attempting to eliminate betting, the province has regulated and benefited from it; lottery revenues, including video lottery terminals (VLT) yields, have accounted for significant levels of funding for community sport in Alberta. In 2001 Premier Ralph Klein suggested a national lottery to help NHL teams, particularly Alberta's, which were struggling to survive. Ironically, the following year the Conservatives allotted $33 million from the provincial lottery fund to support the horse racing industry, which had been in decline due to competition from lotteries and video lottery terminals.[107]

: CONCLUSION

Advocates of youth and amateur sport continue to harbour notions of building character and rehearsing participants for life challenges, but professional sport is a powerful behavioural model for spectators who provide a market for aggressive performance while often decrying its consequences. The competitive ethos in sport, combined with a focus on control over conditions, behaviours, and results, has fostered a climate in which the rewards of winning can justify aggression and illegal performance enhancements At present, the response to violence is usually a call for more effective control through codes of conduct, penalties, and education. However, violence is not simply a sign of isolated personal or regulatory failures; little attention is paid to deeper analyses of the normative culture of sport.[108] Fans continue to express passion in performances echoing those on the field of play, particularly in incidents such as the post-game hockey riots that occurred in November 1983 in Hamilton, in June 1993 in Montreal, June 1994 in Vancouver, 2006 in Edmonton, and 2011 in Vancouver. But the complex of factors shaping risk-taking and aggression in sport draws on deep narratives and mythologies of victory and defeat that reflect broader social dynamics. The role of the mass media in building and stoking a widely shared sport culture is the topic of the next chapter.

10

"THE RAIN UPON OUR SENSES"

SPORT, THE MASS MEDIA, AND MARKETING

MEDIATING THE GAME

*The pleasure in listening to a hockey game, as I do each Saturday
night during the long winter, resides not only in the air of repressed yet
impending violence, but also in the rain upon our senses of those sudden
and glamourous names...Those children of winter are my dream; they race
in the night's dead hours.*

—ROBERT KROETSCH,
The Studhorse Man

The radio pulled fields and rinks into living rooms across the Prairies
in the 1920s and, like the newspaper before it and television afterward,
changed the way games were played, watched, recorded, and sold. In
Alberta, the critical combination of railway, photography, telegraphy,

A crowd waits for an event to begin at the Lake Saskatoon Sports, ca. 1920. [SPRA 2009.39.10]

and mass printing was in place from the late nineteenth century. News of scores and changing statistics circulated frequently enough to sustain excitement about both local and distant events, and photographs of players fostered the growth of fan culture. Telephones, important for relaying event news and scores quickly, were common by 1910. People shared a widening realm of information along with greater physical and social mobility. With longer leisure hours for working people, new markets and communities of interest in sport arose.[1] As the news industry delivered audiences to advertisers, commercial sport and the mass media evolved symbiotically. By the late twentieth century the extent of sports coverage in North American media "frequently surpasse[d] space given to economics, politics or any other single topic of interest."[2]

Media sources are only one component of multidimensional consumption patterns, including attendance at events and discussion with other fans; cultural knowledge of sport circulates through social networks that negotiate the meanings of various activities in everyday life. The construction of the mass media audience for sports in the early twentieth century built on a strong core of existing cultural interest developed over decades of settlement in western Canada. Social organization had bloomed along growing networks of transportation and sporting events drew large live audiences; racing humans and horses were consistently popular.

Telegraphy and the press ensured that individual athletes became national heroes as commercial sport expanded in the latter half of the nineteenth century. Private entrepreneurial interests were active in promoting professional boxing, wrestling, baseball, and horse racing. In the 1870s, crowds paid admission fees to watch pro and semi-pro baseball. Ice hockey required more equipment, facilities, and organization to become a true spectator sport, but local matches were reported and eagerly followed in newspapers from the 1890s.[3] With the convenience of automobiles by the late 1920s, touring theatres, musicians, speakers, and sports teams brought entertainment and culture to Alberta populations. Most of the province had radio reception; Calgary in particular fostered enthusiastic broadcasters. Alberta also received network broadcasts from the United States. As the 1930s began, the population of Alberta was over 700,000, and the Depression led to greater movement between regions than ever before.

Mass media underscored and formalized sport's traditional narrative appeal, built around versions of the performances of powerful characters in struggle with others or with nature. The mass print and broadcast media accordingly developed dramatic sport reporting conventions conveying heroic aspiration, aesthetic achievement, and high performance. Familiar set-ups involving oppositions of gentlemen amateur versus professional or working-class hero, or of communities and diverse social groups, transferred easily to journalism and broadcasting in terms of righteous rivalries and victories.[4] After World War I strengthened Canadians' sense of nationhood, radio, newspapers, and magazines also did a fair job of connecting national pride and identity to winning teams.

The rails carried mail, machinery, and the newspapers that were an
early feature of prairie community life. By 1902 a territorial government
official estimated that newspapers were more widely and carefully read
in Alberta than anywhere else in Canada. The first newspapers were
published in Edmonton, Fort Macleod, and Calgary in the early 1880s;
local news was supplemented with mass "readyprint" inserts.[5] Sports
coverage was an effective way to attract newspapers' core market of
male wage earners and businessmen. Early Alberta papers ran short
accounts or lists of sporting results for both local games and important
competitions elsewhere. These tidbits were scattered amid bulletins
on social and business life, reflecting early journalism practice but also
echoing the way that sport was more casually integrated into daily
life and other community interests. As leisure became more rationally
organized, urban dailies took on promotional roles that helped to build
local communities around sport. In 1895, the *Edmonton Bulletin* called
for a multipurpose sports ground and advised players "to form, boys,
your different athletic clubs for the summer." Fuelling an enduring
tradition, the *Bulletin* exhorted local clubs to "wake up" lest eternal
rival Calgary win hockey and football supremacy.[6]

Specialized newspaper sport sections emerged slowly as more
readers, senior sports organizers, promoters, and entrepreneurs arrived
to larger communities. Papers, both large and small, covered everything from professional play to local minor and recreational events,
including cricket, football, baseball, hockey, and lacrosse, and international boxing, track and field, and more. After Deacon White came
to Edmonton and founded the Western Canada Baseball League in
November 1906, the *Bulletin* introduced a regular sports section, and
most provincial dailies followed by 1910. Newspaper accounts were
often biased due to the prevalent civic boosterism of the era. In 1911
the *Calgary Daily Herald* praised two Edmonton papers "which are now
publishing excellent sensible sport," implying a perceived improvement in objectivity over time.[7]

The January 2, 1907 edition ran three full columns on local hockey scores, as well as suggestions for the management of wildly partisan audiences, and in the spring of the same year the *Bulletin* carried two full columns of regular features on American major league baseball and reported on White's league planning and player signings. But hockey coverage grew in prominence; the *Calgary Daily Herald* detailed provincial leagues and games such as one in 1913 that attracted so many spectators that hundreds were turned away.[8] By 1915, football stories averaged only 2 per cent and baseball about 30 per cent of daily sport coverage in Edmonton newspapers.[9] Some eastern papers carried news of western Canadian sports, and in 1919 the new Lethbridge Municipal Golf Club made national front pages when H.A. McKillop scored one of the first North American holes-in-one and was showered with prizes and gifts from sporting goods dealers. This club later became the Lethbridge Golf Club and then the Henderson Lake Golf Club. In 1932 the Lethbridge Country Club was formed by golf club members who were offended by the 1931 motion to restrict ladies' golf time on Saturdays.[10]

Newspapers, indefatigable civic boosters, pointed out the public benefits of sport and promoted individual star players. The longest item on the *Bulletin*'s March 26, 1907 sport page concerned a benefit game at the Thistle Rink in support of two players who had been injured while "providing gilt-edged sport for the public" with "a superior class of hockey, and incidentally to give the city itself prominence in the athletic arena."[11] In 1908, Edmonton rugby captain Harold Burnham's letters home to Ontario regularly included anecdotes and newspaper clippings about games, including "a very flattering account of my doings in the Calgary game and...an extract from another Calgary paper so you can hardly blame me if my hat doesn't fit now...I feel very much tickled and I've been sending copies of the papers to all my old football companions."[12]

As communications technology advanced, statistics and records were compiled and circulated more quickly and accurately. Readers immersed themselves in "the fantasy of far-away games," and international reports "sometimes filled five sports pages, completely overshadowing—or providing the cultural framework for—local events."[13] Between 1885 and 1915, over 50 per cent of sport coverage in Canadian newspapers was about American teams. Half of the *Bulletin*'s March 26, 1907 sport section featured American and European content. The *Calgary Daily Herald* ran a regular column on "Old Country Football," and the January 13, 1913 edition devoted two pages of sports news to America and England.[14] The *Herald*'s "In the World of Sports" page daily connected contemporary Albertans to continental sporting events. In 1923 the *Herald*'s British coverage outweighed that of either Canadian or American sport, but by the end of World War II, two-thirds of sports coverage in the *Lethbridge Herald* was of Canadian sports, with American coverage at 21 per cent and British topics at 13 per cent.[15]

Alberta athletes, entrepreneurs, and audiences were accordingly encouraged to think of themselves as part of a broader network of sports culture, reflecting trading and communication networks that already shaped local economies. This did not mean simply a more diverse and intense rain of information, more hours spent memorizing statistics, or living vicariously in someone else's very swift skates now and then. The evolution of performance and the business of sport, and thus the fortunes of athletes, were nurtured by the media's appetite for content. In 1912 news photographers were on hand to capture Wop May dropping the first baseball of the season from his biplane over Diamond Park. Over time, sports promoters and managers began to cater to media imperatives such as deadlines, sponsor preferences, and novel content. In one extreme example, in the 1930s Banff Springs Hotel sports director Colonel Phil Moore wanted to promote C P Hotels Golf Week. Accordingly, he invented and staged Bow and Arrow Golf games for news reporters and photographers. Local First Nations people were hired to wear colourful costumes and fire arrows like golf balls over the greens. (These games ended with an arrow's near miss of a regular golfer looking for a ball in the woods.)[16]

Amid the expansion of sports coverage, news of community and regional amateur, minor and major league sport continued strong.

Wop May dropping first ball of the season from a plane, Diamond Park, Edmonton, 1912.
[CEA EA-10-3181-6-4-1]

Editors fed curling audience appetites with detailed coverage, front-page photographs, end-by-end scores, and almost verbatim recounting of bonspiel church sermons.[17] During the Depression, community papers around the province still ran regular, detailed reports on both local and "old country" sport, including hockey, curling, basketball, carpetball, dog racing, boxing, bowling, Olympic skating, badminton, soccer, and more. The *Red Deer Advocate* of January 3, 1934 featured news of hockey and curling matches on the front page.[18] In November 1936, the *Herald* reported a football game between the University of Alberta Polar Bears and the University of Saskatchewan Huskies in which "oddly enough neither Polar Bears nor Huskies relished playing in the snow."[19] The *Albertan* of July 11, 1938 followed a Calgary cricket team's trip to a Vancouver tournament, a double header of senior baseball, a "booming" interest in lacrosse, and a professional golf tournament won by Henry Martell in Edmonton. Tennis was still popular, and several articles described competitions around the province as well as the provincial swimming championships in Sylvan Lake.[20]

Smaller community newspapers usually had no separate sports sections. On January 11, 1939, the *Camrose Canadian* ran sporting news on the front page next to the church bulletins. Topics included a plebiscite on building a swimming pool for local youth, news of the upcoming provincial ski championships, local curling club competition results, skating and hockey schedules, accounts of the senior hockey Camrose Maroons games, and announcements of ski clubs and lessons.[21] Aside from obvious fan interest, the detailed focus of newspapers on sport reflected the fact that so many of their readers and advertisers were involved in sponsoring sport. Newspapers worked hand in hand with businesses, community boosters, and team owners to rally support and generate excitement among both participants and onlookers.

In the longer term, the press also affirmed and reinforced codes of order in sports culture itself. Stories about great crowds of spectators turning out for respectable, high quality performances helped to develop the image of sports as family entertainment, rather than dens of gambling, drinking rowdies.[22] Prairie newspapers published portentous accounts of mighty conflicts kept in check by uniform, standardized rules, and enforcement. Readers were educated by convenient crib sheets on rules and conventions, and advice about how to join and excel in games themselves; during the 1930s, the *Albertan* ran a "Good Golf" instructional column. In July 1938, along with reports following Howard Hughes's bid to fly around the globe, the paper printed the full text of revised national association football (soccer) rules due to go into effect that year.[23] The appearance of regulations in print as they were developed helped to entrench them as intrinsic to the game and resistant to change.

Regular features on players and game rules, like those the *Lethbridge Herald* ran promoting the local Maple Leafs hockey team during the 1940s, gave fans the sense of being insiders and even experts while building their dependence on the press. A contemporary ad in the national *Star Weekly* advised that "before the whistle sounds...and after the field is cleared...games are played and replayed wherever sports fans meet. That's why you want advance news and 'follow up' of the big events."[24] The *Albertan* reached beyond the standard market profile for sports fans when it boasted that its "sport pages are read by everybody. Advertisers realize that women of all ages are just as enthusiastic sports fans as are the men—they all follow their favourite sports through the *Albertan* where all the News breaks first."[25]

During the 1920s, the Canadian mass media helped to fuel the boom in women's sports. Major newspapers and national magazines introduced columns by pioneer women sportswriters such as Alexandrine Gibb, who wrote "No Man's Land of Sports" for the *Toronto Star*. Gibb was also a key organizer of national women's sports organizations. The Edmonton Grads, consistent winners and presentable citizens, were always good copy, and the team, in turn, were publicists for the city as they travelled and were celebrated across the continent and abroad. But as the 1930s brought a backlash against sportswomen, male journalists joined a campaign for segregation and against feminization designed to head off manly behaviours such as aggressive play.[26] For most of the 1930s, coverage of women's sport dwindled in Alberta newspapers. The *Albertan*'s four pages of sport on July 11, 1938 offered only a few items on women's activities, including a track meet in Toronto, softball in BC, lawn tennis in Dublin, and the CNR Tennis Club Tournament in Calgary.[27]

While urban newspapers were engaged in building audiences for major league and pro sport, they continued to cover local athletics in the 1940s. The start of the Red Deer curling season made the city's front page along with war news in early 1944.[28] On November 14, 1945, a few days after the first Remembrance Day ceremonies following the war and as world leaders planned the UN Atomic Energy Commission, the *Advocate*'s front page led with "Red Deer Curling Club Holds Good Banquet," and announced that twelve sheets of ice would be available for the planned Central Alberta bonspiel. Ice making was also in progress for a revival of the intermediate Central Alberta Hockey League.

The paper emphasized that local men only, and no imported talent, would participate. "Twenty boys who have served overseas," some with promising hockey experience, would compete with others for a spot on the Red Deer team.[29]

After World War II, sport became ever more central to popular culture in Canada. Even in smaller local papers, professional sports gained prominence, and distinct sports sections developed. Exceptions were, as now, front-page coverage of local teams making good. With the public eye ever more intently upon them, players were more motivated to intense competition and high performance. Not only newspapers but mail-order catalogues contributed to the emergence of professional stars, who first appeared in their pages during the 1930s. As the game of stardom accelerated, the NHL introduced the system of numbering hockey sweaters for easier identification of individuals. Eaton's and Simpson's catalogues of the 1930s accordingly offered numbers to sew on copies of NHL team jerseys. Stars appeared on catalogue pages endorsing equipment into the 1950s.[30]

Sports spectatorship and news coverage rose sharply in the 1960s as cities acquired semi-pro and pro teams. In the early 1970s, when the WHA came to Edmonton, 46 per cent of the *Journal*'s sports pages were devoted solely to hockey.[31] The popular and lucrative culture of hockey is also reflected in the many consumer artifacts, from toys and player cards to advertising premiums dating to the 1960s and 1970s. The steady commodification of players and the game through the network of mass media and consumer culture meant dwindling illusions that a team or player would reside in and represent a particular community—the logical outcome of early communications links that created imaginary communities of sports fans across a continent and beyond. Nevertheless, the media continues to create narratives of competition based in symbolic ideas of place. The Toronto media, for instance, were particularly hostile toward Edmonton's sustained superiority in sport between the 1978 Commonwealth Games and the Oilers' fifth Stanley Cup in 1990.[32]

BROADCASTING

Sporting events were first broadcast in North American cities via the telegraph. In 1908, Edmonton Eskimos fans gathered at the CNR station to hear the team play Montreal for the Stanley Cup. The telegraph operator would read out text relayed from the rink: "Face Deeton gets it. Gardner takes it gives it to Glass shoots and misses. Glass crosschecked Miller and is put off. Deeton passes to Vair to Miller who loses to Gardner passes to Smith...Edmonton 4 Wanderers 4."[33] Telephones later relayed play-by-play action to distance fans, and those in the early 1920s still depended on newspaper companies to sponsor reliable links. The *Albertan* supplemented print and telephone coverage with a megaphone service from its office building. The *Calgary Herald*'s radio station, CFAC, broadcast games but the paper still installed extra phone lines for playoff games updates, and crowds of over 2,500 gathered outside the building to listen to megaphone reports of Tigers' hockey games. When the team went to the 1924 Stanley Cup playoffs in Winnipeg, plays were telephoned to a CPR telegraph operator who sent them to the newspaper offices where a staff reporter shouted "the story of [the] hockey game" to the crowd waiting in a "howling north wind."[34]

Even after cinema newsreels of major sporting events were available in provincial theatres in the 1920s,[35] fans wanted the immediate experience of the game. Newspaper offices also often provided visuals in the form of a large model of the rink or playing field above the street, with player tokens moved about manually or by electricity in response to telegram reports as the game progressed. The *Calgary Herald* operated one of these boards for large crowds watching important games such as the World Series. The *Edmonton Journal* and others did the same into the 1930s. Mike's News Stand in Edmonton also had a model hockey rink on its marquee for this purpose and employed creative techniques to replicate the action.

Fans on Jasper Avenue watched a glass screen, about ten feet square.
From incoming telegrams Mike [owner John Michaels] called the play

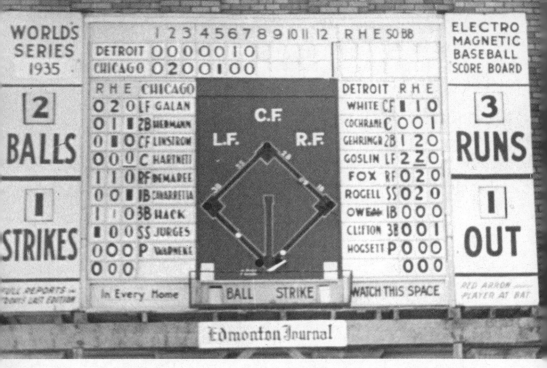

Scoreboard hung on the Edmonton Journal building for the World Series baseball game, 1935.

[CEA EA-160-842]

through a megaphone, while behind the screen Clyde [Hook of Hook Signs] and Colin [Allen of Colin Allen Electric] moved magnetic lights to illustrate the action. When the hated foes were on the attack, fans watched a red puck move toward the Eskimos' end of the ice. When the Eskimos attacked, a green puck would move. Certain players had unique styles well suited to the medium. Bullet Joe Simpson was also known as Corkscrew Joe for his twisting manner or rushing. When Joe was on the move, his progress was shown in a series of S-turns.[36]

The lively imaginations of the spectators would be supplemented by the later newsprint version. Film of events such as the Calgary Stampede were also circulated to theatres and community halls around the province.[37] The complex of sports audiences, journalists, and emerging broadcast technologies was in place.

The first radio sportscasters in the province were not usually professional journalists but fans, coaches, or players themselves. The University of Alberta campus station, CKUA, became the second radio station in Canada to carry live football coverage in 1928 when the Edmonton Eskimos played the Golden Bears. The seminary brothers of St. Joseph's and St. Stephen's Colleges announced intervarsity games, and CKUA also had lines to the university gym for basketball and hockey reports. Covering games in distant cities in the 1920s, broadcasters such as CJCA's Dick Rice still relied on telegrams to get the news home. At home, radio stations broadcast from the arenas, sometimes at centre ice or, like Rice, Jack Makepeace, and Gordon Williamson for CFRN, from the rafters.[38] Restaurant owner Jimmie Condon sponsored Calgary juvenile and junior sports including girls' basketball, hockey, lacrosse, soccer, and bowling teams in Calgary from the 1920s. He also sponsored *Jimmie's Sportlight Review*, the first commercial radio sportscast in the city, from 1929 to 1947.[39] In the late 1940s, CKUA broke new ground when it broadcast women's sports, with nursing student Shirley Stinson as the station's first female sports announcer. Stinson later became the first nurse in western Canada to earn a doctorate and become a U of A professor and a national leader in nursing education.[40] Pearl Edmanson Borgal, a program director at Calgary's CKXL radio, is also cited as possibly the first female sportscaster in Canada. Borgal was also an outstanding athlete, coach, and organizer of sports, including basketball, golf, swimming, speed skating, and hockey. In the 1960s she organized the first all-girls rodeos and became the first director of the Canadian Girls Rodeo Association. Lisa Miller got her start in broadcasting while covering University of Alberta Bears and Pandas games for the student radio station and joined CFRN in 1978 to cover the Commonwealth Games in Edmonton.[41]

Like transportation technologies and newspapers, radio was key to linking organized sport at a regional and national scale. Once live sport was more accessible, both geographically and over the airwaves,

a more spectator-oriented product could emerge and be commodi-
fied, promoted, and sold. Intense sports rivalries, already present, could
be encoded and nurtured, and hometown radio stations roused local
listeners to cheer on the home team. Although professional leagues
and American events like the World Series attracted large audiences
in Alberta, enthusiasm spilled over into participation and support
for local and minor play. When the Calgary Stampeders travelled
to Toronto for the 1948 Grey Cup game, the home town saw a sharp
increase in radio sales, repairs, and rentals. Radios were installed in
many businesses for game day, with earphones made available at every
bed in the Colonel Belcher Hospital. Only bartenders and beer servers
were forced to miss the game, to their chagrin, because liquor regulations banned radio in taverns.[42]

As Paul Rutherford reminds us, television did not create a passion
for sport but added pictures to what it had inherited from the press
and radio. In the 1920s, radio, which was then a solely private enterprise usually owned by newspaper companies, found hockey to be
popular with advertisers.[43] While broadcasting and commercial sport
were linked in a process of commodification, amateur athletics operated on small government grants for international competition and
was primarily heard via state-controlled broadcasting after the formation of the Canadian Broadcasting Corporation (CBC) in 1932. Just as
Canadian public radio in helped to knit a national net of arts awareness and political identity, it also helped to construct the idea of a
shared national popular culture through episodic broadcasts of shared
sporting pastimes. Over time, amateur sport in Canada was aligned
with messages of national unity and international prestige. Richard
Cavanagh argues that the achievements nurtured by Canadian high
performance sport policies and programs were reproduced through
CBC television productions beginning in the 1950s; amateur sport
supplied Canadian programming and generated commercial sponsorship and audiences.[44]

Alberta's first television station was Calgary's CHCT-TV, a CBC affiliate launched in October 1954. The province, with the rest of the nation,

tuned into *Hockey Night in Canada*. CFRN-TV came to Edmonton as
its CBC affiliate a couple of weeks later. Audience demand drove the
overall increase in sport coverage, and in 1958 it accounted for 10 per
cent of CBC broadcasting content. Meanwhile, pro sport developed in
the context of the commercial television industry. Private television
networks such as CTV relied on imported American productions; the
network was established in 1961 by John Bassett, who also owned the
Toronto Telegram and the Toronto Argonauts. A mid-1970s study estimated that Edmonton viewers received thirty to thirty-five hours of
sports broadcasting per week.[45]

Television itself as a medium affected the fortunes of popular sport.
In the 1960s, Marshall McLuhan noted a drop in the popularity of baseball as a mechanical-industrial age shifted into a new era of corporate
and electronic life that valued faster and more aggressive action. In
fact, football began to surpass baseball as a spectator sport in America
in the decades immediately after the wide adoption of television. One
explanation is that the long summer season and slow pace of baseball, as well as its wide field with fixed positions, made it unsuited to
television audiences, who found the fall and winter entertainment of
football worked well with zoom lenses, slow motion, and instant replay
as the camera closely followed action across the field.[46] The development of television and audiovisual equipment in the 1950s and 1960s
also offered new opportunities to monitor athletes and events; in 1964,
for example, a CBC videotape was used to clear a BC skiing competitor
of a disqualifying charge.[47]

Canadian Football League coverage began in 1952 when the league
was very popular; the next year, the Grey Cup was carried live on a
CBC network that extended to Toronto, Montreal, and Ottawa, with
film flown to Sudbury. In 1954 the Grey Cup final received the highest
radio and television coverage of any sports event in Canadian history.
The CBC estimated that 80 per cent of the nation's 900,000 television
sets were tuned to the game. However, only ten cities of twenty-two in
Canada received the live broadcast; for others, including Winnipeg and
"a jubilant city of Edmonton,"[48] whose team had won, Royal Canadian

Air Force jets were intended to deliver immediately-processed film of the game for later broadcast; they were grounded by snow and the film arrived by commercial aircraft that evening. Prime Minister Louis St. Laurent delivered a pre-game speech on the value of the Grey Cup to Canadian unity.[49]

The survival of the CFL today is tied to television revenues. From the 1970s on, cable and satellite gave exposure to national and international sports events, including large amateur competitions. At Edmonton's 1978 Commonwealth Games, over 600 media representatives outnumbered the 220 athletes, who were watched by approximately 20,000 on site and many more on television. The 1978 Commonwealth Games in Edmonton furthered the trend toward the alignment of state-based high performance sport with complex television production. The CBC, for instance, drew an audience of eleven million for certain Games events. CBC revenues for 1978-1979 included $506 million from Commonwealth Games-related advertising.[50]

Television coverage also helped to transform once elite sports like golf and tennis into popular pastimes and later brought attention to women's rodeo. After the 1994 Olympics, the popularity of figure skating rose swiftly; the 1996 World Figure Skating Championships drew a TV audience of 177 million viewers and set attendance records. It was the largest international sporting event held in Edmonton. The new popularity of lacrosse in Canada—participation increased by nearly 30 per cent between 1999 and 2001—is attributed in part to National Lacrosse League television exposure.[51]

Television did not at first alter the nature of hockey, though it may have at first discouraged the violence that disturbed many viewers. After fuelling a rise of interest in hockey in the 1950s, television later influenced its decline; as wide exposure made the sport newly profitable and the television lens magnified its symbolic and spectacular resonance, league expansion led to a decline in quality during the 1970s (though there have been revivals since). Television stepped into the gap with alternatives, including golf, baseball, and football.[52]

The success of curling as a spectator sport lies partly in the fact that so many viewers are also players, and partly in increased television exposure in recent years. In 1954 a record 32,000 spectators watched Matt Baldwin compete live in the Edmonton Brier. Almost ten times that many people attended the 2005 Tim Hortons Brier in Edmonton, but the television broadcast drew almost six million viewers. The final game alone drew the largest curling audience since numbers were first tracked in 1989. Other major events, such as the women's Scott Tournament of Hearts, also attract hundreds of thousands of fans, both live and broadcast. The 2005 Ford men's world championship, where Edmonton's Randy Ferbey rink won a sixth Brier title, attracted more viewers than most NHL games.[53]

Mass media can link fans at a distance to the fortunes of their home team or heroes, which helps to sustain a sense of identification and ownership—an echo of the community basis of early organized sport. But, as Richard Gruneau and David Whitson demonstrate, professional sport today is integrated in the North American entertainment economy, linked to strategies of transnational consumption; commercial pressures to standardize consumption have helped to erode regional sporting identities over the past century. Television played an important part in the delocalizing trend as media owners exploited sports' marketing potential within a complex of international leisure industries and converging media platforms. The Internet furthers mergers between media and entertainment companies that package sport with other online offerings. Today's league product is sold not only to fans but also to media companies who purchase broadcasting rights, communities that build facilities and support clubs, and corporations such as sponsors or owners. All of these processes work against the traditional notion that sport is based in place and identity with regionally distinct sports cultures.[54] At the same time, regional sportswriters and broadcasters keep the home flame burning with close attention to players and events at the local level, with journalists often embodying in their careers the close networks of ties between community, junior, minor, major, and professional level sport.

Amateur sports, apart from the Olympics, are often honoured and memorialized in halls of fame but typically ignored by commercial broadcasters. As a public broadcaster, the CBC to some extent sustains coverage of amateur sport while depending on NHL broadcasts for survival of its television service. But as we become more alienated from wealthy, imported players and as franchises go bankrupt, many predict the decline of pro sports. As the industry that sells sport as entertainment creates passive fans who identify with a particular star athlete rather than with a community, the game becomes just a game, lacking loyalties and the necessary illusion of connection. As we have seen, these are the logical outcomes of processes with deep roots in the history of professional sport. Whether they will eventually erode even Alberta hockey fans' tight grip on the ideal of resident NHL teams remain to be seen.

GATEKEEPERS AND CHEERLEADERS

SPORTS JOURNALISTS

Journalists are the poets, town criers, and messengers between athletes, spectators, and the wider networks of sport culture. Teams themselves commonly control media access, while local dailies depend more on the major franchises than do broadcasters. The cliché of newspaper sportswriters haunting the locker room is therefore based in some reality, as they often become close to teams and coaches, travelling with them and celebrating their victories. In general, though, broadcasters have tended to be boosters of the games and players that they covered, while newspaper writers have been the main source of critical journalism, provoking and challenging owners and managers in ways that would be unacceptable in television, where sport is treated not as news but commercial entertainment. Canadian writers such as Stephen Brunt, Roy MacGregor, and Cam Cole are best known for efforts to foster an objective public understanding of the economic realities of team sport in the 1990s and later.[55]

Journalists often become identified with a particular sport, fostering its growth and profile. Dwayne Erickson knew nothing about rodeo in 1958 when Hal Pawson, sports editor for the *Edmonton Journal*, assigned him to cover an event. Erickson went on to report on rodeo for the *Edmonton Journal*, the *Winnipeg Free Press*, the *Edmonton Sun*, the *Calgary Sun*, CBC-TV, the Canadian Rodeo News and, finally, the *Calgary Herald*. He also spent five years as manager of media relations for the 1978 Commonwealth Games, of which Pawson was a committee member. In 2008, he was inducted into the Alberta Sports Hall of Fame. He remarked that the honour put "rodeo on the same footing with all the other sports, so it's kind of overwhelming....It's really, really nice."[56]

Whether in print or over the air, the strong connection between certain journalists and local teams or particular sports can transform a sportswriter or broadcaster into a prominent community figure. Ted Knight, a Calgary firefighter who was the live announcer for all major city sports activities from 1905 to 1935, also served as Stampede marshal.[57] Don Mackay, a sports commentator with radio CJCJ in Lethbridge, later became mayor of Calgary. Joe Carbury started football and hockey broadcasting in Medicine Hat in 1948 but attributes his high public profile mainly to his longstanding job as a Calgary Stampede announcer. Frank Ryan has covered most amateur sports in most regions of the province, joining the *Red Deer Advocate* in 1976 and incidentally serving as radio hockey announcer, official scorekeeper for senior basketball and fastball leagues, Special Olympics chair, and Lions Speed Skating Club director.[58]

Occasionally journalists would become part of the story. Pawson was at the Edmonton Gardens in June 1960 when a boxing match, featuring champion Dick Tiger and Wilf Greaves, for the British Empire middleweight championship was declared a draw before 3,360 spectators. As Pawson and boxing reporter Tom Harris joined the congestion toward the exits, they passed the boxing commission table and noticed that the scorecards did not tally with the results; when Pawson requested the scorecards be rechecked, an emergency meeting concluded the original decision invalid, and Tiger was declared the loser; the press was informed an hour after the fight was over.[59]

Many sportswriters and broadcasters are particularly involved in local minor and amateur sports. Consequently, there are several public facilities named after journalists, such as Henry Viney, who played, promoted, and refereed sports, including officiating at all the major Grads competitions. Viney also covered sports from radio in the 1920s to television broadcasting at CFCN in Calgary.[60] The significant role of such journalists in community sport is recognized in the Alberta Sports Hall of Fame's Bell Memorial Award. Some members, such as Ernie Afaganis, have also been inducted into national halls of fame. Afaganis, who like Viney came from Lethbridge, was a broadcaster with CFRN and CBC in Edmonton, prominent in CFL coverage from 1955 to 1980. He also covered international games from the 1960s to the 1980s, as well as the Calgary Stampede and NHL playoffs. Afaganis has also devoted much time to supporting amateur sports and charitable groups.[61]

Cecil (Tiger) Goldstick exemplifies the community-minded sports journalist. He was a sportswriter for the *Edmonton Bulletin* in the late 1940s and a trainer or coach with professional teams including the Eskimos baseball and football clubs and the Flyers hockey team. The role of trainer may not have been his best. Terry Jones tells the story of one injured Eskimos player in 1949 calling out, "Don't touch me, Tiger... This one is serious."[62] Strongly dedicated to amateur sports, he started the first peewee hockey league in the city in 1938, coached and refereed various minor sports, ran a regular feature on amateur athletes on CFRN, and founded several charitable programs including Sports Central, which supplies equipment to children. In 1966, Goldstick became a sportscaster with CFRN radio and television. He received the Order of Canada in 1990 and Goldstick Park was named after him in 1986. Goldstick died in 2006.[63]

Probably the best-known sportscaster from Alberta is Ron MacLean of Red Deer, who began broadcasting Calgary Flames games on CFAC-TV in 1984 before becoming a national household name as *Hockey Night in Canada* host with Don Cherry on CBC television. MacLean is dedicated to developing grassroots hockey, hosting the annual Hockey Day in Canada program, and refereeing for the Canadian Amateur Hockey Association. He also "proudly flaunts the Red Deer connection…During Olympic broadcasts he's been known to welcome the…town's Games athletes into his studio roost, and display the front page of the *Red Deer Advocate* newspaper."[64]

Writers and broadcasters who specialize in a certain sport or team often become identified with it. Peter Gzowski's interest in the Edmonton Oilers produced a romantic, reverent treatment of the game and the team in *The Game of Our Lives*. Terry Jones, who became a sportswriter in Edmonton in the 1960s, has covered major international events since the 1970s, but he has most consistently chronicled the Oilers. Rod Phillips, known as The Voice of the Edmonton Oilers, announced a "history-making hockey team" as they won their first Stanley Cup championship in 1984. After calling 3,542 games, he retired in 2011.[65]

Ed Whalen, news and sports director at CHCT-TV in Calgary in the 1950s, became identified with Stu Hart's *Stampede Wrestling* show as a longtime announcer. He was later the telecaster for the Calgary Flames and renowned for charity work in the city. He was also omnipresent in other radio and newspaper sports coverage.[66] Bryan Hall is another well-known Edmonton sports broadcaster as the longtime voice of the Edmonton Eskimos as well as, at various times, the Flyers, Oil Kings, and Oilers hockey teams. Hall has commented that "controversy is the lifeblood of sports. You have to make it interesting for the fan." An increasingly intense and polarized fan response indicates his success. Hall officially retired in 2009.[67] Wes Montgomery, another popular and colourful public figure, began his radio career in Peace River, Lloydminster, and Saskatoon, joining Edmonton's CHED in 1964.

He regularly hosted football dinners and events, did the Eskimos play-by-play for three years, and, for a time, was the team's public address announcer. Montgomery died in 2005. An award in his name providing an educational bursary for an amateur football player was awarded for the first time to Tristan Jones of the Edmonton Wildcats in 2007.[68]

Art Ward was a radio announcer in Calgary during the late 1930s, joined Edmonton's CFRN and became known for his coverage of Flyers games and baseball from Renfrew Park. Ward was CKUA's first sports director in 1947. Sportswriter Don "Buckets" Fleming of the *Edmonton Journal* is best known for curling coverage starting in the 1950s; he was the first to start keeping game statistics and was inducted into the Canadian Curling Hall of Fame in 2005. Fleming was known for his larger-than-life character, including a reputation for heroic levels of alcohol consumption. He once asked John Ducey about standards of decorum in the new Renfrew Park press box and was told, "There'll be none of that in here. You do your drinking elsewhere." He covered horse racing for the *Edmonton Journal* for almost forty years beginning in the 1950s. Upon retirement he became a track publicist and wrote articles for the racing programs under the pseudonyms such as Shudda Haddim and Willie Ketchum. Fleming became a member of the Canadian Horse Racing Hall of Fame.[69]

Paradoxically, although sports journalism has churned out over a century's worth of information about Alberta events, many athletes and teams, famous in their day, have been forgotten. This is partly due to the ephemeral nature of sporting activity and results, which means that yesterday's newsprint or tape quickly seems irrelevant. What is available has been subject to the bias against popular culture that prevailed in historical scholarship until the latter twentieth century. Late-twentieth- and early-twenty-first-century scholars are now interested in sports archives, and contemporary writers, bloggers, and filmmakers often take sport as a popular focus. Hall of fame type museums remain one of the major mass media of sport history, usually appealing to a converted audience of sports fans. Such institutions, of which there are over 300 in Canada, emerged with the escalating media coverage and commercialization of sport, and as social and economic change accelerated in the twentieth century, these kinds institutions became, in part, "responses to the need for collective and personal nostalgia at times of social dislocation and identity crisis." Typical displays organize familiar narratives of stars, victory, and achievement around heroic images and objects, representing established interests such as the NHL. According to Bruce Kidd, however, the selection and contents of displays can omit much of the actually nuanced, diverse histories.[70]

For instance, only 13 per cent of Canada's sports halls of fame inductees are women.[71] At the Alberta Sports Hall of Fame as of 2007, women inductees accounted for less than one-quarter of the facility's represented athletes, and only one female journalist is included. Without concluding that this constitutes deliberate oversight, since conditions of selection vary, some omissions are curious. Arthur Skitch, a member of championship teams in multiple Edmonton sports, who coached girls' track and field for fifteen years among numerous other achievements, is included; his daughter Edith, a record-setting track champion, is not. Member Ken McAuley, considered the "best all-round athlete Edmonton ever produced," played on the Flyers and coached junior teams, including the Oil Kings. Absent is his wife, Mildred Warwick McAuley, who played for the All-American Girls Professional Baseball League during World War II and later was the first women in Edmonton to coach little league baseball.[72] Charlotte Dawes and Norma Chiddy, to name only two of the women track athletes renowned in their day, are also absent, although Chiddy was inducted into the Wetaskiwin Sports Hall of Fame in 2006.[73] However, Helen Nicol, a multi-sport athlete who excelled in softball, baseball, hockey, speed skating, and golf for more than forty years from the 1930s on is present. As a softball pitcher she played for teams in both Edmonton and Calgary, as well as one in Chicago and the All-American Girls Professional Baseball League from 1943 to 1954.[74]

The gender imbalance logically suggests the predominant number of males on selection committees. Halls of fame also typically rely on nominations from the community. At least part of the problem must simply be the relatively larger mass of records available on male athletes and produced by male journalists. The same is true in comparing the vast amount of central Canadian sport history to the relative paucity of that amassed for Alberta. Regional institutions like the Alberta Sports Hall of Fame and Museum can play a crucial role in preserving the public memory of regional and local cultures, in part as starting points for further investigation.

⋮ SPONSORSHIP AND MARKETING

BEER AND BEYOND

Athletes, facilities, and events are the fodder of sports publicity but also serve as media for commercial messages. On both amateur and professional levels, sponsors have looked to profit by directly advertising products and through the indirect benefits of public goodwill for sports teams. Most have also been motivated simply by community spirit and passion for sport. The Lethbridge baseball team Houk's Savages, a "simon-pure club that one year won the Alberta championship," was organized around 1906 by George Houk.[75] He had been a frontier whiskey trader, stagecoach driver, and Pony Express rider before turning respectable liquor merchant in Lethbridge, but he was retired by the time he sponsored the team. His background and contemporary attitudes were reflected in the team's name, as Houk had married a First Nations woman and lived with the local Blood people most of his time.[76] Larger companies also supplied equipment or facilities in the interests of employee morale and loyalty. The CNR hotels offered tennis courts and golf course access for employees in the 1920s and 1930s and sponsored local skiing and climbing organizations. These sponsorships were instituted, ideally, to develop tourist services and attract more people to the mountains.[77]

From the 1930s to 1950s, businesses such as agriculture, oil, liquor, and car dealerships sponsored numerous industrial and mercantile leagues. Edmonton meat-packing plant Gainers hosted the Superiors hockey club, provincial senior champs in 1931, 1933, and 1935, and won the 1933 international championships. Many hockey players played soccer in the summer, and several had successful careers in both sports. James Graham, who was a member of the Edmonton Nationals soccer team that made the western final in 1929, played centre for the Superiors since 1925. He played in the 1932–1933 European tournament and coached the Mercurys hockey team to their win in 1950.[78]

Sponsored teams of the period included the Waterloo Mercurys and Superstein Chevrolet (automobiles), the Calgary Buffaloes (beer), and Calgary Purity 99 (gasoline). The Lethbridge Commercial Basketball League had teams named after furniture stores, the local gas company, and Imperial Motors. The Alberta Wheat Pool supported a team called the Wheat Kernels in the 1920s, and local merchants supplied baseball uniforms for teams in Jasper in the 1950s. The Alberta Oilers' 1950s hockey team colours of blue and orange were calculated to win sponsorship from the Gulf Western oil company, whose logo used those colours, but the deal was cancelled when the company realized that the game was already identified with rival Imperial Oil through *Hockey Night in Canada*. The Oilers kept the colours anyway.[79]

Although mercantile league teams were supported by businesses, strict amateur status forbade any profit taking or player remuneration. But the nature of sponsorship was loosely interpreted at the time, and it was common for commercial firms to cover expenses in return for advertising. In 1938, the Canadian Amateur Basketball Association (CABA) complained that Calgary businesses had sponsored women's basketball teams in order to control players' "freedom to move from team to team."[80] Calgary's managers argued in response that the maximum annual sponsorship of about $150 per team allowed for negligible influence, if any. The Edmonton Grads were the only amateur basketball team not sponsored by commercial interests since they derived funds from paying audiences while "providing the main finances of the Canadian Association through a percentage of the gate."[81] It seems that the CABA was pleased to accept financial support from amateur teams while protesting their right to seek financial support elsewhere.

Relying largely on attendance for financial support was not tenable in the long term. In July of 1938, CABA established a Senior A women's basketball series in an attempt to introduce more serious competition for the Grads. The organization also considered a resolution to allow players to be compensated for time lost from work during playoffs. At the time, Percy Page proposed to the CABA that "any team challenging Grads for the Canadian women's title be required to pay part of their expenses to Edmonton should the series be played here." If competition was good enough to attract gate revenue, visiting teams would be reimbursed.[82] In September 1938, Page announced that poor attendance at Underwood Trophy games in Edmonton threatened survival of the team. He feared that it "might have to disband because it is just too good" and cash customers were "not getting a thrill anymore from watching Grads breeze through to victory after victory."[83] The first game attracted 1,672 cash customers and the Grads won 75-25; only 512 attended the second game, "not enough to gain sufficient finances for the Grads to carry on."[84]

The convoluted nature of sponsorship practices is in part explained by the status of players. Most senior amateurs (and even professionals and semi-pros) expected little financial reward. Future premier Peter Lougheed made only enough for university tuition and spending money during his year with the Edmonton Eskimos football team in the 1940s; a typical baseball player of the early 1950s received a salary of a room and $200 per month. But larger companies could sponsor their teams indirectly by giving the players jobs. Art Maguire, president of the Calgary Exhibition and Stampede that sponsored the team, told Stampeders hockey players in 1946 that "you who have played so well will be able to give the same fine effort to the companies for which you work."[85] This was often a mixed blessing. Jack Altman was one of the imported players for the Lethbridge baseball team in the 1950s; after a day or two at his new job of lifting heavy boulders he quit, saying,

"I don't think I can pitch well if I keep doing this." Another player remarked that he "learned quite a lot about grain elevators." Some Granum players worked for league head George Wesley on his ranch, eating in the cookhouse with the cowboys.[86]

Local papers followed the development of teams in great detail and emphasized their significance to civic life. In 1945 the *Lethbridge Herald* reported approvingly that members of the Maple Leafs hockey team were not interested in professional careers and had all been offered jobs in the town. Therefore, "all hockey-spirited citizens are urged to do what they can to find a room for these players."[87] (The same plea went out for newly arrived Edmonton Eskimos players in fall of 2007, though the problem at that time was that the economic boom in the province had caused a severe housing shortage.)

Tax benefits have, at least in part, been an important impetus for community sports involvement by corporations, including the Calgary Brewing and Malting Company. From the turn of the century, the company supported sports for men, women, and youth in the city, introducing the Brewery Trophy in 1905 to "promote and create an interest in the game of Baseball" and incorporating the Calgary Buffalo Athletic Association (CBAA) in 1942 "to promote, foster and encourage athletics, sports and recreation." At first offered for any organized team in the North-West Territories, provision was made that the trophy would apply only to the province of Alberta after the upcoming inauguration of the province.[88] In the 1920s, an influx of soldiers to a city military base resulted in "intensive sporting activities," and the brewery financed a baseball park. From 1943 onward the CBAA focused on hockey, including a team of mostly professional ex-hockey players called the Calgary Buffaloes, which was intended to raise funds for the "Milk for Britain" program. The team won the Western Canada Intermediate title, coached young players, and developed the CBAA hockey program. The idea was that ballpark revenues would fund hockey development, but by war's end the hockey program, which enjoyed what some considered "an overly generous attitude toward the supply of materials and playing equipment," overshadowed the previously high local interest in baseball.[89] Meanwhile, the Calgary Brewing network of city boosters held regular Malt Room meetings on sports sponsorship to help develop a "corps of salesmen" for the city. (The meetings ceased in the 1960s when the Alberta Liquor Control Board imposed restrictions on the use of the site for imbibing.)[90]

The CBAA was the platform for developing many successful minor, senior, and professional hockey players. In an unofficial battle of the breweries in 1948, the CBAA Junior B hockey team lost a Junior A playoff against the semi-pro Sick's Lethbridge Native Sons. A new Junior A Buffaloes team formed, then lost the 1949 Memorial Cup. Ambitious to expand and succeed, the team began to import and pay some professional players. A flourishing senior (later professional) Buffaloes team was now competing for spectators with junior teams in Calgary. In 1963 the organization helped to incorporate the Alberta Junior Hockey League with five clubs from Calgary and Lethbridge. The junior Buffaloes won the AJHL title each of their first three seasons but, each time, were defeated for the Memorial Cup playoffs by the Edmonton Oil Kings. By 1967, the Toronto Maple Leafs were sponsors of the junior program, drawing accusations that the CBAA organization had become simply a farm operation for the pros.[91]

The CBAA's operating losses steadily increased after its first years. Revenue of almost $40,000 in 1945-1946 yielded a minimal surplus, and both Association and Junior A hockey continued to lose money. After a total 1966 operating loss of $225,832.83, the brewery wrote off a similarly large 1967 advance to the CBAA, and the fixed assets of the stadium and its lands were sold to developers Eau Claire Estates for $420,000. The CBAA reverted to an amateur operation and community teams took over hockey programs.[92]

Sick's Breweries sponsored a 1946 Lethbridge entry in the Western Canada Senior Hockey League, coached by Dave "Sweeney" Schriner. Born in Calgary, Schriner was a junior hockey star for teams including the Calgary Bronks. While playing NHL hockey in the 1930s, he had become "one of the greatest sports figures in Canada," according to the *Lethbridge Herald*.[93] The Maple Leafs quickly became popular; a game

Dave "Sweeney" Schriner, Lethbridge Maple Leafs coach, 1948. Photo: Eric Bland.

against the Stampeders outsold all others in Calgary that season. Fans offering as much as ten dollars for seventy-five-cent seats found few takers. The Leafs also had a hometown booster club, which held fundraisers including parades and N H L game film nights. The Drumheller Miners hockey team had its own booster club in the 1940s, sponsoring fundraising events such as Dominion Day sports meets. Profits beyond those needed by the team would go to charities and war funds.[94]

As well as the Maple Leafs and the Native Sons, Sick's backed juvenile and midget teams. The Sick's Lethbridge brewery was the foundation of a profitable business empire in western Canada and the United States, later acquired by Molson. Emil Sick was a tireless supporter of local sport teams everywhere he lived and conducted business over the years. Chairman Sick urged the community to support local junior and minor hockey by developing training facilities to avoid importing players. Sick's was the main corporate sponsor for the new Lethbridge sports centre in 1949, donating $100,000 toward the Fritz Sick Memorial Arena as well as funding a swimming pool. As Sick put it, "we are in hockey in a big way. We intend to do everything in our power to make Lethbridge one of Canada's best known hockey centres."[95] A principal goal, which was never achieved, was to bring the Memorial Cup for major junior hockey to Lethbridge. Larger companies were generally uninterested in amateur sport sponsorship, but in the period leading to the 1976 Montreal Olympics, private capital (especially brewery companies) suddenly paid more attention to amateur athletics as its profit potential emerged. When Molson became a major sponsor of the Olympic Games, Labatt began to sponsor Canadian Interuniversity Athletic Union athletes.[96]

According to some British sports historians, an "emergent symbiosis between supporting sport and consuming alcohol...further entrenched the masculinity of sporting culture and the exclusion of women from that culture."[97] This argument can certainly be made for North America as well, but in Alberta, in the first half of the twentieth century, breweries happily associated themselves with women's sport. The Calgary Brewing and Malting Co. supported a basketball team

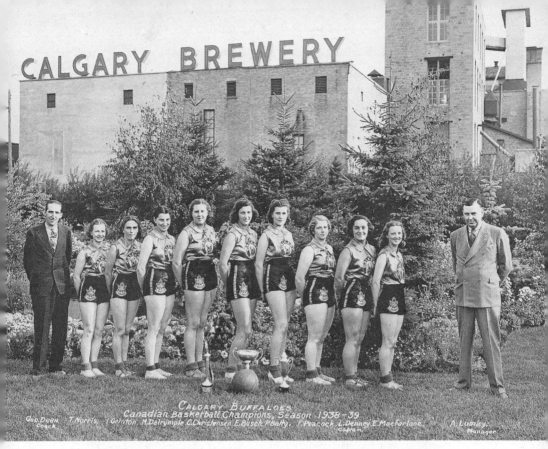

CALGARY BREWERY

CALGARY BUFFALOES
Canadian Basketball Champions, Season 1938-39

Geo.Dean. T.Norris, I.Grinton. M.Dalrymple O.Christensen E.Busch P.Baily, F.Peacock L.Denney E.MacFarlane. A.Lumley.
Coach Captain. Manager

Calgary Buffaloes ca. 1939, the year in which they won the Canadian basketball championship.
[GA NA-3164-389]

called the Buffaloes after the central image in the company's logo. In Lethbridge, packed houses followed four different women's teams. In the 1960s, with laws against liquor advertising, government agency the Alberta Liquor Control Board ruled in 1964 that the Seagram Company must remove its name from the promotion for a sponsored art show. Sports columnist Gorde Hunter pointed out the threat to sport sponsorship if companies like Seagram (golf), the Scotch Whiskey Association (curling), Schenley (football) and even the Grey Cup, after which an Alberta distillery had named a brand of rye, were forced to withdraw their names from all public events and promotions.[98]

Tobacco producers were also important sponsors of both men's and women's teams until Canada's Tobacco Act prohibited sports sponsorship in 2003. In the late 1930s, Reynolds Tobacco donated a trophy for competitive ladies' softball in the Grande Prairie region, although no financial support is recorded.[99] With more substantial contributions, Macdonald Tobacco was long associated with curling, sponsoring the Brier from 1927 until 1979 and the Canadian women's national championship, called the Lassie after the company logo, in the 1970s. And tobacco company ads were prominent in rinks and arenas throughout Alberta.

Local market factors always influenced sponsorship choices. In 1949 the *Edmonton Journal* discouraged any Alberta city from joining a new International Senior Basketball League, arguing that the game "hasn't been worth a quarter at the box office hereabouts since the days of the Edmonton Grads...Basketball has terrific competition from hockey in northern Alberta...[and] in Lethbridge for...many years now."[100] Thirty years later, the Alberta Dusters of Lethbridge became the only pro basketball team in the country when a group of local businessmen imported it from the United States. The team folded in 1987 due to insufficient fan interest and inadequate funding. Media contracts are one of the most important considerations in fielding a pro or semi-pro team today, and in 2004 the American Basketball Association started the Calgary Drillers team, made confident by a deal giving the league several major outlets. Still, the Drillers folded in 2005. The following year, the Edmonton Rush and Calgary Roughnecks lacrosse clubs entered the Pork Sports program in a marketing partnership with Alberta Pork. Building on what it promotes as a natural connection between sports, food, and entertainment, the program aimed to "build relationships with sports audiences" and "reach out to people who value the healthy, active lifestyle" by advertising and selling pork products at sporting events.[101] A more negative association of pork with sport relates to the corporate subsidizing of professional sport by all levels of government, which is discussed in the next chapter.

Ira Gilmour at the Grande Prairie Stampede, 1927. The saddle blanket has an advertisement on it for Hoot Gibson's show. [SPRA 0024.01.09]

Sponsorship has been crucial to professional sport in almost every realm of activity. Ranch owners and international entertainment impresarios commercialized rodeo across the west. While endorsed saddle blankets and arena boards were a form of early mass advertising media, promotional photographs and print ads played an important role in shaping the public image of the sport. American merchants linked cigarettes, liquor, and other products with the romantic figure of Wild West individualism, authenticity, and physical power. The 1966 GWG ad was of Harold Mandeville from Calgary, the previous year's All-Around Canadian Champion Cowboy. GWG's appeals to professional cowboys as upstanding family men extended to women's rodeo wear as well, but, despite the fact that rodeo drew serious female

competitors, marketing to women stressed aesthetics. The 1967
Canadian Girls Rodeo Association program ad reported that the wife of
pictured rodeo champion Tom Bews "likes the smart styling of G W G
[jeans]," while the hero himself was concerned with the toughness of
the fabric.[102] Other ads in rodeo publications suggested the cowboy's
fondness for beer, though one in the 1953 Edmonton Rodeo Souvenir
Program for Orange Crush soda took the riders more seriously, reading,
"Get the healthy habit!...the only soft drink endorsed for use of athletes
by the Sports College of Canada."[103]

In 1945, an American rodeo manager wrote to promote his acts
to the newly-established Edmonton Exhibition Association's (E E A)
annual rodeo. Lisogar Stampede Shows offered top Canadian and
American cowboys as well as wholesome western entertainment,
including Tex Ritter and a "girl trick rider," with "no gambling games
or any such connections."[104] Edmonton Rodeo advertising that year
aimed wide across the province in posters, banners, press, radio, theatre
slides, and buttons. Despite such ambitious promotional campaigns,
E E A director James Paul admitted that the 1950 rodeo was strictly
an agricultural show with chuckwagon races, since no appropriate
grounds yet existed.[105]

But in June 1951, Canadian Stampede Managers Association president Herman Linder sent Paul a list of "the boys," the "cream" of the
selection, signed for the Edmonton show. These included Cam Lansdell
of Turner Valley, Canadian Saddle Riding Champion runner-up for the
North American title of 1950, and Fred Gladstone, Canadian Champion
Calf Roper and "one of the very progressive, efficient and prosperious
[sic] Indians of the Blood Reserve."[106] Concerning his competition,
Linder added that "if some little punkin roller show advertises that
they are going to have something they are not going to have there
isn't much we can do about it, they are not fooling anybody but themselves."[107] The E E A also negotiated with Lisogar for appearances by
celebrity cowboys Hopalong Cassidy and Roy Rogers.[108]

In 1955 Buster Ivory of the Rodeo Cowboys Association (R C A)
complained to Paul that rodeo had become over-commercialized. The

RCA worried that the public, under a barrage of arena advertising and other messages, "can but think of rodeo less as a sport and more as a show."[109] But rodeo continued to be promoted as serious athletic competition; the 1958 Edmonton Rodeo of Champions press party invitation list included sports reporters for all major local broadcasting outlets and newspapers.[110] Around this time, rodeo sponsorship came mainly from companies directly involved in farming, ranching, and tourism. The Edmonton Exhibition Association's 1961 rodeo program attracted ads from the Alberta Wheat Pool, Calgary Power, the Palliser Hotel, Briggs Furrier and Tannery, Riley and McCormick, and others. GWG donated the Canadian All-Around Championship trophy.

During the 1960s, a wider range of sponsors appears to have recognized the appeal of rodeo. In the mid-1960s, these included various independent merchants and broadcaster CKXL as well as the Calgary Brewing and Malt Company, Calgary Tourist and Convention Association, ranch suppliers, and cowboy singer Wilf Carter. In 1968 sponsors included Lakeview Texaco, White Knight Cleaners, Calgary Co-op, Bob's Tire Service, Jennings Drilling, Simpsons Sears, Lewis Stationery, and the Bank of Nova Scotia. CFCN television donated the Canadian Rookie Trophy of the Year. Events in the 1970s and early 1980s were sponsored by department stores and malls, car dealerships, home builders, liquor companies, and media outlets as well as more equine- and bovine-oriented businesses. The trend suggests the recognition of rodeo as an economic engine for host communities beyond the immediate rodeo audience. The Canadian Finals Rodeo generates significant economic returns of more than $50 million to the local community. In 2006, for example, the competition yielded $60 million in economic spinoffs for the host city. Nearly forty of the fifty-eight professional rodeos in the country in 2010 were in Alberta.[111]

Contemporary sponsors benefit from the sport world's huge audiences and defined market segments. While "measuring the results of sports marketing is like trying to nail jelly to a wall," the late twentieth and early twenty-first centuries have witnessed a dramatic rise in corporate spending.[112] Through ambush marketing, a company associates itself with an event to capitalize on its publicity value without actually purchasing advertising or sponsorship. This occurred during the 2001 International Association of Athletics Federations World's championships in Edmonton when a local escort service called itself "World's Class" and copied the distinctive illustration and typographic style of the official event advertising.[113] These ads were quickly quashed, yet during every playoff season hockey teams and stars are invoked in advertisements by local companies with no direct connection to them.

Naming trends are evidence of the growing significance of company sponsorship in professional sport. As curling experienced strong commercial growth from the 1960s on, more national competitions were named after large corporations such as Tim Hortons (the Brier) and Scott (Tournament of Hearts.) Historically, publicly owned arenas and stadiums were named after location or symbol (the Edmonton Gardens), a founding individual (John Ducey Park, McMahon Stadium), or the main tenant. The park named after Ducey, Edmonton's "Mr. Baseball," became TELUS Field in the 1990s. After more than $37 million in renovations in 1994, the Calgary Saddledome became the Pengrowth Saddledome.

In the late twentieth century, private investment trumped the right of public funders to honour public legacies. From 1990 to 1998, the number of facilities in the NHL named after corporations rose from under 5 per cent to over 50 per cent. Companies such as Skyreach and Rexall expect that their names on a city's pro hockey arena will associate them with the team's hoped-for survival. In Red Deer, WHL team the Rebels play in the ENMAX Centrium, the largest indoor venue in central Alberta; the Junior B Vipers still use the arena named after the city. The up-for-sale nature of naming rights means that, in the twenty-first century, all glory is transient. The city of St. Albert put the naming rights to the Mark Messier and Troy Murray Arenas up for sale in 2006. The facilities were named in 1992 to honour the players who had lived in the city and played for the local junior team, but that history was not sufficient to pay for a new $42.7-million leisure centre to incorporate both rinks.[114]

Benefiting from the cultural capital of sports fame, some journalists and team owners have built public profiles in business and politics. Percy Page built a successful public career in part due to his high profile with the Grads. Edmonton Oilers owner Peter Pocklington ran for office in the 1980s, commenting that there was "no better marketing vehicle in this country than Gretzky and this hockey club."[115] For individual elite athletes, of course, endorsements are lucrative incentives. Alberta audiences may be particularly aware of Wayne Gretzky's high post-retirement commercial profile. Occasionally, star power can raise the profile of a sport and generate endorsement deals. When Kurt Browning became world men's figure skating champion in 1989, male skaters were taken more seriously. Browning was the first to win endorsement contracts with major corporations such as Toshiba and Coca-Cola. As the "son of an Alberta rancher and trail guide, Browning's cowboy background was rarely left unmentioned by journalists and television commentators. He was presented as the boy-next-door...an athlete who, had he been bigger, might have had a shot at the NHL."[116]

The women's World Cup soccer final in 1999 drew forty million television viewers, more than the men's games. But most women continue to struggle for sponsors and media coverage, lagging well behind those for professional male athletes even as their sports often attract more athletes and spectators. Exceptions tend to be predictable; assuming the common factor of high performance in their careers, a narrow range of selection criteria seems to prevail. Alberta-based speed skater Catriona Le May Doan won a record fifteen medals at the 1998 Olympics and is also considered "highly marketable" due to her looks and personality.[117] Photogenic young Albertans Jamie Sale and David Pelletier have smiled in tooth-whitening product ads since winning the figure skating pairs medal at the 2002 Olympics. Cyclist Lori-Ann Muenzer, thirty-eight years old at the time and an out lesbian, was

turned down for sponsorship by sports marketing giant I M G before
the 2004 Olympics and was told to "come back when you win a gold
medal."[118] But Muenzer has struggled for sponsorship and visibility
even after her gold medal win. Though this may in part have been
due to the relatively low profile of her sport in Canada, Diane Jones
Konihowski criticized the Canadian Cycling Association itself for not
"promoting [Muenzer] and putting her out there in such a way that we
can get 10,000 kids out...Medals inspire and we need to get Canadians
inspired."[119]

CONCLUSION

Sport storytelling is highly selective, offering a "rain upon the senses"
of words and images of high-profile professional men's team or elite-
level sport, while amateur, minor, or women's sport barely requires an
umbrella. Elite sport performance, as a commodity in an exchange
society, continues to animate the leisure sphere with the values of
economic production. There remains a "marked disconnect between
sports as it is experienced through television, talk radio, and the sports
pages, and the recreational pursuits of those who do not possess world
class, big league skills."[120]

But whether we are participants or consumers, the phenomena
of sport have carried a lot of social and cultural weight on basic
bones of statistics and scores. The mass media have influenced, if
not directly shaped, the performance of this body of cultural meanings and symbols as it has made sports culture a part of everyday life.
As the mass media have worked to construct sport as an object of rapt
attention, sport itself has served as a medium for publicizing selected
aspects, and assets, of our communities. The media have been effective vehicles of the longstanding promotion of team owners' interests
as equivalent to those of the public.[121] The next chapter considers the
ways that sport generates, energizes, and meshes with stories we tell
about ourselves, our communities, and our country.

11

GETTING ON THE MAP

SPORT RAISES THE RAFTERS

IN 1950, the first year of the annual Lacombe Lions Baseball Tournament, Stan Moher of the *Edmonton Bulletin* wrote, "the lid really came off this town. Thousands poured in from points north, south, east and west...Lacombe's prestige as a live-wire central Alberta centre received a big shot in the arm as a result of the successful promotion of their first tourney."[1] More than 9,000 seats were set up, and "ladies of the town and district" mustered to feed large crowds on 300 pounds of tomatoes, 1,000 pies, and more. As was common at sporting events, there were additional attractions, including an RCAF air show, public dances, an industrial exhibition, and a cavalcade of over 100 cars sent by the Edmonton Chamber of Commerce. A civic holiday was declared. The tournament went on to run for thirty years, offering the most base-ball prize money in western Canada.[2] It sounds like a fine time, but why should a baseball tournament enhance the prestige—or the sense of place—of a prairie town? Was it something inherent to the game, the teams, or local fans? What is the connection between sports and civic life or community spirit?

SPORT AND PLACE
"THE SPIRIT OF THE PRAIRIE"

The mythic construction of recorded memory and civic identity is particularly evident in annual sports events.[3] The Calgary Stampede, for example, is a multifaceted festival but the rodeo contests remain at the heart of the brand of both event and city. The history of the Stampede organization underlines the patterns of power prevalent in urban sport culture. Maxwell Foran sees the power structures of the city and the organization as virtually indistinguishable, "rooted in the belief that the latter benefited the former commercially."[4] Edmonton's official city motto is "Industry, Integrity, Progress," but much more publicized is the slogan "City of Champions," first coined in the 1930s to celebrate the Grads basketball team, who had brought international recognition to the city. The slogan didn't stick until the 1980s when the city made a move to counter Calgary's higher profile with a reminder of more northerly hockey and football dynasties, but it was quietly retired in the 2000s when local teams became less competitive.[5] Sports teams have served to embody community spirit and the mythical *genius loci* shared by a population. Coach Percy Page said of the Grads that "the spirit of the Prairie is born and bred in them."[6] The enduring integration of sport into public life was forged early in the context of civic holidays, parades, and ceremonies such as Dominion Day. The province's inauguration events on September 1, 1905 included a range of sport competitions and demonstrations, many of which were cancelled due to unexpected snow. Parades in particular have celebrated and mythologized sport as a populist source of solidarity, strength, and joy in modern life. In Calgary's "Historical Pageant" parade in the 1920s, the "Great Men" floats were followed by a section with thirty different sports. As they had been for decades, these were all directly associated with values of populist strength, prosperity, and military proficiency. The announcer (likely Ted Knight) chanted, "Pass, pass on, visionary people of the mighty growing race. Give way to the sports of the people. Make place for the games where is learned the way to fight when need arises. Pass, baseball and cricket, football and lacrosse; pass, skiing and hunting, fishing and shooting. Forward, skating and hockey, tennis and golf. Forward, onward, into the future, support of a virile race."[7]

This form of street theatre also serves the somewhat narrower stages of team victory celebrations. When the Edmonton Flyers won the Allan Cup in 1948, nearly half of the city's population—between 50,000 and 60,000 people—turned out to welcome them home. The parade was the "wildest demonstration" in history for "this hockey-crazed northern Alberta metropolis."[8] A record "concentration of enthusiastic humanity...jammed Jasper Avenue...and Market Square."[9] Civic officials, the premier, the lieutenant-governor, various MPs, the mayor, sports executives, and Miss Edmonton all attended. Local businesses sponsored parties and presented the players with gifts, including socks, cutlery, HBC blankets, clothing, candy, money, and nylon stockings. (Stockings were still a luxury item a few years after the war.) Menswear merchant Henry Singer presented each player with a new sports jacket, and Captain Gordie Watt was proclaimed mayor for the day. And in 1963, when the Oil Kings won their first ever Memorial Cup, according to Wes Montgomery, "the whole city went nuts and stayed nuts for four years."[10]

It may come down to the fact that victories and champion-ships make "citizens feel good about their towns and themselves."[11] But many fans stay loyal in the slow times as well. A crowd of over 2,000 celebrated the defeated Calgary Tigers and the junior Calgary Canadians hockey clubs upon their return from the Dominion Championships in 1924. In 1934-1935 the Edmonton Athletic Club won the western Canada junior championship but was defeated at the Dominion level. They returned from their loss winning "highest praise for clean play and sportsmanship" to a "monster demonstration [and] gigantic parade" involving the lieutenant-governor, mayor, premier, MLAs, city council, and every sports organization in the city.[12] In 1946 the Calgary Stampeders were the first Alberta team to win the Allan Cup, but even when they lost the following year the *Herald* called the team "winners in the heads of hockey fans," who turned out in large numbers for a welcome parade that "probably surpassed" the greeting of the year before. The mayor called them "ambassadors of goodwill for Calgary."[13]

The intense identification of fans with teams and individual athletes prevails under varying circumstance in towns, cities, regions, and the nation. Although Albertan Kurt Browning failed to win top place at the 1994 Olympics, Canadian fans donated enough gold jewellery to be forged into a large medal presented to him. And after the Edmonton Oilers' last-minute playoff loss in 2006, the team was greeted by thousands of fans, a public celebration was held at City Hall, and the mayor spoke of the "real championship feeling" the team had brought to the city and the pride of "our entire city—indeed all of Canada [in] the passion and character they've shown."[14] In 2005 Edmonton officials celebrated a local team's Brier win by declaring Randy Ferbey Rink Day, calling the players the best representatives of the city.[15] Win or lose, amateur or professional, teams and individual athletes embody the idealized qualities of the collective.

COMMUNITY FACE-OFF

BOOSTERS AND RIVALRIES

For over a century, large and small Alberta municipalities have taken a front seat in the chuckwagon of organized sports, drawing on a tradition of athletics-oriented civic promotion reaching back to ancient Greece. In Great Plains towns in both America and Canada, politicians on town councils and business people on boards of commerce worked together in a conflation of public and private interests. In the ambitions of local councils, sport could unite a diverse population as cities grew, creating, as the *Claresholm Local Press* put it in 1932, a "civic

Turner Valley Oilers, Alberta Senior Hockey League, 1939–1940. [GA NA-4607-2]

consciousness."[16] A high-profile sporting event, team, or facility was also a powerful beacon of status indicating a community that could support jobs, consumer, and tourist spending and infrastructure. After the World War I and the 1920s recession, boards of trade turned from boosting independent business investment to servicing public projects such as sports facilities.[17]

Attracting attention at home and on the road, the names of both amateur and professional teams have been calculated to publicize selected civic histories, wealth, features, and products. In 1949 a new Lethbridge senior men's basketball team was named the Green Acres in order to "publicize Lethbridge and Southern Alberta's vast agricultural resources," including the wonders of modern irrigation in a dry region.[18] The Turner Valley Oilers' promotional materials around 1940 included team pictures arranged around a scene of a gushing oil well reflecting the local landscape. In the 1950s, Alberta sports teams included the Calgary Chinooks, Lethbridge Miners, Medicine Hat Gaslighters, Calgary Bronks, and several incarnations of the Edmonton Eskimos and the Oilers. Edmonton also had teams emphasizing its capital status, such as the Legislators, Capitals, and even the Imperials.[19]

As early as the 1880s, Medicine Hat was glad to be known as a "sporting town."[20] In the early 1900s, the Blairmore paper opined that "a good team in any line of athletics is a splendid advertisement."[21] In 1908, Edmonton department store owner J.H. Morris financed the hockey team's trip to the Stanley Cup to advertise the city in the east. Vulcan offered large cash prizes and excursion trains to attract visitors during its 1915 Stampede. The Drumheller Board of Trade managed all team sports from 1914 to 1919; in 1925 local businessmen sponsored uniforms for the local baseball team. And in the late 1920s the Lacombe Board of Trade honoured the district's champions in sports as well as in farming and business.[22]

The promoters of the Banff Winter Carnival certainly met their goal of promoting winter recreation and tourism in the mountains. The carnival offered annual competitions, but advertising and support

were crucial to extend the season beyond the brief event. In 1931 a
Banff tourism entrepreneur reportedly said, "let's put this man's town
on the map as the winter playground of America."[23] Eleanor Luxton,
of the influential Banff family, wrote a contemporary account of this
"new winter resort" for the University of Alberta *Gateway*, describing the
joys of skiing, hockey, skating, curling, and indoor swimming amid the
beauty of the mountains. Promoters also reminded the public that "the
overlapping of winter and summer sports...in Banff is unique...on this
continent if not in the world." While skiing continued on mountaintops
in May, people below could canoe, swim, and play golf and baseball.[24]
Banff's summer Indian Days, invented to entertain tourists, featured
sports competitions among members of the Stoney band. When
Princess Margaret visited Banff in 1958, she was greeted by a crowd of
5,000, most of whom were attired in summer sports clothing.[25]

Baseball was particularly alluring to boosters, and this proved to be
one of the main reasons for the development of the sport in western
Canada.[26] Press coverage grew rapidly with the advent of semi-pro ball
in the early 1900s, but even amateur baseball competitions attracted
attention to growing towns, and many were specifically mounted for
this reason. In January 1906, Lethbridge held an outdoor baseball game
featuring the home team against Calgary. With the temperature at
fifty-three degrees Fahrenheit (or almost twelve degrees Celsius) in
midwinter, the game attracted 800 spectators and considerable hyper-
bole. The *Calgary Herald* called the game a "big advertisement for the
Banana Belt" that would "establish the claim of Lethbridge to the finest
climate in Canada."[27] (A 1931 ad for a track meet in Wetaskiwin also
cast a wide net with "put your shoulder to the wheel, and 'Let Canada
Know Alberta.'")[28] Meanwhile, the *Bulletin* boasted that "Edmonton has
the fastest bunch of amateurs in the Golden West,"[29] and the *Calgary
Herald* argued that a successful baseball club would be the best kind
of advertising for the city.[30] The town of Bassano, part of the Western
Canada Baseball League in 1912, called their baseball team the Boosters.
In 1920, the *Red Deer Advocate* linked Vulcan's survival to sport, asking
whether it would "stay on the map as a real live baseball town or sink

into oblivion."[31] In Edmonton, the mayor and Alberta's Lieutenant-Governor Dr. William Egbert participated in the ceremonies for an opening season game in the spring of 1926.

Representing a city, or by extension a province or country, was not to be taken lightly. Team owner Jim Christiansen warned the Edmonton Flyers that their performance in the 1948 world championship series would be "blazed in the Press of all the important and sport loving countries of the world" and over the air waves in Canada. Christiansen must have been gratified when European press praised the team for their gentlemanly conduct.[32] Although the city booster committee circulated publicity booklets and advertisements abroad, in 1950 a more effective instrument was the Edmonton Mercurys hockey team, which travelled Europe to win the world amateur hockey championship with plenty of news coverage along the way. The stakes were higher in the late 1980s when Calgary mayor Ralph Klein proclaimed the Olympic Games an opportunity to promote the city as a major international player.[33]

Of course, missteps by teams and players can correspondingly damage a city's reputation. In 1955 the Edmonton Eskimos of the Western Canada Baseball League were Canadian semi-pro champions and were designated national representatives in the eight-nation Global World Series at Milwaukee. Team management had agreed to include five star players from other clubs, but when four Eskimos refused to play under this arrangement the team was replaced for the series by the Saskatoon Gems. Pointing out that all four were American imports, Hal Pawson of the *Journal* chided the players for lack of team spirit, as well as for jeopardizing the status of pro ball in the "city associated with sports": "The four should get along well in organized baseball, if they quit every time a superior makes a decision they don't like….in so doing they hurt the Eskimos, they hurt Edmonton—but fortunately not much because this city is too big in athletics to be hurt by such small men—and they hurt Canadian baseball. Worse than that, they just may have delivered the death blow to baseball in this city."[34] Edmonton survived as a baseball city and continued to field teams in the Western Canada League—and one year in the Canadian-American League—until it folded in 1964.

Nothing affirms the borders of a given community faster than the sight of another on the horizon. As Alberta settlements developed pride in distinct versions of identity, squads of locals out for bragging rights were logical symbols of economic and cultural rivalries. Ongoing conflict between close neighbours, such as Edmonton and South Edmonton (Strathcona), inspired high levels of fan loyalty; approximately one in four citizens attended the teams' 1905 Christmas Day confrontation at the Thistle Rink.[35] The South Side Covered Rink was built in 1904 when "some of the young bloods with hustle and ideas stirred up some of the older bloods, with money," such as John Walter, A.C. Rutherford, and Robert Ritchie.[36] The group sold shares until enough funds were raised for a structure that would allow Strathcona to compete with Edmonton teams, which had the Thistle Rink. Sports facilities in this period were commonly supported by citizens, encouraged by boosters who called for financial contributions and manual labour to build baseball diamonds, ice arenas, and football fields; local businesses were also expected to provide employment for players.[37]

As train connections improved, other towns and cities "worked out their local pride through competition." Feelings between the Calgary Tigers and the Edmonton Eskimos were "so fierce that in 1913 they had to play at Red Deer because neither would even set foot on the other's home ground."[38] In 1948 Mack W. Lyle of Edmonton complained that Calgary fans were so vindictive that they had elected to cheer for Ottawa in a playoff game against their neighbours, the Edmonton Flyers. (Lyle, in his turn, dismissed the Calgary Arena as a dilapidated barn.) When the Flyers won the Allan Cup that year, another observer rejoiced that "Edmonton is a big boy now and this is an opportunity to prove it or kneel humbly hereafter when Calgary is mentioned."[39] With the entry of Edmonton and Calgary to the NHL in 1979 and 1980, the "Battle of Alberta" continued to make headlines as the Oilers and the Flames became rivals for top spot.[40]

"Gearing up for the Grey Cup." Published in The Albertan, *November 25, 1955. Calgary mayor Don Mackay, right, presents a piggy bank to Fred Gardiner of Toronto.* [GA NA-5600-7126J]

The annual Grey Cup game has been marked by the mayors of opposing cities striking personal wagers on the outcome. In 1955 Calgary's Don Mackay wore a First Nations war bonnet for the occasion. The University of Alberta had to wait until 1963 to finally deny hinterland status when the *Gateway* announced that "Alberta is not the backwoods of Canadian college sport."[41] The football team had beaten the top-ranked Queen's University's Golden Gaels, and even the Ontario campus paper agreed that western football had come of age. The *Edmonton Journal*, which usually paid little attention to university sport, covered the game, which was attended by over 8,000 Alberta fans. Decades later, sport was still a pediment for local profile; during the University of Alberta's unsuccessful bid for the 2015 Universiade, committee chairman Eric Newell predicted that hosting the games would "help cement the U of A's position as one of the top twenty universities in the world."[42]

OLD BOYS, ENTREPRENEURS, AND PROMOTERS

Not all taxpayers subscribe to the discourse of sport as the joy and the glue of civic life. Opposition to public funding for elite events and venues has arisen in several host communities, including both Edmonton in 1978 and Calgary in 1988. A corresponding skepticism emerged earlier in the century when the 1920 Alberta Curling Bonspiel was planned for Edmonton. Although the city had granted the event controversially large sums in 1913 and 1914, the mayor now objected that curling was "an expensive sport which only included a small section of the citizens [and he] did not see why those who were going to benefit could not raise the money themselves." Curling supporters and aldermen argued that city stores and other businesses benefited from an influx of people with money, and the city granted $500 to the event. These previous grants by council also caused controversy; the 1914 grant, according to the mayor in 1920, caused "more trouble than any other grant." The newspaper cites $12,000 in 1913 and $1,00 in 1914; both may be typos, since $12,000 would be the equivalent of around a quarter of a million dollars in today's currency, seemingly excessive for event funding; the second figure is probably meant to be $1,000, only twice as much as the 1920 grant.[43]

Not coincidentally, in early prairie cities sports tended to be organized by and for middle-class merchants, professionals, and politicians meeting in their offices and shops. Edmonton's first bicycle club formed in 1895 and was composed of dental surgeon Alexander Hopper Goodwin, physician John Harley Harrison, bank manager George R.F. Kirkpatrick, and barristers Nicholas D. Beck and Pat McNamara. All were also involved in other sports, including tennis, cricket, baseball, lacrosse, and foot racing. The second club, North Star, was also made up of business and professional men, of whom almost half had a direct financial interest in the sale of bicycles. Membership in these clubs was not necessarily exclusive but connections probably didn't hurt. The North Star captain was a clerk at Larue and Picard's large and prominent general store. With the 1896 North American cycling boom, more stores began to stock bicycles, and, by the turn of the century, they appeared in more newspaper ads than any other product; nearly all Edmonton ads were sponsored by prominent club members.[44]

Service clubs, which in general would have included most of the same prominent men, have also long sponsored community and recreational sport. Specialized commercial sports facilities were rarely successful in smaller centres. Skating rinks in Grande Prairie in the 1920s and Drumheller in the 1940s, for example, were all unprofitable. On the other hand, facilities built by service clubs could rely on the necessary capital and sometimes operating funds and were usually built on public land and eligible for other public support. Athabasca's Kinsmen Club has contributed financial assistance for the construction of the local arena, swimming pool, two playgrounds, and a baseball diamond since its formation in 1920. In Grande Prairie, the 1942 Kinsmen objective to "promote and direct fellowship among young men of good character" was reflected in their support of sports. Their first large community project in 1946 was raising $24,000 for a town swimming pool, and then $75,000 for a new arena, followed by other projects.[45] The Edmonton Kinsmen were central to the project to build a facility for the 1983 Universiade, later to become a public sports and fitness venue.

Sports fans also voted with their wallets to support teams and facilities, and early-twentieth-century clubs often incorporated in order to sell shares to players and fans alike. Football player Harold Burnham owned shares in the Capital City Curling Rink, the Edmonton Tennis and Bowling Company, and the Edmonton Country Club from 1908 to 1912.[46] Smaller communities struggled consistently to support teams. In Granum in the mid-1920s, the Elks Club formed a hockey team that later joined a small league under the jurisdiction of the Alberta Amateur Association (AAA). In 1928, all the teams hired a few outside players, and by 1929 most players were paid. That year the Granum team solicited fifty people to co-sign a loan of $5,000 to fund the season, to be repaid through raffles, bake sales, paid admissions, and dances. Survival seemed ensured, but during the Southern Alberta Playoffs, the AAA secretary walked onto the ice and pulled the membership cards of three Granum players despite the fact that the opposing team also had paid members. Demoralized, with its standard of play compromised, the team folded and the league disbanded.[47]

In debates condemning the making of money versus "the making of men,"[48] pro sports promoters were easy targets as amateur athletic unions remained powerful. Successful promoters building intercity competition had the incentive and the funds to import star players, rather than choosing local men. Calls to enforce amateur regulations continued in the 1920s as professional sport expanded, but in practice market factors were inseparable from the survival of any elite team. *Maclean's* magazine of February 15, 1928 questioned whether "by the giving of uniforms, membership, equipment, too liberal travelling allowances, training tables and special comforts, are we not creating in the minds of our athletes, a feeling that they are doing us a favour by playing our games?...It is only a short step across the border to professionalism."[49]

Professional and semi-pro teams organized or were taken on by boards and other operating groups. The success of the Calgary Tigers hockey team in the 1920s was attributed to citizen ownership through the city's Exhibition Board, fostering a "unity of desire to keep the good name of the city to the front," rather than allowing private individuals to "profit by the sporting propensities of the citizens."[50] When the Eskimos became the first western football team to compete in the Grey Cup, manager Moe Lieberman raised $1,800 in loans from the Rotary Club to finance the trip east by promising to advertise Edmonton across the country. (The Elks Club also sponsored in return for renaming the team the "Elks," but the original name stuck.)[51] In Calgary the local Active Club presented the MVP trophy for the 1940–1941 Stampeders hockey season. The first athlete chosen as Sportsman of the Year by the Calgary Booster Club in 1956 was football player Norman Kwong, Alberta's lieutenant-governor from 2005 to 2010.[52]

Over time, the success of booster logic around sports has been such that, in practice, the discourses of commercial and public goods are often inextricable. Government expenditures have been justified by the perceived role of sports in building community, demonstrating the close link between politics, culture, and commerce. Private sports promoters have also worn the hats of public spirit as well as of business since the boom in organized sports activities around 1900 presented new opportunities. As the fortunes of promoters, teams, and communities aligned, a commercial star system emerged; amateur regulators and recreation reformers were eclipsed in the public eye by those focused on building teams and audiences.

Promoters tended to be larger-than-life characters with a genuine passion for sports and not always solely motivated by profit, since most were lucky to break even. Many had longer-term visions of an expanded quality of life along with larger markets, and their tactics were admired, or at least tolerated, in light of their talents for advancing local interests. Tommy Burns of Calgary, as we have seen, got away with creative manoeuvres around contemporary boxing laws. Guy Weadick, founder of the Calgary Stampede, sued the board in 1932 over his firing for drunkenness, and the judge ruled that drinking was, in fact, a part of his job as promoter. (Weadick left town anyway, not returning until the fortieth anniversary of the Stampede in 1952.)[53]

Many promoters shaped regional sporting landscape and culture in the long term. Lloyd Turner, known as "Mr. Hockey" in Calgary, was manager of the Sherman Arena from 1909 until it was destroyed by fire in 1915; he then managed the Crystal Rink, and in 1918 the Horse Show Building, later called Victoria Park Arena. He helped to organize the Western Canada Hockey League, and at various times managed the Tigers hockey team, the Bronks baseball team, and the Calgary Baseball Club. In 1932 he brought artificial ice to Victoria Park Arena, helping to revive Allan Cup competition in the province, and managed the

Stampede Corral facility from 1950 to 1964. Turner became an original member of the Hockey Hall of Fame.[54]

Deacon White, a sports promoter, athlete, coach, and manager who came to Edmonton in 1906, "became the dominant influence on Edmonton sport for some two dozen years" and earned the city a national profile in team sports.[55] White managed Edmonton's first professional sports team—a baseball club called the Legislators in a nod to the city's new capital status—but from 1909 onward all his professional baseball, hockey, and football clubs were called the Edmonton Eskimos, including the 1920s football team that won the Western Canada football championship and played in the Grey Cup. He was also involved in amateur sports and the formation of the Edmonton Amateur Athletic Association in 1913. It was White who, with the support of local business and service clubs, orchestrated the 1923 championship basketball game that launched the Edmonton Grads to international acclaim.[56] John Ducey of Edmonton was another tireless promoter of minor, major, and professional baseball in Edmonton; Ducey became a dominant force in the game's organization in the 1930s and thereafter.

Wild Bill Hunter, remembered as Edmonton's founding father of hockey, helped to invent the World Hockey Association (WHA) to compete with the NHL in cities without a pro team. Although motivated by a sense that the province's cities were shunned by the NHL, Hunter's WHA promotion was nevertheless instrumental in preparing the NHL's path into Alberta. After selling the WHA Oilers in 1976 to Nelson Skalbania (who sold the team the following year to Peter Pocklington) and a failed attempt to bring the St. Louis Blues to Saskatoon, Hunter successfully organized and promoted curling. Inducted into numerous sports halls of fame as well as the Order of Canada, he also received the Canadian Tourism Award. However, perhaps due to his involvement in the "outlaw" WHA, he is not in the Hockey Hall of Fame in Toronto.[57]

Some promoters, like Granum baseball's George Wesley, appeared to the *Lethbridge Herald* sportswriter in 1955 to be "in baseball strictly for

the kicks. There's certainly been no personal gain attached to his operation. It's all been for the fun of it...a new twist in the money-grabbing
sports ventures of today." Because Wesley was reportedly flexible in
negotiating financial arrangements, he was able to "provide fans hereabouts with a pretty fair brand of ball during the past three seasons."[58]
Under Wesley's hands-on management style, teams made sure that
"their uniforms were always clean and their shoes polished...One thing
they all had in common—they must be of good character and always
hustle on the diamond."[59] Wesley went on to become "Mr. Baseball" in
Lethbridge during this period, managing the senior Lethbridge White
Sox, who went semi-pro in 1959 and subsequently won many titles and
championships. Wesley's push for lights in the local stadium helped
to bring Pioneer League baseball to Lethbridge in the 1970s, though the
team was sold in 2000.[60]

Many other promoters also followed their love of the game and the
hometown with investments of time, energy, and money.[61] One of
Alberta's most important rodeo promoters was Johnnie Phelan, who
came to the Prairies from the United States in 1909 to play baseball. As
the owner of a Red Deer hotel in the 1940s, he helped to develop softball
and men's baseball in the city. But he was best known as the sponsor of
a chuckwagon outfit, usually driven by Ron Glass, which won the Calgary
Stampede championship three times and the world championship in
1950 and 1951. In 1949 Red Deer Mayor C.R. Bunn praised Phelan as the
"chuckwagon champion [who] has brought so much fame to his city,"[62]
and the Board of Trade thanked him for "reflecting the honour on all
the city, community and district...publicity of this kind cannot be bought
with money."[63] Phelan's outfit won the top prize of $1,000 in the
Edmonton Exhibition rodeo of July 1952, and the following summer
broke the world chuckwagon record at the Stampede in a race held in
honour of H R H Princess Elizabeth and the Duke of Edinburgh.[64] Meanwhile Phelan continued to work in community sport, and in 1966 he won
the Red Deer Minor Hockey Association Sportsman of the Year award.

Promoters with a persistent vision of Alberta as a viable sports
market include Russell Parker, who brought pro baseball to Calgary

in the late 1970s. He saw Calgary as a "quality baseball town" due to high spectator turnout and excellent facilities. (Foothills Stadium was upgraded by the city in 1985 for the arrival of the new Cannons team at a cost of $2.2 million.) The unpredictable weather, however, was not one of the local advantages. On season opening day, April 19, 1985, Parker posed in a blizzard holding a snow baseball. In 1987 the Cannons were the Pacific Coast League's northern division champions, but year's end marketing evaluation noted ongoing problems: "team not playing well" and "not great weather," although PCL baseball still made sense as an "family entertainment" franchise.[65] The organization optimistically predicted that the 1988 Olympics would focus city spirit and that the league would also benefit from the "intense, long-standing rivalry between Calgary and Edmonton." Neither factor, nor the team's policy of supporting local minor and amateur sports, could guarantee long-term financial survival, and the team was sold after 2002.[66]

While entrepreneurial individuals and community groups are essential to kickstarting organized sport, sustained success is subject to vagaries of economics and public support. The difficulty of ensuring steady funding from municipalities, service clubs, and businesses meant that large league sports like hockey and baseball had to become viable spectator draws. By the 1930s, professional versions of sport such as senior hockey were already feasible only in centres big enough to afford a competitive team. In the early twenty-first century, professional teams came and went as they always had. As well as the Oilers and the Trappers, Peter Pocklington owned the Edmonton Drillers of the North American Soccer League until the team folded in 2000. The Trappers were sold in 2004. Medicine Hat had a Toronto Blue Jays farm team for twenty-seven years but it too was sold in 2002 due, once again, to low community support and high travel costs. As players increasingly relocate to the United States for better salaries, interest in professional ball has declined in Canada.[67]

Team owners take various approaches to ensure survival in small markets. David Mills contrasts the ownership patterns of the Calgary Flames and Edmonton Oilers in the 1970s and 1980s, arguing that, while the Flames managed to embody a spirit and identity "owned" by the community, the Oilers team exemplified the commercial product that professional sport has become. The Flames kept hockey separate from other business ventures, emphasizing the spirit of prairie booster optimism, civic pride, and co-operation between business and local government. Owners were not motivated solely by personal profit but supported amateur sports in order to develop hockey at grassroots levels as had the Calgary Buffalo Athletic Association. (On the other hand, two of the Flames' original owners left in 1994, skeptical of the NHL's financial survival in Canada.) The Flames enjoyed strong fan support.[68]

The Oilers also have a loyal fan base, and sports entrepreneur Pocklington has insisted professional sports franchises are not owned but held it in trust for the community (adding that they also garner it international recognition and roughly $100 million per year).[69] In practice, the team has been primarily a business proposition. When Pocklington bought the WHA Oilers in the late 1970s, it was a money-losing franchise despite high attendance figures. When the NHL expanded into Edmonton, Pocklington negotiated a local TV deal with Molson Breweries, and the Oilers showed a profit in the first year. After the team won its first Stanley Cup in 1984, higher salary demands and rents raised ticket prices, as well as the owner's profits, to among the highest in the league. Although Pocklington was burned in effigy by Edmonton fans when he traded Wayne Gretzky in 1988, the move confirmed the harsh truth that hockey was, in fact, a business rather than a civic ornament. In his poem, "The Trade that Shook the Hockey World," John B. Lee offers an apt simile for the impact of Wayne Gretzky's trade from the Oilers:

> When Gretzky went to LA
> my whole nation trembled
> like hot water in a tea cup when a train goes by.[70]

Later analysis suggested that Gretzky himself was amenable to or even requested his departure, but Canadians, and particularly Albertans, took it personally, feeling in effect that "the best hockey player in the world was ours, and the Americans flew up from Hollywood in their private jet and bought him. It wasn't the Canadian heart that was torn, it was the Canadian psyche that was ripped by an uppercut to the paranoia."[71]

When the value of the Oilers franchise declined after the early 1990s, Pocklington's threats to move the team resulted in the city turning over full control of the Northlands arena, contributing $15 million of federal infrastructure funds, and building a new park for Pocklington's baseball club. Late in 1997, the Alberta Treasury Branches took control of the team in lieu of Pocklington's debt payments and a year later sold it to a coalition of local businesses and companies.[72]

⋮ SPORT PALACES AND MEGA-EVENTS

In 2003, Daryl Katz's pharmacy company signed a sponsorship and marketing deal with the Oilers, renaming the arena Rexall Place. Katz creatively explained that the Oilers were "great ambassadors" for the Rexall brand because they stood for "health and active living." Oilers' CEO Patrick LaForge predicted that the arena would become "a landmark hockey and entertainment facility known across North America."[73] Katz bought the team itself in 2008. That year he and LaForge were named to Alberta Venture magazine's most influential people list. LaForge was chair of the Edmonton Chamber of Commerce as well as Oilers president and a member of the Arena Feasibility Committee that recommended building a new $450 million downtown sports arena complex.[74]

The combined economic, social, and cultural role of sport facilities made their presence seem almost inevitable as the population grew, and prominent arenas and stadiums proclaimed the substantial place of sport in local life. In Edmonton, the Strathcona Skating Rink opened in 1899 and the South Side Covered Rink in 1904. Fur trader, merchant, and Conservative MLA Richard Secord was the main benefactor of the team and chief financier for the indoor Thistle Roller and Ice Rink

built in 1902 with a seating capacity of 2,000.[75] The quality and size of
the building, as well as its eclectic role in local society, is indicated by
the fact that it was also used for events such as the province's inaugural ball in 1905, and the first sitting of the provincial legislature
in 1906.

In the early twentieth century, these initial constructions in small
prairie cities represented aspects of the North American consumer
culture producing quantities of large new buildings dedicated to widely
hyped mass media and entertainment events. But even before the
commercialization of sport, facilities were entrenched as a necessary
component of modern living involving physical culture and healthful,
productive exercise. In the spirit of contemporary democratic leisure
movements, the *Journal* argued in April 1913 that, despite past practices
of exclusivity, "golf is not a rich man's game...and public links on the
flats...would be a great boon."[76] When the public Highlands Golf Course
opened in 1929, Edmonton's mayor Ambrose Bury endorsed the social
importance of recreation and the need for even those of moderate
means to look beyond the necessity of work and material acquisition.
The benefits of leisure in the open air should be available to all citizens,
particularly those working in unhealthy factory jobs.[77] Local booster
clubs, city councils, and provincial governments have all boosted both
arts and sports facilities for occasions like Alberta's 1955 Golden Jubilee
celebrations and later the national centennial. As a civic facility, the
1951 Edmonton Exhibition 8,000-seat grandstand was dedicated "to the
people of the Province of Alberta."[78]

But in the long term, universal healthful recreation would not
suffice as a rationale for investment in building facilities; a community
needed to supplement grassroots sports with winning, ticket-selling
teams as well as a concentration of players and spectators. The importance of local facilities as reliable practice and game spaces became
apparent early on. Medicine Hat came late to organized hockey due to
its unpredictable weather, but after a covered rink was built in 1896 the
local team won the territorial championship, and a regulation rink was
built in 1902. This was still insufficient. After the first curling bonspiel

Mayor Don Mackay greets swimmer Bill Patrick at the opening of the Golden Jubilee pool, sponsored by the Calgary Kiwanis Club, July 1955. Photo: Jack deLorme. [GA NA-5600-6301B]

in Medicine Hat was held on two sheets of ice in January 1903, representatives of curling, lacrosse, cricket, football, baseball, hockey, and other sports formed the Medicine Hat Athletic Association to raise funds for a modern recreation complex. Regular organized hockey was also not possible in Lethbridge until the first covered arena was built in 1914. The small town of Edgerton, which had a one-sheet curling rink in 1912, built a two-sheet rink for the 1919–1920 season, and a local team won the grand challenge event at the Wainwright bonspiel.[79]

In Red Deer, a new skating and curling rink was built in 1903. After the roof collapsed in 1907, it took until 1925 to raise the funds for a new building. But the next spring the men's Red Deer Hockey Club were Intermediate Provincial Champions, the first sports team in the city to achieve a provincial championship. A few years later, the women's hockey team, the Amazons, won the women's provincial championships twice in a row. During the 1940s, Red Deer's A-20 Wheelers hockey team were local heroes in the Central Alberta Garrison Hockey League.[80] A new arena, the Centrium, was built in 1991 and the Red Deer Rebels joined the WHL in 1992, won their first playoff series in 1996, and won the Memorial Cup in 2001; they reached the playoffs in 2002, 2003, 2004, 2005, and 2007.

In the 1920s, the hot ticket was artificial ice, invented in England in the late nineteenth century and developed further in Alberta around 1919 by Elias Bjarni "Ole" Olson, who was motivated by a desire for better curling. The new technology depended on reliable supplies of electricity. Hockey players had first call on available facilities, so, for decades to come, many curlers continued to rely on nature. The 1928 Alberta Curling Association's "Night and Day" bonspiel was so called because of Calgary's warm weather, which resulted in such poor ice conditions that many matches were played at night or early in the morning. In 1936 enthusiasm for a ladies' bonspiel in Drumheller was so fervent that when warm weather caused "sticky ice" to develop later in the day, determined players started as early as 4:30 A.M.[81] The 1937 Alberta curling final at Victoria Arena in Calgary was the first to be played on artificial ice, installed at the arena in 1932 but normally used for hockey. Large bonspiels were particularly difficult to organize; the city's Royal Caledonian Curling Club bonspiel entries declined "to as low as forty rinks" before fourteen sheets of artificial ice became available in 1945. Calgary's 1948 bonspiel, played at the Victoria Arena and the Glencoe club, attracted a record entry of 184 rinks. On the down side, this made it again necessary to play night as well as day matches.[82] In 1946 the Granite Club in Edmonton was the first private curling club in western Canada to install artificial ice.[83]

Olson, who was chairman of the Alberta Curling Association's rock and ice committee, convened three-day ice making schools starting in 1956; in 1958 the session attracted thirty students from all over Alberta, indicating the high level of interest in the sport.[84] Forestburg inaugurated its rink's artificial ice plant with a ceremony in 1960, attended by a representative of the Camrose Curling Club, which had installed its artificial ice in 1954. The curling club at Hay Lakes already had its ice installed and other small communities such as New Norway were "making rapid progress" toward the same goal. That year, the Camrose Kinsmen Club raised $12,000 for a new rink with artificial ice, launched with an exhibition game between the Maroons and the University of Alberta Golden Bears. The mayor of the town dropped the first puck.[85]

Large seating capacity and ice quality were apparently crucial to success; it may be a coincidence, but until the Calgary Saddledome was built in 1983, Edmonton's hockey team beat Calgary every year.[86] The presence of good facilities in a community was not necessarily a guarantor of successful competition, but it obviously didn't hurt. Announcing plans to rebuild the town of Viking's arena after a fire in 2005, the mayor said that "every young hockey player and figure skater dreams of becoming a star, and they know they will have a much better chance of doing it with a local arena."[87] As minor hockey and recreational curling grew more popular after World War II, Alberta communities renewed the drive to construct sports centres. Newspapers, which were often owned by the same interest groups responsible for boosting facility construction, reported regularly on building and renovation activities in the 1940s and 1950s. Lethbridge raised approximately $325,000 to open a new sports centre with a stadium, swimming pool, gyms, and other facilities in 1949.[88]

The spread of electricity that permitted ice making also allowed for artificial light and extended playing times. In 1921 the Edmonton Eskimos rubgy team had had trouble fitting in practice time around players' work schedules due to the short autumn days, and they often practiced by moonlight with a phosphorus-painted ball. In the 1930s floodlights were installed in Calgary and Edmonton football fields. Immediate incentive for the latter improvement was the 1939 Royal Visit, which also left a legacy of 1,500 new seats at Clarke Stadium, built the previous year and named after the mayor. (A popular suggested name had been Grads Park, which indicated the high local prestige of the Edmonton women's basketball team.) Echoing years of claims made during the city's protracted yearning for metropolitan status, sportswriter Terry Jones called the building of the new football stadium in 1978 a sign that Edmonton had reached the "big leagues."[89]

A new rubber composition "fast" track was built at the University of Alberta in 1964, the only one of its kind in western Canada. Expected to "result in a wholesome attack on" provincial records, it attracted the Western Canadian Track and Field Championships to Edmonton for the first time. The majority of the eighty-eight competitors were from Alberta.[90] When the Kinsmen Field House was built in 1968 to host the Canadian Track and Field Championships, it meant that "the budding Alberta athlete can stop talking about the weather and start doing something about it." The severe winter had been blamed for the constricted track and field season and the consequent low percentage of Alberta athletes competing in international games.[91]

For over one hundred years, and during four previous economic booms, the city of Edmonton has considered building new arenas, each imagined as "a showcase for the city."[92] For the Edmonton hockey season opener on Christmas Day 1913, a new arena at Northlands (the Edmonton Exhibition's Livestock Pavilion) debuted at a size that "dwarfed" the Thistle Rink, which had burned down that year. Leased to various organizations and promoters, it became home ice to some of the most successful teams in hockey history. In 1926 the NHL expanded and top Edmonton talent went to American professional teams; the arena served amateur junior and senior and semi-pro hockey. In 1949, after the Flyers won the Allan Cup, the arena was renovated and expanded as the Edmonton Gardens, but a total of 6,800 seats was still insufficient to meet demand for tickets to team games.[93]

New proposals for Edmonton arenas arose every few years during the 1960s. The process was never without controversy or revitalization and booster rhetoric. In the 1960s, an Edmonton group proposed an ambitious omniplex for sport, theatre, trade, and conventions under one roof in downtown Edmonton to "stimulate revitalization of the city core."[94] Alderman Les Bodie argued in 1963 that "the coliseum will be a major factor in attracting interest in our city."[95] In a plebiscite that year, the arena plan was rejected by almost half of taxpayers and Mayor William Hawrelak challenged citizens: "How much do we want Edmonton to lead all Canada in bold, imaginative downtown development?"[96]

In the 1968 municipal election plebiscite, taxpayers voted 72.8 per cent in favour of building the complex at an estimated capital cost of $23 million. However, in the boom time economy, costs rose significantly and the 1970 plebiscite asking voters whether council should borrow over $26 million for construction was defeated. By 1971 the cost rose to over $35 million and the arena was never built, but with the oil boom of that decade, boosters and hockey promoters continued to agitate for a new facility.[97] After the World Hockey Association came to the city in 1972, all three levels of government supported the building of the Coliseum in 1974, "deemed to be the greatest hockey arena of its time." The new arena was key to the Oilers,' and by extension the city's, admission to big league status when the team joined NHL in 1979. Public money also built Commonwealth Stadium in Edmonton and the Saddledome in Calgary in this period.

When new NHL arenas began to go up in other cities in the 1990s, each with a claim to enhancing downtown development, Edmonton began the most recent debate on an arena projected to cost $450 million.[98] In the mid-1990s, federal infrastructure funds underwrote major renovations that mainly added high-cost luxury boxes to the coliseum.[99] In Edmonton, supporters of the 2007 proposal for Rexall's new downtown NHL arena argued that the facility would support not only the faltering Oilers (who, in a rare playoff run the previous year, demonstrated that they were "indispensable when it comes to civic pride and Edmonton's national stature") but also contribute to inner city revitalization.[100] Both city and province denied that any public funding would be involved, although the province did contribute $10 million to Rexall Place for upgraded dressing rooms in 2007. Early in 2011, the city began focused negotiations with the Katz Group of Companies, which forecast benefits to the city through real estate development around the new facility. Recalling the arguments of his predecessor in 1963, Mayor Stephen Mandel argued that "either we build a new arena or we become a second-class city."[101] In hundreds of similar cases across the continent, taxpayers have usually participated directly in the run for the shiny new goalposts, and in times of economic or social change, a new stadium or arena proposal typically describes social benefits expanding outward from the site. Over the last century, rationales of both market support for championship teams and democratic recreation access have helped legitimize the expenditure of public funds. According to the prevailing logic, winning teams and franchises equal city pride and identity; facilities for those teams generate high consumer satisfaction among all sports fans, whether live or broadcast; and facilities resulting from major sporting events are a community legacy. But more critics are examining the knots in this circuit that tend to choke off trickle-down benefits to citizens and bids for big buildings and big events alike continue to come under scrutiny. In October 2011, Edmonton City Council voted to support a new framework for a funding agreement with Katz that would still mean provincial and federal contributions would be necessary to build the arena. Public interest and participation in debate about the plans were high, with opinions generally addressing the cost to taxpayers in light of other perceived priorities, the contribution of the building to the city's stature and quality of life, and the arrogance of the Katz Group in demanding public funds for what would be a private revenue generating enterprise.[102]

The debate foregrounds the entwined roles of symbolic and economic significance of hallmark events and buildings. Special events have been particularly significant to prove local metropolitan recognition and status. In 1921 the Hamilton Tigers came to Alberta to acquaint westerners with the eastern style of football. A local newspaper glowed at the attention: "The fact that they are coming shows that Edmonton is getting to be a centre of importance, big enough to attract the best in everything. Four thousand people should be at that game on Thursday. Think of it, a game of rugby against the best team in Canada, that has travelled 3,000 miles! Rubby...draws bigger crowds than any other game played."[103]

"I've noticed that more and more since Calgary got the nod for the winter Olympics bid."
Cartoon by Tom Innes, Calgary Herald, *October 30, 1979. Preparations for the outdoor Olympic events were haunted by the unpredictable local weather that had been a problem a century before. [GA M-8000-484]*

As developed nations have increasingly fused tourism campaigns with sporting events, Canadians have orchestrated a greater number and variety of multi-sport festivals than anyone else. Western provinces have hosted the most major international events, Alberta with the Commonwealth Games (1982), World University Games (1983), Winter Olympics (1988), IAAF World Athletics Championship (2001), and World Masters Games (2005). Apart from tourism and economic infusions, legacy infrastructure has been one of the most common arguments for hosting major sporting events. When Lethbridge hosted the Canada Games in 1975, the city and its partner communities in the region received public funds for improvements to existing facilities and a new $4 million Sportsplex. According to Games president

Maury Van Vliet, the University of Alberta's Aquatic Centre, built for the 1978 Commonwealth Games and later named for Van Vliet, would be the "jewel in Edmonton's facilities crown." The *Financial Post* predicted that it would "do for the city what the University usually does only for its students." A skeptical volunteer doubted that impact but thought it would be a nice place to go in winter. In 2009 Edmonton made a $400 million bid to host the 2015 Universiade with an eye on community facility legacies.[104]

The enormous effort and expenditure needed for mega-event bids and hosting requires the enthusiastic assent of civic leaders, business, and other keen booster groups. Significantly, Alberta has earned a reputation for turning out hordes of eager volunteers for these events. Mass volunteer participation can go a long way toward countering fears of elitist control, as occurred when Calgary hosted the 1988 Olympics. City elites promised long-term rewards, including federally funded infrastructure, tourism, and investment benefits. In a period of economic recession, getting the Games gave the city "a material and psychological boost in the arm and infused a climate of positivism."[105] Compared to other Olympic cities, which often seem to view it "as a licence to pour concrete, Calgary did a good job resisting" over-expenditure on facilities.[106] Nevertheless, Alberta taxpayers contributed $461 million for buildings that were later sold off to private interests for a dollar. Although organizers claimed a profit overall, when these government subsidies for game venues were figured into costs, the Games ultimately took a significant financial loss.[107]

The promise of facilities and tourism may have focused civic hopes but, according to one analysis, Calgary's sense of collective ownership and passion for the Games most effectively capitalized on existing culture, identity, heritage, and traditions of western hospitality, for example. Kevin Wamsley and Michael Heine discuss the effective campaign of "civic training" that drew volunteers and citizens into support for the Olympics in Calgary. In the long term, this prepared citizens for an ongoing urban planning regime dependent on tax hikes.[108] The Alberta public's role in decision making about long-term consequences has been limited. A century and more after an emerging commercial sports culture aligned with tenets of civic progress, massive public subsidies and tax concessions appear to benefit mostly elite and professional sport. University event driven facilities, for instance, do provide benefits for students, but as Cora McCloy points out, these remain elite institutions not easily accessible to the public. Raymond Keating calls "sports pork" the reward of special interest politics taxing the many for the needs of an elite few team owners and players.[109] The 1978 Commonwealth Games brought Edmonton a new arena for the Oilers that was not used for the event itself; it also funded a new $23 million stadium for the Eskimos. In Calgary, the Olympic bid specified a professional-quality hockey arena for the new Flames, and the Games yielded an endowment fund to advance high performance sport.[110]

It is also true that, like other corporations, major sports franchises and events operate effective community foundations and projects supporting local minor sport, among other causes. The history of public enthusiasm for building projects, parades, and festivals must also be recognized, though tempered by recognition of its transience. However, as successful investment, building programs, and events broaden a city's capacity to attract elite sports, local traditions of fan support can wither when teams are obviously transient imports and when build-ings are generic copies of distant others.

As Richard Gruneau and David Whitson demonstrate, what were once distinct professional and elite amateur sports have merged in the context of global markets for sport products. Regional sports cultures have been more or less absorbed into a monoculture.[111] In an often turbulent economic climate, debates about the place of sport in civic and provincial life continue. Like other jurisdictions, Alberta sports policy and that of its municipalities attempts to balance public community sport, elite amateur, and professional spheres. It must do so amid the vagaries of a resource-based economy with boom and bust cycles that determine funding levels. In the years after the province's implemented a sport development strategy in 1984 to co-ordinate a

sport delivery system in the province, government support for cultural
and social programs fell with a severe economic recession. In 2008, on
what seemed a stable wave of oil prosperity, a new sports plan established priorities including participation, excellence, business, funding,
and facilities. Programs were tied to delivery through communities,
volunteer organizations, and educational institutions.[112]

However, the 2008 provincial budget allocation for public recreation and sport fell from $51,505,000 in 2008-2009 to $31,106,000 for
2010-2011.[113] It remains to be seen whether the plan will result in
higher citizen participation in sport and how much emphasis will be
placed on selecting and training athletes with elite potential. The 2008
budget also announced new funding for high performance athletes
and training facilities, as part of the national push for success in the
Olympic Games. The Podium Alberta program will receive $1.5 million
annually, supplementing federal funding to athletes. The 2008 Alberta
budget also put $20 million toward the creation of a Canadian Centre of
Sport Excellence, including a new facility at Olympic Park in Calgary.
The preparation for the 2010 Olympics was also geared toward the
opportunity to use athletic success to promote the province's tourism
economy.[114]

CONCLUSION
THOUGHTS IN OVERTIME

The promotion of "world class" events and products, including
professional leagues and facilities, influences the urban politics of
competition in leisure commodities. In practice, it is difficult to assess
the benefits of sport to local economies; we can point to cases where,
for instance, arena funding takes away from other community projects,
and question how much of the team's revenue actually remains in the
community. How would spending that currently goes to sport affect
the number and quality of local jobs if directed to other areas of public
recreation such as minor sport, the arts, and so on?[115] A focus on sport's
potential to attract global markets and investments naturally weakens

claims that major league teams are community and national institutions, even though public debate about keeping professional teams in Canadian markets often involves genuine emotional attachment to a franchise and legitimate concern for the economic health of a city.

Another trend aligning tourism and sports is the development of "retro" venues exploiting ticket buying potential among those nostalgic for past (simpler, amateur, local) urban sports cultures. Modern sport spaces by contrast are often placeless, eliminating factors of climate and locale, with business practices that alienate teams from the community. Old-fashioned rinks and ballparks, like Edmonton's TELUS Field, can also establish continuity with the history of a local team, franchise, or tradition even as their local names are erased for corporate labels. The 2003 Heritage Classic game between the Canadiens and the Oilers was an apparent reversal of elite sport on bricks and mortar. The game, played in the open winter air on an outdoor rink created in the football stadium, offered not a new building but a new landscape created from "a pastiche of images, traditions, history, nostalgia and fiction." The inclusion of hay bales and pickup trucks produced dream images of an ideal sports landscape that had nothing to do with the past of professional hockey but with reinforcing emotional links to mass audiences.[116]

After the game, as we continue to stand on the frozen pond and gaze at the empty nets, we have more time to consider origin myths. These tend to combine ideas of what still exists as everyday recreation with the vague sense that spectator sport was also once simply a bigger, faster version of what we played ourselves. As the recorded history stands, though, organized sport in Alberta moved swiftly into modernity. Radios, automobiles, and artificial ice soon made it possible to export sports like curling, figure skating, and hockey into global markets regardless of climate or sports cultures. The Heritage Classic game was a powerful origin story of friends and neighbours getting together to enliven summer days and winter nights with friendly games, edged with transformative dreams of shooting stars and big city lights that would contain the nature of play forever.

Sport has been viewed as a secular religion and as a frivolous diversion. It can be both, and many other things, depending on who is playing, watching, or organizing. An underlying question is always, what is at stake? A sports fan might answer most easily that it is the outcome of a particular game or competition, but for the rest of us, there is still much to count. Robert Trumpbour notes that the role of mythmaking in historical memory is particularly evident in sport,[117] a powerful vehicle of messages about people and place. Sport is "invented" in the same way that other spheres of culture are, through a process of selection and incremental action. Among all the grains of possibility that gather into patterns of cultural identity, sport is a hardy instance of how passions, more or less rational or irrational, take root and flourish in the imagination.

Of course, the components of players, games, fans, and spectators form a particular sports culture only in certain contexts, and sport in Alberta reflects the contemporary modern history of technology, mass culture, bureaucracy, and the marketplace. The haphazard organization of the late-nineteenth-century era yielded to a more formal culture of leisure controlled less by participants than by sports promoters, owners, and suppliers in the early twentieth century. The commercialization of popular culture, including sports, returns everyday practices to the people among whom they originated, but as products for paying spectators.[118] The development of organized sport has paralleled other aspects of cultural transformation as the province became a predominantly urban, industrial society. These include the increasing competition for resources and consequent balancing of public and private interests in the production of culture.

In November 1963, a University of Alberta *Gateway* writer lamented the disproportionately high funding dispensed to sport on campus and beyond. As sport had "become a big business" all over the country, he argued, the city of Edmonton could not support "even one professional theatre," and university facilities for fine arts were neglected and inadequate. Were citizens "placing too much emphasis on sports and not enough on the Arts? Do we want our country to have a culture, or team spirit?"[119] The two need not be mutually exclusive. Cities in Alberta went on to develop thriving (though still underfunded) arts scenes as well as sports champions. Considering the broader sense of "culture" as a "whole way of life," city councils argue that a strong sports presence actually fosters sufficient confidence, population, and leisure facilities to support arts production and audiences as well. This is part of the argument for public investment in professional teams and facilities, but we can also argue that within sport discourses a range of important themes touching on how we think about and construct identity and meaning in broader areas of everyday life have also been articulated.

In political terms, sport has served as one of the expressions of shared identity and pride for community and region. The popular meanings of sport have been shaped from the beginning in Alberta by the mass media, but in terms of social and cultural life, sport is still interwoven on a community level with the leisure time of people of all ages and experience. Of all the range of leisure activities available in Alberta, sport was and still is one of the most pervasive and visible. It is difficult to go through a typical day of work, socializing, and monitoring mass media without once encountering a reference to sports, whether a passing anecdote about family life or a radio commentary about the pro team's chances in the playoffs. Sports pages and broadcasts continue to deliver not just game scores but messages about economic life, political aspirations, gender relationships, cultural interests, and social belief systems. Decoding these messages tells us much about ourselves. Sport is important in part because, like other aspects of cultural activity, it "helped create a sense of identity in the province and fostered the evolution of that identity over the last century to produce Albertans."[120]

Sport is a social and cultural product created within contingent historical circumstances. The history of this territory in the northwest of the continent is rich in the meeting of immigrant peoples and Indigenous cultures, spectacular geography, and extreme climate. To ask why the history of sport might be important considering the myriad more significant claims on our attention is to ask why people busy with important tasks would pause to play or watch games. We might also wonder why so many community leaders and business people have focused so much passion and energy in sport. For players and spectators, any given sporting event can provide at least diversion. For social and political institutions, sport is also one area in which the boundaries of discipline and social control are effectively delineated. And for entrepreneurs, Alberta was a branch of North American spectator sports that became "one of the most commercially promising forms of popular culture...not least because they organized and celebrated skills and passions that had long been familiar features of male recreation."[121] Amid the reality of life in an essentially utilitarian, imported culture, and resource-based society, people worked hard and looked for fun. Sporting activities blossomed and entered the marketplace of popular cultural products.

The languages and practices of sport in Alberta still have great power to give meaning to social life, to "build communities, to demarcate social, political, and cultural struggles, to simultaneously connect and disconnect individuals and groups, to construct genders, to sell goods, propositions and ideologies."[122] This is one sketch of the history of sport in Alberta; other versions will continue to emerge.

PART I

INVENTING ALBERTA SPORTS CULTURE

1. Hughson, "Cultural History and the Study of Sport," 3.
2. "Lesson Plans: Heroes," *History by the Minute*, Historica, accessed January 12, 2011, http://www.histori.ca/minutes/lp.do;jsessionid=203E4C67ACF2363 CC8C12199A574AC94.tomcat1?id=13051.

1 SPORT AS CULTURAL IDENTITY

1. *Canadian Encyclopedia*, s.v. "North-West Territories 1870-1905," by David J. Hall, accessed February 3, 2012, http://www.thecanadianencyclopedia.com/articles/northwest-territories-18701905; MacGregor, *A History of Alberta*.
2. Dunning, *Sport Matters*.
3. Williams, *The Long Revolution*, 364.
4. Hughson, "Making of Sporting Cultures," 1-2.
5. Donnelly, Knight, and MacNeill, "Only in Canada, Eh!"

6.   "Council to Stop Sports Playing McConkey Park," *Drumheller Review*, June 20, 1940, 1.

7.   Cross, *A Social History of Leisure Since 1600*, 4.

8.   Caillois, *Jeux et sports*; Guttmann, *From Ritual to Record*.

9.   Guttmann, *From Ritual to Record*. While modern industrialized society extends back several centuries, in this discussion the term is associated more narrowly with the period of cultural modernity of the latter nineteenth and first part of the twentieth century; see Howell, *Blood, Sweat, and Cheers: Sport and the Making of Modern Canada*.

10. Metcalfe, *Canada Learns to Play*.

11. Bourdieu, "Sport and Social Class"; Bourdieu, "How Can One be a Sports Fan?"; White and Wilson, "Distinctions in The Stands."

12. Kidd, "The Making of a Hockey Artifact."

13. Adria, *Technology and Nationalism*.

14. McCartney, "Mavericks: Examining Glenbow Museum's Presentation of Alberta History," *Seven Oaks*, 2007, accessed June 14, 2009, http://www.sevenoaksmag.com/features/mavericks.html; van Herk, *Mavericks*.

15. See Don Morrow and Kevin Wamsley, *Sport in Canada: A History*; Bryan Palmer, *The Descent into Discourse*; Douglas Booth, "Escaping the Past? The Cultural Turn and Language in Sport History"; Bob Phillips, *Honour of Empire*.

2   FROM INDIGENOUS GAMES TO CITIES OF CHAMPIONS

1.   Ferguson, "Edmonton," 283.

2.   See Howell, *Blood, Sweat, and Cheers*; Cross, *A Social History*; Cox et al., "Sport in Canada, 1868–1900."

3.   Penz, "Ballgames of the North American Indians and in Late Medieval Europe"; see Mott, ed., *Sports in Canada*.

4.   Haslip, "A Treaty Right to Sport?"; Cosentino, *Afros, Aboriginals and Amateurs*; Pakes, "Skill to Do Comes of Doing"; Dewar, "Runners of the Plains," 3–4.

5.   Forsyth and Wamsley, "'Native to Native...We'll Recapture Our Spirits'"; Forsyth, "The Indian Act and the (Re)shaping of Canadian Aboriginal Sport Practices."

6. J. Wingrove, "Traditional Sport Breathes Life Into Native Communities," *Edmonton Journal*, June 10, 2007.

7. Forsyth and Wamsley, "'Native to Native...We'll Recapture Our Spirits.'"

8. Indigenous Sport Council Alberta, accessed September 4, 2009, http://www.aboriginalsports.org/home.html; Alberta Sport, Recreation, Parks and Wildlife Foundation, Future Leaders Program, accessed July 12, 2010, http://www.asrpwf.ca/recreation-active-living/future-leaders-program.aspx.

9. J. Hargreaves, *Heroines of Sport: The Politics of Difference and Identity*. Examples of Canadian Heritage agencies are the Canadian Association for the Advancement of Women and Sport and Physical Activity (CAAWS) and the Aboriginal Sport Circle.

10. Palmer and Palmer, *Alberta: A New History*.

11. Fudge, "The North West Mounted Police," 17-18.

12. Wilson, "Medicine Hat—'The Sporting Town'"; Fudge, "North West Mounted Police."

13. Wilson, "Medicine Hat—'The Sporting Town,'" 15.

14. Palmer and Palmer, *Alberta*, 117, 207.

15. Burnet, *Next Year Country*; Palmer and Palmer, *Alberta*.

16. Wetherell and Kmet, *Useful Pleasures*. By 1941, three-quarters of Alberta's population was still of British origin.

17. Jameson, "The Social Elite of the Ranch Community and Calgary," 66.

18. Palmer, "Immigrants and Other Settlement 1880-1920."

19. "Towns Should Arrange Non-conflicting Dates for Sports Events," *Macleod Gazette*, May 30, 1889: 4; Betke, "Winter Sports in the Early Urban Environment"; Dawe, *Red Deer*.

20. Mills, "100 Years," 203; Wetherell, "Making New Identities"; Artibise, "The Urban West."

21. David Leonard, "Popular Culture in Edmonton During the Second World War," in Ken Tingley, ed., *For King and Country: Alberta in the Second World War* (Edmonton: Provincial Museum of Alberta), 1995, available online, *World War II: The Homefront in Alberta*, Heritage Community Foundation, accessed November 9, 2006, http://www.albertasource.ca/homefront/feature_articles/popular_culture.html.

22. Short, "Hockey's Final Shining Days"; Palmer and Palmer, *Alberta*.

23. Bumsted, *Peoples of Canada*.

24. Vantour, *The Fabulous Flyers*; Wetherell, "Making New Identities"; Palmer and Palmer, *Alberta*; C. Spencer, "Political footballs," *Edmonton Journal*, July 7, 2007, B2.

25. For a study of government involvement in sport up to the 1970s, see R.S.P. Baka, "A History of Provincial Government Involvement in Sport in Western Canada," (M A thesis, University of Alberta, 1978).

26. Palmer and Palmer, *Alberta*; Wamsley and Heine, "Tradition, Modernity and the Construction of Civic Identity"; MacAloon, "Festival, Ritual and Television."

27. Baker, Lodge, and Tagg, *Weddings, Work and War*. See photograph P58000E5, City of Lethbridge Archives.

28. Bogle and Howe, "Women's Soccer."

29. Pitters-Caswell, "Women's Participation in Sporting Activities."

30. Status of Women Canada, "Women and Sports in Canada: A Historical Overview," 2003, accessed March 19, 2005, http://www.swc-cfc.gc.ca/dates/ whm/2002/history_e.html.

31. American Committee of the Y W C A, "The Physical Department," ca. 1900, Portland Y W C A Archives, qtd. in Salcedo, "Best of Intentions," 184.

32. Field, "Safe Haven," 7; Melnyk, "A Century of Solidarity"; Harshaw, *When Women Work*; Salcedo, "Best of Intentions."

33. Jose and Rannie, *The Story of Soccer in Canada*, 35.

34. Kidd, "Missing: Women from Sports Halls of Fame."

35. Minutes, A G M A A H A, Calgary, November 11, 1931, J.B. Long fonds, Red Deer and District Archives; Howell and Howell, *History of Sport*; Bogle and Howe, "Women's Soccer in Canada."

36. Kidd, "Women's Amateur Athletic Federation."

37. Harrigan, "Intercollegiate Sport, National Culture."

38. *The Albertan*, July 11, 1938, 14–16.

39. See, for instance, *Edmonton Journal*, "Once Great in Edmonton, Track, Field Languishes," September 1, 1955, newspaper clipping, H.E. Mildren Collection, M S 38, City of Edmonton Archives.

40. Lynn, *Women's Liberation*, 96.

41. D. Layzell, "Sports Women Reach Another Milestone," *Herald Magazine*, April 29, 1966: 11. Doreen Ryan won the group's first annual provincial award for all-round athlete in 1963.

42. Canadian Advisory Council, *Ten Years Later: An Assessment of the Federal Government's Implementation made by the Royal Commission on the Status of Women.*

43. Canadian Association for the Advancement of Women and Sport and Physical Activity (CAAWS), accessed April 24, 2007, http://caaws.ca/influentialwomen/. See also M.A. Hall, *The Girl and the Game*; Helen Lenskyj, *Out of Bounds*; Alberta Sports Hall of Fame and Museum, 2005.

44. Kidd, *Struggle for Canadian Sport*, 261.

45. Wamsley, "Power and Privilege in Historiography."

46. Kidd, "Making of a Hockey Artifact."

47. Freund, McGuire, and Podhurst, eds., *Health, Illness, and the Social Body*; Grierson, "Inscribing the Social Body"; Lock and Scheper-Hughes, "A Critical-interpretive Approach in Medical Anthropology"; Poovey, *Making a Social Body*.

3   FENCING THE FIELDS

1. May, "The Sportsman, an Edmonton Childhood Memoir." May, a successful businessman, and his friend, later better known as Lou Hyndman, Edmonton lawyer and chancellor of the University of Alberta, both managed to do quite well for themselves after all.

2. Bourdieu, "The Forms of Capital," 248.

3. McFarland, *The Development of Public Recreation in Canada*; Wetherell and Kmet, *Useful Pleasures*.

4. Guttmann, *Games and Empires*, 2; Dunning, *Sport Matters*.

5. Elizabeth Bailey Price, "Children on the Streets," *The Albertan*, July 3, 1912, (repr. in *Alberta History* 51, no. 3 [2003]: 24).

6. Bumsted, *Peoples of Canada*; Bouchier, *For the Love of the Game*; Cashman, "The First Alberta Marathon."

7. "Sport as a Social Force," *Edmonton Journal*, February 13, 1914, 4.

8. Kidd, "Muscular Christianity and Value-centred Sport"; Putney, *Muscular Christianity*; Bell, "History of Tennis at the University of Alberta." On Alberta context, see Howell, *Blood, Sweat, and Cheers* and Wetherell and Kmet, *Useful Pleasures*.

9. Until the mid-1960s, Alberta's Sunday observance laws prohibited charging for sporting and recreational activities, barring professional sport and community facility charges. G. Hunter, "One Man's Opinion,"

Calgary Herald, March 26, 1958, 36; "City Council, Legislature, Debate on Sunday Sport Issue," *Calgary Herald*, February 6, 1962, 17.

10. "Harry Duke Seeks New Fields For His Cagers to Conquer," *Vancouver Sun*, February 27, 1924, 5.

11. Bicket, *The Canadian Curler's Manual*, vi.

12. "Need of Reliance on God," *New York Times*, January 20, 1896, 3.

13. Pezer, *Stone Age*.

14. McLeod, *My First Bonspiel*, memoir recorded by Robert E. Gard.

15. Pezer, *Stone Age*.

16. Schissel, *Beiseker's Golden Heritage*, 43.

17. Coulter, "Patrolling the Passions of Youth."

18. Edmonton Federation of Community Leagues. "Historical Timeline," 2008, accessed April 24, 2009, http://www.efcl.org/EFCL/EFCLHistoricalTimeline/tabid/58/Default.aspx.

19. Mills, "100 Years."

20. von Heyking, "An Education for 'Character' in Alberta Schools, 1905–45"; von Heyking, *Creating Citizens*; Osborne, "Public Schooling and Citizenship Education in Canada"; Thomas, *Ryerson of Upper Canada*; Cosentino, *History of Physical Education in Canada*; *Canadian Encyclopedia*, s.v. "Physical Education (Kinesiology)," by Don Morrow, accessed 29 February 2012, http://www.thecanadianencyclopedia.com/index.cfm?PgNm=TCE&Params=A1ARTA0006272.

21. Prokop, "Canadianization of Immigrant Children," 5; von Heyking, *Creating Citizens*; Osborne, "Public Schooling."

22. Prokop, "Canadianization," 8; Gruneau and Whitson, *Hockey Night in Canada*, and Wetherell and Kmet, *Useful Pleasures*, also make the point that amateur sports was a means for immigrants and other community members to integrate socially.

23. Zeman, *Alberta on Ice*; Mills, "100 Years."

24. Alberta Schools Athletic Association, "Historical Overview," 2007, accessed April 25, 2008, http://www.asaa.ca/new/aboutasaa.php.

25. Canadian Interuniversity Sport, "History," accessed February 29, 2012, http://www.universitysport.ca/e/about/history.cfm.

26. Harrigan, "Women's Agency and the Development of Women's Intercollegiate Athletics"; Lamont, *We Can Achieve*.

27. M. Hirji, "Pandas Pioneer Strives to Recreate History," *The Gateway*, March 28, 2011, http://thegatewayonline.ca/articles/sports/2011/03/23/pandas-pioneer-strives-recreate-history.

28. "Basketball History was Made Saturday When Grads Suffered Defeat," *Edmonton Journal*, March 2, 1926 qtd. in Johns, *History of University of Alberta*, 102.

29. Helen Beny Gibson fonds, accession nos. 72-204, 78-135, University of Alberta Archives.

30. "Alberta Records go at Edmonton," *Calgary Daily Herald*, July 2, 1930, 7.

31. Harrigan, "Women's Agency"; Lamont, *We Can Achieve*.

32. Harrigan, "Women's Agency."

33. Statistics Canada, "W340-438, Full-time university enrolment, by sex, Canada and provinces, selected years, 1920 to 1975, Alberta and Saskatchewan," Government of Canada, 2008, accessed April 30, 2009, http://www.statcan.gc.ca/pub/11-516-x/sectionw/4147445-eng.htm.

34. Sanctioned activities and national championship areas now include a wide range of men's and women's sport. Alberta Colleges Athletic Conference, "An Introduction to the Alberta Colleges Athletic Conference," 2011, accessed November 24, 2011, http://www.acac.ab.ca/pages/about-us.php.

35. Harrigan, "Women's Agency"; Lamont, *We Can Achieve*.

36. Harrigan, "Women's Agency"; J. Jenkins, "Title XI Opponents a Bunch of Sad Sacks," *Washington Post*, June 24, 2002, D1.

37. Harrigan, "Women's Agency."

38. Lamont, *We Can Achieve*; Harrigan, "Women's Agency"; Morrow et al., *Concise History of Sport in Canada*.

39. University of Alberta, "Sports," accessed December 11, 2011, http://www.uofaweb.ualberta.ca/facts/nav01.cfm?nav01=94758; University of Calgary Dinos, "BLG Awards," 2007, accessed April 12, 2008, http://www.godinos.com/sports/2008/7/23/BLG.aspx?tab=blgawards; Kubish, "Great Teams at the University of Alberta."

40. M. Hirji, "Alberta teams top Gateway rankings," *The Gateway*, March 30, 2011, http://thegatewayonline.ca/articles/sports/2011/03/30/alberta-teams-top-gateway-rankings.

41. Kubish, "Great Teams"; Drager, "Clare Drake," 17.

42. "Excellence in Sport and Recreation Nets Alberta Centennial Awards for Faculty's Profs, Alumni," Faculty of Physical Education and Recreation, University of Alberta, 2005, accessed June 23, 2006, http://www.physedandrec.ualberta.ca/news.cfm?story=41075.

43. Morrow et al., *Concise History*; Harrigan, "Women's Agency."

44. "The Crystal Gazer," *The Gateway*, February 12, 1920, 1, http://repository. library.ualberta.ca/newspapers/.

45. "The Game's the Thing," *The Gateway*, January 9, 1930, 2, http://repository. library.ualberta.ca/newspapers/.

46. "School Spirit," *The Gateway*, January 23, 1930, 2, http://repository.library. ualberta.ca/newspapers/.

47. "The Game's the Thing," *The Gateway*, 2.

48. "School Spirit," *The Gateway*, 2.

49. "Czajkowski on Sport," *The Gateway*, September 19, 1969, http://repository. library.ualberta.ca/newspapers/.

50. In 1961-1962, almost $60,000 was spent to send teams to the Western Canada Intercollegiate Athletic Union competition. The hockey budget alone was $9,550, or $530 per player, and football's budget was $9,750. "Money Wasted on Sport?" *The Gateway*, November 17, 1961, 4, http://repository.library.ualberta.ca/newspapers/; Johns, *History of the University of Alberta*; ACAC, "Introduction," 2011, accessed November 24, 2011, http://www.acac.ab.ca/pages/about-us.php.

51. Smyth, "Sound Body, Sound Mind."

52. Cashman, "The First Alberta Marathon"; Bouchier, *For the Love of the Game*.

53. Bumsted, *Peoples of Canada*, 108-09.

54. H. Ballantyne, "Beginnings of the Amateur Athletic Union," *Edmonton Capital*, January 14, 1911, repr. in *Alberta History* 52, no. 3 (2004): 26.

55. Newspaper clipping, untitled, n.d., ca. 1910, Harold Burnham fonds, 75.79, Provincial Archives of Alberta.

56. Ballantyne, "Beginnings of Amateur Athletic Union."

57. "Busy Day in Edmonton on Saturday," *Calgary Daily Herald*, November 6, 1914, 10.

58. Amateur Athletic Union of Canada, Alberta Branch, M 6553, Glenbow Archives; Sport Alberta fonds, Glenbow Archives.

59. Mott, "British Protestant Pioneers."

60. Morrow et al., *Concise History.* During the pivotal interwar years, four groups were central to struggles of control: the Amateur Athletic Union of Canada; the Women's Amateur Athletic Federation; the Workers Sports Association; and the National Hockey League. Kidd, *Struggle for Canadian Sport.*

61. Betke, "Winter Sports," 64.

62. Brunt, "Changing Face of Sport."

63. Betke, "Winter Sports"; Cross, *A Social History.*

64. Wetherell and Kmet, *Useful Pleasures.*

4 "THE WEST HAS MADE FAIRLY GOOD HEADWAY"

1. University of Calgary Lacrosse Centre, "History," http://www.strc.ucalgary.ca/lacrosse/h.html. See also Morrow et al., *Concise History*; Cosentino, *Afros, Aboriginals and Amateur Sport.*

2. Fisher, *Lacrosse,* 5, 173.

3. Poulter, "Snowshoeing and Lacrosse."

4. Fisher, *Lacrosse.*

5. Beers, *Lacrosse,* vii.

6. Salter, "The Indian Athlete"; Cosentino, *Afros, Aboriginals and Amateur Sport*; Pakes, "Skill to Do Comes of Doing"; Unwin, "Who Do You Think I Am?"; Zeman, *To Run with Longboat.*

7. *Calgary Herald,* June 5, 1884 qtd. in "The Start of Lacrosse," *Calgary Herald,* September 15, 2008, http://www2.canada.com/calgaryherald/news/theeditorialpage/story.html?id=c2817948-f750-48d5-a51c-37533dbcfd18; Morrow et al., *Concise History*; University of Calgary Lacrosse Centre, "History," accessed February 29, 2012, http://www.kin.ucalgary.ca/strc/lacrosse/h.html.

8. *Edmonton Bulletin,* May 23, 1892 qtd. in Hess, "A Social History of Cycling in Edmonton."

9. Morrow et al., *Concise History*; Metcalfe, *Canada Learns to Play.*

10. Carl Carter, "Is Lloyd Loving Lacrosse?" *Lloydminster Meridian Booster,* April 2009, http://www.meridianbooster.com/ArticleDisplay.aspx?e=1499148; "Lacrosse is in a State of Crisis" CBC Archives, April 2, 1957, http://www.cbc.ca/archives/categories/sports/lacrosse/lacrosse-a-history-of-canadas-game/lacrosse-is-in-a-state-of-crisis.html; Metcalfe, *Canada Learns to Play.*

11. Angela Hill, "Lacrosse Season Starts," *High River Times*, April 2009, http://www.highrivertimes.com/ArticleDisplay.aspx?e=1435296.

12. "Taking the Commonwealth Games by Storm," CBC Archives, August 9, 1978, http://archives.cbc.ca/500f.asp?id=1-41-824-4869.

13. University of Calgary Lacrosse Centre, accessed January 29, 2005, http://www.kin.ucalgary.ca/strc/lacrosse/h.html.

14. "New Battle of Alberta is Born," Calgary Roughnecks, May 4, 2005, accessed September 29, 2007, http://www.calgaryroughnecks.com/html/prmay405.htm.

15. "Roughnecks Among League Elite," Calgary Roughnecks, accessed September 29, 2007, http://www.calgaryroughnecks.com/default.asp?webpage=467.

16. Associated Press, "NLL Cancels 2008 Season After Failing to Reach Labor Agreement," *Minnesota Daily*, October 17, 2007, http://www.mndaily.com/articles/2007/10/17/72163896.

17. Rees, *Polo*; Southern Alberta Pioneers and Their Descendants, "Wilmont, Edmond Meade," *Pioneer Profiles* (2004), accessed July 9, 2007, http://www.pioneersalberta.org/profiles/w2.html.

18. Evans, *The Bar U and Canadian Ranching History*; "Polo: 1st game of Macleod Polo Club," *Macleod Gazette* (Fort Macleod, AB), August 13, 1891, 3.

19. Reid, "Sports and Games in Alberta Before 1900."

20. Sheep Creek Polo Cup, Collections and Research, PI-19899 A-B, Glenbow Museum, http://www.glenbow.org/collections/museum/history/leisure.cfm; "Polo Association Should be Formed to Settle Disputes Between Clubs," *Macleod Gazette* (Fort Macleod, AB), October 5, 1894, 1.

21. Varty, "Polo and British Settlement."

22. HCF *Alberta Online Encyclopedia*, s.v. "Bar U Ranch Part 4: Gee Bong Polo Club," by Cheryl Croucher, accessed January 12, 2007, http://www.abheritage.ca/pasttopresent/en/rural_life/395_BarU_P4.html.

23. Roller skating polo team, Calgary, 1880s, NA-1075-21, Glenbow Archives.

24. Young, "The Reins in Their Hands."

25. Patton, "Good Old Glenmore School Days," 16.

26. *Wickets in the West* is the title of one of the first cricket tour books published to mark the Marylebone Cricket Club Canadian tour of 1872. Fitzgerald, *Wickets in The West*.

27. Birley, *A Social History of Cricket*, 96.

28. Johnes, "'Poor Man's Cricket.'"

29. *Victoria Daily Colonist*, March 16, 1863, qtd. in Sarah Pugh, Kathryn Gibbons, and Chris Adams, "Cricket: Colonial Keepsake or Canadian Cast-out?" Cricket in the British Empire, University of Victoria, 2002, accessed April 23, 2008, http://web.uvic.ca/vv/student/cricket/empire/canada.html.

30. "April 20, 1879: A Comparison of Cricket in England and America," *Brentano's Aquatic Monthly and Sporting Gazetteer*, qtd. in Dreamcricket USA, "History of American Cricket Part V, 1870s," April 23, 2008, http://www.dreamcricket.com/dreamcricket/news.hspl?nid=8923&ntid=4.

31. Western Canada Cricket Association Tournament program, Edmonton, August 2-7 1926, Bill Holmes Collection, Box 1, 97.393, Provincial Archives of Alberta.

32. Minute Book, Edmonton Cricket Club, September 27, 1957, Bill Holmes Collection, Box 1. 97.393, Provincial Archives of Alberta.

33. Edmonton and District Cricket League fonds, City of Edmonton Archives; "Lethbridge Cricket Club Formed," *Lethbridge News*, June 4, 1886, 3.

34. Barraclough, *From Prairie to Park*; Nick Lees, "Loonie for the Loss Campaign Gains Momentum, Higher Profile," *Edmonton Journal*, March 26, 2008, http://www2.canada.com/edmontonjournal/news/story.html?id=02ae560d-1960-4c89-b6c8-637122fcb4e6&p=1.

35. Marylebone Cricket Club Goodwill Tour, Official Souvenir Programme, August 13-14, 1937, Riley Park, Calgary and District Cricket League, Bill Holmes Collection, Box 1, 97.393, Provincial Archives of Alberta; Cooper, "Canadians Declare 'It Isn't Cricket'"; James, *Beyond a Boundary*.

36. Western Canada Cricket Association Tournament program, Edmonton August 2-7, 1926, Bill Holmes Collection, Box 1, 97.393, Provincial Archives of Alberta.

37. T. Pasternak, "Alberta Bound," Alberta Cricket Association, 2005, accessed June 23, 2006, http://www.cricket.ab.ca/aca/.

38. Cooper, "Canadians Declare 'It Isn't Cricket'"; Sandiford, *Cricket and the Victorians*.

39. Cooper, "Canadians Declare 'It Isn't Cricket.'"

40. ECL, Edmonton, February 26, 1963 to C.D. Lester, Calgary re: Alberta Cricket Association, letter, Edmonton and District Cricket League fonds, MS 326, Class 1, File 1, City of Edmonton Archives.

41. "Appeal Started by Cricketers," *Calgary Daily Herald*, July 7, 1930, 6.

42. As of 2010, the Edmonton Cricket Club was one of the few clubs in Canada with its own private ground, located in St. Albert. Edmonton and District Cricket League fonds, MS 326, Class 4, File 1, File 2, and Class 5, File 1, City of Edmonton Archives.

43. Minute Book, Edmonton Cricket Club, October 4, 1960, Bill Holmes Collection, Box 1, 97.393, Provincial Archives of Alberta.

44. M. Ahuja, personal communication, July 11, 2005; Salim Kara Cricket Co-ordinator Agakhan Sports Club, letter, Edmonton and District Cricket League fonds, MS 326 Class 1, City of Edmonton Archives; M.G. Gibb, Managing Director Alberta Sport Council, Edmonton to D.H. Holder, letter, Calgary, October 1, 1984, ACA.

45. Embry, "Transplanted Utah."

46. Mitchelson, "The Evolution of Men's Basketball in Canada, 1892–1936"; Embry, "Transplanted Utah"; Bowie and Day, "Sport and Religion"; Palmer and Palmer, *Alberta.*

47. Mary Nemeth, "A Patch of Hoops Heaven," *Maclean's,* March 20, 1995, 2.

48. "Outlaws and Altas are Winners in Two Exciting Games in 'Y' Hoop Leagues," scrapbook, newspaper clippings, November 29, 1923, Doris Neale Chapman fonds, MS 416, City of Edmonton Archives.

49. "International Cage League Will Be Discussed Sunday," *Edmonton Journal,* September 8, 1949, 11; "International Cage Circuit is Formed," *Edmonton Journal,* September 12, 1949, 8.

50. B. Johnson, "My Nickel's Worth," *Spokane Daily Chronicle,* June 8, 1954, 23.

51. "Outlaws and Altas are Winners in Two Exciting Games in 'Y' Hoop Leagues," scrapbook, newspaper clippings, November 29, 1923, Doris Neale Chapman fonds, MS 416, City of Edmonton Archives.

52. White, "Basketball in the Twenties," 137.

53. Tickets, Arthur Reid Lawrence fonds, MS 421, File 6, City of Edmonton Archives; Doris Neale Chapman fonds, MS 416, City of Edmonton Archives; Brochure, 1933, The Senior Girls Baseball League fonds, MS 574, City of Edmonton Archives; Mills, "100 Years"; "Alberta Gets Meet," *Montreal Gazette,* November 4, 1930, 16.

54. G. Nagel, "Growing up in McKernan," *Edmonton: A City Called Home,* accessed July 5, 2006, http://www.epl.ca/edmonton-a-city-called-home/ edmonton-a-city-called-home-story?id=747.

55. C. Macdonald, "The Edmonton Grads: Canada's Most Successful Team."

56. "Edmonton Grads: 25 Years of Basketball Championships, 1915-1940," 1975, http://www.archive.org/stream/edmontongrads25y00cana#page/n1/mode/2up.

57. "Sitting on Top of the World, 1915-1940: The Amazing Record of the Edmonton 'Grads,'" Edmonton Commercial Grads, 1940, accessed July 5, 2006, http://peel.library.ualberta.ca/bibliography/6357.html.

58. Terry Jones, "The Greatest Canadian Team," *Edmonton Centennial*, Sun Media, 2004, 26.

59. Official Programme and Score Card, International Basketball Championship, Edmonton Arena, October 25 and 27, 1927, 96.611, Provincial Archives of Alberta; Jack Manson fonds, File 7, Provincial Archives of Alberta.

60. "Jimmies Clash With Comets in Hoops Playdowns," *Calgary Daily Herald*, March 11, 1936, 6.

61. "Edmonton Grad Was an Icon in Her Day," *Edmonton Journal*, May 15, 2008, http://www.canada.com/edmontonjournal/news/sports/story.html?id=db5deef3-a882-496e-a307-36880b57bba1.

62. "Women's Best Basketball Team Quits," *Spokesman-Review* (Spokane, WA), April 10, 1940, 24. The article cited overall team wins of 516 games out of 540.

63. "Percy Page Announces New Team Will Succeed Edmonton's Grads," *Calgary Herald*, October 16, 1940, 7.

64. "Comets Shooting for Interprovincial Basketball Title Here Next Week," *Edmonton Journal*, April 9, 1941, 10.

65. "Grad-Comets Ad [*sic*] Another Record," *Calgary Herald*, April 7, 1942, 11.

66. Calgary 88s fonds, M-8067, Glenbow Archives.

67. Curtis J. Phillips, "Drillers Hope to Open a Door," October 14, 2004, American Basketball Association, *Our Sports Central*, http://www.oursportscentral.com/services/releases/?id=3092876; "Edmonton Owners Pull Plug on Playoff Trip, *Edmonton Journal*, June 29, 2010.

68. Metcalfe, *Canada Learns to Play*.

69. McLuhan, "Games: Extensions of Man."

70. McLennan, *Sport in Early Calgary*, 69; photograph of Edmonton baseball teams holding baby, 10-23, City of Edmonton Archives, repr. in Duccy, *Rajah of Renfrew*, 27.

71. *Lethbridge News*, July 19, 1900; City of Lethbridge, accessed August 26, 2006, http://www.lethbridge.ca/home/City+Hall/Departments/Leisure+and+Recreation+Services.

72. The Senior Girls Baseball League fonds, City of Edmonton Archives; Brochure, 1933, M S 574, City of Edmonton Archives; *The Albertan*, May 8, 1931, 5; Ted Knight fonds, M 8414 0s, Glenbow Archives; "Sporting Periscope," *Edmonton Journal*, August 28, 1930, 8.

73. Bumsted, *Peoples of Canada*, 22.

74. "Western Canada Baseball League: New League is formed in Alberta," *Morning Telegram* (Winnipeg), September 18, 1906, 14, repr. in *Western Canada Baseball 1907*, accessed November 8, 2007, http://www.attheplate.com/wcbl/1907_1.html.

75. Lamb, "Deacon White, Sportsman"; Mills, "100 Years"; Ducey, *Rajah of Renfrew*; Gilpin, *Edmonton*; See also, City of Edmonton Archives, *Deacon White, Founder of Modern Sport in Edmonton* (1995).

76. Stubbs, *Shoestring Glory*.

77. Stubbs, *Shoestring Glory*, 6.

78. Ducey, *Rajah of Renfrew*; Lamb, "Deacon White"; Humber, *Diamonds of the North*.

79. Broadfoot, *Ten Lost Years: 1929–1939*, 267.

80. Newspaper clipping, no title, *Edmonton Journal*, March 20, 1937, Women's Sports files, City of Edmonton Archives.

81. B. Sheridan, "From the Sportsbox," *The Plaindealer* (Drumheller), June 3, 1937, 6.

82. J. Wall, personal communication, Edmonton, July 29, 2005.

83. Photograph 524-43, City of Edmonton Archives, repr. in Ducey, *Rajah of Renfrew*, 250; Lamb, "Deacon White"; *Reach's Official Score Book*, J.B. Long fonds, Red Deer and District Archives.

84. Tingley, *City of Champions*.

85. Jay-Dell Mah, "1955...Last again, but wait'll next year," Western Canada Baseball, accessed March 17, 2008, http://www.attheplate.com/wcbl/1955_1.html.

86. John Ducey, "Interview with Mr. John Ducey, Edmonton's 'Mr. Baseball,' conducted by John McIsaac, 1979," Edmonton Parks and Recreation, City of Edmonton Archives; Stubbs, *Shoestrings*.

87. Mah, "1955...Last again," Western Canada Baseball, accessed March 17, 2008, http://www.attheplate.com/wcbl/1955_1.html.

88. Mah, "1955...Last again."

89. Hal Pawson, "The Sporting Periscope," Edmonton Journal, September 15, 1955, qtd. in Mah, "1955...Last again." The league included Lloydminster, Edmonton, Saskatoon, Moose Jaw, North Battleford, Moose Jaw, and Regina.

90. Taylor, "Sports in Review."

91. Taylor, "Sports in Review," 25; Mah, "Western Canada Baseball," Western Canada Baseball, 2011, www.attheplate.com/wcbl.

92. Mah, "1954, A Team of Our Own," Western Canada Baseball, accessed March 17, 2008, http://www.attheplate.com/wcbl/1954_1.htm; Mah, "1957... Nearly World Champs," Western Canada Baseball, 2009, http://www.attheplate.com/wcbl/1954_1.htm.

93. "Lethbridge Mounties," Bullpen, Baseball-reference.com, modified January 17, 2012, http://www.baseball-reference.com/bullpen/Lethbridge_Mounties.

94. Humber, Diamonds of the North, 62–74; McKenna, "History of Baseball."

95. Calgary Cannons fonds, M7989, Glenbow Archives. Parker also served as commissioner of the Alberta Major Baseball League.

96. "Edmonton Snowbirds," International Women's Professional Softball, updated April 25, 2011, http://sites.google.com/site/iwpsoftball/the-teams/edmonton-snowbirds.

97. "Father and Daughter Inducted into Hall of Fame," Alberta Sweetgrass, January 10, 2002, 3. Joan French of Alberta is also a member of the Canadian Softball Hall of Fame. Brian Swayne, "Capitals Will Pay Tribute to Edmonton Trappers," Edmonton Examiner, n.d. [August 2011.]

98. Horton, "They're Outta Here," Edmonton Journal, September 3, 2004.

99. Dan Barnes, "Lack of Attendance Costing Cracker-Cats Some of Their Nine Lives," Edmonton Journal, August 2, 2007.

100. Jessica Chen, "Rough Ice," Forbes, March 8, 2011, http://www.forbes.com/forbes/2011/0328/billionaires-11-possessions-daryl-katz-edmonton-oilers.html.

101. Brent Parker qtd. in G. Harder, "Parker reliving his baseball past," Leader-Post (Regina), August 10, 2007.

102. Cosentino, Canadian Football.

103. Lamb, "Rugby"; C F L, "History of the Edmonton Eskimos," accessed
January 5, 2007, http://www.cfl.ca/page/his_teams_edm; "Football a
Favorite Pastime in Lethbridge," *Lethbridge News*, March 26, 1886, 3;
"Lethbridge Football Club Organizational Meeting Called," *Lethbridge News*,
September 5, 1888, 3.

104. Dempsey "Calgary vs. Edmonton," 1.

105. Wolley-Dod qtd. in Dempsey, "Calgary vs. Edmonton," 2.

106. Dempsey, "Calgary vs. Edmonton," 10.

107. McLennan, "Sport in Early Calgary."

108. Lamb, "Rugby."

109. Cosentino, *Canadian Football.*

110. *Toronto Globe* author qtd. in Cosentino, *Canadian Football*, 49.

111. Calgary Canucks Rugby Club fonds, Glenbow Archives; Morrow et al.,
Concise History.

112. "New Western Rugby Football Body May be Organized Today," *Edmonton
Journal*, October 25, 1941, 10.

113. Alberta Rugby Union fonds, 1960-1983, M6930, Glenbow Archives. In the
spring of 1958, the teams involved were Edmonton Rugby Club (Pirates),
the Calgary Barbarians Rugger Club, the Edmonton Wanderers Rugby
Club, and the Penhold R C A F; Edmonton Rugby Football Club, "A Look Back
at 50 Years of Pirates History," Pirates Rugby, accessed June 21, 2008, http://
www.piratesrugby.ca/history/; Lamb, "Deacon White."

114. Lamb, "Deacon White."

115. Alberta Soccer Centennial, "100 Year History Timeline," 2009, accessed
August 3, 2009, http://albertasoccer100.ca/main.php?p=history.

116. Ted Knight fonds, Glenbow Archives.

117. A. Melville, "Footballers Made An Important Move by Declaring
Themselves," *Calgary Daily Herald*, November 25, 1913, 8.

118. R.C. Taylor, "Soccer Sounds her Challenge," *The Gateway*, November 1, 1920, 3.

119. "Last of the Original Esks, Mendryk Hangs Up Cleats," *Edmonton Journal*,
October 8, 1958, 9.

120. "R.E. Watkins, "A History of Canadian University Football," Canadian
University Sport, revised May 2006, http://www.cisfootball.org/history/
wirfu.html; "Golden Bears Football History," Faculty of Physical Education
and Recreation, University of Alberta, Edmonton, 2010, http://www.bears.
ualberta.ca/Football/men.

121. Colin Jose, "Alberta: The Early Years. History of Canadian Soccer 1876–1940," Canadian Soccer History, accessed February 13, 2012, http://www.canadiansoccerhistory.com/Alberta/Alberta-%20The%20Early%20Years.html.

122. "Alberta Soccer to Foster Junior Game Next Season," *Calgary Herald*, December 12, 1949, 20.

123. "1st DFC Victoria Soccer Club News 1965," Edmonton Cycle Club Record Book 1963–65, MS 194, City of Edmonton Archives.

124. Derek van Diest, "Alberta Soccer Honours Petrone," *Edmonton Sun*, December 9, 2009, http://www.edmontonsun.com/sports/soccer/2009/12/09/12089556-sun.html.

125. Alberta Soccer Centennial, "100 Year History Timeline," accessed January 12, 2009, http://albertasoccer100.ca/main.php?p=history.

126. Scott McKeen, "Indoor Soccer Rivals Hockey in Alberta," *Vancouver Sun*, January 16, 1999, B1, B4; G. Prince, "Pro Soccer in Edmonton...A Look Through the Years," Edmonton Drillers Archive, 2011, http://drillersarchive.com/index2.php?option=com_content&do_pdf=1&id=494.

127. Maurice Tougas, "Women's Soccer Team Kickstarts Interest," *Business Edge* 3, no. 39 (October 30, 2003), http://www.businessedge.ca/archives/article.cfm/pro-soccer-pitched-to-fans-as-solid-investment-4283.

128. Tougas, "Women's Soccer Team Kickstarts Interest."

129. Scott McKeen, "Indoor Soccer Rivals Hockey in Alberta," *Vancouver Sun*, January 16, 1999, B1, B4; Litterer, "Canadian Soccer League," 1996, accessed January 12, 2008, http://www.sover.net/~spectrum/csl.html; Gerry Prince, "Pro soccer in Edmonton, A Look Through the Years," 2004, accessed January 12, 2008, http://drillersarchive.com/index.php?option=com_content&task=view&id=494&Itemid=2; Canadian Major Indoor Soccer League, Press Release, "Canadian Major Indoor Soccer League Concludes Showcase Season Before Capacity Crowd," April 1, 2007, http://www.cmisl.com/.

130. Alberta Soccer Association, 2004, accessed January 23, 2008, http://www.albertasoccer.com.

131. "Our Club: Club Beginnings," Calgary Blizzard Soccer Club, accessed March 10, 2012, http://www.calgaryblizzard.com/index.php/history/96; Beckett, *History of Soccer in Alberta*.

132. "Soccer: The Canadian Soccer Association," NCAA, accessed April 29, 2008, http://www1.ncaa.org/membership.

133. Alberta Soccer Association, accessed April 29, 2008, www.albertasoccer. com/index; McKeen, "Indoor Soccer Rivals Hockey."

134. Alberta Soccer Association, accessed April 29, 2008, www.albertasoccer. com/index; McKeen, "Indoor Soccer Rivals Hockey."

135. "Argonauts Are Rugby Champions," *The Leader* (Regina), December 5, 1921, 10.

136. *Manitoba Free Press* qtd. in Cosentino, *Canadian Football*, 53.

137. Cashman, "Clarence Richards."

138. Cosentino, *Canadian Football*.

139. Mills, "100 Years," 218; J. Deacon, "Three-down nation," *Maclean's*, November 22, 2004, 43.

140. Cashman, "Clarence Richards"; Mills, "100 Years."

141. Cosentino, *Canadian Football*.

142. "Johnny Bright," *Edmonton Journal*, October 3, 2004, 33.

143. Edmonton Eskimos, "History," 2009, http://www.esks.com/page/history.

144. Terry Jones, "The Team that Time Forgot," *Edmonton Sun*, September 27, 2002.

145. Don Mackay qtd. in *Edmonton Journal*, October 30, 1952, qtd. in Eckert, "Development of Organized Recreation," 162.

146. "About Football Alberta," Football Alberta, 2008, www.footballalberta.ab.ca.

5   "LOVE AND HOMETOWN GLORY"

1. Bicket, *The Canadian Curler's Manual*, vii.

2. Adams, "Freezing Social Relations," 57.

3. B. Weeks, "Rock stars," *Globe and Mail*, April 2, 2005, D15; Pezer, *Stone Age*.

4. Norman McLeod, *My First Bonspiel*, memoir recorded by Robert E. Gard, n.d. (ca. 1940), University of Alberta Libraries: Alberta Folklore and Local History Collection, Alberta Folklore and Local History Collection 96-93-532, http://folklore.library.ualberta.ca/dspCitation.cfm?ID=132.

5. "Curliana," *Calgary Herald*, November 30, 1883 qtd. in Redmond, *The Sporting Scots of Nineteenth-Century Canada*, 134-35.

6. Redmond, *The Sporting Scots*, 135.

7. Wieting and Lamoureux, "Curling in Canada."

8. Adams, "Freezing Social Relations," 57.

9. "The Calgary Bonspiel," *The Albertan*, February 3, 1900, 1.

10. "Lethbridge's First Covered Rink Opens," *Lethbridge Daily News*, December 10, 1914, 2; Wilson, "Medicine Hat."

11. Pezer, *Stone Age*, 119.

12. Pezer, *Stone Age*, 75–86.

13. Pezer, *Stone Age*, 98–107.

14. City of Lethbridge, accessed September 23, 2008, http://www.lethbridge.ca/home/City+Hall/Departments/Leisure+and+Recreation+Services; Millet Ladies' Curling Club fonds, Millet and District Museum and Archives.

15. Pezer, *Stone Age*, 105.

16. Pezer, *Stone Age*, 107; Melissa Bell, "Ines Sainz and A Short History of Female Reporters in Locker Rooms," (blog) *Washington Post*, September 15, 2010, http://voices.washingtonpost.com/blog-post/2010/09/ines_sainz_and_a_short_history.html.

17. Calgary North Hill Curling Club, constitution and by-laws, qtd. in Pezer, *Stone Age*, 101.

18. Mills, "100 years," 205.

19. Dominion Curling Association, "Alberta Curling Association," *Rule Book of the Dominion Curling Association*, 69-73; Maxwell, *Canada Curls*.

20. Maxwell, *Canada Curls*; R. Lappage, "The Canadian Scene and Sport 1921–1939," in Howell and Howell, *History of Sport*.

21. "The Roots of Curling in Camrose," Alberta Scotties Tournament of Hearts, accessed February 2, 2011, http://www.2011albertascotties.com/default.aspx?p=clubhistory.

22. "Roots of Curling in Camrose," Alberta Scotties Tournament of Hearts.

23. "Administrative History/Biographical Sketch," Edmonton B'nai Brith Lodge No. 732 fonds, Archives Canada, archivescanada.ca; B'nai Brith Menorah Curling Club fonds, 1947-1999, Provincial Archives of Alberta.

24. Maxwell, *Canada Curls*.

25. "Innocents Aboard," clipping, January 18, 1961, newspaper photograph of E. Lees and E. Morton boarding train, Ethel Lees fonds, 94.31, Red Deer and District Archives; D. Scott, "Lees, Baillie Rinks Reach Curling Final," *Calgary Herald*, February 11, 1960, 53.

26. Pezer, *Stone Age*.

27. J.R.S. Hambly, "Behind the Glass," *Camrose Canadian*, December 14, 1960, 2.

28. Pezer, *Stone Age*, 102.

29. "Curling Statistics," Alberta Sport History Project, updated November 6, 2010, http://libguides.ucalgary.ca/content.php?pid=83876&sid=1378965.

30. J.R.S. Hambly, "Behind the Glass," *Camrose Canadian*, December 14, 1960, 2.

31. Pezer, *Stone Age*.

32. Edmonton Heritage Council, "Edmonton's Curling Legacy," 2009, http://www.edmontonheritage.ca/go/programs1/heritage-exhibits/.

33. Pezer, *Stone Age*, 254; Wood and King, "Sweeping Up: Alberta Curling."

34. "Curling Statistics," Alberta Sport History Project, updated November 6, 2010, http://libguides.ucalgary.ca/content.php?pid=83876&sid=1378965.

35. J. Morris, "Alberta's Kevin Martin Wins Tim Hortons Brier," City News, March 16, 2008, http://www.citynews.ca/news/news_20669.aspx; Canadian Curling Association, "Alberta's Kevin Martin Claims Brier Crown," March 16, 2008, http://www.curling.ca/content/NewsAndFeatures/news7.asp; "Ferbey to Martin: 'Get over it, Kevin,'" *Edmonton Journal*, February 7, 2007; K. Gilchrist, "Fitness Regimens No Longer Being Swept Aside by Curlers," *The Province* (BC), March 10, 2009; Wieting and Lamoureux, "Curling in Canada."

36. "CBC to Restructure Curling Coverage for Brier After Scott Debacle," *Edmonton Journal*, March 6, 2005; "Brier Final Draws 1.499 Million CBC Viewers," *Globe and Mail*, March 14, 2005; Alan Maki, "Curling Rocks," *Globe and Mail*, April 9, 2005, F2.

37. Jesse Kohl, "As Curling Heats Up, Eyeball Wars in the Offing," Media in Canada, March 22, 2007, http://www.mediaincanada.com/articles/mic/20070322/curling.html.

38. Moore qtd. in Kohl, "As Curling Heats Up."

39. Wieting and Lamoureux, "Curling in Canada."

40. Dryden and MacGregor, *Home Game*, 2.

41. J. Holubitsky, "New Ice Age Here for Avid Hockey Town," *Edmonton Journal*, August 16, 2007.

42. "Mayerthorpe Arena Burns to the Ground," CBC News, July 29, 2008, http://www.cbc.ca/canada/edmonton/story/2008/07/29/arena-fire.html.

43. Dryden and MacGregor, *Home Game*, 9.

44. Hughes-Fuller, "Am I Canadian?" 27; Batistella, *Shinny: The Hockey in All of Us*.

45. Gruneau, "Modernization or Hegemony."

46. Gruneau and Whitson, *Hockey Night*, 26.

47. Dryden and MacGregor, *Home Game*, 20.

48. "From Saturday's Daily," *Calgary Weekly Herald*, January 4, 1893.

49. "The Curling Rink," *Calgary Weekly Herald*, March 22, 1893, 8; Sandor, *Battle of Alberta*.

50. Newspaper clipping, Mrs. John Darley Harrison fonds, City of Edmonton Archives.

51. Norton, *Women on Ice*, 53; Zeman, *Alberta on Ice*.

52. *Calgary Daily Herald*, January 13, 1911, 9.

53. O'Riordan, "The 'Puck-Eaters.'"

54. Ray Turchansky, "Once the Fans were Caged the Game Could Start," *Edmonton Journal*, October 3, 2004, 55.

55. Wood and King, "Amateur Hockey in Alberta," 198–99; Sandor, *Battle of Alberta*, 126.

56. Sandor, *Battle of Alberta*, 19.

57. Sandor, *Battle of Alberta*, 16.

58. *Edmonton Bulletin*, March 1934, newspaper clipping, Monarchs file, H.E. Mildren Collection, MS 38, City of Edmonton Archives.

59. Christina McKnight, untitled, H.E. Mildren Collection, Monarchs file, MS 38, City of Edmonton Archives; "Monarchs play Regents on Monday," clippings, February 1917, "Ladies Play Another Tie Hockey Game," n.d., ca. 1916–1917, and "Girls' Teams to Play Hockey Friday Night," n.d., ca. 1916, H.E. Mildren Collection, Monarchs file, MS 38, City of Edmonton Archives.

60. Norton, *Women on Ice*, 108, 125; Clippings files, Monarchs file, H.E. Mildren Collection, MS 38, City of Edmonton Archives.

61. Zeman, *Alberta on Ice*; Dawe, *Red Deer*.

62. Kossuth, "Hockey on the Margins," 70–77.

63. Zeman, *Alberta on Ice*.

64. Robinson, *Crossing the Line*, 64.

65. Zeman, *Alberta on Ice*.

66. G. Moysa, "Lords of the Ring," *See Magazine* (Edmonton), November 27–December 3, 2003. Joan and Reg Woods were instrumental in building the sport in Alberta.

67. Betke, "Winter Sports"; Mills, "100 Years."

68. Harold Atkins, "Cross-Canada Sports Snippings," *The Standard* (Montreal), November 13, 1948.

69. R. Hayden, "Elaborate Scouting System Spreads to Alberta's Open Rinks," *Calgary Herald*, January 6, 1939, 7.

70. Ken Dryden, "Soul on Ice," *The Beaver* 80, no. 6, December 2000–January 2001, 18–25.

71. "Alberta Junior Hockey League: History," Alberta Junior Hockey League, 2006, http://ajhl.ca/league/about_ajhl.html.

72. City of Edmonton, "George S. Hughes South Side Arena honours a lifetime of community and sport contributions," October 24, 2008, http://www. edmonton.ca/city_government/news/7677.aspx.

73. Wood and King, "Amateur Hockey," 199.

74. "Why Here is Gordon Watt," clipping, n.d., ca. 1939, Alex Watt fonds, MS 541, City of Edmonton Archives.

75. Turchansky, "Oil Kings Once Ruled Western Junior Hockey," *Edmonton Journal*, September 17, 2007; *Edmonton Exhibition Association 1906–1964*, vol. 1, *Archives Special Collection*, 1989, City of Edmonton Archives.

76. Paula Simons, "Former Oil King Captain Will Get Medal He Helped Canada Win," *Edmonton Journal*, May 3, 2005, B1; Smallwood, *In the Hearts of Kings*.

77. "Alberta Junior Hockey League: History," Alberta Junior Hockey League, 2006, http://ajhl.ca/league/about_ajhl.html; Hunter and Weber, *Wild Bill*; D. Erickson, "Puck Patter," Official Program, Edmonton Oil Kings, Memorial Cup 1962–63, MS 366, A84-89, City of Edmonton Archives.

78. Turchansky, "Oil Kings Once Ruled"; Turchansky, "Oil Kings Lose"; Drinnan, "WHL History"; Hunter and Weber, *Wild Bill*; Montgomery, "Ken McAuley"; Erickson, "Puck Patter," Official Program, Edmonton Oil Kings, Memorial Cup 1962–63, MS 366, A84-89, City of Edmonton Archives.

79. "Alberta Junior Hockey League: History," Alberta Junior Hockey League, 2006, http://ajhl.ca/league/about_ajhl.html.

80. "Team History," Golden Bears and Pandas Athletics, University of Alberta, 2012, http://www.bears.ualberta.ca/en/Teams/PandasHockey/Team %20History.aspx.

81. Hockey League History, "Amateur and Senior Hockey Leagues," accessed January 30, 2009, http://hockeyleaguehistory.com/amateur_leagues.htm.

82. Edmonton Oilers Heritage, accessed January 30, 2009, http://www. oilersheritage.com/index2.html.

83. Sandor, *Battle of Alberta*, 22–24.

84. Zeman, *Alberta on Ice*. See Allan Cup, http://www.allancup.ca.

85. F.M. Gerrie, "Eskimos Win Championship in Thrilling Overtime Struggle," *Edmonton Journal*, March 17, 1923, 28.

86. Edmonton Oilers Heritage, accessed January 30, 2009, http://www.oilersheritage.com/index2.html; Sandor, *Battle of Alberta*.

87. McGillis, "North Side Story," 202.

88. Riley Mullen to Dave "Sweeney" Schriner, letter, October 22, 1946, qtd. in Vantour, *The Fabulous Flyers*, 5.

89. Edmonton Oilers Heritage, accessed January 30, 2009, http://www.oilersheritage.com/index2.html.

90. D. Matthews, "Leafs Retain Alberta Senior Hockey Championship," *Lethbridge Herald*, March 25, 1942.

91. Jack Manson's Hockey Scrapbook, A 97-171, City of Edmonton Archives; Sandor, *Battle of Alberta*, 88.

92. *Edmonton Exhibition Association*; Fay Faehrer fonds, M S 372, Provincial Archives of Alberta.

93. T. Jones, "Mercurys Rising," *Edmonton Sun*, December 11, 2001. Jack Manson's Hockey Scrapbook, clippings, "Big Parade to Welcome Mercurys," *Edmonton Bulletin*, n.d.; "Cheer Mercurys Tomorrow," *Edmonton Journal*, April 5, 1950, A 97-171, City of Edmonton Archives.

94. *Canadian Encyclopedia*, s.v. "Edmonton Mercurys," by F. Cosentino, accessed April 21, 2001, http://www.thecanadianencyclopedia.com/articles/edmonton-mercurys.

95. M. Mandel, "Mercurys Were Kings in 1952," *Toronto Sun*, February 27, 1994.

96. *Canadian Encyclopedia*, s.v. "Edmonton Mercurys," by F. Cosentino, accessed April 21, 2001, http://www.thecanadianencyclopedia.com/articles/edmonton-mercurys.

97. Wood and King, "Amateur Hockey in Alberta," 201; Lacombe and District Chamber of Commerce "Sports and Recreation," in *Lacombe: The First Century*, 369-406.

98. Short, "Shining Days," 284-88; Wong, "It's a Free Country," 5-6.

99. Jack Manson's Hockey Scrapbook, A 97-171, City of Edmonton Archives; Zeman, *Alberta on Ice*.

100. J. Short, "Out of Sham Amateurs came Frank Professionalism," in Byfield, ed., *Alberta in the Twentieth Century*, vol. 5, 244-88.

101. Betke, "Winter Sports," 64; Art Gagne fonds, M S 514, A87-134, City of Edmonton Archives.

102. Duhatschek et al. Hockey Chronicles; Sandor, *Battle of Alberta*, 93.

103. "NHL Digs Ralph," *Calgary Sun*, June 16, 2001, 3.

104. "Edmonton Investors Group Ltd.—A Last-minute Reprieve," Edmonton Oilers Heritage, accessed January 12, 2008, http://www.oilersheritage.com/legacy/contributions_owners_EIG.html; G. Lamphier, "Katz Bids to Buy Oilers," *Edmonton Journal*, May 5, 2007.

105. E. Weiner, "Canada Gains Expansion Value With Loonie," *New York Sun*, September 27, 2007, http://www.nysun.com/sports/canada-gains-expansion-value-with-loonie/63509/; K. Allen, "With NHL's Salary Cap Comes a Leveling of the Ice," *USA Today*, September 29, 2009, http://www.usatoday.com/sports/hockey/nhl/2009-09-28-nhl-salary-cap_N.htm.

106. Bumsted, *Peoples of Canada*, 109.

107. Rutherford, *When Television was Young*, 251.

108. Rutherford, *When Television was Young*, 271.

109. Bowling, "Na Na Na Na, Hey Hey Hey, Goodbye," 47.

110. R. Litwinowich, personal communication, Edmonton, May 20, 2006.

111. Photograph of girls' hockey school, Calgary, Alberta, September 1974, NA-2864-26082, Glenbow Archives.

112. Charlie Gillis, "Girls Give Hockey a Badly Needed Lift," *Maclean's*, March 8, 2004.

113. "Honouring Women's Hockey," *Montreal Gazette*, November 12, 2010.

114. Hockey Alberta Foundation, "News Release: Hockey Alberta Foundation Continues to Preserve Alberta Hockey History," December 9, 2005, http://www.hockeyalbertafoundation.ca/UserFiles/File/Ed%20Flyers%20NR.pdf.

115. Evan Daum, "Minor Hockey Week a Family Affair," *Edmonton Journal*, January 23, 2012, http://www.edmontonjournal.com/sports/Minor+Hockey+Week+family+affair/6035054/story.html.

116. Ramshaw and Hinch, "Place Identity and Sport Tourism"; Mason, Duquette, and Scherer, "Heritage, Sport Tourism and Canadian Junior Hockey."

117. Terry Jones, "Heritage and Heart: Minor Hockey Has a Special Feeling This Year," *Edmonton Sun*, January 14, 2004.

118. University of Alberta, "Golden Bears Ice Hockey History," Golden Bears Hockey, http://www.bears.ualberta.ca//pdfs/2006-BearsHockey.pdf; University of Calgary, Dinos Hockey Program, University of Calgary

Athletics, accessed October 19, 2009, http://www.godinos.com/
sports/2008/7/21/MHK_0721081458.aspx?path=mhockey.

119. Dronyk, "The Puck Artist," 74.

6 SPORT AND THE SINGLE ATHLETE

1. van Herk, *Mavericks*, 325.

2. C. Stock, "Calgary Stampede," *You Bet* (blog), *Edmonton Journal*, November 11, 2006, www.canada.com/edmontonjournal/news/blog/stock.html?post=5238.

3. L. Drake, "Liberal Leader Wants Rodeo to be Alberta's Official Sport," *Edmonton Journal*, November 6, 2008.

4. "Quebec 'Snub' Misinterpreted," *Montreal Gazette*, October 1, 1965, 1.

5. Wetherell, "Making Tradition," 24-28.

6. Wetherell, "Making Tradition," 23-26; Silversides, *Shooting Cowboys*.

7. T. Babiak, "A Free Man Rides Off Into History," *Edmonton Journal*, February 20, 2011; University of Calgary, "Black Immigrants," Calgary and Southern Alberta, Applied Research Group, 1997, http://www.ucalgary.ca/applied_history/tutor/calgary/black.html; MacEwan, *John Ware's Cow Country*.

8. Faulkner, *Turn Him Loose!*, 1-3.

9. Herman Linder fonds, M 3973, file 9, NA 3252, Glenbow Archives; Dewar, "Herman Linder," 38-39.

10. John Douglas McCulloch fonds, Pete Knight materials, Glenbow Archives; Knight, *Pete Knight*; HCF *Alberta Online Encyclopedia*, s.v. "Wilf Carter," accessed April 24, 2010, http://www.abheritage.ca/albertans/people/atlantic_wilf.html.

11. Silversides, *Shooting Cowboys*; Town of Raymond, September 19, 2008, http://www.townofraymond.com/stampede/mainstampede.html; Wetherell and Kmet, *Useful Pleasures*.

12. Foran, "More Than Ten Days of Fun," 179; Wetherell, "Making Tradition," 24-27; Foran, "The Stampede in Historical Context."

13. Maxwell Foran qtd. in *Dreamers and Doers, A Documentary on 100 Years of Arts and Culture in Alberta* (DTMI, 2004), http://www.dreamersanddoers.ca/transcripts2.htm.

14. Wetherell, "Making Tradition," 30; Seiler and Seiler, "The Social Construction of the Canadian Cowboy," 304.

15. *The Albertan*, July 12, 1938, 1.

16.   Herman Linder, Calgary, July 31, 1951 to James Paul, EEA, Edmonton, letter, EEA M5322, Class 70, s/c 5, File 1, City of Edmonton Archives.

17.   EEA M5322, Class 70, s/c 5, File 5, City of Edmonton Archives. Media organizations included CJCA, CHED, CHFA, CBX, CKUA, *Edmonton Journal*, and *Edmonton Sun*.

18.   James Paul, EEA, July 21, 1953 to Guy Weadick, Arizona, letter, EEA M5322, Class 70, s/c 5, File 4, City of Edmonton Archives.

19.   Edmonton Rodeo 1957 Official Program (7th annual), *Edmonton Rodeo of Champions*, April 29–May 4, Edmonton Gardens, EEA M5322, Class 70, s/c 5, File 6, City of Edmonton Archives.

20.   EEA M5322, Class 70, s/c 5, File 1, City of Edmonton Archives; Rodeo Committee Minutes May 30, 1960, EEA M5322, Class 70, s/c 5, File 6, City of Edmonton Archives; EEA M5322, Class 70, s/c 5, Files 3, 4, and 6, City of Edmonton Archives; M. Male, "Canadian Finals Rodeo (CFR) Attendance Numbers," MasterMaq (blog), November 17, 2009, http://blog.mastermaq. ca/2009/11/17/canadian-finals-rodeo-cfr-attendance-numbers/.

21.   Wetherell, "Making Tradition," 42.

22.   Canadian Professional Rodeo Association fonds, Canadian Girls Rodeo Association fonds, Glenbow Archives; Silversides, *Shooting Cowboys*; Gunderson, *The Linder Legend*, 20–23.

23.   "Managers Feel Too Many Rodeos Being Staged," *Calgary Herald*, December 7, 1950, 17.

24.   Canadian Girls' Rodeo Association fonds, 1959–1990, M7703/65, Glenbow Archives.

25.   Cowgirls' Super Challenge program, 1981, 7, Canadian Girls' Rodeo Association fonds, M7703/65, Glenbow Archives.

26.   Canadian Girls' Rodeo Association fonds, M7703/65, Glenbow Archives; "Sponsors," Canadian Girls Rodeo Association, accessed February 18, 2012, http://www.canadiangirlsrodeoassociation.com.

27.   "Group Gets Cash, Seeks Volunteer Labour For New Soccer Fields," *Provost News*, April 16, 2003, http://www.provostnews.ca/thenews/arch/2003/ april_16.html.

28.   Burgess, "Canadian 'Range Wars'"; Wetherell, "Making Tradition"; Dewar, "The Canadian Indian Cowboy," 26.

29.   Indian Days Cover Feature," *Crag & Canyon*, June 17, 1955, 1.

30.   Furniss, "Cultural Performance as Strategic Essentialism," 23–40.

31. "Indian Rodeo Associations," Rodeo, Canadian Museum of Civilization, updated April 1, 2010, http://www.civilization.ca/cmc/exhibitions/aborig/rodeo/rodeo91e.shtml; Iverson and MacCannell, *Riders of the West.*

32. Penrose, "When All the Cowboys are Indians," 703–05.

33. "Down the Road," Rodeo, Canadian Museum of Civilization, updated April 1, 2010, http://www.civilization.ca/cmc/exhibitions/aborig/rodeo/rodeo96e.shtml.

34. Terry Lust, "Alberta Cowboys Rake in Most of the Big Bucks," *Alberta Sweetgrass,* January 13, 2000, 11.

35. "What Makes Native Rodeo Different?" Rodeo, Canadian Museum of Civilization, updated April 1, 2010, http://www.civilization.ca/cmc/exhibitions/aborig/rodeo/rodeo90e.shtml.

36. van Herk, *Mavericks*; Eckert, "Development of Organized Recreation."

37. "Api-Kai-Ees, Deerfoot," Honoured Members, Alberta Sports Hall of Fame and Museum, accessed February 18, 2012, http://www.albertasportshalloffame.com/component/zoo/item/deerfoot; HCF *Alberta Online Encyclopedia,* s.v. "The Siksika Nations Profiles: Deerfoot," accessed July 24, 2009, http://www.albertasource.ca/treaty7/traditional/siksika_deerfoot.html.

38. Dewar, "Alex Wuttunee Decoteau," 54; Edmonton Public Library, "Alex Decoteau Historical Timeline," *Edmonton: A City Called Home,* accessed July 24, 2009, http://www.epl.ca/edmonton-a-city-called-home/edmonton-a-city-called-home-story?id=251. Alex Latta Jr. fonds and G.R. Bowen fonds, City of Edmonton Archives.

39. *Wetaskiwin Free Press* advertisement, 1931, Carl Walin fonds, WET-98.10, City of Wetaskiwin Archives.

40. "Alberta Track and Field Stars Return," *Calgary Daily Herald,* September 14, 1937, 6; "George Sutherland," Honoured Members, Alberta Sports Hall of Fame and Museum, accessed February 18, 2012, http://www.albertasportshalloffame.com; B. Ibsen, Track and Field, EA-302-65, City of Edmonton Archives.

41. "Edmonton's Skitch Arrives in Montreal," *Edmonton Journal,* March 20, 1948, clipping, H.E. Mildren Collection, MS 38, City of Edmonton Archives.

42. *Canadian Encyclopedia,* s.v. "Jones Konihowski, Diane," by Ted Barris, accessed March 10, 2012, http://www.thecanadianencyclopedia.com/articles/diane-jones-konihowski.

43. 1932 Canadian Olympic Team Trials Official Program, Charlotte Medvard Dawes Collection, MS 139 File 1, City of Edmonton Archives.

44. "Women's Participation," program, British Empire Games, Hamilton, Canada, August 16-23, 1930; "Charlotte Daws [*sic*] Gives Edmonton Olympic Club 3 Wins in South," *Edmonton Bulletin*, September 17, 1931, newspaper clipping, Charlotte Medvard Dawes Collection, MS 139 File 2, City of Edmonton Archives.

45. "Three Records Shattered by Edmonton Athlete at Highland Games Meet," n.d., ca. 1930s, Charlotte Medvard Dawes Collection, MS 139, File 4, City of Edmonton Archives; "Once great in Edmonton, Track, Field Languishes," *Edmonton Journal*, September 1, 1955, newspaper clipping, H.E. Mildren Collection, MS 38, City of Edmonton Archives.

46. "Rivet, Vera (nee Barilko)," obituary, *Edmonton Journal*, August 25, 2004; "Albertans Dominate Local Speed Skating Meet," *Saskatoon StarPhoenix*, February 18, 1947, 11; "Raymond Cagers Take Lead in Girls' Provincial Final," *Edmonton Journal*, April 1, 1950, 16.

47. J. Soltek, "Bearcat Murray to be Honoured by Hall of Fame," *Western Wheel* 34, no. 15 (November 12, 2008), 1. Murray is listed as Annabelle McLean in the Alberta Sports Hall of Fame, http://www.albertasportshalloffame.com.

48. See, for example, newspaper report on a Calgary prep school, "Education in Alberta," *The Leader* (Regina), August 25, 1898, 8.

49. "Once Great in Edmonton, Track, Field Languishes," *Edmonton Journal*, September 1, 1955, clipping, H.E. Mildren Collection, MS 38, City of Edmonton Archives.

50. Norcliffe, *Ride to Modernity*; Hess, "Social History of Cycling."

51. Klassen, "Bicycles and Automobiles," 2; "Bicycle Club Organized at Lethbridge" *Lethbridge News*, May 4, 1893, 3.

52. Hess, "A Social History of Cycling"; Klassen, "Bicycles and Automobiles"; "Bicycle Club Organized at Lethbridge," *Lethbridge News*, May 4, 1893, 3; Wilson, "Medicine Hat."

53. Klassen, "Bicycles and Automobiles"; Edmonton Cycle Club Record Book, 1963-1965, MS 194, City of Edmonton Archives.

54. Ernest Brown photograph collection, Provincial Archives of Alberta.

55. "Mr. J.H. Wrigley, Lethbridge, Wins Bicycle Championship at Regina," *Macleod Gazette*, July 27, 1894, 4; "J.H. Wrigley Explains Unfair Treatment at Regina Turf Club," *Lethbridge News*, August 1, 1894, 2; "Mr. Wrigley,

Lethbridge, Barred for 2 Years by Winnipeg Turf Association," *Macleod Gazette*, August 17, 1894, 4.

56. Klassen, "Bicycles and Automobiles"; Hess, "Social History of Cycling"; Glass, "Cycling in the Province of Alberta."

57. Klassen, "Bicycles and Automobiles"; Lindsay and Hess, "Sporting Elites in Late Nineteenth Century Edmonton," 42–43; Hess, "Social History of Cycling."

58. Norcliffe, *Ride to Modernity*, 192–93.

59. Hess, "Social History of Cycling," 23.

60. Hess, "Social History of Cycling," i.

61. "Not How 'Cheap' But How 'Good,'" *Calgary Daily Herald*, May 19, 1919, 20.

62. Edmonton Exhibition Parade July, 1939, E A-160-1158, City of Edmonton Archives; Northern Alberta Bicycle Association, July, 1937, E A-160-1173, City of Edmonton Archives; H. A. Hollingworth, "Northern Alberta Bicycle Association Bicycle Race," July, 1937, E A-160-1178, City of Edmonton Archives; "Paul Smith Looks Over the Bulletin Trophy," August 28, 1950, EA-600-4939, City of Edmonton Archives; "Fairgrounds and Race Track," Didsbury, Alberta, 1909, N A-2135-2, Glenbow Archives.

63. F. Taylor, "Cycle Race Site Switched," *Edmonton Journal*, June 1, 1963; Edmonton Cycle Club Record Book, 1963–1965, M S 194, City of Edmonton Archives.

64. C. Vallentgoed, personal communication, Edmonton, April 20, 2005.

65. L. Arrowsmith, "Olympic Gold Medallist Lori-Ann Muenzer Announces Retirement from Cycling," C B C Sports, October 30, 2006, http://www.cbc.ca/cp/sports/061030/s103066.html; J. Korobanik, "J. Muenzer Wheels into Retirement," *Edmonton Journal*, October 31, 2006.

66. J. MacKinnon, "Whitten's Winning Ways Bringing in Big Bucks," *Edmonton Journal*, March 21, 2011.

67. Bell, "History of Tennis"; Eckert, "Development of Organized Recreation."

68. Hendriks, *William Bleasdell Cameron*, 171.

69. Newspaper clipping, *The Albertan*, July 18, 1938, Beverley Alexander file, Galt Museum Archives.

70. Bell, "History of Tennis."

71. Bell, "History of Tennis"; Garneau Tennis and Beach Volleyball, "History," accessed February 18, 2012, http://www.garneau-tennis.com/about-us.

72. "Provincial Net Tournament Opens at Lethbridge," *Calgary Herald*, July 17, 1939, 6; "Sports of All Sorts," *Edmonton Bulletin*, June 17, 1921; "Highlands Lawn Tennis Tourney Now Under Way," *Edmonton Bulletin*, June 27, 1916, newspaper clipping, H.E. Mildren Collection, MS 38, City of Edmonton Archives.

73. Bell, "History of Tennis"; D. Fleming, Sport column, *Edmonton Journal*, November 19, 1982.

74. B. Cheevers, "First Aid Veteran Wanted to be Ready," *Calgary Herald*, November 27, 1976; "St. John Ambulance Wins Dominion First Aid Prizes," *Calgary Herald*, October 28, 1947, 6.

75. Wamsley, "Strangers in the Eighteenth Hole"; Kenneth L. Crockett, "The Early History of the Mayfair Golf and Country Club," Address on sixtieth anniversary, May 29, 1982, Kenneth Crockett fonds, MS 447 A 82-76, City of Edmonton Archives.

76. Wamsley, "Strangers in the Eighteenth Hole"; McLennan, *Sport in Early Calgary*.

77. "Ladies Form Golf Branch for Alberta," *Calgary Daily Herald*, April 19, 1928, 6.

78. Wamsley, "Strangers in the Eighteenth Hole," 5.

79. J.W. McClung, "The Tradition," *Edmonton Country Club*, November 1995, http://www.edmontoncountryclub.com/The-Club-%281%29/The-Early-Years.aspx.

80. McClung, "Edmonton Country Club."

81. McClung, "Edmonton Country Club."

82. K.L. Crockett, "The Early History of the Mayfair Golf and Country Club," Address on sixtieth anniversary, May 29, 1982, Kenneth Crockett fonds, MS 447 A 82-76, City of Edmonton Archives; Alberta Golf Association 1935–1981, Glenbow Archives.

83. Alberta Golf Association fonds, M 627, Glenbow Archives; Wamsley, "Strangers in the Eighteenth Hole."

84. Redmond, *The Sporting Scots*, 240.

85. Barraclough, *From Prairie to Park*, 77; Lawrence Herzog, "Canada's First Municipal Golf Course," *It's Our Heritage* 20, no. 32, August 8, 2002, http://www.rewedmonton.ca/content_view2?CONTENT_ID=167.

86. Banff Springs Golf Club, Ladies Section fonds, Whyte Museum of the Canadian Rockies Archives.

87. "Golf Notes," *Camrose Canadian*, July 21, 1948, 1.

88. J. Robbie et al., "History," Highlands Golf Club, written 1989, accessed February 29, 2012, http://highlandsgolfclub.memberstatements.com/tour/tours.cfm?tourid=67260; Wamsley, "Strangers"; "Henry Martell," Canadian Professional Golfers Association, accessed February 29, 2012, http://www.pgaofcanada.com/site_search/view.aspx?1 =0,1128,1131,1144.

89. Jim Matheson, "Golf Phenom Went on to Blaze Trail for Women," *Edmonton Journal*, October 3, 2004, 62; "A Local Golfer's Legacy," Amateur Golf, Golf Canada, October 12, 2011, http://www.golfcanada.ca/amateur-competition/amateur-championships/article6727.ece; Crockett, "Early History."

90. D. Scott, "Fine Effort," *Calgary Herald*, May 11, 1963, 18.

91. Tingley, *City of Champions*.

92. "Swimming Champions Compete Tonight for the Alberta Honors," *Calgary Daily Herald*, September 28, 1911, 8.

93. Byl, "Directing Physical Education in the Canadian YWCAS"; YWCA of Edmonton, accessed April 20, 2007, http://www.ywcaofedmonton.org/aboutus/history.htm.

94. Newspaper clippings from the *Calgary Herald*, October 16, 1942, Helen Woodside fonds, M 1341, Glenbow Archives; Harry Scott, "Calgary Swimmers Clean up in Championship Meet held at Banff Winter Carnival," n.d., ca. 1924; "Prairie Maiden Wins Laurels as Swimmer," *Moose Jaw Evening Times*, July 20, 1926; "Tickets on Sale for Hoop Game," *Calgary Daily Herald*, April 20, 1928, 6.

95. Barraclough, *From Prairie to Park*, 65, 73, 90; "Swimming in Alberta: The Early Years," Swim Alberta, accessed February 29, 2012, https://www.swimming.ca/SwimAlberta.

96. First Alberta Open Swimming and Diving Championships, Mill Creek Pool in Edmonton, program, August 22, 1959, Club fonds, 82.25/54, Provincial Archives of Alberta.

97. "Patrick, Bill," Alberta Sports Hall of Fame and Museum, accessed February 29, 2012, http://www.albertasportshalloffame.com.

98. South Side Swim Club fonds, 82.25/27, Provincial Archives of Alberta; South Side Swim Club fonds, 82.25/54, Provincial Archives of Alberta.

99. South Side Swim Club fonds, 82.25, file 48, Provincial Archives of Alberta; "Sporting Lives: Graham Smith," Library and Archives Canada, accessed April 22, 2007, http://www.archives.ca/05/0527/05270606_e.html.

100. *Canadian Encyclopedia*, s.v. "Mark Tewksbury," accessed February 29, 2012, http://www.thecanadianencyclopedia.com/articles/mark-tewksbury.

101. Tingley, *City of Champions*.

102. "The Great Waldo," *New Straits Times* (Malaysia), October 1, 1988, 11; Canada's Sports Hall of Fame, "Honoured Members: Debbie Muir," accessed February 29, 2012, http://www.sportshall.ca/honoured-members/27828/debbie-muir/; Synchro Swim Alberta fonds, Glenbow Archives.

103. "Mrs. Ollie Olga Currie," City of Edmonton, Salute to Excellence Awards Hall of Fame, accessed November 12, 2011, http://www.edmonton.ca/for_residents/programs/ollie-olga-currie.aspx.

104. Skate Canada, "Our History," accessed November 12, 2011, http://www.skatecanada.ca/en-us/aboutus/history.aspx.

105. Red Deer College, "Kevin Sirois," Future Students, accessed November 4, 2010, http://www.rdc.ab.ca/future_students/continuing_education/fitness_and_wellness/kevin_sirois.html; "Keen Rivalry for Skating Meet," *Edmonton Journal*, March 5, 1953, 14.

106. Tingley, *City of Champions*; CAAWS, http://www.caaws.ca/e/awards/article.cfm?id=177.

107. Ryan, "The Development of Speed-skating in Western Canada from a Personal Perspective," in Corbet and Rasporich, *Winter Sports*.

108. S.V. Lloyd, "Pat Underhill," Speed Skating BC, November 2001, accessed April 22, 2007, http://www.speed-skating.bc.ca/leading/oct2001/Pat%20Underhill.doc.

109. "Auch Calls it a Speedskating Career," CBC Sports, December 10, 2002, http://www.cbc.ca/sports/story/2002/12/09/auch021209.html; Catriona Le May Doan, "Biography," accessed January 24, 2010, http://www.catrionalemaydoan.ca/bio.html. Demonstrating the athletic versatility that characterizes many other female athletes through Alberta's history, Auch also placed fourth in qualifying for the national cycling team in 2000.

110. Barraclough, *Prairie to Park*.

111. "Statistics Canada General Social Survey: Most Popular Sports," Statistics Canada, 1998, qtd. in McGarry, "Passing as a 'Lady.'"

112. Carl Walin fonds, WET-98.37-49-48, City of Wetaskiwin Archives; "Revue Has Space Theme," *Edmonton Journal*, March 4, 1959, 53.

113. Medicine Hat Figure Skating Club fonds, Esplanade Archives, Medicine Hat.

114. "Walter Kaasa Heart and Soul of Local Culture," *Edmonton Journal*, July 14, 2008.

115. Although access to ice became less exclusive, competition for time is still a politically charged issue. See Adams, "Freezing."

116. Mrs. Lilley, North Glenora Community Club, to Archie Zarisky, letter, December 12, 1961, personal collection, A. Zarisky.

117. "Hanna Skater With Ice Show," *Calgary Herald*, January 29, 1960, 45; "Enthusiasm High For Blade School," *Calgary Herald*, June 22, 1957, 18.

118. "Glencoe Club Sports Begun Friday Night," *Calgary Herald*, November 23, 1931, 3; *The Albertan*, January 28, 1954, 10.

119. I. MacDonald, "Poshness in Edmonton—The Club Fever," *Calgary Herald*, January 31, 1962, 5.

120. Personal communication, Archie Zarisky, Edmonton, July 10, 2009; Royal Glenora Club fonds, Provincial Archives of Alberta.

121. Terry Jones, "Glenora Skaters Leave Their Mark at National," *Edmonton Sun*, February 9, 1997.

122. 1996 World Figure Skating Championships. Edmonton, Canada, competition notes, March 17–24, 1996, Ice Skating International Online, http://www.iceskatingintnl.com/archive/results_worlds/world96.htm.

123. J. Deacon, "Skating Scandal at 2002 Winter Olympics," *Maclean's*, February 25, 2002, in *Canadian Encyclopedia*, 2011, http://www.thecanadianencyclopedia.com/index.cfm?PgNm=TCE&Params=M1ARTM0012372.

124. "2001 Skate Canada Fact Sheet," Skate Canada, accessed February 29, 2012, www.skatecanada.ca.

125. Dahlie, "Skiing For Identity and Tradition."

126. Peach, *Thanks for the Memories*; Wheeler, "'We Want Your Pictures So Kodak As you Go.'"

127. Minutes, December 13, 1954, Banff Ski Runners of the Canadian Rockies fonds, M431, Whyte Museum of the Canadian Rockies Archives.

128. Lund, "Development of Skiing in Banff"; Lund, "Recreational Skiing in the Canadian Rockies."

129. "Ski Chatter," *Calgary Herald*, December 22, 1950, 20.

130. K. Francis, "Weekend Ski Jump Activity Recalls Stories of Glory, Fame," *Edmonton Journal*, January 27, 1962, 9.

131. C. Mitchell, "The first 25 Years of the Calgary Skiing Club 1935-1960," typescript, 1985, Calgary Skiing Club fonds, M 8092, Glenbow Archives; Peach, *Thanks for the Memories.*

132. "New Ski Course Ready in Canada," *Milwaukee Journal*, December 3, 1939, 15.

133. Lund, "Development"; Mitchell, "Calgary Skiing Club"; Calgary Skiing Club fonds, M8092, Glenbow Archives.

134. A. Loeb, "Canada Extends Her Travel Frontiers: New Concrete Trails Open to the Visitor Many Remote Areas of the Dominion," *New York Times*, June 9, 1940, 1; National Parks Association of Canada, "The Outdoor Holiday Habit," *NPAC Circular* 142, April 15, 1948, 2; "N.B. Zimmerman, "Canadian Rockies: Jasper and Banff National Parks Expect To Be Jam-Packed Again This Summer," *New York Times*, June 6, 1948, 33; R. Francis, "Canada's High Runs: Popular Winter-Sport Areas in the Rockies Continue to Provide New Facilities," *New York Times*, December 14, 1952, 34; "Alberta Sets Pace in Ski Boom," *Calgary Herald*, December 2, 1966.

135. "Trudeaus Enjoy Alberta Slopes," *Calgary Herald*, February 11, 1975. Trudeau had been skiing at Sunshine since 1940, well before intensive commercial development.

136. "Calgary Ski Club Captures Cross Trophy," *Calgary Daily Herald*, February 7, 1938, 6; "Edmonton Skiers Win Cross Trophy," *Calgary Herald*, February 24, 1941, 7.

137. Mitchell, "The first 25 Years of the Calgary Skiing Club 1935-1960," typescript, 1985, M8092, Glenbow Archives.

138. "Alberta Sets Pace in Ski Boom," *Calgary Herald*, December 2, 1966.

139. K. Francis, "Weekend Ski Jump Activity Recalls Stories of Glory, Fame," *Edmonton Journal*, January 27, 1962, 9.

140. Derksen, "Living History."

141. C. Stock, "Karen Percy-Lowe Shares Memories from a Magical Olympics 20 Years Ago," *Edmonton Journal*, February 24, 2008.

142. "The Mom of All the Ski Racers," obituary, Dee Read 1926-2004, *Globe and Mail*, August 7, 2004; "Read, Ken," Alberta Sports Hall of Fame and Museum, accessed July 29, 2008, http://www.albertasportshalloffame.com/default.aspx?p=member&mid=222.

143. "Centre Combats Athlete Shortage," *Star Phoenix* (Saskatoon), January 3, 1968, 24.

144. H. Walker, "World of Sport," *Calgary Herald*, March 22, 1973, 69; "Calgary Honors Three Hockey Teams Tonight," *Morning Leader* (Calgary), April 11, 1924, 12; C. Cotton, "Games Bid Began With Idle Talk," *Calgary Herald*, April 27, 1981, 36.

145. Robidoux, *Men at Play*; Ducey, *Rajah of Renfrew*; O'Riordan, "The 'Puck-Eaters'"; *Edmonton Exhibition Association 1906–1964*, vol. 1, Archives Special Collection, 1989, City of Edmonton Archives.

146. Kirwin, "A Colony Within a Colony," 76–77; Ducey, *Rajah of Renfrew*.

147. Calhoun, *Sport, Culture and Personality*.

148. Dryden, "Soul on Ice"; Howell, *Blood, Sweat, and Cheers*; W. Houston, "Viewer Numbers Give the NHL Reason to Worry," *Globe and Mail*, January 16, 2007.

149. Abdel-Shehid, "'Who Got Next?'"; Dryden, "Soul on Ice."

150. The highest numbers of Alberta immigrants come from Asian countries. Statistics Canada, 2006 Census, "Ethnic Origin, Visible Minorities, Place of Work and Mode of Transportation," *The Daily*, April 2, 2008, http://www.statcan.gc.ca/daily-quotidien/080402/dq080402a-eng.htm.

151. See, for example, Nauright and White, "Mediated Nostalgia, Community and Nation"; Gruneau and Whitson, "Upmarket Continentalism," Gruneau and Whitson, *Hockey Night*; Kidd, *Struggle for Canadian Sport*.

PART III

THE SOCIAL BODY

1. R. Turchansky, "Gretzky Hoisting the Stanley Cup, Underdog Eskimos on Top, Grads' Quarter-century Reign," *Edmonton Journal*, October 3, 2004, 64.

2. Fullerton, "Not Playing Fair"; Robinson, *She Shoots, She Scores*.

3. Bourdieu, "How Can One be a Sports Fan?"; Bourdieu, *Distinction*; Sugden and Tomlinson, "Theorizing Sport, Status and Social Class."

4. Howell, *Blood, Sweat, and Cheers*, 5.

5. Coakley and Donnelly, *Sport in Society*.

6. Veenstra, "Who the Heck is Don Bradman?"; Erickson, "Culture, Class, and Connections."

1. "Good Leadership for Boys and Men Provided by the Calgary YMCA,"
   Calgary Daily Herald, June 18, 1921, 7; Douglas Stinson, "Community
   Celebrates Colourful Past," Bridgeland Riverside Community
   Association, 2011, December 18, 2011, http://www.calgaryarea.com/ne/
   bridgelandriverside/communitynews/history.htm.

2. "Good Leadership for Boys and Men Provided by the Calgary YMCA,"
   Calgary Daily Herald, June 18, 1921, 7; Stinson, "Community Celebrates";
   McFarland, *The Development of Public Recreation in Canada*.

3. Killam Memorial Arena Opening Program, Killam, Alberta, February 18,
   1961.

4. Foucault, "Nietsche, Genealogy, History," 53.

5. Freund, McGuire, and Podhurst, eds., *Health, Illness, and the Social Body*;
   Grierson, "Inscribing the Social Body"; Lock and Scheper-Hughes, "A
   Critical-interpretive Approach in Medical Anthropology."

6. Grant, *Short History of Classical Civilization*; Forbes, *Greek Physical Education*;
   Barrow and Brown, *Man and Movement*; Austin, "Cult of the 'Body
   Beautiful'"; Peter Stothard, "Greeks Baring All," *Globe and Mail*, August 7,
   2004, D4.

7. Matthews, "A Historical Study of the Aims, Contents, and Methods";
   Reischer and Koo, "The Body Beautiful."

8. Friedrich. L. Jahn, *A Treatise on Gymnastics* qtd. in "Friedrich Ludwig Jahn,
   "The German Art of Gymnastics, Part II," Gym Media, updated July 18,
   2001, http://www.gymmedia.com/jahn/E_Jahn2.htm.

9. Laski, "The Life Beautiful"; Reischer and Koo, "Body Beautiful"; Gienow-
   Hecht, "Review of *The Cult of Health and Beauty in Germany*"; Turner, *The Body
   and Society*; McFee and Tomlinson, "Riefenstahl's *Olympia*."

10. Hughson points out that, though Arnold is more or less credited with
    ideas of muscular Christianity, it was actually invented and codified later
    in Thomas Hughes's book *Tom Brown's School Days*.

11. Kidd, "Muscular Christianity and Value-centred Sport"; Putney, *Muscular
    Christianity*; MacAloon, "Introduction: Muscular Christianity After 150
    Years."

12. "Muscular Christianity Gets Workout in Winnipeg," CBC News, May
    16, 2005, http://www.cbc.ca/news/canada/story/2005/05/16/wrestling-
    church050516.html.

13. Jhally, "The Spectacle of Accumulation"; Chisholm, "Incarnations and Practices of Feminine Rectitude"; Weisman, "Two Centuries of Women's Health Activism"; Kidd, *Struggle for Canadian Sport*.

14. "On Time," *Calgary Daily Herald*, June 18, 1921, 28.

15. "Will Take Off Excess Fat," *Edmonton Bulletin*, January 1, 1920, 6.

16. Hoeger and Hoeger, *Principles and Labs for Fitness and Wellness*.

17. Barbara Curry Mulcahy, "Hard Times Cop: Jerry Mulcahy's Years Walking the Beat During the Depression," in *Edmonton: A City Called Home*, http://www.edmontonhistory.ca/prelaunch/citycalledhome/remember/i_page.php?SSKey=5204&SectionKey=250&ScreenKey=1044; "1930 City Police Softball Team," in *Edmonton: A City Called Home*, http://www.edmontonhistory.ca/prelaunch/citycalledhome/resources/rwindow.php?ResourceKey=5353.

18. Heritage Community Foundation, "Midlandvale," When Coal was King: Coal Mining in Western Canada," accessed January 12, 2009, http://wayback.archive-it.org/2217/20101208160312/http://www.coalking.ca/; Kuban, *Edmonton's Urban Villages*.

19. Bell, "History of Tennis"; Men's Athletic Association fonds, 1909-1943, University of Alberta Archives. The University of Alberta established a separate campus in Calgary in 1960 and it became an autonomous institution, the University of Calgary, in 1960.

20. Driard Hotel Gymnasium, April 1, 1931, Carl Walin fonds, WET-Free-1-4-31, City of Wetaskiwin Archives.

21. Canadian National Parks Association, "Outdoor recreation," *CNPA Circular* 40, Progress Report, January 3, 1938, GAIA M2169 F5, http://openarchive.acadiau.ca/cdm/singleitem/collection/CNPA/id/697.

22. Harshaw, *When Women Work*; Meller, *Leisure and the Changing City*; Kidd, *Struggle for Canadian Sport*; Hosgood, "Negotiating Lower-middle-class Masculinity"; Edmonton YMCA, accessed January 12, 2007, http://www.edmonton.ymca.ca/about_the_y/1.6_history.htm.

23. Martens, "Young Man! When You're Low on Your Dough."

24. McQuarrie, "The Struggle Over Worker Leisure."

25. McQuarrie, "The Struggle Over Worker Leisure"; Kidd, "Radical Immigrants"; Wheeler, "Organized Sport and Organized Labour"; Melchers, "Sports in the Workplace."

26. Kidd "Radical Immigrants," 212.

27. McFarland, *Development of Public Recreation*.

28. Markham-Starr and Delamere, "Canada Needs You"; Forsyth and Heine, "'A Higher Degree of Social Organization.'"

29. Mah qtd. in Ducey, *Rajah of Renfrew*.

30. Burstyn, *Rites of Men*.

31. NPAC, "The Outdoor Holiday Habit," *NPAC Circular*, 142, April 15, 1948, 2, NAC RG 29, vol. 844 f222-1-167, accessed January 25, 2008, http:// openarchive.acadiau.ca/cdm/singleitem/collection/CNPA/id/637.

32. McFarland, *Public Recreation*.

33. "Five Basic eXercises," *Getting Physical: Canada's Fitness Movement*, originally broadcast August 16, 1961, CBC Archives, 2006. http://archives.cbc.ca/ IDC-1-41-615-3304/sports/fitness/clip2.

34. "Five Basic eXercises"; "Committing armchair suicide," *Getting Physical: Canada's Fitness Movement*, originally broadcast July 16, 1968, CBC Archives, 2006, http://archives.cbc.ca/IDC-1-41-615-3305/sports/fitness/clip3.

35. Cavanagh, "The Development of Canadian Sports Broadcasting."

36. McNeill, "Social Marketing, Gender, and the Science of Fitness"; ParticipACTION: The Mouse That Roared: A Marketing and Health Communications Success Story, Ontario Health Promotion E-Bulletin, OHPE Bulletin 374, vol. 2004, no. 374, accessed March 3, 2012, http://www. ohpe.ca/node/259.

37. R. Coleman, *The Cost of Obesity in Alberta*, GPI Atlantic, 2000, http://www. gpiatlantic.org/pdf/health/obesity/ab-obesity.pdf; Government of Alberta, *Active Alberta: A Recreation, Active Living and Sport Policy*, May 2010, http://tpr. alberta.ca/activealberta/docs/ActiveAlbertaPolicy.pdf.

38. Photograph 82.0101.19b, opening of UAC Gym, Physical Education Building, March 1962, University of Calgary Archives; see Bumsted, *A History of the Canadian Peoples*, 3rd ed.; Glassford, "Active Living."

39. CR92-029, CalA CR-92-029-179, City of Calgary Archives.

40. White and Young, "Health and the New Age Aesthetic," 109.

41. Sport Canada, "Sport Participation in Canada, 1998 Report Highlights," Canadian Heritage, modified November 22, 2008, http://www.pch.gc.ca/ pgm/sc/info-fact/1998-psc-spc/1998-fs-h-eng.cfm.

42. J. Berkowitz, "Study by McGill prof confirms super-sizing of NHL," *Ottawa Citizen*, June 5, 2006.

43. Burstyn, *Rites of Men*; White, "Muscles Don't Make the Man."

44. Photo 82.010_1.19b, University of Calgary Archives.

45. McFarland, *Development of Public Recreation*. Later in the twentieth century, Fijians, Guyanese, Trinidadians, Ismailis, and Pakistanis were active in organizing cricket, soccer, badminton, and Ping-Pong in Alberta cities. Buchignani, "South Asians."

46. Dallaire, "Sport's Impact on the Francophoness"; Heritage Community Foundation, "Alberta's Francophone Heritage, Francophone Games," 2004, http://www.abheritage.ca/francophone/en/culture/francophone_games. html; Bruno Mercier, personal communication, Edmonton, June 5, 2009.

47. Palmer and Palmer, *Alberta*; Wetherell, "Making New Identities."

48. Palmer and Palmer, *Peoples of Alberta*.

49. Solomon, "Jews and Baseball"; "Invictus 'A' defeats Jewish Hustlers 5 to 1 in a Classy Contest," *Edmonton Bulletin*, February 9, 1924, 7; Albert Stein, "The Jewish Farm Colonies of Alberta," *Outlook*, March/April 2001, http://www.vcn.bc.ca/outlook/library/articles/CdnJewishExperience/p05Farm Colonies.htm.

50. Ichikawa, "A Test of Religious Tolerance."

51. "Judo Tests Completed," *Calgary Herald*, October 27, 1959, 12.

52. L. Watson, "Quebec Gymnast the Golden One," *Edmonton Journal*, August 16, 1974, 23; Judo Alberta, "Yoshio Katsuta, Yosio Senda, Allan Sattin named Alberta Centennial Salute Award Winners by Province," October 2005, http://www.judoalberta.com/pdf/newsletters/october2005.pdf.

53. *The Albertan*, May 18, 1956, 13; Ramsay Community Association, *Ramsay Newsletter*, December 2006, http://www.ramsaycommunity.ab.ca/ newsletter/RCA_Newsletter_2006-09_scrn.pdf.

54. "The Honourable Norman L. Kwong, CM, AOE," Alberta Heritage Community Foundation, 2005, http://www.heritagecommunityfdn.org/ documents/norman_kwong_bio.pdf.

55. McLennan, *Sport in Early Calgary*, 6; "Great Bronc Riders Hail From Alberta," *Calgary Herald*, July 5, 1939, 22; S. Aizenman, "Name Change Requested for Nigger John 4-H Club," *Calgary Herald*, August 20, 1960, 22.

56. *Grey River Argus*, January 28, 1911, 4.

57. HCF *Alberta Online Encyclopedia*, s.v. "Discrimination," Alberta's Black Pioneer Heritage, accessed March 3, 2012, http://wayback.archive-it. org/2217/20101208162254/http://www.albertasource.ca/blackpioneers/

history/1907-1912/discrimination.html; "A Hard Price for Freedom—in the Alberta Wilderness," *Calgary Herald*, August 16, 1974, 74.

58. McLennan, *Sport in Early Calgary*, 6.

59. Cui and Kelly, "'Our Negro Citizens'"; H C F *Alberta Online Encyclopedia*, s.v. "Boxing and Rodeo," Alberta's Black Pioneer Heritage, accessed March 3, 2012, http://wayback.archive-it.org/2217/20101208162317/http://www. albertasource.ca/blackpioneers/cultural/leisure/boxing_rodeo.html.

60. Penley, "Russ Gideon."

61. Stubbs, *Shoestring Glory*, 35–38.

62. H C F *Alberta Online Encyclopedia*, s.v. "Baseball," Alberta's Black Pioneer Heritage, accessed March 3, 2012, http://wayback.archive-it. org/2217/20101208162315/http://www.albertasource.ca/blackpioneers/ cultural/leisure/baseball.html.

63. "Lacombe Plans Huge Ball Event," *Calgary Herald*, June 12, 1950, 23; "Now Almost Assured for Berth in Final," *Edmonton Journal*, June 21, 1950, 11.

64. "Champion Ball Team to Play at Camrose Saturday, August 7th," *Camrose Canadian*, July 21, 1948, 1.

65. *Lethbridge Herald*, August 14, 1952, qtd. in Mah, "1952: Southern Alberta Baseball League," Western Canada Baseball, accessed June 22, 2008, http:// www.attheplate.com/wcbl/1952_10i.htm.

66. Pope, "Review, *Ethnicity and Sport in North American History and Culture*."

67. Mah, "1956...One game away from the championship," Western Canada Baseball, 2010, http://www.attheplate.com/wcbl/1956_1.html.

68. Dewar, "Scabby Dried Meat and Bad Dried Meat."

69. H C F *Alberta Online Encyclopedia*, s.v. "The Siksika Nation Profiles: Deerfoot," Treaty 7 Past and Present, accessed March 3, 2012, http://wayback. archive-it.org/2217/20101208161901/http://www.albertasource.ca/treaty7/ traditional/siksika_deerfoot.html; Dempsey, "Deerfoot and Friends."

70. Zeman, *To Run with Longboat*; Sam Laskaris, "Humble Pitcher Gets Third Hall of Fame Induction," *Alberta Sweetgrass* 18, no. 4 (2011), http://www. ammsa.com/publications/alberta-sweetgrass/humble-pitcher-gets-third-hall-fame-induction. The article indicates his membership in the Edmonton Sports Hall of Fame and the Alberta Sports Hall of Fame but as of 2012 his name does not appear on their websites.

71. Baillargeon, "Aboriginal Rodeo Cowboys"; "Indian Stars Steer Tagging," *The Albertan*, July 12, 1938, 1.

72. "Hundred Thousand People Witnessed Stampede Events," *Calgary Herald*, September 7, 1912, 7; "Tom Three Persons," Alberta Settlement, Collections Canada, accessed March 3, 2012, http://www.collectionscanada.gc.ca/eppp-archive/100/200/301/ic/can_digital_collections/pasttopresent/settlement/aa_Tom_Three_Persons.html.

73. Candace Savage, "It's Cold in Them Thar Hills...," *Globe and Mail*, February 14, 1998.

74. Burgess, "Canadian 'Range Wars'"; Joudrey, "Expectations of a Queen."

75. W.W. Parker, "Sundre Stampede," ca. 1940, Alberta Folklore and Local History Collection, University of Alberta Libraries, accessed March 3, 2012, http://folklore.library.ualberta.ca/dspImage.cfm?ID=162&Current=1.

76. J. Klaszus, "How the West Went Wild: Dissecting Calgary's Stampede," *Alberta Views*, July/August 2007, 10–11.

77. Mikkelsen, "Indians and Rodeo," 17; Penrose, "All the Cowboys."

78. *Cowgirls' Super Challenge* 1981 program, 7, Canadian Girls' Rodeo Association fonds, M7703/65, Glenbow Archives; "Shelli Currie Yellowbird," Indian Cowgirls, Indian Rodeo News, 2008, accessed April 28, 2009, http://indianrodeonews.com/HallofFame.htm.

79. Donnelly, "Scapegoating the Indian Residential Schools"; Fay, "A Historiography of Recent Publications On Catholic Native Residential Schools"; Scott-Brown, "The Short Life of St. Dunstan's Calgary Indian Industrial School."

80. Robidoux, "Narratives of Race Relations."; Paraschak, "Variations in Race Relations."

81. "Biography—Chief Wilton Littlechild," Aboriginal Affairs and Northern Development Canada, modified August 12, 2011, http://www.ainc-inac.gc.ca/ai/mr/nr/m-a2009/bio000000348-eng.asp.

82. Palmer and Palmer, "The Black Experience"; Forsyth, "Native to Native."

83. Shogan, "Social Construction of Disability," 75.

84. *Canadian Encyclopedia*, s.v. "Robert Daniel Steadward," by C.J. Peterson, accessed March 3, 2012, http://www.thecanadianencyclopedia.com/articles/robert-daniel-steadward; McPherson and Mohapatrab, "The Paralympics: A Strategic Social Enterprise," unpublished paper, n.d., ca. 2008, http://pdffinder.net/THE-PARALYMPICS:-A-STRATEGIC-SOCIAL-ENTERPRISE.html.

85. Peers qtd. in J. Hurly, "Vanier Graduate Scholarship for Danielle Peers," *Express News*, University of Alberta, May 22, 2009, http://www.physedandrec.ualberta.ca/news.cfm?story=91298; Depauw, "Girls and Women with Disabilities in Sport."

86. Hurly, "Peers"; D. Woog, "Fighting for the Crips and the Queers," *Outsports*, September 14, 2007, http://www.outsports.com/columns/outfield/070914.htm.

87. M. Brown, "Paralympics Support Tour Makes Stop at U of A," *Folio*, 48, no. 19, May 23, 2008, http://www.folio.ualberta.ca/articlecfm?v=94250&i=79371&a=14; N W B A, "History of Wheelchair Basketball" accessed March 3, 2012, http://www.nwba.org/index.php?option=com_content&view=article&id=13&Itemid=120.

88. Terry Jones, "Special Games' Success Assured," *Edmonton Journal*, May 26, 1971, 81.

89. N. Lees, "Bob Steadward Believes We Haven't Embraced Our Inner Cowboy," *Edmonton Journal*, November 5, 2010.

90. Peers, "(Dis)empowering Paralympic Histories."

91. Coakley and Donnelly, *Sport in Society*; Shogan, "Social Construction."

8   "RED-BLOODED SPORTS" AND "MASCULINE FACSIMILIES"

1. Howell, *Northern Sandlots*, 97.

2. Reverend James W. Kramer, qtd. in Howell, *Northern Sandlots*, 105.

3. Wetherell and Kmet, *Useful Pleasures*, 127.

4. "Student Athletics," *The Gateway*, February 1, 1912, 10–11.

5. Putney, *Muscular Christianity*; Mott, "The British Protest Pioneers"; D. Brown, "Northern Character Theme"; Coulter, "Teenagers in Edmonton"; Coulter, "Patrolling the Passions of Youth."

6. Robidoux, "Historical Interpretations of First Nations Masculinity."

7. Oxley, *My Strange Rescue*, 344; Robidoux, "Historical Interpretations of First Nations Masculinity."

8. *Calgary Herald* qtd. in Mills, "100 Years," 215.

9. Danysk, *Hired Hands*.

10. Messner, "The Life of a Man's Seasons"; Christopher Dummitt, "Review, Jeffery Vacante, The Manly Modern: Masculinity in Postwar Canada,"

H-Canada, H-Net Reviews, May 2008, http://www.h-net.org/reviews/ showrev.php?id=14480.

11. "Football an Art of War," *Calgary Herald*, June 5, 1894.

12. Nauright and Chandler, *Making Men*, 2–3; Nauright, "Sustaining Masculine Identity."

13. *Alberta Plaindealer*, February 16, 1900, qtd. in O'Riordan, "The 'Puck-Eaters,'" 11.

14. "400 Demonstrate Youth Training," *Edmonton Journal*, April 24, 1941, 13.

15. K. McConnell, "12,000 Fans Thrilled as Maple Leafs Defeat Notre Dame 18–5," *Edmonton Journal*, October 14, 1941, 11.

16. Frederick B. Watt, "Tribute to the Grads," 1940, 70.25/5, Provincial Archives of Alberta.

17. Don Fleming, *Edmonton Journal*, January 20, 1979, C2.

18. Alan Maki, "Curling Rocks," *Globe and Mail*, April 9, 2005, F2.

19. Donna Spencer, "Days of Smoking, Drinking Long Gone at the Brier as Curlers Dream of Olympics," *Prince George Citizen*, March 9, 2009.

20. Seiler and Seiler, "Social Construction of the Canadian Cowboy."

21. Bannerman, "'Cowboys' of the Canadian West," 52; Silversides, *Shooting Cowboys*; Seiler and Seiler, "The Social Construction of the Canadian Cowboy"; Rusted, "'A Wonderful Picture'"; Russell, *The Canadian Cowboy*; Dempsey, *Golden Age of the Canadian Cowboy*.

22. "Cowboys Hit Town in Full Regalia," *Montreal Gazette*, May 13, 1934, 13.

23. "South American Junket Sours American Cowboys," *Ellensburg Daily Record* (WA), May 2, 1940.

24. Canadian Girls' Rodeo Association fonds, M7703/65, Glenbow Archives; Cathy Roy, "GWG and the Rodeo," in *Piece by Piece: The GWG Story*, Royal Alberta Museum, 2010, http://www.royalalbertamuseum.ca/virtualExhibit/ GWG/en/marketing/cowboys.html; Katherine Milliken, "Selling the Frontier Style," in *Piece by Piece: The GWG Story*, Royal Alberta Museum, 2010, http://www.royalalbertamuseum.ca/virtualExhibit/GWG/en/ marketing/frontierstyle.html. The term "cowboyography" was coined by singer Ian Tyson as the title of his 1986 album.

25. Filax, "Producing Homophobia in Alberta."

26. GayWired, "GLISA Takes Part in Global Initiatives Against Homophobia in Sport," December 7, 2005, http://www.connexion.org/newsstory. cfm?id=3908&returnurl=news.cfm. For more coverage of this and other

events, see Gordon Laird, "Bucking the System," *Globe and Mail*, July 12, 2003, F4, F5; Brenda Barnes, "Wide World of Sports: Gay Games (Un)Covered," *Fuse* 14, no. 3 (1991): 5–6; Brian Pronger, "Fear and Trembling: Homophobia in Men's Sport," in White and Young, *Sport and Gender*; Anderson, *In the Game: Gay Athletes and the Cult of Masculinity*.

27. "First North America OutGames 2007 On-site Attendee Survey" and "Final Report, Calgary OutGames—A Research Legacy," Zinc Research, August 26, 2007, accessed July 15, 2008, http://zincresearch.wordpress.com/2007/08/26/calgary-outgames-a-research-legacy/; " D. Vox, "Calgary Gets a Gay Face Lift with OutGames," Gay Sports, accessed November 5, 2007, http://www.gaysports.com/page.cfm?Sectionid=44&typeofsite=storydetail&ID=931&storyset=yes.

28. "History," Alberta Rockies Gay Rodeo Association, accessed July 8, 2007, http://www.argra.org/culture_history.php.

29. "Rodeo Events," Alberta Rockies Gay Rodeo Association, accessed December 20, 2009, http://www.argra.org/rodeo_events.php; First North America OutGames, "Team Calgary Gears up for the OutGames!," February 11, 2007, http://www.calgary2007.com/documents/Release_Feb11.pdf.

30. S. Hoult, "Achieving Tolerance Through...Curling," *Fast Forward Weekly* (Calgary) 11, no. 19, April 20, 2006, http://www.ffwdweekly.com/Issues/2006/0420/life.htm.

31. K. Allen, "Calgary's Western Cup a Growing Success," *Xtra* (Vancouver), April 26, 2006, http://www.xtra.ca/public/Vancouver/Calgarys_Western_Cup_a_growing_success-1618.aspx.

32. Hoult, "Achieving Tolerance Through...Curling." For further reading on homosexuality in sport, see Davison and Blye, "Sexualities, Genders, and Bodies in Sport: Changing Practices of Inequity"; Griffin, "Changing the Game: Homophobia, Sexism, and Lesbians in Sport"; D.E. Johnston, "Sites of resistance, sites of strength"; Pronger, "Outta My Endzone: Sport and the Territorial Anus"; Robinson, "The Love of a Strong Woman: The Lesbian Athlete."

33. C. Zdeb, "Jocks Prefer Female M DS, Study Suggests," *Edmonton Journal*, April 30, 2007; "Sports," *Perceptions* 18, no. 6 (September 13, 2000): 13, http://library2.usask.ca/srsd/perceptions/2271.html; "Camp for Gay, Lesbian Youth Branching Out," *Edmonton Journal*, August 3, 2008.

34. "Edmonton Public School Board Approves Sexual Orientation Policy,"
    Edmonton Journal, March 9, 2011; T. Audette, "Alta. to Enshrine Gay
    Protections—But Let Parents Pull Kids from Class," *Montreal Gazette*, April
    28, 2009.

35. J. Deacon, "Sex Sells, to a Point: While Katarina Witt Can Flaunt Her
    Sexuality, Many Gay Athletes Hide Theirs," *Maclean's*, November 30, 1998.

36. *glbtq: An Encyclopedia of Gay, Lesbian, Bisexual, Transgender, and Queer Culture*,
    s.v. "Orser, Brian," by Linda Rapp, accessed January 20, 2010, http://www.
    glbtq.com/arts/orser_b.html; "Orser: 'I've Never Had to Lie about It,'" *Globe
    and Mail*, December 9, 1998, A1, A13; "Gay Magazine Editor Wants Major-
    league Boyfriend to Come Out," CBC sports, June 9, 2001, http://www.cbc.
    ca/sports/story/2001/06/09/gaysinsport010609.html.

37. "Rainbow Warriors: Gay and Lesbian Athletes," CAAWS, accessed July 10,
    2009, http://www.caaws.ca/e/advocacy/caaws.cfm?ID=8.

38. Wamsley and Heine, "Tradition, Modernity and the Construction of Civic
    Identity"; J. Lee, "Gay Athletes to Get Home of Their Own at Olympics,"
    Vancouver Sun, May 9, 2009. G. Filax, "Post-Vriend—the Human Face,"
    Parkland Post, Summer 1998.

39. Cahn, "From the 'Muscle Moll' to the 'Butch' Ballplayer"; Caitlin Cranshaw,
    "Calendar Girls Don't Give Athletes a Sporting Chance," *Express News*,
    August 13, 2006, University of Alberta, http://www.uofaweb.ualberta.ca/
    researchandstudents/news.cfm?story=49161; Knight and Giuliano, "Blood,
    Sweat, and Jeers."

40. T. Kerr, "Queermonton," *Vue Weekly* (Edmonton) 650, April 3, 2008.

41. Jhally, "Spectacle of Accumulation."

42. Montgomery Brothers window display for "Fleet Foot" shoes, WET-98.37-
    173, City of Wetaskiwin Archives; "Boys and Girls Join the Fleet Foot
    Athletic Club," *Montreal Gazette*, May 15, 1930; "Fleet Foot for Every Sport
    and Recreation," *Vancouver Sun*, June 25, 1920, 14.

43. "Club Chat About Sports," *New York Times*, March 8, 1896. The Rational
    Dress Society established in England in 1881 rejected all forms of women's
    clothing constricting and artificially shaping the body.

44. "Before E-commerce: A History of Canadian Mail-order Catalogues,"
    Canadian Museum of Civilization, updated October 22, 2009, http://www.
    civilization.ca/cmc/exhibitions/cpm/catalog/cat00o0e.shtml; Cathy Roy,
    personal communication, April 23, 2009, Edmonton, Alberta.

45. Bear Brand, *Bucilla and Glossilla Blue Book*, vol. 25, 9 Jack Manson fonds, 96.611, Provincial Archives of Alberta.

46. Pauline Weston Thomas and Guy Thomas, "Dress Emancipation for Women Through Sports," Fashion-Era, accessed December 18, 2011, http://fashion-era.com/sports_fashion_until_1960.htm.

47. LeCompte, *Cowgirls of the Rodeo.*

48. Girls' hockey team, Mount Royal College, Calgary, 1925, NA-1105-70, Glenbow Archives.

49. Dewar, "Edmonton Grads"; "The Edmonton Grads (1915–1940)," *Celebrating Women's Achievements: Women in Canadian Sport*, Library and Archives Canada, Collections Canada, accessed September 23, 2008, http://www.collectionscanada.gc.ca/women/002026-229-e.html.

50. Smallwood, dir., *In the Hearts of Kings.*

51. Stacy Lorenz and Rod Murray, "NBA Dress Code Smacks of Racism," *University of Alberta Express News*, December 22, 2005.

52. "Style, Work Clothes Prairie Earners," *Financial Post*, June 12, 1954, 38.

53. Burstyn, *Rites of Men.*

54. "Alberta Sets Pace in Ski Boom," *Calgary Herald*, December 2, 1966.

55. Mark Spector, "They'd Rather Fight Than Switch," *National Post*, November 6, 2004, A1. Since the late 1990s, when the Federation Internationale de Volleyball adopted new uniform standards, inseam lengths have been shrinking in both shorts and tops for women's teams.

56. McGarry, "Passing as a 'Lady'"; "Young Calgary Skater Passes CFSA Gold Test," *Calgary Herald*, August 31, 1953, 6.

57. McGarry, "Passing as a 'Lady.'"

58. "Figure Skating No Sissy Sport," *Edmonton Journal*, January 24, 1964, 22.

59. L. Weinlos, "Ten Girls for Every Boy Makes Practicing a Joy," *Edmonton Journal*, November 13, 1964, 53.

60. Adams, "So What's the Problem with Wussy Sports?"

61. Adams, "So What's the Problem with Wussy Sports?"

62. P. White, "Figure Skating Gets Tough," *Globe and Mail*, February 4, 2009, 2.

63. Nauright and Chandler, *Making Men.*

64. Sandoz and Winans, eds., *Whatever it Takes.*

65. Kidd, *Struggle for Canadian Sport*, 114.

66. Mills, "100 Years of Sports," 204.

67. *Badminton Magazine* 1919, qtd. in Dunning, *Sport Matters*, 123.

68. Ladies' Home Journal qtd. in Elizabeth Talbot, "Athleticism, the Female Body and History," National Centre for History Education, Australian Government, accessed March 21, 2010, http://www.hyperhistory.org/index. php?option=displaypage&Itemid=711&op=page#art.

69. "Are Women's Hands Bigger?" *The Albertan*, February 3, 1900, 2.

70. Beecher, *Educational Reminiscences and Suggestions*, 85–86.

71. Todd, *Physical Culture and the Body Beautiful*.

72. Ferguson, *Janey Canuck*, 290.

73. "Wives for Westerners," *The Albertan*, February 3, 1900, 3.

74. Jameson, "Women in the Southern Alberta Ranch Community."

75. LeCompte, "Home on the Range."

76. Seiler and Seiler, "Social Construction of the Canadian Cowboy"; Bannerman, "'Cowboys' of the Canadian West."

77. M.A. Hall, "Women's Sport in Canada Prior to 1914"; Patterson, "Beyond Empire"; Bell, "History of Tennis."

78. "Swimming Champions Compete Tonight for the Alberta Honors," *Calgary Daily Herald*, September 28 1911, 8.

79. "Prairie Maiden," *Moose Jaw Evening Times*, 1926, newspaper clipping, Helen Woodside fonds, M1341, Glenbow Archives.

80. *Calgary Herald*, October 16, 1942, newspaper clipping, Helen Woodside fonds, M1341, Glenbow Archives.

81. Status of Women Canada, "Women's History Month," 2002, accessed April 27, 2007, http://www.swc-cfc.gc.ca/dates/whm/2002/history_e.html.

82. "How You Can Change...For the Better At Your YWCA," ca. late 1940s, Portland YWCA Archives, qtd. in Salcedo, "Best of Intentions," 186.

83. C. Mitchell, "The First 25 Years of the Calgary Skiing Club 1935-1960," type-script, 1985, M8092, Calgary Skiing Club fonds, Glenbow Archives.

84. "BSR to Hold Fashion Show and Dance," clipping, n.d., ca.1950s; Minutes, December 13, 1954; Minutes, November 9, 1960, Banff Ski Runners of the Canadian Rockies fonds, M431, Whyte Museum of the Canadian Rockies Archives.

85. Pedersen, "The Photographic Record of the Canadian YWCA."

86. Burstyn, *Rites of Men*; Lynn, Hardin, and Walsdorf, "Selling (Out) the Sporting Woman."

87. M.A. Hall, *The Girl and the Game*; Jim Trautman, "The Barbara Ann Scott Skating Doll, Reliable Toys (1948-1954)," Antique 67, accessed April

21, 2010, http://www.antique67.com/articles/BarbaraAnnScott_dolls/
BarbaraAnnScott_dolls.php; Alberta Sports Hall of Fame and Museum,
http://www.albertasportshalloffame.com/.

88. MacKinnon, "'Just an Ordinary Person.'"

89. A. Hu, "These Ladies Could Kick Your Ass," *The Gauntlet* (University of
     Calgary), November 1, 2007, http://gauntlet.ucalgary.ca/story/11847.

90. Macdonald, "The Edmonton Grads"; "The Edmonton Grads," "Women in
     Canadian Sport," Library and Archives Canada, 2005, accessed April 21, 2007,
     http://www.collectionscanada.gc.ca/women/002026-229-e.html.

91. Dewar, "Edmonton Grads"; Lenskyj, *Out of Bounds.*

92. *Edmonton Journal,* qtd. in C. Betke, "The Social Significance of Sport in the
     City," 226; Wetherell, *Useful Pleasures.*

93. Chalus, "Edmonton Commercial Graduates"; Short, "Hockey's Final
     Shining Days," 285.

94. "Bobbed-Headed Athletes Menace Male Supremacy," *Toronto Star Weekly,*
     April 24, 1926, qtd. in Chalus, "Edmonton Commercial Graduates," 74.

95. Chalus, "Edmonton Commercial Graduates," 81.

96. Edith Stone qtd. in Dewar, "Edmonton Grads."

97. Wamsley, "Power and Privilege." Wamsley particularly critiques Chalus,
     who argues that the Grads themselves accepted certain roles, for ignoring
     the cultural pressures on women that would have shaped their accounts.

98. J. MacDonald, "Alma Mater Whence Came Superstars, Heroes, Stalwarts,"
     n.d., ca. 1980s, *Edmonton Journal,* newspaper clipping, Edward R. Musteca
     fonds, File 3, MS 352, City of Edmonton Archives.

99. Noel MacDonald, "Windows in Home Make Personality," *Edmonton
     Journal,* March 20, 1937, newspaper clipping, Women's Sports files, City
     of Edmonton Archives; "Percy Page," Legislative Assembly of Alberta,
     accessed April 25, 2009, http://www.assembly.ab.ca/lao/library/lt-gov/page.
     htm.

100. Jose and Rannie, *Soccer Story in Canada;* "Women's Soccer Alive and
     Kicking," *Toronto Star,* August 8, 1995, 76; Wetherell and Kmet, *Useful
     Pleasures.*

101. "Women Invade the Soccer Field," *Province* (Vancouver), March 2, 1980, 10.

102. "Women's Soccer Alive and Kicking," *Toronto Star,* August 8, 1995, 76.

103. Bogle and Howe, "Women's Soccer in Canada"; "Women's National Teams Making Strides," *Toronto Star*, March 17, 1995, F5; Alberta Soccer Association, accessed April 24, 2009, http://www.albertasoccer.com/.

104. Photo A11820, Alberta Department of Health fonds, G R 1968.031, Provincial Archives of Alberta. This photo was part of a public health education and promotion series distributed throughout rural Alberta in the 1920s and 1930 by the Department of Health's travelling clinics.

105. Burstyn, *Rites of Men*.

106. O'Reilly, "Canadian Advertising Success Stories: Budweiser"; Joyce, "A Nation of Employees."

107. Danysk, *Hired Hands*; Bishop, introduction to *Mountain Masculinity*.

9 A "GREAT SLAUGHTER ON THE FIELD"

1. *Medicine Hat News*, August 21, 1890.

2. "Worst Baseball Fiasco in Local History Staged at Mewata Park," n.d., ca. 1920, newspaper clipping, Lloyd Turner fonds, M S 5767, Glenbow Archives.

3. "Spark Plugs Lose," "Misfits Win," n.d., ca. 1920s, newspaper clippings, Alice Faulkner fonds, 1915–1926, Glenbow Archives.

4. Farha Rajabali et al., "Sports Injuries Among Youth as Seen in Four Emergency Departments," BC Injury Research and Prevention Unit, n.d., http://www.injuryresearch.bc.ca/Publications/Posters/EDISS%20Poster. pdf.

5. "Small Boy Dies After Being Hit on Head by Ball," *Calgary Daily Herald*, June 18, 1921, 11.

6. Mitchell, "Gym Class Ruling Overturned," 6. In various accounts of the incident, the victim's name is spelled as both McCabe and MacCabe.

7. Leon Craig qtd. in C. Yu, "$4-million Mistake in Phys. Ed.: All Four Safety Rules Were Ignored in the (Margaret) MacCabe Gym Accident," *Alberta Report*, October 26, 1998, 21.

8. Russell, *The Social Psychology of Sport*, 181.

9. Brunt, "How Sport Became a Religion"; Metcalfe, *Canada Learns to Play*.

10. Burstyn, *Rites of Men*; Elias, "The Genesis of Sport as a Sociological Problem"; Young, "Violence, Risk, and Liability in Male Sports Culture."

11. Lorenz and Osborne, "'Talk About Strenuous Hockey.'"

12. Mason and Duquette, "Newspaper Coverage of Early Professional Ice Hockey."

13. Metcalfe, *Canada Learns to Play*.

14. Dufresne, "A Study of the Incidence, Nature, and Cause of Football Injuries."

15. Findlay, "Breaks of the Game," 75; Michener, *Sports in America*.

16. Mummery and Spence, "Rate and Frequency of Sport and Recreational Injuries."

17. K. Williamson, "Friend of Fallen Player Recalls Hit," *Calgary Herald*, November 17, 2005; Beamish and Ritchie, "From Fixed Capacities to Performance-Enhancement."

18. *Edmonton Bulletin*, May 7–14, 1893, qtd. in Lindsay and Hess, "Sporting Elites."

19. Hess, "Social History of Cycling"; "Mirror For a Bicycle," *Calgary Herald*, June 5, 1894, 4.

20. HCF *Alberta Online Encyclopedia*, s.v. "Ski Release Harness (Patent No: 789422)," Alberta Inventors and Inventions, accessed January 24, 2009, http://www.abheritage.ca/abinvents/database/description.php?ID=4497; HCF *Alberta Online Encyclopedia*, s.v. "Curling Ice Shaver (Patent No: 662457)," Alberta Inventors and Inventions, accessed January 24, 2009, http://www.abheritage.ca/abinvents/database/description.php?ID=4497; "Fred Longo and Lloyd Cowie Model New Riding Helmuts [*sic*], Which Appear for the First Time on a Canadian Track," *The Albertan*, May 19, 1956, 17.

21. Rosandich, "Sports Equipment and Technology"; University of Alberta, Faculty of Engineering, "Engineering and Sport," October 12, 2000, http://www.engineering.ualberta.ca/news.cfm?story=17742.

22. Ryan, "Development of Speed-skating."

23. "BSR to Hold Fashion Show and Dance," n.d., ca. 1950s, clipping; Minutes, December 13, 1954; Minutes, November 9, 1960, Banff Ski Runners of the Canadian Rockies fonds, M 431, Whyte Museum of the Canadian Rockies.

24. C. Mitchell, "The First 25 Years of the Calgary Skiing Club 1935–1960," type-script, 1985, Calgary Skiing Club fonds, M8092, Glenbow Archives.

25. "A 'Phenomenal' Boom Has Made Skiing Canada's Fastest-Growing Winter Sport," *Calgary Herald*, February 21, 1959, 61.

26. Yeo, "Making Banff a Year-round Park."

27. Alex Baumann qtd. in J. MacKinnon, "$318 million Worth of Sports Infrastructure Attached to City's Universiade Bid," *Edmonton Journal*, April 3, 2009.

28. Brown, "The Hypocrisy Game," 24–25. Shortly before the 2010 Olympics, Sport Canada initiated a medal-oriented program called Own the Podium. See Allinger and Allinger, "Own the Podium 2010."

29. Canadian Sport Centre Calgary, accessed March 3, 2012, http://www.canadiansportcentre.com/index.php.

30. Butterwick and Meeuwisse, "Bull Riding Injuries in Professional Rodeo."

31. Silversides, *Shooting Cowboys*; Foran, "The Stampede in Historical Context."

32. van Herk, *Mavericks*, 325.

33. *The Albertan*, July 12, 1938, 1.

34. A. Maki, "Still Tall in the Saddle," CareCure Community (online forum), July 5, 2003, http://sci.rutgers.edu/forum/showthread.php?t=45852.

35. "Rounding Up Rodeo Injuries Helps Prevention," *ScienceDaily*, July 13, 2007, http://www.sciencedaily.com/releases/2007/07/070713131144.htm.

36. "Rodeo Injuries Common but Preventable," Reuters.com, October 5, 2007, http://www.reuters.com/article/healthNews/idUSKIM56572320071005.

37. MacEwan, *Calgary Cavalcade*; Wamsley and Whitson, "Celebrating Violent Masculinities."

38. Wamsley and Whitson, "Celebrating Violent Masculinities," 419.

39. Wamsley and Whitson, "Celebrating Violent Masculinities"; McCaffery, *Tommy Burns*.

40. Wamsley and Whitson, "Celebrating Violent Masculinities"; MacEwan, *Calgary Cavalcade*.

41. *Calgary Herald*, April 21, 1922, newspaper clipping, Ted Knight fonds, M 8414 os, Glenbow Archives.

42. "Stewart Throws Kent, Leathers Pins Russell in Wild Mat Game," *Calgary Herald*, November 2, 1936.

43. "Eliminations for Provincial Boxing Tonight," *Calgary Daily Herald*, n.d., ca. 1920s, newspaper clipping, Ted Knight fonds, Glenbow Archives; AAUC fonds, file 4, M 655.3, Glenbow Archives.

44. *Calgary Herald*, April 21, 1922, newspaper clipping, Ted Knight fonds, M 8414 os, Glenbow Archives.

45. "Mitt Association All Set," *Lethbridge Herald*, n.d., ca. 1949, newspaper clipping, 19750017000. G M 975.17, Galt Museum Archives.

46. "$75 More for Boxing Fund," *Lethbridge Herald*, October 7, 1949; "Fine Gymnasium Opened in Sports Centre for Boxers," *Lethbridge Herald*, n.d., ca. 1949, newspaper clippings, 19750017000. G M 975.17, Galt Museum Archives.

47. MacEwan, *Calgary Cavalcade*.

48. "Wrestling Canadian Hall of Fame: Ed Whalen," Slam Sports, accessed April 21, 2008, http://slam.canoe.ca/SlamWrestlingBios/whalen.html.

49. Mondak, "The Politics of Professional Wrestling; Barthes, "Le monde ou l'on catche."

50. Greg Oliver, "The Stu Hart Interview, Part 2," Slam Sports, accessed April 21, 2008, http://slam.canoe.ca/SlamWrestlingArchive/hartstu_interview2.html.

51. "Stu Hart Discovers Talent," *StarPhoenix* (Saskatoon), July 29, 1978, 60.

52. Greg Oliver, "The Stu Hart Interview, Part 1," Slam Sports, accessed April 21, 2008, http://slam.canoe.ca/SlamWrestlingArchive/hartstu_interview1.html.

53. "Stu Hart Discovers Talent," *StarPhoenix* (Saskatoon), July 29, 1978, 60.

54. N.G. Moore, "Review of *Hitman: My Real Life in the Cartoon World of Wrestling* by Bret Hart," *Globe and Mail*, November 10, 2007, D11.

55. Dawn Walton, "A Wrestler's Hart-rending Battle to Win Disability Benefits," *Globe and Mail*, November 5, 2005, A12; Marc Ciampa, "Pro Wrestler Owen Hart's Unnecessary Death," *Sports Renaissance* 3, no. 6, June 1999, http://www.renaissancemag.com/sports/default.asp?article=0699.

56. Oliver and Johnson, *The Pro Wrestling Hall of Fame*, 72.

57. "Slam Wrestling: Gene Kiniski Chat," Slam Sports, accessed April 21, 2008, http://slam.canoe.ca/SlamWrestlingChats/nov10_kiniski-can.html.

58. Oliver and Johnson, *The Pro Wrestling Hall of Fame*.

59. Rutherford, *When Television was Young*.

60. Nicholas C. Vallentgoed, personal communication, Edmonton, Alberta, 2009.

61. McCoy, *Pain and Passion*.

62. O'Riordan, "The 'Puck-Eaters.'"

63. "Protection of Spectators at Sports: Do Away with Foul Language at Sporting Events," *Lethbridge News*, June 23, 1911, 4.

64. *Edmonton Bulletin*, January 14, 1897, qtd. in O'Riordan, "Puck-Eaters," 8; Cashman, "The Thistle Rink," 71-72.

65. *Medicine Hat News*, February 2, 1905 qtd. in Wilson, "Medicine Hat," 24; Cashman, *The Edmonton Story*.

66. Ray Turchansky, "Once the Fans were Caged the Game Could Start," *Edmonton Journal*, October 3, 2004, 55; "The Battle of Alberta: The 'Eye' of the

Storm," Edmonton Oilers Heritage, accessed February 26, 2012, http://www.
oilersheritage.com/history/early_events_battle_alberta.html.

67. "Dominions Whitewash Shermans" and "McCarty Defeats Palzer,"
    Edmonton Bulletin, January 2, 1913, 9.

68. D.L. Moore et al., Final Report of the Alberta Department of Youth:
    Submitted to the Honourable Robert C. Clark, Minister of Youth, November
    15, 1967, qtd. in Fortna, "'A Firm Referee That Will Make Both Sides Abide by
    the Rules,'" 22.

69. Bumsted, *History of the Canadian Peoples*, 22.

70. Petition in support of Eddie Shore, Edmonton, Alberta, 1933, N D-3-6561,
    Glenbow Archives; "Eddie Shore: The Edmonton Express," Edmonton
    Oilers Heritage, accessed February 26, 2012, http://www.oilersheritage.com/
    history/early_players_eddieshore.html.

71. "New Emphasis on Skating, Stick Work, Draws Praise," *StarPhoenix*
    (Saskatoon), January 22, 1958, 26.

72. Watson and Rickwood, "'Stewards of Ice Hockey.'"

73. G. Fisher, "Helmets Prove Unpopular," *Edmonton Journal*, March 9, 1966, 44.

74. "Only Game in Town: Saddle Lake's Junior B Warriors Give the Indian
    Reserve Something to Cheer, and Young Players a Reason to Leave," *Alberta
    Report* 25, no. 14 (March 23, 1998): 26–30.

75. "Only Game in Town," *Alberta Report*.

76. Robidoux, "First Nations Masculinity"; Robidoux and Bocksnick, "Playing
    Beyond the Glass"; Robidoux, "Narratives of Race Relations."

77. R. McKinley, "U P S Delivers the Goods to Advance Sport," *Windspeaker*,
    December 1997, 23.

78. B. Morgan, "Sandy McCarthy Talks to Native Americans," *Sports Illustrated
    for Kids*, February 1997, 18.

79. Robinson, *Crossing the Line*; Robidoux, *Men at Play*.

80. Smallwood, *In the Hearts of Kings*; W. Overland, "C A H A Ruling Will Kill
    Many Boys' Education," *Edmonton Journal*, March 9, 1966, 44.

81. "Alberta Scrutinizes its Hockey Situation," *Edmonton Sun*, March 1968, 17.

82. Stubbs, *Shoestring Glory*; Lucht, "Scobey's Touring Pros."

83. Lloyd Turner fonds, *Calgary Herald*, 1920, newspaper clipping, M S 5767,
    Glenbow Archives.

84. "Serious Sport," *Calgary Herald*, September 20, 1946, 19.

85. Mah, "1958...American College Kids Take the Canadian Title," *Western Canada Baseball*, accessed March 3, 2012, http://www.attheplate.com/wcbl/1958_1.htm.

86. *Edmonton Journal*, June 13, 1957 qtd. in Mah "1958...American College Kids Take the Canadian Title."

87. *Edmonton Journal*, June 13, 1957 qtd. in Goyette and Roemmich, *Edmonton In Our Own Words*, 294. The umpire in question, Rollan Natter, was a McGowan School for Umpires grad.

88. John McIsaac, "Interview with Mr. John Ducey, Edmonton's 'Mr. Baseball,'" 1979, Edmonton Parks and Recreation, City of Edmonton Archives.

89. Scott Zerr, "Basebrawl: Cracker-Cats Go at it With Hated Calgary Vipers in Cowtown Dust-up," *Edmonton Sun*, June 15, 2006; "Busch, Bevington and Seven Players Suspended," *Northern League*, June 16, 2006, http://www.northernleague.com/news/?id=4453; Adam Wazny, "Battle of Alberta, Baseball Style," *Edmonton Sun*, June 15, 2006.

90. "On to Canmore," newspaper clipping, n.d., Alice Faulkner fonds, M 364/V 197, Whyte Museum of the Canadian Rockies.

91. "Spark Plugs Lose," newspaper clipping, Alice Faulkner fonds, M 364/V 197, Whyte Museum of the Canadian Rockies.

92. "Canmore Bluebirds Win," n.d., ca. 1915–1926, newspaper clipping, Alice Faulkner fonds, M 364/V 197, Whyte Museum of the Canadian Rockies.

93. "New Year Game Was a Good One," n.d., ca. 1915–1926, newspaper clipping, Alice Faulkner fonds, M 364/V 197, Whyte Museum of the Canadian Rockies.

94. "Alberta Gets Meet," *Montreal Gazette*, November 4, 1930, 16.

95. Korkia, "Drugs in Sport."

96. Haraway, *Simians, Cyborgs and Women*; Hoberman, *Mortal Engines*; Hughson, "Science, Culture, and the Sporting Body."

97. Mike Celizic, "WWE's Chairman Calls Benoit a 'Monster,'" Today.com, June 25, 2007, http://today.msnbc.msn.com/; H. McCoy, "Grappler Learned Ropes in Calgary," *Calgary Herald*, June 26, 2007.

98. Terry Jones, "Good on ya, Graham!," *Edmonton Sun*, April 20, 2002, 32.

99. M. Clarkson, "Beckie Finally Gets Gold: This is a Victory for the Little Guy," *Toronto Star*, December 19, 2003.

100. Brunt, "Changing Face of Sport."

101. Stacy Lorenz, "Who's to Blame for Drugs in Sports? Before We Condemn the Next Abuser, We Should First Examine Our Own Values," *Edmonton Journal*, December 20, 2004, A 14; Burstyn, *Rites of Men*.

102. Voisey, *Vulcan*; Hosgood, "Poker and the Police in Early Twentieth Century Alberta."

103. "First Champions," *Olds Gazette*, December 31, 1959, 8.

104. "Bettors Iced by Lockout," *Edmonton Journal*, September 28, 2004, S2.

105. "Calgary Fair July 9, 10, 11, 12 Racing Program," *Calgary Eye Opener*, June 29, 1907, 1; Wetherell, "Making Tradition."

106. Janice Sather, "50 Fast Years, 50 Great Stories," Alberta Quarter Horse Racing Association, accessed April 21, 2008, http://www.aqhra.ca/50years.htm; "Charge Pair Robbed Dead," *Camrose Canadian*, June 15, 1955, 25; Northlands Park, "Racing," Memories Worth Keeping, April 22, 2008, http://www.northlands.com/memories/.

107. "Klein to Push N H L Lottery to Bettman," C T V News, June 15, 2001, http://www.ctv.ca/CTVNews/CTVNewsAt11/20010615/ctvnews91188/; "Putting Slots in the Saddle," *Edmonton Journal*, April 21, 2002, D 8, 9, 13; Edmonton Northlands, "Racing," Memories Worth Keeping, accessed April 22, 2008, http://www.northlands.com/memories/community_events/racing.html.

108. Vaz, "Institutionalized Rule Violation."

10 "THE RAIN UPON OUR SENSES"

1. Morrow et al., *Concise History of Sport*; Lorenz, "In the Field of Sport at Home and Abroad"; Lowes, *Inside the Sports Pages*.

2. Gorn and Oriard, "Taking Sports Seriously," 20.

3. *Calgary Daily Herald*, January 13, 1911, 9; Metcalfe, *Canada Learns to Play*; Lorenz, "In the Field."

4. Lowes, "Sports Pages"; Mason and Duquette, "Newspaper Coverage.

5. Strathern, *Alberta Newspapers*.

6. *Edmonton Bulletin*, March 14, 1895, qtd. in Hess, "Social History of Cycling," 54.

7. "Swimming Champions Compete Tonight for the Alberta Honors," *Calgary Daily Herald*, September 28, 1911, 8; Hess, "Social History of Cycling."

8. "Sport," *Edmonton Bulletin*, January 2, 1907, 8; Ducey, *Rajah of Renfrew*; *Calgary Daily Herald*, January 13, 1911, 9; Lorenz, "Sports Coverage."

9. Lorenz, "Bowing Down to Babe Ruth," 22-23.

10. Sports clippings files, Galt Museum Archives.

11. "Benefit Hockey Tonight," *Edmonton Bulletin*, March 26, 1907, 5.

12. Harold Burnham, to "Florence," November 21, 1908, Harold Burnham fonds, 75.79, Provincial Archives of Alberta.

13. Betke qtd. in Lorenz, "In the Field of Sport," 154.

14. "In the World of Sports," *Calgary Daily Herald*, January 11, 1913; "Sport," *Edmonton Bulletin*, March 26, 1907.

15. Baker, Lodge, and Tagg, *Weddings, Work and War*.

16. Macdonald et al., "Radical Sports."

17. Pezer, *Stone Age*.

18. "Curling Results," *Red Deer Advocate*, January 3, 1934, 1.

19. "Saskatchewan Turns Back Alberta's Bid in College Football," *Calgary Daily Herald*, November 2, 1936, 6.

20. *The Albertan*, July 11, 1938, 15–16.

21. *Camrose Canadian*, January 11, 1939, 1.

22. Lorenz, "Sports Coverage."

23. "Soccer Rules as Revised by National Association Officials," *The Albertan*, July 11, 1938, 15.

24. *Star Weekly*, n.d., ca. 1940, 13, newspaper clipping, Helen Pilon fonds, box 1, file 2, M 7955, Glenbow Archives.

25. *The Albertan*, ca. 1940–1941, newspaper clipping, box 1, file 2, Helen Pilon fonds, M 7955, Glenbow Archives.

26. M.A. Hall, "Alexandrine Gibb"; Howell, *Blood, Sweat, and Cheers*.

27. *The Albertan*, July 11, 1938, 15–18.

28. "Curlers Start Season," *Red Deer Advocate*, January 5, 1944, 1.

29. "Red Deer Curling Club Holds Good Banquet," *Red Deer Advocate*, November 14, 1945, 1; "Declaration on Atomic Bomb By President Truman and Prime Ministers Attlee and King," November 15, 1945, Nuclearfiles.org, accessed June 23, 2011, http://www.nuclearfiles.org/menu/key-issues/ nuclear-energy/history/dec-truma-atlee-king_1945-11-15.htm.

30. John Willis, "Professional Hockey and the Mail-order Catalogue," Canadian Museum of Civilization, updated October 22, 2009, http://www. civilization.ca/cmc/exhibitions/cpm/catalog/cat2207e.shtml.

31. Macintosh, Bedecki, and Franks, *Sport and Politics in Canada*.

32. Kelly, *Hanging it Out on Camera 3*.

33. Goyette and Roemmich, *Edmonton In Our Own Words*, 214. The quotation is an unattributed illustration of a telegram on the page.

34. "Vast Crowd Listens to Story of Hockey Game," *Calgary Daily Herald*, n.d., ca. 1924, 16, newspaper clipping, Lloyd Turner fonds, MS 5767, Glenbow Archives.

35. Lorenz, "Bowing Down to Babe Ruth."

36. Cashman, "Mike's News Stand," 163.

37. "These Recent Programs Pleased Audiences for Miles Around," *Edmonton Journal*, March 18, 1941, 8.

38. Zeman, *Alberta on Ice*.

39. D. Scott, "Benefactor," *Calgary Herald*, January 12, 1963, 13.

40. University of Alberta Centennial, "People: Shirley Stinson," University of Alberta, 2008, http://www.ualbertacentennial.ca/people/displaybio.php?bio_id=651. Today CKUA carries no sports coverage. This in itself is an attraction for many non-sports fans who weary of the sports bulletins carried by the other available public broadcaster, namely the CBC. CKUA Sound Archives, CKUA Radio, accessed April 19, 2008, http://66.244.199.219/CKUA_Archives/eng/people.

41. Sanderson, "Pearl Edmanson Borgal, 1911–1993," 82; "Lisa Miller," Alberta Sports Hall of Fame and Museum, accessed March 3, 2012, http://www.albertasportshalloffame.com/component/zoo/item/miller-lisa.

42. "Beer Waiters Protest at Not Hearing Game," *Calgary Herald*, November 27, 1948, 1; Lorenz, "Bowing Down to Babe Ruth"; Palmer and Palmer, *Peoples of Alberta*.

43. Rutherford, *When Television was Young*.

44. Cavanagh, "Development of Canadian Sports Broadcasting."

45. Rutherford, *When Television was Young*; Cavanagh, "Development of Canadian Sports Broadcasting."

46. McLuhan, "Games: Extensions of Man"; Marannis, *When Pride Still Mattered*.

47. B. Mellor, "Movies May Bring Skiing Changes," *Ottawa Citizen*, March 3, 1964, 5.

48. B. Dufresne, "Millions Attend Game By Person and TV," *Leader-Post* (Regina), November 29, 1945, 4.

49. "'54 Grey Cup Game to Be Well Covered" *Calgary Herald*, November 24, 1954, 32.

50. Cavanagh, "Development of Canadian Sports Broadcasting."

51. D. Chezzi, "What's Old is New," *Maclean's*, August 27, 2001, 46–47. Audience access is also a reason for attention to the game, as it costs about ten to thirty-five dollars to see a top lacrosse team compared to as much as $145 for an NHL game.

52. Rutherford, *When Television was Young*.

53. B. Weeks, "Another Edmonton Dynasty," *Globe and Mail*, March 14, 2005.

54. Gruneau and Whitson, "Upmarket Continentalism."

55. Whitson and Gruneau, ed., introduction to *Artificial Ice*; Rutherford, *When Television was Young*; Gasher, "Review of M.D. Lowes, *Inside the Sports Pages*."

56. "Herald Rodeo Scribe to be Feted," *Calgary Herald*, March 12, 2008.

57. Clipping, Ted Knight fonds, Glenbow Archives.

58. "Last Call for 'They'rrrre off' as Voice of Stampede Chuckwagon Race Retires," CBC News, July 12, 2008, http://www.cbc.ca/news/canada/calgary/story/2008/07/12/stampede-carbury.html; "Joe Carbury," and "Frank Ryan," Alberta Sports Hall of Fame and Museum, 2012, http://www.albertasportshalloffame.com/.

59. H. Pawson, "Sporting Periscope," *Edmonton Journal*, June 23, 1960; Adeyinka Makinde, "Dick Tiger—Not a Visiting Apprentice," *Wail! The CBZ Journal*, accessed January 23, 2010, http://cyberboxingzone.com/boxing/w7x-dt.htm.

60. Henry Joseph Viney, 1910-1945, phonotape, 79.17/3a, 3b, Provincial Archives of Alberta.

61. Sport Media Canada, "Ernie Afaganis," accessed January 27, 2010, http://www.sportsmediacanada.com/ernie_afaganis.html.

62. T. Jones, "A Real Tiger," Slam Sports, February 4, 2006, http://slam.canoe.ca/Slam/Columnists/Jones/2006/02/04/1425994-sun.html.

63. T. Jones, "A Real Tiger"; Laurence Herzog, "The Tough Guy with the Soft Heart," *Alberta Real Estate Weekly* 24, no. 6 (February 9, 2006); "Tiger Goldstick" Alberta Sports Hall of Fame and Museum, accessed February 27, 2012, http://www.albertasportshalloffame.com/.

64. C. Young, "In Red Deer, MacLean's Simply 'Our Guy,'" *Toronto Star*, October 4, 2002, E6.

65. J. MacKinnon, "The Voice Part of Oilers History," *Edmonton Journal*, March 30, 2011, http://www.edmontonjournal.com/sports/Voice+part+Oilers+history/4526619/story.html; Gzowski, *The Game of Our Lives*; "Ron MacLean

bio," *Hockey Night in Canada*, CBC Sports, accessed January 29, 2008, http://
www.cbc.ca/sports/hockey/hnic/bios-ron.shtml; Alberta Sports Hall of
Fame and Museum, "Ron MacLean" accessed February 27, 2012, http://
www.albertasportshalloffame.com/.

66. "Ed Whalen," Slam Sports, accessed January 29, 2008, http://slam.canoe.ca/
SlamWrestlingBiosW/whalen_01dec05-sun3.htm.

67. "Bryan Hall—A Year to Remember," Edmonton Oilers Heritage, accessed
February 28, 2012, http://www.oilersheritage.com/legacy/contributions_
announcers_bryanhall.html.

68. S. O'Donnell, "Montgomery a Morning Legend," *Edmonton Journal*, April 26,
2005; J. Huntington, "Jones Captures First-ever Wes Award," *Edmonton Sun*,
October 26, 2006, SP6.

69. R. Turchansky, "Riding High in 'Buckets" Seat," *Edmonton Journal*, August
21, 2006.

70. Kidd, "Making of a Hockey Artifact," 2.

71. Kidd, "Missing: Women." Furthermore, there are only two women—Diane
Jones Konihowski and Susan Nattrass—among thirteen selectors at
Canada's Sports Hall of Fame.

72. C. Clark, "Bringing History to the World Cup of Women's Baseball,"
Edmonton Woman Magazine, 2007, http://www.edmontonwoman.com/
baseball.php; "Ken McAuley," Alberta Sports Hall of Fame and Museum,
accessed July 13, 2007, http://www.albertasportshalloffame.com/.

73. "2006 Induction Ceremony," Wetaskiwin Sports Hall of Fame, accessed
July 23, 2007, http://wetaskiwinsportsfame.com/photo_gallery_2006.htm.

74. "Helen Nicol," Alberta Sports Hall of Fame and Museum, accessed July 23,
2007, http://www.albertasportshalloffame.com/.

75. Tiffin, "George Washington Houk."

76. Baker, Lodge, and Tagg, *Weddings, Work and War*.

77. Spears, "'Siding 29' or the Role of the Canadian Pacific Railway," 60.

78. C. Jose, "Alberta, the Early Years," Provincial Histories, Canadian Soccer
History, accessed March 3, 2012, http://www.canadiansoccerhistory.
com/Alberta/Alberta-%20The%20Early%20Years.html. He also won the
Edmonton senior men's golf championships from 1960 to 1962.

79. "Commercial Cagemen Start Activities Tomorrow Night," *Lethbridge Herald*,
November 30, 1949; Hunter and Weber, *Wild Bill*. Lethbridge also had the
Army, Navy, and Air Force Veterans in 1949.

80. *The Albertan*, July 12, 1938, 15.

81. *The Albertan*, July 12, 1938, 15.

82. "Asks New Cage Deal," *Windsor Daily Star*, July 12, 1938, 18; "Seek Stronger Competition for Edmonton Girl Cagers," *Windsor Daily Star*, July 12, 1938, 18.

83. "Edmonton Grads, Facing Disbandment, Open Three Game Series with Wichita," *Calgary Herald*, September 28, 1938, 6.

84. "End of Edmonton Grads Forecast Unless Fans' Interest Improves," *Montreal Gazette*, September 22, 1938, 28.

85. *The Albertan*, July 12, 1938.

86. Mah, "1955…Last Again," Western Canada Baseball, 2010, http://www. attheplate.com/wcbl/1955_1.html.

87. "Need Accommodation," *Lethbridge Herald*, June 27, 1946, newspaper clipping, Sick's Breweries files, 19901008007, Galt Museum Archives.

88. Rules Governing the Brewery Trophy, August 1, 1905, Molson Breweries Western Division, M 8581/592, Glenbow Archives.

89. J. Kerr, "The Calgary Buffaloes Athletic Association," n.d., ca. 1967, Molson Breweries Western Division, M 8581/594, Glenbow Archives. Peter Lougheed was a player on the minor league hockey team.

90. Kerr, "Calgary Buffaloes"; E. Luxton, "A Winter Dissertation," *The Gateway*, March 20, 1930, 29.

91. Kerr, "Calgary Buffaloes."

92. Calgary Buffalo Athletic Association, Molson Breweries Western Division, M8581/593, 594, Glenbow Archives.

93. Newspaper clippings, *Lethbridge Herald*, "League Prexy," *Lethbridge Herald*, "Schriner Lethbridge Coach," June 1, 1946, Sick's Breweries files, 19901008007, Galt Museum Archives.

94. Newspaper clipping, *Drumheller Review*, June 17, 1940, 1, Sick's Breweries files, Galt Museum Archives.

95. "Sick's Backs Native Sons," *Lethbridge Herald*, April 23 1949; "Fine Sports Stadium Built Without Debt," *Lethbridge Herald*, October 18, 1949, Sick's Breweries files, Galt Museum Archives.

96. Cavanagh, "Development of Canadian Sports Broadcasting."

97. Hughson, "Cultural History and the Study of Sport," 12.

98. G. Hunter, "Gorde Hunter," *Calgary Herald*, January 25, 1964, 16.

99. "Twilight Ladies Softball League, 1937-1949," South Peace Regional Archives, accessed March 3, 2012, http://www.southpeacearchives.org/fonds/fonds110.htm.

100. Don Pilling column, *Lethbridge Herald*, n.d., ca. 1949; J. Brooke, "Five O'Clock Shadow," *Lethbridge Herald* n.d., ca. 1949, newspaper clippings, 19750017000 G M 975.17, Galt Museum Archives.

101. Edmonton Rush Lacrosse Club, "Edmonton Rush Joins Marketing Partnership with Alberta Pork," news release, January 16, 2006, http://www.edmontonrush.com/news/2006/january/16.php; Alberta Dusters Professional Basketball Team Yearbook 1980-1981, 19881037018, Galt Museum Archives.

102. Canadian Girls' Rodeo Association fonds, M7703/65, Glenbow Archives.

103. Edmonton Rodeo Souvenir Program, 1953, Edmonton Exhibition Association (E E A) M 5322, Class 70, s/c 5, file 1, City of Edmonton Archives.

104. Roy Lisogar to E E A, March 24, 1945, letter, E E A M 5322, Class 70, s/c 5, file 1, City of Edmonton Archives. Lisogar's company had produced over thirty-five rodeos and Stampedes in Canada since 1937.

105. Managing director E E A to E. J. Tyne of Edmonton, October 2, 1950, letter, E E A M 5322, Class 70, s/c 5, file 1. City of Edmonton Archives. Markets included Tofield, Stettler, Wetaskiwin, Camrose, Vegreville, Ponoka, Fort Saskatchewan, Grande Prairie, Vermilion, and Red Deer as well as larger cities.

106. Herman Linder, Calgary, June 4, 1951 to James Paul, E E A, Edmonton, letter, E E A M 5322, Class 70, s/c 5, file 1, City of Edmonton Archives.

107. Herman Linder, Calgary, June 4, 1951 to James Paul, E E A, Edmonton, letter, E E A M 5322, Class 70, s/c 5, file 1, City of Edmonton Archives. See Herman Linder fonds, Glenbow Archives.

108. E E A M 5322, Class 70, s/c 5, file 1, City of Edmonton Archives.

109. B. Ivory, Denver Colorado, February 22, 1955 to James Paul, E E A, Edmonton, letter, E E A M 5322, Class 70, s/c 5, file 3, City of Edmonton Archives.

110. E E A M 5322, Class 70, s/c 5, file 5, City of Edmonton Archives.

111. J. Hawkins, "Rodeo Predicts $60M in Spinoffs," *Edmonton Journal*, November 1, 2006; J. Bell and D. Blumhagen, "Rodeo: Alberta's Passion," *The Gateway*, May 6, 2010, http://thegatewayonline.ca/articles/features/2010/05/06/rodeo-albertas-passion.

112. Wilson, "Does Sport Sponsorship Have a Direct Effect?"

113. World Class Escort Service advertisement, *Edmonton Journal*, August 2001; Doust, "Ethics of Ambush Marketing."

114. B. Mah, "Alberta City Dumps Players' Names from Arena," Canada.com, July 30, 2006, http://www.canada.com/topics/sports/story. html?id=859d248b-0a7a-414e-84df-8147bb441b8b&k=53496.

115. Mills, "Peter Pocklington and the Business of Hockey," 309.

116. Adams, "So What's the Problem with Wussy Sports?."

117. Crystal Kingwell, "A Gold Medal is Worth its Weight in Endorsements," Media Awareness Network, accessed March 5, 2012, http://www.media-awareness.ca/english/resources/educational/teachable_moments/ gold_medal_endorsements.cfm; Veltri and Long, "A New Image: Female Athlete-endorser."

118. T. Jones, "Another Joy Ride For Canadian Cyclist Lori-Ann Muenzer," *Edmonton Sun*, September 29, 2004.

119. Judy Monchuk, "Olympic Golden Girl Muenzer Rolls On with Little Fanfare, Sponsorship," Canada.com, December 8, 2004, http://www.canada. com/sports/story.html?id=a9517a96-21fb-404c-a837-23a4605c77b5.

120. Brunt, "Changing Face of Sport."

121. Whitson and Gruneau, *Artificial Ice*.

11 GETTING ON THE MAP

1. Mah, "1950...Sceptre, the Mohawks, the Rockets & the ManDak League," Western Canada Baseball, accessed March 2, 2012, http://www.attheplate. com/wcbl/1950_1.html.

2. *Lacombe Globe*, June 8, 1950.

3. Trumpbour, "Rituals, Invented Traditions."

4. Foran, "More than Partners," 152.

5. Lightbody, "City Campaigns on the Cusp"; Wetherell, "Making New Identities"; McHugh, "The Tourism Tiger."

6. Page qtd. in Mills, "100 Years," 217.

7. *Calgary Daily Herald*, May 19, n.d., ca. 1920s, newspaper clipping, Ted Knight fonds, Glenbow Archives.

8. "50,000 to see Champions Parade; City Hails our Flyers," *Edmonton Bulletin*, May 10, 1948, 1.

9. Ray Turchansky, "Once the Fans were Caged the Game Could Start," *Edmonton Journal*, October 3, 2004, 55.

10. Smallwood, *Hearts of Kings*; Vantour, *The Fabulous Flyers*.

11. Ducey, *Rajah of Renfrew*, 10.

12. "Triumphantly into Final Junior," *Edmonton Journal*, April 12, 1934, 16.

13. *Calgary Herald*, n.d., ca. 1947, newspaper clipping, Helen Pilon fonds, M7955, box 1, file 2, Glenbow Archives.

14. Canwest News Service, "Oilers Arrive at Edmonton Airport," June 20, 2006, Canada.com, http://www.canada.com/topics/sports/hockey/playoffs2006/story.html?id=17137d8a-6a73-4bb0-b27d-2faafd5ba43e.

15. "Edmonton Rally Honours Randy Ferbey Rink," *Globe and Mail*, March 14, 2005; Maki, "Curling rocks," *Globe and Mail*, April 9, 2005, F2.

16. *Claresholm Local Press* qtd. in Wetherell and Kmet, *Useful Pleasures*, 267–68.

17. Wetherell, "Making New Identities."

18. "Green Acres is Name of City Senior Cagers," *Lethbridge Herald*, n.d., ca. 1949, newspaper clipping, 19750017000 GM 975.17, Galt Museum Archives.

19. Ducey, *Rajah of Renfrew*. When he acquired the Edmonton Oil Kings in 1956, Bill Hunter changed the name only slightly to the Alberta Oilers to keep the central association with the region's black gold.

20. Wilson, "Medicine Hat," 18.

21. Wetherell and Kmet, *Town Life*, 268.

22. Lamb, "Deacon White"; Lorenz, "Sports Coverage"; Wetherell and Kmet, *Town Life*.

23. N. Vernon-Wood, "Us Winter Sports," *The Sportsman* (January 1931): 44–45 qtd. in *Mountain Masculinity*, eds. Gow and Rak, 72.

24. "Summer and Winter Sports Going on at Banff the Same Time," *Calgary Herald*, May 20, 1929, 8.

25. "Princess to Rest at Banff," *The Age*, July 28, 1958, 3.

26. Ducey, *Rajah of Renfrew*.

27. Baker, Lodge, and Tagg, *Weddings, Work and War*, 75.

28. *Wetaskiwin Free Press* advertisement for the Women's Dominion Championships and the Boys' Provincial Championships, Wetaskiwin, Alberta, August 12, 1931, Carl Walin fonds, WET-98.10, City of Wetaskiwin Archives.

29. *Edmonton Bulletin* qtd. in Lorenz, "Sports Coverage," 152.

30. Wetherell and Kmet, *Town Life*.

31. Voisey, *Vulcan*, 60; Lorenz, "Sports Coverage."

32. Jack Manson's Hockey Scrapbook, newspaper clipping, ca. 1948, A 97-171, City of Edmonton Archives.

33. Wamsley and Heine, "Tradition, Modernity and the Construction of Civic Identity"; DyckFehderau, "The Magnificent 'Rogue' of the Miracle Mile."

34. Hal Pawson, "The Sporting Periscope," *Edmonton Journal*, September 15, 1955, qtd. in Mah, "1955...Last again," Western Canada Baseball, 2010, http://www.attheplate.com/wcbl/1955_1.html.

35. O'Riordan, "The 'Puck-Eaters.'"

36. Cashman, *The Edmonton Story*, 222.

37. Voisey, *Vulcan*; Wetherell, "Making Tradition."

38. van Herk, *Mavericks*, 331.

39. "50,000 to See Champions Parade; City Hails our Flyers," *Edmonton Bulletin*, May 10, 1948, 1; M.W. Lyle, "Deplores Attitude of Calgary Fans," *Edmonton Journal*, n.d., ca. 1948, newspaper clippings, Helen Pilon fonds, box 1, file 2, M 7955, Glenbow Archives.

40. Cuhatscheck et al., *Hockey Chronicles*; Byfield, *Alberta*, vol. 2; Falla, Johnson, and Batten, *Quest for the Cup*.

41. "Underrated but Supreme," *The Gateway*, November 19, 1963, 4.

42. Sheila Pratt, "City's Universiade Bid Enters Home Stretch," *Edmonton Journal*, April 29, 2009.

43. "Civic grant of $500 is given for bonspiel, *Edmonton Bulletin*, January 1, 1920, 1.

44. *Edmonton Bulletin*, June 10, 1895 and November 25, 1898 qtd. in Hess, "Social History of Cycling," 87.

45. Kinsmen Club of Grande Prairie fonds, Grande Prairie Regional Archives; Kinsmen Club of Athabasca fonds, Athabasca Archives.

46. "Why Hockey Succeeds Here—Tiger Club is Owned by Citizens," n.d., ca. 1924, newspaper clipping, Lloyd Turner fonds, Glenbow Archives; Harold Burnham fonds, Provincial Archives of Alberta.

47. Kellicut, "Early History of Sports in the Granum Area," 126.

48. Betke, "Winter Sports," 64.

49. *Maclean's* qtd. in Bell, "History of Tennis," 87.

50. Lloyd Turner fonds, "Why Hockey Succeeds," pamphlet, Glenbow Archives.

51. Cosentino, *Canadian Football*.

52. "New Trophy Presented by Local Active Club," n.d., ca. 1941, newspaper clipping, Helen Pilon fonds, Glenbow Archives.

53. van Herk, *Mavericks*; Betke, "Winter Sports." Burns left the city after the fatal McCarty-Pelkey fight in 1913.

54. Scrapbook, Lloyd Turner fonds, MS 5767, Glenbow Archives.

55. Lamb, "Deacon White," 33.

56. Lamb, "Deacon White."

57. D. Mclellan, "Bill Hunter, 82. Founder of World Hockey Assn," *Los Angeles Times*, September 21, 2002, http://articles.latimes.com/2002/dec/21/local/me-hunter21; "'Wild' Bill Hunter Dead at 82," CBC Sports, December 17, 2002, http://www.cbc.ca/sports/story/2002/12/17/hunter021217.html; *Canadian Encyclopedia*, s.v. "Hunter, William Dickenson," by B. Weber, accessed March 4, 2012, http://www.thecanadianencyclopedia.com/articles/william-dickenson-hunter.

58. D. Pilling, *Lethbridge Herald*, 1955, qtd. in Mah, "The Granum/Lethbridge Reunion, 2000" Western Canada Baseball, accessed March 4, 2012, http://www.attheplate.com/wcbl/2000_lethbridge_reunion.html.

59. Kellicut, "Early History of Sports in the Granum Area," 127.

60. Humber, *Diamonds of the North*; Lethbridge Sports Hall of Fame, "Inductees: George Wesley," accessed January 15, 2009, http://www.lethbridgesportshalloffame.ca/Bio.aspx?ID=WESLEYGEORGEAward1991.

61. Familiar names include Edmonton's Jack Agrios, Jim Wheatley, Rick LeLacheur, Bill Smith, Jim Hole, Bruce Saville, Cal Nichols, Ron Hayter. D. Barnes, "Heart and a Healthy Sports Ego," *Edmonton Journal*, November 2, 2003, 45.

62. Newspaper clipping, n.d., ca. 1947–1949, Phelan fonds, Red Deer and District Archives.

63. Red Deer Board of Trade, Geo. A. Nechkin, Secretary to J. Phelan, Red Deer, July 19, 1949, letter, Phelan fonds, Red Deer and District Archives.

64. "Red Deer Driver Wins Wagon Race," *Calgary Herald*, July 18, 1949; F. Kennedy, "Agricultural Alberta," *Calgary Herald*, July 17, 1952, 16; *Edmonton Journal*, July 21, 1952, 13, newspaper clippings, Phelan fonds, Red Deer and District Archives.

65. "Calgary Cannons Media Guide 1987"; A. Thomas, "Play ball!," magazine clipping, n.d., ca. 1985, Calgary Cannon fonds, M7989, Glenbow Archives.

66. Manuscript, n.d., ca. 1987, Calgary, Calgary Cannons fonds, M7989, Glenbow Archives; Cochrane Cruisers Hockey Club, letter March 20, 1989, to

Calgary Cannons Baseball Club in thanks for donation to a Novice hockey tournament.

67. Humber, *Diamonds of the North*.

68. Mills, "100 Years."

69. Mills, "100 Years."

70. Lee qtd. in Heidi L.M. Jacobs, "Hockey Writing in Canada: a Profile," *Northwest Passages*, accessed March 4, 2012, http://www.nwpassages.com/hockeylit.asp.

71. Jim Taylor, "A Nation in Mourning: A Canadian Writes of Gretzky and His Country's Grief," *Sports Illustrated*, August 22, 1988, http://sportsillustrated.cnn.com/vault/article/magazine/MAG1067655/index.htm; Brunt, *Gretzky's Tears*.

72. G. Lamphier, "Katz Bids to Buy Oilers," *Edmonton Journal*, May 5, 2007.

73. "Katz, Edmonton Oilers Sign Promotional Deal," *Chain Drug Review* 25, no. 21 (December 15, 2003): 3.

74. Tracy Hyatt et al., "Alberta's 100 Most Influential People, Patrick LaForge," *Alberta Venture*, July 1, 2008, http://www.albertaventure.com/?p=453.

75. Turchansky, "Once the Fans Were Caged"; Trumpbour, "Rituals"; O'Riordan, "The 'Puck-Eaters.'"

76. Wamsley, "Strangers on the Eighteen Hole," 6.

77. Robbie et al., "History, Highlands Golf Club."

78. Inscription on dedication plaque, photograph, EA-10-2569, July 6, 1951, City of Edmonton Archives.

79. "Lethbridge's First Covered Rink Opens," *Lethbridge Daily News*, December 10, 1914, 2; Wilson, "Medicine Hat."

80. Dawe, *Red Deer*.

81. *The Plaindealer* (Drumheller), March 12, 1936. The Drumheller club won the bonspiel.

82. "Heavy Ice Makes Curling Hard Work," *Edmonton Journal*, February 10, 1928, 1; B. Mamini, "Sport-O-Scope," *Calgary Herald*, December 28, 1939, 6; "Artificial Ice Will Permit Curling Despite Weather," *Calgary Herald*, January 10, 1945, 11; "Around-the-clock Curling Seen Likely," *Calgary Herald*, January 14, 1948, 1. In 1945, Edmonton's Granite Club installed the city's first artificial ice.

83. Tingley, *City of Champions*.

84. "Ice-makers Start School Today," *Edmonton Journal*, October 8, 1958, 9.

85. J.R.S. Hambly, "Behind the Glass," *Camrose Canadian*, December 14, 1960, 2; "Golden Bears Victors in Opening Exhibition," *Camrose Canadian*, December 14, 1960, 2.

86. Wood and King, "Amateur Hockey"; van Herk, *Mavericks*.

87. J. Holubitsky, "New Ice Age Here for Avid Hockey Town," *Edmonton Journal*, August 16, 2007.

88. "New Swimming Pool Proves Popular on its Opening Day," *Lethbridge Herald*, September 6, 1949, Sports clippings files, Galt Museum Archives.

89. T. Jones, "The Magnificent Stadium," Clarke Stadium 1938–1978, *Edmonton Eskimos Souvenir Program*, August 23 1978, 5; Morrow et al., *Concise History*. Total seating was now 3,500.

90. "Weekend Meet Opens New 'Rubber' Track," *StarPhoenix* (Saskatoon), July 24, 1964, 15.

91. "Centre Combats Athlete Shortage," *StarPhoenix* (Saskatoon), January 3, 1968, 24.

92. David Staples, "Is Edmonton Ready to Take a Risk on a New Hockey Arena?" *Edmonton Journal*, December 13, 2009.

93. Lamb, "Deacon White"; Betke, *Winter Sports*; Wood and King, "Amateur Hockey in Alberta," 198; Vantour, *The Fabulous Flyers*, 18; Edward R. Musteca fonds, M S 352, file 1, City of Edmonton Archives.

94. Lawrence Herzog, "Edmonton's Lost Omniplex," *Alberta Real Estate Weekly*, 25, no. 32 (August 9, 2007), http://www.rewedmonton.ca/content_view_rew?CONTENT_ID=1933.

95. *Edmonton Journal*, September 12, 1963, Coliseum Complex, file 1, 1963–1974, City of Edmonton Archives.

96. Hamly Press, n.d., Coliseum Complex, file 1, 1963–1974, City of Edmonton Archives.

97. Herzog, "Edmonton's Lost Omniplex"; *Edmonton Journal*, October 17, 1963, Coliseum Complex, file 1, 1963–1974, City of Edmonton Archives.

98. D. Staples, "Is Edmonton Ready to Take a Risk on a New Hockey Arena?" *Edmonton Journal*, December 13, 2009.

99. Gruneau and Whitson, "Upmarket Continentalism."

100. "Mayor Ready to Study New Downtown Arena," C B C News, April 18, 2007, http://www.cbc.ca/canada/edmonton/story/2007/04/18/arena-edmonton.html; S. McKeen, "New Arena Would be a Boon for the City, Despite Fear and Pessimism," *Edmonton Journal*, April 27, 2007.

101. J. Markusoff, "Door Not Quite Shut on Provincial Aid," *Edmonton Journal*, March 25, 2008; G. Kent, "Edmonton Council Votes to Enter Formal Arena Negotiations with Katz Group," *Edmonton Journal*, January 18, 2011; M.D. Male, "Will Edmonton be a Second-class City Without the New Arena?" *MasterMaq* (blog), March 7, 2011, http://blog.mastermaq.ca/2011/03/07/will-edmonton-be-a-second-class-city-without-the-new-arena.

102. Elise Stolte, "Standing-room Only at City Hall as 110 Speakers Weigh in on Arena Debate," *Edmonton Journal*, October 25, 2011, http://www.globaltvedmonton.com/standing-room+only+at+city+hall+as+110+speakers+weigh+in+on+arena+debate/6442508008/story.html.

103. Cosentino, *Canadian Football*, 50.

104. J. MacKinnon, "$318 million Worth of Sports Infrastructure Attached to City's Universiade Bid," *Edmonton Journal*, April 30, 2009; A. Edinborough, "New Beginning for Edmonton," *Financial Post*, August 15, 1978, 2; "1975 Lethbridge Winter Games," Jeux du Canada Games, accessed January 23, 2008, http://cms.nortia.org/Org/Org38/Content/Games/1975%20Lethbridge.asp?mnu=3.

105. M. Foran qtd. in M. Janofsky, "Games Help Calgary Solve Hard Times," *New York Times*, January 28, 1988, http://www.nytimes.com/1988/01/28/sports/games-help-calgary-solve-hard-times.html?pagewanted=all.

106. K. Brookes, "Vancouver is All Hyped Up for the Olympics Letdown," December 29, 2008, *SkyscraperCity* (online forum), http://www.skyscrapercity.com/archive/index.php/t-776802.html.

107. M. Milke, "Bread, Circuses, and Olympic Questions," Canadian Taxpayers Federation, accessed June 23, 2008, http://www.taxpayer.com/ltts/bc/June14-02.htm; T. Walkom, "The Olympic Myth of Calgary: Making Money," *Toronto Star*, February 8, 1999.

108. Wamsley and Heine, "Tradition, Modernity, and the Construction of Civic Identity"; C.M. Hall, *Hallmark Tourist Events*. See also H. Lenskyj, *Inside the Olympic Industry*; Roche, *Mega-events and Modernity*.

109. Keating, "Sports Pork"; Trumpbour, "Rituals, Invented Traditions"; McCloy, "Hosting"; Gruneau and Whitson, "Upmarket Continentalism." Before the Depression, subsidies were not common, as they became afterward.

110. Whitson and Macintosh, "Global Circus"; Whitson and Macintosh, "Becoming a World-Class City."

111. Gruneau and Whitson, *Hockey Night in Canada*.

112. Alberta's Sport Plan Task Force, *A New Century for Amateur Sport: From Participation to Excellence. A Sport Plan for Alberta*, Government of Alberta, 2008.

113. Ministry of Tourism, Parks and Recreation. *Tourism, Parks and Recreation Business Plan 2008–2011*, Alberta Provincial Budget 2008.

114. Government of Alberta, "In Pursuit of Olympic Excellence, Alberta Increases Support for Athletes and Training Facilities," news release, April 30, 2008, http://www.winsportcanada.ca/files/coda-media-releases/Budget-2008-athlete-funding-announcement_NR-FINAL_20080430.pdf.

115. Whitson, "Pro Sports: Who Pays the Price?"

116. Ramshaw, "Nostalgia, Heritage, and Imaginative Sports Geographies." In 2003 and 2005 non-stop pond hockey games were held to raise funds for cancer research; a Guinness World Record was set and intense public interest generated.

117. Trumpbour, "Rituals, Invented Traditions and Shifting Power."

118. Bourdieu, "Sport and Social Class."

119. "Spectrum," *The Gateway*, November 19, 1963, 4.

120. Mills, "100 Years," 231.

121. Gruneau and Whitson, "Upmarket Continentalism," 237.

122. D. Booth, "Escaping the Past?" 104; Phillips, *Honour of Empire*.

LIBRARY COLLECTIONS

UNIVERSITY OF ALBERTA LIBRARIES

Alberta Folklore and Local History Collection. http://folklore.library.ualberta.ca

Newspapers. *The Gateway*. http://repository.library.ualberta.ca/newspapers/GAT

ACADIA UNIVERSITY

Digital Archives. Vaughan Memorial Library, Esther Wright Collection.
    http://library.acadiau.ca/ContentDM/digitalArchives.html

BROADCAST ARCHIVES

Canadian Broadcasting Corporation Archives

CKUA Sound Archives. http://66.244.199.219/CKUA_Archives/eng/people

PUBLIC ARCHIVES COLLECTIONS

ATHABASCA ARCHIVES

Kinsmen Club of Athabasca fonds

Mothers Auxiliary to the Athabasca Hockey Association fonds

CITY OF EDMONTON ARCHIVES

B'nai Brith Menorah Curling Club fonds

G.R. Bowen fonds

MS 416, Doris Neale Chapman fonds

MS 447, A 82-76, Kenneth Crockett fonds

Edmonton and District Cricket League fonds

MS 194, Edmonton Cycle Club Record Book 1963–1965

M 5322, Edmonton Exhibition Association fonds

Edmonton Exhibition Association 1906–1964, vol. 1, Archives Special Collection, 1989

Edmonton Parks and Recreation fonds

MS 514, Art Gagne fonds A 87-134

Mrs. John Darley Harrison fonds

Alex Latta Jr. fonds

MS 421, Arthur Reid Lawrence fonds

A 97-171, Jack Manson's Hockey Scrapbook

MS 711, A 98-70, Bill Morrissey fonds

MS 38, H.E. Mildren Collection

MS 352, File 1, Edward R. Musteca fonds

MS 574, 1933, The Senior Girls Baseball League fonds

MS 541, Alex Watt fonds

CITY OF WETASKIWIN ARCHIVES

W ET-98.10, Carl Walin fonds

GALT MUSEUM ARCHIVES

9881037018, Alberta Dusters Professional Basketball Team Yearbook, 1980–1981

19891016127.128, Alexander Johnston papers

19750017000, Scrapbook G M 975.17

19901008007, Sick's Breweries files

Sports (clippings files)

GLENBOW ARCHIVES

M 627, Alberta Golf Association, 1935–1981

M 6930, Alberta Rugby Union fonds

M 655.3, Amateur Athletic Union of Canada, Alberta Branch fonds

M 120, Albert Boyd fonds

Mrs. H.O. Boyd papers

M 7989, Calgary Cannons fonds

M 8092, Calgary Skiing Club fonds

M 7703, Canadian Girls Rodeo Association fonds

M 6636, Canadian Ladies Golf Association, Alberta Branch

M 6512, M 7072, Canadian Professional Rodeo Association fonds

M 5982, Marjorie Eustace fonds

M 8414 os, Ted Knight fonds

M 3973, Herman Linder fonds

M 2717, John Douglas McCulloch fonds

M 8581/594, Molson Breweries fonds, Western Division

M-9028-1277, Everett Soop fonds

M 8069, Sport Alberta fonds

Synchro Swim Alberta fonds

M 2187, Tiger Hockey Club fonds

MS 5767, Lloyd Turner fonds

M 1341, Helen Woodside fonds

GRANDE PRAIRIE REGIONAL ARCHIVES

Kinsmen Club of Grande Prairie fonds

Twilight Ladies Softball Team fonds

PROVINCIAL ARCHIVES OF ALBERTA

75.79, Harold Burnham fonds

PR 1970.27, Edmonton Commercial Graduates Basketball Team fonds

MS 372, Fay Faehrer fonds

97.393, Bill Holmes Collection, Box 1

82.25/54, South Side Swim Club fonds

70.25/5, Tribute to the Grads, Frederick B. Watt, 1940

RED DEER AND DISTRICT ARCHIVES

94.31, Ethel Lees fonds

J.B. Long fonds

Johnnie Phelan fonds

UNIVERSITY OF ALBERTA BOOK AND RECORD DEPOSITORY

Helen Beny Gibson fonds, 72-204, 78-135

UNIVERSITY OF CALGARY ARCHIVES

WHYTE MUSEUM OF THE CANADIAN ROCKIES

M 431, Banff Ski Runners of the Canadian Rockies fonds

Archives, Banff Springs Golf Club, Ladies Section

M 364/V 197, Alice Faulkner fonds

Abdel-Shehid, Gamal. "'Who Got Next?' Raptor Morality and Black Public Masculinity in Canada." In *Who Da Man?: Black Masculinities and Sporting Cultures*, 128–39. Toronto: Canadian Scholars' Press, 2005.

Adams, Mary Louise. "Freezing Social Relations: Ice, Rinks, and the Development of Figure Skating." In *Sites of Sport: Space, Place, Experience*, edited by P. Vertinsky and J. Bale, 57–72. London: Routledge, 2004.

———. "So What's the Problem with Wussy Sports?" *Borderlines* 46 (1998): 12–15.

Adelman, Melvin L. "Spectators and Crowds in Sport History: A Critical Analysis of Allen Guttmann's Sports Spectators." *Journal of Sport History* 14, no. 2 (1987).

Adria, Marco. *Technology and Nationalism*. Montreal and Kingston: McGill-Queen's University Press, 2008.

Alberta Alcohol and Drug Abuse Commission. *Position on Performance and Appearance Enhancing Drugs*. Edmonton, June 2004,

http://corp.aadac.com/content/corporate/about_aadac/position_
performance_appearance_enhancing_drugs.pdf.

Allinger, C.P., and T. Allinger, "Own the Podium 2010: Final Report with
Recommendations of the Independent Task Force for Winter NSOS and
Funding Partners." Own the Podium Task Force, September 10, 2004. http://
www.sportmatters.ca/Groups/SMG%20Resources/Sport%20and%20PA%20
Policy/otp_report_-_final_-_e.pdf.

Anderson, Eric. *In the Game: Gay Athletes and the Cult of Masculinity.* New York:
SUNY Press, 2005.

Appadurai, Arjun. "Disjuncture and Difference in the Global Cultural Economy."
In *Global Culture: Nationalism, Globalism and Modernity,* edited by
M. Featherstone, 295-310. London: SAGE, 1990.

Armstrong, Jerry. "How the Calgary Stampede Began." *Old West* 6, no. 3 (1970):
30-33, 86-87.

Artibise, Alan F.J. "Continuity and Change: Elites and Prairie Urban
Development 1914-1950." In *The Usable Urban Past: Planning and Politics in the
Modern Canadian City,* edited by A.F.J. Artibise and G. Stelter, 130-54. Toronto:
Macmillan of Canada, 1977.

———. "The Urban West: The Evolution of Prairie Towns and Cities to 1930."
Prairie Forum 4, no. 2 (1979): 237-62.

Austin, April. "Cult of the 'Body Beautiful.'" *Christian Science Monitor,* August 13,
2004.

Avery, Joanna, and Julie Stevens. *Too Many Men on the Ice: Women's Hockey in
North America.* Victoria, BC: Polestar, 1997.

Bailey, Elizabeth. "Children on the Streets." *The Albertan,* July 3, 1912. Reprinted
in *Alberta History* 51, no. 3 (2003): 24.

Bailey, Peter. *Leisure and Class in Victorian England: Rational Recreation and the
Contest for Control, 1830–1885.* Oxford: Oxford University Press, 1990.

Baillargeon, Morgan. "Aboriginal Rodeo Cowboys: The Good Times and the Bad."
In *Hidden in Plain Sight: Contributions of Aboriginal People to Canadian Identity
and Culture,* edited by D. Newhouse, C. Voyageur, and D. Beavon, 379-99.
Toronto: University of Toronto Press, 2005.

Baka, Richard S.P. "A History of Provincial Government Involvement in Sport in
Western Canada." MA thesis, University of Alberta, 1978.

Baker, William M., William J. Lodge, and James Tagg. *Weddings, Work and War: Lethbridge 1914-1945: A Scrapbook History.* Lethbridge, AB: History 3704 Scrapbook Publishing Consortium, 1994.

Baker, William J. *Sports in the Western World.* Urbana: University of Illinois Press, 1988.

Ballantyne, H. "Beginnings of the Amateur Athletic Union." *Edmonton Capital,* January 14, 1911. Reprinted in *Alberta History* 52, no. 3 (2004): 26.

Bannerman, Sheila, "'Cowboys' of the Canadian West: Re-orienting a Disoriented Mythology." *English Quarterly* 40, nos. 1/2 (2008): 51-57.

Barnes, Brenda. "Wide World of Sports: Gay Games (Un)Covered." *Fuse* 14, no. 3 (1991): 5-6.

Barney, R.K. "Hallowed Halls and Baseball History: The Evolution of the Canadian and American Baseball Halls of Fame." *Nine: A Journal of Baseball History and Social Policy Perspectives* 4, no. 1 (1995): 11-33.

Barraclough, Morris. *From Prairie to Park: Green Spaces in Calgary.* Calgary: Century Calgary Publications, 1975.

Barrow, Harold M., and Janie P. Brown. *Man and Movement: Principles of Physical Education.* 4th ed. Philadelphia: Lea & Febiger, 1988.

Barthes, Roland. "Le monde ou l'on catche." *Mythologies.* Paris: Éditions du Seuil, 1957.

Batistella, David, dir. *Shinny: The Hockey in All of Us.* National Film Board of Canada, 2001. Film, 72 min. 51 s.

Beamish, Rob, and Ian Ritchie. "From Fixed Capacities to Performance-Enhancement: The Paradigm Shift in the Science of 'Training' and the Use of Performance-Enhancing Substances." *Sport in History* 3 (2005): 412-33.

Beckett, Brad. *The History of Soccer in Alberta.* Edmonton: Alberta Soccer Association, 1986.

Beecher, Catherine. *Educational Reminiscences and Suggestions.* New York: J.B. Ford, 1874.

Beers, William G. *Lacrosse: The National Game of Canada.* New York: Townsend & Adams, 1869.

Bell, Robert J. "A History of Tennis at the University of Alberta." M ED thesis, University of Alberta, 1994.

Bercuson, David. "Regionalism and the 'Unlimited Identity' in Western Canada." *Journal of Canadian Studies* 15, no. 2 (1988): 121-26.

Bergman, Brian. "When Girls Ruled." *Maclean's,* July 9, 2001, 28-29.

Betke, Carl. "The Social Significance of Sport in the City: Edmonton in the 1920s." In *Cities in the West: Papers of the Western Canadian Urban History Conference.* Mercury Series Paper no. 10, edited by A.R. McCormack and I. MacPherson. Ottawa: National Museum of Man, 1975.

———. "Sports Promotion in the Western Canadian City: The Example of Early Edmonton." *Urban History Review* 12, no. 2 (1983): 47-56.

———. "Winter Sports in the Early Urban Environment of Prairie Canada." In *Winter Sports in the West,* edited by E.A. Corbet and A.W. Rasporich, 52-68. Calgary: Historical Society of Alberta, 1990.

Bianchi, Cristina. "Sports History? Sports Archives!" *Journal of Olympic History* 7, no. 1 (1999): 28-29.

Bicket, James. *The Canadian Curler's Manual.* Toronto: The British Colonist, 1840.

Birley, Derek. *A Social History of Cricket.* London: Aurum Press, 1999.

Bishop, Ted. Foreword to *Mountain Masculinity: The Life and Writing of Nello "Tex" Vernon-Wood in the Canadian Rockies, 1906–1938.* Edited by Andrew Gow and Julie Rak, 1-8. Edmonton: Athabasca University Press, 2008.

Blackburn, Cecil R. "The Development of Sports in Alberta, 1900-1918." M A thesis, University of Calgary, 1974.

Bloom, Michael, Michael Grant, and Douglas Watt. *Strengthening Canada: The Socio-Economic Benefits of Sports Participation in Canada.* Conference Board of Canada, 2005. Available at http://www.sportmatters.ca/.

Bogle, Meredith, and Bruce Howe. "Women's Soccer in Canada: A Slow Road to Equity." Paper presented at Connections Conference, University of Victoria Faculty of Education Research, 1998.

Booth, Douglas. "Escaping the Past? The Cultural Turn and Language in Sport History." *Rethinking History* 8, no. 1 (2004): 103-25.

Bordo, Susan. "Anorexia Nervosa: Psychopathology as the Crystallization of Culture." *Food and Culture: A Reader* 17, no. 2 (1985): 226-50.

Bouchier, Nancy B. *For the Love of the Game: Amateur Sport in Small-Town Ontario 1838–1895.* Montreal and Kingston: McGill-Queen's University Press, 2003.

Bourdieu, Pierre. "The Forms of Capital." In *Handbook of Theory and Research for the Sociology of Education,* edited by J.G. Richardson, 241-58. New York: Greenwood Press, 1986.

———. "How Can One Be a Sports Fan?" In *The Cultural Studies Reader,* edited by Simon During, 339-55. London: Routledge, 1993.

———. "Sport and Social Class." *Social Science Information* 17 (1978): 819-40.

Bowie, Gary W., and James A.P. Day. "Sport and Religion: The Influence of the Mormon Faith on Sport in Alberta." Paper presented at the Second World Symposium in the History of Sport and Physical Education, Banff, Alberta, 1971.

Bowling, Tim. "Na Na Na Na, Hey Hey Hey, Goodbye." *Alberta Views*, December 2005/January 2006, 47.

"Boys' Physical Self-perception." *Perceptual and Motor Skills* 93, no. 3 (2001): 626–30.

Brittain, Melisa, dir. *G.I.M.P. Bootcamp*. Canada, 2008.

Brown, Douglas. "The Hypocrisy Game." Review of *Fastest Highest Strongest: A Critique of High-Performance Sport* by R. Beamish. and I. Ritchie. *Literary Review of Canada* 15, no. 9 (2007): 24–25.

———. "Modern Sport, Modernism and the Cultural Manifesto: De Coubertin's Revue Olympique." *International Journal of the History of Sport* 18, no. 2 (2001): 78–109.

———. "Mountain Vista, Geographical Signifier, and the Meaning of Distinction: The Emergence of Physical Recreation and Outdoor Pursuits Culture in Calgary, 1884–1930." *North American Society For Sport History Proceedings & Newsletter* (1998): 8–9.

———. "Northern Character Theme and Sport in Nineteenth-century Canada," *Canadian Journal of the History of Sport/Revue canadienne de l'histoire des sports* 20, no. 1 (1989): 47–56.

———. "Waterton National Park and the Sporting Culture of South Western Alberta Between 1910 and 1940: An Intersection and Interdependency of National and Regional Discourses." *North American Society For Sport History Proceedings & Newsletter* (1999): 86–87.

Brown, Ken. "Life After Hockey." In *Five from the Fringe: A Selection of Five Plays*, edited by Nancy Bell. Edmonton: NeWest Press, 1986.

Brunt, Stephen. "The Changing Face of Sport: From Hometown Heroes to Supermen and Superwomen." In *Canadian Centre for Ethics in Sport Symposium: The Sport We Want*, 80–87. Ottawa: Canadian Centre for Ethics in Sport, 2003.

———. *Gretzky's Tears: Hockey, Canada, and the Day Everything Changed*. New York: Random House, 2010.

———. "How Sport Became a Religion." In *Taking Sport Seriously: Social Issues in Canadian Sport*. 2nd ed., edited by P. Donnelly, 12–14. Toronto: Thompson Educational Publishing, 2004.

Buchignani, Norman. "South Asians." In *Peoples of Alberta: Portraits of Cultural Diversity*, edited by Howard Palmer and Tamara Palmer, 413–36. Saskatoon: Western Producer Prairie Books, 1985.

Bumsted, J.M. *A History of the Canadian Peoples*. 3rd ed. Toronto: Oxford University Press, 2007.

———. *The Peoples of Canada: A Post-Confederation History*. Toronto: Oxford University Press, 1992.

Burckhardt, Jacob. *The Greeks and Greek Civilization*, edited by Oswyn Murray. New York: St. Martin's Griffin, 1999.

Burgess, Marilyn. "Canadian 'Range Wars': Struggles over Indian Cowboys." *Canadian Journal of Communication* 18, no. 3 (1993).

Burnet, Jean R. *Next Year Country: A Study of Rural Social Organization in Alberta*. Toronto: University of Toronto Press, 1951.

Burns, N.L., "Title IX is Making a Difference." *Generation Woman*, 2003. Accessed March 19, 2006. http://www.generationwoman.com/article. php3?story_id=162.

Burroughs, Catherine B., and Jeffrey Ehrenreich. *Reading the Social Body*. Iowa City: University of Iowa Press, 1993.

Burstyn, Valda. *The Rites of Men: Manhood, Politics and the Culture of Sport*. Toronto: University of Toronto Press, 1999.

Butterwick, D.J., and W.H. Meeuwisse. "Bull Riding Injuries in Professional Rodeo: Data for Prevention and Care." *Physician and Sportsmedicine* 31, no. 6 (2003): 37–41.

Byfield, Mike. "Health (16% of Severe Sports-Related Injuries Were From Snowmobiling)." *The Report* 30, no. 4 (February 17, 2003): 33.

Byfield, Ted, ed. *Alberta in the Twentieth Century*. Vol. 2, *The Birth of the Province 1900–1910*. Edmonton: United Western Communications Ltd., 1995.

———. *Alberta in the Twentieth Century*. Vol. 3, *The Boom and the Bust 1910–1914*. Edmonton: United Western Communications Ltd., 1995.

———. *Alberta in the Twentieth Century*. Vol. 4, *The Great War and its Consequences, 1914–1920*. Edmonton: United Western Communications Ltd., 1995.

———. *Alberta in the Twentieth Century*. Vol. 5, *Brownlee and the Triumph of Populism, 1920–1930*. Edmonton: United Western Communications, 1995.

———. *Alberta in the Twentieth Century*. Vol. 7, *Aberhart and the Alberta Insurrection, 1935–1940*. Edmonton: United Western Communications Ltd., 1995.

———. *Alberta in the Twentieth Century*. Vol. 9, *Leduc, Manning and the Age of Prosperity 1946–1963*. Edmonton: United Western Communications Ltd., 1995.

Byl, J. "Directing Physical Education in the Canadian YWCAs." *Sport History Review* 27, no. 2 (1996): 139–54.

Cady, Elizabeth H. "Pop Art and the American Dream." In *Sport Inside Out*, edited by D.L. Vanderwerken and S.K. Wertz. Fort Worth: Texas Christian University Press, 1985.

Cahn, Susan K. *Coming on Strong*. New York: Free Press, 1994.

———. "From the 'Muscle Moll' to the 'Butch' Ballplayer: Mannishness, Lesbianism, and Homophobia in U.S. Women's Sport." *Feminist Studies* 19, no. 2 (1993): 343–68.

Callois, Roger. *Les jeux et les hommes*. Paris: Gallimard, 1958.

———. *Jeux et sports*. Tours: Gallimard, 1967.

Calhoun, D.W. *Sport, Culture and Personality*. 2nd ed. Champaign, IL: Human Kinetics, 1987.

Canada. Ministry of Supply and Services. *Sport Canada Policy on Women in Sport*. Ottawa: Government Printing Office, 1986.

Canadian Academy of Sport Medicine Safety Committee. "Position Statement: Violence and Injuries in Ice Hockey." Canadian Academy of Sport Medicine, 1988.

Canadian Advisory Council. *Ten Years Later: An Assessment of the Federal Government's Implementation made by the Royal Commission on the Status of Women*. Ottawa: Canadian Advisory Council on the Status of Women, 1979.

Canadian Public Health Association, *ParticipACTION: The Mouse That Roared: A Marketing and Health Communications Success Story*. Accessed July 21, 2009. http://www.cpha.ca/english/inside/mediarm/newsrel/mouse_e.html.

Canevacci, Massimo. "The Anthropological Interpretation of Sport: A Task for Museums." *Museum* 43, no. 20 (1991): 86–88.

Carter, Sarah. *The Importance of Being Monogamous: Marriage and Nation Building in Western Canada to 1915*. Edmonton: University of Alberta Press and Athabasca University Press, 2008.

Cashman, Tony. "Clarence Richards: Fondly Remembered." In *Edmonton On Location: River City Chronicles*, edited by Heather Zwicker, 78-82. Edmonton: NeWest Press, 2005.

——. *The Edmonton Story: The Life and Times of Edmonton, Alberta*. Edmonton: The Institute of Applied Art, 1956.

——. "The First Alberta Marathon." In *Edmonton: Stories from the River City*, 134-37. Edmonton: University of Alberta Press, 2002.

——. "Mike's News Stand." In *Edmonton: Stories from the River City*, 159-68. Edmonton: University of Alberta Press, 2002.

——. "The Thistle Rink." In *The Best Edmonton Stories*, 71-72. Edmonton: Hurtig, 1976.

Cavanagh, Richard P. "The Development of Canadian Sports Broadcasting 1920-78." *Canadian Journal of Communication* 17, no. 3 (1992). http://www.cjc-online.ca/index.php/journal/article/viewArticle/677/583.

Chalus, Elaine. "The Edmonton Commercial Graduates: Women's History, An Integrationist Approach." In *Winter Sports in the West*, edited by E.A. Corbet and A.W. Rasporich. Calgary: Historical Society of Alberta, 1990.

Chezzi, D. "What's Old is New." *Maclean's*, August 27, 2001, 46-47.

Chisholm, Ann. "Incarnations and Practices of Feminine Rectitude: Nineteenth-century Gymnastics for U.S. women." *Journal of Social History* 38, no. 3 (2005): 737-63.

Ciampa, Marc. "Pro Wrestler Owen Hart's Unnecessary Death." *Sports Renaissance* 3, no. 6 (June 1999).

"The CITC Interview: Dan Smith, DG of Sport Canada." *Canadian Issues/Themes canadiens* (Autumn 1999): 27-29.

Clark, C. "Bringing History to the World Cup of Women's Baseball." *Edmonton Woman Magazine* (2007). Accessed January 24, 2008. http://www.edmontonwoman.com/baseball.php.

Coakley, Jay, and Peter Donnelly. *Sport in Society: Issues and Controversies—First Canadian Edition*. Toronto: McGraw-Hill, 2004.

Coleman, R. "The Cost of Obesity in Alberta." *GPI Atlantic*. December 2000. http://www.gpiatlantic.org/pdf/health/obesity/ab-obesity.pdf.

Collins, Andrea. "CKUA, The Mouse That Roared." *University of Alberta Engineer Magazine*. Faculty of Engineering, University of Alberta (Winter 2006). http://www.engineering.ualberta.ca/uofaengineer/article.cfm?article=40322&issue=40307.

Cooper, David. "Canadians Declare 'It Isn't Cricket': A Century of Rejection of the Imperial Game, 1860-1960." *Journal of Sport History* 26, no. 1 (1999): 51-81.

Copeland, R., W. Frisby, and W. McCarville. "Understanding the Sport Sponsorship Process From a Corporate Perspective." *Journal of Sport Management* 10, no. 1 (1996): 32-48.

Corbet, Elise A., and Anthony W. Rasporich, eds. *Winter Sports in the West.* Calgary: Historical Society of Alberta, 1990.

Cosentino, F. *Afros, Aboriginals and Amateur Sport in pre-World War One Canada.* Ottawa: Canadian Historical Association/Department of Canadian Heritage, Government of Canada, 1998.

——. *Canadian Football: The Grey Cup Years.* Toronto: Musson, 1969.

——. *A History of Physical Education in Canada.* Toronto: General Publishing Co., 1971.

Coulter, Rebecca P. "Patrolling the Passions of Youth." In *Edmonton: The Life of a City,* edited by Bob Hesketh and Frances Swyripa, 150-60. Edmonton: NeWest Press, 1995.

——. "Teen-agers in Edmonton 1921-1931: Experiences of Gender and Class." PHD diss., University of Alberta, 1987.

Cox, Alan E. "A History of Sports in Canada 1868-1900." PHD diss., University of Alberta, 1969.

Cox, Alan E., B.N. Noonkester, Maxwell L. Howell, and Reet A. Howell. "Sport in Canada, 1868-1900." In *History of Sport in Canada.* Rev. ed., edited by Maxwell Howell and Reet A. Howell. Champaign, IL: Stipes Pub. Co., 1985.

Creelman, W.A. *Curling, Past and Present.* Toronto: McClelland & Stewart, 1950.

Cross, Gary S. *A Social History of Leisure Since 1600.* State College, PA: Venture Publishing, 1990.

Cui, D., and J.R. Kelly. "'Our Negro Citizens': An Example of Everyday Citizenship Practices." In *The West and Beyond: New Perspectives on an Imagined Region,* edited by Alan Finkel, Sarah Carter, and Peter Fortna, 253-77. Edmonton: Athabasca University Press, 2010.

Dahlie, J. "Skiing For Identity and Tradition: Scandinavian Venture and Adventure in the Pacific Northwest, 1900-1969." In *Winter Sports in the West,* edited by E.A. Corbet and A.W. Rasporich, 99-111. Calgary: Historical Society of Alberta, 1990.

Dallaire, Christine. "Sport's Impact on the Francophoness of the Alberta Francophone Games (AFG)." *Ethnologies* 25 no. 2 (2003): 33-58.

Dallaire, Christine, and Claude Denis. "Asymmetrical Hybridities: Youths at Francophone Games in Canada (1) (Alberta Francophone Games)." *Canadian Journal of Sociology* 30 (2005): 143-68.

Dallaire, Christine, and Jean Harvey. Introduction to "Sport, Identity and Social Division in Canada / Sport, identités et clivages sociaux au Canada." Edited by C. Dallaire and J. Harvey. Special issue, *International Journal of Canadian Studies / Revue internationale d'études canadiennes* 35 (2007): 1-2.

Danysk, Cecilia. *Hired Hands: Labour and the Development of Prairie Agriculture, 1880-1930.* Toronto: University of Toronto Press, 1995.

Darbasie, Pat. *West Indian Diary: From Possibility to Actuality. The Story of Caribbean Immigration into Alberta.* Edmonton: Ground Zero Productions, 2011.

Davison, Kevin G., and Frank W. Blye. "Sexualities, Genders, and Bodies in Sport: Changing Practices of Inequity." In *Sport and Gender in Canada.* 2nd ed., edited by Phillip White and Kevin Young, 178-93. Toronto: Oxford University Press, 2006.

Dawe, Michael J. *Red Deer: An Illustrated History.* Red Deer: Red Deer and District Museum Society, 1996.

Deacon, J. "Sex Sells, to a Point: While Katarina Witt Can Flaunt Her Sexuality, Many Gay Athletes Hide Theirs." *Maclean's*, November 30, 1998, 78.

——. "Three-down Nation." *Maclean's*, November 22, 2004, 43.

Dempsey, Hugh A. "Calgary vs. Edmonton: First Rugby Football Games." *Alberta History* (Winter 2010). http://findarticles.com/p/articles/mi_hb3289/is_1_58/ai_n55089761/?tag=content;col1.

——. *Calgary: Spirit of the West.* Calgary: Fifth House, 1994.

——. "Deerfoot and Friends." In *The Amazing Death of Calf Skin and Other Blackfoot Stories*, 161-85. Calgary: Fifth House, 1994.

——. *The Golden Age of the Canadian Cowboy: An Illustrated History.* Calgary: Fifth House, 1995.

——. *Tom Three Persons: Legend of an Indian Cowboy.* Saskatoon: Purich Publishing, 1997.

den Otter, A.A. "Social Life of a Mining Community: The Coal Branch." *Alberta Historical Review* 17, no. 4 (1969): 1-11.

Depauw, Karen P. "Girls and Women with Disabilities in Sport." *JOPERD—The Journal of Physical Education, Recreation & Dance* 70 (1999).

Derksen, Jeremy. "Living History: Edmonton Ski Club Celebrates its 100th Anniversary." *Vue Weekly* (Edmonton) 790, December 8, 2010, 17.

Dewar, John. "Alex Wuttunee Decoteau: An Indigenous Olympian." *North American Society for Sport History Proceedings & Newsletter* (1992): 54.

———. "The Canadian Indian Cowboy." *North American Society for Sport History Proceedings & Newsletter* (1987): 26.

———. "The Edmonton Grads: The Team and Its Social Significance from 1915-1940." In *Her Story in Sport: A Historical Anthology of Women in Sports,* edited by R. Howell 541-47. West Point, NY: Leisure Press, 1982.

———. "Herman Lindner, Canada's Champion Cowboy." *North American Society for Sport History Proceedings & Newsletter* (1984): 38-39.

———. "Runners of the Plains." *North American Society for Sport History Proceedings & Newsletter* (1988): 3-4.

———. "Scabby Dried Meat and Bad Dried Meat: Blackfoot Brothers of the Wind." *North American Society for Sport History Proceedings & Newsletter* (1995): 39.

Digital Time Machine Incorporated. "Dreamers and Doers, A Documentary on 100 Years of Arts and Culture in Alberta." Transcript. 2004. http://www.dreamersanddoers.ca/transcripts2.htm.

Dominion Curling Association. "Alberta Curling Association." *Rule Book of the Dominion Curling Association,* 1945.

Donnelly, P., ed. *Taking Sport Seriously: Social Issues in Canadian Sport.* Toronto: Thompson, 1997.

———. "Scapegoating the Indian Residential Schools." *Alberta Report* 25, no. 6 (January 26, 1998): 6-12.

Donnelly, P., Graham Knight, and Margaret MacNeill. "'Only in Canada, Eh!': Media, Multiculturalism, and National Identities at the 2002 World Cup." *m/c reviews* (2002). http://reviews.media-culture.org.au/modules.php?name=News&file=article&sid=1861.

Doust, Denise. "The Ethics of Ambush Marketing." *Cyber-Journal of Sport Marketing* 1, no. 3, (1997). http://fulltext.ausport.gov.au/fulltext/1997/cjsm/v1n3/doust.htm.

Drager, Derek. "Clare Drake: Undercover Agent of Change." *New Trail* 62, no. 3 (2007): 17.

Dronyk, Levi. "The Puck Artist." In *Our Game: An All-Star Collection of Hockey Fiction,* edited by D. Beardsley, 61-75. Victoria, BC: Polestar, 1997.

Dryden, Ken. "Soul on Ice." *The Beaver* 80, no. 6 (December 2000/January 2001).

Dryden, Ken, and Roy MacGregor. *Home Game: Hockey and Life in Canada.* Toronto: McClelland & Stewart, 1989.

Ducey, Brant. *The Rajah of Renfrew: The Life and Times of John E. Ducey, Edmonton's "Mr. Baseball."* Edmonton: University of Alberta Press, 1998.

Dufresne, Lawrence W. "A Study of the Incidence, Nature, and Cause of Football Injuries in the City of Edmonton During 1969." M A thesis, University of Alberta, 1971.

Duhatschek, Eric, Trent Frayne, Lance Hornby, Gord Miller, and Al Strachan. *Hockey Chronicles: An Insider History of National Hockey League Teams.* Toronto: Key Porter, 2000.

Dunning, Eric. *Sport Matters: Sociological Studies of Sport, Violence and Civilization.* New York: Routledge, 1999.

Dunning, E.G., Joseph A. Maguire, and R.E. Pearton, eds. *The Sports Process: A Comparative and Developmental Approach.* Champaign, IL: Human Kinetics, 1993.

DyckFehderau, Ruth. "The Magnificent 'Rogue' of the Miracle Mile." In *Edmonton On Location: River City Chronicles,* edited by Heather Zwicker. Edmonton: NeWest Press, 2005.

Dyer, Kenneth F. *Challenging the Men: The Social Biology of Female Sporting Achievement.* St. Lucia: University of Queensland Press, 1982.

Earle, N. "Hockey as Canadian Popular Culture: Team Canada 1972, Television and the Canadian Identity." In *Slippery Pastimes: Reading the Popular in Canadian Culture,* edited by J. Nicks and J. Sloniowski, 321–44. Waterloo, ON: Wilfrid Laurier University Press, 2002.

Eckert, H.M. "The Development of Organized Recreation and Physical Education in Alberta." M ED thesis, University of Alberta, 1980.

"Edmonton Gamblers." *Alberta History* (Winter 2005). http://findarticles.com/p/articles/mi_hb3289/is_/ai_n29155332.

Edmonton Heritage Council. "Edmonton's Curling Champions." N.d. http://www.edmontonheritage.ca/default/assets/File/pane16_v5.pdf.

Edmonton Public Library. "Alex Decoteau Historical Timeline." In *Edmonton: A City Called Home.* Edmonton Public Library, 2004. http://www.epl.ca/edmonton-a-city-called-home/edmonton-a-city-called-home-story?id=251.

Eksteins, Modris. *Rites of Spring: The Great War and the Birth of the Modern Age.* Toronto: Lester and Orpen Dennys, 1989.

Elias, Norbert. "The Genesis of Sport as a Sociological Problem." In *The Sociology of Sport: A Selection of Readings,* edited by E. Dunning, 85–132. Toronto: University of Toronto Press, 1972.

Elias, Norbert, and E. Dunning, eds. *Quest for Excitement: Sport and Leisure in the Civilizing Process.* Oxford: Basil Blackwell, 1986.

Embry, Jessie L. "Transplanted Utah: Mormon Communities in Alberta." *Oral History Forum d'histoire orale* 18 (1998). http://www.oralhistoryforum.ca/index.php/ohf/issue/view/18.

Erb, Marsha. *Stu Hart, Lord of the Ring.* Toronto: ECW Press, 2002.

Evans, Simon. *The Bar U and Canadian Ranching History.* Calgary: University of Calgary Press, 2004.

Falla, Jack, Lance Hornby, George Johnson, and Jack Batten. *Quest for the Cup: A History of the Stanley Cup Finals, 1893-2000.* Toronto: Key Porter, 2001.

Faulkner, Cliff. *Turn Him Loose! Herman Linder, Canada's Mr. Rodeo.* Saskatoon: Western Producer Prairie Books, 1977.

Fay, T.J. "A Historiography of Recent Publications On Catholic Native Residential Schools." *Historical Studies* 61 (1995): 79-97.

Ferguson, Emily. "Edmonton." In *Janey Canuck in the West.* 4th ed. London: Cassell and Company, 1910.

Field, Dorothy. "Safe Haven." *Legacy* 12, no. 2 (2007): 7.

Filax, Gloria. "Post-Vriend—the Human Face." *Parkland Post* (Summer 1998).

——. "Producing Homophobia in Alberta, Canada in the 1990s." *Journal of Historical Sociology* 17, no. 1 (2004): 87-120.

Findlay, S. "Breaks of the Game." *U.S. News & World Report* 103 (October 5, 1987): 75-77.

Finkel, Alvin, Sarah Carter, and Peter Fortna, eds. *The West and Beyond: New Perspectives on an Imagined Region.* Edmonton: Athabasca University Press, 2010.

Fisher, Donald M. *Lacrosse: A History of the Game.* Baltimore: Johns Hopkins University Press, 2002.

Fitzgerald, Robert A. *Wickets in The West.* London: Tinsley Bros., 1873.

Foothills Cowboys' Association. *Rodeo: The West in Action.* Calgary: Calgary Brewing and Malting Company Limited, 1971.

Foran, Maxwell. "More Than Partners: The Calgary Stampede and the City of Calgary." In *Icon, Brand, Myth: The Calgary Stampede,* edited by Maxwell Foran, 147-67, Edmonton: Athabasca University Press, 2008.

——. "More Than Ten Days of Fun: The Calgary Exhibition and Stampede." In *Alberta: A State of Mind,* edited by Sidney Sharpe, Robert Gibbons, and James H. Marsh, 177-80. Toronto: Key Porter, 2005.

———. "The Stampede in Historical Context." In *Icon, Brand, Myth: The Calgary Stampede*, edited by M. Foran, 1-20. Edmonton: Athabasca University Press, 2008.

Forbes, C.A. *Greek Physical Education*. New York: The Century Company, 1929.

Forsyth, Janice. "The Indian Act and the (Re)shaping of Canadian Aboriginal Sport Practices." In "Sport, Identity and Social Division in Canada / Sport, identités et clivages sociaux au Canada." Edited by C. Dallaire and J. Harvey. Special issue, *International Journal of Canadian Studies / Revue internationale d'études canadiennes* 35 (2007): 95-111.

———. "Native to Native: Canadian Assimilation Policy and the Emergence of Indigenous Games." *North American Society For Sport History Proceedings & Newsletter* (2000): 77-78.

Forsyth, Janice, and Michael Heine. "'A Higher Degree of Social Organization': Jan Eisenhardt and Canadian Aboriginal Sport Policy in the 1950s." *Journal of Sport History* 35, no. 2 (2008): 261-77.

Forsyth, Janice, and Kevin B. Wamsley. "'Native to Native...We'll Recapture Our Spirits': The World Indigenous Nations Games and North American Indigenous Games as Cultural Resistance." *International Journal of the History of Sport* 23, no. 2 (2006): 294-314.

Fortna, Peter. "'A Firm Referee That Will Make Both Sides Abide by the Rules': Gentlemanly Status and Hockey Referees in Edmonton, Alberta 1893-1907." *Past Imperfect* 12 (2006): 1-23.

Foucault, Michel. *Discipline and Punish: The Birth of the Prison*. Translated by A. Sheridan. Harmondsworth, UK: Penguin, 1977.

———. "Nietzsche, Genealogy, History." In *The Foucault Reader*, edited by P. Rabinow, 76-100. Harmondsworth, UK: Penguin, 1984.

———. *Power/Knowledge, Selected Interviews and Other Writings 1972-1977*. Edited by C. Gordon. New York: Pantheon, 1980.

Fowles, Jib. "Mass Media and the Star System." In *Communication in History: Technology, Culture and Society*. 4th ed., edited by D. Crowley and P. Heyer, 194-98. Toronto: Pearson Education, 2003.

Francis, R. Douglas. *Images of the West*. Saskatoon: Western Producer Prairie Books, 1989.

———. "In Search of a Prairie Myth: A Survey of the Intellectual and Cultural Historiography of Prairie Canada." In *Riel to Reform: A History of Protest in Western Canada*, edited by G. Melnyk, 20-42. Saskatoon: Fifth House, 1992.

Freedman, Lawrence. "The Changing Roles of Military Conflict." *Survival* 40,
no. 4 (1998): 39–56.

Freund, Peter, Meredith McGuire, and Linda Podhurst, eds. *Health, Illness, and the
Social Body: A Critical Sociology.* 4th ed. Toronto: Pearson, 2003.

"From Vice to Popular Pastime: A History of Gambling in Alberta." *Research
Reveals* 3, no. 21. University of Calgary, 2003. http://dspace.ucalgary.ca/
bitstream/1880/339/6/RR-Issue1-vol3-2003.pdf.

Fudge, Paul H. "The North West Mounted Police and Their Influence on Sport
in Western Canada, 1873–1905." *North American Society for Sport History
Proceedings & Newsletter* (1981): 17–18.

Fullerton, Romayne S. "Not Playing Fair: Coverage of Women and Minorities
in the Sports Pages." *SIMILE: Studies in Media and Information Literacy
Education* 6, no. 2 (2006): 1–13.

Furniss, Elizabeth. "Cultural Performance as Strategic Essentialism: Negotiating
Indianness in a Western Canadian Rodeo Festival." *Humanities Research* 3
(1998): 23–40.

Gasher, Mike. "Review of *Inside the Sports Pages: Work Routines, Professional
Ideologies and the Manufacture of Sports News* by Mark Lowes." *Canadian
Journal of Communication* 26, no. 2 (2001): 323–24.

Gienow-Hecht, Jessica C.E. "Review of *The Cult of Health and Beauty in Germany:
A Social History, 1890–1930* by Michael Hau." *Journal of Social History* 39, no. 1
(2005): 275–77.

Gillespie, Greg. "'Wickets in the West': Cricket, Culture, and Constructed Images
of Nineteenth-century Canada." *Journal of Sport History* 27, 1 (Spring 2000):
51–66.

Gillis, Charlie. "Girls Give Hockey a Badly Needed Lift." *Maclean's,* March 8, 2004.

Gilpin, John F. *Edmonton: Gateway to the North.* Woodland Hills, CA: Windsor
Publications 1984.

Glass, D.J. "Cycling in the Province of Alberta 1885–1960." *Alberta Museums Review*
12, no. 1 (1988).

Glassford, Gerry. "A Way of Life: The Emergence of Active Living." *Wellspring*
11, no. 1 (Spring 2000): http://www.centre4activeliving.ca/publications/
wellspring/2000/Spring/WayOfLife.html.

Gorn, Elliot J., and Michael Oriard. "Taking Sports Seriously." In *Taking Sport
Seriously: Social Issues in Canadian Sport,* edited by P. Donnelly. Toronto:
Thompson, 1997.

Government of Alberta. *Active Alberta: A Recreation, Active Living and Sport Policy.*
  2011. http://tpr.alberta.ca/activealberta/default.aspx.

Gow, Andrew, and Julie Rak, eds. *Mountain Masculinity: The Life and Writing of*
  Nello "Tex" Vernon-Wood in the Canadian Rockies, 1906–1938. Edmonton:
  Athabasca University Press, 2008.

Goyette, Linda, and Carolina J. Roemmich. *Edmonton In Our Own Words.*
  Edmonton: University of Alberta Press, 2004.

Grant, Michael. *A Short History of Classical Civilization.* London: Weidenfeld and
  Nicolson, 1991.

Grierson, Elizabeth. "Inscribing the Social Body: Economies of Image/Text
  in the Public Domain." Working Papers for Art, Science and the Body
  Research Cluster, Catalogue Essay to accompany BODY Exhibition, Project
  Space. RMIT School of Art: Melbourne, 2009. Accessed April 25, 2010.
  http://schoolofartgalleries.dsc.rmit.edu.au/PSSR/exhibitions/2009/body/
  inscribing-the-social.pdf.

Griffin, Pat. "Changing the Game: Homophobia, Sexism, and Lesbians in Sport."
  Quest 44, no. 2 (1992): 251–65.

Grossberg, Lawrence. *Bringing It All Back Home: Essays on Cultural Studies.*
  Durham, NC: Duke University Press, 1997.

———, ed. "On Postmodernism and Articulation: An Interview with Stuart Hall."
  In *Stuart Hall: Critical Dialogues in Cultural Studies,* edited by David Morley
  and Kuan-Hsing Chen, 131–50. London: Routledge, 1996.

Gruneau, Richard. "Modernization or Hegemony: Two Views on Sport and Social
  Development." In *Not Just a Game: Essays in Canadian Sport Sociology,* edited
  by Jean Harvey and Hart Cantelon, 9–32. Ottawa: University of Ottawa
  Press, 1988.

Gruneau, Richard, and David Whitson. *Hockey Night in Canada: Sport, Identities*
  and Cultural Politics. Toronto: Garamond Press, 1993.

———. "Upmarket Continentalism: Major League Sport, Promotional Culture,
  and Corporate Integration." In *Continental Order?* edited by Vincent Mosco
  and Dan Schiller, 235–64. New York: Rowan & Littlefield, 2001.

Gunderson, Harald. *The Linder Legend: The Story of Pro Rodeo and Its Champion.*
  Calgary: Sagebrush, 1996.

Guttmann, Allen. *From Ritual to Record: the Nature of Modern Sports.* 2nd ed. New
  York: Columbia University Press, 2004.

———. *Games and Empires: Modern Sports and Cultural Imperialism.* New York: Columbia University Press, 1994.

———. *Sports Spectators.* New York: Columbia University Press, 1986.

Gzowski, Peter. *The Game of our Lives.* Toronto: McClelland & Stewart, 1981.

Hall, Colin M. *Hallmark Tourist Events: Impacts, Management and Planning.* London: Belhaven Press, 1992.

———. "Sport Tourism and Urban Regeneration." In *Sport Tourism: Interrelationships, Impacts and Issues,* edited by B.W. Ritchie and D. Adair, 192-206. Toronto: Channel View Publications, 2004.

Hall, M. Ann. "Alexandrine Gibb: In 'No Man's Land of Sport.'" *International Journal of the History of Sport* 18, no. 1 (2001): 149-72.

———. *Fair Ball: Toward Sex Equality in Canadian Sport.* Ottawa: Canadian Advisory Council on the Status of Women, 1982.

———. *The Girl and the Game: A History of Women's Sport in Canada.* Peterborough, ON: Broadview Press, 2002.

———. "Women's Sport in Canada: Have we Achieved Gender Equity?" Speaking notes, keynote speech at the 5th Annual Congress of the Japan Society for Sport and Gender Studies, Kyoto, July 1-2, 2006. http://www.jssgs. org/English/e-Conference/e-Congress/Files%202006/5th%20JSSGS%20 Speaking%20Notes.pdf.

———. "Women's Sport in Canada Prior to 1914." M A thesis, University of Alberta, 1971.

Hall, M. Ann, Trevor Slack, Gary Smith, and David Whitson. *Sport in Canadian Society.* Toronto: McClelland & Stewart, 1991.

Hall, Stuart. "The Problem of Ideology: Marxism Without Guarantees." In *Stuart Hall: Critical Dialogues in Cultural Studies,* edited by D. Morley and K.H. Chen, 24-45. London: Routledge, 1996.

Hankins, Gerald W. *Rolling On: The Story of the Amazing Gary McPherson.* Edmonton: University of Alberta Press, 2003.

Hansen, Warren. *Curling: The History, the Players and the Game.* Toronto: Key Porter, 1999.

Haraway, Donna J. *Simians, Cyborgs and Women: The Reinvention of Nature.* London: Free Association Books, 1991.

Hargreaves, Jennifer. "Aboriginal Sportswomen: Heroines of Difference or Objects of Assimilation?" In *Heroines of Sport: The Politics of Difference and Identity,* edited by J. Hargreaves, 78-128. London: Routledge, 2000.

———. "Sport and Hegemony: Some Theoretical Problems." In *Sport, Culture and the Modern State*, edited by D. Whitson and R. Gruneau, 103–40. Toronto: University of Toronto Press, 1982.

Harrigan, Patrick J. "Intercollegiate Sport, National Culture, and Federal Sport Policy in Canada since 1961." North American Society for Sport History Proceedings & Newsletter (2000): 112–14.

———. "Women's Agency and the Development of Women's Intercollegiate Athletics, 1961–2001." *Historical Studies in Education/Revue d'histoire de l'éducation* 15, no. 1 (Spring 2003): 37–77.

Harshaw, Josephine P. *When Women Work Together: A History of the Young Women's Christian Association in Canada, 1870–1966.* Toronto: Ryerson Press, 1966.

Harvey, J., and H. Cantelon, eds. *Not Just a Game: Essays in Canadian Sport Sociology.* Ottawa: University of Ottawa Press, 1988.

Haslip, Susan. "A Treaty Right to Sport?" *E-Law* 8, no. 2 (June 2001). http://www.murdoch.edu.au/elaw/issues/v8n2.

Hendriks, Robert W. *William Bleasdell Cameron: A Life of Writing and Adventure.* Edmonton: Athabasca University Press, 2008.

Herzog, Lawrence. "Canada's First Municipal Golf Course." *It's Our Heritage. Edmonton Real Estate Weekly* 20, no. 32, August 8, 2002.

———. "Edmonton's Lost Omniplex." *Alberta Real Estate Weekly* 25, no. 32, August 9, 2007.

———. "The Tough Guy with the Soft Heart." *Alberta Real Estate Weekly* 24, no. 6, February 9, 2006.

Hess, Robert M. "A Social History of Cycling in Edmonton 1890–1897." M A thesis, University of Alberta, 1991.

Hickok, Ralph. *The Encyclopedia of North American Sports History.* 2nd ed. New York: Facts on File, 2002.

Hoberman, John. *Mortal Engines: The Science of Performance and the Dehumanization of Sport.* New York: Free Press/Macmillan, 1992.

Hoeger, Walter, and Sharon A. Hoeger. *Principles and Labs for Fitness and Wellness.* 5th ed. Englewood, NJ: Morton Publishing Company, 1999.

Hosgood, Christopher. "Negotiating Lower-middle-class Masculinity in Britain: The Leicester Young Men's Christian Association, 1870–1914." *Canadian Journal of History* 37, no. 2 (2002): 253–73.

———. "Poker and the Police in Early Twentieth Century Alberta." Paper presented at the Western Social Science Association, Las Vegas, April 10,

2003. http://www.abgaminginstitute.ualberta.ca/documents/research/
Policing_Alberta.pdf.

Howell, Colin. *Blood, Sweat, and Cheers: Sport and the Making of Modern Canada.*
Toronto: University of Toronto Press, 2001.

———. *Northern Sandlots: A Social History of Maritime Baseball.* Toronto: University
of Toronto Press, 1995.

Howell, Maxwell L., and Reet A. Howell, eds. *History of Sport in Canada.* Rev. ed.
Champaign, IL: Stipes Pub. Co., 1985.

Howell, R., ed. *Her Story in Sport: A Historical Anthology of Women in Sports.* West
Point, NY: Leisure Press, 1982.

Huggins, Jessica, L. Brass, and K. Brass, dirs. *How the West Went Wild.* Calgary,
2007.

Hughes-Fuller, Patricia. "Am I Canadian?: Hockey as 'National' Culture." Paper
presented at Culture and the State Conference, May 2-5, 2003, University of
Alberta. http://www.arts.ualberta.ca/cms/hughes.pdf.

Hughson, John. "Cultural History and the Study of Sport." *Sport in Society* 12,
no. 1 (2009): 3-17.

———. "The Making of Sporting Cultures: Introduction." *Sport in Society* 12, no. 1
(2009): 1-2.

———. "Science, Culture and the Sporting Body." *Sport in Society* 12, no. 1 (2009):
36-52.

Huizinga, Johan. *Homo Ludens: A Study of the Play Element in Culture.* Boston:
Beacon Press, 1950.

Humber, William. *Diamonds of the North: A Concise History of Baseball in Canada.*
Toronto: Oxford University Press, 1995.

Hunter, Bill, and Bob Weber. *Wild Bill: Bill Hunter's Legendary 65 Years in Canadian
Sport.* Calgary: Johnson Gorman Publishers, 2000.

Ichikawa, Akira. "A Test of Religious Tolerance: Canadian Government and Jodo
Shinshu Buddhism During the Pacific War, 1941-1945." *Canadian Ethnic
Studies* 26, no. 2 (1994): 46-69.

"Information to Die For." *Marketing Health Services* 22, no. 1 (2002): 40-42.

Iverson, P., and L. MacCannell. *Riders of the West: Portraits from Indian Rodeo.*
Seattle: University of Washington Press, 1999.

Jahn, F.L. *A Treatise on Gymnastics.* Northampton, MA: Simon Butler, 1828.

James, C.L.R. *Beyond a Boundary.* Durham, NC: Duke University Press, 1993.

Jameson, Shielagh S. "The Social Elite of the Ranch Community and Calgary." In *Frontier Calgary: Town, City and Region 1875-1914*, edited by A.W. Rasporich and H. Klassen, 57-70. Calgary: McClelland & Stewart, 1975.

———. "Women in the Southern Alberta Ranch Community 1881-1914." In *The Canadian West: Social Change and Economic Development*, edited by H.C. Klassen, 63-78. Calgary: University of Calgary, 1977.

Jhally, Sut. "The Spectacle Of Accumulation: Material and Cultural Factors in The Evolution of The Sports/Media Complex." *The Insurgent Sociologist* 12, no. 3 (1984): 41-57.

Johnes, Martin. "'Poor Man's Cricket': Baseball, Class and Community in South Wales, c. 1880-1950." *International Journal of the History of Sport* 17 no. 4 (2000): 153-66.

Johns, Walter. *A History of the University of Alberta, 1908-1969*. Edmonton: University of Alberta Press, 1981.

Johnson, A.T., and J.H. Frey, eds. *Government and Sport: The Public Policy Issues*. Totowa, NJ: Rowman and Allanheld, 1985.

Johnston, D.E. "Sites of Resistance, Sites of Strength: The Construction and Experience of Queer Space in Calgary." MA thesis, University of Calgary, 1999.

Jose, Colin, and William Rannie. *The Story of Soccer in Canada*. Lincoln, NE: W.F. Publishers, 1982.

Joudrey, Susan. "Expectations of a Queen: Identity and Race Politics in the Calgary Stampede." In *The West and Beyond: New Perspectives on an Imagined Region*, edited by A. Finkel, S. Carter and P. Fortna, 133-55. Edmonton: Athabasca University Press, 2010.

Joyce, Thomas A. "A Nation of Employees: The Rise of Corporations and the Perceived Crisis of Masculinity in the 1950s." *Graduate History Review* 3, no. 1 (2011): 24-28.

Karolides, Nicholas J., and Melissa Karolides. *Focus on Fitness*. Santa Barbara, CA: ABC-CLIO, 1993.

"Katz, Edmonton Oilers Sign Promotional Deal." *Chain Drug Review* 25, no. 21 (December 15, 2003): 3-4.

Keating, Raymond J. "Sports Pork: The Costly Relationship Between Major League Sports and Government." *Policy Analysis* 339 (April 5, 1999). http://www.cato.org/pubs/pas/pa339b.pdf.

Kellicut, B. "Early History of Sports in the Granum Area." In *Leavings by Trail, Granum by Rail*, 124-33. Granum, AB: Granum History Book Committee, 1977.

Kelly, Malcolm. *Hanging it Out on Camera 3: Canadian Sports in the Media Era* Toronto: Prentice Hall Canada, 2001.

Kidd, Bruce. "The Making of a Hockey Artifact: A Review of the Hockey Hall of Fame. (Museum Review)." *Journal of Sport History* 23, no. 3 (1996): 328-34.

——. "Missing: Women From Sports Halls of Fame." *CAAWS Action Bulletin* (Winter 1995). http://www.caaws.ca/e/milestones/women_history/missing_print.cfm.

——. "Muscular Christianity and Value-centred Sport: The Legacy of Tom Brown in Canada." *International Journal of the History of Sport* 5 (2006): 701-13.

——. "Radical Immigrants and the Workers' Sports Federation of Canada, 1924-37." In *Ethnicity and Sport in North American History and Culture*, edited by G. Eisen and D.K. Wiggins, 201-20. Westport, CT: Greenwood Press, 1994.

——. *The Struggle for Canadian Sport*. Toronto: University of Toronto Press, 1996.

——. "The Women's Amateur Athletic Federation: For 37 Years—The Canadian Parliament of Women's Sport." *CAAWS Action Bulletin* (Winter 1994).

Kidd, Bruce, and John McFarlane. *The Death of Hockey*. Toronto: New Press, 1972.

Kirwin, Bill. "A Colony Within a Colony: The Western Canada Baseball League of 1912 or Imperialistic Rhapsodies in D Minor." *North American Society for Sport History Proceedings & Newsletter* (1994): 76-77.

Klassen, Henry C. "Bicycles and Automobiles in Early Calgary." *Alberta History* 24, no. 2 (1976): 1-8.

——. "Life in Frontier Calgary." In *Frontier Calgary: Town, City and Region 1875-1914*, edited by Anthony W. Rasporich and H.C. Klassen, 43-57. Calgary: McClelland & Stewart West, 1975.

Klaszus, Jeremy. "How the West Went Wild: Dissecting Calgary's Stampede." *Alberta Views*, July/August 2007, 10-11.

Knight, Darrell. *Pete Knight: The Cowboy King*. Bartlett: Wild Horse Press, 2004.

Knight, Jennifer L., and Tracy A. Giuliano. "Blood, Sweat, and Jeers: The Impact of the Media's Heterosexist Portrayals on Perceptions of Male and Female Athletes." *Journal of Sport Behavior* 26, no. 3 (2003): 272-84.

Knupp, Lillian. *Life and Legends: A History of the Town of High River*. Calgary: Sandstone Publishing, 1982.

Kondro, Wayne. "Canada Starts Renewed Effort Against Tobacco-industry
Advertising." *The Lancet* 351, no. 9118 (June 13, 1998).

Korkia, P. "Drugs in Sport." *Journal of Substance Use* 4, no. 4 (2000): 125-27.

Kossuth, Robert S. "Hockey on the Margins: Women's Hockey in Rural Southern
Alberta before World War II." *Journal of the West* 47, no. 4 (2008): 70-77.

———. "Men on the Closing Range: Early Rodeo Competition in the Southern
Northwest Territories/Alberta." *North American Society for Sport History
Proceedings & Newsletter* (2005): 32-33.

Kroetsch, Robert. "Alberta, Twenty-Five Years after *Alberta*." Preface to *Alberta*,
2nd ed., by Robert Kroetsch, 49-50. Edmonton: NeWest Press, 1993.

———. *The Studhorse Man*. Edmonton: University of Alberta Press, 2004.

Kuban, Ron. *Edmonton's Urban Villages: The Community League Movement*.
Edmonton: University of Alberta Press, 2005.

Kubish, Shelagh. "Great Teams at the University of Alberta." *New Trail* 62, no. 3
(Autumn 2007): 11-16.

Lacombe and District Chamber of Commerce. "Sports and Recreation." In
Lacombe: The First Century, 369-406. Lacombe, AB: Lacombe and District
Chamber of Commerce, 1982.

Lamb, Patrick. *Deacon White, Founder of Modern Sport in Edmonton*. Edmonton: City
of Edmonton Archives, 1995.

———. "Deacon White, Sportsman." *Alberta History* 37, no. 1 (1989): 23-27.

———. "The North West Mounted Police Force and the Development of Rugby
Football in Western Canada 1873-1908." *North American Society for Sport
History Proceedings & Newsletter* (1987): 9-10.

Lamont, Kate. *We Can Achieve: Women in Sport at the University of Alberta: A
Report*. Edmonton: Campus History Group of the Faculty Women's Club,
University of Alberta, 1986.

Lappage, R.S. "The Canadian Scene and Sport 1921-1939." In *History of Sport in
Canada*, edited by M.L. Howell and R.A. Howell, 244-302. Champaign, IL:
Stipes Pub. Co., 1985.

———. "Sport as an Expression of Western and Maritime Discontent in Canada
Between the Wars." *Canadian Journal of History of Sport & Physical Education*
8, no. 1 (May 1977): 50-71.

Lash, Scott, and John Urry. *Economies of Signs and Space*. London: SAGE, 1994.

Laski, M. "The Life Beautiful." *Notes and Queries* 8, no. 9 (1961): 341-43.

Lassiter, Collette, and Jill Oakes. "Ranchwomen, Rodeo Queens and Nightclub Cowgirls: The Evolution of Cowgirl Dress." In *Standing on New Ground: Women in Alberta*, edited by Catherine A. Cavanaugh and Randi R. Warne, 55-70. Edmonton: University of Alberta Press, 1993.

LeCompte, Mary Lou. *Cowgirls of the Rodeo: Pioneer Professional Athletes.* Urbana: University of Illinois Press, 1995.

———. "Home on the Range: Women in Professional Rodeo, 1929-1947." *Journal of Sport History* 3 (1990): 318-46.

Lenskyj, Helen. *Inside the Olympic Industry: Power, Politics, and Activism.* Albany: SUNY Press, 2000.

———. *Out of Bounds: Women, Sport and Sexuality.* Toronto: Women's Press, 1986.

Lightbody, Jim. "City Campaigns on the Cusp and the Edmonton Mayoralty Election of 1992." *Journal of Canadian Studies* 32, no. 11 (1997): 112-34.

Lindsay, Peter L., and Robert Hess. "Sporting Elites in Late Nineteenth Century Edmonton: The Case of Cycling." *North American Society for Sport History Proceedings & Newsletter* (1990): 42-43.

Lock, Margaret, and Nancy Scheper-Hughes. "A Critical-interpretive Approach in Medical Anthropology: Rituals and Routines of Discipline and Dissent." In *Medical Anthropology: Contemporary Theory and Method*, edited by T.M. Johnson and C.F. Sargent, 41-70. New York: Praeger, 1990.

Lorenz, Stacy L. "'Bowing Down to Babe Ruth': Major League Baseball and Canadian Popular Culture, 1920-1929." *Canadian Journal of the History of Sport/Revue canadienne de l'histoire des sports* 26, no. 1 (1995): 22-39.

———. "In the Field of Sport at Home and Abroad: Sports Coverage in Canadian Daily Newspapers 1850-1914." *Sport History Review* 34, no. 2 (2003): 133-67.

———. "'A Lively Interest on the Prairies': Western Canada, the Mass Media and 'A World of Sport' 1870-1939." Paper presented at Northern Great Plains History Conference, Brandon, Manitoba, September 1995.

———. "Local Teams in a World of Sport: Sports Coverage and Community Identity in Canadian Daily Newspapers, 1850-1900." *North American Society for Sport History Proceedings & Newsletter* (2000): 62-63.

Lorenz, Stacy L., and Geraint G. Osborne. "'Talk About Strenuous Hockey': Violence, Manhood, and the 1907 Ottawa Silver Seven-Montreal Wanderer Rivalry." *Journal of Canadian Studies* 40, no. 1 (2006): 125-56.

Lowes, Mark D. *Inside the Sports Pages: Work Routines, Professional Ideologies and the Manufacture of Sports News.* Toronto: University of Toronto Press, 1999.

Lucht, Gary. "Scobey's Touring Pros: Wheat, Baseball and Illicit Booze." *Historical Society of Montana* 30, no. 3 (1970): 88-93.

Luke, Bob. "Hall of Famer: Bill McGowan Umpired with Vigor and Style— Baseball." *Baseball Digest* (February 2002): 2.

Lukowich, Ed, Eigel Ramsfjell, and Bud Somerville. *The Joy of Curling.* Toronto: McGraw-Hill Ryerson Limited, 1990.

Lund, Rolf T. "Development of Skiing in Banff." *Alberta History* 25, no. 4 (1977): 25-30.

———. "Recreational Skiing in the Canadian Rockies." *Alberta History* 26, no. 2 (1978): 30-34.

Lynn, Mary. *Women's Liberation in the Twentieth Century.* Toronto: John Wiley and Sons, 1975.

Lynn, Susan, Marie Hardin, and Kristie Walsdorf. "Selling (Out) the Sporting Woman: Advertising Images in Four Athletic Magazines." *Journal of Sport Management* 18, no. 4 (2004): 335-49.

Kelly, Malcolm. *Hanging it Out on Camera 3: Canadian Sports in the Media Era.* Toronto: Prentice Hall Canada, 2001.

MacAloon, John J. "Festival, Ritual and Television (Los Angeles 1984)." In *The Olympic Movement and the Mass Media: Part 6,* edited by Roger Jackson and Tom McPhail, 21-40. Calgary: Hunford Enterprises, 1989.

———. "Introduction: Muscular Christianity After 150 Years." In "Muscular Christianity and the Colonial and Post-colonial World," edited by J.J. MacAloon. Special issue, *International Journal of the History of Sport* 23, no. 5 (2006): 687-700.

Macdonald, Catherine. "The Edmonton Grads: Canada's Most Successful Team: A History and Analysis of Their Success." M A thesis, University of Windsor, 1976.

MacEwan, Grant. *Calgary Cavalcade: From Fort to Fortune.* Saskatoon: Western Producer Prairie Books, 1975.

———. *John Ware's Cow Country.* Saskatoon: Western Producer Prairie Books, 1976.

MacGregor, James. *A History of Alberta.* Edmonton: Hurtig, 1981.

Macintosh, Donald, Donna Greenhorn, and David Black. "Canadian Diplomacy and the 1978 Edmonton Commonwealth Games." *Journal of Sport History* 1 (1992): 26-55.

Macintosh, Donald, Thomas Bedecki, and C.E.S. Franks. *Sport and Politics in Canada: Federal Government Involvement Since 1961*. Montreal and Kingston: McGill-Queen's University Press, 1988.

MacKinnon, Doris. "'Just an Ordinary Person': The History of Dr. Ethel Taylor" Unpublished paper. N.d. Athabasca University. http://www2.athabascau.ca/wgst/forms/MacKinnon.doc.

MacNeill, Margaret. "Social Marketing, Gender, and the Science of Fitness: A Case-study of ParticipACTION Campaigns." In *Sport and Gender in Canada* 2nd ed., edited by P. White and K. Young, 215-31. Toronto: Oxford University Press, 2006.

Mair, Alex. *Gateway City: Stories from Edmonton's Past*. Calgary: Fifth House, 2000.

Marannis, David. *When Pride Still Mattered: A Biography of Vince Lombardi*. New York: Touchstone, 2000.

Marinetti, Filippo T. *Critical Writings*. Edited by D. Thompson. New York: Farrar, Straus and Giroux, 2006.

Markham-Starr, Susan, and T. Delamere. "'Canada needs you': The Jan Eisenhardt Story." Abstracts of papers presented at the Eleventh Canadian Congress on Leisure Research. Edited by T. Delamere, C. Randall, and D. Robinson, 385-90. Malaspina University College, BC, 2005.

Marshall, Penny, dir. *A League of Their Own*. Columbia/Tristar Studios, 1992.

Martens, J.W. "Young Man! When You're Low on Your Dough: The Depression and YMCA's Leisure Time League." *Alberta History* 52, no. 4 (2004).

Mason, Dan S. "What is the Sports Product and Who Buys It? The Marketing of Professional Sports Leagues." *European Journal of Marketing* 33, no. 3/4 (1999): 401-19.

Mason, Dan S., and G.H. Duquette, "Newspaper Coverage of Early Professional Ice Hockey: The Discourses of Class and Control." *Media History* 10, no. 3 (2004): 157-73.

Mason, Dan S., G.H. Duquette, and J. Scherer. "Heritage, Sport Tourism and Canadian Junior Jockey: Nostalgia for Social Experience or Sport Place?" *Journal of Sport and Tourism* 10, no. 4 (2005): 253-71.

Matthews, D.O. "A Historical Study of the Aims, Contents, and Methods of Swedish, Danish, and German Gymnastics." Proceedings of the National College Physical Education Association for Men, 72nd, n.p., January 1969.

Maxwell, Doug. *Canada Curls: The Illustrated History of Curling in Canada*. North Vancouver: Whitecap Books, 2002.

———. *Tales of a Curling Hack*. North Vancouver: Whitecap Books, 2006.

May, Denny. "The Sportsman, an Edmonton Childhood Memoir From the 1940s." In *Edmonton: A City Called Home*. Edmonton: Edmonton Public Library, 2004. Accessed July 25, 2005. http://www.epl.ca/edmonton-a-city-called-home/edmonton-a-city-called-home-story?id=1439.

McCaffery, Dan. *Tommy Burns: Canada's Unknown World Heavyweight Champion*. Toronto: Lorimer, 2000.

McCarthy, Larry M., and Richard Irwin. "Names in Lights: Corporate Purchase of Sport Facility Naming Rights." *Cyber-Journal of Sport Marketing* 2, no. 3 (July 1998).

McCloy, Cora. "Hosting International Sport Events in Canada: Planning for Facility Legacies." *The Global Nexus Engaged: Sixth International Symposium for Olympic Research* (2002): 135-42. http://www.la84foundation.org/SportsLibrary/ISOR/ISOR2002q.pdf.

McCoy, Heath. *Pain and Passion: The Story of Stampede Wrestling*. Toronto: ECW Press, 2005.

McFarland, Elsie. *The Development of Public Recreation in Canada*. Ottawa: Canadian Parks/Recreation Association, 1978.

McFarlane, Brian. *One Hundred Years of Hockey*. Toronto: Deneau, 1989.

McFee, Graham, and Alan Tomlinson. "Riefenstahl's Olympia: Ideology and Aesthetics in the Shaping of the Aryan Athletic Body." *International Journal of the History of Sport* no. 2 (1999): 86-106.

McGarry, Karen. "Passing as a 'Lady': Nationalist Narratives of Femininity, Race, and Class in Elite Canadian Figure Skating." *Genders* 41 (2005). http://www.genders.org/g41/g41_mcgarry.html.

McGillis, Ian. "North Side Story." In *Edmonton On Location: River City Chronicles*, edited by Heather Zwicker. Edmonton: NeWest Press, 2005.

McKenna, Jennifer. "History of Baseball." Unpublished paper, Red Deer College, Recreation Administration, 2004.

McKinley, Rob. "UPS Delivers the Goods to Advance Sport." *Windspeaker* 15, no. 8 (December 1997): 23.

McLennan, William M. *Sport in Early Calgary*. Calgary: Fort Brisebois Pub., 1983.

McLeod, Norman. *My First Bonspiel*. Memoir recorded by Robert E. Gard. N.d., ca. 1940. University of Alberta Libraries, Alberta Folklore and Local History Collection, Alberta Folklore and Local History Collection 96-93-532. http://folklore.library.ualberta.ca/dspCitation.cfm?ID=132.

McLuhan, Marshall. "Games: Extensions of Man." In *Understanding Media: The Extensions of Man*, 254-66. Cambridge, MA: MIT Press, 2000.

McPherson, Gary W., and Siddharth Mohapatrab."The Paralympics: A Strategic Social Enterprise." Unpublished paper. N.d., ca. 2008. http://pdffinder.net/THE-PARALYMPICS:-A-STRATEGIC-SOCIAL-ENTERPRISE.html.

McQuarrie, Fiona A.E., "The Struggle Over Worker Leisure: An Analysis of the History of the Workers' Sports Association in Canada." *Canadian Journal of Administrative Sciences/Revue canadienne des sciences de l'administration* 27, no. 4 (2010): 391-402.

Meili, Diane. "Cree Hero Runs Again." *Legacy* 6, no. 3 (2001): 18-19.

Melchers, Ronald. "Sports in the Workplace." In *Not Just a Game: Essays in Canadian Sport Sociology*, edited by J. Harvey and H. Cantalon, 51-68. Ottawa: University of Ottawa Press, 1988.

Meller, Helen E. *Leisure and the Changing City, 1870–1914*. London: Routledge, 1976.

Melnyk, Olga. "A Century of Solidarity." *Legacy* 12, no. 2 (2007): 25-27.

Messner, M. "The Life of a Man's Seasons: Male Identity in the Life-course of the Jock." In *Changing Men*, edited by M.S. Kimmel, 53-67. London: SAGE, 1987.

Metcalfe, Alan. *Canada Learns to Play: The Emergence of Organized Sport, 1807–1914*. Toronto: McClelland & Stewart, 1987.

Michener, James A. *Sports in America*. Greenwich, CT: Fawcett, 1987.

Mikkelsen, Glen. "Indians and Rodeo." *Alberta History* 35, no. 3 (1987): 13-19.

Mills, David. "100 Years of Sports." In *Alberta: A State of Mind*, edited by S. Sharpe, R. Gibbons, J.H. Marsh, and H.B. Edwards, 197-231.Toronto: Key Porter, 2005.

———. "Peter Pocklington and the Business of Hockey." In *Edmonton: The Life of a City*, edited by Hesketh, B. and F. Swyripa, 306-15. Edmonton: NeWest Publishers, 1995.

Milton, Nora J. "The Scots in Alberta." In *Peoples of Alberta: Portraits of Cultural Diversity*, edited by H. Palmer and T. Palmer, 109-22. Saskatoon: Western Producer Prairie Books, 1985.

Mitchell, Teresa. "Gym Class Ruling Overturned." *Law Now* 26, no. 3 (2001): 6.

Mitchell, W.O. *The Black Bonspiel of Wullie MacCrimmon*. Toronto: McClelland & Stewart, 1993.

Mitchelson, Edward B. "The Evolution of Men's Basketball in Canada, 1892–1936." MA thesis, University of Alberta, 1968.

Morgan, B. "Sandy McCarthy Talks to Native Americans." *Sports Illustrated for Kids*, February 1997, 18.

Morrison, Elsie C., and P.N.R. Morrison. *Calgary, 1875–1950: A Souvenir of Calgary's Seventy-fifth Anniversary.* Calgary: Calgary Publishing Co., 1950.

Morrow, Don. "A Case Study in Amateur Conflict: the Athletic War in Canada 1907–1908." *British Journal of Sports History* 3, no. 2 (1986): 183–90.

Morrow, Don, Mary Keyes, Wayne Simpson, F. Cosentino, and R. Lappage. *A Concise History of Sport in Canada.* Toronto: Oxford University Press, 1989.

Morrow, Don, and Kevin B. Wamsley. *Sport in Canada: A History.* Don Mills, ON: Oxford University Press, 2005.

Mott, Morris. "Bonspiel Sermons, 1894–1970." *North American Society For Sport History Proceedings & Newsletter* (1990).

——. "The British Protestant Pioneers and the Establishment of Manly Sports in Manitoba 1870–1886." *Journal of Sport History* 3, no. 3 (1980): 25–36.

——. ed., *Sports in Canada.* Toronto: Copp Clark Pitman 1989.

Mondak, J.J. "The Politics of Professional Wrestling," *Journal of Popular Culture* 23 (1989): 139–50.

Mulcahy, Barbara C. "Hard Times Cop: Jerry Mulcahy's Years Walking the Beat During the Depression." In *Edmonton: A City Called Home.* Edmonton: Edmonton Public Library, 2004. http://www.edmontonhistory.ca/ prelaunch/citycalledhome.

Mummery, W.K., and J.C. Spence. "Rate and Frequency of Sport and Recreational Injuries: Results from the 1995 Alberta Sport and Recreation Injury Survey." *Research Update* 4, no. 1 (September 1996). http://www. centre4activeliving.ca/publications/research-update/1996/sept-injury.htm.

Nagel, Gladys. "Growing up in McKernan." In *Edmonton: A City Called Home.* Edmonton: Edmonton Public Library, 2004. http://www.epl.ca/ edmonton-a-city-called-home/edmonton-a-city-called-home-story?id=747.

Nauright, John. "Colonial Manhood and Imperial Race Virility: British Responses to Post-Boer War Rugby Tours." In *Making Men: Rugby and Masculine Identity,* edited by J. Nauright and T.J.L. Chandler, 121–39. London: Frank Cass, 1996.

——. "Sustaining Masculine Identity: Rugby and the Nostalgia of Masculinity." In *Making Men: Rugby and Masculine Identity,* edited by J. Nauright and T.J.L. Chandler, 227–44. London: Frank Cass, 1996.

Nauright, John, and Phillip White. "Mediated Nostalgia, Community and Nation: The Canadian Football League in Crisis and the Demise of the Ottawa Rough Riders, 1986–1996." *Sport History Review* 33, no. 2 (2002): 120–37.

Navalkowski, Anna. "Shandro School." *Alberta Historical Review* 18, no. 4 (1970): 8–14.

Nemeth, Mary. "A Patch of Hoops Heaven." *Maclean's*, March 20, 1995, 48.

Noll, Roger G., and Andrew Zimbalist. "Sports, Jobs, and Taxes: Are New Stadiums Worth the Cost?" *The Brookings Review* 15, no. 3 (1997): 35–39.

Norcliffe, Glen. *The Ride to Modernity: The Bicycle in Canada, 1869–1900.* Toronto: University of Toronto Press, 2001.

Norton, Wayne. *Women on Ice: The Early Years of Women's Hockey in Western Canada.* Vancouver: Ronsdale Press, 2009.

Oliver, Greg, and Steve Johnson. *The Pro Wrestling Hall of Fame: The Heels.* Toronto: ECW Press, 2007.

"Only Game in Town: Saddle Lake's Junior B Warriors Give the Indian Reserve Something to Cheer, and Young Players a Reason to Leave." *Alberta Report* 25, no. 14 (March 23, 1998): 26–30.

O'Reilly, Michael. "Canadian Advertising Success Stories: Budweiser." Canadian Congress of Advertising, 1997. http://cassies.ca/content/caselibrary/winners/Budweiser.pdf.

Oriard, Michael. *Reading Football: How the Popular Press Created an American Spectacle.* Chapel Hill: University of North Carolina Press, 1995.

O'Riordan, Terence. "The 'Puck-Eaters': Hockey as a Unifying Community Experience in Edmonton & Strathcona 1894-1905." *Alberta History* 49, no. 2 (2001): 2–11.

Osborne, K. "Public Schooling and Citizenship Education in Canada." *Canadian Ethnic Studies* 32 no. 1 (2000): 8–37.

Oxley, J. Macdonald. *My Strange Rescue and Other Stories of Sport and Adventure in Canada.* London: T. Nelson, 1895.

Pakes, Fraser. "'Skill to Do Comes of Doing': Purpose in Traditional Indian Winter Games and Pastimes." In *Winter Sports in the West,* edited by E.A. Corbet and A.W. Rasporich, 26–37. Calgary: Historical Society of Alberta, 1990.

Palmer, Bryan. *The Descent into Discourse: The Reification of Language and the Writing of Social History.* Philadelphia: Temple University Press, 1990.

Palmer, Howard. "Patterns of Immigration and Ethnic Settlement 1880-1920." In *Peoples of Alberta: Portraits of Cultural Diversity,* edited by H. Palmer and T. Palmer, 1–27. Saskatoon: Western Producer Prairie Books, 1985.

Palmer, Howard, and Tamara Palmer. *Alberta: A New History.* Edmonton: Hurtig,
    1990.

———. "The Black Experience in Alberta." In *Peoples of Alberta: Portraits of Cultural
    Diversity,* edited by H. Palmer and T. Palmer, 365–93. Saskatoon: Western
    Producer Prairie Books, 1985.

———. "The Icelandic Experience." In *Peoples of Alberta: Portraits of Cultural
    Diversity,* edited by H. Palmer and T. Palmer, 174–94. Saskatoon: Western
    Producer Prairie Books, 1985.

———, eds. *Peoples of Alberta: Portraits of Cultural Diversity.* Saskatoon: Western
    Producer Prairie Books, 1985.

Paraschak, Victoria. "Variations in Race Relations: Sporting Events for Native
    Peoples in Canada." *Sociology of Sport Journal* 14, no. 1 (1997): 1–21.

Parker, P. *The Feather and the Drum: The History of Banff Indian Days 1889–1978.*
    Calgary: Consolidated Communications, 1990.

Patterson, Martha H. "Beyond Empire: The New Woman at Home and Abroad."
    Journal of Women's History 21, no. 1 (2009): 180–84.

Patton, Clarence. "Good Old Glenmore School Days." *Alberta History* 52, no. 3
    (2004): 11–16.

Peach, Jack. *Thanks for the Memories: More Stories from Calgary's Past.* Saskatoon:
    Fifth House, 1994.

Pealo, Wayne, and Gerald Redmond. *Canadian Sport Tourism: An Introduction.*
    Nanaimo, BC: Malaspina University College, 2003.

Pedersen, Diana. "The Photographic Record of the Canadian YWCA, 1890–1930:
    A Visual Source for Women's History." *Archivaria* 24 (Summer 1987): 10–35.

Peers, Danielle. "(Dis)empowering Paralympic Histories: Absent Athletes and
    Disabling Discourses." *Disability & Society* 24, no. 5 (2009): 653–65.

Penley, Ken. "Russ Gideon: Athlete and Business Leader." *Alberta History* (March
    22, 2006).

Penrose, Jan. "When All the Cowboys Are Indians: The Nature of Race in
    All-Indian Rodeo." *Annals of the Association of American Geographers* 93, no. 3
    (2003): 687–705.

Penz, Otto. "Ballgames of the North American Indians and in Late Europe."
    Journal of Sport & Social Issues 15 (1991): 43–58.

Pezer, Vera. *The Stone Age: A Social History of Curling on the Prairies.* Markham, ON:
    Fifth House, 2003.

Phillips, Bob. *Honour of Empire, Glory of Sport: The History of Athletics and the Commonwealth Games.* Manchester: Parrs Wood, 2000.

Pitters-Caswell, Marian. "Women's Participation in Sporting Activities as an Indication of a Feminist Movement in Canada between 1867-1914." *Proceedings of the Canadian Symposium on the History of Sport and Physical Education.* Halifax: Dalhousie University, 1974.

Poovey, Mary. *Making a Social Body: British Cultural Formation 1830–1864.* Chicago: University of Chicago Press, 1995.

Pope, Steven W. "Review, *Ethnicity and Sport in North American History and Culture*, edited by George Eisen and David K. Wiggins (Greenwood Press, Westport, 1994)." *Sporting Traditions: Journal of the Australian Society for Sport History* 12, no. 2 (May 1996): 99-105.

——, ed. "Sport History: Into the New Century," *Journal of Sport History* 25, no. 1 (1998): i-x.

Poulsen, David A. *Wild Ride! Three Journeys Down the Rodeo Road.* Toronto: Balmur Book Publishing, 2000.

Poulter, Gillian. "Snowshoeing and Lacrosse: Canada's Nineteenth Century 'National Games.'" *Culture, Sport, Society,* 6, nos. 2/3 (2003): 293-320.

Prokop, Manfred. "Canadianization of Immigrant Children: The Role of the Rural Elementary School in Alberta 1900-1930." *Alberta History* 37, no. 2 (1989): 5-17.

Pronger, Brian. "Fear and Trembling: Homophobia in Men's Sport." In *Sport and Gender in Canada.* 2nd ed., edited by P. White and K. Young, 182-97. Toronto: Oxford University Press, 2006.

——. "Outta My Endzone: Sport and the Territorial Anus." *Journal of Sport and Social Issues* 23, no. 4 (1999): 373-89.

Putney, Clifford. *Muscular Christianity: Manhood and Sports in Protestant America, 1880–1920.* Cambridge, MA: Harvard University Press, 2001.

Ramshaw, Greg. "Nostalgia, Heritage, and Imaginative Sports Geographies: Sport and Cultural Landscapes." Paper Presented at the Forum UNESCO University and Heritage 10th International Seminar. Newcastle upon Tyne, UK, April 2005.

Ramshaw, Greg, and Tom Hinch. "Place Identity and Sport Tourism: The Case of the Heritage Classic Ice Hockey Event." *Current Issues in Tourism* 9, nos. 4 and 5 (2006): 399-418.

Rasporich, A.W., and H.C. Klassen. *Frontier Calgary: Town, City and Region 1875–1914.* Calgary: McClelland & Stewart West, 1975.

Redmond, Gary. "The Development of Curling in Western Canada." In *Winter Sports in the West,* edited by E.A. Corbet and A.W. Rasporich, 112–23. Calgary: Historical Society of Alberta 1990.

———. *The Sporting Scots of Nineteenth-Century Canada.* Rutherford, NJ: Fairleigh Dickinson University Press, 1982.

Rees, Tony. *Polo: The Galloping Game.* Calgary: University of Calgary Press, 2001.

Reichwein, PearlAnn. "'Enjoyment, Health and Safety': The Legacy of Queen Elizabeth Swimming Pool." *The Strathcona Plaindealer Annual* 23 (2000): 11–14.

Reid, John E. "Sports and Games in Alberta Before 1900." M A thesis, University of Alberta, 1969.

Reischer, Erin, and Kathryn Koo. "The Body Beautiful: Symbolism and Agency in the Social World." *Annual Review of Anthropology* 33 (2004): 297–317.

Robertson, Sheila. "Changing the System." *Canadian Journal for Women in Coaching* 2, no. 4 (March 2002). Accessed January 12, 2004. http://www.coach.ca/WOMEN/e/journal/mar2002/pg6.htm#Changing.

Robidoux, Michael A. "Historical Interpretations of First Nations Masculinity and its Influence on Canada's Sport Heritage." *International Journal of the History of Sport* 23, no. 2 (2006): 267–84.

———. "Imagining a Canadian Identity Through Sport: A Historical Interpretation of Lacrosse and Hockey." *Journal of American Folklore* 456, no. 1 (2002): 209–25.

———. *Men at Play: A Working Understanding of Professional Hockey.* Montreal and Kingston: McGill-Queen's University Press, 2001.

———. "Narratives of Race Relations in Southern Alberta: An Examination of Conflicting Sporting Practices." *Sociology of Sport Journal* 21 (2004): 287–301.

Robidoux, Michael A., and J. Bocksnick. "Playing Beyond the Glass: How Parents Support Violence in Minor Hockey." In *Sexual Sports Rhetoric,* edited by Linda K. Fuller, 45–61. New York: Peter Lang, 2010.

Robinson, Laura. *Black Tights: Women, Sport and Sexuality.* Toronto: Harper Collins, 2002.

———. *Crossing the Line: Violence and Sexual Assault in Canada's National Sport.* Toronto: McClelland & Stewart, 1998.

———. *She Shoots, She Scores: Canadian Perspectives on Women in Sport.* Toronto: Thomson Educational Publishers, 1997.

Roche, Maurice. *Mega-events and Modernity: Olympics and Expos in the Growth of Global Culture*. London: Routledge, 2000.

Rose, David, and Geoffrey Lawrence. "Beyond National Sport: Sociology, History and Postmodernity." *Sporting Traditions* 12, no. 2 (1996): 3-16.

Routledge, Penelope D. "The North West Mounted Police and Their Influence on the Sporting and Social Life of the North-West Territories, 1870-1904." M A thesis, University of Alberta, 1978.

Rowe, Ashley, and Wayne Pealo. "The World Masters Games 2005: Implications for Canadian sport tourism research." In *Papers Presented at the Eleventh Canadian Congress on Leisure Research*. May 17-20, 2005, edited by T. Delamere, C. Randall and D. Robinson. Canadian Association for Leisure Studies, 2005.

Russell, Andy. *The Canadian Cowboy: Stories of Cows, Cowboys and Cayuses*. Toronto: McClelland & Stewart Ltd., 1995.

Russell, Gordon W. *The Social Psychology of Sport*. New York: Springer-Verlag, 1993.

Rusted, Brian. "'A Wonderful Picture': Western Art and the Calgary Stampede." In *Icon, Brand, Myth: The Calgary Stampede*, edited by M. Foran, 271-92. Edmonton: Athabasca University Press, 2008.

Rutherford, Paul. *When Television was Young: Primetime Canada 1952-1967*. Toronto: University of Toronto Press, 1990.

Ryan, D. "The Development of Speed-skating in Western Canada from a Personal Perspective." In *Winter Sports in the West*, edited by E.A. Corbet and A.W. Rasporich, 124-31. Calgary: Historical Society of Alberta, 1990.

Salcedo, Marissa. "The Best of Intentions: Upbuilding Through Health at the Portland Y W C A, 1908-1959." *Journal of Women's History* 15, no. 3 (2003): 183-89.

Salter, Michael A. "The Indian Athlete: Exploiting or Exploited?" *North American Society For Sport History Proceedings & Newsletter* (1976). http://www.la84foundation.org/SportsLibrary/NASSH_Proceedings/NP1976/NP1976w.pdf.

Samler, Johanta, and Franie Ford. "Can This Sport be Liberated?" *Branching Out* 5, no. 4 (1978): 37-38.

Sanderson, Kay. "Pearl Edmanson Borgal, 1911-1993." In *200 Remarkable Alberta Women*, edited by Hilda Hauschildt, 82. Calgary: Famous Five Foundation, 1999.

———. "Rose Pearson Kohn, 1900-1967." In *200 Remarkable Alberta Women*, edited by Hilda Hauschildt, 64. Calgary: Famous Five Foundation, 1999.

Sandiford, Keith. *Cricket and the Victorians.* Aldershot, UK: Scolar Press, 1994.

Sandor, Steven. *The Battle of Alberta: A Century of Hockey's Greatest Rivalry.* Surrey, BC: Heritage House, 2006.

Sandoz, Joli, and Joby Winans, eds. *Whatever it Takes: Women on Women's Sport.* New York: Farrar, Straus and Giroux, 1999.

Schissel, Wendy. *Beiseker's Golden Heritage.* Beiseker, AB: Beiseker Historical Society, 1977.

Scott-Brown, Joan. "The Short Life of St. Dunstan's Calgary Indian Industrial School, 1896-1907." *Canadian Journal of Native Education* 14, no. 1 (1987): 41-49.

Seiler, R.M., and T.P. Seiler. "The Social Construction of the Canadian Cowboy: Calgary Exhibition and Stampede Posters, 1952-1972." In *Icon, Brand, Myth: The Calgary Stampede,* edited by M. Foran, 293-324. Edmonton: Athabasca University Press, 2008.

Sharpe, Sydney, Roger Gibbons, James H. Marsh, and Heather B. Edwards, eds. *Alberta: A State of Mind.* Toronto: Key Porter, 2005.

Shogan, Debra. "The Social Construction of Disability in a Society of Normalization." In *Adapted Physical Activity,* edited by Robert D. Steadward, E. Jane Watkinson, and Garry D. Wheeler, 65-74. Edmonton: University of Alberta Press, 2003.

Short, John. "Hockey's Final Shining Days." In *Alberta in the Twentieth Century.* Vol. 5, *Brownlee and the Triumph of Populism, 1920-1930,* edited by Ted Byfield, 284-88, Edmonton: United Western Communications Ltd., 1995.

———. "Out of Sham Amateurs Came Frank Professionalism." In *Alberta in the Twentieth Century.* Vol. 5, *Brownlee and the Triumph of Populism, 1920-1930,* edited by Ted Byfield, 282. Edmonton: United Western Communications Ltd., 1995.

Silverman, Elaine L. *The Last Best West: Women on the Alberta Frontier 1880-1930.* Montreal: Eden Press, 1984.

Silversides, Brock. *Shooting Cowboys: Photographing Cowboy Culture 1878-1965.* Markham, ON: Fifth House, 1998.

Skrine, Agnes. "A Lady's Life on a Ranche." In *A Flannel Shirt and Liberty: British Emigrant Gentlewomen in the Canadian West 1880-1914,* edited by S. Jackel, 95-110. Vancouver: University of British Columbia Press, 1982. Originally published in *Blackwood's Edinburgh Magazine* 163, no. 987 (January 1898).

Smallwood, R., dir. *In the Hearts of Kings.* Edmonton: Hole in the Wall Productions, 2007.

Smith, Garry J. "The Noble Sports Fan." *Journal of Sport & Social Issues* 12, no. 1
(1988): 54-65.

Smyth, J.E. "Sound Body, Sound Mind." In *Taking Sport Seriously: Social Issues in
Canadian Sport*, edited by Peter Donnelly. Toronto: Thompson, 1997.

Solomon, Eric. "Jews and Baseball: A Cultural Love Story." In *Ethnicity and Sport
in North American History and Culture*, edited by G. Eisen and D.K. Wiggins,
75-102. Westport, CT: Greenwood Press, 1994.

Spears, Betty. "'Siding 29' or the Role of the Canadian Pacific Railway in the
Development of Canadian Rocky Mountain Sport." *North American Society
for Sport History Proceedings & Newsletter* (1990): 60.

Stein, Albert. "The Jewish Farm Colonies of Alberta," *Outlook* (March/April 2001).
http://www.vcn.bc.ca/outlook/library/articles/CdnJewishExperience/
p05FarmColonies.htm.

Stiles, J.A. "Descended from Heroes: The Frontier Myth in Rural Alberta." *Alberta*
20, no. 20 (1990): 27-46.

Strathern, Gloria H. *Alberta Newspapers, 1880–1982: An Historical Directory.*
Edmonton: University of Alberta Press, 1988.

Stubbs, Lewis. *Shoestring Glory: Semi-Pro Baseball on the Prairies 1886–1994.*
Winnipeg: Turnstone Press, 1996.

Sugden, J., and A. Tomlinson. "Theorizing Sport, Status and Social Class." In
Handbook of Sports Studies, edited by J. Coakley and E. Dunning, 309-21.
London: SAGE, 2000.

Takach, Geo. *Will the Real Alberta Please Stand Up?* Edmonton: University of
Alberta Press, 2010.

Taylor, Jim. "A Nation in Mourning: A Canadian Writes of Gretzky and His
Country's Grief." *Sports Illustrated*, August 22, 1988.

Tenenbaum, Gershon, Evan Stewart, Robert N. Singer, and Joan Duda.
"Aggression and Violence in Sport: an ISSP Position Stand," *International
Society of Sport Psychology*. N.d., ca. 1995. http://www.issponline.org/
documents/aggressionstatement.pdf.

Thomas, Clara. *Ryerson of Upper Canada*. Toronto: Ryerson Press, 1969.

Tollestrup, Mary. "George Washington Houk." *Water Works Wonders: A History
of the White, Wilson, McMahon, River Junction School Districts*, 343-45.
Lethbridge, AB: McNally Seniors, 1995.

Tingley, Ken. *The City of Champions: Highlights from Edmonton's Sport History.*
Edmonton: City of Edmonton, United Cycle and Edmonton Sport

Council. N.d., ca. 2005. http://www.unitedcycle.com/images/about/
EdmontonSportHistory.pdf.

———, ed. *For King and Country: Alberta in the Second World War*. Edmonton:
Reidmore Books and Alberta Community Development, 2005.

Todd, Jan. *Physical Culture and the Body Beautiful: Purposive Exercise in the Lives of
American Women 1800–1875*. Macon, GA: Mercer University Press, 1998.

Tougas, Maurice. "Women's Soccer Team Kickstarts Interest." *Business Edge* 3,
no. 39 (October 30, 2003). http://www.businessedge.ca/archives/article.cfm/
pro-soccer-pitched-to-fans-as-solid-investment-4283.

Trainer, Yvonne. *Tom Three Persons: A Multimedia Poetry Sequence*. Calgary:
Frontenac House: Quartet 2002 Series, 2002.

Trumpbour, Robert C. "Rituals, Invented Traditions, and Shifting Power: The
Role of Communication in the History of Stadium Construction." *Journal of
Communication Inquiry* 31, no. 4 (2007): 310–30.

Turner, Bryan. *The Body and Society: Explorations in Social Theory*. 2nd ed. London:
SAGE, 2007.

Unwin, Peter. "Who Do You Think I Am?: A Story of Tom Longboat." *The Beaver*
81, no. 2 (April–May 2001): 20–26.

Vacante, Jeffrey. "Review of Dummitt, Christopher, *The Manly Modern:
Masculinity in Postwar Canada*." H-Canada, H-Net Reviews, May 2008. http://
www.h-net.org/reviews/showrev.php?id=14480.

van Herk, Aritha. *Mavericks: An Incorrigible History of Alberta*. Toronto: Penguin
Canada, 2002.

Vantour, James. *The Fabulous Flyers*. Edmonton: Hockey Alberta Foundation and
United Cycle, 2005.

Varty, John F. "Polo and British Settlement in Alberta 1880–1930." *Alberta History*
43, no. 3 (1995): 7–15.

Vaz, E.W. "Institutionalized Rule Violation and Control in Professional Hockey:
a Perspective." *Journal of the Canadian Association of Health* 43, no. 3 (1977):
6–16.

Veenstra, Gerry. "Who the heck is Don Bradman? Sport Culture and Social Class
in British Columbia, Canada." *Canadian Review of Sociology and Anthropology*
14, no. 3 (2007): 319–43.

Veltri, F.R., and S.A. Long. "A New Image: Female Athlete-Endorser." *Cyber-
Journal of Sport Marketing* 2, no. 4 (1998).

Vertinsky, Patricia, and John Bale. Introduction to *Sites of Sport: Space, Place, Experience*. Edited by Patricia Vertinsky and John Bale, 1-7. New York: Routledge, 2004.

Visek, Amanda, and Jack Watson. "Ice Hockey Players' Legitimacy of Aggression and Professionalization of Attitude." *Sport Psychologist* 12, no. 2 (2005): 178-92.

Voisey, Paul. *Vulcan: The Making of a Prairie Community.* Toronto: University of Toronto Press, 1988.

von Heyking, Amy. *Creating Citizens: History and Identity in Alberta's Schools, 1905 to 1980.* Calgary: University of Calgary Press, 2006.

———. "An Education for 'Character' in Alberta Schools, 1905-45." In *Aspenland 1998: Local Knowledge and a Sense of Place*, edited by David Goa and David Ridley. Red Deer, AB: Central Alberta Museums Network, Provincial Museum of Alberta, Red Deer and District Museum, 1998. http://www. albertasource.ca/aspenland/eng/society/article_education_character.html.

Wamsley, Kevin B. "Power and Privilege in Historiography: Constructing Percy Page." *Sport History Review* 28, no. 2 (1997): 146-55.

———. "Strangers in the Eighteenth Hole: The Evolution of Golf in Edmonton and the Establishment of Canada's First Municipal Golf Course 1896-1914." *Canadian Journal of the History of Sport/Revue canadienne de l'histoire des sports* 20, no. 2 (1989).

Wamsley, Kevin B., and Michael Heine. "Tradition, Modernity and the Construction of Civic Identity: The Calgary Olympics." *OLYMPIKA: The International Journal of Olympic Studies* 5 (1996): 81-90.

Wamsley, Kevin B., and D. Whitson. "Celebrating Violent Masculinities: The Boxing Death of Luther McCarty." *Journal of Sport History* 25, no 3. (1998): 419-31.

Watson, Ronald D., and Gregory D. Rickwood. "'Stewards of Ice Hockey': A Historical Review of Safety Rules in Canadian Amateur Ice Hockey." *Sport History Review* 30, no. 1 (1999): 30-33.

Weisman, Carol. "Two Centuries of Women's Health Activism." Seminar: The History and Future of Women's Health. Office on Women's Health and PHS Co-ordinating Committee on Women's Health, US Department of Health and Human Services, June 1998.

Welch, Paula D. *History of American Physical Education and Sport.* 3rd ed. Springfield, IL: C.C. Thomas, 2004.

Wetherell, Donald Grant. "Making New Identities: Alberta Small Towns Confront the City, 1900–1950." *Journal of Canadian Studies* 39, no. 11 (2005): 175–97.

——. "Making Tradition: The Calgary Stampede, 1912–1939." In *Icon, Brand, Myth: The Calgary Stampede*, edited by M. Foran, 21–45. Edmonton: Athabasca University Press, 2008.

——. "A Season of Mixed Blessings: Winter and Leisure in Alberta Before World War II." In *Winter Sports in the West*, edited by E.A. Corbet and A.W. Rasporich, 38–51. Calgary: Historical Society of Alberta, 1990.

Wetherell, Donald Grant, and Irene Kmet. *Town Life: Main Street and the Evolution of Small Town Alberta, 1880–1947.* Edmonton: University of Alberta Press, 1995.

——. *Useful Pleasures: The Shaping of Leisure in Alberta 1896–1945.* Regina: Canadian Plains Research Center, 1990.

Wheeler, Laura. "'We Want Your Pictures So Kodak As you Go': Promoting Winter Recreation in Banff in the 1920s." *Past Imperfect* 15 (2009): 6–35.

Wheeler, Robert F. "Organized Sport and Organized Labour: The Workers' Sports Movement." *Journal of Contemporary History* 13, no. 1 (1978): 191–210.

White, Helen. "Basketball in the Twenties." *Along the Fifth: A History of Stony Plain and District.* Stony Plain, AB: Stony Plain Historical Society, 1982.

White, P. "Muscles Don't Make the Man." In *Taking Sport Seriously: Social Issues in Canadian Sport*, edited by P. Donnelly. Toronto: Thompson, 1997.

White, P., and B. Wilson, B. "Distinctions in the Stands: An Investigation of Bourdieu's 'Habitus,' Socieoconomic Status and Sport Spectatorship in Canada." *International Review for the Sociology of Sport (IRSS)* 34, no. 3 (1999): 245–64.

White, P., and K. Young. "Health and the New Age Aesthetic." In *Taking Sport Seriously: Social Issues in Canadian Sport*, edited by P. Donnelly. Toronto: Thompson, 1997.

White Pine Pictures. "A Farmer from Amber Valley: J.D. Edwards." In *A Scattering of Seeds: The Creation of Canada.* Accessed June 15, 2010. http://www.whitepinepictures.com/seeds/iv/45/index.html.

Whitson, David. "Pro Sports: Who Pays the Price?" In *Taking Sport Seriously: Social Issues in Canadian Sport*, edited by P. Donnelly. Toronto: Thompson, 1997.

———. "Sport and Hegemony: On the Construction of the Dominant Culture." *Sociology of Sport Journal* 1 no. 1 (1984): 64-78.

Whitson, David, and R. Gruneau, eds. *Artificial Ice: Hockey, Culture and Commerce.* Peterborough, ON: Broadview Press, 2006.

———. *Sport, Culture and the Modern State.* Toronto: University of Toronto Press, 1982.

Whitson, David, and D. Macintosh. "Becoming a World-Class City: Hallmark Events and Sport Franchises in the Growth Strategies of Western Canadian Cities." *Sociology of Sport Journal* 10, no. 3 (1993): 224-25.

———. "The Global Circus: International Sport, Tourism, and the Marketing of Cities." *Journal of Sport and Social Issues* 20, no. 3 (1996): 270-85.

Whorton, J. *Crusaders for Fitness: The History of American Health Reformers.* Princeton: Princeton University Press, 1982.

Whyte, J. *Indians in the Rockies.* Banff: Altitude Publishing, 1985.

Wieting, Stephen G., ed. *Sport and Memory in North America.* London: Frank Cass, 2001.

Wieting, Stephen G., and Danny Lamoureux. "Curling in Canada." In *Sport and Memory in North America,* edited by S.G. Wieting, 1-20. London; Frank Cass, 2001.

Williams, Raymond. *The Long Revolution.* Harmondsworth, UK: Penguin, 1965.

Wilson, G.A. "Does Sport Sponsorship Have a Direct Effect on Product Sales?" *Cyber-Journal of Sport Marketing* 1, no. 1 (1997).

Wilson, L.J. Roy. "Medicine Hat—'The Sporting Town,' 1883-1905." *Canadian Journal of Sport History* 16, no. 2 (1985): 15-32.

Wong, John. "It's a Free Country: The Demise of Major League Hockey in the West." *North American Society for Sport History Proceedings & Newsletter,* edited by C.M. Parratt (2000): 5-6.

Wood, L., and K. King. "Amateur Hockey in Alberta." In *Alberta: A State of Mind,* edited by S. Sharpe, R. Gibbons, J.H. Marsh, and H.B. Edwards, 198-202. Toronto: Key Porter, 2005.

———. "Sweeping Up: Alberta Curling." In *Alberta: A State of Mind,* edited by S. Sharpe, R. Gibbons, J.H. Marsh, and H.B. Edwards, 206-09. Toronto: Key Porter, 2005.

Wood, Tex. "Us Winter Sports." In *Mountain Masculinity: The Life and Writing of Nello "Tex" Vernon-Wood in the Canadian Rockies, 1906-1938,* edited by Andrew Gow and Julie Rak, 71-75. Edmonton: Athabasca University Press, 2008.

Woog, Dan. "Fighting for the Crips and the Queers." *Outsports*, September 14, 2007. http://www.outsports.com/columns/outfield/070914.htm.

Wuest, Deborah A., and Charles A. Bucher. *Foundations of Physical Education and Sport*. St. Louis, MO: Mosby, 1995.

Yeo, William B. "Making Banff a Year-round Park." In *Winter Sports in the West*, edited by E. A. Corbet and A.W. Rasporich, 87-98. Calgary: Historical Society of Alberta, 1990.

Young, Kevin. "Embodied Sport: Pleasure, Betrayal, and Disability." *Disability Studies Quarterly* 12, no. 2 (1992): 41-46.

———. "Violence, Risk, and Liability in Male Sports Culture." *Sociology of Sport Journal* 10, no. 4 (1993): 373-96.

Young, Nancy. "The Reins in Their Hands: Ranchwomen and the Horse in Southern Alberta 1880-1914." *Alberta History* 52, no. 1 (2004): 2-8.

Zeman, Brenda. *To Run with Longboat: Twelve Stories of Indian Athletes in Canada*. Edmonton: GMS2 Ventures, 1988.

Zeman, Gary W. *Alberta on Ice: The History of Hockey in Alberta Since 1893*. Edmonton: Westweb Press, 1985.

Note regarding names of teams and facilities: These are indexed under place, e.g., Lethbridge and Red Deer; except for Calgary and Edmonton. The latter are indexed under the name of the team and facility, in order to distinguish them from the many other subheadings under Calgary and Edmonton.

Abbott Cup, 115–16

Abdel-Shehid, Gamal, 179

Abdullah the Butcher, 277

able-bodied people's sports, focus on, 184–85

Aboriginal athletes/players
    Bow and Arrow Golf and, 296

and foot racing, 144

and lacrosse, 60–61, 227–28

Aboriginal athletes/players, 213–17
    baseball, 214
    basketball, 216
    and elite/professional levels, 216–17
    hockey, 216, 217, 281–82
    rodeo, 214–16
    and rodeo, 135, 139, 141–43
    running, 213–14
    and sport, 17–19
    See also names of individual groups

Aboriginal peoples
    assimilation of, 18, 216

colonial appropriation of
identity, 60
exclusion of, 60
marginalization of, 184-85
as models of masculinity, 227-28
reserves, 60, 200
residential schools, 200, 216
acrobatics, WSA and, 199
Active Living Alliance, 219
Adams, Mary Louise, 97, 246
Afaganis, Ernie, 310
African-Americans. See colour,
people of
aggression
spectatorship and, 281, 289
and sporting culture, 264
See also violence
agricultural exhibitions, 21
Alberta All-Stars, 87
Alberta Amateur Association (AAA),
342-43
Alberta Amateur Baseball
Association, 81
Alberta Amateur Hockey
Association (AAHA), 27, 48,
109, 110, 118, 279
women's council, 113
Alberta Amateur Softball
Association, 80
Alberta Amateur Sports Hall of
Fame, 166
Alberta Associated Football League
(AAFL), 85. See also Alberta
Soccer Association
Alberta Association for the Mentally
Retarded, 219

Alberta Colleges Athletic Conference
(ACAC), 43, 46
Alberta Cricket Association (ACA),
68
Alberta Curling Association, 38,
100, 352
Alberta Female Football League, 255
Alberta Football Association, 85, 87
Alberta Football League, 85-86
Alberta Francophone Games, 207
Alberta Future Leaders program, 18
Alberta Girls' Curling Association,
102
Alberta Golf, 160
Alberta Golf Association (AGA), 157,
160
Alberta Junior Hockey League
(AJHL), 115, 117, 282, 318
Alberta Ladies Golf Association, 160
Alberta Liquor Control Board, 318,
321
Alberta Major Soccer League, 89
Alberta Native Provincial
Championships, 282
Alberta Nordic Juniors, 175
Alberta Northern Lights men's
wheelchair basketball team,
219
Alberta Oilers. See Oilers, Alberta
(later Edmonton Oilers)
Alberta Olympic Game Plan, 146
Alberta Open Swimming and
Diving Championships, 165
"Alberta Pearl," Linder as, 136
Alberta Plaindealer, use of hockey
metaphor for Boer war, 230

Alberta Pork, 322

Alberta Professional Chuckwagon
    and Chariot Association, 135

Alberta Rockies Gay Rodeo
    Association (ARGRA), 237

Alberta Rugby Football Union, 82

Alberta Rugby Union (ARU), 82, 84

Alberta Schools' Athletic
    Association (ASAA), 40

Alberta Senior Hockey League, 116

Alberta Soccer Association, 85,
    89, 90, 259. See also Alberta
    Associated Football League
    (AAFL)

Alberta Sport, Recreation, Parks and
    Wildlife Foundation, 68

Alberta Sport Council, 48, 68, 146

Alberta Sports Hall of Fame and
    Museum, 147, 166, 254, 309,
    313, 314

    Bell Memorial Award, 310

Alberta Stampede Company, 136

Alberta Treasury Branches (ATB),
    124-25, 349

Alberta Wheat Pool, 315

Alberta Wheelchair Sports
    Association, 220

Alberta Winter Games, 1st, 1968, 48

Alberta Women's Major Soccer
    League, 89

Alberta Women's Rugby Union, 85

Albertan
    about own sports pages, 299
    on chuckwagon racing, 270
    on golf, 298
    megaphone sports coverage, 301

school closing montage in, 41*fig.*

sports coverage, 297

and women's sports, 27, 299

alcohol consumption
    and exclusion of women, 320-21
    and promotion, 344
    sponsorship and, 318-21
    at university games, 46
    Ward and, 312

Alexander, Keith, 161

Alfred Blythe Studios Trophy, 71

All Indian Rodeo Cowboys
    Association (AIRCA), 142*fig.*,
    143, 215. See also Indian Rodeo
    Cowboy Association (IRCA)

All-American Girls Professional
    Baseball League, 77-78

Allan Cup, 118, 119, 120, 120*fig.*, 121,
    122, 229, 333, 334, 339, 344, 354

All-Star Wrestling, 277

Alpine Cup, 110, 112

Altman, Jack, 316-17

Amateur Athletic Union of Canada
    (AAUC), 26, 27, 47, 48, 49,
    85, 272. See also Canadian
    Amateur Athletic Union
    (CAAU)

Amateur Speed Skating Association
    of Canada, 167

amateur sports/amateurism
    and behaviour, 48
    broadcasting and, 304, 308
    collective purpose, 49-50
    and cricket, 66
    definition of amateurs, 47
    discourse of, 49

and elite players, 49

employed vs. unemployed
players and, 49

exclusions from competitive
events, 47–48

and exploitation, 282–83

and football, 84, 92

and hockey, 109–10, 118–21

marginalization of, 184–85

in newspapers, 296–97

organization of, 48–49

principles of, 48

professional vs., 49, 177, 343

and rodeo, 135

and soccer, 89–90

sponsorship and, 202, 315–16

sports journalists and, 310

and tennis, 156

university sports and, 45

Amateur Synchronized Swimming
Association of Canada, 166

Amber Valley Giants baseball team,
211–12, 211*fig*.

American Basketball Association,
73, 322

Anderson, Nettie, 146

Anthracite, curling in, 97

Api-Kai-Es. *See* Deerfoot (runner)

Apollo Friends in Sport, 236

Aquabelles (Calgary), 166

arenas
hockey, 105, 115
professionalism of hockey and,
113
See also names of individual arenas

Argonauts, 84

Argyll Velodrome, 152

Armitt, Bob, 145

Army and Navy softball team, 74

Arnison, Mr. (golfer), 157

Arnold, Paddy, 162

Arnold, Thomas, 193–94

Ashmead, Sid, 145

assimilation
of Aboriginal peoples, 216
of First Nations, 18
of immigrants, 39–40
sport and, 207

Athabasca
black settlers in, 211–12
Colored Giants, 212
Kinsmen club, 342

athletics. *See* track and field

Atlanta Flames, 124

Auch, Susan, 169

automobiles, 102, 164, 174, 293, 361

Aviak, 18

Aviators, 88–89

Bad Dried Meat, 213

Bagley, Ray, 264

Bailey, Ace, 280

Bailey, Elizabeth, 35

Bailey, Harvey, 210

Baldwin, Matt, 103, 307

Banff
basketball in, 285
curling in, 97
golf in, 160, 161
hockey in, 110
Indian Days, 141, 215, 337
Ladies Golf Club, 161

Ski Club, 172

skiing in, 172-73, 173-74, 268

Spark Plugs basketball team, 285

speed skating in, 167

swimming in, 164

Winter Carnival, 110, 111*fig.*, 112,
164, 172, 251, 336-37

Banff Springs Hotel

golf at, 160, 161

winter opening and activities,
173

Bannerman, Sheila, 233

Bar Tenders (Calgary baseball team),
74

Bar U Ranche team (polo), 64-65

Barbers (Calgary baseball team), 74

Barnett, Ethel, 42, 146

Barthes, Roland, 274-75

baseball, 74-81, 283-85

African-Americans in, 210-13

amateur/minor as thriving, 81

American players, 78, 79

boosterism and, 337-38

CBAA and, 317-18

cricket compared to, 67

Depression and, 76-77

domination of men's game, 75

first annual Lacombe Lions
tournament, 331-32

gambling and, 65, 287

imported players, 316-17

injuries, 266, 284

integration of, 213

masculinity and, 226

in newspapers, 295, 296, 297

professional, 80-81, 178-79

promotion of, 345-47

soccer vs., 87

and social integration, 207-08

as spectator sport, 67

spectators, 283-84

sponsorship, 315

television and, 305

violence in, 283, 284-85

women and, 77-78

as working class sport, 67

See also softball

Baseball Alberta, 81

basketball, 68-73

Aboriginal players, 216

African-American players, 212-13

clothing/dress for, 241-42

"girls' rules" for, 256

history of, 68-69

hockey compared to, 71-72

injuries, 285

leagues, 68

media and, 72

Mormons and, 37, 69

naming of teams, 336

promotion of, 345

in schools, 216

semi-pro, 73

sponsorship of, 70-71, 320-21, 322

travel funds for, 73

University of Alberta, 42

violence in, 263, 285

women and, 42, 70-71, 255-58,
315-16

See also wheelchair basketball

Bassano Boosters (baseball team),
75-76, 337

Bassett, John, 305

Battle of Alberta (Sandor), 128

Battleford Industrial School, 144

"Battles of Alberta," 82, 92, 100, 237,
    339–41

Bay, The. *See* Hudson's Bay Company
    (HBC)

Beattie, John, 120

Beatty, E.W., 67

Beavers (Edmonton hockey team),
    115

Beck, Nicholas D., 341

Beddoes, Dick, 277

Beecher Howe, Catherine, 248

Beers, W. George, 60

behaviour
    amateur sports and, 48
    clothing/dress and, 242, 244–45
    control over, 259
    of cowboys, 233, 234
    masculinities and, 227
    social classes and, 265
    women and, 245

Beiseker
    baseball in, 74
    curling club, 38

Bennett, R.B., 66

Benoit, Chris, 286

Berube, Emile, 80

Best, Lyle, 128–29

Betty Stanhope-Cole Park
    (Edmonton), 162

Bews, Tom, 324

Big Four Inter City League, 78

Big Four league (hockey), 118

Big Six League (baseball), 79

Big Six League (hockey), 280

Birks jewellers, 67

*The Black Bonspiel of Wullie
    MacCrimmon* (Mitchell), 95

black people. *See* colour, people of

Blackfoot (Siksika) people, 20*fig.*, 21,
    144, 213

Blairmore
    on teams as advertisement for
        town, 336
    YCL in, 199

Bleasdell, W.B., 154

Blood people
    Houk and, 314
    and rodeo, 215
    and running, 213

B'nai Brith Lodge (Edmonton),
    curling at, 101

Bodie, Les, 354

bodies, human
    body beautiful movement, 192–93
    bodybuilding, 204–06
    as commodities, 196
    and concept of social body, 192
    and difference, 206–07
    discipline of, 194
    Enlightenment and, 193
    Greeks and, 193
    healthy minds within, 193
    male athletes as ideal, 206
    Nazi regime and, 193
    police, 196
    sexuality and, 204
    size of, 196, 205–06
    social change and perceptions
        of, 204

Boer war, 230

Bohne, Richard, 69

Boomers (Calgary soccer team), 89

boosterism, 334-41, 344, 350

Borden Ladner Gervais Awards, 44

Borden Park cricket team
    (Edmonton), 66

Borgal, Pearl Edmanson, 303

Borst, Cathy, 102

Boston
    Bloomers, 74
    Bruins, 118, 120, 124, 280
    Gardens, 138

Botterill, Tom, 148

Bourbonnais, Roger, 116

Bourdieu, Pierre, 33-34, 185-86, 187

Bow and Arrow Golf games, 296

Bowden, curling in, 99

Bowling, Tim, 126

Bowness Park swimming pool, 164

boxing, 271-73
    Aboriginal youth and, 273
    black people and, 210
    and bodily characteristics, 206
    children and, 225
    injuries, 266
    and masculinity, 226, 271
    muscular Christianity and, 272
    and violence, 271
    YCL and, 199

Bradley, Carman, 165

Braemar Badminton Club, 170

Breaker, Shawn, 282

Brewery Trophy, 317

Brewster, Fern, 161

Brickmen, 88

Brier national curling
    championship, 103, 104, 232,
    307, 322, 326, 334

Bright, Johnny, 91

British Columbia Provincial
    Recreation Programme (Pro-
    Rec), 200

British Empire Games (BEG), 145,
    146, 147

broadcasting, 301-08. *See also* radio;
    television; *and names of*
    individual stations/channels

Bronks (Calgary football team;
    later Stampeders), 91, 177,
    318, 336, 344. *See also* Calgary
    Stampeders

Brookins, Dick, 210-11

Brooks, Medicine Hat and District
    League, 79

Brooks hockey team, 282

Brown, Cliff, 211*fig.*

Brown, Ernest, 149

Brown, J.B., 211*fig.*

Brown, Miss (Edmonton golfer),
    157, 160

Browning, Kurt, 171-72, 238, 246, 327,
    334

Bruised Head, Pete, 214

Brunt, Stephen, 49-50, 264-65, 287,
    308-09

Bucyk, Bill, 116

Bucyk, John, 116, 128

Buddhism, 208

Budweiser, 259-60

Buffalo, Todd, 143

Buffaloes (Calgary basketball team), 315, 317–18, 320–21

Bunn, C.R., 346

Burnham, Harold, 48, 295, 342

Burnham-Frith Electric Company, 48

Burns, Tommy, 271, 272, 344

Burstyn, Valda, 254

    Rites of Men, 265

Bury, Ambrose, 350

businesses/corporations

    and employee sport

        participation, 196–97

    radios in, 304

    spending by, 325–26

    as sponsors, 314–15

    sports programs provided by, 199

    See also sponsorship

Butterwick, Dale, 270

Cahn, Susan, 239

Caledonian Games, 21, 147

Caledonians ("Callies"; Calgary

    soccer team), 86, 89

Caledonians (Calgary football team), 83*fig.*

Calgary

    Active Club, 343

    baseball/softball in, 80, 210, 211, 284–85, 346–47

    basketball in, 70

    bicycle clubs, 148

    black settlers in, 209

    Booster Club, 344

    boxing in, 271–72

    CFRN-TV in, 304–05

Corral, 103

cricket in, 66, 67

curling in, 97, 98, 99–100, 102, 103, 352

cycling in, 149, 152

Deerfoot Trail, 214

Elbow Park, 173

figure skating in, 169, 170, 171

football in, 81, 82, 91, 210, 254–55, 353

Foothills Stadium, 347

gay/lesbian athletes in, 236

Golden Jubilee Pool, 351*fig.*

golf in, 157, 159, 160–61

historical pageant parade, 332–33

hockey in, 107–08, 109, 110, 112, 115, 117, 118, 120–21, 122, 123, 124, 125, 137, 348

judo in, 208

Kiwanis Club, 351*fig.*

lacrosse in, 61–62, 63

National Sport Centre, 146

newspapers in, 294

Olympic Oval, 168

polo in, 65

Premier Cycle and Sports, 253

radio in, 293

Riverside area, 191–92

rugby in, 82, 84

running in, 213–14

skating school, 170

skiing in, 173–74, 174–75

soccer in, 86, 88, 89

softball in, 75

speed skating in, 168–69

Stampede Corral, 171, 345

swimming in, 163–64, 164–65, 351*fig.*

tennis in, 154, 155

Victoria Arena, 352

Winter Olympics, 1988, 23, 104, 122, 347, 357, 357*fig.*, 358, 359

World Ski Jumping Championships, 173

YCL in, 199

YWCA, 26

Calgary 88s, 73

Calgary Amateur Athletic Association, 47

Calgary and District Cricket Association, 67

Calgary Avenue Grills, 112

Calgary Baseball Club, 344

Calgary Blizzard Soccer Club, 89

Calgary Booster Club, 28, 177

Calgary Boxing and Wrestling Commission, 276

Calgary Brewing and Malting Company, 175, 317, 318, 320–21, 325

Calgary Buffalo Athletic Association (CBAA), 317–18, 348

Calgary Citywide Softball League, 75

Calgary Curling Club, 99, 237

Calgary Daily Herald

bicycle advertisements in, 196

on Edmonton newspapers, 294

on hockey, 295

"In the World of Sports," 296

international coverage, 296

on soccer, 85

Calgary Exhibition and Stampede, Indian race, 8*fig.*

Calgary Exhibitions, 288

Board, 343

rodeo in, 135, 137

Calgary Eye Opener, and horse racing, 288

Calgary Fire Brigade hockey team, 278–79

Calgary Golf and Country Club, 157, 159

Calgary Herald

on baseball, 283, 337

broadcasting of games, 301

on cowboys, 233

on curling, 97

football in, 229, 297

on hockey, 126, 278–79

on horse racing, 288

on lacrosse, 61

on Lethbridge baseball game, 337

rodeo in, 309

on skiing clothes, 244

women's sports in, 28, 251

Calgary Indian Industrial School, 83*fig.*

Calgary Lacrosse Club, 61

Calgary Ladies Softball Association, 75

Calgary Lawn Tennis Club, 155

Calgary minor pro Stampeders, 121, 122

Calgary Normal Schools ladies' hockey teams, 40

Calgary North Hill Curling Club, 99–100

Calgary Rugby Football Union, 82

Calgary Saddledome, 326, 353, 355

Calgary Ski Club, 174, 175

Calgary Sports Women Association, 28

Calgary Stampede, 134, 136, 137, 214–15, 232, 233–34, 236, 270, 302, 332, 344

Calgary Sun, rodeo in, 309

Calhoun, D.W., 179

calisthenics, 248

Callies (Calgary soccer team). *See* Caledonians ("Callies"; Calgary soccer team)

Calvert, Miss (cyclist), 149

Cameron, Douglas, 154

Cameron, Michelle, 166

Camp Slim-Teen, 202

Camrose
baseball in, 78, 212
Curling Club, 101, 352–53
curling in, 101, 103
Kinsmen Club, 353
ladies' golf tournament, 161
Maroons, 298
new recreation complex (1967), 101

Camrose Canadian
on baseball game including African-American players, 212
on curling, 102
on horse racing, 288
sporting news in, 298

Canada Bicycle Week, 151

Canada Cup

curling, 102, 103

soccer, 89

Canada West All-Stars, 44

Canada Winter Games, Lethbridge (1975), 167, 174, 357

Canadian Amateur Athletic Union (CAAU), 47
Alberta Branch (AAAU), 47, 48
See also Amateur Athletic Union of Canada (AAUC)

Canadian Amateur Basketball Association (CABA), 69, 315–16

Canadian Amateur Hockey Association (CAHA), 117, 279, 280, 311

Canadian Amateur Swimming Association, 163, 164

Canadian Association for Health, Physical Education and Recreation, 239

Canadian Association for the Advancement of Women and Sport and Physical Activity (CAAWS), 28, 168, 238–39

Canadian Barrel Racing Association, 139

Canadian Centre of Sport Excellence, 360

Canadian Cricket Association, 66

Canadian Curler's Manual, 37, 96

Canadian Curling Association, 104, 232

Canadian Curling Hall of Fame, 312

Canadian Cycling Association, 152, 328

Canadian Figure Skating
    Association (CFSA), 167, 170,
    245. *See also* Skate Canada
Canadian Finals Rodeo, 134, 138,
    221, 325
Canadian Football League (CFL).
    See CFL (Canadian Football
    League)
Canadian Girls' Rodeo Association
    (CGRA), 139, 303, 324. *See also*
    Women's Professional Rodeo
    Association
Canadian Hockey Association, 118
Canadian Horse Racing Hall of
    Fame, 312
Canadian Indian Rodeo Cowboys
    Association (CIRCA), 216
Canadian Interprovincial Cricket
    Championship, 68
Canadian Interuniversity Athletic
    Union (CIAU), 40, 43, 44, 320
Canadian Interuniversity Sport
    (CIS), 44, 128–29
Canadian Ladies Curling
    Association, 102
Canadian Ladies Gold Union
    (CLGU), Alberta Branch, 157,
    159
Canadian Major Indoor Soccer
    League, 89
Canadian National Gay Rodeo
    (CNGR), 237
Canadian National Parks
    Association, 197

Canadian National Railway Tennis
    Club tournament, Calgary,
    154
Canadian Northern Railway, 55
Canadian Olympic Hall of Fame, 122
Canadian Pro Rodeo Association,
    138, 139
Canadian Rugby Football Union,
    82, 84
Canadian Ski Hall of Fame, 177
Canadian Soccer Association, 258
Canadian Soccer League, 88
Canadian Softball Hall of Fame, 80
Canadian Sports Centre, 269
Canadian Stampede Manager's
    Association, 139
Canadian Wheelmen's Association,
    148, 149
Canadian Women's Intercollegiate
    Athletic Union (CWIAU),
    43, 44
Canadian Women's Track and Field
    Championships
    1933, New Westminster, 146
    1947, Edmonton, 147
Canadians (Calgary hockey team),
    115, 333
Canmore
    basketball in, 263
    Bluebirds, 285
    golf course, 162
    hockey in, 110
    Red Wings, 285
    skiing in, 174
Cannons (Calgary baseball team),
    80, 347

Canucks (Calgary rugby football team), 84

Capital City Curling Rink (Edmonton), 342

Capital Tennis Championship, 155

capitalism
masculinity and, 228
rodeo and, 138
and sport, 9
and sports culture, 194

Capitals (Edmonton baseball team), 80

Capitals (Edmonton hockey team), 116. *See also* Oil Kings (Edmonton hockey team)

Carbury, Joe, 309

Cardinals (baseball team), 80

Cardston
basketball in, 69
rodeo in, 138

Carnegie Commission, 45

Carrier, Roch, 106

Carter, Wilf, 136, 325

Carvel, baseball in, 77

Carver, Lindsay, 156

Castor, skiing in, 173

Cavanagh, Richard, 304

CBC (Canadian Broadcasting Corporation), 304-05, 310, 311
and amateur sports, 308
and curling, 104
and rodeo, 309
television coverage, 304, 305, 306

Centennial awards, 45

Central Alberta Baseball League, 76

Central Alberta Garrison Hockey League, 352

Central Alberta Hockey League, 299-300

Central Grads (Calgary Central Collegiate Institute basketball team), 164, 165

CFAC, 301, 311

CFCN, 310, 325

CFL (Canadian Football League), 92, 305-06
Kwong and, 209
sponsorship/funding and, 105
television and, 306

CFRN radio, 303, 310, 312

Chapman, Doris (Neale), 70

Chateau Lake Louise. *See under* Lake Louise

CHCT-TV, 304-05, 311

CHED radio, 311

Cherry, Don, 311

Chicago Blackhawks, 118

Chiddy, Norma, 145, 313

children
and boxing, 225
exercise for, 193
"fat camps" for, 202, 203*fig.*
and fitness, 201
and hockey, 114-15
playgrounds for, 34, 35
and soccer, 90
socialization of, 33-34, 35
and swimming, 162-63
and television, 201
YMCA/YWCA and, 191-92

Children's Aid (Calgary), 192

Chill (Edmonton basketball team; later Edmonton Energy), 73

Chimos (Edmonton women's hockey team), 113, 123

Chinese-Canadians, 209

Chinooks (Calgary lacrosse team), 61–62, 336

Chrétien, Jean, 106

Christiansen, Jim, 116, 121–22, 338

chuckwagon races, 135–36, 138, 270, 346

churches, and sport, 36–38

cinema, 301

citizenship
  physical education and, 45
  sport and, 191

City of Edmonton Track and Field awards, 147

Civil Services Athletic Association, 39

CJCA radio, 303

CJCJ radio, 309

CKUA radio, 303, 312

CKXL radio, 303, 325

Claresholm, curling in, 103

Claresholm Local Press, on civic consciousness, 334, 336

Clark, Mrs. (Calgary golfer), 157, 160

Clarke Stadium, 87, 88, 91, 353

Clarkson, Adrienne, 106

classes, social. See social classes

Claxton's Star Rink, 97

Cleveland Favorite-Knits, 241–42

climate/weather
  and baseball/softball, 76
  and curling, 97, 101

and cycling, 150–51

and hockey, 106

and participation in sports culture, 177

clothing/dress
  basketball, 241–42
  and behaviour, 242, 244–45
  curling, 243, 243fig.
  cycling, 240
  development of specialized, 267
  figure skating, 244fig., 245
  golf, 240
  for gymnasiums, 241
  hockey, 241
  and male athletes, 242
  production methods, 243
  rodeo, 241
  skiing, 240, 244, 251, 252fig.
  and social control, 242
  team uniforms, 242
  textiles/fabrics, 243–44
  women's, 240–42, 243, 244–45

CNR hotels, 314

Coaldley, Jay, 221

Coalspur, tennis in, 154, 154fig.

Cobb, Ty, 226

Cole, Betty Stanhope, 161–62

Cole, Cam, 308–09

Coleman, Jim, 277

collective mobilization/organization
  amateur sport and, 49–50
  and solo sport athletes, 176
  sport and, 6

colonialism
  and appropriation of Aboriginal peoples' identity, 60

and cricket, 66–67

and muscular Christianity, 194

colour, people of, 209–13

Columbus (Calgary hockey team), 118

Comets (Edmonton basketball team), 72, 73

Comets (Raymond), 69

commodities

    hockey players as, 282, 300

    human bodies as, 196

    sport as, 9

Commonwealth Games

    1978 Edmonton, 23, 63, 165–66, 300, 303, 309, 358, 359

    1982, 357

    1986, 166

    1990, 166

    2010, 153

    television and, 306

Commonwealth Stadium (Edmonton), 89, 355

community/-ies

    amateur sports and, 49–50

    boosterism by, 334–41

    competition and pride between, 339–41

    curling and, 104

    hockey and, 105, 118, 125–26

    leagues, 38–39, 169

    mass media and, 307

    parades, 332–34

    professional sport and, 50

    rivalry between neighbouring, 339

    roles of groups/organizations in, 177

    sport as beacon of status, 336

    sport as uniting diversity within, 334, 336

    sports journalists as figures in, 309

    teams embodying spirit of, 332

    teams/players representing, 338–39

    and track and field athletics, 144–45

Condon, Jimmie, 303

Confederation, and national identity, 67

Confederation of North, Central American and Caribbean Association Football, 127–28

Connaught Cup, 86

Continental Basketball Association, 73

Corsan, George H., 162

Corsan, H.H., 162

Cotton, Joe "Dad," 210

country clubs, 170

Coven Women's Rugby Football Club, 85

cowboys, 233–35

Cowboys (Calgary hockey team), 124

Cowboys' Insurance Association, 138

Cowboys Protective Association, 234–35

Cowgirls' Super challenge, 139

CP Hotels Golf Week, 296

CPR, 81, 174

INDEX

Cracker-Cats (Edmonton baseball
team), 80, 284-85
Craig, Leon, 264
Cranshaw, Caitlin, 239
Crazy Canucks (Canadian skiing
team), 176
Crescents (Calgary women's hockey
team), 110, 112
Crestwood Community League, 39,
101
Crestwood Curling Club, 103
cricket, 65-68
baseball compared to, 67
British imperialism and, 66-67
compared to gambling sports, 65
elite connotations, 66-67
in Medicine Hat, 19
in newspapers, 297
playing grounds, 67
social classes and, 65
Crowfoot, 213
Crystal Rink (Calgary), 344
Crystals (Calgary hockey team), 115
CTV, 305
Cubs (Edmonton basketball team),
72
cultural capital, 33
defined, 185-86
hockey and, 106
sports journalists and, 327
cultural identity, sport as, 5-13
culture, sport and traditional, 216
curling, 95-105
advantages of participation, 96
artificial ice and, 352-53

bonspiels, 37, 38, 98, 99, 100, 103,
232, 237, 341, 350-51, 352
brooms, 231-32
"carspiels," 102-03
churches and, 37-38
climate/weather and, 97, 101
clothing/dress for, 243, 243fig.
as collective celebration, 104
and community life, 104
corporate sponsorship, 102-03
facilities, 350-53
history of, 96-97
hockey vs., 96, 104, 352
ice and, 97, 98
international interest in, 103-04
Jewish people and, 39
liquor and, 232
masculinity and, 231-32
media coverage, 312
military association with, 97
mixed gender teams, 98-99, 102
in newspapers, 297, 299
promotion of, 345
public funding for, 341
and public profiles as serious
athletes, 103
rinks, 39, 100, 101
smoking during, 232
social aspects, 38
spectatorship of, 307
sponsorship of, 105, 322
television and, 307
women and, 98-100, 99fig., 101-
02, 231, 243fig.
youth and, 104-05

curling clubs
   Beiseker, 38
   chaplains for, 37
Currie, Frank, 170
Currie, Olga (Ollie), 167
Currie, Peggy, 170
Currie, Sonja, 170
cycling, 148–53
   and access to golf clubs, 157
   and access to other sporting
      events, 150–51
   clothes for, 240
   clubs for, 61, 148–49, 152, 341–42
   and commuting, 150
   and democracy, 151
   drugs in, 286
   elite and, 148, 149
   history of, 148–49
   machine development and, 149,
      267
   as mode of transport, 150–51
   profile of, 148
   races, 151–52
   recreational, 151
   safety bicycles and, 149–50
   ten-speed models and, 152
   and transport to country roads,
      151
   velodromes, 152
   women and, 149, 150, 152–53, 240,
      327–28

Daines, Cheryl, 270
Daines, Duane, 270
Dallaire, Christine, 207
Dallas Cowboys, 88
Dan, Etta, 73

Danysk, Cecilia, 229
Davis, Violet, 70, 111*fig.*, 251
Davis Cup, 154
Dawes, Charlotte, 146, 313
de Jong, Gerry, 152
Decôteau, Alex Wuttunee, 144
Deerfoot (runner), 144, 213–14, 287
Deerfoot Classic Relay race, 214
democracy
   cycling and, 151
   recreation and, 192
   sport and, 30
   team sports and, 35
demographics
   and sports culture, 179
   See also population
Dempsey, Hugh, 81
Depression, 23, 49
   baseball and, 76–77
   and curling, 101
   and mobility, 293
   physical education during, 200
   and polo, 65
   relief and physical health, 197
   rodeo during, 137
   sports in newspapers during, 297
   and swimming, 164
   and women's involvement in
      sport, 251
   YMCA and, 198
Derrick club (Edmonton), 170
Detroit Cougars, 118
Detroit Red Wings, 121
   farm team, 116–17
Dewar, John, 213

Diamond Park (Edmonton), 37, 75,
    76, 110, 296, 297*fig. See also*
    Renfrew Park (Edmonton)
Diefenbaker, John, 91
Dinos (University of Calgary), 128-29
Dirt Girls (women's cycling), 152
disabled athletes, 184-85, 218-21
distances, and participation in
    sports culture, 177
diving, 163, 164
Dodgers (Calgary baseball team), 210
Doll, L.H., 148
Dominion Basketball Association,
    285
Dominion Curling Association, 100
Dominion Interprovincial Cricket
    Tournament, 68
Dominion Soccer Association, 258
Dominion Women's Amateur
    Hockey Association, 112
Dominions (hockey team), 118, 279
Donaldson, Gail, 170
Donnelly, Peter, 221
Dragon Cups, 88
Drake, Clare, 44-45
Drillers (Calgary basketball team),
    73, 322
Drillers (Edmonton soccer team),
    88, 347
drugs, 286-87
Drumheller
    Athletics (baseball team), 75
    baseball in, 75
    Board of Trade, 336
    coal mine operators'
        sponsorship, 197

creation of dedicated sports field
    in, 7
curling in, 352
hockey in, 122
Miners, 118, 122, 320
skating rink, 342
softball in, 77
WSA in, 200
YCL in, 199
Dryden, Ken, 106, 179
Ducey, Brant, 76
Ducey, John, 78, 200, 284, 312, 326, 345
Dunning, Eric, 6

Eagle Toddies (softball team), 74
Eaton's
    and softball, 75
    and women's curling
        championships, 101-02
economic capital, 33, 186
economics
    obstacles to participation in
        sport, 187-88
    and sport, 23-24
Edgerton curling rink, 351
Edinburgh, Duke of, 346
Edinburgh Cup, 122
Edmonton
    arenas, 354-56
    baseball/softball in, 75, 76, 77, 78,
        80, 200, 214, 284-85, 345
    basketball in, 69, 70, 71, 345
    bicycle clubs in, 61, 341-42
    black settlers in, 209
    Boyle Street Park, 71, 74, 75, 78*fig.*
    Canadian Finals Rodeo in, 138

Central Community League
   basketball team, 69
CFRN-TV in, 305
as "city of champions," 332
Coliseum, 171, 354-55
Commonwealth Games in, 23, 63,
   357, 358, 359
community leagues, 38-39
cricket in, 65-66, 67-68
curling in, 97, 98, 100, 101, 102,
   103, 341, 352
cycling in, 148, 149, 150-52, 150fig.
Elks Club, 343
facilities in, 350
figure skating in, 170, 171
football in, 82, 90, 91-92, 255, 345,
   353, 354
golf in, 157, 158fig., 159-60, 161-62
hockey in, 108-10, 112, 113-14,
   115-17, 118, 119-21, 123, 124-25,
   126, 278, 279, 345, 348-49, 354-
   55
hockey/football dynasties of
   1970s/1980s, 24
judo in, 208
lacrosse in, 61, 63
leisure activity in, 15
McDougall Commercial High
   School, 71
newspapers in, 294
omniplex, 354
population, 23
Rodeo of Champions, 138
rugby in, 82, 84
skiing in, 173, 174-75
soccer in, 86-88, 88-89

softball in, 74-75
speed skating in, 167-68
Stampede Rodeo, 137
swimming in, 162, 163, 164, 165
TELUS Field, 361
tennis in, 155, 156
Thanksgiving Day sports meet,
   1941, 230-31
track and field in, 354
Winter Carnival, 175
YCL in, 199
Edmonton Amateur Athletic
   Association, 345
Edmonton and District Cricket
   League, 67
Edmonton Aquadettes Synchronized
   Swimming Club, 166
Edmonton Athletic Club, 115-16,
   333-34
Edmonton Baseball Association, 75
Edmonton Bulletin
   on baseball, 295
   on benefit game at Thistle Rink,
      295
   and boosterism, 337
   on curling, 97
   on cycling, 150-51
   Goldstick and, 310
   on hockey, 278, 279
   international coverage, 296
   overfatness pills advertised in,
      196
   promotion of sports, 294
   sports section, 294
   on tennis, 155
Edmonton Capital, on AAAU, 47

Edmonton Commercial Graduates.
   See Edmonton Grads

Edmonton Country Club, 159, 342

Edmonton Cricket Club, 66, 68

Edmonton Curling Club, 38, 97

Edmonton Dominion Furriers club,
   118, 119

Edmonton Eskimos, 301, 339
   White's various clubs all named,
     345
   See also Eskimos (Edmonton
     baseball team); Eskimos
     (Edmonton football team);
     Eskimos (Edmonton hockey
     team)

Edmonton Exhibition, 346
   Association (EEA), 116, 121, 138,
     288, 324–25
   grandstand, 350
   Livestock Pavilion, 354
   races at, 144

Edmonton Federation of
     Community Leagues (EFCL),
     38–39

Edmonton Figure Skating Club
     (EFSC), 170

Edmonton Gardens, 118, 119, 170,
     326, 354

Edmonton Girls' Curling
     Association, 102

Edmonton Hardware Company, 149

Edmonton Journal
   on college sport, 340
   on cycling, 148
   depictions of women, 251
   on girls' softball, 77
   on golf, 350
   and hockey, 116, 300
   horse racing in, 312
   Learn to Swim events, 163
   on masculinity and figure
     skating, 245–46
   on men's vs. women's sports,
     127–28
   on muscular Christianity, 36
   rodeo in, 309
   scoreboard on building, 302*fig.*
   on top ten historical events in
     sport, 183
   on women's basketball, 42
   women's sports in, 27

Edmonton Junior Hockey League,
   121

Edmonton Kinsmen, 177

Edmonton Ladies Hockey Team,
   108–09

Edmonton Minor Soccer
     Association, 89

Edmonton Never Sweats (baseball
     team), 74

Edmonton Parks and Recreation,
     and cricket, 68

Edmonton Pavilion, 109

Edmonton Ringette Club, 113

Edmonton Rodeo of Champions, 325

Edmonton Rugby Football Club,
   82, 84

Edmonton Senior Girls Baseball
     League, 74

Edmonton Ski Club, 175

Edmonton Sports Hall of Fame, 168

Edmonton Sun, rodeo in, 309

Edmonton Tennis and Bowling
Company, 342

education. *See* schools/education

Edward, Prince of Wales, 76

Edwards, Alonzo, 211*fig.*

Edwards, Booker, 211*fig.*

Edwards, Kenny, 211*fig.*

Egbert William, 159–60, 338

Eisenhardt, Jan, 200

Eisler, Laurie, 245

elite (social class)
and cycling, 148, 149
golf and, 159
sporting interests, 185–87

elite sports
Aboriginal players and, 216–17
amateur sports and, 49
athletes as role models in, 266
campaign for production of
· performance, 260
cricket as, 66–67
curling as, 232
drug use in, 286
health/aesthetic training vs., 202
hockey as, 106, 113, 129
public policy and, 269
recreational vs., 47

Elizabeth II, Queen, 175, 346

Elks Club, 342, 343

Embry, Jessie, 69

employers. *See* businesses/
corporations

Empress, curling in, 103

Energy (Edmonton basketball team;
formerly Edmonton Chill), 73

environmentalism, 34–35

Erickson, Dwayne, 309

Ermineskin band, 139, 216

Escoe, Vern, 210

Eskimo Girls (baseball team), 74

Eskimo Girls (basketball team), 70, 71

Eskimo Ski Club (ESC), 175

Eskimos (Edmonton baseball team),
79, 80, 284, 338

Eskimos (Edmonton football team),
23, 86, 88, 90, 91–92, 275–76, 312,
316, 317, 343

Eskimos (Edmonton hockey team),
109–10, 116, 118, 119, 123, 279–
80, 311, 359

Eskimos (Edmonton rugby football
team), 84, 353

Esquimaux (Edmonton rugby team),
82

Eustace, Marjorie Collinge, 28, 156

Evans, Simon, 63

The Fabulous Flyers (Vantour), 128

facilities, 349–56
boosterism and, 350
and competition success, 353
electricity for, 352, 353
entrenchment as healthy
recreation, 350
floodlights, 353
and juvenile delinquency, 192
for male vs. female sport, 44
modern vs. old-fashioned, 361
as practice/game spaces, 350–51
public funds for, 356
"retro" venues, 361
for special events, 357–59

and substantiality of place of
sport in local life, 349–50
use/control of public spaces and,
7
fairgrounds, 21
FC Edmonton, 89
Federation Figure Skating Club, 170
Fédération Internationale de
Football Association (FIFA),
89, 258–59
femininity
competitiveness and, 257
and figure skating clothing, 245
and Grads basketball team,
256–58
and women's involvement in
sport, 251, 254
YWCA advertising regarding
women, 253–54
Ferbey, Randy, 104, 307, 334
Ferguson, Emily, 248–49
Ferguson, Scott, 282
Fernie Swastikas, 110
films, 302
Fire Department (Calgary baseball
team), 74
First Nations. See Aboriginal peoples
First Nations Hockey Association,
281
First Presbyterian Church, Victoria
Girls Hockey Team, 37
Fisher, Donald, 59–60
fitness
of children, 201
declining levels of, 260
physical education and, 202

promotion of, 197
and social capital, 201
and social integration, 207
and social/financial success, 196
of soldiers, 201
and wars, 230
women and, 28, 248
Fitness and Amateur Sport Act, 201
Flames (Calgary hockey team), 124,
125, 209, 282, 311, 339, 347–48,
359
Fleming, Don "Buckets," 312
Fleming, Pat, 28, 29fig.
Flyers (Edmonton hockey team), 116,
118, 119–20, 121, 170, 311, 312,
333, 338, 339, 354
foot racing. See running
football, 81–92, 83fig.
amateur, 92
American players, 92
association (see soccer)
as business, 92
Canadian, 81
contests between eastern vs.
western teams, 90
facilities, 353–54
gay/lesbian athletes in, 238
history of, 81
injuries, 266
leagues, 91
minor, 92
in newspapers, 295, 297
professional, 92
promotion of, 345
protective gear, 267
television and, 305

and wars, 229

women and, 254-55

See also Grey Cup; rugby

Football Alberta, 92

Foothills Stadium, 347

Foothills-Wheatbelt League, 79

Foran, Maxwell, 137, 332

Foran-Woodward, Gail, 156

Foran-Woodward, Shannon, 156

Ford, Johnny, 284

Forestburg, artificial ice in, 352-53

Forsyth, Janice, 18

Fort Edmonton

cricket in, 66

football in, 81

Fort Macleod

curling in, 97

golf club, 160

Midnight Rodeo, 214

newspapers in, 294

polo in, 63-64, 228*fig.*

sport in, 19

Fort McMurray, rugby in, 84

Fort Saskatchewan

black settlers in, 209

cricket in, 66

Fortna, Peter, 279

forts, sport at, 19

Fortune, Rev., 37

Fox, Stephen, 216

Francis, Emile, 284

francophones, 207

Francophonie jeunesse de l'Alberta
(FJA), 207

Fritz Sick Memorial Arena, 320

Fullerton, Romayne, 184-85

funding

high levels of, 362-63

public, 356, 358, 359

and spectatorship, 347

See also sponsorship

Fur Trappers (basketball team), 70

Furniss, Elizabeth, 141

The Futurist Manifesto, 286

Fyfe, Ken, 267-68

Gadoury, Shelley Berube, 80

Gainers Superiors, 87, 120, 315

Galusha, Cathy, 162

gambling, 287-89

and baseball, 287

and cricket, 65

on Grey Cup outcome, 341

and hockey, 109, 287-88

on horse racing, 287, 288-89

and rise of spectator sports, 143

and risk-taking, 267

video lottery terminals (VLTS),
288-89

The Game of Our Lives, 311

Gateway

on Alberta college sport, 340

on funding of sport, 362-63

on role of sports in university,
45-46

on soccer, 86

on university sport, 44

Gay and Lesbian International Sport
Association (GLISA), 236

Gay Games, 236

gay/lesbian athletes

in curling, 237

events, 236
  in football, 238
  in hockey, 238
  marginalization of, 238
  and Olympic Games, 239
  provincial government and
    rights of, 236
  in rodeo, 237
  in skating, 238
  sponsorship of, 238
Geary, Benny, 210
Gee Bong Polo Club, 64
gender
  equality, 43-44
  figure skating and, 245
  and halls of fame, 313-14
  identity in sport, 246-47
  wild vs. domesticated identity,
    259-60
  See also masculinity; women
Gervais, Hector (Hec), 103
Getty, Don, 23
Gibb, Alexandrine, 71, 299
Gibson, Helen Beny, 42
Gibson, Hoot, 323*fig.*
Gibson Girls, 70
Gideon, Russ, 210
Gideon family, 210
Gillespie, Beatrice, 146
Gillespie, Vera, 70
Gilmour, Ira, 323*fig.*
girls
  and curling, 102
  and hockey, 113, 114, 126-27
Girls' City League (Edmonton), 69, 70

Girls' Rodeo Association. *See*
    Canadian Girls' Rodeo
    Association (CGRA);
    Women's Professional Rodeo
    Association
Gladstone, Fred, 324
Gladstone, Jim, 215-16
Gladue, Gary, 282
Glass, Ron, 346
Glencoe Club, 101, 170, 171, 244*fig.*,
    245, 352
Glenora Skating and Tennis Club,
    170. *See also* Royal Glenora
    Club
Global World Series, 79, 338
Globe and Mail, focus on professional
    sports, 184
Golden Bears (University of Alberta
    hockey team), 44-45, 88, 117,
    155, 353
Golden Jubilee (1955), 164, 350
Goldstick, Cecil (Tiger), 310
Goldstick Park, 310
golf, 157-62, 158*fig.*
  clothing, 157, 161, 240
  clubs, 157, 159
  elite and, 159
  equipment, 159
  facilities, 350
  in newspapers, 295, 297
  television and, 306
  transport for access to, 157
  women and, 157, 159, 160, 161-62
Goodstriker, Rufus, 216
Goodwin, Alexander Hopper, 341
Gorrie, Jim, 99

Grad-Comets, 73

Gradettes, 72

Grads (Edmonton basketball team), 23, 42, 70, 71–73, 165, 231, 241–42, 255–58, 299, 310, 315–16, 322, 332, 345, 353

Grads Park, 353

Graham, James, 315

Graham, Jimmy, 86–87

Granato, Cammi, 128

Grande Prairie

    Kinsmen club, 342

    skating rink, 342

    skiing in, 173

    softball in, 322

    Stampede, 323fig.

Grandi, Thomas, 176

Granite Club (Edmonton), 352

Granum

    baseball in, 79, 284, 317

    Elks Club, 342

    hockey team, 342–43

    White Sox, 79

Great West Garment Company (GWG), 234–35, 323–24, 325

Greaves, Wilf, 309–10

Gretzky, Wayne, 124, 141, 327, 348–49

Grey Cup, 23, 72, 84, 90, 91, 92, 304, 305–06, 321, 340, 343

Gruneau, Richard, 307, 359

Gulf Western oil company, 315

GutsMuths, Johann, 193

gymkhanas, 135

gymnasiums

    clothing for, 241

University of Alberta in Calgary, 205fig.

gymnastics

    history/regimes of, 193

    women and, 248

    WSA and, 199

Gzowski, Peter, 311

Hague, C.W., 160

Hall, Bryan, 311.

Hall, Glenn, 128

Hall, Rosemary, 245

halls of fame, 30, 312–14. See also names of individual halls of fame

Hamilton Tigers, 356

Hand Hills Lake Stampede, 136

Hanna

    golf club, 161

    organized sports in, 20

    rodeo, 235fig.

Haraway, Donna, 286

Hardy, W.H., 44

Hardy Cup, 44

Harmon, Mrs. Byron, 161

Harper, Doug, 210

Harrigan, Patrick, 42, 43, 44

Harris, Tom, 309–10

Harrison, John Harley, 341

Hart, Bret "Hitman," 276

Hart, Owen, 276

Hart, Stu, 275–76, 311

Hart family, 286

Hawaiian players, 213

Hawrelak, William, 355

Hay Lakes curling club, 353

Heil, Jenn, 175

Heine, Michael, 239, 358

Heisler, Pat, 162

Henderson Lake Golf Club, 295

Henry House Flats, rodeo at, 137

Heritage Classic games, 128, 361

Hess, Robert, 150–51

Hi Grads, 90

High River

    Blackfoot (Siksika) people at

        races, 20*fig.*

    horse racing at, 21

    lacrosse in, 61, 63

    polo in, 64

high schools

    basketball in, 73

    curling in, 104

    football in, 92

    hockey in, 110

    sport in, 40

    sports injuries in, 266

Highland Games, 147

Highlands Golf Course (Edmonton),

    161, 162, 175, 350

Highlands Lawn Tennis Tourney

    (Edmonton), 155

Hinton, Horace, 211*fig.*

Hitmen (Calgary hockey team), 282

Hobbema

    baseball in, 214

    lacrosse in, 18

    Northern Alberta Native

        Cowboys Association, 216

    Panee Memorial Agriplex, 139,

        143, 216

    Rattlesnake from, 214

    rodeo in, 139, 143

Hoberman, John, 286

hockey, 278–83

    Aboriginal players, 216, 217, 281–

        82

    advertisers and, 304

    arenas, 105, 115

    audience riots, 117

    basketball compared to, 71–72

    body contact in, 279–80

    books on, 128

    as business, 125, 348–49

    CBAA and, 317–18

    children and, 114–15

    climate/weather and, 97

    clothing/dress for, 241

    and collective identity, 106

    commodification of players, 282,

        300

    and community, 105, 118, 125–26

    in culture, 106

    curling vs., 96, 104, 352

    domination of media coverage,

        107

    elite and, 106, 113, 129

    equipment, 114*fig.*, 115, 128

    facilities, 353, 354–56, 359

    fighting in, 117, 280

    figure skating compared to, 246

    finances, 116–17, 124–25

    gambling on, 109, 287–88

    gay/lesbian athletes in, 238

    girls and, 126–27

    helmets/faceguards, 267, 280–81

    Heritage Classic, 361

    in high schools, 110

    history of, 106–08

importance in Alberta, 129

injuries, 266, 279, 280

intercollegiate, 117-18, 129

junior, 115-16, 117-18, 282

lacrosse and, 61, 62

leagues, 113-14, 117, 123

loosening of hold on
　imagination, 179

lottery for, 125

masculinity and, 226, 228-29

mass media and, 300

media and, 119, 125

minor, 123, 128, 282-83

mixed gender teams, 113

muscular Christianity and, 278

mythology of, 139, 141

in newspapers, 295, 297, 298-99,
　299-300

as northern hemisphere game,
　179

in Olympic Games, 122

ownership and, 282

players' education, 282

pond, 128-29

populism of, 106

post-game riots, 289

professionalism in, 49, 113, 117,
　121

promotion of, 345

racism and, 281

radio and, 115, 291

recreational, 113-14

recruitment within, 114-15

in residential schools, 216

rinks, 109, 350

rodeo and, 137

salaries, 124

senior amateur, 118-21

skating vs., 169

small-market teams leaving
　Canada, 124

soccer compared to, 90

sponsorship, 315, 318-20

television and, 115, 117, 306

violence in, 278, 279

and wars, 229-30, 231

winter and, 106

women and, 40, 42, 108-09, 110,
　112-13, 117-18, 123, 126-27, 129,
　247, 351-52

youth involvement in, 115, 126

See also Stanley Cup

Hockey Alberta Foundation, 128

Hockey Day in Canada, 311

Hockey Hall of Fame, 128, 345

Hockey Night in Canada, 121, 305, 311,
　315

Hollies (Calgary women's hockey
　team), 112

horse racing

　early origins of, 135

　gambling on, 288-89

　helmets, 267

　at High River, 21

　Japanese-Canadians and, 209

　in newspapers, 312

Horse Show Building (Calgary),
　344. See also Victoria Park
　(Calgary)

Horton, Marc, 80

Houk, George, 314

Houk's Savages, 314

Howell, Colin, 186, 226

Hudson's Bay Company (HBC)

    Athletic Grounds, 70

    and basketball, 70

    and curling, 21

    and Fur Trappers, 70

    and golf, 21, 157, 160

    and roots of sport, 19

    and softball, 74

Hughes, George, 115

Hunter, Bill ("Wild Bill"), 117, 282, 345

Hunter, Gorde, 321

Hunter, Jim, 176

Hyatt, Edith, 146

Hyatt, Kathleen, 146

Hyndman, Jerry, 33

ice

    artificial, 97, 100, 352-53

    and curling, 97-98

    See also rinks

Ice Breaker tournament, 237

Ice Capades, 170

IMG, 328

immigrants

    assimilation of, 39-40

    and cricket, 68

    Eastern European, 22

    importation of home-country

        sports, 198-99, 207

    Irish, 21

    numbers of, 179

    and rugby, 84

    Scottish, 21

    and soccer, 87, 207

    YMCAS and, 197-98

Imperial Motors, 315

Imperial Oil, 315

imperialism. *See* colonialism

Imperials (Edmonton baseball

    team), 75

imported players, 308, 316-17, 343

Inamasu, Kemo, 208-09

Indian Days. *See under* Banff

Indian Head Rockets (baseball

    team), 212

Indian National Finals Rodeo, 215-16

Indian Rodeo Cowboy Association

    (IRCA), 143, 215. *See also* All

        Indian Rodeo Cowboys

        Association (AIRCA)

Indigenous Sport Council Alberta, 18

injuries

    baseball, 266, 284

    basketball, 285

    boxing, 266

    football, 266

    hockey, 266, 279, 280

    rodeo, 266, 269-70

    rugby, 266-67

    and sporting culture, 265

    in youth sports, 266

Innes, Tom, 357*fig.*

Inter-Allied Sports Council, 77

intercollegiate sport

    budget for, 46

    development of, 40, 42

    football, 86

    hockey as, 117-18

    intramural sports vs., 46

    women in, 42, 43-44

International Amateur Ice Hockey Federation, 122

International Association of Athletics Federation (IAAF)
Edmonton hosts championships, 147
World Athletics Championship, Edmonton, 2001, 326, 357

International Basketball Association, 73

International Olympic Committee, 172

International Paralympic Committee, 218

International Skating Union (ISU), 167, 171-72

International Women's Professional Softball League, 80

Internet, 307

Interprovincial Cricket Tournament, 66

Irish Athletic Club, 144

Ivory, Buster, 324-25

Jamerson, Leon, 135

James, Angela, 128

Jamieson, Hazel, 102

Japanese-Canadians, 79, 208-09

Jasper
baseball in, 315
golf courses, 160
rodeo in, 137
skiing in, 174

Jasper Park Lodge golf course, 160

Jasper Place
hockey in, 112

Rustlers, 112

J.B. Cross slalom trophy, 174-75

Jewish Hustlers, 208

Jewish people
and baseball, 208
and curling, 39, 101
sports clubs and, 39

Jimmie's Sportlight Review, 303

John A. McDougall Commercial High School, 71

John Ducey Park (Edmonton), 326

Johnson, Ben, 166

Johnson, Dot, 256fig.

Johnson, Gus, 172

Johnson, Jack, 271

Jones, Jesse, 145-46

Jones, Terry, 310, 311, 354

Jones, Tristan, 312

Jones Konihowski, Diane, 146, 328

journalists, sports, 308-14
as community figures, 309
and cultural capital, 327
identification with particular sports/players, 309, 311-12
and minor/amateur sports, 310
as part of story, 309-10

Joyce, Thomas, 259

judo, 208

Judo Alberta, 208

juvenile delinquency, 192

Juventus (Calgary cycling club), 152

Juventus (Edmonton cycling club), 152, 153

Juventus Sports Club (Calgary), 152

Kaasa, Walter, 169

Kain, Conrad, 172

Kainai Chiefs, 281

Kainai News, cartoon of urban
Indian, 233*fig.*

Kainai reserve, and rodeo, 143

Kariya, Paul, 208

Katsuta, Yoshio, 208

Katz, Daryl, 80, 125, 349, 356

Katz Group of Companies, 355, 356

Keating, Raymond, 359

Keats, "Duke," 118, 123

Kent, Harry, 272

Keyano club (Edmonton), 165. *See
also* South Side Swim Club
(Edmonton)

Keys, Hector, 103

Keys, Jack, 103

Keys, Stan, 103

Kickers (Calgary football team), 89

Kidd, Bruce, 27, 30, 36, 313

Killam Memorial Arena, 192

Kinasewich, Ray, 116, 280

Kiniski, Gene, 276–77

Kinsmen clubs
Athabasca, 342
Camrose, 353
Edmonton, 90, 177, 342
Field House, Edmonton, 354
Grande Prairie, 342

Kirkpatrick, George R.F., 341

Kirwin, Bill, 178

Kiwanis Club, 164

Klein, Ralph, 125, 204, 288, 338

Kmet, Irene, *Useful Pleasures,* 136

Knight, Pete, 136

Knight, Ted, 309, 333

Konihowski, Diane Jones. *See* Jones
Konihowski, Diane

Kossuth, Robert, 112

Kroetsch, Robert, *The Studhorse Man,*
291

Kwong, Norman (Normie) L., 23, 91,
192, 209, 344

Labatt, 320

Lacombe
baseball in, 78, 79, 212, 331–32
Board of Trade, 336
hockey in, 122, 278, 287–88
Lions Baseball Tournament, 331
Rockets, 122

lacrosse, 59–63
Aboriginal peoples and, 60–61,
227–28
Alberta League, 61–63
box, 62
clubs, 59
duality of, 59–60
financial issues, 63
history of, 17
hockey and, 61, 62
junior league, 62–63
lack of promotion, 63
as national game, 59
in newspapers, 297
television and, 306
violence in, 263

Ladies Hockey Club, 27

Ladue, Flores, 249

LaForge, Patrick, 349

Lake Louise
Chateau, 163*fig.,* 173

skiing at, 174, 269

Lake Saskatoon sports, 292*fig.*

Lalonde report, 202

LaMarsh, Judy, 28

Lamoureux, Danny, 105

Lansdell, Cam, 324

Larue and Picard, 342

Lassie (women's curling award), 322

Laval University students, 134

Lay, Mrs. J.M., 159

Le May Doan, Catriona, 168-69, 327

leagues
    baseball/softball, 75, 76, 77-78
    basketball, 68
    development of, 21-22
    football, 91
    formation of professional, 49
    hockey, 113-14, 117, 123
    soccer, 85
    and violence, 265

LeClerc, Leo, 242, 282

Lee, Gayle, 102

Lee, John B., "The Trade that Shook
    the Hockey World," 348

Lee-Gartner, Kerrin, 176

Lees, Ethel, 102

Legislators (Edmonton baseball
    club), 345

lesbianism, 219, 327-28

Lethbridge
    Alberta Dusters basketball team,
      73, 322
    Amateur Boxing Association
      (LABA), 272-73
    baseball/softball in, 74, 75, 78, 79,
      80, 283, 314, 337, 345-46

basketball in, 70, 322, 336

boxing in, 272-73

Broncos, 117

Canada Winter Games in, 167,
    174, 357

Chinook Cycle Club, 149

Commercial Basketball League,
    315

Country Club, 157, 295

cricket in, 66

curling in, 96-97, 98, 243*fig.*

cycling in, 148, 149

football in, 81, 255

Fritz Sick Memorial Arena, 320

golf in, 157, 160, 295

Green Acres basketball team, 336

hockey in, 97, 117, 121, 122, 318-20

Hurricanes, 282

IRCA and, 215

Jamboree tennis club, 154

judo in, 208

Kyodokan Judo Club, 208

lacrosse in, 61

Maple Leafs hockey team, 121,
    122, 298-99, 317, 318-20, 319*fig.*

Miners, 336

Mounties, 79

Municipal Golf Club, 157, 295

Native Sons, 122, 318, 320

new sports centre (1949), 353

Nisseis baseball team, 79

rodeo in, 143

rugby in, 84

soccer in, 86, 87

softball in, 24, 25*fig.*

Sportsplex, 357

Supinas, 86

tennis in, 154

Three Persons at fair in, 214

White Sox, 346

YCL in, 199

Lethbridge Herald

on hockey, 298-99, 317

international coverage, 296

on Wesley and baseball, 345-46

Lethbridge News

on baseball, 74

on hockey, 278

Lieberman, Moe, 343

Lilley, Mrs., 169-70

Linder, Herman, 136, 138, 324

Lionel Conacher Award, 171

Lipscombe, Nathaniel, 210

Lipscombe, Ozzie, 211*fig.*

Lipscombe, Richard, 210

Lisogar Stampede Shows, 324

Little Plume (runner), 144

Littlechild, J. Wilton, 217

Lloyminster

baseball in, 200

Border Kings, 122

hockey in, 122

Locke, Bobby, 160

Lorenz, Stacy, 242, 287

Los Angeles Kings, 124

Lou Marsh Award, 166, 168-69

Lougheed, Peter, 23, 91, 174, 316

Louis Bull band, 18

Lount, Mayor (Beiseker), 38

Lucht, Gary, 283

Ludtke, Frank, 152

Lukowich, Ed, 103, 104

Luscar Indians, 156

Luxton, Eleanor, 161, 337

Lyle, Mack W., 339

MacCabe, Margaret, 264

Macdonald, Catherine, 71

MacDonald, Noel, 72, 73, 258

Macdonald Tobacco, 97, 102, 232, 322

MacGregor, Bruce, 242

MacGregor, Roy, 106, 308-09

Mackay, Don, 92, 309, 340, 340*fig.*,
351*fig.*

Mackay Trophy, 157, 160

MacKenzie, Shelby, 102

MacLean, Ron, 311

Maclean's magazine, 343

Macleod Gazette, on polo, 63-64

Macrae, Kate, 70, 257

MacRae, Rev. Dr., 37-38, 85

Mac's World Invitational A A A
Midget Hockey Tournament,
128

MacTavish, Craig, 281

Magnussen, Karen, 254

Magrath

baseball in, 79

basketball in, 69

Maguire, Art, 316

mail-order catalogues, 300

Makepeace, Jack, 303

Manahan, Cliff, 103

Mandel, Stephen, 355-56

Mandeville, Harold, 323

Manitoba Free Press, on football, 90

Manitoba-Dakota League, 78

Manley, Elizabeth, 254

Manson, Jack, 121

Maple Leaf Football Club (Calgary soccer), 85

Maple Leafs (Edmonton hockey team; later Mets), 117

Maple Leafs (Edmonton junior rugby team), 230–31

Maple Leafs (Lethbridge). *See under* Lethbridge

Maple Leafs (Toronto hockey team), 318

Margaret, Princess, 337

Marinetti, Filippo, 286

market size, and survival, 347–48

Maroons, 353

Martell, Henry, 161, 297

Martens, James, 198

martial arts, 208

Martin, Kevin, 104

Marylebone Cricket Club, 65, 66

masculinity
of Aboriginal hockey, 281
in advertisements, 240
and behaviour, 227
boxing and, 271
cowboys and, 232–35
and curling, 231–32
and figure skating, 245–46
First Nations models of, 227–28
of frontier, 228
and hockey, 228–29
mobility of, 226
and organized sport, 229
pioneer farm workers and, 229
rodeo and, 232–35
and spectatorship, 227

sports associated with, 226
types of, 226–27
western athletes and, 229

mass entertainment, 22–23

mass media
and basketball, 72
construction of audience, 293
contracts, 322
extent of sports coverage, 292
and hockey, 107, 119, 125, 300
and identification/ownership of teams, 307
and male vs. female sport, 44
and narrative appeal of sport, 293
as one component of multidimensional consumption, 292–93
and professional sports, 183–85
and skating, 171
and spectatorship, 304
and women's sports, 27, 30
and women's vs. men's sport, 127–28
See also broadcasting; newspapers

mass participation in sport, 201, 202

Massey-Ferguson, 102–03

May, Denny, 33, 225, 226

May, Wilfrid Reid "Wop," 76, 226, 296, 297*fig.*

Mayerthorpe hockey arena, 105

Mayfair Gold Club, 157

Mayfair Golf and Country Club, 159–60

McAuley, Ken, 313

McAuley, Mildred Warwick, 313

McCarthy, Sandy, 282

McCarty, Luther, 271-72, 279

McCloy, Cora, 359

McDonald, Lewis, 200

McDonald and McLeod (law firm), 97

McDougall Commercial High
    School, 71

McDougall, John, 144

McGarry, Karen, 245

Mcgavin, Bruce, 175

McKenzie, Kenny, 123

McKillop, H.A., 295

McKnight, Christina, 110

McLennan, William, 209

McLeod, Norman, 38, 96-97

McLuhan, Marshall, 74, 305

McMahon, Vince, 286

McMahon Stadium, 326

McNamara, Pat, 61, 149, 341

McNamara, Sam, 149

McPherson, Gary, 219

McQuarrie, Myrna, 102

McQueen, Rev. Dr., 38

Medicine Hat
    baseball/softball in, 75, 79-80,
        210-11
    cricket in, 19
    curling in, 97, 350-51
    cycling in, 148
    facilities in, 350-51
    Figure Skating Club, 169
    Gaslighters, 336
    golf courses, 160
    hockey in, 97, 112
    lacrosse in, 61, 263
    organized hockey in, 350-51
    rodeo in, 136

rugby in, 84

as "sporting town," 336

Athletic Association, 351

Toronto Blue Jays farm team in,
    347

Medicine Hat News, on hockey, 278

Medlock, Fordie, 211*fig.*

mega-events, 358

Melnyk, Gary, 116

Memorial Cup, 115, 117, 318, 320, 333,
    352

Mendryk, Steve, 86

Menorah Curling Club, 101

Mercantile Basketball League, 70

Mercurys hockey team. *See* Waterloo
    Mercurys hockey team
    (Edmonton)

Messier, Doug, 121

Messier, Mark, 117, 121, 326-27

Metcalfe, Alan, 74

Mets (Edmonton hockey team), 117

Mewata Stadium, 147

Mewata Swim Club, 165

middle classes. *See under* social
    classes

Midnight Rodeo, 214

Mike's News Stand, 301-02

Miles, Rollie, 88

Mill Creek pool, 164

Millarville
    Cricket Club, 66
    horse racing in, 288
    polo in, 250*fig.*

Miller, Lisa, 303

Millet, curling in, 98

Mills, David, 347-48

Mills, Ike, 251

Minor Hockey Week, 128

minority athletes

    acculturation of, 207

    exclusion of, 206–07

    marginalization of, 184–85

    media and, 183

Misener Cup, 110

Mitchell, W.O., *The Black Bonspiel of Wullie MacCrimmon*, 95

modernity/modernization

    and organized sport, 361

    and social identity, 49–50

    and sport, 9, 10

Moher, Stan, 331

Molson Breweries, 320, 348

Monarchs (Edmonton women's hockey team), 110, 111*fig.*, 112, 251

Mondak, Jeffrey, 274

Montgomery, Wes, 231–32, 268, 311–12, 333

Montreal Canadiens, 110, 128, 361

Montreal Expos, 79

Montreal Gazette, on recognition for elite women athletes, 128

Moore, Phil, 296

Moore, Scott, 104

Moose Jaw, baseball in, 283

Moosewah, Larry, 281

Mooswa (runner), 144

Morinville, black settlers in, 209

Morley stampede, 141

Mormons, and basketball, 37, 69

Morris, J.H., 336

Morris School of Physical Culture, 70, 195*fig.*

Morrison, Jim, 174

Morton, Jack, 270

Mossop, Harry, 96

Movers (Edmonton hockey team; later Mets), 117

Moving to Inclusion series, 219

Muenzer, Lori-Ann, 152–53, 327–28

Muir, Debbie, 166

Mullen, Cary, 176

Mullen, Riley, 120

municipal governments, and sport/recreation, 202, 204

Murdoch, J.N., 69–70

Murphy, Emily, 15

Murray, Annabelle, 147

Murray, Athol, 231

Murray, Rod, 242

Murray, Troy, 326–27

muscular Christianity, 36, 194

    and boxing, 272

    hockey as, 278

    pacifism and, 194

    and wrestling, 194

Muskogee Cardinals, 212

Muttart Lumber, 74–75

Nagel, Gladys, 71

Naismith, James, 25, 256

Nanton, skiing in, 173

National Basketball League, 73

National Conference on Women and Sport, 1st, 1974, 28

National Council of Women, 55

National Girls' Team, 37, 110

National Hockey Association (NHA), 110, 265

National Hockey League (NHL). *See*
NHL (National Hockey League)
National Lacrosse Association, 59,
60–61
National Lacrosse League, 63, 306
National Parks Association of
Canada (NPAC), 201
National Physical Fitness Act, 201
National Professional Soccer
League, 88
Native Sons (Edmonton lacrosse
team), 61
Native Sport and Recreation
Program, 216
Negro Leagues, 78, 213
New Kiev, YCL in, 199
New Norway, artificial ice in, 353
*A New Perspective on the Health of
Canadians*, 202
Newcast, YCL in, 199
Newell, Eric, 341
Newman, Potts, 110
newspapers, 294–300
American teams in, 296
international reports in, 296
photographers, 296
and public benefits, 295
separate sports sections, 298
smaller community, 298
specialized sports sections, 294
and sports culture, 298
and sports statistics, 295–96
on star players, 295
and women's sports, 27–28, 299
writers as source of critical
journalism, 308–09

*See also titles of individual
newspapers*
NHL (National Hockey League)
2004–2005 lockout, 104, 125, 128
as Canadian institution, 125
Drake and, 45
Edmonton/Calgary joining, 124
farm teams, 123
formation of, 279
Hockey Night in Canada and, 121
Keats as player for, 118
as main period in pro hockey
history, 123
and minor hockey, 283
salary cap, 125
scouts, 115
Sutter brothers in, 105
weight of players in, 206
WHA vs., 345
Nicol, Helen, 313
Nigger John 4-H Beef Club, 209
Noble, Bunty, 244*fig.*
Norquay, Mount, 173, 174, 176, 268, 269
Norris, Thelma, 145, 146
North American Indigenous Games,
217
North American Soccer League
(NASL), 88, 89, 347
North Battleford Beavers, 284
North Star Cycle Club, 148, 149,
341–42
North West Mounted Police
(NWMP), 19, 21
and cricket, 67
and curling, 96

and football, 81, 82
and golf, 157
and gymkhanas, 135
and hockey, 107-08, 278
and tennis, 153, 155
Northcott, Ron, 103
Northern Alberta Bicycle
    Association, 151
Northern Alberta Ladies' Hockey
    League, 113
Northern Alberta Native Cowboys
    Association, Hobbema, 216
Northern Indian Cowboys
    Association, 215
Northlands arena (Edmonton), 349,
    354
Northlands Park (Edmonton), 288
North-West Rebellion, 60
North-West Territories, 5
Notre Dame Hounds, 230-31

obesity, 202, 203*fig.*, 260
O'Connor, Marilyn, 162
oil
    discovery of, 23, 84
    and Hobbema reserve, 139
Oil Kings (Edmonton hockey team),
    115, 116-17, 121, 242, 280, 282,
    311, 318, 333. *See also* Capitals
    (Edmonton hockey team)
Oilers (Edmonton baseball team),
    78, 80
Oilers (Edmonton hockey team), 121,
    124-25, 206, 281, 282, 300, 311,
    334, 339, 345, 347-49, 359, 361

Oilers, Alberta (later Edmonton
    Oilers), 124, 315
Okotoks
    baseball/softball in, 80
    hockey in, 110
Olson, E.B., 267
Olson, Elias Bjarni "Ole," 352
Olympic Games
    1904 St. Louis, 286
    1908 London, 47
    1912 Stockholm, 144
    1936 Berlin, 193
    1952 Oslo, 121-22
    1956 Melbourne, 165
    1976 Montreal, 320
    1980 Lake Placid, 45
    1988 Calgary, 146, 166, 167, 176
    1992 Albertville, 176
    1994 Lillehammer, 171, 306
    2002 Salt Lake City, 122, 172
    2004 Athens, 328
    2012 London, 153
    Alberta Olympic Game Plan, 146
    Edmonton Grads at, 72
    Paralympics and, 218, 220
    Podium Alberta program, 360
    speed skating in, 168
    See also Paralympic Games;
        Winter Olympics
origin myths, 361
O'Riordan, Terence, 109
Orser, Brian, 238
OutGames, 236
Outlaws (Calgary basketball team),
    73

Oval X-tremes (Calgary women's
hockey team), 123

Pacific Coast Hockey League
(PCHL), 123, 124, 347
Pacific Coast League (PCL)
(baseball), 80
pacifism, 194
Page, J. Percy, 23, 71, 72, 204, 256, 257,
258, 316, 327, 332
Page, Patricia, 146
Palliser, John, 143-44
Palmer, Howard, 19
Palmer, Tamara, 19
Pan-American Games, 166
Pandas (University of Alberta
women's sports teams), 44,
129, 244-45
Panee Memorial Agriplex, Hobbema,
139, 143, 216
Paralympic Games, 167, 218, 219,
220, 221
Paraschak, Victoria, 217
Parker, Brent, 81
Parker, Jackie, 91, 134
Parker, Russell, 80, 346-47
ParticipACTION, 202
Patrick, Bill, 165, 351fig.
Patrick, Frank, 123
Patrick, Lester, 110
Pats, 70, 71
Patton, Clarence, 65
Paul, James, 324
Pawson, Hal, 309-10, 338
Peacock, Fay, 145
Pearson, Robert, Rev., 36, 45

Peden, Sandy, 152
Peden, Torchy, 151, 152, 243
Pedersen, Blaine, 141
Pederson, Diana, 254
Peers, Danielle, 218-19, 221
Peigan people, and running, 213
Pekisko Polo Club, 64-65
Pelkey, Arthur, 271-72
Pelletier, David, 171, 172, 327
Pengrowth Saddledome. See Calgary
Saddledome
Penrose, Ian, 143
People's Shield, 86
Percival, Lloyd, 201
Percy, Karen, 176
Perley, H.A., 148
Petrone, Joe, 88
Pezer, Vera, 96, 98
Phelan, Johnnie, 346
Phillips, Rod, 311
Phillips, Tom, 110
physical capital, 186
physical culture, and social order,
192
physical education
and citizenship, 45
as compulsory, 197
development of programs in, 193
and sports/games vs. holistic
fitness, 202
for unemployed, 200
at University of Alberta, 86, 197
Picture Butte
baseball in, 79
Indians, 213

Pincher Creek
  cricket in, 66
  Dominoes, 212
  polo in, 64
Pioneer League (baseball), 79–80, 346
playgrounds
  children's, 34, 35
  movement, 191–92
  See also facilities
Plume, Clay, 282
Pocklington, Peter, 80, 88, 124–25, 327,
    345, 347, 348–49
Podium Alberta, 360
Podivinsky, Ed, 176
Poile, Bud, 280
Polkinghorn, Nora, 157
polo, 26, 63–65, 64, 135, 228fig., 250fig.
Ponoka
  figure skating in, 169
  Stampede, 135
  swimming pool, 164
Pope, Steven, 212
population
  of Alberta, 23, 293
  of Edmonton, 23
  growth, 22
  and participation in sports
    culture, 177
Pork Sports, 322
post-secondary institutions
  academic vs. sporting
    achievement in, 46
  basketball in, 73
  enrolment in, 43
  and football, 86
  and hockey, 117–18, 129

role of sport in, 40, 42–46
  and rugby, 85
  tennis in, 155
  See also university sport
Poulter, Gillian, 60
Powder Puff football game, 254
power interests
  Calgary Stampede and, 332
  and hockey, 282
  mainstream sports discourse
    and, 179
  and sport, 10, 30, 217
  and sporting interests, 185–86
  and sports culture, 178
press coverage. See mass media
Primrose, Neil, 170
Primrose, Philip, 170
Prince of Wales Cup, 136
professional players/teams
  development of, 23
  hockey, 109–10, 113, 117, 121
  rodeo, 135
  tennis, 156
  women and, 30
professional sport(s)
  amateur vs., 49, 177, 343
  baseball as, 75
  community and, 50
  condemnation of, 49
  decline of, 308
  economic centres vs. regions
    and, 178–79
  entertainment economy and, 307
  football, 92
  growth of, 293
  hockey as, 49, 113, 117, 121

marginality of franchises/
    leagues, 179
    press coverage of, 183–85
    soccer, 88–89
    sponsorship of, 322–26
    wrestling as, 273–75
    promoters, 344–47
A Proposed Sports Policy for Canadians,
    201–02
Pro-Rec, 200, 201
provincial government
    and baseball, 81
    budget for recreation/sport, 360
    and gay/lesbian rights, 236,
      237–38
    and sport/recreation, 39, 202, 204
    and tennis, 155
Puckettes, 42
Purity 99 (Calgary baseball team),
    315
Purvis, Doug, 114*fig.*
Purvis, Fred, 114*fig.*

Queen Elizabeth Pool (Edmonton),
    165
Queen's Birthday sports days, 35

Rabbit Hill, 175
race/racism
    clothing/dress and, 242
    and football, 91–92
    in hockey, 281
radio, 293
    and decline of professional sport,
      22–23
    and hockey, 115, 291

sportscasters, 303–04
railway
    and curling, 100
    and football, 81
    and skiing, 173–74
Ramsay, James, 159
ranch life
    and polo, 64
    and sport, 21
Ranchland Hockey League, 281
Rattlesnake, Jimmy ("Chief"), 214
Raymond
    baseball in, 79
    basketball in, 69
    Buddhist temple in, 208
    Comets, 69
    judo in, 208
    rodeo in, 136
    Union Jacks, 69
Read, Dorothy (Dee), 176, 177
Read, Jim, 176
Read, Ken, 176–1777
Reader's Digest, and Indian Days, 141
Recreation Canada, 202
Recreation Development Act, 202
recreational sport
    cycling and, 151
    as democratic right, 192
    elite sports vs., 47
    hockey as, 113–14
    post-secondary institutions and,
      46
    public, 38–39
    swimming, 162
    tennis, 155

and transition to organized
leagues/professional teams,
75
World War I and, 77
Red Deer
A-20 Wheelers hockey team, 352
Amazons women's hockey team,
112, 351–52
baseball/softball in, 75, 346
competitive team sports in, 21
curling in, 102, 299
ENMAX Centrium, 326, 352
Football Club, 87*fig.*
hockey in, 109, 110, 112, 299–300,
351
MacLean and, 311
Rebels, 326, 352
recreational facilities for
women/girls, 254
rugby in, 84
Sims Auction Mart, 274*fig.*, 275*fig.*
skiing in, 173
Skookums women's hockey
team, 112
soccer in, 86, 87*fig.*
speed skating in, 168
sports facilities, 351–52
Stars women's hockey team, 112
Red Deer Advocate
MacLean and, 311
sports journalism in, 297, 309
on Vulcan and sport, 337–38
Rees, Tony, 63
Reeves, Mary Ann, 166
Regents (Calgary women's hockey
team), 110, 112

Regina
Bonepilers, 210–11
football in, 91
Regina *Leader*, on rugby, 90
Reid, MacKenzie, 282
Reilly, Jack, 102
Renfrew Park (Edmonton), 77, 312.
See also John Ducey Park
(Edmonton)
Rexall
company, 326
Place, 349, 355
Reynolds Tobacco, 322
Rice, Dick, 303
Richard, Maurice "Rocket," 140*fig.*,
141
Richards, Clarence, 90
Riel, Louis, 60
Riley, Ezra H., 66
Rinehardt, Jack, 197, 198*fig.*
ringette, 113
rinks, 350–53
curling, 39, 100, 101
hockey and, 109, 114
outdoor, 128–29, 361
professionalism of hockey and,
113
See also names of individual rinks
risk
and courage, 264
physical activities and, 264
schools and, 264
societal consequences of, 264
technology and, 267
Ritchie, Robert, 339
Rites of Men (Burstyn), 265

River City Roundup, 221

Rivet, Vera (Barilko), 147

Robertson, Annie Laurie, 108

Robertson, Jean, 70

Robidoux, Michael, 217, 227-28, 281

Robinson, Billy, 277

Robinson, Laura, 113

Robinson, Lorna, 185

Rockers (Edmonton women's
    football team), 85

Rocky Mountain House, baseball in,
    283-84

Rocky Mountain national parks,
    promotion of, 197

rodeo, 134-43

    Aboriginal peoples and, 141-43,
        214-16

    affordability of, 136

    amateur, 135

    Canadian Finals, 134, 138

    and capitalism, 138

    clothing/dress for, 241

    commercialization of, 135

    cowboy strikes, 138

    First Nations and, 139

    frontier image/mythology of, 137,
        138

    growth of, 135

    in Hanna, 235fig.

    history of, 134-37

    and hockey, 137

    injuries, 266, 269-70

    journalism on, 309

    mainstream vs. gay, 237

    masculinity and, 232-35

    mythology of, 139, 141

organizations, 138-39

professionals in, 135

promoters, 346

protective equipment, 270

sponsorship of, 139, 323-25

stars, 135-36

women and, 139, 249, 306, 323-24

wrestling compared with, 234

Rodeo Association of America, 139

Rodeo Cowboys' Association (RCA),
    138, 324-25

Rosedale, YCL in, 199

Ross, Jean, 166

Ross, Mrs. Fred, 149

Rotary Club, 343

Roughnecks (Calgary lacrosse
    team), 63, 322

Royal and Ancient Golf Club of St.
    Andrews Scotland, 160

Royal Caledonian Curling Club
    (RCCC), 98, 100, 352

Royal Canadian Air Force, 305-06

    5BX and 10BX exercises, 201

Royal Commission on the Status of
    Women, 28, 43-44

Royal Curling Club, 170

Royal Glenora Club, 170-71

Royal Visit 1939, 353

Royals (Edmonton baseball team),
    214

rugby, 82-85, 90, 356

    and amateurism, 84

    elite vs. workers' versions of, 82

    immigrants and, 84

    injuries, 266

    junior, 84

in newspapers, 295

rules differences in Canadian, 82

women and, 85

Rugby Canada National Festival, 85

Rumsey

baseball in, 208

Jews in, 208

running

Aboriginal athletes and, 213-14

and drug use, 286

First Nations and, 17

See also track and field

Rush (Edmonton lacrosse team), 63, 322

Ruskin, John, 193

Russell, Bob, 272

Rutherford, A.C., 339

Rutherford, Paul, 126, 304

Ruttan, R.A., 159

Ryan, Doreen McLeod, 146-47, 167-68, 169, 268

Ryan, Frank, 309

Ryan, Pat, 103

Ryerson, Egerton, 39

Saddle Lake Warriors, 281

Saints (Calgary rugby football team), 84

salaries, players', 316-17

Salcedo, Marissa, 253

Sale, Jamie, 171, 172, 327

Sandor, Steven, *Battle of Alberta*, 128

Saracens (Calgary rugby football team), 84

Sargent, Kristy, 171

Saskatchewan River Bank Snowbirds, 175

Saskatoon

baseball in, 78

Gems, 79, 338

soccer in, 88

St. Louis Blues and, 345

Saunders, Arthur, 211*fig*.

Savage, Candace, 215

Scabby Dried Meat. *See* Deerfoot (runner)

Schenley, 321

Schmirler, Sandra, 96

schools/education

and assimilation of immigrants, 39-40

basketball in, 216

gay/lesbian rights in, 238

hockey players and, 282

risk and, 264

rugby in, 84

sport as cultural capital in, 33

sport in, 39-40

track and field athletics in, 147

See also high schools; post-secondary institutions; residential schools *under* Aboriginal peoples

Schriner, David "Sweeney," 120, 192, 318-20, 319*fig*.

Scotch Cup (curling), 103

Scotch Whiskey Association, 321

Scott, Barbara Ann, 169, 254

Scott, Beckie, 286-87

Scott Tournament of Hearts, 102, 307, 326

Seagram Company, 321

Secord, Richard, 98, 349

Seitz, Susan, 102

Semple, Bessie, 70

Senior Amateur Football Championship, 82

service clubs, 342, 343

Setoguchi, Dale, 208

Setoguchi, Devin, 208

settlers, sport of, 15-16

sexual preference/orientation, 235-36. *See also* gay/lesbian athletes

Shade, Dean, 282

Shaganappi Club (Calgary), 160-61

Shamrocks
    rink, 109
    Strathcona hockey team, 229-30
    Strathcona women's hockey team, 110

Sharples, William, 229-30

Shaw, George Bernard, 193

Shaw, Miss (London *Times* correspondent), 249

Sheep Creek Polo Cup, 64

Sheppard, Russ, 18

Sherman Arena (Calgary), 344

Shermans (Calgary hockey team), 110, 279

Shore, Eddie ("Edmonton Express"), 124, 257, 279-80

Sick, Emil, 320

Sick's Breweries, 318-20

Silver Hawks Bicycle Club, 151-52

Silverberg, Doug, 161

Silversides, Brock, 136

Simon, Chris, 282

Simpson, Rae Milligan, 162

Singer, Henry, 333

Sirens (Edmonton women's cycling team), 152

Sirois, Kevin, 167

Skalbania, Nelson, 89, 124, 345

Skate Canada, 167, 172, 246. *See also* Canadian Figure Skating Association (CFSA)

skating
    clubs, 169
    equipment, 170
    figure, 167, 169-72, 244*fig.*, 245-46, 306, 327, 353
    finances of, 168
    gay/lesbian athletes in, 238
    speed, 167-69, 327
    television and, 306

Ski Runners of the Canadian Rockies, 172-73, 253, 268

skiing, 172-76
    benefits of, 253
    clothing/dress for, 240, 244, 251, 252*fig.*
    clubs, 173
    cross-country, 172, 199, 286-87
    downhill racing, 172, 173, 268
    equipment, 173
    golfification of, 269
    history, 172-73
    jumps, 172, 173, 175
    by physically challenged skiers, 220*fig.*

rope tows, 174

specialized equipment/clothing
for, 268-69

sponsorship, 174-75

transportation to, 173-74

women and, 172, 244, 251

Skimeisters, 175

Skitch, Arthur, 313

Skitch, Edith, 146, 313

Skyhawks (Edmonton basketball
team), 73

Skyreach, 326

Smith, Connie, 256*fig.*

Smith, Graham, 165-66, 286

Smith, Gwen, 286

Smith, Rebecca, 166

Smith, Sandra, 166

Smith, Sue, 166

Smith, W. Donald, 165

Smyth, J.E., 46

Snowbirds (Edmonton softball
team), 80

soccer

amateur, 89-90

baseball vs., 87

growth in popularity, 179

history of, 85-86

hockey compared to, 90

immigrants and, 87, 207

leagues, 85

minor, 89-90

participation rates, 89

professional, 88-89

as southern hemisphere game,
179

women and, 88, 89-90, 127-28,
258-59, 327

YCL and, 199

social capital

defined, 33-34

fitness and, 201

physical capital and, 186

sportswomen and, 251, 253

social classes

and behaviour, 265

British upper-middle leisure
culture in sport, 21

clothing/dress and, 242

and cricket, 65

middle classes and outdoor
leisure, 157

middle-class urban people, 23

polo and, 64-65

and rural-urban sports rivalries,
200

sport cutting across lines of, 22

and tennis, 153, 154, 156

and violence in sport, 278

women's sport and, 245

See also elite (social class);
working classes

social control/order

bodily control and, 204

clothing/dress and, 242

and cultural/economic capital,
33

exercise and, 259

institutions and, 35-36

of leisure, 264

need for, vs. excitement of
unruliness/unpredictability,
265
physical culture and, 192
of sexuality, 259
sport and, 9, 34–36
of violence, 289
women in sports and, 247
social identity
of Alberta, 10
hockey and, 106
modernization of sport and,
49–50
socialization
of children, 33–34, 35
environmentalism and, 34–35
sport and, 40
softball, 24, 25*fig.*, 74–81
promoters, 346
sponsorship of, 322
women and, 74–75, 78*fig.*, 80
solo sport athletes, 176
Solomon, Eric, 207–08
Sons of England (Edmonton cricket
team), 66
Sons of Scotia (Calgary curling
team), 97
Soop, Everett, 233*fig.*
Souray, Sheldon, 282
South Side Arena (Edmonton), 179
South Side Covered Rink
(Edmonton), 339, 349
South Side Swim Club (Edmonton),
165. *See also* Keyano club
South Side Terrors (softball team), 75
Southam, John, 173

Sparkes, Bernie, 103
special events, 356–60
Special Games, 177, 219
Special Olympics Alberta, 219
spectacle, sport as, 9
spectator sports
attraction of, 264–65
recreation compared to, 361
wagering and, 143
spectatorship/viewership
aggression from, 281
and aggressiveness in
performance, 289
and athletic bodies, 206
of baseball/softball, 76, 283–84
of basketball, 72, 73
of curling, 98, 104, 307
financial support of teams/
facilities, 342–43
funding and, 347
of hockey, 109, 113, 118, 119
and identification with teams/
players, 334
masculinities and, 227
mass media and, 304
of men at women's sports, 247
organic link with athletes, 49–50
of soccer, 89
television and, 305, 307
at university games, 227
university students and, 45–46
women, 247
of women's sport, 247
World War I and, 77
Speed Skating Canada, 168
Spencer, Herbert, 193

sponsorship, 314-28

   and advertising, 197

   and amateurism, 315-16

   of basketball, 320-21

   of CFL, 105

   of cricket, 67

   of curling, 102-03, 105, 322

   of elite vs. amateur sport, 202

   employment of players, 316-17

   factors influencing, 178

   of gay/lesbian athletes, 238

   of lacrosse, 322

   local markets and, 322

   and naming, 326-27

   of professional sport, 322-26

   of rodeo, 139, 323-25

   of skiing, 174-75

   of softball, 322

   and status of players, 316-17

   tax benefits and, 317

   tobacco and, 322

   of women, 327-28

   of women's basketball, 70-71

   of working-class sports, 187

sport

   capitalism and, 9

   churches and, 36-38

   and collective mobilization, 6

   as commodity, 9

   co-ordination of, 35

   as cultural identity, 5-13

   and democracy, 30

   First Nations and, 17-19

   gender identity in, 246-55

   history of, 8-10, 19-31

   importation into Alberta, 8-9

   invention/mythmaking of, 362

   modernization and, 9, 10

   power interests and, 10, 30

   quantification of, 9

   scholarship, 11

   of settlers, 15-16

   and social control, 9, 34-36

   social value of, 30

   and socialization, 40

   as spectacle, 9

   themes of, 129-30

   urbanization and, 9, 10

   war vs., 265

   women in, 246-55

Sport Alberta, 48

Sport Canada, 202, 269

sports culture(s)

   aggression and, 264

   of Alberta, 362

   backstage performances and, 176

   capitalism and, 194

   characteristics of, 47-48

   climate and participation in, 177

   demographics and, 179

   development of, 19-20

   distances and participation in, 177

   injuries and, 265

   as monoculture, 359

   newspapers and, 298

   population size and participation in, 177

   power brokers and, 178

Spring Coulee, baseball in, 79

Spruce Grove

   hockey in, 117

Mets, 117

Saints, 117

St. Albert

    hockey in, 117

    Mark Messier Arena, 326–27

    Saints, 117

    Troy Murray Arena, 326–27

St. Andrews golf club (Calgary), 160

St. Dunstan's Indian Industrial

    School (Calgary), 216

St. Kitts-Nevis-Edmonton Cricket

    Association, 68

St. Laurent, Louis, 306

St. Louis Blues, 345

St. Mary's reserve school, 216

St. Paul's residential school (Blood

    reserve), 216

Stampede Grandstand (Elbow Park,

    Calgary), 173

Stampede Wrestling, 276, 286

Stampede Wrestling, 273–74, 277, 311

Stampeders (Calgary football team;

    earlier, Bronks), 23, 91, 92,

    118, 119, 120, 120*fig.*, 122, 209,

    304, 316, 334. *See also* Calgary

    Bronks

Stanley, Jack, 172

Stanley Cup, 71, 72, 110, 123, 124, 300,

    301, 311, 336, 348

Starlets, 72–73

Starr Acme Club, 109

Stars on Ice, 171

Steadward, Robert, 220–21

Stettler, figure skating in, 169, 170

Stevenson, Margaret, 251

Stewart, Bobby, 272

Stinson, Shirley, 303

Stirling, basketball in, 69

Stockyard Bulls (Edmonton baseball

    team), 214

Stojko, Elvis, 238, 246

Stone Sutton, Edith, 72, 257

Stoney band, and Banff Indian Days,

    215, 337

Stony Plain

    basketball in, 70

    Eagles, 118, 122

    hockey in, 122

Storey, Fred, 103

Strathcona

    black settlers in, 209

    cricket in, 66

    hockey in, 109, 110, 278, 279

    Hotel, 109

    lacrosse in, 61

    Skating Rink, 349

street celebrations, 332–34

Strong, Myrtle, 70

Strong, O. F., 279

The Studhorse Man (Kroetsch), 291

Sundre Stampede, 215

Sunshine Village

    gondola, 269

    skiing in, 174, 269

Superstein Chevrolet, 315

Sutherland, George, 145

Sutter, Brian, 117

Sutter brothers, 105

Swastika skating club (Calgary), 110

Swastikas (Edmonton women's

    hockey team), 110, 241, 241*fig.*

swimming, 162–67, 351*fig.*

children and, 162–63

clubs, 164

competitive, 164, 165–67

holes, 164

in newspapers, 298

pools, 162, 164

profile of, 162

public campaigns, 163

recreational, 162

synchronized, 166, 254

women and, 163–64, 250

Sylvan Lake, YCL in, 199

Synchro Swim Alberta, 166

Taber

baseball in, 79

hockey in, 109–10

Taft, Kevin, 134

Taylor, Ethel, 254

Taylor, Jack, 89

Team Canada, 106, 122

Team Edmonton, 237

team sports, 278–85

Arnold and, 193–94

and democracy, 35

employers and, 196–97

forts/trading posts vs. local

communities, 19

and union solidarity, 197

technology

and hazardous play, 267

and performance enhancement,

267–68

and risk, 267

telegraphy, 293, 301–02, 303

telephones, 292, 301

television, 304–08

children and, 201

commercial vs. private, 305

and hockey, 115, 117

and objectification of bodies, 244

and popularity of different

sports, 305

sport as entertainment vs.

critical journalism, 308

and university sport, 43

TELUS Field, 326, 361

tennis, 153–56, 154*fig.*

amateurs, 156

churches and, 37

clubs, 155

courts, 155

districts, 155

employers and, 153

equipment, 153

history of, 153

in newspapers, 297–98

professionals, 156

recreational, 155

social classes and, 153, 154, 156

social mobility and, 154

stars, 156

television and, 306

Universiade and, 155

in universities, 155

women and, 154, 156, 249

Tewksbury, Mark, 166, 238

Thirsty Thugs, 74

Thistle Curling Club (Edmonton), 98

Thistle Rink (Edmonton), 109, 278,

295, 339, 349–50, 354

INDEX

Thistles (Edmonton hockey team),
     109, 278-79, 295
Thompson, Stanley, 160
Thomson, Olive, 258
Thornhill Fitness Centre, 204
Three Persons, Tom, 141, 214-15
Tiger, Dick, 309-10
Tigers (Calgary football team), 83*fig.*,
     210
Tigers (Calgary hockey team), 118,
     119, 123, 229, 301, 333, 339, 343,
     344
Tigers (Calgary rugby football team),
     82, 84
Tim Horton, 326
Tobacco Act, 322
tobacco sponsorship, 97, 102, 232, 322
Toronto Blue Jays, 347
     farm team in Medicine Hat,
     79-80
Toronto Globe, on rugby, 84
Toronto Granites, 122
Tory, H.M., 159
Tournament of Hearts. *See* Scott
     Tournament of Hearts
Tournament of Pearls, 102
Tournament of Roses, 102
Town Boys (Calgary hockey team),
     107
track and field
     Aboriginal peoples and, 144
     in British Empire Games, 145
     community and, 144-45
     early contests, 144
     facilities, 354
     finances, 145-46

history, 143-44
     public holidays and, 144-45
     in schools, 147
     women in, 42, 146-47
     See also running
"The Trade that Shook the Hockey
     World" (Lee), 348
training institutes, sport in, 40
Trappers (Edmonton baseball team),
     80, 347
Trochu, baseball in, 208
Trottier, Bryan, 117
Trudeau, Pierre, 167, 174
Trumpbour, Robert, 362
Turner, Lloyd, 344-45
Turner Valley
     golf club, 161
     Oilers, 335*fig.*, 336
     organized sports in, 20
     skiing in, 173
Tweedsmuir, John Buchan, Lord,
     8*fig.*
Twinn, Walter, 273
Two Youngman, Jake, 141

Ullman, Norm, 116, 128
Underhill, Pat, 168, 169
Underwood Trophy, 71-72, 242, 316
union solidarity, and sport
     participation, 197
United States
     African-Americans, 210-13
     baseball players, 78, 79, 210-13
     football players, 92
     players relocating to, 317, 348-49
     teams in newspapers, 296

Title IX, 43-44

Universiade

1983, 23, 155, 269, 357

2015, 340-41, 358

University of Alberta

    Aquatic Centre, 358

    basketball, 42

    Centennial awards to coaches, 45

    CKUA radio, 303

    Faculty of Physical Education

        and Recreation, 45

    hockey in, 129

    and intervarsity competition, 44

    intervarsity football, 86

    Men's Athletic Association, 197

    national championships won, 44

    as no longer sports backwoods,

        340

    and physical education, 197

    physical education at, 86

    Polar Bears, 297

    Puckettes, 42

    rugby football, 84

    soccer at, 87

    and spectators at games, 227

    Steadward Centre, 220

    summer camp for GLT youth, 237

    and swimming, 163

    teachers/coaches, 44-45

    and tennis, 155

    track and field facilities, 354

    University Athletic Board, 197

    and wheelchair games, 219

    women's rugby, 85

    and women's sports, 42

University of Alberta in Calgary. *See*

    University of Calgary

University of Calgary

    and Borden Ladner Gervais

        Awards, 44

    Centennial awards to coaches, 45

    Dinos, 128-29

    gym opening, 204

    gymnasium, 205*fig.*

    registry for catastrophic injuries

        in pro rodeo, 270

    women students in football

        helmets, 254-55

    and women's sports, 42

University of Saskatchewan

    Huskies, 297

university sport

    and alcohol consumption, 46

    funding, 46

    role of, 45-46

    spectatorship for, 45-46

Urban, Bruce, 63

urbanization

    and men's vs. women's hockey,

        113

    and sport, 9, 10

Useful Pleasures (Wetherell; Kmet),

    136

Uyeyama, Hiromi, 209

Vajda, Peter, 174

van Herk, Aritha, 10, 134, 143

Van Vliet, Maury, 43, 358

Vancouver *Province*, on women's

    soccer, 258

Vancouver Sun, on Edmonton as
    basketball centre, 37
Vantour, James, *The Fabulous Flyers*,
    128
Varsconas, 42
Varsity Arena, 44
Varsity Rink, 170
Varsity Ski Club, 175
Varty, John, 64
velodromes, 152
Velo-Sport Edmonton, 152
Vics (Calgary hockey team), 118, 120
Victoria Arena (Calgary), 352
Victoria *Daily Colonist*, on cricket, 65
Victoria Girls Hockey Team
    (Edmonton), 37
Victoria High School girls'
    basketball team (Edmonton),
    147
Victoria Park (Calgary)
    Arena, 344
    Athletic Club, 210
    ski jump in, 173
Victoria Park golf course
    (Edmonton), 158*fig.*, 159, 160
Victoria Pavilion (Calgary), 272
Victoria Soccer Club (Edmonton),
    87–88, 152
Victorias (Edmonton high school
    girls' hockey team), 110
Viking
    arena, 353
    Carena, 105
    figure skating in, 353
    hockey in, 105, 353
    multi-use facility in, 105

Viney, Henry, 310
violence
    in achievement of goals, 265
    in baseball, 283, 284–85
    in basketball, 263, 285
    boxing and, 271
    control of, 289
    in hockey, 278, 279
    in lacrosse, 263
    leagues and, 265
    in non-contact sport, 265–66
    racism and, 281
    regulation of, 265, 279
    in wrestling, 275, 277
Vipers (Calgary baseball team), 80
visible minorities
    numbers of, 179
    See also colour, people of;
        minority athletes
Voisey, Paul, 287
volleyball, 244–45
Vulcan, 337–38
    curling in, 103
    Stampede, 1915, 336

wagering. *See* gambling
Wainwright
    Bisons, 281
    bonspiel, 351
Wait, Norton, 244*fig.*
Waldo, Caroline, 166
Walker, James, 98
Walter, John, 339
Wamsley, Kevin B., 18, 239, 257, 358
Ward, Art, 312
Ware, Bob, 210

Ware, John, 135, 209, 210

wars, sport vs., 265

Waterloo Mercurys hockey team
(Edmonton), 87, 121-22, 315,
338

Watson, Whipper Billy, 277

Watt, Gordon (Gordie), 116, 333

Weadick, Guy, 137, 249, 344

weather. *See* climate/weather

Webster, George H., 163*fig.*

Wepsala, Gertrude, 174

Wesley, George, 79, 317, 345-46

Western Canada Baseball League
(WCBL), 75-76, 79, 200, 211, 283,
294, 338-39

Western Canada Cricket
Association, 66

Western Canada Cricket
Tournament, 67, 68

Western Canada Hockey League
(WCHL), 117, 119, 121, 123, 280,
344

Western Canada Junior Hockey
League (WCJHL), 116

Western Canada Rugby Football
Union (WCRFU), 82, 91, 177

Western Canada Senior Hockey
League, 124

Western Canadian Intercollegiate
Athletic Union (WCIAA), 43

Western Canadian Interuniversity
Athletic Union, 86

Western Canadian Major Junior
Hockey League, 117

Western Canadian Ski Association,
174

Western Cricket Association, 65-66

Western Cup, 237

Western Football Conference, 91, 92

Western Hockey League (WHL), 116,
120-21, 122, 124, 280

Western Inter-College Conference,
43

Western Intercollegiate Athletic
Association (WIAA), 40, 42

Western Intercollegiate Athletic
Union, 117

Western Intercollegiate Football
League, 86

Western Intercollegiate Rugby
Football Union, 86

Western International League
(WIL), 76, 78-79

Western Interprovincial Football
Union (WIFU), 91

Western Major Baseball League, 80

Western Women's Canadian
Football League, 255

Wetaskiwin
baseball in, 214
Braves, 214
Driard Hotel Gymnasium, 198*fig.*
figure skating in, 169
Montgomery Brothers store, 240
Old Stars, 214
Rinehardt's physical culture
classes for boys in, 197, 198*fig.*
Sports Hall of Fame, 214, 313
track and field in, 144-45, 337

Wetherell, Donald Grant, *Useful
Pleasures*, 136, 138

Whalen, Ed, 274, 277, 311

Wheat Kernels, 315

wheelchair basketball, 218–19

wheelchair sports, 220

Whistler, Mount, skiing on, 174

White, Deacon, 75, 84, 294, 295, 345

Whitson, David, 307, 359

Whitten, Charlotte, 28

Whitten, Tara, 153

Whyte, Clifford, 172–73

Wieting, Stephen, 105

Wildcat, Lawrence, 139, 216

Wildwood, black settlers in, 211

Williams, Raymond, 6

Williams, Upton, 212

Williams Lake Stampede, 141

Wilmot, E.M., 63

Wilson, Dr. (Edmonton cricket club president), 66

Winnipeg
    Blue Bombers, 84
    cricket in, 66
    football in, 91
    hockey in, 117
    'Pegs, 84
    soccer in, 88
    Turf Association, 149

Winnipeg Free Press, rodeo in, 309

Winter Olympics
    1988 Calgary, 23, 104, 122, 347, 357, 358, 359
    1994 Lillehammer, 334
    2010 Vancouver, 104, 221, 239, 360
    women's hockey teams in, 128

Wolley-Dod, A.G., 81

Wolosinka, Garry, 105

women
    alcohol consumption, and exclusion of, 320–21
    and baseball, 77–78
    and basketball, 42, 70–71, 255–58, 315–16
    body size through sport participation, 196
    as cheerleaders, 247
    clothing/dress, 240–42, 243, 244–45
    and curling, 98–100, 99*fig.*, 101–02, 231, 243, 243*fig.*
    and cycling, 149, 150, 152–53, 327–28
    enrolment in post-secondary education, 43
    equal opportunity in sport for, 254
    equity, 24
    femininity of, 240, 253–54
    feminism and, 250
    and figure skating, 169–70
    fitness movements and, 28
    and football, 254–55
    funding/sponsorship and, 168, 327–28
    in gay rodeo, 237
    and golf, 157, 159, 160, 161–62
    and gymnastics, 248
    in halls of fame, 30, 313–14
    hand size, 247–48
    and hockey, 40, 42, 108–09, 110, 112–13, 117–18, 123, 126–27, 129, 247, 351–52
    and horse riding, 248–49
    in intercollegiate sport, 42–44

marginalization of, 184–85

media and, 27-28

and nation building, 247

in newspapers, 299

and organized sport, 24-30

perceptions of beauty of, 204

physical attributes, 146–47

physical fitness for, 248

and polo, 26, 64

in prairie farm society, 248-49

and professional careers, 30

in public sphere, 24, 247

purposive exercise for, 248

reproductive systems, 248

and rodeo, 139, 215, 249, 306, 323-24

and rugby, 85

and skiing, 172, 244, 251

and soccer, 88, 89-90, 127-28, 258-59, 327

and social capital, 251, 253

social image of, 24

and softball, 24, 25*fig.*, 74-75, 78*fig.*, 80

as spectators, 247

and speed skating, 167-68

and sport, 41*fig.*, 45, 246-55

as sports announcers, 303

stereotypes regarding, 43, 239

students, 42, 43-44

and swimming, 163-64, 250

and tennis, 154, 156, 249

in track and field, 42, 146–47

WCIAA and, 43

World War I and, 26

World War II and, 231

and wrestling, 274*fig.*

YWCA advertising regarding, 253-54

Women's Amateur Athletic Association of Canada, 71, 285

Women's Amateur Athletic Foundation (WAAF), 27, 30

Women's Intercollegiate Athletic Union (WIAU), 43

Women's Professional Rodeo Association, 139. *See also* Canadian Girls' Rodeo Association (CGRA)

Woods Ringette Tournament, 113

Woodside, Helen, 163-64, 163*fig.*, 165, 250

Workers' Sports Association (WSA), 199-200

working classes

and baseball, 67

and boxing, 210

and cricket, 65

and excellence in sport, 200

non-British sport and, 21

playground movement and, 34

and polo, 64-65

rejection of British-dominated sports, 178

YMCA/YWCA and, 191–92, 197-98

World Aquatic Championships, 166

World Basketball League, 73

World Curling Federation, 103

World Figure Skating Championships, 171, 306

World Hockey Association (WHA), 123, 124, 345, 355

World Indigenous Games, 217

World Masters Games, 357

World Open Bonspiel, 103

World Ski Jumping Championships,
173

World University Games. *See*
Universiade

World War I
athletes in military during, 22
and baseball/softball, 76
and curling, 101
and football, 84, 86
and spectator sports, 77
sport as conditioning for, 229
and women in public life, 26

World War II
fitness of soldiers, 201
and football, 90, 91
and hockey, 112, 115, 231
and soccer, 87
women and, 231

World Wrestling Federation, 276, 286

wrestling, 273-77, 274*fig.*, 275*fig.*
and bodily characteristics, 206
drug use in, 286
and masculinity, 226
muscular Christianity and, 194
professional, 273-75
rodeo compared with, 234
violence and, 275, 277
women and, 274*fig.*
WSA and, 199
YCL and, 199

Wrigley, J.H., 149

Wynn, Don, 168

Yamaguchi, Kristi, 171, 172

Yellowbird, Shelli, 216

Yellowhorn, Colton, 282

Yeo, William, 269

YMCAS, 191-92
and basketball, 69
Calgary, 163, 164, 191, 197, 198, 250
and citizenship, 191
and Depression, 198
Edmonton, 197
and football, 82
goals/audience of, 197-98
Hoop League games, 69
and immigrant youth, 197-98
and judo, 208
and juvenile delinquency, 192
Leisure Time League, 198
and muscular Christianity, 36
and physical culture, 192
police at, 196
and swimming, 163, 164, 165, 250
and tennis, 155
and women, 250
and working classes, 197-98
WSA and, 199
and youth, 197-98

Young, Harvey "Pug," 119-20

Young Communist League (YCL),
199

Young Men's Hebrew Association,
208

youth
Aboriginal, 273, 282
acculturation of, 207
and cricket, 68
and curling, 104-05
GLBT, 237

and hockey, 115-16, 126

organized activities for, 38

promotion of fitness for, 197

and recreational facilities, 165

and soccer, 89

sports injuries, 266

WSA and, 200

YMCAS and, 197-98

See also children; girls

YWCAS, 191-92

and basketball, 69

and boxing, 272

brochure for women

participants, 251, 253

Calgary, 26, 164, 166

and citizenship, 191

Edmonton, 162, 253-54

and heterosexual identity, 253

images of women, 253-54

and swimming, 162, 164

and synchronized swimming,
166

and tennis, 155

and women in sport, 26

Zarisky, Archie, 170

Other Titles from The University of Alberta Press

THE GRADS ARE PLAYING TONIGHT!

The Story of the Edmonton Commercial Graduates Basketball Club

M. ANN HALL

TERRY JONES, *Foreword*

384 pages | 100 B&W photographs, foreword, notes, bibliography, appendices, index

978-0-88864-602-6 | $29.95 (T) paper

978-0-88864-612-5 | $23.99 (T) EPUB

978-0-88864-636-1 | $23.99 (T) Kindle

Sports History/Women in Sports/Edmonton

TAKING THE LEAD

Strategies and Solutions from Female Coaches

SHEILA ROBERTSON, *Editor*

DRU MARSHALL, *Introduction*

312 pages | B&W images, tables

978-0-88864-542-5 | $34.95 (T) paper

978-0-88864-586-9 | $27.99 (T) EPUB

978-0-88864-653-8 | $27.99 (T) Kindle

Sports/Leadership/Women's Studies

THE RAJAH OF RENFREW

The Life and Times of John E. Ducey, Edmonton's "Mr. Baseball"

BRANT DUCEY

520 pages | B&W photographs, notes, bibliography, index

978-0-88864-314-8 | $29.95 (T) paper

Biography